D1261250

EVERYMAN,
I WILL GO WITH THEE,
AND BE THY GUIDE,
IN THY MOST NEED
TO GO BY THY SIDE

WILLIAM SHAKESPEARE

Histories

with an Introduction by Tony Tanner
General Editor – Sylvan Barnet

VOLUME 1

EVERYMAN'S LIBRARY

177

First included in Everyman's Library, 1906

These plays are published by arrangement with New American
Library, a division of Penguin Books USA, Inc.

ISBN 1-85715-177-1

A CIP catalogue record for this book is available from the
British Library

Published by David Campbell Publishers Ltd., 79 Berwick Street,
London W1V 3PF

Distributed by Random House (UK) Ltd.,
20 Vauxhall Bridge Road, London SW1V 2SA

Typeset by MS Filmsetting Limited, Frome, Somerset

Printed and bound in Germany by
Mohndruck Graphische Betriebe GmbH, Gütersloh

HISTORIES

CONTENTS

———

INTRODUCTION

When Richard, then Duke of Gloucester, and the Duke of
Buckingham are 'persuading' the young Prince Edward to
'sojourn' in the Tower of London, whence he will never
emerge, prior to his 'coronation', which of course will never
take place, there occurs this rather strange exchange:

> *Prince.* I do not like the Tower, of any place.
> Did Julius Caesar build that place, my lord?
> *Buck.* He did, my gracious lord, begin that place,
> Which since succeeding ages have re-edified.
> *Prince.* It is upon record, or else reported
> Successively from age to age, he built it?
> *Buck.* Upon record, my gracious lord.
> *Prince.* But say, my lord, it were not regist'red,
> Methinks the truth should live from age to age,
> As 'twere retailed to all posterity,
> Even to the general all-ending day.
> *(Richard III, III, i, 68–78)*

This moment is entirely Shakespeare's invention; there is
nothing remotely like it in his sources. It might strain credulity
to think that Prince Edward, rightly very apprehensive on
being unrefusably urged into the Tower, should pause for a
brief discussion concerning matters of historical authentic-
ation and verifiability. But, at this moment, that is exactly
what Shakespeare chooses to foreground. Julius Caesar was
indeed in London in 55 and 54 BC, and fortified buildings were
erected there in Roman times. But the Tower of London was
built during the reign of William the Conqueror (possibly over
a Roman bastion), and extended by Henry III. Buckingham –
'the deep-revolving, witty Buckingham' – is certainly no
historian, but presumably he will say anything to mollify the
young prince at this point, since his only objective is to bed
him down – terminally – in the Tower. But the prince has
good and pertinent questions: recorded or reported; registered
or retailed? Not just – what happened? But – how do we *know*

what happened? Did you *hear* it: or did you *read* it? Julius Caesar, the prince goes on, was 'a famous man':

> With what his valor did enrich his wit,
> His wit set down to make his valor live.
> Death makes no conquest of this conqueror,
> For now he lives in fame, though not in life.
>
> (III, i, 85–8)

Caesar was not only a valorous *doer*, he was also a 'witty' *writer*; and so – 'now he lives in fame, though not in life'. At a climactic point in his Histories – the lawful king of England, though not yet crowned, is being led away to be murdered – Shakespeare, as it were, turns his play to face the audience and asks the spectators to consider how things – facts, names, deeds, events – are handed on, handed down; how do they come through to us? How, *when* they do, do they leave life only to enter 'fame'? All the etymologies of 'fame' (Latin *fama*, Greek *pheme*) refer to speaking and speech – a saying, report, rumour, hence reputation and renown. That would certainly cover 'reporting' and 'retailing', but – the prince has a point, though it is a singularly strange time to make it – they are not quite the same as 'recording' and 'registering'. This is the reverse of a trivial matter. The Elizabethans were becoming very interested in matters of historiography; and Shakespeare, as this crucial little exchange indicates, was clearly aware of the rich problems (or ambiguities, or what you will) inhering in his own position of a *reader* of chronicles and a *listener* to legends, *writing plays* which, though he could hardly have expected this, will almost certainly be both *read* and *spoken* 'even to the general all-ending day'. *History* is 'knowing', and how did *Shakespeare* know what he knew – or thought he knew? – when he came to write his Histories?

Here is Sir Philip Sidney in his *Apologie for Poetrie* (1580, about ten years before Shakespeare started writing history plays):

The historian, loden with old mouse-eaten records; authorising himself for the most part upon other histories, whose greatest authorities are built upon the notable foundation of hear-say; having

much ado to accord differing writers and to pick truth out of
partiality ...

Sidney is mocking historians in order to promote the superior
merits of poetry. But even as he intends an irony he is making
an important point – history *is* ultimately 'built upon the
notable foundation of hear-say'. If you go far enough back, *hear-
say* (an engagingly accurate compound phrase) always and
inevitably precedes *read-write* (if I may be permitted the comple-
mentary nonce term). History may end in registers and records,
but it starts in 'tails' and tales (tells), retailings and reportings.
We perhaps tend to forget how comparatively recent printing,
indeed literacy, was for the Elizabethans. The first official
English printed Bible (the Miles Coverdale translation) dates
from 1535 – thirty years before the birth of Shakespeare. The
earlier shift, from memorizing things to writing them down,
can be marked by the date of 1199 when chancery clerks began
to keep copies, on parchment, of the main letters sent out under
the great seal. From then on it meant that the whole population
was, in Kenneth Morgan's phrase, 'participating in literacy'
(*The Oxford History of Britain*, pp. 124–5). By the beginning of
the sixteenth century, it is estimated that more than fifty per cent
of Englishmen were literate (and that meant *English* English –
French was in marked decline before the end of the fourteenth
century). To illustrate the significance of the shift, historians
compare the two popular uprisings of the later Middle Ages –
the Peasants' Revolt (1381) and John Cade's rebellion (1450).
'In 1381 the complaints of the peasantry from Kent and Essex
were (as far as we know) presented to Richard II orally, and all
communications with the king during the revolt appear to have
been by word of mouth. Compare this with 1450, when the
demands of Cade's followers, also drawn from Kent and the
south-east, were submitted at the outset in written form, of
which several versions were produced and circulated.' (Morgan, p. 246). (Cade's revolt features in *Henry VI* Part 2, though
Shakespeare curiously makes it seem more like Wat Tyler's
rising of 1381. But more of this in due course.) The Elizabethans, of course, had writings; but they also still had 'tellings'
– myths, apocrypha, legends, and a very active oral tradition.

When Shakespeare began writing, then, 'history' was hear-say *and* read-write. Higden (a fourteenth-century monk) ends his *Polychronicon* with the reign of Edward III, but starts with the Creation: Holinshed comes up to Henry VIII, but starts with Noah. They both include entirely legendary material from Geoffrey of Monmouth's *Historia Regum Britanniæ* (first half of the twelfth century), which purports to give an account of 'the kings who dwelt in England before the incarnation of Christ' and especially of 'Arthur and the many others who succeeded him after the incarnation'. This included the story of Gorboduc, stemming from the legend of the Trojan Brute, descended from Aeneas, who founded Troynovant, or London, the first of a long line of glorious British kings (which included Lear). In general, the Elizabethans, and this included many of their historians, had no very clear idea where the myths ended and what we would think of as the facts began.

*

Shakespeare wrote ten English history plays. Leaving aside *King John* and *Henry VIII*, the remaining eight plays cover the period from 1399 (the deposition of Richard II) to 1485 (the death of Richard III at the battle of Bosworth and the accession of Henry VII). They fall into two tetralogies – in terms of historical chronology they run *Richard II*, *Henry IV*, Parts 1 and 2, *Henry V*; and *Henry VI*, Parts 1, 2, and 3, and *Richard III*. Oddly, Shakespeare wrote the second tetralogy first (1590), and the first one second (1595–9). But perhaps not so oddly. Out of the chaos of the Wars of the Roses between the Lancastrians and Yorkists had emerged the Tudor dynasty, bringing much-needed peace and stability (relatively speaking) to England. By the 1590s the Elizabethans were becoming increasingly worried about who would succeed their childless queen – and how the succession would come about. The troubles had all started when Richard II died, also leaving no son and heir, thereby triggering nearly a century of contesting usurpations and the nightmare of prolonged civil war. It is perhaps not surprising that Shakespeare should first choose to make a dramatic exploration of how that nightmare

came about, and how it ended with the establishment of
Tudor order. These were comparatively recent events for
Shakespeare and his contemporaries, and questions of succession were matters of real urgency. Shakespeare's first tetralogy
could be seen as dramatizing a warning and concluding with a
hope. In the event, the accession of James VI of Scotland to
Elizabeth's throne was peaceful enough – though of course the
nightmare duly returned with the Civil War of 1642–9. But
that is another story.

Before considering how and where Shakespeare found his
'history', and what sort of historiography was available to
him, I intend to set down some basic historical details for those
who, like myself, have some difficulty in getting, and keeping,
straight some of the whos and whens and whys involved in the
historical period he is dramatizing. More securely grounded
historians may safely skip the next few paragraphs. It is worth
remembering that, after Roman Britain, the country fell into a
number of kingdoms with many 'kings'. (It is possible that in
AD 600 English kings could be counted in dozens.) Alfred the
Great (871–99) was more truly 'king of the English' than any
ruler before him. (He was the first writer known to use the
word 'Angelcynn' – land of the English folk. 'Englaland' does
not appear for another century.) From the time of the Norman
Conquest there was a line of legitimate and legitimated kings
until the deposition of Richard II. Richard II, it is important
to remember, was the last king ruling by undisputed hereditary right, in direct line from William the Conqueror – 'the
last king of the old medieval order', Tillyard calls him. (In
1327 Edward II was deposed, thus breaking the inviolability
of anointed kingship; but his son was crowned in his place,
thus maintaining the hereditary principle.) Of course, what
'legitimated' William was primarily successful conquest. If
you follow 'legitimation' far enough back, you will invariably
come upon some originating or foundational act of appro-
priating violence which, once in position and in possession,
seeks means (call them mystifications if you will) of retro-
spective self-legitimation. But that is too large a matter for
consideration here. Suffice it say that, for the Elizabethans,
Richard II was the last truly legitimate king, to be followed by

over a century of more and less successful usurpers who ruled *de facto* rather than *de jure*.

Not surprisingly, then, the fifteenth century was a particularly turbulent time. War and murder were seldom far away. 'Towards the end of the fifteenth century, French statesmen were noting with disapproval Englishmen's habit of deposing and murdering their kings and the children of kings (as happened in 1327, 1399, 1461, 1471, 1483, and 1485) with a regularity unmatched anywhere else in Western Europe' (Morgan, p. 192). There was a growing emphasis on the king's sovereign authority which was reinforced by the principle (from 1216) that the crown should pass to the eldest son of the dead monarch. The centralization of power with the king was at the expense of the feudal, regional power of the great landowners – those barons and magnates who are forever jostling around the throne in Shakespeare's history plays. If there was intermittent uneasiness and struggle in the court, there was more serious trouble further afield for, under Edward I (1272–1307), England entered an era of perpetual war. 'From Edward I's reign onwards, there was no decade when Englishmen were not at war, whether overseas or in the British Isles. Every generation of Englishmen in the later Middle Ages knew the demands, strains, and consequences of war – and more intensely than their forbears' (Morgan, p. 194). With France alone there was what has been called the Hundred Years War (1337–1453), never mind problems with the Welsh, Scots, and Irish. Following on from that was the period of dynastic struggle known as the Wars of the Roses. And here we need a bit of detail.

Richard II finally alienated too many powerful people by his behaviour and that of his discredited favourites, and in 1399 he was dethroned. As he was childless, the question was who should now be king? Who had the strongest claim – who had the most power? 'Custom since 1216 had vested the succession in the senior male line, even though that might mean a child-king (as in the case of Henry III and Richard II himself). But there was as yet no acknowledged rule of succession should the senior male line fail. In 1399 the choice by blood lay between the seven-year-old Earl of March, descended through his grandmother from Edward III's second son, Lionel, and Henry Bolingbroke, the thirty-three-year-old son of King Edward's third son, John. Bolingbroke seized the crown after being assured of support from the Percy family whom Richard had alienated. But in the extraordinary circumstances created by Richard II's dethronement and imprisonment, neither March nor Bolingbroke had obviously the stronger claim. No amount of distortion, concealment, and argument on Bolingbroke's part could disguise what was a *coup d'état*. Hence, as in the twelfth century, an element of dynastic instability was injected into English politics which contributed to domestic turmoil and encouraged foreign intrigue and intervention in the following century' (ibid, p. 221). For Bolingbroke read 'Lancastrian'; for March read 'Yorkist'; and for 'dynastic instability' read – finally – 'the Wars of the Roses'. It should also be remembered that, though 'the Tudor myth' would have it otherwise, in fact Henry VII had no stronger claim to the throne than Bolingbroke. The Tudors were simply the third of the three usurping dynasties of the fifteenth century who seized the crown by force.

The Lancastrians ruled from 1399 to 1461 and in many ways enjoyed considerable success both at home and in France. Under Henry V, and with famous victories at Agincourt (1415), Cravant (1423), and Verneuil (1424), the English acquired a considerable portion of France. But under Henry VI, who reigned from 1422 to 1461 (he briefly reigned again from 1470 to 1471, in which year he was, almost certainly, murdered in the Tower), the Lancastrian rule disintegrated; nearly all the land in France was lost; and, what with viciously squabbling magnates, and a popular uprising in 1450, everything was going wrong. The Yorkists took over in 1461, and throughout the 1470s, under Edward IV, England enjoyed a period of relative stability and peace. But, when Edward IV died in 1483, his son and heir, also Edward, was only twelve. After nearly a century in which the most ruthless dynastic ambition had manifested itself in the bloodiest of ways, the time was ripe for the emergence of the most unprincipled schemer of them all, Richard of Gloucester, who made no bones about having his nephew murdered and seizing his crown – to become, of course, Richard III. His brutal reign lasted only two years before he was killed at Bosworth Field on 22 August 1485 – by Henry Tudor, from Wales by way of France. Henry VII, as he was to become, had two signal advantages. He was the only one of the fifteenth-century usurpers to kill his childless predecessor in battle. And, most importantly, he was supported by the Yorkists who had become disillusioned with the increasingly impossible Richard. But we should heed the historian's point. 'The Wars of the Roses came close to destroying the hereditary basis of the English monarchy, and Henry Tudor's seizure of the crown hardly strengthened it. Henry posed as the represent-ative and inheritor of both Lancaster and York, but in reality he became king, and determined to remain king, by his own efforts' (Morgan, p. 236).

Having said which, we may also note the historian's opinion that 'there is much to be said for the view that England was economically healthier, more expansive, and more optimistic under the Tudors than at any time since the Roman occupa-tion of Britain'. When Henry VIII died in 1547, there was another of those dreaded power vacuums at the centre, and for the next two years there was rioting nearly everywhere, and there were many disturbances during the short reigns of Edward VI and Mary. It is perhaps not surprising that when Elizabeth was crowned in 1558 her coronation slogan was 'concord'. And perhaps not surprising, too, that, in the 1590s, with her death just around the corner, so to speak (she was born in 1533), many people fearfully wondered whether they might not be in for another packet of upheaval and dissension – like the Wars of the Roses. When Shakespeare was writing his history plays, 'Englaland' was very far from being a complacent country. Stability, peace, and 'concord' could by no means be taken for granted. If anything, just the reverse was true.

In this connection, one other momentous historical event should be mentioned here. Between 1533 and 1536, by a series of Acts (including the Act of Supremacy and the First Act of Succession – 1534; and, finally, the Act against the Pope's Authority – 1536), Henry VIII and his parliament broke free of Rome, so that all English jurisdiction, both secular and religious, henceforward came from the king, and the last traces of Papal power were eliminated. England became a Protestant nation (soon to produce its own schism in the fiery post-Reformation form of the disaffected 'Puritans'). But Catholics and Catholicism did not disappear overnight. Far from it. It is worth remembering that Catholicism still predominated at the time of Elizabeth's accession, and throughout her reign there were constant fears of Catholic intrigue and an awareness of the real dangers of a Catholic coalition (which could bring in the Papacy, Spain, and France) against England. Mary Stuart was finally executed in 1587, a year before the defeat of the Spanish Armada. But the possibility of other Catholic plots was felt to be a constant one. *That* was where the next Wars of the Roses might come from. And it is just around this time – two years after the Armada – that Shakespeare began to write his history plays.

*

Such are the bare historic facts, as near as it is possible to ascertain, set down as neutrally and untendentiously as possible – uninterpreted, unarranged, with a minimum of narrative consequentiality. But Shakespeare did not acquire his history in this way or this form, and we must briefly consider how history was written in the Tudor period. The Tudors themselves initiated a new historiography, which can be said to begin in 1501 when Henry VII commissioned an Italian scholar, Polydore Vergil, to write a history of England – a history which would establish the right of the Tudors to the throne. So, according to Vergil, the Tudor dynasty emerged *of necessity*, with God punishing the various crimes of the Lancastrians and Yorkists, and guiding Henry through exile to the crown. This was history as (Tudor) propaganda, and it would influence history writing for the rest of the century. But not only propaganda. Tillyard calls Vergil 'the first chronicler of English history to be seriously concerned with cause and effect' and, as one of the authors of the later *A Mirror for Magistrates* (published 1559 and also very important for Shakespeare) would write:

But seeing causes are the chiefest things
That should be noted of the story writers,
That men may learn what ends all causes brings,
They be unworthy the name of chroniclers
That leave them clean out of the registers
Or doubtfully report them ...

The difference between history as memorial – an iterated commemoration of events and deeds – and history which explores causes, is also the difference between ritual and drama, and it is in Shakespeare that we see history finally emerge from ritual into drama (there are, of course, antecedent attempts which I will mention later). Vergil starts his *Anglica Historia* (not published until 1534) with fabled, misty beginnings. Where he does discern (impose? – hard to separate the two cognitive activities) a specific pattern in English history is, precisely, the period from Richard II to Henry VII.

Much more influential was the work of Edward Hall who, in 1548, published *The Union of the two Noble and Illustre Famelies of Lancastre and Yorke*, a work which was to have a direct influence on the sense of history in Shakespeare's plays. Hall was a convinced Protestant who firmly believed in the autocracy of the Tudors as recently established by Henry VIII. He built on the work of Vergil, complete with its propaganda, and made an evolving moral drama out of the dissensions between 'the two noble and illustre famelies of Lancastre and Yorke' and the final triumphant resolution of that strife in 'the reign of the high and prudent prince King Henry the Eighth, the indubitable flower and very heir of the said lineages'. Hall imposed a secular, rather than a sacred, pattern on his material: as Tillyard says, 'Hall's chief importance is that he is the first English chronicle-writer to show in all its completeness that new moralizing of history which came in with the waning of the Middle Ages, the weakening of the Church, and the rise of nationalism.' And I must take one more point from Tillyard. Hall's work is divided into eight chapters, one for each king from Henry IV to Henry VIII. Each chapter title characterizes the nature of that king's reign – 'The unquiet time of', 'The troublous season of', 'The prosperous reign of', 'The pitiful life of' and so on. But two titles stand out. 'The

victorious *acts* of King Henry the Fifth' and 'The tragical *doings*
of King Richard the Third' (my italics). Tillyard is surely right
to point to the deliberately dramatic implications of these
titles, and indeed Hall presents these reigns in an unusually
dramatic way. Shakespeare would certainly have noticed this,
and 'acts' and 'doings', victorious and tragical, are the very
stuff of his history plays (and, of course, his tragedies).

The other major source for Shakespeare, and arguably the
most influential, was the *Chronicles of England, Scotlande and
Irelande* by Raphael Holinshed, first published in 1577 but
appearing in an altered second edition in 1587, the edition
Shakespeare drew on. Holinshed was, by common consent,
less of an artist and more of a compiler than Hall; but he used
the work of Hall and covered more history than the earlier
writer. His history was less 'providential' than Hall's – though
it should be noted that in the 1587 edition of Holinshed
(prepared by Abraham Fleming after Holinshed's death) the
sense of history as being a working out of God's scheme was
more strongly stressed than in the earlier Holinshed or in Hall.
But Elizabethan historiography was not exclusively 'providential'. Irving Ribner explains that 'we can isolate two distinct
trends which exerted an influence upon Elizabethan historiography: a humanist trend essentially classical in origin, and a
medieval trend based upon the premises of Christian belief.
We cannot suppose, however, that in the minds of the Elizabethans there was any clear distinction between these two
lines of influence. The English Renaissance, in most intellec-
tual areas, shows an easy merging of the medieval and
humanist' (*The English History Play in the Age of Shakespeare*,
pp. 21–2). Humanist history, as written by Leonardo Bruni,
Francesco Guicciardini, and above all Niccolo Machiavelli,
was didactic, instructional, and nationalistic – more secular-
ized, rationalistic, and 'political' than Christian history, which
tended to be providential, apocalyptic, and universal. Is
history made by man, or decreed by God? The Elizabethans
seemed to have felt that it was something of both.

The subject matter of Renaissance historiography was the
life of the state – in Fulke Greville's words 'the growth, state
and declination of princes, change of government, and laws,

vicissitudes of sedition, faction, succession, confederacies, plan-
tations, with all other errors or alterations in public affairs'.
The purposes for which these matters were treated by writers
of history are usefully summarized by Irving Ribner under
two headings. 'Those stemming from classical and humanist
philosophies include (1) a nationalistic glorification of England; (2) an analysis of contemporary affairs, both national
and foreign so as to make clear the virtues and the failings of
contemporary statesmen; (3) a use of past events as a guide to
political behaviour in the present; (4) a use of history as
documentation for political theory; and (5) a study of past
political disaster as an aid to Stoical fortitude in the present.
Those stemming from medieval Christian philosophy include:
(6) illustration of the providence of God as the ruling force in
human – and primarily political – affairs, and (7) exposition of
a rational plan in human events which must affirm the wisdom
and justice of God' (op. cit., p. 24). All of these uses of history
may be found in Shakespeare's plays – whether just glanced
at, provisionally entertained, seriously questioned, or hope-
fully embraced. But there is one purpose which has not been
mentioned so far.

Between the end of Roman Britain and the Norman Conquest, there had evolved (in the eleventh century) and
decayed (in the fourteenth and fifteenth centuries) a unique
form of society – feudalism, which had its own economic
system, social hierarchy, codes of value and conventions of
behaviour. To what *extent* Shakespeare knew about the details
of this society we cannot know; but we can be sure that he was
aware of historical *discontinuity* and social *change* in Britain's
past. It is sometimes maintained that Shakespeare's history
plays are indirectly (or directly) addressed to matters concerning contemporary Tudor Britain, either as loyal propaganda
or adversarial critique according to the reading. But to the
extent that this is true, it is certainly only partly true.
Shakespeare is manifestly interested in the past *as* past – as
different from the present. Graham Holderness has written well
about this, and I will simply quote his main contention.

Shakespeare's plays of English history are chronicles of feudalism:

xxii

INTRODUCTION

they offer empirical reconstruction and theoretical analysis of a social formation firmly located in the past, and distinctly severed from the contemporary world. In this historiographical reconstruction, which focuses on the decline of feudalism in the fourteenth and fifteenth centuries, society is seen as a historical formation built on certain fundamental contradictions, and incapable of resolving or overcoming them within the framework of political and ideological determinants provided by the historical basis itself. As the vision of feudal society is historically specific, the disclosure of contradictions cannot be defined as reversion to medieval pessimism or a compliance with Machiavellian pragmatism: if a conception of the past admits the possibility of fundamental social change, the contradictions of a particular historical formation cannot be identified with 'the human condition' ...

(*Shakespeare Recycled*, p. 19)

There is no suggestion that this was a merely antiquarian exercise for Shakespeare, and of course 'universals' can be (perhaps may best be) discovered by studying an 'historically specific' society, event, place, person. By exploring how we lived *then*, we may – this is perhaps the tacit hope in all historiography – the better understand the way we live *now*. And – who knows? – perhaps improve it.

The earliest English drama – the Miracle plays, the Christian 'cycles' (probably a twelfth-century development) – emerged out of the static liturgy of the Church. Literally emerged as well, leaving the church for the streets. Towards the end of the fourteenth century a new kind of play can be found – the Morality play; a kind of play still being performed in the time of Elizabeth. The Miracle play necessarily dealt with 'universals' – the universal truths of the Catholic Church (when Henry VIII assumed the role of head of the Church, the cycles were suppressed – too Roman). The Morality play also dealt in universals, allegorically presenting the conflict of opposing powers (as it might be, Mischief and Mercy) for the soul of Man – as in *Mankynd* and *Everyman*. But this genre had an important potentiality – as A. P. Rossiter puts it, 'a potential frame for a life-story: not of mankind as *Humanum Genus*, but the human-kind as revealed in One Man' (*English Drama*, p. 99). More than that. 'The Morality not only got at

xxiii

the dramatic essential of protracted conflict in a world of
jarring wills, but also arrived at one of the simple formulae for
play-making.' Simply, the 'moral' had to have a point towards
which the action moved, and that meant – *plot*. In the
sixteenth century and with the coming of the Renaissance,
there is a narrowing of focus and a growing interest in more
political matters concerning rule and policy, princecraft and
governorship. In Skelton's *Magnyfycence* (1516), for instance,
the hero is a prince. He is confused and led astray by such
incomparably named figures as Counterfeit Countenance,
Crafty Conveyance, Cloaked Collusion, and Courtly Abusion.
We will meet such figures in the Histories, except that there
they will be called Buckingham – or Richard. (The prince, I
may say, is tempted to suicide by Despair, but is saved by
Good Hope who administers the Rhubarb of Repentance!)
From the prince generic to the king specific is but a step, and
with the assertion of Tudor autocracy the figure of the king
takes on a special interest since he is now the absolute power.

Sure enough, by 1536 we have *Kynge Johan* (altered in 1539,
surviving only in a revision of 1561). In this play, John is a
Christian hero who stood up against the Pope. The play is not
very concerned with historical accuracy, but it was just what
the Tudors wanted, or perhaps ordered (the Act of Supremacy, remember, was 1534). The important thing about this
play is that it shows a way of using history for a predetermined
purpose. (We will see what Shakespeare made of King John.)
In Rossiter's words, 'the point of *Kynge Johan* is that it suggests
a method by which any not-wildly-unsuitable "chronicle" stuff
can be made into a history-play: by beginning with "what you
want to prove" and patternizing history in accordance with
set dogmas' (ibid., p. 122). With this sense that history can be
patterned for a purpose (which, of course, need not necessarily
be didactic or propagandist), we are close to the history play
proper. But it is important to bear in mind that, even when we
move to drama that is historically specific (*Richard II*, not
Mankynd), we will find traces, or after-glimpses, of the Morality pattern, as the plays still present struggles between opposed
abstractable qualities, albeit now locked together *inside* human
consciousness. Rossiter quotes the contemporary Thomas

Lodge who, in his 'A Defense of Plays' of 1580, says that the
dramatists 'dilucidate and well explain many darke obscure
histories, imprinting them in men's minds in such indelible
characters that they can hardly be obliterated'. Rossiter
comments: 'the suggestion of an allegoric shadow-show behind
the historic characters, on another plane than the clash of
transient personalities, was an essential part of that
"dilucidation"' (ibid., p. 155).

Gorboduc (1561) is regarded as the first English history-
tragedy, but the subject was taken from the legendary chronicles of early Britain, and the play was something of a neo-
classical Senecan exercise. This was not to be Shakespeare's
way. But by the time Shakespeare started writing his history
plays, Marlowe's *Tamburlaine the Great* had been published.
This not only marked a revolutionary step in the use of blank
verse; it brought a new Renaissance type of amoral hero to the
English stage. Marlowe's plays manifest that fear of man's
potentialities which seems to increase towards the end of the
Elizabethan period when writers, Shakespeare supremely,
began to contemplate what kind of figure man might become
'given freedom from all the Christian and medieval restraints'
(ibid.). But while Tudor drama is very much a phenomenon
and product of the English Renaissance, it is still very
involved, as I have tried to stress, in what we call the Middle
Ages. As we turn to Shakespeare, we might bear in mind
Rossiter's simple but suggestive generalization that much of
Elizabethan drama consists of 'the adventures of Renaissance
Man in a Medieval World-Order'.

*

HENRY VI PART 1
> Henry the Sixth, in infant bands crown'd King
> Of France and England, did this king succeed;
> Whose state so many had the managing,
> That they lost France and made this England bleed:
> Which oft our stage hath shown ...
> *(Henry V*, V, ii, 9–13)

At the end of this second tetralogy, Shakespeare looks back
to where he began the first. He started with the funeral of

HISTORIES

Henry V, accompanied by dark forebodings and ominous
portents, and went on to dramatize the losses and bleedings
which England suffered during the reign of Henry VI – 'which
oft our stage hath shown'. Henry V was the last great heroic
warrior-knight king; thereafter came 'declension' – disagree-
ment, dissention, disorder – 'jars'; then, disintegration and
degeneration until, in Part 3, England has collapsed into a
'slaughter house'. Henry Tudor arrives to tidy up the shambles. But the *Henry VI* trilogy is really about – as far as England
is concerned – diminution, dissolution, loss. Joan of Arc's
words are both lyrically fitting and historically accurate:

> Glory is like a circle in the water,
> Which never ceaseth to enlarge itself
> Till by broad spreading it disperse to nought.
> With Henry's death the English circle ends;
> Dispersèd are the glories it included.

> (I, ii, 133–7)

The *Henry VI* plays survey (and inquire) how England's
glories – after the death of Henry V – 'disperse to nought'.

That this did happen, and the trajectory of its happening, is
of course inscribed in the Chronicles. Hall announced, clearly
enough, that his theme was 'what mischief hath insurged in
realms by intestine division … what calamitee hath ensued in
famous regions by domestical discord & unnatural controversy'; while Holinshed states, succinctly enough, 'through
dissention at home, all lost abroad'. The first, if not the prime,
cause of the trouble, was that king 'in infant bands' – 'woe to
the nation whose king is a child' was a familiar adage for the
Elizabethans. But that alone could not account for England's
collapse into ungloried chaos. The Chronicles record that this
did happen. Shakespeare sets out imaginatively to recreate the
occasions – the causes – of its happening. And to transform
'chronicle' into 'drama', he had to set about 'patterning' his
material. This he did so freely, and to such effect, that
Bullough – the great master of Shakespeare's sources – gives
his opinion that what Shakespeare finally produced is 'not so
much a Chronicle Play as a fantasia on historical themes'.

In no other history play does Shakespeare so freely disrupt

and alter the time sequence of his Chronicle material. He brings events together that were years apart; he inverts the order of their happening; he makes sudden what was slow; he makes simultaneous what was separate. He expands and contracts; he omits – and invents. As Andrew Cairncross well puts it in his introduction to the Arden edition of the play, Shakespeare throws 'the events of thirty years into the melting-pot' and, just because he makes so free with chronology, he has to 'avoid precise indications of time' (there are no dates) – 'events must happen, as it were, in a great sea of time with no fixed points of reference but the death of Henry V behind and the Wars of the Roses before'. Just to give a few examples of the liberties Shakespeare took with his material: the episodes in the play cover more than thirty years, from the start of Henry's reign (1422) to the death of the heroic Talbot (at Bordeaux in 1453); but, from the start, disparate events are yoked together – thus, the siege of Orléans (1428–9) is depicted as taking place during the funeral of Henry V (seven years earlier). Joan was burned in 1431, while Talbot was buried in 1453 – yet in the play, she lives to see him dead. Joan was captured in 1430, though not by York as in the play. In the play, this is *immediately* followed by the (completely fictitious) capture and wooing of Margaret by Suffolk. In fact, negotiations for Henry's marriage did not take place until 1444. Burgundy's defection from the English takes place over twenty years in Hall. In the play, it is effected on the instant as a result of a patriotic appeal by Joan (quite unhistorical – she had been burned some years previously). And so on. Shakespeare is tightening his pattern – pointing up the conflict between the once heroic English and the devious, effeminate French; the undermining of chivalric ideals, the decay of feudal loyalties, and loss of old values; the fading of the old, noble heroic ethos, and the rise of a generation driven by ruthlessness, expediency, and cunning; and (this is not so commonly noted) the capitulation – on certain fronts – of the masculine to the feminine. Everywhere, ceremony is, if not drowned, then disrupted, spoiled, profaned. The sense of growing disaster and impending dissolution is relentless. Chaos is not quite come again; but it is surely not far away.

We might start by considering interrupted ceremony, since that is how the play starts. A history play dealing with kingly matters is bound to contain a lot of pageantry – processions, flourishes, drums, flags. This is the very panoply of the feudal courtly world – its binding ritual: everyone in their place; hierarchy and degree visibly enacted; order celebrated and power and authority manifested. So this play opens with the great solemn Dead March at Henry V's funeral. But the dignified exequies and formal lamentations are almost immediately disrupted by a most unseemly squabble between Gloucester and Winchester, signs of a bitter rivalry which will dominate the first part of the play. Bedford seeks to turn their attention away from private rancour and back to the public ritual – 'cease these jars ... Let's to the altar' (I, i, 44–5). ('Jars' is a recurrent word in this long study of discord.) Bedford tries to invoke and prolong the spirit of the dead king:

> Henry the Fifth, thy ghost I invocate:
> Prosper this realm, keep it from civil broils,
> Combat with adverse planets in the heavens!
> A far more glorious star thy soul will make
> Than Julius Caesar or bright –
>
> (I, i, 52–6)

But just there, with the name of Julius Caesar on his lips, he is interrupted by a messenger with tidings 'Of loss, of slaughter, and discomfiture' – more specifically, with news of the loss of seven towns in France. 'What treachery was used?' asks incredulous Exeter. 'No treachery, but want of men and money' (I, i, 69). This is important. Throughout, it is made clear that, for all the talk of the diabolical French and witchcraft, for every setback and loss, England has only itself to blame. 'Through dissention at home, all lost abroad.' A second messenger brings 'letters full of bad mischance' (the Dauphin has been crowned king). Then a *third* messenger brings the 'dismal' news of Talbot's capture. I stress 'three' because the play is full of triads (observed by Lawrence V. Ryan and others). I will come back to this. The scene ends, interestingly, exactly as it began – that is, it starts with speeches from Bedford, Gloucester, Exeter, Winchester, and it ends with speeches from them in the same order, as they variously exit. The king being an infant, they are responsible for managing the realm. They leave to take up their duties – except for Winchester. He remains behind to give the first soliloquy in the history plays:

> Each hath his place and function to attend;
> I am left out; for me nothing remains.
> But long I will not be Jack out of office.
> The king from Eltham I intend to send
> And sit at chiefest stern of public weal.

(I, i, 173–7)

The repetition witnessed in the entrances and exits suggests order, an ordering; things and people in their proper sequences. But the amoral candour, the revealed personal ambition of the voice alone, offers a violation and threat to that order. As disorder and disarray increase, so do the soliloquies and asides; while ritual, processional confidences and enactments wane.

The play has sometimes been described as the tragedy of Talbot, the honest old English hero whose destruction is engineered by the wily French witch, Joan. So much is there but to see it that way makes, I think, for an uncomfortably coarse, not to say jingoistic, play. And it ignores the fact that Talbot dies at the end of Act IV and clearly, quite deliberately, Shakespeare concludes his play, not just with the death of Joan, but also – and instantly ensuant on that death – the (unhistorical) wooing of Margaret by Suffolk, and his persuading Henry to break a previous contract of marriage and instead take Margaret (a critical act of 'oath-breaking' which anticipates many more). Joan, the 'scourge of the English', is dead. Long live Margaret, who will be a scourge of the English for years to come (she is the only character to appear in every play of the tetralogy).

But let me turn to the matter of threes and triads. There are, most obviously from the start, three heroic English generals – Salisbury, Bedford, Talbot; grey-haired and ageing, they seem like increasingly isolated survivors from another, simpler, nobler age. They meet their deaths in battle at the three

French towns which figure in the play – respectively, Orléans, Rouen, Bordeaux. (Talbot, I might mention, has 'three attendants,/Lean Famine, quartering Steel, and climbing Fire': IV, ii, 11.) Correspondingly, three ruthlessly ambitious and distinctly *ig*noble nobles emerge in the course of the play – Winchester, York, and Somerset – representing a new breed of men who know the chivalric gestures, and postures, and words, but have none of the old chivalric sense of duty, obligation, and loyalty. Between them, they are preparing the wars and discords of the morrow. There are three interrupted ceremonies. The funeral, already mentioned: the parliament-house where the young king makes his first appearance in the play (III, i), only to have the occasion violently disrupted by Gloucester's and Winchester's fighting serving-men: and the king's coronation in Paris (IV, i), which is marred, first by Talbot's stripping of the Garter from cowardly Falstaff (no relation) – Talbot accompanies this act with what amounts to an elegy for the old heroic knightly virtues; secondly, by the news of Burgundy's treacherous defection; and thirdly by the request by Vernon and Basset – 'presumptuous vassals' – to be allowed the right to combat. They are serving-men belonging to York and Somerset, who do nothing to contain and curb this grossly unseemly behaviour on the part of their servants. The stains of discord are seeping down through the ranks of society.

But, perhaps most importantly, there are three women, all French, and the only women in the play. There are three scenes in which each of them exercises her seductive wiles on a man in a superior position of power – twice with complete success, but once, most instructively, to no avail. The first encounter is between Joan and the Dauphin in the second scene in the play. She appears here as 'a holy maid' with 'the spirit of deep prophecy'. The encounter is recorded in the Chronicles. What Shakespeare adds is their engaging in a round of single combat, which opens itself to sexual *double entendre* – 'thou shalt buckle with me', etc. The Dauphin's abject capitulation to her – 'Let me thy servant and not sovereign be ... thy prostrate thrall' (I, ii, 111, 117) – represents a dramatic inversion – male king craving the

domination of a peasant girl – which the Elizabethans would
find shocking, or perhaps amusing (that's the French for you!).
Very different is the strange little incident involving the
Countess of Auvergne and her attempt to trap Talbot in her
castle (II, iii). This scene is completely Shakespeare's invention. Tillyard dismissed it as an 'irrelevant anecdote' intro-
duced as fun for the audience. It is rather more interesting
than that. The countess has asked to entertain Talbot, who has
graciously – he *is* a knight – accepted. Upon seeing him, the
countess evinces surprise that he is so small and un-heroic
looking – 'What! Is this the man?'

> I see report is fabulous and false.
> I thought I should have seen some Hercules ...
> Alas, this is a child, a silly dwarf!
>
> (II, iii, 18–22)

After this piece of opening politeness, the countess announces
that he is her prisoner (such is her plot). She adds that, in a
way, he has been her 'prisoner' for a long time.

> Long time thy shadow hath been thrall to me,
> For in my gallery thy picture hangs.
> But now the substance shall endure the like,
> And I will chain these legs and arms of thine ...
>
> (II, iii, 36–9)

Talbot simply laughs, as well as he might since half his army is
waiting outside the door. But he goes on to say that she never
had more than his shadow anyway.

Countess. Why, art not thou the man?
Talbot. I am indeed.
Countess. Then have I substance too.
Talbot. No, no, I am but shadow of myself:
   You are deceived, my substance is not here,
   For what you see is but the smallest part
   And least proportion of humanity.

> (II, iii, 48–53)

And the countess finds this a riddle:

> He will be here, and yet he is not here.
>
> (II, iii, 58)

The countess's mistake is to identify bodily presence – which in this case is relatively puny – with true 'substance'. But Talbot's real – male – 'substance' is in his name, his fame, and the power at his disposal. Just as he is, there alone in the countess's room, temporarily reduced to his body, he is effectively, like his painted image, a 'shadow' (doubly so, since 'shadow' was also a word for an actor – Shakespeare is already beginning to exploit the available ironic analogies between history and theatre). The countess recognizes her mistake:

> Victorious Talbot, pardon my abuse;
> I find thou art no less than fame hath bruited
> And more than may be gathered by thy shape.
> (II, iii, 67–9)

This episode represents a complete defeat of the feminine. The virile old English knight is immune to the effeminizations of France. But he is a dying breed.

The third male encounter with a French female – again, Shakespeare's invention – takes place in the last Act between Suffolk and Margaret. Suffolk enters holding Margaret's hand and gazing at her, even as the other captured French female, Joan, is led off. It is immediately clear that he has been entirely captivated by her beauty and charm. And she uses no (obvious) seductive arts: in this play she is passive and decorous throughout her appearances. Suffolk, desperate somehow to keep Margaret close to him, conceives the plan of persuading Henry to take her as his bride. In this, he is successful, and the last lines of the play see him happily setting off for France again, to bring Margaret to England. The lines could hardly be more ominous.

> Thus Suffolk hath prevailed, and thus he goes,
> As did the youthful Paris once to Greece,
> With hope to find the like event in love,
> But prosper better than the Trojan did.
> Margaret shall now be queen, and rule the king;
> But I will rule both her, the king, and realm ...
> (V, v, 103–8)

INTRODUCTION

Since Britain was, mythically, descended from Troy, the proposed importation of a second Helen into the realm presages an interminable period of disaster.

Can anything legitimately be made of these recurrent triads? Not, certainly, anything to do with whatever mystic properties might be thought to be associated with the number three. I think it has to do with that 'patterning' which the dramatist has to impose on his material. Historically, things happen just once. But if, in a representation of it, things seem to come in threes, you get the sense that perhaps there are echoes, recurrencies, repetitions, symmetries which, while you live through the actual day, you never notice. As Philip Brockbank well says, Shakespeare's Histories 'give us the sense of being close to the event together with a sense of knowing its consequences ... The rhythm between pattern and process is maintained; the play like the history must be both reflected upon and lived through, its moral shape apprehended but its clamor and hurly-burly wracking the nerves' (*On Shakespeare*, p. 83). This is why we are afforded long backward – and forward-looking vistas, from Mortimer's long genealogical speech tracing the succession from Edward III, to the many speeches of foreboding and prophecy which Shakespeare inserts, often at the end of a scene. One example: the Temple Garden scene – again, completely Shakespeare's invention – serves in an almost heraldic way to give a sharp and high-lighted beginning to the Wars of the Roses proper (this is nothing like so clear in the Chronicles). Warwick declares:

> And here I prophesy: this brawl today,
> Grown to this faction in the Temple garden,
> Shall send, between the red rose and the white,
> A thousand souls to death and deadly night.
>
> (II, iv, 124–8)

Shakespeare uses prophecies, and later curses and dreams, not just to relate and bind together the three parts of the trilogy, but to suggest that English history does *have* a perceptible pattern. Albeit, for a while it is a pattern of accelerating disaster.

Much of the play does concentrate on the struggle between Talbot and Joan. Talbot is certainly the noble old heroic soldier from another age – English, virile, unquestioningly loyal, implacably ferocious in battle. Just there we might pause, for there is in fact something barbaric, atavistic, about his fury. 'Your hearts I'll stamp out with my horse's heels,/And make a quagmire of your mingled brains' (I, iv, 108–9). This doesn't, to me, have the smack of chivalry about it. Similarly, he reveals that, when a prisoner of the French, 'I with my nails digged stones out of the ground' to hurl at his captors. Brave, perhaps. But this is just how the mob which interrupts parliament behaves: they

> Have filled their pockets full of pebble stones
> And banding themselves in contrary parts
> Do pelt so fast at one another's pate
> That many have their giddy brains knocked out.

> (III, i, 80–83)

Talbot, one feels, would be a good man in a mob action – on either side. He is one of those archaic warrior figures, seemingly dominated by a disposition of unrelenting ferocity, who recur throughout Shakespeare (Coriolanus is, of course, the last). He has much to say about the French 'fiends'; but to the French, *Talbot* is the 'fiend'. 'I think this Talbot be a fiend of hell' (II, i, 46). Who is 'saviour' and who is 'fiend' clearly depends on what side you are on. And, for all the talk of witchcraft and diabolical assistance of the French, the death of Talbot is shown to be, four-squarely, the fault of England. York and Somerset won't send him the help they were pledged to provide, because they are jealous of each other. As Lucy – another Shakespearian invention – says to them:

> Thus, while the vulture of sedition
> Feeds in the bosom of such great commanders,
> Sleeping neglection doth betray to loss ...
>   Whiles they each other cross,
> Lives, honors, lands, and all hurry to loss
> ...
> The fraud of England, not the force of France,
> Hath now entrapped the noble-minded Talbot;

INTRODUCTION

> Never to England shall he bear his life,
> But dies betrayed to fortune by your strife.
>
> (IV, iii, 47–53: IV, iv, 36–9)

Talbot is, in fact, very much at sea in this new world which fights by rules, or guiles and stratagems, that he does not understand. Lost and bewildered in one battle, he says despairingly:

> My thoughts are whirlèd like a potter's wheel;
> I know not where I am, nor what I do.
>
> (I, v, 19–20)

There is no way such a figure could survive.

But he survived a good deal longer than Shakespeare allows him to, so that – quite anachronistically – Joan is in at his death. This is a crucial scene; but, before looking at it, we must briefly consider Shakespeare's Joan. In the early part of the play, she is allowed some speeches of (from the French point of view) impeccable patriotism, which Shakespeare could only have approved. But he is soon allowing an equivocation on 'Pucelle or pussel' (virgin or whore). He allows her a scorching indictment of English hypocrisy (V, iv, 36 ff.), but also portrays her in converse with evil spirits. She – damnably – denies her peasant father, and finally loses all credibility and dignity as she casts around, admitting to any sexual liaison, to avoid the stake. There are, of course, English and French versions of Joan, and Shakespeare finally endorses an English one. But the English are in no point exempted from the chaos they have caused, the deteriorations they have permitted. Concerning a final judgment of Joan, I prefer the humane exhortation of Holinshed – 'cast your opinions as ye have cause'.

At the death of Talbot, Lucy gives a long commemorative speech which spells out all his titles:

> Valiant Lord Talbot, Earl of Shrewsbury,
> Created, for his rare success in arms,
> Great Earl of Washford, Waterford, and Valence,
> Lord Talbot of Goodrig and Urchinfield,
> Lord Strange of Blackmere, Lord Verdun of Alton,
> Lord Cromwell of Wingfield, Lord Furnival of Sheffield,

The thrice victorious Lord of Falconbridge,
Knight of the noble order of Saint George,
Worthy Saint Michael, and the Golden Fleece,
Great Marshal to Henry the Sixth
Of all his wars within the realm of France.

(IV, vii, 61–71)

To which Joan comments:

Here's a silly stately style indeed!
The Turk, that two and fifty kingdoms hath,
Writes not so tedious a style as this.
Him that you magnifi'st with all these titles
Stinking and fly-blown lies here at our feet.

(IV, vii, 72–6)

Interestingly, it has been established that Lucy's words are taken from an actual historical monument, Talbot's tomb at Rouen. A lapidary speech indeed – words of stone, words in stone. The true identity – 'substance' – of the man is asserted to exist and persist in his name and fame. Look for the man in the monument. Joan, the woman, concentrates on the rotting physical body (rotting rather quickly, as has been pointed out: Shakespeare wants the stark contrast of the male/female attitudes). Joan is defeated, and Talbot's name lives on. But her mockery of the male 'silly stately style' leaves its mark, sows its doubt. Leaving monuments to the English heroes who die in France is very important in this play. And one result of the disastrous marriage between Henry and Margaret is that all historical records and monuments may well be lost. As Gloucester says to his fellow nobles at the beginning of the next play:

Fatal this marriage, canceling your fame,
Blotting your names from books of memory,
Razing the characters of your renown,
Defacing monuments of conquered France,
Undoing all, as all had never been.

(Part 2, I, i, 99–103)

The whole record and celebration of heroic England is under threat of erasure. That would be Joan's revenge indeed. History is just corpses.

Henry is the man of peace and piety, preferring meditation to action, and prayer to policy. He has too much 'lenity' to control and govern the warring factions springing up around him. He is something of a saint, and he certainly becomes a martyr. But he is a disastrously ineffectual king, and some of his innocence may be held to be culpable. His last speeches in the play, in which he allows himself to be swayed by Suffolk's descriptions of Margaret, portend disaster:

> So am I driven by breath of her renown
> Either to suffer shipwreck or arrive
> Where I may have fruition of her love.
>
> (V, v, 7-9)

The pilot of the ship of state should not even countenance 'shipwreck'.

> I feel such sharp dissension in my breast,
> Such fierce alarums both of hope and fear,
> As I am sick with working of my thoughts.
>
> (V, v, 84-6)

If there is 'sharp dissension' *within* the oscillating, unstable king, what hope that he can control the 'sharp dissensions' that are beginning to spread through the land?

In one of his late soliloquies, the besotted Suffolk thinks how much he wants Margaret, but pulls himself up, realizing he must try to persuade Henry to take her for his wife:

> O wert thou for myself! But, Suffolk, stay;
> Thou mayst not wander in that labyrinth;
> There Minotaurs and ugly treasons lurk.
> Solicit Henry with her wondrous praise ...
>
> (V, iii, 187-90)

He does enter that labyrinth, and for most of the next three plays, it seems that England does, too. And the real Minotaur, lurking to emerge, will prove to be the monstrous, misshapen Machiavel – Richard.

*

HENRY VI PART 2

Given that he was so hopelessly inadequate and ineffectual as a king, Henry VI's reign was a surprisingly long one – about fifty years if we include his short, second reign. During that time, all manner of political events occurred, but, as it might be felt, in a random and disconnected way. It was all very rambling and scattered. Shakespeare simply had to take hold of a chunk of that time and make it appear as a self-explanatory sequence, all contributing to a single dramatic line. He fixed on the period from 1444, when Henry welcomes his French queen Margaret to England, to 1455, the battle of St Albans, and the final, unambiguous emergence of York as an intending usurper. To achieve the concentration and focus he wanted, Shakespeare omitted a large amount of Chronicle material which would not have served his purpose; he tightens and emphasizes causes by linking what was historically unlinked (thus, both the Armourer scenes, and the Cade rebellion, are directly related to York's treason); he conflates with ruthless economy (the subversion of Salisbury and War- wick dragged on for twenty years – it is here reduced to a single scene – II, ii); he reaches into other periods for what he wants (Eleanor, Duchess of Gloucester, in fact fell four years *before* Margaret landed from France; Shakespeare clearly wants them contemporary). More remarkably, when it comes to the Jack Cade rebellion, Shakespeare ignores most of his Chronicle material, and goes back to sources concerning Wat Tyler and the Peasants' Revolt of 1381. This play will show the tragic fall of Gloucester, and the irresistible rise of York.

In the first part of the trilogy, England lost its old heroes. In this second part, it loses (in the symbolic form of one man) its law-givers. The fall of Gloucester effectively occupies the play until his murder in the middle of Act III. Gloucester is a strong and active man (he is not a feeble relic like John of Gaunt). The play opens with high ceremony as Henry's French queen is welcomed to the English court. It must be stressed that this marriage is seen as the triggering disaster behind the events of the play. Gloucester, it should be remem- bered, had proposed an eminently sensible, diplomatic mar- riage to which the young king had at first agreed. Then he

INTRODUCTION

succumbed to Suffolk's guile – 'which fact,' says Hall, 'engendered such a flame, that it never went out, till both the parties
with many other were consumed and slain, to the great
unquietness of the king and his realm'. This is the marriage
which Gloucester says will wipe out England's old heroic
history. His first task in the scene – he is Protector – is to read
out the contracted articles pertaining to the marriage. When
he comes to the quite shameful surrender of Anjou and Maine,
he lets the paper fall from his hand and can read no more.
Power and authority have begun – literally – to slip from his
hands, as other plots – out of his cognizance and control –
begin to seethe around him. Almost as soon as he leaves, a
small group is planning to 'quickly hoise Duke Humphrey
from his seat' (I, i, 169). And when they have gone we are left
with York – alone. He speaks the first of a series of long –
dangerously long – soliloquies. Dangerous because the more
time and space are, as it were, arrogated by the private voice
going over its own intentions and devices, the less time and
space seem to be committed to publicly performed, orderly,
communal life. This voice is not remotely interested in
'common-wealth'.

> Then, York, be still awhile, till time do serve:
> Watch thou and wake, when others be asleep,
> To pry into the secrets of the state;
> Till Henry surfeit in the joys of love
> ...
> And, force perforce, I'll make him yield the crown,
> Whose bookish rule hath pulled fair England down.
>> (I, i, 248–51, 258–9)

We have already seen man plotted-against (Gloucester); and
man-plotting (York). The die is cast. And we are heading for a
period during which England as a whole will fall under the
sway of – 'force perforce'.

For two Acts we see Gloucester administering law with
robust confidence and justice (which is perhaps a little severe).
The business of Simpcox and the false miracle, and the
fighting armourers, presumably shows him looking after the
law of the land. While he is there, there is still some social

order. But the plot to set up his ambitious wife, and bring her to disgrace on account of her trafficking in black magic (here arranged by Suffolk for the queen), effectively brings him down as well. This is presumably why Shakespeare wanted both events brought together. When Eleanor is arraigned, he is bowed down by the 'dishonour', and, in tears, asks the king's permission to leave. Surrendering his staff of office, he shuffles off – suddenly an old man. (He is not old in the Chronicles. It is as if, while in the first part Shakespeare saw heroes to be a dying breed, so in this part he sees 'honour' fading out of England.)

But Gloucester is still confident that he remains outside of the reach of the law ('I must offend before I be attainted': II, iv, 59 – already a touchingly old-fashioned trust). When Gloucester arrives at the abbey in Bury, and Suffolk arrests him 'of high treason', he is unmoved:

> Well, Suffolk, thou shalt not see me blush,
> Nor change my countenance for this arrest:
> A heart unspotted is not easily daunted.
> The purest spring is not so free from mud
> As I am clear from treason to my sovereign.
>
> (III, i, 98–102)

But then the false accusations mount up against him, and he realizes the case is lost.

This occasions two of the most important speeches of the play, concerning the positive values which, the play suggests, are certainly under threat, if not in the process of being dismantled. Gloucester turns to the king:

> Ah, gracious lord, these days are dangerous:
> Virtue is *choked* with foul ambition,
> And charity chased hence by rancor's hand;
> Foul subornation is predominant,
> And equity exiled your Highness' land.
> I know their complot is to have my life,
> And if my death might make this island happy,
> And prove the period of their tyranny,
> I would expend it with all willingness.
> But mine is made the prologue to their play:
> For thousands more, that yet suspect no peril,

Will not conclude their plotted tragedy.

(III, i, 142–53 – my italics)

He tells the king he has thrown away his 'crutch':

> Thus is the shepherd beaten from thy side,
> And wolves are gnarling who shall gnaw thee first.

(III, i, 191–2)

At first, Henry seems to touch the bottom of his abject, concessionary hopelessness – 'My lords ... do or undo' ... Do what you like. But then, in a speech of high passion, of which there is not a trace in the Chronicles, Henry laments Gloucester and turns on his queen. It is his most sustained piece of oratory, and as one must feel, one of his most heart-felt, in the trilogy. As Gloucester recedes, it is as if Henry sees more clearly all the values he embodied.

> Ah, uncle Humphrey, in thy face I see
> The map of honor, truth, and loyalty;
> And yet, good Humphrey, is the hour to come
> That e'er I proved thee false or feared thy faith?
> What louring star now envies thy estate,
> That these great lords, and Margaret our Queen
> Do seek subversion of thy harmless life?
> Thou never didst them wrong, nor no man wrong:
> And as the butcher takes away the calf,
> And binds the wretch, and beats it when it strays,
> Bearing it to the bloody slaughter-house,
> Even so remorseless they have borne him hence;
> And as the dam runs lowing up and down,
> Looking the way her harmless young one went,
> And can do nought but wail her darling's loss,
> Even so myself bewails good Gloucester's case
> With sad unhelpful tears, and with dimmed eyes
> Look after him and cannot do him good,
> So mighty are his vowèd enemies.
> His fortunes I will weep, and 'twixt each groan
> Say "Who's a traitor? Gloucester he is none."

(III, i, 202–22)

He leaves. It is a final flaring, a last attempt to express his sense of what is happening around him. Henceforward he is effectively extinct, politically impotent. But he is absolutely right, of course. England *is* headed for the 'slaughter-house'. Meanwhile Suffolk articulates the complete lack of interest in ceremony or law, or anything else which constrains and guides conduct:

> And do not stand on quillets how to slay him:
> Be it by gins, by snares, by subtlety,
> Sleeping or waking, 'tis no matter how,
> So he be dead.

(III, i, 261–4)

Just *kill* him – any way at all. Force perforce.

We do not see the murder – that is night-time, secret work. The butcher's shop, or slaughter-house, is now open for a new sort of business. But, in a gruesome scene – which feels like something in a medieval Morality – Gloucester's corpse is exposed on stage. For a second time, the audience is invited to consider the dead body of an old Englishman, whose world is being supplanted by one dominated by people who are immeasurably littler, and inexpressibly meaner. The spectacle is macabre – grotesque – and a minute description follows. This is the real close-up of Death in the play. From the black face and starting eyes, it is clear he has been strangled. Gloucester's earlier Morality abstraction has been terribly literalized. 'Virtue' really *has* been '*choked* with foul ambition'.

After the death of Gloucester, Shakespeare allows things to happen very quickly; or rather, things seem to tumble pell-mell towards disintegration. Holinshed emphasizes that Gloucester's murder brought about the end of the rule of law: 'while the one partie sought to destroie the other, all care of the common-wealth was set aside, and justice and equitie clearlie exiled'. Hall makes clear what an unmitigated disaster the death was – not least, indeed, for the queen herself. She 'procured and consented to the death of this noble man, whose only death brought to pass that thing, which she fain would have eschewed ... if this Duke had lived, the Duke of York durst not have made title to the crown: if this Duke had lived, the nobles had not conspired against the king, nor yet the commons had not rebelled: if this Duke had lived, the house of

INTRODUCTION

Lancastre had not been defaced and destroyed.' If this Duke
had lived – perhaps, no War of the Roses. But this Duke died –
look at the stage – and the roads to chaos are open.

Eruption is the word. The dangerously buzzing commons
threaten to erupt against Suffolk, who is summarily exiled for
Gloucester's murder (no more trials now). This is immediately
followed by the completely unexpected death of Cardinal
Beaufort, raving mad in his bed, as if the pent-up guilt of a
lifetime of ruthless greed and ambition has finally burst within
him. ('So bad a death argues a monstrous life.') Then, the
people erupt in the streets, and at sea. Pirates and mobs
completely dominate the whole of Act IV. The pirates who
capture Suffolk are pure anarchy. Perhaps rather bravely,
Suffolk maintains his contemptuous and haughty 'obscure and
lousy swain' tone with the pirates throughout – or perhaps he
just realizes that nothing he says can help him now. But the
'lieutenant' of the pirates is not your average marauder of the
high seas. Before sending Suffolk off to be killed, he addresses a
long speech to him:

> Ay, kennel, puddle, sink, whose filth and dirt
> Troubles the silver spring where England drinks.
> Now will I dam up this thy yawning mouth
> For swallowing the treasure of the realm;
> Thy lips, that kissed the Queen, shall sweep the ground;
> And thou that smil'dst at good Duke Humphrey's death
> Against the senseless winds shalt grin in vain,
> Who in contempt shall hiss at thee again.
> And wedded be thou to the hags of hell,
> For daring to affy a mighty lord
> Unto the daughter of a worthless king,
> Having neither subject, wealth, nor diadem.
>
> (IV, i, 71–82)

Twenty lines follow, showing a remarkable knowledge of what
has been going on in England since Henry's marriage,
concluding:

> The commons here in Kent are up in arms;
> And, to conclude, reproach and beggary
> Is crept into the palace of our King,

xliii

And all by thee. Away! Convey him hence.

(IV, i, 100–104)

It is as if he is aware of himself as an agent in a scheme of ruthless retributive morality (the Christian cult of *Vindicta Dei*). It is as if *some* sort of law, however archaic, has caught up with Suffolk. He has much to answer for, and we recognize a certain kind of justice as he is hauled off to be beheaded. But as the attendant gentleman comments, the murder is also a 'barbarous and bloody spectacle'. In the world into which we are moving, acts of 'retribution', like the crimes which provoke them, take place in a sickening miasma of evil.

And Jack Cade. Shakespeare's Cade hardly resembles the 'young man of goodly stature and pregnant wit', 'the subtle captain' portrayed by Hall. And, whereas Hall's Cade appreciated 'teachers' and 'privy schoolmasters', Shakespeare's Cade is violently against *all* forms of literacy. Similarly in Holinshed, Cade is 'of goodlie stature and right pregnant wit', and his 'fair promises of reformation' and his (written) 'Complaint of the Commons of Kent' are responsible and sensible. There is none of this in Shakespeare. Shakespeare's Cade and his merry men are a very, very crude lot. Some think this is more evidence of Shakespeare's personal antipathy – he loathed mobs. Perhaps that is not so very hard to understand. But there must be a little more to it than that. *At this point in his pattern*, having shown all English law and order gone to the grave with Humphrey, Shakespeare hardly wants the sudden appearance of a reasonable, civilized, and literate mob-leader, with a manifest respect for law and letters. As Brockbank says, this rebellion must appear as a direct evil consequence of misrule, specifically the misrule of Suffolk (we see this starting when he cruelly tears up the petitions of the conscientious citizens, in I, iii) and the forces of negation which that helped to release. So Shakespeare turned back to the Wat Tyler rebellion of 1381, and took just what he needed for his plan – the killing of the lawyers, the destruction of the Savoy and the Inns of Court, and the burning of the records of the realm. The death of Cade in Iden's all-too-perfect pastoral retreat is not very interesting. Iden is a little mannikin of Tudor order

INTRODUCTION

and degree, and hardly credible. But the way Cade's followers
turn against him is more interesting. Confronting the mob,
Clifford invokes Henry V, with obscure relevance. The mob
immediately cries to follow Clifford. Cade is justified in his
appraisal. 'Was ever feather so lightly blown to and fro, as this
multitude? The name of Henry the Fifth hales them to an
hundred mischiefs and makes them leave me desolate' (IV,
viii, 56–9). Clifford has not dealt with the problem of mob
violence. He has simply found a way to divert it in another
direction. Brockbank is surely right to see distant promise in
this early scenario:

It is assimilated into a firm comprehensive structure, a version of
political and historical tragedy that will serve later as the ground of
Julius Caesar – another play which moves through the plotting and
execution of an assassination, through the generation of lynch law in
the streets, to the deflection of that violence into civil war.

(op. cit., p. 95)

Pirates, mobs, and York and his sons – these are the pheno-
mena which emerge in the post-Humphrey lawless wasteland
of England. As far as Henry is concerned, some 'pirate' is
trying to board his ship of state (IV, ix, 33) – Cade or York, it
hardly matters. Since York started Cade on, it might be felt he
will serve as the representative figure. York, we must feel
(historically this is very unjust), is an adequate progenitor of
that entirely new animal in English history and politics –
Richard. Young Clifford has an eye for the Yorks. 'Why, what
a brood of traitors have we we here!' – and specifically for
Richard:

Hence, heap of wrath, foul indigested lump,
As crooked in thy manners as thy shape!

(V, i, 157–8)

Clifford will become an arguably insane figure of violence in
the next Part. But it is Clifford who speaks some of Shakespeare's most awesome lines about war, starting with an
utterance about the general chaos of war, and moving on to a
long lament for his father whose corpse he has just found (V, ii,
31–65).

xlv

> Shame and confusion! All is on the rout;
> Fear frames disorder, and disorder wounds
> Where it should guard.
>
> (V, ii, 31–3)

These famous lines are not clear to me. The idea of 'fear' 'framing' – arranging, putting in order – anything, hardly sits easily, though when you take into account the fact that the verb could more generally mean simply 'shapes', then it presents no problems. And what should 'disorder' 'guard'? Does it mean that those forces which should be protecting are wounding those in their care? Perhaps. Things are becoming unsettled in the mists of war. And what about the king, whose play this is – what has he been doing? As you might expect, very little. We last see him hopelessly trying to keep up with events until the queen says with pardonable exasperation – 'What are you made of? You'll nor fight nor fly' (V, ii, 74). Clifford helps to pack him off. But he will have to endure a whole further play, during which uncertainties come inseparable from atrocities. It will be the worst.

*

HENRY VI PART 3

The most vivid image of *Henry VI* Part 3 is of a figure of mad energy fighting to escape from a wild wood:

> And I – like one lost in a thorny wood,
> That rends the thorns and is rent with the thorns,
> Seeking a way and straying from the way,
> Not knowing how to find the open air,
> But toiling desperately to find it out –
> Torment myself to catch the English crown:
> And from that torment I will free myself,
> Or hew my way out with a bloody ax.
>
> (III, ii, 174–81)

The old chivalric heroes have gone; the great law-givers have been removed; anarchy is the 'order' of the day. England is ready for the emergence of its most monstrous creation – Richard.

The first two Acts concern the battles of 1460–61, when

Henry was still king, in name. Acts III and IV concern the
manoeuvring of the various parties of nobles with their rival
kings; while the last Act presents the campaigns of 1471 – all
war. Shakespeare had a morass of more or less shapeless
material in front of him, suggesting no one particular dramatic
or moral plan – just victories and defeats, victories and defeats.
(One or two events *did* have an inherent dramatic significance
– the breach of faith of Edward's marriage to Lady Grey; the
perfidiousness of side-changing Clarence; and these Shakespeare duly exploited.) He compressed, streamlined,
amalgamated, telescoped, until the play became a sharpened
study of anarchy – in state, family, and individual – and
disorder itself. The characters appear to have no inner life;
they move like masks through this disintegrating world, and
hardly seem responsible for what they do. They are driven by
primary passions – fury, hate, ambition, lust – and see nothing
outside their own dominant passion and its aims. They
resemble Morality types – vengeful Clifford, holy Henry,
lustful Edward, perjured Clarence, ambitious Richard, she-
wolf Margaret – and seem to be as unchanging. They whirl
around, as if oblivious of the chaos that is their world –
custom, trust, duty, self-control, all forgot. I must here cite an
important point made by Brockbank concerning this
dehumanizing 'characterisation':

So long as the characterisation is neutral the first tetralogy displays a
barbarous providence ruling murderous automatons whose reactions
are predictable in terms of certain quasi-Hobbesian assumptions
about human nature: when argument fails men resort to force; when
an oath is inconvenient they break it; their power challenged, they
retort with violence; their power subdued they resort to lies, murder
or suicide; their honor impugned, they look for revenge; their enemies
at their mercy, they torture and kill them; and if a clash of loyalties
occurs they resolve it in the interest of their own survival. Such might
be the vision of the play's pantomime, but its dimensions are not
confined to its pantomime and to its shallower rhetoric. The anar-
chic, egocentric impulses are not presented as the inescapable laws of
human nature; they are at most manifestations of forces that automa-
tically take over when the constraints of government are withheld.
Law and order cease to prevail when men cease to believe in them,

xlvii

and the process by which this comes about is explored in the play's dominant characters.

(op. cit., p. 98)

The play opens with York and his gang strolling into the parliament house and simply taking possession. Richard throws the head of the Duke of Somerset on the floor, and there is much showing of bloody swords. Indeed, they decide to call it 'the bloody parliament' and resolve to stay there, still in their armour. There is no longer any pretence at, or interest in, public ritual. Henry enters, and his followers immediately want to fall on the Yorkists; but, peace-loving and shrinking from action as always, Henry will not let them 'make a shambles of the Parliament House'. After another of those unresolvable arguments as to who has the stronger title or better claim, Henry suddenly capitulates and offers a shameful deal, saying to York: 'Let me for this my lifetime reign as king ... Enjoy the kingdom after my decease' (I, i, 171, 175). The dismayed reactions of his followers cover the implications of what he has done:

> What wrong is this unto the Prince your son?
> What good is this to England and himself!
> Base, fearful, and despairing Henry!
> How hast thou injured both thyself and us!

(I, i, 176–9)

Henry will remain a curiously isolated figure – in or out of captivity – throughout the play until his death. But while he stands as a permanent protest against the horrors of civil war, and there is a permanent pathos in his continuously disappointed faith in the political efficacy of mercy, pity, and peace, his indisputable 'virtue' ('I'll leave my son my virtuous deeds behind': II, ii, 49) is catastrophic for England at large. It is this betrayal and the craven disinheritance of his son, Edward, that goads the mother, Queen Margaret, to show herself for the Fury she is, as she effectively banishes Henry ('get thee gone': I, i, 258) and, with her son, takes over control of his forces and allies.

Richard soon persuades his father to abandon his promise to allow Henry to see out his life as king:

> And, father, do but think
> How sweet a thing it is to wear a crown,
> Within whose circuit is Elysium
> And all that poets feign of bliss and joy.
>
> (I, ii, 28–31)

Clearly, the actual crown – easy to fetishize – had a disturbing magic and allure all of its own. York says: 'Richard enough; I will be King or die' (I, ii, 35). But what is another act of perjury in a world in which allegiances, loyalties, and the keeping of words, have gone out of fashion?

But Margaret is on the move, along with the mad nihilist Clifford, and we soon see what sort of war we are in for. Clifford finds York's youngest son, Rutland, with his chaplain. He bundles the chaplain out of the way, and turns to little Rutland:

> The sight of any of the house of York
> Is as a Fury to torment my soul;
> And till I root out their accursèd line
> And leave not one alive, I live in hell.
> Therefore –
>
> (I, iii, 30–34)

Therefore, he stabs him to death. This is immediately followed by the capture, and the prolonged baiting and mockery, of York. He is made to stand on a molehill in a vaguely crucifixion pose; he is crowned with a paper crown; and offered a napkin stained with the blood of his freshly murdered son, Rutland. It is an outrageous profanation and mutilation of the ideals (and idols) of kingship, knighthood, fatherhood, womanhood – everything concerning family and state. Margaret evinces a powerful sadistic pleasure in her prolonged mental torturing of York, who is nevertheless allowed a long, powerful speech of recrimination ('She-wolf of France, but worse than wolves of France') of nearly sixty lines, before Margaret and Clifford stab him to death. Shakespeare is just following his sources in showing this whole atrocity as a prolonged, blasphemous inverted ritual. But he clearly wants it to carry more general implications concerning the brutal, anti-chivalric nature of this civil war.

A similar scene is almost re-enacted when, later, Clifford falls in battle. The York boys gather round, as they 'devise fell tortures' for their number one enemy. Fortunately for Clifford, he is already dead though the Yorks, thwarted of their anticipated ghoulish pleasures, can hardly accept the fact. Richard:

> 'Tis but his policy to counterfeit,
> Because he would avoid such bitter taunts
> Which in the time of death he gave our father.
>
> (II, vi, 65–7)

Ideally, Clifford and Richard would like to go on taunting each other, and fighting each other, forever. As psychopaths, they are evenly matched. But Clifford has dropped from the field. And there will be no one else who can take on Richard for a long time.

Henry has been kept entirely apart from the action, so when he appears, he speaks as a solitary, melancholy observer, able to subsume the surgings of the war into the great struggles of nature:

> This battle fares like to the morning's war,
> When dying clouds contend with growing light,
> What time the shepherd, blowing of his nails,
> Can neither call it perfect day nor night.
> Now sways it this way, like a mighty sea
> Forced by the tide to combat with the wind.
> Now sways it that way, like the selfsame sea
> Forced to retire by fury of the wind.
> Sometime the flood prevails, and then the wind;
> Now one the better, then another best;
> Both tugging to be victors, breast to breast,
> Yet neither conqueror nor conquerèd:
> So is the equal poise of this fell war.
> Here on this molehill will I sit me down.
> To whom God will, there be the victory!
>
> (II, v, 1–15)

This is, at least theatrically, the same molehill on which York was mocked, so it is a good site for kingly meditation. And there, Henry draws out his pastoral fantasy:

> O God! methinks it were a happy life,
> To be no better than a homely swain;
> To sit upon a hill, as I do now,
> To carve out dials quaintly, point by point,
> Thereby to see the minutes how they run –
> How many makes the hour full complete,
> How many hours brings about the day,
> How many days will finish up the year,
> How many years a mortal man may live;
> When this is known, then to divide the times –
> So many hours must I tend my flock,
> So many hours must I take my rest,
> So many hours must I contemplate,
> So many hours must I sport myself,
> So many days my ewes have been with young,
> So many weeks ere the poor fools will ean,
> So many years ere I shall shear the fleece.
> So minutes, hours, days, months, and years,
> Passed over to the end they were created,
> Would bring white hairs unto a quiet grave.
> Ah, what a life were this! how sweet! how lovely!
>
> (II, v, 21–41)

It is a dream of a world slowed down to its lowest pulse-rate; a life reduced to seasons and cycles and their repetitions and recurrencies. A life and a world which history does not penetrate and violate. But then, as if in a tableau, two figures carrying corpses enter from different directions. Only now do they realize that one is a father who has just killed his own son; the other a son who has killed his own father. The grief is very stylized and antiphonal, and the theme was a common one, showing up:

> What stratagems, how fell, how butcherly,
> Erroneous, mutinous and unnatural,
> This deadly quarrel daily doth beget!
>
> (II, v, 89–91)

It allows Henry to lament over the whole war:

> Woe above woe! grief more than common grief!
> O that my death would stay these ruthful deeds!
> O, pity, pity, gentle heaven, pity!

li

> The red rose and the white are on his face,
> The fatal colors of our striving houses:
> The one his purple blood right well resembles;
> The other his pale cheeks, methinks, presenteth:
> Wither one rose, and let the other flourish!
> If you contend, a thousand lives must wither.
>
> (II, v, 94-102)

Henry's recipe for peace – 'wither one rose' – has no future, though his desire for peace is manifestly heart-felt. But this rather dream-like little heraldic, or emblematic, tableau-interlude is soon over, and we are back among the real fighting.

In this play that means pre-eminently with Richard. His father, York, had already started to develop the potentialities, and exploit the privileges, of the soliloquy – getting the audience on your side, tapping into its willingness to take a low view of human nature and a completely cynical attitude to politics. In an astonishing speech, Richard shows that he has appropriated the soliloquy prerogative, and is capable of developing it in entirely new ways for his own ends. Nothing would have prepared the audience for this speech, and they would have heard nothing like it in the theatre before. King Edward (as he now is – though the crown shifts between Edward and Henry for the rest of the play) has just announced his determination to marry Lady Grey – he must have his will, and that's that. He exits, looking like a figure for whom kingship means primarily the chance to pursue sexual plea-sure. Henry, we are told, has just been taken to the Tower. Richard stands back and begins to reveal himself:

> Ay, Edward will use women honorably.
> Would he were wasted, marrow, bones and all,
> That from his loins no hopeful branch may spring,
> To cross me from the golden time I look for!
> And yet, between my soul's desire and me –
> The lustful Edward's title burièd –
> Is Clarence, Henry, and his son young Edward,
> And all the unlooked-for issue of their bodies,
> To take their rooms, ere I can place myself:
> A cold premeditation for my purpose!

> Why then, I do but dream on sovereignty;
> Like one that stands upon a promontory,
> And spies a far-off shore where he would tread,
> Wishing his foot were equal with his eye,
> And chides the sea that sunders him from thence,
> Saying, he'll lade it dry to have his way:
> So do I wish the crown, being so far off;
> And so I chide the means that keeps me from it;
> And so (I say) I'll cut the causes off,
> Flattering me with impossibilities
> . . .
> I'll make my heaven to dream upon the crown,
> And, whiles I live, t' account this world but hell,
> Until my misshaped trunk that bears this head
> Be round impalèd with a glorious crown.
> And yet I know not how to get the crown,
> For many lives stand between me and home...
>
> (III, ii, 124–143, 168–173)

Then follow the lines I quoted at the start of this section, about fighting his way out of a wild wood with a bloody axe, hinting at some monstrous, unnatural birth. But it is the final lines that are the most astonishing:

> Why, I can smile, and murder while I smile,
> And cry "Content" to that which grieves my heart,
> And wet my cheeks with artificial tears,
> And frame my face to all occasions.
> I'll drown more sailors than the mermaid shall;
> I'll slay more gazers than the basilisk;
> I'll play the orator as well as Nestor,
> Deceive more slily than Ulysses could,
> And, like a Sinon, take another Troy.
> I can add colors to the chameleon,
> Change shapes with Proteus for advantages,
> And set the murderous Machiavel to school.
> Can I do this, and cannot get a crown?
> Tut, were it farther off, I'll pluck it down.
>
> (III, ii, 182–95)

Richard reveals that he has at his disposal the energies and proclivities of all the other characters – York's steely ambition and crown-hunger; Clifford's dedication to pure violence and

killing; Edward's soft, indulgent pruriences; Margaret's soar-
ing ruthlessness, and so on. And those last lines are addressed
to the audience. He will outplay all the famous dissemblers
and shape-changers of legend and epic. Indeed, he promises
them a performance the like of which has never been seen
before. He will treat history as his theatre, which he will
dominate because he is capable of playing any and every role.
The ground is here laid for the mood and atmosphere of the
first three Acts of *Richard III*.

*

Almost the last atrocity we have to witness is the death of
brave young Prince Edward (Henry's son), who is systemati-
cally stabbed by King Edward, then Richard, then Clarence.
It is brutal butchery, but not, it has to be admitted, so very
different from the stabbing of Rutland at the beginning. The
play is *all* one long butchery. Queen Margaret is so distraught
at the killing of her child that she asks to be killed as well.
Richard, of course, is instantly willing to oblige, but Edward
stays his hand, prompting Richard to say: 'Why should she
live, to fill the world with words?' (V, v, 44). It is a line we may
well have occasion to remember in the next play.

The ultimate confrontation of the play, of the whole trilogy,
is between Henry and Richard. These are the two extreme
products of the terrible years covered by the plays – the
Martyr and the Machiavel, as Brockbank designates them.
Richard has gone to Henry in the Tower, to murder him as
Henry well divines. And, speaking with great moral force and
authority, Henry utters his indictment of Richard:

> And thus I prophesy, that many a thousand,
> Which now mistrust no parcel of my fear,
> And many an old man's sigh and many a widow's,
> And many an orphan's water-standing eye –
> Men for their sons, wives for their husbands,
> Orphans for their parents' timeless death –
> Shall rue the hour that ever thou wast born.
> The owl shrieked at thy birth – an evil sign;
> The night-crow cried, aboding luckless time;
> Dogs howled and hideous tempest shook down trees;

> The raven rooked her on the chimney's top,
> And chatt'ring pies in dismal discords sung.
> Thy mother felt more than a mother's pain,
> And yet brought forth less than a mother's hope,
> To wit, an undigested and deformèd lump,
> Not like the fruit of such a goodly tree.
> Teeth hadst thou in thy head when thou wast born,
> To signify thou cam'st to bite the world.
> And, if the rest be true which I have heard,
> Thou cam'st –
>
> (V, vi, 37–56)

This is quite enough for Richard. 'I'll hear no more. Die, prophet, in thy speech.' And stabs him. One feels that it is the only way this kind of uncompromising moral force can be stopped – pure principle silenced by pure power. This is the final issue of these wars. The prophet dying in his speech may not be quite a tragic death, but it has a dignity not accorded to any of the other victims of the play.

Richard – it is his last soliloquy in this play – accepts the birth, identity, and destiny outlined for him by Henry. He remembers being told he was born with teeth:

> which plainly signified
> That I should snarl and bite and play the dog.
> Then, since the heavens have shaped my body so,
> Let hell make crook'd my mind to answer it.
> I have no brother, I am like no brother;
> And this word 'love', which graybeards call divine,
> Be resident in men like one another
> And not in me: I am myself alone.
>
> (V, vi, 76–83)

I am myself alone. This is the first time but far from the last, that these words are heard in Shakespeare. A certain kind of hard, Renaissance individualism is beginning to speak out, and it can take frightening forms.

The very last scene shows King Edward comfortably enthroned – 'Now am I seated as my soul delights' – talking of autumn and harvests and 'lasting joy'. He points to his young baby who will reap the gain of their labours. Richard has his own ideas about that, as expressed in an aside to the audience:

> I'll blast his harvest, if your head were laid,
> For yet I am not looked on in the world.
> This shoulder was ordained so thick to heave,
> And heave it shall some weight, or break my back.
> Work thou the way, and that shalt execute.
>
> (V, vii, 21–5)

And when he is invited to kiss the baby, he is ready – with the Judas kiss.

> And, that I love the tree from whence thou sprang'st,
> Witness the loving kiss I give the fruit.
> [*Aside*] To say the truth, so Judas kissed his master,
> And cried, "All hail!" whenas he meant all harm.
>
> (V, vii, 31–4)

Richard, unashamedly intending 'all harm', can, by this time, hardly wait to take over the whole historic show. And, by this time, the audience, perhaps, can hardly wait to watch him do it.

*

RICHARD III

Edward IV reigned for quite a long time – some twenty years in all. When Henry VI finally died (was murdered), in 1471, Edward was at last secure and undistracted on the throne; and for the dozen years until his death he was quite a popular king reigning over a stable and recovering England. I mentioned that Hall had a different epithet for the reigns of each of the kings he deals with, and it is worth noting that 'The troublesome season of King Henry the Sixth' is followed by 'The prosperous reign of King Edward the Fourth'. There is *nothing* of this in Shakespeare, and he lets all Edward's good kingly years quietly drop away. Shakespeare's Edward performs effectively only two significant acts – he capitulates shamelessly to his lust for Lady Grey and marries her, and, near the start of *Richard III*, he dies. And that is all. This is seldom commented on, and, indeed, it is hard, *now*, to imagine an *Edward IV* coming between *Henry VI*, and *Richard III*. Yet it is worth a moment's speculation. Perhaps Shakespeare found Edward dramatically uninteresting. But we can be certain that he wanted nothing – for example, a tolerably successful pragmatist – to get in the way of the dramatic contrast between the two extreme types engendered by the wars – meek martyr Henry, and monster Machiavel Richard. At the start of *Richard III*, Henry VI is finally dead and, *as if immediately following this* (in fact it was ten years later), Richard takes over centre-stage, and starts to run literally everything. And there is one more consideration. If Richard was just a singularly nasty historical interruption (to a decade of peace and recovery under Edward), rather than the culmination and final flower of a long-gathering evil (as Shakespeare wants us to feel), then Richmond is less the agent of God, finally bringing peace and reconciliation, and, frankly, more just another Machiavellian, moving in to take over a land in a mess. For all sorts of reasons, Shakespeare does not want his tetralogy to conclude on such a note. His Richmond *is* part of a larger pattern. But, as we contemplate the triumphalist end, it might be worth remembering that the other, less providential, account was probably nearer to the truth of the matter.

*

Richard III is Shakespeare's longest history play. Indeed, it is longer than any of his plays except *Hamlet*, and it is entirely dominated by Richard, rising and falling. He appears in fourteen out of twenty-five scenes, and even when he is not actually present, his shadow hangs over everything. He speaks nearly a third of the lines – i.e. about one thousand out of some three thousand, six hundred. This is completely Richard's play. Shakespeare actually devises more villainies for him than the sources offered. Apart from that, the only scenes which Shakespeare invented are – the wooing of Anne, Clarence's dream, the wailing queens, and the second wooing scene. But it should be noted from the outset that, although the play covers two years of multiplying and accelerating horrors, we see none of them – nothing which might give rise to direct pathos or horror – on stage. Indeed, the only person who actually dies on stage is Richard himself; and that takes place in a flash of dumb-show at the start of the last scene – no death speech for Richard – so that one would be justified in wondering if one had actually seen it. Richard is a very violent man; and yet the play resolutely refuses to allow any of that violence to leak on to the stage. Whatever else, Shakespeare clearly wanted to forestall and prevent any simple 'oh my God, whatever next?' sort of response on the part of the audience. There is nothing to blur and shake us out of sustained, intelligent appreciation.

Early in the third Act, Richard openly acknowledges his theatrical-historical legacy from the Morality play: 'Thus, like the formal Vice, Iniquity, I moralize two meanings in one word' (III, i, 82–3). The Vice was the self-avowed mischief-maker, if not chaos-bringer, and we should remember that one of his satanic privileges was to inveigle the audience into laughing at evil. The figure of the Vice was clearly invaluable to Shakespeare when it came to depicting inexplicable evil, evil which seems gratuitous, unmotivated, simply for its own sake. From any point of view, Richard's behaviour is profoundly irrational, and is finally both horrifying and incomprehensible even to his closest accomplices (in fact, no one is close to him at all; simply, some accompany him further into his evils than others). Richard is, as he has told us, an expert Machiavel; he is also a Senecan tyrant and a Marlovian villain (closest to Barabas in *The Jew of Malta*). But he is primarily a Vice. However – and this is crucial – he is a Vice who acquires (no matter how foully) the legitimate robes of a king. 'On the face of it, he is the demon-Prince, the cacodemon born of hell, the misshapen toad, etc. (all things ugly and ill). But through his prowess as actor and his embodiments of the comic Vice and impish-to-fiendish humour, he offers the false as more attractive than the true (the actor's function), and the ugly and evil as admirable and amusing (the clown's game of value reversals)' (A. P. Rossiter, *Angel with Horns*, p. 20).

Shakespeare emphasizes Richard the actor. When Richard and Buckingham 'dress up' in 'rotten armor, marvellous ill-favored', as if having prepared in desperate haste to defend themselves against an armed plot, Richard briefs Buckingham:

> Come, cousin, canst thou quake and change thy color,
> Murder thy breath in middle of a word,

> And then again begin, and stop again,
> As if thou wert distraught and mad with terror?

Buckingham knows the game:

> Tut, I can counterfeit the deep tragedian,
> Speak and look back, and pry on every side,
> Tremble and start at wagging of a straw,
> Intending deep suspicion. Ghastly looks
> Are at my service, like enforcèd smiles;
> And both are ready in their offices
> At any time to grace my stratagems.
>
> (III, v, 1–11)

Buckingham is, of all the nobles, most fitted to be Richard's henchman and accomplice in crime. Though, of course, Richard finally has his head cut off as well.

We might just stay with the death of Buckingham, since in some ways it is exemplary of an important part of the atmosphere of the play. Asked by the dying King Edward to swear devotion to Queen Elizabeth and the children, Buckingham formulates a rather elaborate oath. He turns to the queen:

> Whenever Buckingham doth turn his hate
> Upon your Grace ...
>   God punish me
> With hate in those where I expect most love!
> When I have most need to employ a friend,
> And most assurèd that he is a friend,
> Deep, hollow, treacherous, and full of guile
> Be he unto me! This do I beg of God,
> When I am cold in zeal to you or yours.
>
> (II, i, 32–40)

This is *exactly* what happens, when Richard, to whom his dedication has been complete, murderously turns on him. Buckingham recognizes this terrible irony:

> That high All-seer which I dallied with
> Hath turned my feignèd prayer upon my head
> And given in earnest what I begged in jest.
>
> (V, i, 20–22)

lix

Something very similar happens to Anne. Confronted by
Richard's preposterous proposal of marriage, she makes a
mighty curse of misery for any future wife of Richard's. She
becomes that wife and discovers she has 'proved the subject of
mine own soul's curse' (IV, i, 80). She is finally whisked off to
death so quietly, you could be forgiven for not noticing it had
happened. Such dire reversals of intention are characteristic.
They are, suggests Rossiter, 'on precisely the pattern of the
repeated reversals of human expectation, the reversals of
events, the anticipated reversals (foreseen only by the
audience), which makes "dramatic irony" '. Rossiter mentions
Buckingham, whose words 'have been reversed into actuality',
and goes on: 'The same irony plays all over *Richard III*. It lurks
like a shadow behind the naively self-confident Hastings; it
hovers a moment over Buckingham when Margaret warns
him against "yonder dog" (Richard), and, on Richard's
asking what she said, he replies, "Nothing that I respect, my
gracious lord" (I, iii, 295) – and this at a time when
Buckingham is under no threat whatever. Its cumulative effect
is to present the personages as existing in a state of total and
terrible uncertainty.' It *is* a terrible state, spreading out like a
toxic fog to affect the ordinary citizens, one of whom says:

> Truly, the hearts of men are full of fear.
> You cannot reason, almost, with a man
> That looks not heavily and full of dread.

(II, iii, 38–40)

Mostly, the people stand silently – waiting for the worst.

*

Richard starts the play with forty lines on his own, and he has
a number of important soliloquies in the first three scenes. The
stage is his. His first speech affords us an important insight into
the man. Everything is fine, now, in Edward's court, and
everyone is happy:

> But I, that am not shaped for sportive tricks
> Nor made to court an amorous looking glass;
> I, that am rudely stamped, and want love's majesty
> To strut before a wanton ambling nymph;

INTRODUCTION

> I, that am curtailed of this proportion,
> Cheated of feature by dissembling Nature,
> Deformed, unfinished, sent before my time
> Into this breathing world scarce half made up,
> And that so lamely and unfashionable
> That dogs bark at me as I halt by them;
> Why, I, in this weak piping time of peace,
> Have no delight to pass away the time
> Unless to spy my shadow in the sun
> And descant on mine own deformity.
> And therefore, since I cannot prove a lover
> To entertain these fair well-spoken days,
> I am determinèd to prove a villain
> And hate the idle pleasures of these days.

(I, i, 14–31)

These are not the words of a man seething with anger, or boiling with resentment. He is as cool as could be. He is *bored*. He is capable of changes of mood of lightning-like suddenness and unpredictability – always disturbing. But – until he becomes king – he is always icily in control. He is elegant, mannered, even fastidious – you will never find a drop of blood on *his* hands. He just wants something fully to engage his intelligence and energies. He wants his fun, and it's going to be dark fun.

> As I am subtle, false, and treacherous,
> This day should Clarence closely be mewed up ...

(I, i, 3–8)

Sit back and watch. Richard's play is about to begin.

His first 'scene' is almost too easy. Clarence is on his way to the Tower, and Richard sympathizes deeply, though he faked the 'evidence' and contrived the arrest. Clarence has no idea what is going on, and as, all-bemused, he is led away, Richard permits himself a joke:

> Simple plain Clarence, I do love thee so
> That I will shortly send thy soul to heaven,
> If heaven will take the present at our hands.

(I, i, 118–20)

Clarence, alas, is a knock-over. But what follows offers a

supreme, histrionic challenge. He determines to woo and win
the hand of Anne, whose husband and father-in-law he
personally murdered. As a project, it sounds not only deeply
distasteful, but utterly impossible. Richard rises to the challenge. (Anne, incidentally, is depicted as taking the body of
Henry VI from St Paul's to the abbey at Chertsey. Although
Henry has been long dead, Shakespeare wants, as I have
suggested, to give us the sense of passing almost immediately
from Henry dead to Richard rampant. Anne's sense of outrage
certainly seem very fresh.) How Richard wins over Anne, who
only has reasons to loathe and execrate him, involves a
dazzling, bravura performance on Richard's part (and on
Shakespeare's – it is all his invention). You've never seen
anything quite like that. Breathtaking. Richard is even rather
impressed at himself.

> Was ever woman in this humor wooed?
> Was ever woman in this humor won?
> I'll have her, but I will not keep her long.
> What! I that killed her husband and his father
> To take her in her heart's extremest hate,
> With curses in her mouth, tears in her eyes,
> The bleeding witness of my hatred by,
> Having God, her conscience, and these bars against me,
> And I no friends to back my suit at all
> But the plain devil and dissembling looks,
> And yet to win her, all the world to nothing!
> Ha!

(I, ii, 227–38)

There's the satisfaction – that of the supreme gambler. The
odds against his success must have been thousands to one – no,
everything to nothing. Yet he pulled it off! Ha!

Richard shows himself in yet another role – the injured
innocent – in the next scene. Queen Elizabeth and some
nobles are wondering gloomily what will happen if Edward
dies and Richard takes over as Protector, when Richard bursts
in, almost beside himself, as it seems, with aggrieved fury.

> They do me wrong, and I will not endure it!
> Who is it that complains unto the King

That I, forsooth, am stern, and love them not?
By holy Paul, they love his Grace but lightly
That fill his ears with such dissentious rumors.
Because I cannot flatter and look fair,
Smile in men's faces, smooth, deceive, and cog,
Duck with French nods and apish courtesy,
I must be held a rancorous enemy.
Cannot a plain man live and think no harm
But thus his simple truth must be abused
With silken, sly, insinuating Jacks?
...
When have I injured thee? When done thee wrong?
Or thee? Or thee? Or any of your faction?
A plague upon you all!

(I, iii, 42–58)

And he scatters accusations and imputations all over them.
It is all shameless, outrageous stuff, of course – a farrago of
nonsense from out of nowhere. But the ferocity of the performance leaves his listeners helpless, and quite unable to answer
in any adequate way. And indeed, subjected to such a mad
torrent of simulated suspicions and fantasized outrage, it is
hard to think where they would begin. Frightening, really.
Out of nothing this man can do anything. (I will note here
that it is in this scene that old Queen Margaret starts to speak
out against Richard. Hers is the voice Richard can never
silence, and she haunts him throughout the play. This is quite
anachronistic, since she died in 1482 and in fact never
returned to England after being ransomed years before. But I
will return to the importance of Queen Margaret.) Richard is
sufficiently pleased at how things went, as he soliloquizes:

I do the wrong, and first begin to brawl.
The secret mischiefs that I set abroach
I lay unto the grievous charge of others
...
But then I sigh, and with a piece of Scripture
Tell them that God bids us do good for evil;
And thus I clothe my naked villainy
With odd old ends stol'n forth of holy writ,
And seem a saint when most I play the devil.

(I, iii, 323–5, 333–7)

This man turns evil into an art.

*

For the first time in the play Richard is absent, for the last
scene of the first Act. This is entirely as it should be, since, for
the first and only time, we see one of his murderous orders
being executed. Usually, all we see is the almost ritual
marching off of people to what will be called in *Henry VIII* 'the
long divorce of steel'. Here we see some of Richard's nasty
business being done for him, as the two murderers enter the
Tower to deal with Clarence. Clarence's dream, which he
describes to his keeper before the arrival of the murderers, is
another of Shakespeare's extraordinary inventions. In dreaming that Richard actually pushed him overboard to drown on
a turbulent Channel crossing, Clarence reveals the accuracy of
his unconscious fears. He describes the horror of drowning,
and the greater horrors that awaited him in the realm after
death as the reproachful ghosts gathered:

> "Clarence is come, false, fleeting, perjured Clarence,
> That stabbed me in the field by Tewkesbury.
> Seize on him, Furies, take him into torment!"
>
> (I, iv, 55-7)

It is like a massive explosion of conscience as the denied guilt of
an evil life comes flooding into the helpless mind. I take it that
Shakespeare thought the case of Clarence would serve as
exemplary of what must have been the hidden state of mind of
many of those around Richard.

Clarence sleeps, and the murderers enter. The Second
Murderer seems disinclined to go through with the job – he
feels 'a kind of remorse' and is resolved to let Clarence live. He
wants to go ahead, but is impeded by 'some certain dregs of
conscience ... yet within me' (I, iv, 122). Then the First
Murderer reminds him of the promised reward, and the
Second Murderer immediately regains his resolve. The
exchange that follows is very important:

First M. Where's thy conscience now?
Second M. O, in the Duke of Gloucester's purse.

First M. When he opens his purse to give us our reward, thy conscience flies out.

Second M. 'Tis no matter, let it go. There's few or none will entertain it.

First M. What if it come to thee again?

Second M. I'll not meddle with it; it makes a man a coward. A man cannot steal, but it accuseth him; a man cannot swear, but it checks him; a man cannot lie with his neighbor's wife, but it detects him. 'Tis a blushing shamefaced spirit that mutinies in a man's bosom. It fills a man full of obstacles. It made me once restore a purse of gold that, by chance, I found. It beggars any man that keeps it. It is turned out of towns and cities for a dangerous thing, and every man that means to live well endeavors to trust himself and live without it.

(I, iv, 129–46)

What *has* happened to conscience in this world? Has it been turned out of towns and banished the land? There seems precious little of it around, though there are vestigial flashes and 'dregs' of it, as in the Second Murderer, and these become increasingly important. The light of conscience never quite goes out entirely. The Murderers finally manage to stab Clarence (the only stabbing we see on stage in this play – contrast the *Henry VI* trilogy), though he presumably expires off-stage in his famous butt of malmsey. But the Second Murderer does not stab, and deplores 'this most grievous murder'. To the First Murderer he says: 'Take thou the fee ... For I repent me that the Duke is slain' (I, iv, 280–81). He may not wish to 'meddle' with conscience, but he cannot prevent conscience from meddling with him.

Shakespeare was clearly fascinated by the question of whether there could be a man *completely* devoid of conscience (i.e. not conscience totally repressed, but just nothing there at all). Iago appears to be his only concession that such a monstrous aberration might occur. Richard seems another candidate, and he certainly shows no trace or hint of conscience throughout the play. But on the eve of the battle of Bosworth (when he will die), in a dream-troubled night of which Clarence's nightmare seems an early adumbration, the avenging ghosts of Richard's victims return to accuse him and he finds his conscience tormentingly awake:

O coward conscience, how dost thou afflict me!
…
My conscience hath a thousand several tongues,
And every tongue brings in a several tale,
And every tale condemns me for a villain.

(V, iii, 180, 194–6)

There was a Richard who would have been quite unmoved by
any inward voice telling him he was a villain. Indeed, it was
his chosen ambition. But this Richard is a broken man, and he
cannot cope with a sudden outburst of something he had never
looked to have.

*

How and why does Richard collapse? It is certainly something
in Richard, since there is not a figure in the play, up to his
gaining of the crown, who is capable of mounting anything
remotely like significant opposition to him. Richard carries on
with his plottings and ordered beheadings – ever the dark
play-master – until he is finally crowned in Act IV. But it
should be noticed that at every step, some accomplice seems to
hold back. The defection of the Second Murderer is the first
sign; then Hastings refuses to see him crowned; Buckingham
baulks at murdering the princes. They are finally murdered by
Tyrrel who, in a long speech, expresses his horror at 'the
tyrannous and bloody act … [this] deed of piteous massacre'
(IV, iii, 1–2). Such compunction is completely alien to the
pitiless Richard, who is unmoved by the deed. He has become
very frightening. But, as he climbs, he empties his world. In *A
Kingdom for a Stage* Robert Ornstein puts it well: 'each of
Richard's triumphs is purchased with a diminishing Machiavellian capital, and though his political debts are self-
liquidating, so too are his political assets. When he gains the
pinnacle of power, he stands alone, isolated from other men by
his criminality, and hated by those whose allegiance he
nominally commands.' As a matter of fact, Richard begins to
crack up the very minute he ascends to the throne, but just
prior to that we have had two unmistakable signs that he has
hit his limit.

In a very short scene, a Scrivener comes on stage with a

paper in hand. It is the entirely false 'indictment of the good Lord Hastings', whom Richard has had beheaded. The Scrivener is revolted by his task:

> Who is so gross
> That cannot see this palpable device?
> Yet who so bold but says he sees it not?
> Bad is the world, and all will come to nought
> When such ill dealing must be seen in thought.
>
> (III, vi, 10–14)

The moral outrage of anonymous servants at the cruel and shameless doing of their 'superiors' is very important in Shakespeare (absolutely crucial in *King Lear*), and at this moment we realize that the whole world is beginning to see through Richard. In the next scene, Buckingham reports back to Richard concerning the response of the London citizens to the proclamation that Richard will be king. 'The citizens are mum, say not a word … they spake not a word,/But like dumb statues or breathing stones/Stared each on other and looked deadly pale' (III, vii, 3, 24–6). This bodes very badly for Richard, since without the 'acclaim' of the people of London, no man could truly be king of England, whatever his claim. Richard will never *really* be king.

As Buckingham hands Richard to the throne, Richard's very first words are:

> But shall we wear these glories for a day?
> Or shall they last, and we rejoice in them?
>
> (IV, ii, 5–6)

This is something new, and potentially fatal, in Richard – anxiety, loss of nerve. He immediately, and utterly pointlessly, decides to test Buckingham, the one man above all others who helped him to the throne. He asks him to murder the princes. 'Shall I be plain? I wish the bastards dead' (IV, ii, 18). Even Buckingham draws back at this – 'Give me some little breath, some pause, dear lord' (IV, ii, 24)' – and Richard immediately, insanely, catastrophically, sets down Buckingham in his mind as an enemy. He has gratuitously alienated his most loyal accomplice. And he is letting his uncertain emotions show: 'The King is angry. See he gnaws his lip' (IV, ii, 27). He becomes permanently irritable, something quite different from the earlier cool, controlled master of his moods. He responds indecisively to news of invasions, and, disastrous for an actor-director, seems to be forgetting his lines:

Ratcliffe. What, may I please you, shall I do at Salisbury?
Rich. Why, what wouldst thou do there before I go?
Rat. Your Highness told me I should post before.
Rich. My mind is changed.

(IV, iv, 453–6)

He no longer knows his own mind: his usually deft plotting hand is faltering. He tries one more wooing, but it entirely lacks the old panache (he thinks he has succeeded, but there is every reason to think that Elizabeth is simply playing for time). He begins to rely on wine:

> Give me a bowl of wine.
> I have not that alacrity of spirit
> Nor cheer of mind that I was wont to have.

(V, iii, 72–4)

He used to be *all* 'alacrity of spirit', and for such a figure to be reduced to relying on stimulants is a terrible falling-off. His desperate attempts to cheer himself up with false jocular bravado – 'Norfolk, we must have knocks; ha, must we not?' (V, iii, 5) – are simply embarrassing. Where is the imperturbable satanic wit of yester-year? He is finally reduced to the supreme indignity of spying on his own troops, to see if any are disloyal:

> Under our tents I'll play the easedropper
> To see if any mean to shrink from me.

(V, iii, 222–3)

This hopeless creature is not even a shadow of his former self. (There are just one or two Macbeth-like hints – 'But I am in/ So far in blood that sin will pluck on sin' (IV, ii, 62–3); and his anger at the messengers who bring him bad news – 'Out on ye, owls! Nothing but songs of death?' (IV, iv, 507). But Richard, while he has also been a bad man and a king, has nothing of Macbeth's extraordinary, searching subjectivity.)

lxviii

INTRODUCTION

When he wakes up from his dreadful dream, the night before the battle of Bosworth, he reveals a state of almost total mental disintegration:

> What do I fear? Myself? There's none else by.
> Richard loves Richard: that is, I am I.
> Is there a murderer here? No. Yes, I am.
> Then fly. What, from myself? Great reason why!
> Lest I revenge. What, myself upon myself?
> Alack, I love myself. Wherefore? For any good
> That I myself have done unto myself?
> O no! Alas, I rather hate myself
> For hateful deeds committed by myself.
> I am a villain. Yet I lie, I am not.
> Fool, of thyself speak well. Fool, do not flatter.
>
> (V, iii, 183–93)

'I am myself alone.' Whatever happened? Is this where such proud, supreme individualism, or impossible egoism, ends? Call it schizophrenia, call it what you like, but this is the self in complete tatters and fragments. Richard, himself alone, the supreme impresario of evil, is ending in gibberish.

Richard was at his best, his most brilliantly adroitly active, in reaching out for a seemingly impossibly remote crown. But he is a completely hopeless king. The minute he takes on that role, he suffers a vertiginous loss of control. Clearly, all his genius is for plotting: he has none at all for ruling. John Danby once made the point that 'in Richard ... the corruption of his time is made aware of itself. This is the ambiguity of his role: to be the logical outcome of his society, and yet a pariah rejected by his society; a hypocrite, yet more sincere in his self-awareness than those he ruins and deceives.' There is an important point here, though it is overstated. In no way is Richard *representative* of his society – he is an aberration, a monster, a permanent outsider. He seems not even to understand what society might be for. But it is true that everyone in the play (except, of course, the princes – and Richmond) is in some way guilty, tainted by the times. It is certainly significant that the word 'guilty' occurs more times in this play than in any other by Shakespeare. Richard manipulates an already fairly rotten world.

lxix

*

As well as Richard's darting, flashing, seemingly improvised way of talking, there is another kind of rhetoric which runs continuously throughout the play, against which Richard's individual voice is heard. This is a formal, incantatory, marmorealizing, ritualized, choric rhetoric of lamentation and mourning, most closely associated with the wailing queens. Dominant here is Queen Margaret, a Senecan Fury, a hideous archaic figure howling for revenge, who is in some ways the voice of the past – of all the treachery and pitiless cruelty and bloody butchery of the long years of civil war. She haunts Richard, who can ignore, but not silence, her. Every word she speaks drips with blood, and she merely hates Richard as a dog rather than condemning him for being a villain. Some quite other voice is needed if England is to break through into a different future.

That voice, of course, is Richmond's. He has been untouched, uncontaminated by the civil wars – this was an important part of the Tudor myth – and can enter as a clean figure, with unbloodied hands. Shakespeare had prepared his audience for the important role Richmond would play, in *Henry VI*, in which King Henry singles out the young Earl of Richmond:

> Come hither, England's hope. (*Lays his hand on his head.*)
>   If secret powers
> Suggest but truth to my divining thoughts,
> This pretty lad will prove our country's bliss.
> His looks are full of peaceful majesty,
> His head by nature framed to wear a crown,
> His hand to wield a scepter, and himself
> Likely in time to bless a regal throne.
> Make much of him, my lords, for this is he
> Must help you more than you are hurt by me.
>
> (*Henry VI*, Part 3, IV, vi, 68–76)

And Somerset immediately resolves to send Richmond away from the gathering anarchy of England:

> Forthwith we'll send him hence to Brittany,
> Till storms be past of civil enmity.
>
> (IV, vi, 97–8)

He is thus the appropriate person to come back back to England, finish off Richard, clear up his mess, and restore peace and concord to the land. Marrying Elizabeth, he is the pious reconciler. As he makes clear in the last speech of the play:

> And then, as we have ta'en the sacrament,
> We will unite the White Rose and the Red.
> Smile heaven upon this fair conjunction,
> That long have frowned upon their enmity!
> What traitor hears me and says not amen?
> England hath long been mad and scarred herself;
> The brother blindly shed the brother's blood,
> The father rashly slaughtered his own son,
> The son, compelled, been butcher to the sire.
> All this divided York and Lancaster,
> Divided in their dire division,
> O, now let Richmond and Elizabeth,
> The true succeeders of each royal house,
> By God's fair ordinance conjoin together!
> . . .
> Now civil wounds are stopped, peace lives again;
> That she may long live here, God say amen!
> (V, v, 18–31, 40–41)

So ends the play, and so begins the Tudor peace. So much was orthodox Elizabethan history, and Shakespeare is happy enough to bring his tetralogy to a conclusion in this way. But it is worth saying one or two things about Shakespeare's Richmond. Although he notionally overcomes Richard, we see no battle (only Richard, famously crying for a horse), and Richmond can hardly be said to 'defeat' Richard who, indeed, rises and falls all by himself. We see nothing of Richmond as a soldier or general, and, indeed, he is hardly individuated at all. He is a curiously transparent figure – more like a principle of Good than a man of action. It is important that he justifies himself as *God's* soldier, fighting against 'God's enemy', 'a bloody tyrant and a homicide' – if a king was a 'tyrant', there was justification for insurrection against him. Richmond must represent his campaign as a crusade and not a coup. He does not offer any genealogical claims to the throne (he had none), and his (doubtful) legitimacy rests on his moral and religious authority. He is not a chivalric hero of the old school – no need to be back to *that*. Something new and post-feudal is called for. He seems to come more from a spiritual realm than a political one. Most importantly, he is just what England needs – someone untouched by the dynastic feuds which have ruined the country. He promises the indispensable fresh start.

I do not want to suggest that Shakespeare is undermining or mocking the Tudor myth (he is perhaps attenuating it), and its insistence that there was a providential pattern running through English history which had to culminate in the blessed arrival of the Tudors. He respects and accepts the frame of that orthodoxy – it is hard to see how he could not have – and Richmond duly takes over. But as we watch the play, we hardly feel we are seeing God's long plan working itself out through English history (the feeling of the whole tetralogy is much more Aeschylean than biblical). As an individual, Richard is too irruptive, disruptive, to participate in, or confirm, any pattern. With his demonic humour and uncontainable energies, he threatens to make a nonsense of the wished-for processional solemnities of history. He challenges all framings and certainties, and with his effortless inversion of any accepted moral order, he brings in ironies and ambiguities everywhere. He has brought Shakespeare to write a new form of what Rossiter calls 'comic history', and, in time, he will develop into Iago, and then Macbeth – as Shakespeare seems to discover that the real truth of history is tragedy.

*

KING JOHN
If *Richard III* and the three parts of *Henry VI* lead up to the Tudor triumph, *King John* foreshadows it in complex ways. It is not surprising that Shakespeare took the reign of King John (1199–1216) as the subject for a history play. As far as the Tudors were concerned, John was the one British king before Henry VIII who had defied the Pope, and the Protestant chroniclers had made a pre-Reformation hero out of him. (Catholic writers stressed John's subsequent re-surrender of

his crown to the Pope, which meant that Henry VIII was only a vassal and his Reformation a civil and ecclesiastical rebellion.) John Bale's *Kynge Johan*, first written in 1536 (two years after Henry VIII's Act of Supremacy), is arguably the first time the history play begins to emerge from the Morality play, as it concentrates on an actual king in a specific historical moment (that Bale's King John bears little resemblance to what we know of the actual John is not, here, relevant). It was a violently anti-Catholic play which praised John for his opposition to the Pope, and his attack on the abuses of the Church. *The Troublesome Raigne of King John of England* was published anonymously in 1591, and it supports Bale's picture of John as a victim of papal and French plots and ambition. But it also, following Holinshed's more critical account of John, shows him to be a weak and violent man, who could alternate between a resourceful alacrity of response and a fatal inertia. After John expediently submits to the Pope's legate, Pandulph, everything goes wrong for him, until he is poisoned by a monk (for Protestant apologists, this made him a martyr to the Catholics). Most scholars have regarded this as Shakespeare's source-play, which he studied and re-wrote.

There were also perceived similarities between the reigns of John and Elizabeth which gave the play a topical bite. Like John, Elizabeth defied the Pope and was excommunicated, with the Pope promising her murderer canonization; and, like John, she was attacked by a Catholic monarch (Philip II of Spain) who tried to invade England, but whose armada was destroyed at sea (as is the armada of Philip of France in the play). In addition, neither John nor Elizabeth were entirely secure in their claims to the throne, and both had rivals supported by Catholics. John's rival claimant was Arthur, son of his elder brother Geoffrey, who was supported by King Philip of France and the Papacy. Elizabeth's rival was Mary Stuart, Queen of Scots, supported by the Spanish King and Papacy (and many English Catholics). Both claimants or pretenders were barred from the crown by a royal will. John's desire for Arthur's death, and subsequent remorse for it, could be seen as comparable to Elizabeth's handling of the problem of Mary Stuart – by execution – and subsequent troubled feelings (Irving Ribner says that 'adherents of the cause of Mary ... had traditionally used John's treatment of Arthur as an example of usurpation parallel to Elizabeth's treatment of Mary Stuart'). There were further similarities – between the position of Hubert, ordered by John to murder Arthur and then violently blamed by the King for having (as he thinks) done it; and Secretary Davidson, who was rumoured to have been persuaded by Elizabeth to have Mary murdered, but who was subsequently made a scapegoat, fined and imprisoned. Bullough thinks that some of these allusions, or similarities, were too dangerous for Shakespeare to have intended them; but, for the informed eye, they were – and are – undoubtedly there to see.

*

King John has been called Shakespeare's most unhistorical play. It certainly plays fast and loose with facts and time. It is incredibly compressed. One scene, for instance (Act IV, ii), brings together events which cover just about John's whole reign: the seeing of the five moons (1200); the death of Constance (1201); the (rumoured) death of Arthur and the second coronation of John (1202); the death of John's mother, Elinor (1204); the Peter of Pomfret episode (1213); and the landing of the French (1216). In the last century, one P. A. Daniel pointed out that the whole reign is made to seem a matter of a few months, and that the action actually requires only seven separate days, with intervals. Shakespeare sometimes liked to collapse and foreshorten historic time in this dramatic way (most notoriously in *Othello*), and here it serves to jam cause and effect very tightly together.

To what end? John emerges as a very defective king. At times, he fulfills his traditional, dignified monarchical role and issues ringing defiance to his enemies. But for the most part he is shown as weak and treacherous – mean, manipulative, and opportunistic – before his final collapse into utter impotence, and poisoned madness. He does defy the Pope – but for purely political and financial reasons; and he is quick to hand his crown back to Pandulph, the papal legate, when expediency demands. The increasingly discontented barons duly defect from John and go over to the French, and England is consequently, and shamefully, invaded. (It is notable that Shakespeare never mentions Magna Carta (1215), forced on John by the nobles to retain their ancient rights.) England is finally saved by the timely sinking of the French supply ships, the adroit political manoeuvring of Pandulph, and the revelation of the French lord Melun which sends the rebellious English barons hurrying back to the English side. No great victories: no outstanding heroes.

John Masefield thought the play to be primarily a study in treachery, and, indeed, it is full of traitors and turncoats; changing sides, yielding to shifting solicitations and pressures, breaking oaths as soon as they have made them, abandoning sworn loyalties as the wind changes. Some examples of completely hollow rituals of allegiance would include: Arthur willingly embracing Austria (who killed his father); the cynical marriage of Lewis and Blanche; Philip's oath to Constance ('In her right we came,/Which we, God knows, have turned another way,/To our own vantage': II, i, 548–50); John forcing new oaths of allegiance out of his nobles at his second coronation; John's show of renewed allegiance to the Pope as he hands his crown back to Pandulph; and the revelation of the dying Melun to the English lords which, though a good deed in itself (he confesses that the French intend to kill the defecting English lords once victory has been achieved), does break his oath to the Dauphin, who in turn intended to break his oath to the English nobles, who had already broken their oaths of loyalty to the English king – showing, graphically enough, how one broken oath leads to another!

This aspect of the atmosphere of the play is best exemplified by the exchange between the French king, Philip, and the papal legatee, Pandulph. Peace between England and France has just been sealed by the marriage of Blanche and the Dauphin. Pandulph enters, demanding to know why John has spurned the Pope's choice in the appointing of the new Archbishop of Canterbury. John is peremptorily dismissive – 'no Italian priest/Shall tithe or toll in our dominions' etc. (this was the sort of defiant stuff the English Protestants loved). Pandulph duly curses and excommunicates John (though, of course, he will later help him); and he orders the Catholic Philip to turn his forces against the English king. To his credit, Philip is torn:

> I am perplexed, and know not what to say
> ...
> This royal hand and mine are newly knit,
> And the conjunction of our inward souls
> Married in league, coupled and linked together
> With all religious strength of sacred vows;
> The latest breath that gave the sound of words
> Was deep-sworn faith, peace, amity, true love
> Between our kingdoms and our royal selves
> ...
> And shall these hands, so lately purged of blood,
> So newly joined in love, so strong in both,
> Unyoke this seizure and this kind regreet?
> *Play fast and loose with faith?* so jest with heaven,
> *Make such unconstant children of ourselves*
> As now again to snatch our palm from palm,
> *Unswear faith sworn,* and on the marriage bed
> Of smiling peace to march a bloody host,
> And make a riot on the gentle brow
> Of true sincerity?
>
> (III, i, 147, 152–8, 165–74 – my italics)

Surely not. It would be intolerable so to turn the back on all the values a Christian king is supposed to believe in. But Pandulph is adamant. Let go of England's hand, and prepare to fight. Philip still complains, resists:

> I may disjoin my hand, but not my faith.

To which Pandulph replies with a masterpiece of casuistry which is one of the central speeches of the play.

> So mak'st thou faith an enemy to faith,
> And like a civil war set'st oath to oath,
> Thy tongue against thy tongue ...
> What since thou swor'st is sworn against thyself
> And may not be performèd by thyself,
> For that which thou has sworn to do amiss
> Is not amiss when it is truly done;
> And being not done, when doing tends to ill,

The truth is then most done not doing it.
The better act of purposes mistook
Is to mistake again; though indirect,
Yet indirection thereby grows direct,
And falsehood falsehood cures, as fire cools fire
Within the scorchèd veins of one new burned.
It is religion that doth make vows kept,
But thou hast sworn against religion
(By what thou swear'st against the thing thou swear'st)
And mak'st an oath the surety for thy truth
(Against an oath the truth); thou art unsure
To swear – swears only not to be forsworn,
Else what a mockery should it be to swear!
But thou dost swear only to be forsworn,
And most forsworn, to keep what thou dost swear ...

(III, i, 189–213 – my italics)

and endlessly more of the same. This was the kind of Jesuitical 'equivocation' which drove Elizabethan Protestants mad. Philip duly capitulates – 'England, I will fall from thee'. In an atmosphere in which such a speech can dominate and prevail, it is going to be very hard to work out, or hold onto, what might genuinely constitute 'honour', 'loyalty', 'true duty', not to mention 'majesty' and 'nobility'. It is all very unedifying.

*

If this is all there was to it, it would be a lowering play indeed; and one might well have asked – what was Shakespeare trying to show – if not, more simply, why did he write the play? But I have yet to mention its most important feature – the invention of the Bastard, Philip Faulconbridge, supposedly the illegitimate son of Richard Coeur de Lion, the previous king. There is simply a brief reference in Holinshed to the effect that 'Philip, bastard sonne to king Richard ... killed the vicount of Limoges, in revenge of his father's death.' The author of *The Troublesome Raigne* developed this hint into a dynamic character who both brings comic relief, and manifests heroic energy. Shakespeare took this figure and, in turn, developed him into, arguably, his most powerfully original creation to date. Critics and commentators have compared and related him to

numerous other Shakespearian characters: these include –
Petruchio, Berowne, Mercutio, Falstaff, Touchstone, Jacques,
Autolycus, and Henry V (he is contrasted with the bad
bastards, Don John and Edmund). Of these, the most relevant
as far as I am concerned are – it sounds a curious conjunction
– Falstaff and Henry V. But Shakespeare has clearly created a
complex, multi-faceted character who is in many ways seminal
for his own work.

Before considering the Bastard, I must point to two highly
relevant changes Shakespeare made to his sources. In the play,
John is a self-acknowledged usurper (he does not object when
Chatillion rudely refers to his 'borrowed majesty' – I, i, 4; and
his mother reminds him of 'your strong possession much more
than your right' – I, i, 40), while Arthur is offered as having
much more 'right' to the crown. But historically – the chroniclers agree – John's claim to the throne was quite as strong as
Arthur's, and, since Richard I had named him as his heir,
possibly stronger. (In medieval times, primogeniture was not
the sole justification for succession. The 'designation' by the
previous, dying, king of his preferred successor could be
equally important.) And, while Arthur is a young warrior in
Holinshed, Shakespeare turns him into a feeble, helpless child.
Thus, not only do we have 'possession' versus 'right'; we have
a *de facto* king who turns out not to have the qualities to make a
good ruler, and we have a *de jure* 'king' who would clearly
prove hopeless and disastrous were he to be installed on the
throne. This leaves the way clear for the appearance of a
character who, though having neither 'right' nor 'possession',
manifests the desirable, requisite kingly characteristics. And
this, indeed, is one of the Bastard's roles. He develops and
holds onto a true concept of 'honour'; he renews the proper
meaning of 'loyalty' and 'duty' by remaining unflaggingly
steadfast in his support of king and country; he doesn't turn his
coat or change his side, and he never 'plays fast and loose with
faith' or, indeed, anything else. If this were all he was, he
would simply be an idealized stereotype of patriotism etc. But
he is a good deal more complex and interesting than that.

We first encounter him when he and his legitimate half-
brother, Robert, are brought before the king, who is asked to

adjudicate in an argument they are having over the inheriting of the Faulconbridge lands. The Bastard's first words – to the king – are 'Your faithful subject' (I, i, 50), and so, importantly, he proves to be. Indeed, when, later, the English nobles defect to the French, it is as if he is the *only* 'faithful subject' remaining loyal to the king. He knows that John is a bad and defective king – indeed, he has to take over from him when the French invade ('Have thou the ordering of this present time,' says the helpless John – V, i, 77) – but he remains faithful to the kingly office (let's say the symbol more than the man), and never permits himself any thoughts of removing or supplanting the king. Even when the present order is weakened and in disarray, he defends it against any insidiously, or treacherously, suggested alternative. In the quarrel with his half-brother, he gives up his claim quite cheerfully, with a characteristic insouciance and unusual indifference to possessions – 'Brother, take you my land, I'll take my chance' (I, i, 151). The king immediately knights him – 'Arise Sir Richard, and Plantagenet' (I, i, 162) – and the Bastard is happier to have the 'honor' of being the knighted son of Richard Coeur de Lion than to inherit any lands. His developing conception of 'honor' – he is still learning – is crucial to the play, peopled as it is, for the most part, with varyingly dishonourable characters. And he has a touch of that Renaissance sense of the reality and integrity of his own identity – 'And I am I, howe'er I was begot' (I, i, 175). Whatever else, he is clearly his own man.

Shortly after, he has his first soliloquy. It starts, understandably enough, with a bit of summarizing musing:

> A foot of honor better than I was,
> But many a many foot of land the worse.
>
> (I, i, 182–3)

But what follows is rather remarkable:

> Well, now can I make any Joan a lady.
> "God den, Sir Richard!" – "God-a-mercy, fellow" –
> And if his name be George, I'll call him Peter,
> For new-made honor doth forget men's names:
> 'Tis too respective and too sociable

For your conversion. Now your traveler,
He and his toothpick at my worship's mess,
And when my knightly stomach is sufficed,
Why then I suck my teeth and catechize
My pickèd man of countries: "My dear sir" –
Thus, leaning on mine elbow, I begin ...

(I, i, 184–94)

and so he goes on, fantasizing a posturing, pretentious
encounter. Shakespeare does this elsewhere – has a character
on-stage now, in front of us, going through, in imagination,
future scenarios in which he exercises and deploys some new-
won position and power; but, to my knowledge, this is the first
time he attempts it, and the effect is curiously arresting – it
adds a dimension to the character. Here it is comic of course;
the Bastard is having fun with imagining the possibilities
opened up by his new title. More seriously, it suggests he
might be preparing for a career of courtly affectation and
ambition. This impression is both strengthened and qualified
by some important lines which follow:

But this is worshipful society,
And fits the mounting spirit like myself;
For he is but a bastard to the time
That doth not smack of *observation*.
And so am I, whether I smack or no:
And not alone in habit and device,
Exterior form, outward accoutrement,
But from the inward motion to deliver
Sweet, sweet, sweet poison for the age's tooth,
Which, *though I will not practice to deceive,
Yet, to avoid deceit, I mean to learn*;
For it shall strew the footsteps of my rising.

(I, i, 205–16 – my italics)

This certainly seems to suggest that he is preparing for a career
of calculated social climbing ('mounting'). The determination
to deliver a triply sweet 'poison' to 'the age's tooth', should
indicate a commitment to limitless ingratiation and flattery. If
he is going to move into a world of deceit, he will out-deceive
them all. But although 'observation' can mean obsequiousness, it can also mean straightforward, vigilant, clear-eyed

INTRODUCTION

attention. And the lines I have italicized could well mean –
though I have no intention to be dishonest myself, I am
certainly going to watch out for, and self-protectively learn, all
the dishonest tricks going on around me. He could be resolving
to lead an honest life in a world in which everything seems to
make against such an intention. Although the Bastard will
come to embrace what seem like simplicities – king and
country; he is not, as I have indicated, a simple character.

For the next two Acts, as the English and French kings and
nobles spar for positions in France, the Bastard is something of
a loose cannon. He makes ironic, realistic comments (he is,
indeed, an 'observer'), in particular mocking and goading the
Duke of Austria, to the latter's mounting irritation and
discomfiture (Austria would be wearing the famous lion skin
of Richard Coeur de Lion whom he had killed, which is
provocation enough for Richard's spirited son who will,
shortly, kill Austria and retrieve the skin). His caustic comments on the follies of the main players have made some critics
deem him a cynic (hence the Touchstone, Jacques compari-
sons, etc.), but this seems to me wrong. He is more of a
potential Falstaff, an ironic realist, contemptuous of the
rhetorical hypocrisies and mendacities circulating around
him. At the impasse in front of Angiers when, after some
pointless but bloody fighting, both kings claim victory and the
right of entrance, the Bastard comments:

Ha, majesty! How high thy glory tow'rs
When the rich blood of kings is set on fire!
O now doth death line his dead chaps with steel;
And now he feasts, *mousing the flesh of men
In undetermined differences of kings.*

(II, i, 350–55 – my italics)

The compressed power of those last two lines is, I think,
something new in Shakespeare, and marks a sudden step
closer to his mature style. Certainly, at times the speech of the
Bastard represents a qualitatively new burst of linguistic
energy. This is nowhere more clear than in the Bastard's
reaction to the cynically proposed, politic marriage of Blanche
and the Dauphin. Hubert of Angiers, who suggests the mar-

riage, conceals the motivating cynicism under an excessively cosmetic, hyperbolic rhetoric. This way of talking is anathema to the Bastard, who is ever a plain speaker:

> Here's a large mouth, indeed,
> That spits forth death and mountains, rocks and seas
> ...
> Zounds! I was never so bethumped with words
> Since I first called my brother's father dad.
>
> (II, i, 457–8, 466–7)

But it is the marriage itself that repels him. First, because the Dauphin, with his empty, insincere and formulaic love rhetoric, strikes him as horrible ('In such a love so vile a lout as he' – II, i, 509). Secondly, because Blanche in her honesty – 'Further I will not flatter you, my lord' (II, i, 516) – and her obedience – she will do, she says, 'That she is bound in honor still to do' (II, i, 522) – reveals to the Bastard a notion of 'honor' which nothing he has so far seen can match. At the end of the scene, he sums up what he feels about all the manoeuvrings he has been watching. This is the famous 'Commodity' soliloquy (it is the first time Shakespeare used the word) and it is one of the most important speeches in early Shakespeare – again, it is a new step. The speech should be studied in its entirety (II, i, 561–98), but some lines must be singled out. After his opening comprehensive comment – 'Mad world! Mad kings! Mad composition!' – the Bastard goes over what he has seen, and decides on a word for the kind of unprincipled self-interest which seems to determine almost everyone's actions. It is 'that sly devil ... That daily break-vow' –

> That smooth-faced gentleman, tickling commodity,
> Commodity, the bias of the world,
> The world, who of itself is peisèd well,
> Made to run even upon even ground,
> Till this advantage, this vile drawing bias,
> This sway of motion, this commodity,
> Makes it take head from all indifferency,
> From all direction, purpose, course, intent.
> And this same bias, this commodity,
> This bawd, this broker, this all-changing word ...
>
> (II, i, 573–82)

INTRODUCTION

There is a reference to bowling in *The Taming of the Shrew*, but this is Shakespeare's first extended use of what was to become a favourite metaphor. Since, in bowls, the ball always had a 'bias' or weight in one side, it never went straight. The possibilities of the image are many and obvious. To the Bastard's eye, apart from pawns like Blanche and victims like Arthur, everybody has a built-in 'bias' which he calls 'commodity' – self-servingness, expediency, compliance, casuistry, opportunism, compromise, vow-breaking; it has a hundred names – and nobody maintains a straight course, variously abandoning fixed resolves, and deviating from set intentions. And note – 'this all-changing word'. A casuist like Pandulph can, with the 'right', specious words, change 'treachery' into 'loyalty' – and vice versa – in a matter of seconds. The implications are frightening. Anything can be changed into anything. What, then, becomes of stable values, or indeed any of the settled meanings by which we orient ourselves? That way, chaos.

The Bastard has seen – and learned – a lot: his 'observing' has carried him far. But then come some unexpected lines which have confused some critics:

> And why rail I on this commodity?
> But for because he hath not wooed me yet:
> Not that I have the power to clutch my hand,
> When his fair angels would salute my palm,
> But for my hand, as unattempted yet,
> Like a poor beggar, raileth on the rich.
> Well, whiles I am a beggar, I will rail
> And say there is no sin but to be rich;
> And being rich, my virtue then shall be
> To say there is no vice but beggary.
> Since kings break faith upon commodity,
> Gain, be my lord, for I will worship thee!

> (II, i, 587–98)

This seems plain enough – since Commodity reigns, he will submit to its rule. But this is to miss the tone, which is more like – 'I'm probably going on like this because I've never actually been directly tempted; very likely, given the chance, I'd jump at the offer of some corrupt money. Probably, this is

lxxxiii

all envy and, if I became rich, I might well change my tune. Anyway, seeing what kings do, I'd better prepare for a comparable change in myself.' The Bastard is growing in self-knowledge and self-awareness; and there is a lot of protective, excessive self-honesty in these lines – the kind of honesty that over-accuses itself, damns itself in advance, in order to guard against self-righteous, self-deceiving complacency. We are watching, and hearing, the Bastard learn. This man will never be a hypocrite.

The next episode in which the Bastard plays a major role, shows him to considerable advantage. It follows the sequence in which Hubert goes to put out Arthur's eyes; decides to let Arthur live; and then Arthur, trying to escape, jumps to his death from the castle walls. The English nobles, already disaffected from King John, now pretend to uncontainable horror at what they assume to be the murder of Arthur ordered by the King. As their simulated outrage approaches hysteria, the Bastard counsels calm – and good manners:

> Whate'er you think, good words, I think were best.
> ... 'twere reason you had manners now.
>
> (IV, iii, 28, 30)

When they find Arthur's corpse, the nobles leap to the worst conclusions and try to outdo each other in hyperbolic expressions of horror. Only the Bastard keeps balance and sanity:

> It is a damnèd and a bloody work,
> The graceless action of a heavy hand,
> *If that it be the work of any hand.*
>
> (IV, iii, 57–9 – my italics)

He, and he alone, wisely reserves judgement. When Hubert appears, the nobles simply want to 'cut him to pieces'. The Bastard maintains order – 'Keep the peace, I say'; and to the over-inflamed Salisbury – 'Your sword is bright, sir; put it up again' (IV, iii, 79 – a memorable line anticipating, of course, Othello at his initially most authoritative). The nobles leave with their tails between their legs, heading for the French. It is a very impressive performance on the Bastard's part. This is indeed a mature, stalwart, authoritative figure – as solid as rock.

Left alone with Hubert, he says – *if* in fact you *did* do the murder –

> do but despair,
> And if thou want'st a cord, the smallest thread
> That ever spider twisted from her womb
> Will serve to strangle thee! A rush will be a beam
> To hang thee on.
> . . .
> I do suspect thee very grievously.
>
> (IV, iii, 126–30, 134)

But he accepts Hubert's protestations of innocence, and tells him to carry away Arthur's body. There follows a moment of bemusement, and another crucial speech.

> I am amazed, methinks, and lose my way
> Among the thorns and dangers of this world.
> . . .
> Now for the bare-picked bone of majesty
> Doth doggèd war bristle his angry crest
> And snarleth in the gentle eyes of peace:
> Now powers from home and discontents at home
> Meet in one line, and vast confusion waits,
> As doth a raven on a sick-fall'n beast,
> The imminent decay of wrested pomp.
> Now happy he whose cloak and center can
> Hold out this tempest. Bear away that child,
> And follow me with speed: I'll to the King.
> A thousand businesses are brief in hand,
> And heaven itself doth frown upon the land.
>
> (IV, iii, 140–41, 148–59)

He is briefly lost, and is not sure where he stands; then – the images are very powerful – he surveys the imminent chaos and loss of centre as the rebellious English lords join up with the French; then – crucially – he decides upon immediate action (lots to be done), and a resolute direction and commitment – 'I'll to the King'. This is a man now capable of making up his mind in the midst of 'vast confusion'. Invaluable.

Throughout the last act, the Bastard, in effect, takes over

trying to organize the defence of England against the French. First he attempts to rouse the king to kingly behaviour:

> But wherefore do you droop? Why look you sad?
> Be great in act, as you have been in thought;
> Let not the world see fear and sad distrust
> Govern the motion of a kingly eye;
> Be stirring as the time; be fire with fire.

(V, i, 44–8)

To no avail – the king has handed power over to Pandulph to try to arrange an agreed peace. This is 'inglorious' to the Bastard, who does not think that England should

> make compromise,
> Insinuation, parley, and base truce
> To arms invasive.

(V, i, 67–9)

He is for direct, honest confrontation – 'stirring' and meeting fire with fire – and he now speaks for the king and with a king's voice. It is notable that when he goes to speak to the French directly, he says:

> According to the fair-play of the world,
> Let me have audience ...

(V, ii, 119–20)

There is precious little 'fair-play' in the world we have seen, and it is almost as if he is appealing to some forgotten ideal – an ideal which, however, he himself has come to embody. 'Fair-play' is what you respect if you haven't gone over to 'commodity'. To the French he says:

> Now hear our English king,
> For thus his royalty doth speak in me ...

(V, ii, 128–9)

and he duly utters a long speech of kingly defiance (this is his Henry V side). By this time, he *is* to all intents and purposes 'king', and we feel him to be such – though historically we know this cannot happen. Shakespeare here takes his play as near to the radical re-writing of history – pushing it off in another direction – as it was possible for him to go.

This is the point of the final scene, in which Prince Henry, John's son and legitimate heir to the throne, suddenly appears. Not only have we not seen him before; no mention has been made of him (nor, indeed, of John's wife, Isabel). It is as if Shakespeare has been deliberately holding him back while we watch the unimpeded growth of the Bastard into the true kingly figure which, in the event, England did not get (or, at least, not until Henry V). To the end, the Bastard sees his job as:

> To push destruction and perpetual shame
> Out of the weak door of our fainting land ...
>
> (V, vii, 77–8)

But, with the appearance of the true heir, he abdicates his leadership, and turns and kneels:

> To whom, with all submission, on my knee,
> I do bequeath my faithful services
> And true subjection everlastingly.
>
> (V, vii, 103–5)

He is a figure, now, of truly selfless loyalty. Prince Henry's task, says Salisbury, referring to the mess John has made of England, is

> To set a form upon that indigest
> Which he hath left so shapeless and so rude.
>
> (V, vii, 26–7)

The Bastard, we feel, would be a better man for that job. But real history makes its impositions, and marches on. Still, it is given to the Bastard to voice the concluding sentiment of the play – a very important one to the Elizabethans, always afraid of the possibility of civil war:

> Naught shall make us rue
> If England to itself do rest but true!
>
> (V, vii, 117–18)

King John is a new kind of history play for Shakespeare. There is no shadow of the Morality play in the background; nor are there any ritual elements – in the action or in the language (we hear none of the antiphonal exchanges audible in *Richard III*). I have not mentioned some of the elements of the play – the pathos of young Arthur pleading with Hubert not to put out his eyes; the hysterical, though often powerful, complaints and laments of the demented Constance (she dies 'in a frenzy') – in her speeches a descendant of Queen Margaret. But it is clear to me that by far its most important feature is the development of the imaginary character, the Bastard. It *is* worth noting, as E. A. J. Honigman pointed out in his magisterial edition, that certain key words occur more often in this play than in any other Shakespeare play. These include 'blood' (40 times) and 'right' (28 times). The recurrence of 'right' is perhaps hardly surprising since much of the play consists of endless debating about what, in this world where the 'morality' of politics is discussed in terms of games ('Have I not here the best cards for the game/To win this easy match played for a crown?' – V, ii, 105–6) and one good treachery deserves another ('Paying the fine of rated treachery/Even with a treacherous fine of all your lives' – V, iv, 37–8), 'right' actually is, and what *is* 'right'. Perhaps only the Bastard gets and keeps a fast hold on this. 'Blood' lines up with other frequently occurring words referring to parts of the body – 'hand' (52), 'eye' (47), 'arm' (27), 'breath' (18), 'mouth' (14), 'foot' (12), 'brow' (11), 'bosom' (10), 'tooth' and 'teeth' (5), 'spleen' (4), 'bowels' (3) – this is a lot in a comparatively short (2,600 lines) play. It certainly indicates that this is an intensely corporeal play: the emphasis is very much on the body and there is very little sense of the transcendent or the spiritual. In a world dominated by 'commodity', the body is, as it were, the central commodity. Again, this is a new feeling in Shakespeare. But I stay and end with the Bastard as the crucial invention and innovation. He represents the introduction of a new (and fictitious) comic-heroic element into the history play, which will enable Shakespeare to progress to his supreme achievements in the genre – *Henry IV*, Parts 1 & 2.

King's College, Cambridge   Tony Tanner

SELECT BIBLIOGRAPHY

BIOGRAPHY

The standard biography is now Samuel Schoenbaum, *William Shakespeare: A Documentary Life*, Oxford University Press, Oxford, 1975. A shortened version of this excellent volume was published in 1977. For those interested in Shakespearian mythology, Schoenbaum has also produced *Shakespeare's Lives*, Clarendon Press, Oxford, 1970, a witty dissection of the myriad theories concerning the playwright's identity and the authorship of the plays. Rather in the same vein is Anthony Burgess, *Shakespeare*, Penguin, London, 1972, a lively introduction to the presumed facts of the poet's life, enhanced by novelistic licence.

BIBLIOGRAPHY

Among the vast quantity of Shakespeare criticism it is probably only useful to list texts which are both outstanding and easily available. This I do below. For further information the serious student may consult the bibliographies of works listed. There are also three major journals which record the flow of critical work: the *Shakespeare Quarterly*; and the *Shakespeare Survey* and *Shakespeare Studies* which are published annually.

CRITICISM

The two indispensable Shakespearian critics are Johnson and Coleridge. Their dispersed comments are collected in *Samuel Johnson on Shakespeare*, ed., H. R. Woodhuysen, Penguin, London, 1989, and S. T. Coleridge, *Shakespearian Criticism*, two vols., Everyman's Library, London, 1960.

THE HISTORY PLAYS: GENERAL

BROCKBANK, J. P., *On Shakespeare*, 1989.
BURDEN, DENNIS H., 'Shakespeare's History Plays: 1952–1983', *Shakespeare's Studies* (1985).
CAMPBELL, LILY B., *Shakespeare's Histories: Mirrors of Elizabethan Policy*, 1947.
DANBY, J. F., *Shakespeare's Doctrine of Nature*, 1961.
DOLLIMORE, JONATHAN, *Political Shakespeare*, 1985.
HAMILTON, A. C., *The Early Shakespeare*, 1967.
HOLDERNESS, GRAHAM, *Shakespeare Recycled*, 1992.
KANTOROWITZ, E. H., *The King's Two Bodies*, 1957.

HISTORIES

KELLY, H. A., *Divine Providence in the England of Shakespeare's Histories*, 1970.

KERNAN, ALVIN B., '*The Henriad*: Shakespeare's major history plays', in *Modern Shakespeare Criticism*, ed. Alvin Kernan, 1970.

KNIGHT, G. WILSON, *The Olive and the Sword*, 1944.

KNIGHTS, L. C., *Some Shakespearean Themes*, 1959.

ORNSTEIN, ROBERT, *A Kingdom for a Stage: the achievement of Shakespeare's history plays*, 1972.

PALMER, JOHN, *Political Characters of Shakespeare*, 1945.

PATER, WALTER, 'Shakespeare's English Kings' in *Appreciations*, 1889.

PIERCE, ROBERT B., *Shakespeare's History Plays: The Family and the State*, 1971.

PRIOR, MOODY E., *The Drama of Power*, 1973.

REESE, MAX MEREDITH, *The Cease of Majesty: A Study of Shakespeare's Plays*, 1961.

RIBNER, IRVING, *The English History Play in the Age of Shakespeare*, 1957.

ROSSITER, A. P., *Angel with Horns*, 1961.

SACCIO, PETER, *Shakespeare's English Kings: History, chronicle and drama*, 1977.

TENNENHOUSE, LEONARD, *Power on Display*, 1986.

TILLYARD, E. M. W., *The Elizabethan World Picture*, 1943.

TILLYARD, E. M. W., *Shakespeare's History Plays*, 1944.

WHIGHAM, FRANK, *Ambition and Privilege*, 1984.

On particular plays the following commentaries are all helpful:

HENRY VI – Parts 1, 2, 3

BERMAN, RONALD S., 'Fathers and Sons in the Henry VI plays', *Shakespeare Quarterly* 13 (1962).

BERRY, EDWARD I., *Patterns of Decay: Shakespeare's Early Histories*, 1975.

BEVINGTON, DAVID, 'The Domineering Female in *1 Henry VI*', *Shakespeare Studies* 2 (1966).

BROCKBANK, J. P., 'The Frame of Disorder – *Henry VI*' in *On Shakespeare*, op. cit.

CLEMEN, WOLFGANG, 'Anticipation and Foreboding in Shakespeare's Early Histories', *Shakespeare Survey* 6 (1953).

DASH, IRENE G., 'The Paradox of Power: The Henry VI–Richard III Tetralogy' in *Wooing, Wedding, and Power: Women in Shakespeare's Plays*, 1981.

RIGGS, DAVID, *Shakespeare's Heroical Histories: 'Henry VI' and Its Literary Tradition'*, 1971.

SWANDER, HOMER D., 'The Rediscovery of *Henry VI*', *Shakespeare Quarterly* 29 (1978).

SELECT BIBLIOGRAPHY

TURNER, ROBERT Y., 'Shakespeare and the Public Confrontation Scene in Early History Plays', *Modern Philology* 72 (1964).

RICHARD III
BRADBROOK, M. C., *English Dramatic Form*, 1965.

BROOKE, NICHOLAS, *Shakespeare's Early Tragedies*, 1968.

BROOKES, HAROLD F., '*Richard III*: antecedents of Clarence's Dream', *Shakespeare Survey* 32 (1979).

BROOKS, HAROLD F., '*Richard III*: unhistorical amplifications: the women's scenes and Seneca', *MLR* 75 (October 1980).

CHAMPION, LARRY S., *Perspective in Shakespeare's Histories*, 1980.

HASSEL, R. CHRIS, *Songs of Death: Performance, Interpretation, and the Text of 'Richard III'*, 1987.

KENDALL, PAUL MURRAY, *Richard the Third*, 1955.

ROSS, CHARLES, *Richard III*, 1981.

ROSSITER, A. P., 'Angel with Horns – the unity of *Richard III*', in *Angel with Horns*, op. cit.

SPIVACK, BERNARD, *Shakespeare and the Allegory of Evil*, 1958.

URE, PETER, 'Character and role from *Richard III* to *Hamlet*' in his *Elizabethan and Jacobean Drama*, 1974.

VAN LAAN, THOMAS F., *Role-Playing in Shakespeare*, 1978.

WILSON, F. P., Marlowe and the Early Shakespeare, 1953.

KING JOHN
BONJOUR, ADRIEN, 'The Road to Swinstead Abbey: A Study of the Sense and Structure of *King John*', *ELH* 18 (1951).

CALDERWOOD, JAMES L., 'Commodity and Honour in *King John*', *University of Toronto Quarterly* 29 (1960).

CLEMEN, WOLFGANG, *The Development of Shakespeare's Imagery*, 1951.

ELLIOT, JOHN R., 'Shakespeare and the Double Image of King John', *Shakespeare Studies* I (1965).

HONIGMANN, E. A. J., Introduction to the Arden edition of *King John*.

PETTET, E. C., 'Hot Irons and Fever: A Note on Some Imagery of *King John*', *Essays in Criticism* 4 (1954).

VAUGHAN, VIRGINIA MASON, 'Between Tetralogies: *King John* as Transition', *Shakespeare Quarterly* 35 (1984).

WAITH, EUGENE M., '*King John* and the Drama of History', *Shakespeare Quarterly* 29 (1978).

BACKGROUND AND SOURCES
Shakespeare scholarship is massive and exhaustive, covering every imaginable aspect of the writer's work, life and times. Most editions of

the text, including the Everyman Shakespeare, are now supplied with notes which are more than adequate for all normal purposes. However, those who wish to explore questions of Shakespearian language further may care to consult John Bartlett, *A New and Complete Concordance to Shakespeare*, Macmillan, New York, 1894, and C. T. Onions, *A Shakespearian Glossary*, Oxford University Press, London, 1911 (and frequently reprinted). Between them, these texts define and explain every single word Shakespeare uses, citing the places where they appear and exploring obsolete usages.

The thorny questions of textual transmission are covered in W. W. Greg's *The Shakespeare First Folio*, Oxford University Press, New York and London, 1955. This gives a detailed history of the first collected edition of the plays which appeared in 1623.

Finally, a word on sources. Most individual editions of the plays include a note on particular sources, together with extensive quotation. The most readily available and accessible general book on this matter is Kenneth Muir's *Shakespeare's Sources*, Methuen, London, 1957. Muir was one of the most distinguished scholar-critics of his time and his book throws fascinating light on the whole field of Shakespeare studies.

Even more comprehensive – though considerably more daunting – are the eight volumes of Geoffrey Bullough's *Narrative and Dramatic Sources of Shakespeare*, Routledge & Kegan Paul, London, and Columbia University Press, New York, 1957–75.

CHRONOLOGY

DATE	AUTHOR'S LIFE	LITERARY CONTEXT
1564	Born in Stratford, Warwickshire, the eldest surviving son of John Shakespeare, glover and occasional dealer in wool, and Mary Arden, daughter of a prosperous farmer.	Birth of Christopher Marlowe.
1565	John Shakespeare elected Alderman of Stratford.	Clinthio: *Hecatommithi*. Edwards: *Damon and Pythias*.
1566	Birth of Shakespeare's brother Gilbert.	Gascoigne: *Supposes*.
1567		Udall: *Roister Doister*. Golding: *The Stories of Venus and Adonis and of Hermaphroditus and Salamcis*.
1568	His father is elected bailiff.	Gascoigne: *Jocasta*. Wilmot: *Tancred and Gismunda*. Second Edition of Vasari's *Lives of the Artists*.
1569	Probably starts attending the petty school attached to the King's New School in Stratford. Birth of his sister Joan.	
1570	His father involved in money-lending.	
1571	John Shakespeare is elected Chief Alderman and deputy to the new bailiff.	
1572		Whitgift's *Answer* to the 'Admonition' receives Cartwright's *Reply*, beginning the first literary debate between Anglicans and Puritans.
1573		Tasso: *Aminta*.
1574	Probably enters the Upper School (where studies include rhetoric, logic, the Latin poets, and a little Greek). Birth of his brother Richard.	

HISTORICAL EVENTS

Death of Michelangelo. Birth of Galileo.

Rebellion against Spain in the Netherlands. Birth of the actor Edward Alleyn.
Birth of the actor Richard Burbage.

Mary Stuart flees to England from Scotland.

Northern Rebellion.

Excommunication of Elizabeth. *Baïf's* Academy founded in Paris to promote poetry, music and dance.
Ridolfi Plot. Puritan 'Admonition' to Parliament.

Dutch rebels conquer Holland and Zeeland. Massacre of St Bartholomew's Day in Paris.

Accession of Henry III and new outbreak of civil war in France. First Catholic missionaries arrive in England from Douai. Earl of Leicester's Men obtain licence to perform within the City of London.

HISTORIES

DATE	AUTHOR'S LIFE	LITERARY CONTEXT
1575		*Gammer Gurton's Needle* is printed.
1576		Castiglione's *The Book of the Courtier* banned by the Spanish Inquisition. George Gascoigne: *The Steel Glass*.
1577		John Northbrooke's attack in *Treatise wherein Dicing, Dancing, Vain Plays etc are reproved*.
1578	Shakespeare family fortunes are in decline, and John is having to sell off property to pay off his increasing debts.	Sidney writes *The Lady of May* and begins the 'Old' *Arcadia*. George Whetstone: *Promos and Cassandra*. John Lyly: *Euphues, the Anatomy of Wit*. Pierre de Ronsard, leader of the Pléiade, publishes his *Sonnets pour Hélène*. He is said to have exercised a considerable influence on the English sonnet-writers of the sixteenth century.
1579		Spenser: *The Shepherd's Calendar*. North: translation of Plutarch. Gossen: *The School of Abuse, and Pleasant Invective against Poets, Pipers, Players etc*.
1580	Birth of Shakespeare's brother Edmund.	Sidney: *Apologie for Poetrie*. Lodge: *Defense of Plays*.
1581		John Newton's translation of Seneca's *Ten Tragedies*. Barnaby Rich: *Apolonius and Silla*.
1582	Shakespeare marries Anne Hathaway, a local farmer's daughter, 7 or 8 years his senior, who is already pregnant with their first child.	Tasso: *Gerusalemme Liberata*. Watson: *Hekatompathia* (First sonnet sequence published in England). Whetstone: *Heptameron of Civil Discourses*. Sidney begins *Astrophel and Stella* and the 'New' *Arcadia*. Lope de Vega writing for the Corrals in Madrid.

HISTORICAL EVENTS

Kenilworth Revels.

Restricted by the City of London's order that no plays be performed within the City boundaries, James Burbage of The Earl of Leicester's Men builds The Theatre only just outside the boundaries in Shoreditch. The Blackfriars Theatre is built. End of civil war in France. Observatory of Uraniborg built for the Danish astronomer, Tycho Brahe. Death of Titian.
Drake's circumnavigation of the world. The Curtain Theatre built. Birth of Rubens.

First visit to England of the duc d'Alençon as a suitor to Elizabeth, provoking much opposition to a French match. The Corral de la Cruz built in Madrid.

Spanish conquest of Portugal. Jesuit mission arrives in England from Rome led by Edmund Campion and Parsons.
Stricter enforcement of treason laws and increased penalties on recusants. Campion captured and executed. Northern provinces of the Netherlands renounce their allegiance to Phillip II, and invite the duc d'Alençon to be their sovereign.
Sir Walter Ralegh established in the Queen's favour. The Corral del Principe built in Madrid.

DATE	AUTHOR'S LIFE	LITERARY CONTEXT
1583	Birth of their daughter Susanna.	
1583-4	The players' companies of the Earls of Essex, Oxford and Leicester perform in Stratford.	Giordarno Bruno visits England.
1584		Bruno publishes *La cena de le Ceneri* and *Spaccio della bestia trionfante*. Reginald Scott: *The Discovery of Witchcraft*.
1585	Birth of Shakespeare's twins Hamnet and Judith. The following years until 1592 are the 'Lost Years' for which no documentary records of his life survive, only legends such as the one of deer-stealing and flight from prosecution, and conjectures such as ones that he became a schoolmaster, travelled in Europe, or went to London to be an actor as early as the mid 1580s.	Death of Pierre de Ronsard. Bruno: *De gli eroici furori*, dedicated to Sidney.
1586		Timothy Bright: *A Treatise of Melancholy*.
1586-7	Five players' companies visit Stratford, including the Queen's, Essex's, Leicester's and Stafford's.	
1587		Holinshed: *Chronicles of England, Scotland and Ireland*. Marlowe: First part of *Tamburlaine the Great* acted. New edition of *The Mirror for Magistrates*.
1588		Marlowe: Second part of *Tamburlaine*. Thomas Kyd: *The Spanish Tragedy*. Lope de Vega, serving with the Armada, writes some of *The Beauty of Angelica*.

CHRONOLOGY

First meeting of the Durham House Set led by Ralegh, Northumberland and Harriot, to promote mathematics, astronomy and navigation. Archbishop Whitgift leads more extreme anti-Puritan policy. Throckmorton plot, involving the Spanish ambassador.

Death of d'Alençon. Assassination of William of Orange. The Teatro Olimpico, Vicenza, built by Palladio.

England sends military aid to the Dutch rebels under the command of Leicester. Ralegh organizes the colonization of Virginia.

Babington plot. Death of Sir Philip Sidney. Rise of the Earl of Essex. Colonization of Munster.

Execution of Mary Stuart. Drake's raid on Cadiz.

Defeat of the Armada. Death of the Earl of Leicester. The first of the Puritan Marprelate Tracts published.

DATE	AUTHOR'S LIFE	LITERARY CONTEXT
1589	The earliest likely date at which Shakespeare began composition of his first plays (1 *Henry VI, The Taming of the Shrew*) when he would have been working as an actor at The Theatre, with Burbage's company.	Marlowe: *The Jew of Malta.* Thomas Nashe: *The Anatomy of Absurdity.* Richard Hakluyt: *Principal Navigations, Voyages and Discoveries of the English nation.*
1590	2 *Henry VI*, 3 *Henry VI.*	Spenser: first 3 books of *The Faerie Queen.* Publication of Sidney's 'New' *Arcadia.* Nashe: *An Almond for a Parrot,* one of the Marprelate Tracts. Greene: *Menaphon.* Guarina: *The Faithful Shepherd.*
1590–91	*King John* written.	
1590–92	Performances of *Henry VI*, parts 2 and 3, *Titus* and *The Shrew* by the Earl of Pembroke's Men.	
1591	*Richard III* and *The Comedy of Errors* written.	Spenser's *Complaints* which includes his translation of fifteen of Joachim du Bellay's sonnets – du Bellay was a member of the Pléiade and responsible for its manifesto. Sir John Harington's translation of *Orlando Furioso.* Publication of Sidney's *Astrophel and Stella.*
1592	First recorded reference to Shakespeare as an actor and playwright in Greene's attack in *The Groatsworth of Wit* describing him as 'an upstart crow'.	Samuel Daniel: *Delia.* Marlowe's *Edward II* and *Doctor Faustus* performed. *Arden of Feversham* printed. Nashe: *Strange News.*
1592–4	*Titus Andronicus* written.	
1593	Publication of *Venus and Adonis*, dedicated to the Earl of Southampton. The *Sonnets* probably begun.	Marlowe: *Massacre of Paris.* *The Phoenix Nest*, miscellany of poems including ones by Ralegh, Lodge and Breton. Barnabe Barnes: *Parthenophil and Parthenope.* George Peele: *The Honour of the Garter.* Lodge: *Phillis.* Nashe: *Christ's Tears over Jerusalem.*

CHRONOLOGY

DATE	AUTHOR'S LIFE	LITERARY CONTEXT
1593–4	*The Two Gentlemen of Verona.*	
1593–6		John Donne writing his early poems, the Satires and Elegies.
1594	*The Rape of Lucrece* dedicated to his patron Southampton. *The Comedy of Errors* and *Titus Andronicus* performed at the Rose. Shakespeare established as one of the shareholders in his company, The Chamberlain's Men, which performs before the Queen during the Christmas festivities.	Daniel: *Cleopatra.* Spenser: *Amoretti* and *Epithalamion.* Drayton: *Idea's Mirror.* Nashe: *The Terrors of the Night, The Unfortunate Traveller.* Greene: *Friar Bacon and Friar Bungay.*
1594–5	*Love's Labour's Lost* and *Romeo and Juliet* written.	
1595	*Richard II.*	Daniel: *The First Four Books of the Civil Wars between the two houses of Lancaster and York.* Sidney: *Defence of Poesy* published. Ralegh: *The Discovery of the Empire of Guiana.*
1595–6	*A Midsummer Night's Dream.*	
1596	Death of his son, Hamnet. *The Merchant of Venice.* Shakespeare living in Bishopsgate ward. His father, John, is granted a coat of arms.	Lodge: *Wits Miserie.* First complete edition of Spenser's *Faerie Queen.*
1597	*Henry IV* Part 1. First performance of *The Merry Wives of Windsor.* Shakespeare's company now under the patronage of the new Lord Chamberlain, Hunsdon. In Stratford, Shakespeare buys New Place, the second largest house in the town, with its own orchards and vines.	John Donne writes 'The Storme' and 'The Calme'. Francis Bacon: first edition of *Essays.* Jonson and Nashe imprisoned for writing *The Isle of Dogs.*
1597–8	*Henry IV* Part 2.	
1598	Shakespeare one of the 'principal comedians' with Richard Burbage, Heminge and Cordell in Jonson's *Every Man in his Humour.* For the second year, Shakespeare is listed as having failed to pay tax levied on all householders.	Publication of Sidney's *Works* and of Marlowe's *Hero and Leander* (together with Chapman's continuation). *Seven Books of the Iliads* (first of Chapman's Homeric translations). Meres: *Palladis Tamia.*

CHRONOLOGY

Henry of Navarre accepted as King in Paris. Rebellion in Ireland. The London theatres re-open. The Swan Theatre is built. Ralegh accused of blasphemy.

France declares war on Spain. Failure of the Indies voyage and death of Hawkins. Ralegh's expedition to Guiana.

England joins France in the war against Spain. Death of Drake. Raid on Cadiz led by Essex. In long-standing power struggle with Essex, Robert Cecil is appointed Secretary of State.

Islands Voyage led by Essex and Ralegh. The government suppresses the *Isle of Dogs* at the Swan and closes the theatres. Despite the continued hostility of the City of London, they soon re-open. James Burbage builds the second Blackfriars Theatre. Death of James Burbage.

Peace between France and Spain. Death of Philip II. Tyrone defeats the English at Armagh. Essex appointed Lord Deputy of Ireland.

HISTORIES

DATE	AUTHOR'S LIFE	LITERARY CONTEXT
1598 *cont.*		New edition of Lodge's *Rosalynde*. Lope de Vega: *La Arcadia*. James VI of Scotland: *The True Law of Free Monarchies*.
1598–9	*As You Like It*.	
1598–1600	*Much Ado About Nothing*.	
1599	*Henry V, Julius Caesar*. Shakespeare one of the shareholders in the Globe Theatre. He moves lodgings to Bankside. Publication of *The Passionate Pilgrim*, a miscellany of 20 poems, at least 5 by Shakespeare.	Jonson: *Every Man out of his Humour*. Dekker: *The Shoemaker's Holiday*. Sir John Hayward: *The First Part of the Life and Reign of King Henry IV*. Greene's translation of *Orlando Furioso*.
1600		'England's Helicon'.
1600–1	*Hamlet* (performed with Burbage as the Prince and Shakespeare as the Ghost).	
1601	*The Phoenix and the Turtle*. The Lord Chamberlain's Men paid by one of Essex's followers to perform *Richard II* on the day before the rebellion. Death of John Shakespeare.	
1601–2	*Troilus and Cressida*.	
1602	Shakespeare buys more property in Stratford.	
1602–4	*Alls Well That Ends Well*.	
1603	Shakespeare's company now under the patronage of King James. Shakespeare is one of the principal tragedians in Jonson's *Sejanus*.	Montaigne's *Essays* translated into English. Thomas Heywood: *A Woman Killed with Kindness*.
1604	Shakespeare known to be lodging in Silver Street with a Huguenot family called Mountjoy. *Othello*; first performance of *Measure for Measure*.	Chapman: *Bussy d'Ambois*. Marston: *The Malcontent*.
1604–5	Ten of his plays performed at court by the King's Men.	

CHRONOLOGY

The Burbage brothers, Richard and Cuthbert, pull down The Theatre and, with its timbers, build the Globe on Bankside. Essex's campaign fails in Ireland, and after returning without permission to court he is arrested. The government suppresses satirical writings, and burns pamphlets by Nashe and Harvey.

Essex released but still in disgrace. The Fortune Theatre built by Alleyn and Henslowe. Bruno executed for heresy by the Inquisition in Rome.

Essex's Rebellion. Essex and Southampton arrested, and the former executed. Spanish invasion of Ireland. Monopolies debates in Parliament.

Spanish troops defeated in Ireland.

Death of Elizabeth, and accession of James I. Ralegh imprisoned in the Tower. Plague in London. Sir Thomas Bodley re-founds the library of Oxford University.

Peace with Spain. Hampton Court Conference.

DATE	AUTHOR'S LIFE	LITERARY CONTEXT
1605	First performance of *King Lear* at the Globe, with Burbage as the King, and Robert Armin as the Fool. Shakespeare makes further investments in Stratford, buying a half interest in a lease of tithes.	Cervantes: *Don Quixote* (part one). Bacon: *The Proficience and Advancement of Learning*. Jonson and Inigo Jones: *The Masque of Blackness*. Jonson and co-authors imprisoned for libellous references to the court in *Eastward Ho*.
1605–6		Jonson: *Volpone*.
1606	First performance of *Macbeth*.	John Ford's masque *Honour Triumphant*.
1607	*Antony and Cleopatra*. Susanna marries John Hall, a physician. Death of Shakespeare's brother Edmund, an actor.	Tourneur's *The Revenger's Tragedy* printed. Barnes: *The Devil's Charter*.
1607–8	*Timon of Athens, Coriolanus, Pericles*.	
1608	Shakespeare one of the shareholders in the Blackfriars Theatre. Death of his mother.	Lope de Vega: *Peribanez*. Beaumont and Fletcher: *Philaster*. Jonson and Jones: *The Masque of Beauty*. Donne writes *La Corona*. Twelve books of Homer's *Iliad* (Chapman's translation).
1609	Publication, probably unauthorized, of the quarto edition of the *Sonnets* and *A Lover's Complaint*.	Jonson and Jones: *The Masque of Queens*. Donne's 'The Expiration' printed; 'Liturgie' and 'On the Annunciation' written. Bacon: *De Sapientia Veterum*. Lope de Vega: *New Art of Writing Plays for the Theatre*.
1609–10	*Cymbeline*.	
1610		Donne: *Pseudo-Martyr* printed and *The First Anniversarie* written. Jonson: *The Alchemist*. Beaumont and Fletcher: *The Maid's Tragedy*.
1610–11	*The Winter's Tale*.	
1611	*The Tempest* performed in the Banqueting House, Whitehall. Simon Forman records seeing performances of *Macbeth, The Winter's Tale* and *Cymbeline*.	Beaumont and Fletcher: *A King and No King, The Knight of the Burning Pestle*. Tourneur: *The Atheist's Tragedy*.

CHRONOLOGY

HISTORICAL EVENTS

Gunpowder Plot.

Monteverdi: *Orfeo*.
Bacon appointed Solicitor General.

Galileo's experiments with the telescope confirm the Copernican theory.
Kepler draws up 'Laws of Planetary Motion'. Twelve-year Truce between
Spain and Netherlands.

Galileo: *The Starry Messenger*. Assassination of Henry IV of France.
Parliament submits the Petition of Grievances.

The Inquisition of Rome begins investigating Galileo.

DATE	AUTHOR'S LIFE	LITERARY CONTEXT
1611 *cont.*		Jonson and Jones: *Masque of Oberon*. Authorized Version of the Bible. Sir John Davies: *The Scourge of Folly*. Donne writes the *The Second Anniversarie* and a 'A Valediction: forbidding mourning'.
1612	Shakespeare appears as a witness in a Court of Requests case involving a dispute over a dowry owed by his former landlord, Mountjoy, to his son-in-law, Belott. Death of his brother Gilbert.	Webster: *The White Devil* printed. Tourneur: *The Nobleman*. Lope de Vega: *Fuente Ovejuna*.
1613	At a performance of his last play, *Henry VIII*, the Globe Theatre catches fire and is destroyed. As part of the court celebrations for the marriage of Princess Elizabeth, The King's Men perform 14 plays, including *Much Ado*, *Othello*, *The Winter's Tale* and *The Tempest*. Death of his brother Richard.	Sir Thomas Overbury: *The Wife*. Donne: 'Good Friday' and 'Epithalamion' on Princess Elizabeth's marriage. Cervantes: *Novelas ejemplares* – a collection of short stories.
1614	In Stratford, Shakespeare protects his property interests during a controversy over a threat to enclose the common fields.	Jonson: *Bartholomew Fair*. Webster: *The Duchess of Malfi*. Ralegh: *The History of the World*.
1615	The Warwick Assizes issue an order to prevent enclosures, which ends the dispute in Stratford.	Cervantes publishes 8 plays and *Don Quixote* (part two).
1616	Marriage of his daughter Judith to Thomas Quincy, a vintner, who a month later is tried for fornication with another woman whom he had made pregnant. Death of Shakespeare (23 April).	Jonson: *The Devil is an Ass*. Jonson publishes his *Works*.
1623	The players Heminge and Condell publish the plays of the First Folio.	

CHRONOLOGY

HISTORICAL EVENTS

Death of Henry, Prince of Wales.

Marriage of Princess Elizabeth to Frederick, Elector Palatine. Bacon appointed Attorney-General.

The second Globe and the Hope Theatre built.

Inquiry into the murder of Sir Thomas Overbury in the Tower implicates the wife of the King's favourite, Somerset.

Ralegh released from the Tower to lead an expedition to Guiana; on his return he is executed.

WILLIAM SHAKESPEARE

THE FIRST PART OF HENRY THE SIXTH

Edited by Lawrence V. Ryan

KING HENRY THE SIXTH
EDWARD, Prince of Wales, his son
LEWIS XI, King of France
DUKE OF SOMERSET
DUKE OF EXETER
EARL OF OXFORD
EARL OF NORTHUMBERLAND
EARL OF WESTMORELAND
LORD CLIFFORD
RICHARD PLANTAGENET, Duke of York
EDWARD, Earl of March, afterwards King
    Edward IV
EDMUND, Earl of Rutland   } his
GEORGE, afterwards Duke of Clarence   } sons
RICHARD, afterwards Duke of Gloucester
DUKE OF NORFOLK
EARL OF WARWICK
MARQUESS OF MONTAGUE
EARL OF PEMBROKE
LORD HASTINGS
LORD STAFFORD
SIR JOHN MORTIMER   } uncles to the Duke of York
SIR HUGH MORTIMER
HENRY, Earl of Richmond, a youth
LORD RIVERS, brother to Lady Grey
SIR WILLIAM STANLEY
SIR JOHN MONTGOMERY
SIR JOHN SOMERVILLE
TUTOR TO RUTLAND
MAYOR OF YORK and ALDERMEN
MAYOR OF COVENTRY
LIEUTENANT OF THE TOWER
A NOBLEMAN
TWO KEEPERS
A HUNTSMAN
A SON THAT HAS KILLED HIS FATHER

A FATHER THAT HAS KILLED HIS SON
THE FRENCH ADMIRAL
QUEEN MARGARET
LADY ELIZABETH GREY, afterwards Queen to Edward IV
BONA, sister to the French Queen

SOLDIERS, ATTENDANTS, MESSENGERS, WATCHMEN, etc.
Scene: England and France]

THE FIRST
PART OF
HENRY THE SIXTH

ACT I

Scene I. [*Westminster Abbey.*]

*Dead March. Enter the Funeral of King Henry the
Fifth, attended on by the Duke of Bedford, Regent of
France; the Duke of Gloucester, Protector; the Duke of
Exeter, Warwick, the Bishop of Winchester, and the
Duke of Somerset, [with Attendants].*

BEDFORD Hung be the heavens with black, yield day
    to night!
Comets, importing change of times and states,
Brandish your crystal tresses in the sky,
And with them scourge the bad revolting stars
That have consented unto Henry's death!   5
King Henry the Fifth, too famous to live long!
England ne'er lost a king of so much worth.

GLOUCESTER England ne'er had a king until his time.
Virtue he had, deserving to command;
His brandished sword did blind men with his
10   beams;
His arms spread wider than a dragon's wings;
His sparkling eyes, replete with wrathful fire,
More dazzled and drove back his enemies
Than midday sun fierce bent against their faces.
15   What should I say? His deeds exceed all speech:
He ne'er lift up his hand but conquerèd.

EXETER We mourn in black; why mourn we not in
blood?
Henry is dead and never shall revive.
Upon a wooden coffin we attend,
20   And death's dishonorable victory
We with our stately presence glorify,
Like captives bound to a triumphant car.
What! shall we curse the planets of mishap
That plotted thus our glory's overthrow?
25   Or shall we think the subtle-witted French
Conjurers and sorcerers that, afraid of him,
By magic verses have contrived his end?

WINCHESTER He was a king blessed of the King of
Kings.
Unto the French the dreadful judgment day
30   So dreadful will not be as was his sight.
The battles of the Lord of Hosts he fought;
The church's prayers made him so prosperous.

GLOUCESTER The church! Where is it? Had not churchmen prayed,
His thread of life had not so soon decayed.
35   None do you like but an effeminate prince,
Whom, like a schoolboy, you may overawe.

10 his its   16 lift lifted   17 in blood i.e., by shedding blood, probably of the
French in order to avenge the king's death (see lines 25–27)   19 wooden
unfeeling   22 car chariot   23 of mishap causing misfortune

WINCHESTER Gloucester, whate'er we like, thou art
    Protector
    And lookest to command the prince and realm.
    Thy wife is proud; she holdeth thee in awe
    More than God or religious churchmen may.   40

GLOUCESTER Name not religion, for thou lov'st the
    flesh,
    And ne'er throughout the year to church thou go'st
    Except it be to pray against thy foes.

BEDFORD Cease, cease these jars and rest your minds
    in peace;
    Let's to the altar. Heralds, wait on us.   45
    Instead of gold, we'll offer up our arms,
    Since arms avail not now that Henry's dead.
    Posterity, await for wretched years,
    When at their mothers' moistened eyes babes shall
    suck,
    Our isle be made a nourish of salt tears,   50
    And none but women left to wail the dead.
    Henry the Fifth, thy ghost I invocate:
    Prosper this realm, keep it from civil broils,
    Combat with adverse planets in the heavens!
    A far more glorious star thy soul will make   55
    Than Julius Caesar or bright—

Enter a Messenger.

MESSENGER My honorable lords, health to you all!
    Sad tidings bring I to you out of France,
    Of loss, of slaughter, and discomfiture:
    Guienne, Champagne, Rheims, Orleans,   60
    Paris, Guysors, Poictiers, are all quite lost.

BEDFORD What say'st thou, man, before dead Henry's
    corse?

---

37 **Protector** governor of the realm during the king's minority   38 **lookest**
expect   44 **jars** quarrels   46 **arms** weapons   50 **nourish** nurse   53 **broils**
disorders   56 **Julius Caesar** (whose soul, according to Ovid, *Metamorphoses*, xv.
843-51, became a star in the heavens after his assassination)   62 **corse** corpse

Speak softly, or the loss of those great towns
Will make him burst his lead and rise from death.

65 GLOUCESTER Is Paris lost? Is Rouen yielded up?
If Henry were recalled to life again,
These news would cause him once more yield the
ghost.

EXETER How were they lost? What treachery was
used?

MESSENGER No treachery, but want of men and
money.
70 Amongst the soldiers this is mutterèd,
That here you maintain several factions,
And whilst a field should be dispatched and fought,
You are disputing of your generals:
One would have ling'ring wars with little cost;
75 Another would fly swift, but wanteth wings;
A third thinks, without expense at all,
By guileful fair words peace may be obtained.
Awake, awake, English nobility!
Let not sloth dim your honors new begot;
80 Cropped are the flower-de-luces in your arms;
Of England's coat one half is cut away.

EXETER Were our tears wanting to this funeral,
These tidings would call forth her flowing tides.

BEDFORD Me they concern; Regent I am of France.
85 Give me my steelèd coat; I'll fight for France.
Away with these disgraceful wailing robes!
Wounds will I lend the French, instead of eyes,
To weep their intermissive miseries.

---

64 **lead** lining of the coffin 67 **These** (Since *news* was originally plural)
71 **factions** (trisyllabic; the endings *-ion* and *-ions* are often pronounced as two
syllables in Shakespeare) 79 **new begot** recently obtained 80 **flower-de-luces**
fleur-de-lis, or lilies of France (heraldic symbol of the French monarchs) 81 **coat**
coat of arms (the English royal family, as a sign of its pretensions to the throne of
France, included the fleur-de-lis in its coat of arms from the fourteenth through
the eighteenth centuries) 82 **wanting** lacking 83 **her** i.e., England's 84 **Regent**
ruler in the king's absence 88 **intermissive** coming at intervals

Enter to them another Messenger.

SECOND MESSENGER Lords, view these letters full of
     bad mischance.
  France is revolted from the English quite,   90
  Except some petty towns of no import.
  The Dolphin Charles is crownèd king in Rheims;
  The Bastard of Orleans with him is joined;
  Reignier, Duke of Anjou, doth take his part;
  The Duke of Alençon flieth to his side.   *Exit.*   95

EXETER The Dolphin crownèd king? All fly to him?
  O, whither shall we fly from this reproach?

GLOUCESTER We will not fly, but to our enemies'
     throats.
  Bedford, if thou be slack, I'll fight it out.

BEDFORD Gloucester, why doubt'st thou of my for-
     wardness?   100
  An army have I mustered in my thoughts,
  Wherewith already France is overrun.

Enter another Messenger.

THIRD MESSENGER My gracious lords, to add to your
     laments,
  Wherewith you now bedew King Henry's hearse,
  I must inform you of a dismal fight   105
  Betwixt the stout Lord Talbot and the French.

WINCHESTER What? Wherein Talbot overcame, is't so?

THIRD MESSENGER O no, wherein Lord Talbot was
     o'erthrown.
  The circumstance I'll tell you more at large.
  The tenth of August last, this dreadful lord,   110
  Retiring from the siege of Orleans,
  Having full scarce six thousand in his troop,

---

91 **import** importance   92 **Dolphin** Dauphin, title of the heir to the French
throne   97 **reproach** disgrace   104 **bedew** moisten   109 **The circumstance
... large** I shall tell you the details at greater length   112 **full** all told (?)

By three and twenty thousand of the French
Was round encompassèd and set upon.
115 No leisure had he to enrank his men;
He wanted pikes to set before his archers;
Instead whereof, sharp stakes plucked out of hedges
They pitchèd in the ground confusedly,
To keep the horsemen off from breaking in.
120 More than three hours the fight continuèd;
Where valiant Talbot, above human thought,
Enacted wonders with his sword and lance.
Hundreds he sent to hell, and none durst stand him;
Here, there, and everywhere, enraged he slew.
125 The French exclaimed the devil was in arms;
All the whole army stood agazed on him.
His soldiers, spying his undaunted spirit,
"A Talbot! a Talbot!" cried out amain,
And rushed into the bowels of the battle.
130 Here had the conquest fully been sealed up,
If Sir John Falstaff had not played the coward.
He, being in the vanward, placed behind
With purpose to relieve and follow them,
Cowardly fled, not having struck one stroke.
135 Hence grew the general wrack and massacre:
Enclosèd were they with their enemies.
A base Walloon, to win the Dolphin's grace,
Thrust Talbot with a spear into the back,
Whom all France, with their chief assembled
        strength,
140 Durst not presume to look once in the face.

BEDFORD Is Talbot slain then? I will slay myself
For living idly here in pomp and ease
Whilst such a worthy leader, wanting aid,
Unto his dastard foemen is betrayed.

---

115 **enrank** set in ranks   116 **pikes** stakes with sharpened iron points, set in the ground to impale the enemy's horses if the mounted troops charged the archers   119 **off** (apparently redundant, and inserted for metrical purposes)   126 **agazed** astounded (probably a variant of aghast)   128 **amain** with all their might   132 **vanward** vanguard   137 **Walloon** inhabitant of the region between northeastern France and the Netherlands

THIRD MESSENGER O no, he lives, but is took prisoner,   145
  And Lord Scales with him and Lord Hungerford;
  Most of the rest slaughtered or took likewise.

BEDFORD His ransom there is none but I shall pay.
  I'll hale the Dolphin headlong from his throne;
  His crown shall be the ransom of my friend;   150
  Four of their lords I'll change for one of ours.
  Farewell, my masters, to my task will I;
  Bonfires in France forthwith I am to make
  To keep our great Saint George's feast withal.
  Ten thousand soldiers with me I will take,   155
  Whose bloody deeds shall make all Europe quake.

THIRD MESSENGER So you had need, for Orleans is
    besieged;
  The English army is grown weak and faint;
  The Earl of Salisbury craveth supply
  And hardly keeps his men from mutiny   160
  Since they, so few, watch such a multitude.

EXETER Remember, lords, your oaths to Henry sworn:
  Either to quell the Dolphin utterly
  Or bring him in obedience to your yoke.

BEDFORD I do remember it and here take my leave   165
  To go about my preparation.   *Exit Bedford.*

GLOUCESTER I'll to the Tower with all the haste I can
  To view th' artillery and munition,
  And then I will proclaim young Henry king.
                   Exit Gloucester.

EXETER To Eltham will I, where the young king is,   170
  Being ordained his special governor,
  And for his safety there I'll best devise.   *Exit.*

WINCHESTER Each hath his place and function to
    attend;
  I am left out; for me nothing remains.

154 **Saint George's feast** April 23   154 **withal** with   163 **quell** destroy
166 **preparation** (five syllables)   167 **Tower** Tower of London

175   But long I will not be Jack out of office.
       The king from Eltham I intend to send
       And sit at chiefest stern of public weal.

                                    Exit [with Attendants].

              Scene II. [*France. Before Orleans.*]

       *Sound a Flourish. Enter Charles [the Dauphin], Alençon,
          and Reignier, marching with Drum and Soldiers.*

       DAUPHIN Mars his true moving, even as in the
              heavens,
              So in the earth, to this day is not known.
              Late did he shine upon the English side;
              Now we are victors; upon us he smiles.
5   What towns of any moment but we have?
              At pleasure here we lie near Orleans;
              Otherwhiles the famished English, like pale ghosts,
              Faintly besiege us one hour in a month.

       ALENÇON They want their porridge and their fat bull-
              beeves:
10   Either they must be dieted like mules
              And have their provender tied to their mouths,
              Or piteous they will look, like drownèd mice.

       REIGNIER Let's raise the siege; why live we idly here?
              Talbot is taken, whom we wont to fear;
15   Remaineth none but mad-brainèd Salisbury,

---

175 **Jack out of office** a person deprived of official function 177 **And ... weal**
and maintain control of the government I.ii.s.d. **Flourish** fanfare of
trumpets 1 **Mars his** Mars's 5 **moment** importance 7 **Otherwhiles** at
times 9 **bull-beeves** (eating of bull-beef was believed to give one courage)
10 **dieted** fed 11 **provender** food 14 **wont** were accustomed

12

And he may well in fretting spend his gall;
Nor men nor money hath he to make war.

DAUPHIN Sound, sound alarum! we will rush on
    them.
Now for the honor of the forlorn French!
Him I forgive my death that killeth me   20
When he sees me go back one foot or fly.   *Exeunt.*

Here alarum; they are beaten back by the English with
great loss. Enter Charles [the Dauphin], Alençon, and
Reignier.

DAUPHIN Who ever saw the like? What men have I?
Dogs! cowards! dastards! I would ne'er have fled,
But that they left me 'midst my enemies.

REIGNIER Salisbury is a desperate homicide;   25
He fighteth as one weary of his life.
The other lords, like lions wanting food,
Do rush upon us as their hungry prey.

ALENÇON Froissart, a countryman of ours, records
England all Olivers and Rowlands bred   30
During the time Edward the Third did reign.
More truly now may this be verified,
For none but Samsons and Goliases
It sendeth forth to skirmish. One to ten!
Lean raw-boned rascals! who would e'er suppose   35
They had such courage and audacity?

DAUPHIN Let's leave this town, for they are
    hare-brained slaves,
And hunger will enforce them to be more eager.
Of old I know them; rather with their teeth
The walls they'll tear down than forsake the siege.   40

16 **gall** bitterness of spirit   17 **Nor** neither   18 **alarum** call to arms   28 **their hungry prey** prey for which they hunger   29 **Froissart** chronicler of fourteenth-century French, English, and Spanish affairs   30 **Olivers and Rowlands** heroes of the French medieval epic, *La Chanson de Roland*   33 **Goliases** Goliaths   35 **rascals** lean, inferior deer   38 **enforce** compel   38 **eager** (1) hungry (2) fierce

REIGNIER I think, by some odd gimmors or device
        Their arms are set, like clocks, still to strike on;
        Else ne'er could they hold out so as they do.
        By my consent, we'll even let them alone.

45 ALENÇON Be it so.

                Enter the Bastard of Orleans.

BASTARD Where's the Prince Dolphin? I have news
        for him.

DAUPHIN Bastard of Orleans, thrice welcome to us.

BASTARD Methinks your looks are sad, your cheer
        appaled.
        Hath the late overthrow wrought this offense?
50   Be not dismayed, for succor is at hand;
        A holy maid hither with me I bring,
        Which by a vision sent to her from heaven
        Ordainèd is to raise this tedious siege
        And drive the English forth the bounds of France.
55   The spirit of deep prophecy she hath,
        Exceeding the nine sibyls of old Rome:
        What's past and what's to come she can descry.
        Speak, shall I call her in? Believe my words,
        For they are certain and unfallible.

DAUPHIN Go, call her in. [*Exit Bastard.*] But first, to
60   try her skill,
        Reignier, stand thou as Dolphin in my place;
        Question her proudly; let thy looks be stern:
        By this means shall we sound what skill she hath.

        Enter [the Bastard of Orleans, with] Joan [la] Pucelle.

REIGNIER Fair maid, is't thou wilt do these wondrous
        feats?

---

41 **gimmors** (variant of *gimmals*) connecting parts for transmitting motion
48 **cheer appaled** countenance pale with fear   54 **forth** beyond   56 **nine sibyls**
nine books of prophetic utterances offered to King Tarquin of Rome by the sibyl at
Cumae   59 **unfallible** infallible   63 **sound** test   63 s.d. **la Pucelle** the virgin

PUCELLE Reignier, is't thou that thinkest to beguile me?   65
  Where is the Dolphin? Come, come from behind;
  I know thee well, though never seen before.
  Be not amazed, there's nothing hid from me;
  In private will I talk with thee apart.
  Stand back, you lords, and give us leave awhile.   70

REIGNIER She takes upon her bravely at first dash.

PUCELLE Dolphin, I am by birth a shepherd's daughter,
  My wit untrained in any kind of art.
  Heaven and our Lady gracious hath it pleased
  To shine on my contemptible estate.   75
  Lo, whilst I waited on my tender lambs,
  And to sun's parching heat displayed my cheeks,
  God's mother deignèd to appear to me
  And in a vision full of majesty
  Willed me to leave my base vocation   80
  And free my country from calamity.
  Her aid she promised and assured success;
  In complete glory she revealed herself;
  And, whereas I was black and swart before,
  With those clear rays which she infused on me   85
  That beauty am I blessed with which you may see.
  Ask me what question thou canst possible,
  And I will answer unpremeditated;
  My courage try by combat, if thou dar'st,
  And thou shalt find that I exceed my sex.   90
  Resolve on this, thou shalt be fortunate
  If thou receive me for thy warlike mate.

DAUPHIN Thou hast astonished me with thy high
      terms;
  Only this proof I'll of thy valor make,
  In single combat thou shalt buckle with me,   95
  And if thou vanquishest, thy words are true;
  Otherwise I renounce all confidence.

71 She ... dash she acts bravely at the first encounter 73 wit mind 74 our
Lady the Virgin Mary 80 vocation occupation 84 swart dark-complexioned
85 infused shed 91 resolve on this be assured of this 92 mate (1) comrade
(2) sweetheart (?) 93 high terms i.e., mastery of the grand rhetorical style
95 buckle (1) grapple (2) embrace as lovers

PUCELLE I am prepared: here is my keen-edged sword,
  Decked with fine flower-de-luces on each side,
  The which at Touraine, in Saint Katherine's
100 churchyard,
  Out of a great deal of old iron I chose forth.

DAUPHIN Then come, a God's name, I fear no
  woman.

PUCELLE And while I live, I'll ne'er fly from a man.

  Here they fight, and Joan la Pucelle overcomes.

DAUPHIN Stay, stay thy hands! thou art an Amazon
105 And fightest with the sword of Deborah.

PUCELLE Christ's mother helps me, else I were too
  weak.

DAUPHIN Whoe'er helps thee, 'tis thou that must help
  me:
  Impatiently I burn with thy desire;
  My heart and hands thou hast at once subdued.
110 Excellent Pucelle, if thy name be so,
  Let me thy servant and not sovereign be;
  'Tis the French Dolphin sueth to thee thus.

PUCELLE I must not yield to any rites of love,
  For my profession's sacred from above;
115 When I have chasèd all thy foes from hence,
  Then will I think upon a recompense.

DAUPHIN Meantime look gracious on thy prostrate
  thrall.

REIGNIER My lord, methinks, is very long in talk.

ALENÇON Doubtless he shrives this woman to her
  smock;
120 Else ne'er could he so long protract his speech.

---

102 **a** in 105 **Deborah** prophetess who delivered Israel from oppression by the
Canaanites (Judges 4–5) 110 **if thy name be so** if you really are a virgin
111 **servant** lover 112 **sueth to** woos 117 **thrall** slave 119 **shrives ...
smock** (1) questions her closely (2) hears her confession to the most minute detail

REIGNIER Shall we disturb him, since he keeps no
     mean?

ALENÇON He may mean more than we poor men do
     know:
     These women are shrewd tempters with their
     tongues.

REIGNIER My lord, where are you? What devise you
     on?
     Shall we give o'er Orleans, or no?   125

PUCELLE Why, no, I say, distrustful recreants!
     Fight till the last gasp; I'll be your guard.

DAUPHIN What she says I'll confirm: we'll fight it out.

PUCELLE Assigned am I to be the English scourge.
     This night the siege assuredly I'll raise;   130
     Expect Saint Martin's summer, halcyon's days,
     Since I have enterèd into these wars.
     Glory is like a circle in the water,
     Which never ceaseth to enlarge itself
     Till by broad spreading it disperse to nought.   135
     With Henry's death the English circle ends;
     Dispersèd are the glories it included.
     Now am I like that proud insulting ship
     Which Caesar and his fortune bare at once.

DAUPHIN Was Mahomet inspirèd with a dove?   140
     Thou with an eagle art inspirèd then.
     Helen, the mother of great Constantine,
     Nor yet Saint Philip's daughters, were like thee.

121 **keeps no mean** does not control himself 124 **devise you on** are you
deliberating 126 **recreants** cowards 131 **Saint Martin's summer** Indian
summer (named after the feast of Saint Martin of Tours, November 11)
131 **halcyon's days** peaceful times (the ancients believed that the bird called the
halcyon nested on the sea and that the waters remained calm during its breeding
season) 138 **insulting** insolently triumphant 139 **bare** bore 141 **eagle** i.e.,
like Saint John the Evangelist, with the highest source of inspiration 142 **Helen**
Saint Helena, inspired by a vision to find the cross of Jesus 143 **Saint Philip's
daughters** (who had the gift of prophecy; see Acts 21:9)

Bright star of Venus, fall'n down on the earth,
145   How may I reverently worship thee enough?

ALENÇON Leave off delays, and let us raise the siege.

REIGNIER Woman, do what thou canst to save our
        honors;
        Drive them from Orleans and be immortalized.

DAUPHIN Presently we'll try. Come, let's away about
        it;
150   No prophet will I trust, if she prove false.   *Exeunt.*

Scene III. [*London. Before the Tower.*]

Enter Gloucester, with his Servingmen [in blue coats].

GLOUCESTER I am come to survey the Tower this
        day:
        Since Henry's death, I fear, there is conveyance.
        Where be these warders, that they wait not here?
        Open the gates; 'tis Gloucester that calls.

FIRST WARDER [*Within*] Who's there that knocks so
5   imperiously?

GLOUCESTER'S FIRST [SERVING] MAN It is the noble Duke
        of Gloucester.

SECOND WARDER [*Within*] Whoe'er he be, you may not
        be let in.

GLOUCESTER'S FIRST [SERVING] MAN Villains, answer you
        so the Lord Protector?

149 **Presently** immediately I.iii.s.d. **blue coats** (blue clothing was customary for
servants) 1 **survey** inspect 2 **conveyance** underhand dealing 3 **warders**
guards 4 **Gloucester** (trisyllabic here and often, for metrical purposes, elsewhere
in the play)

18

FIRST WARDER [*Within*] The Lord protect him! so we
   answer him;
   We do no otherwise than we are willed.   10

GLOUCESTER Who willèd you? Or whose will stands
   but mine?
   There's none Protector of the realm but I.
   Break up the gates, I'll be your warrantize;
   Shall I be flouted thus by dunghill grooms?
               Gloucester's men rush at the Tower gates, and
                    Woodville the Lieutenant speaks within.

WOODVILLE What noise is this? What traitors have
   we here?   15

GLOUCESTER Lieutenant, is it you whose voice, I hear?
   Open the gates; here's Gloucester that would enter.

WOODVILLE Have patience, noble duke, I may not
   open;
   The Cardinal of Winchester forbids:
   From him I have express commandment   20
   That thou nor none of thine shall be let in.

GLOUCESTER Faint-hearted Woodville, prizest him 'fore
   me?
   Arrogant Winchester, that haughty prelate,
   Whom Henry, our late sovereign, ne'er could
   brook?
   Thou art no friend to God or to the king;   25
   Open the gates, or I'll shut thee out shortly.

SERVINGMEN Open the gates unto the Lord Protector,
   Or we'll burst them open, if that you come not
   quickly.

   Enter to the Protector at the Tower gates Winchester
         and his men in tawny coats.

13 **warrantize** pledge of security 14 **dunghill grooms** vile servingmen
20 **commandment** (trisyllabic; spelled *commandement* in the Folio) 22 **prizest
him 'fore me** rank him above me 24 **brook** endure 28 **if that** if
28 s.d. **tawny coats** (servants of churchmen traditionally wore tawny, or brownish-
yellow, coats)

WINCHESTER How now, ambitious Humphrey, what
        means this?

GLOUCESTER Peeled priest, dost thou command me to
30   be shut out?

WINCHESTER I do, thou most usurping proditor,
        And not Protector, of the king or realm.

GLOUCESTER Stand back, thou manifest conspirator,
        Thou that contriv'dst to murder our dead lord,
35   Thou that giv'st whores indulgences to sin;
        I'll canvas thee in thy broad cardinal's hat,
        If thou proceed in this thy insolence.

WINCHESTER Nay, stand thou back, I will not budge
        a foot;
        This be Damascus, be thou cursèd Cain,
40   To slay thy brother Abel, if thou wilt.

GLOUCESTER I will not slay thee, but I'll drive thee
        back;
        Thy scarlet robes as a child's bearing-cloth
        I'll use to carry thee out of this place.

WINCHESTER Do what thou dar'st, I beard thee to
        thy face.

GLOUCESTER What! am I dared and bearded to my
45   face?
        Draw, men, for all this privilegèd place,
        Blue coats to tawny coats. Priest, beware your
        beard;
        I mean to tug it, and to cuff you soundly.
        Under my feet I stamp thy cardinal's hat;

30 **Peeled** tonsured, bald   31 **proditor** traitor   35 **indulgences** (the brothels
near the theaters on the south bank of the Thames were within the jurisdiction of
the Bishops of Winchester)   36 **canvas ... hat** toss you in your wide-brimmed
ecclesiastical hat as if it were a blanket   39 **Damascus** (supposed to have been
built in the place where Cain killed Abel)   40 **brother** (Winchester was half-
brother to Gloucester's father, King Henry IV)   42 **bearing-cloth** christening
robe   44 **beard** defy   46 **for ... place** (even though drawing of weapons is
forbidden under pain of death in royal residences)

In spite of pope or dignities of church,   50
Here by the cheeks I'll drag thee up and down.

WINCHESTER Gloucester, thou wilt answer this before
    the pope.

GLOUCESTER Winchester goose, I cry, a rope! a rope!
Now beat them hence; why do you let them stay?
Thee I'll chase hence, thou wolf in sheep's array.   55
Out, tawny coats! out, scarlet hypocrite!

*Here Gloucester's men beat out the Cardinal's men, and
enter in the hurly-burly the Mayor of London and his
Officers.*

MAYOR Fie, lords! that you, being supreme
    magistrates,
Thus contumeliously should break the peace!

GLOUCESTER Peace, mayor! thou know'st little of my
    wrongs:
Here's Beaufort, that regards nor God nor king,   60
Hath here distrained the Tower to his use.

WINCHESTER Here's Gloucester, a foe to citizens,
One that still motions war and never peace,
O'ercharging your free purses with large fines,
That seeks to overthrow religion   65
Because he is Protector of the realm,
And would have armor here out of the Tower
To crown himself king and suppress the prince.

GLOUCESTER I will not answer thee with words,
    but blows.   *Here they skirmish again.*

MAYOR Nought rests for me in this tumultuous strife   70
But to make open proclamation.

50 **dignities of church** your high ecclesiastical rank   53 **Winchester goose**
(1) venereal infection (2) prostitute (see note to line 35)   53 **rope** hangman's
cord   56 **scarlet** (a derisive allusion to the red robes of the cardinal)   56 s.d.
hurly-burly tumult   57 **magistrates** administrators of the kingdom   58 **contumeliously** insolently   61 **distrained** seized   63 **still motions** always
proposes   64 **O'ercharging ... fines** overburdening you with excessive special
taxes   68 **suppress** depose

Come, officer, as loud as e'er thou canst,
Cry.

[OFFICER] All manner of men assembled here in arms
75 this day against God's peace and the king's, we
charge and command you, in his highness' name,
to repair to your several dwelling-places; and not
to wear, handle, or use any sword, weapon, or
dagger henceforward, upon pain of death.

80 GLOUCESTER Cardinal, I'll be no breaker of the law,
But we shall meet, and break our minds at large.

WINCHESTER Gloucester, we'll meet to thy cost, be
sure:
Thy heart-blood I will have for this day's work.

MAYOR I'll call for clubs, if you will not away.
85 This cardinal's more haughty than the devil.

GLOUCESTER Mayor, farewell; thou dost but what thou
mayst.

WINCHESTER Abominable Gloucester, guard thy head,
For I intend to have it ere long.   *Exeunt.*

MAYOR See the coast cleared, and then we will depart.
Good God, these nobles should such stomachs
90   bear!
I myself fight not once in forty year.   *Exeunt.*

---

77 **repair** return   77 **several** own   79 **pain** penalty   81 **break ... large** reveal
our thoughts fully   84 **call for clubs** i.e., summon the apprentices of the city to
come with clubs and assist the officers in putting down the riot   90 **these ... bear**
that these noblemen should have such quarrelsome tempers

Scene IV. [*Orleans.*]

Enter the Master Gunner of Orleans and his Boy.

MASTER GUNNER Sirrah, thou know'st how Orleans is
    besieged,
  And how the English have the suburbs won.

BOY Father, I know, and oft have shot at them,
  Howe'er, unfortunate, I missed my aim.

MASTER GUNNER But now thou shalt not. Be thou ruled
    by me: 5
  Chief master-gunner am I of this town;
  Something I must do to procure me grace.
  The prince's espials have informèd me
  How the English, in the suburbs close intrenched,
  Went through a secret grate of iron bars   10
  In yonder tower to overpeer the city
  And thence discover how with most advantage
  They may vex us with shot or with assault.
  To intercept this inconvenience,
  A piece of ordnance 'gainst it I have placed,   15
  And even these three days have I watched
  If I could see them. Now do thou watch,
  For I can stay no longer.
  If thou spy'st any, run and bring me word,
  And thou shalt find me at the governor's.   *Exit.*   20

BOY Father, I warrant you, take you no care;
  I'll never trouble you, if I may spy them.   *Exit.*

    Enter Salisbury and Talbot on the turrets, with
  [*Sir William Glansdale, Sir Thomas Gargrave, and*] *others.*

I.iv.1 **Sirrah** a term used in addressing children or inferiors 7 **grace** favor
8 **espials** spies 11 **overpeer** look down upon 14 **intercept** stop 15 **piece of
ordnance** cannon

SALISBURY Talbot, my life, my joy, again returned!
How wert thou handled, being prisoner?
25   Or by what means gots thou to be released?
Discourse, I prithee, on this turret's top.

TALBOT The Earl of Bedford had a prisoner
Called the brave Lord Ponton de Santrailles;
For him was I exchanged and ransomèd.
30   But with a baser man of arms by far
Once in contempt they would have bartered me;
Which I disdaining scorned and cravèd death
Rather than I would be so pilled-esteemed.
In fine, redeemed I was as I desired.
35   But O! the treacherous Falstaff wounds my heart,
Whom with my bare fist I would execute,
If I now had him brought into my power.

SALISBURY Yet tell'st thou not how thou wert entertained.

TALBOT With scoffs and scorns and contumelious
taunts,
40   In open marketplace produced they me,
To be a public spectacle to all:
Here, said they, is the terror of the French,
The scarecrow that affrights our children so.
Then broke I from the officers that led me,
45   And with my nails digged stones out of the ground
To hurl at the beholders of my shame.
My grisly countenance made others fly;
None durst come near for fear of sudden death.
In iron walls they deemed me not secure;
50   So great fear of my name 'mongst them were spread
That they supposed I could rend bars of steel
And spurn in pieces posts of adamant.
Wherefore a guard of chosen shot I had

---

25 **gots thou** did you manage   26 **Discourse** relate   26 **prithee** pray thee
30 **baser** less well born   33 **pilled-esteemed** poorly valued   34 **In fine** finally
43 **affrights** frightens   47 **grisly** grim   52 **adamant** indestructible material
53 **chosen shot** picked marksmen

That walked about me every minute while,
And if I did but stir out of my bed,   55
Ready they were to shoot me to the heart.

Enter the Boy with a linstock.

SALISBURY I grieve to hear what torments you endured,
But we will be revenged sufficiently.
Now it is supper-time in Orleans;
Here, through this grate, I count each one   60
And view the Frenchmen how they fortify;
Let us look in; the sight will much delight thee.
Sir Thomas Gargrave, and Sir William Glansdale,
Let me have your express opinions
Where is best place to make our batt'ry next.   65

GARGRAVE I think at the north gate, for there stands
  lords.

GLANSDALE And I, here, at the bulwark of the bridge.

TALBOT For aught I see, this city must be famished,
Or with light skirmishes enfeeblèd.   *Here they
          shoot, and Salisbury [and Gargrave] fall down.*

SALISBURY O Lord, have mercy on us, wretched
  sinners!   70

GARGRAVE O Lord, have mercy on me, woeful man!

TALBOT What chance is this that suddenly hath
  crossed us?
Speak, Salisbury; at least, if thou canst speak,
How far'st thou, mirror of all martial men?
One of thy eyes and thy cheek's side struck off!   75
Accursèd tower! accursèd fatal hand
That hath contrived this woful tragedy!
In thirteen battles Salisbury o'ercame;
Henry the Fifth he first trained to the wars;

54 every minute while incessantly   56 s.d. linstock staff to hold the match for
lighting a cannon   64 express precise   65 make our batt'ry direct our fire
67 bulwark fortification   69 enfeeblèd weakened   72 crossed thwarted
74 mirror of model for   76 fatal hand hand of fate

80   Whilst any trump did sound, or drum struck up,
        His sword did ne'er leave striking in the field.
        Yet liv'st thou, Salisbury? Though thy speech doth
            fail,
        One eye thou hast, to look to heaven for grace.
        The sun with one eye vieweth all the world.
85   Heaven, be thou gracious to none alive
        If Salisbury wants mercy at thy hands!
        Bear hence his body; I will help to bury it.
        Sir Thomas Gargrave, hast thou any life?
        Speak unto Talbot; nay, look up to him.
90   Salisbury, cheer thy spirit with this comfort:
        Thou shalt not die whiles—
        He beckons with his hand and smiles on me,
        As who should say, "When I am dead and gone,
        Remember to avenge me on the French."
95   Plantagenet, I will; and like thee, [Nero,]
        Play on the lute, beholding the towns burn.
        Wretched shall France be only in my name.

        Here an alarum, and it thunders and lightens.

        What stir is this? What tumult's in the heavens?
        Whence cometh this alarum, and the noise?

        Enter a Messenger.

        MESSENGER My lord, my lord, the French have gath-
100   ered head:
        The Dolphin, with one Joan la Pucelle joined,
        A holy prophetess new risen up,
        Is come with a great power to raise the siege.

        Here Salisbury lifteth himself up and groans.

        TALBOT Hear, hear how dying Salisbury doth groan!
105   It irks his heart he cannot be revenged.

---

80 **trump** trumpet 86 **wants** lacks 91 **whiles** until 93 **As who** as if he
95 **Plantagenet** (though Salisbury's name was Thomas Montacute, he was related
to the royal family, which adopted the name Plantagenet in the fifteenth
century) 97 **only in** merely at the sound of (?) 98 **stir** commotion
100 **gathered head** raised forces

26

Frenchmen, I'll be a Salisbury to you.
Pucelle or pussel, Dolphin or dogfish,
Your hearts I'll stamp out with my horse's heels,
And make a quagmire of your mingled brains.
Convey me Salisbury into his tent,   110
And then we'll try what these dastard Frenchmen
     dare.
                                        Alarum. Exeunt.

Scene V. [*Orleans.*]

*Here an alarum again, and Talbot pursueth the Dauphin,
and driveth him. Then enter Joan la Pucelle, driving
Englishmen before her [and exit after them]. Then [re-]enter
Talbot.*

TALBOT Where is my strength, my valor, and my
     force?
Our English troops retire, I cannot stay them;
A woman clad in armor chaseth them.

                    Enter [La] Pucelle.

Here, here she comes. I'll have a bout with thee;
Devil or devil's dam, I'll conjure thee: 5
Blood will I draw on thee, thou art a witch,
And straightway give thy soul to him thou serv'st.

PUCELLE Come, come, 'tis only I that must disgrace
     thee.   *Here they fight.*

TALBOT Heavens, can you suffer hell so to prevail?
My breast I'll burst with straining of my courage   10

---

107 **pussel** lewd woman, strumpet   110 **convey me** carry   I.v.5 **dam** (1) mistress
(2) mother   5 **conjure thee** i.e., back to hell whence you came   6 **Blood ...
thee** (whoever could draw blood from a witch was free of her power)   8 **only** with
no other assistance

And from my shoulders crack my arms asunder,
But I will chastise this high-minded strumpet.

> *They fight again.*

PUCELLE Talbot, farewell; thy hour is not yet come;
I must go victual Orleans forthwith.

> *A short alarum. Then enter the town with soldiers.*

15   O'ertake me if thou canst; I scorn thy strength.
Go, go, cheer up thy hungry-starvèd men;
Help Salisbury to make his testament;
This day is ours, as many more shall be.   *Exit.*

TALBOT My thoughts are whirlèd like a potter's wheel;
20   I know not where I am, nor what I do.
A witch, by fear, not force, like Hannibal,
Drives back our troops and conquers as she lists;
So bees with smoke and doves with noisome stench
Are from their hives and houses driven away.
25   They called us for our fierceness English dogs;
Now, like to whelps, we crying run away.

> *A short alarum.*

Hark, countrymen! either renew the fight,
Or tear the lions out of England's coat;
Renounce your soil, give sheep in lions' stead:
30   Sheep run not half so treacherous from the wolf,
Or horse or oxen from the leopard,
As you fly from your oft-subduèd slaves.

> *Alarum. Here another skirmish.*

It will not be. Retire into your trenches.
You all consented unto Salisbury's death,
35   For none would strike a stroke in his revenge.
Pucelle is entered into Orleans
In spite of us or aught that we could do.

---

12 **high-minded** arrogant   14 **victual** bring provisions into   14 **forthwith**
immediately   21 **Hannibal** (who terrified the Romans by driving among them
oxen with lighted torches fixed to their horns)   22 **lists** pleases   26 **whelps**
puppies   28 **lions** heraldic royal symbol of England   29 **soil** (possibly a misprint
for *style;* the line appears to mean: replace the lions in your royal coat of arms with
sheep)   30 **treacherous** fearfully

O, would I were to die with Salisbury!
The shame hereof will make me hide my head.
                              Exit Talbot. Alarum. Retreat.

Scene VI. [*Orleans.*]

*Flourish. Enter on the walls [La] Pucelle, Dauphin,
Reignier, Alençon, and Soldiers.*

PUCELLE Advance our waving colors on the walls;
Rescued is Orleans from the English.
Thus Joan la Pucelle hath performed her word.

DAUPHIN Divinest creature, Astraea's daughter,
How shall I honor thee for this success?   5
Thy promises are like Adonis' garden
That one day bloomed and fruitful were the next.
France, triumph in thy glorious prophetess!
Recovered is the town of Orleans;
More blessèd hap did ne'er befall our state.   10

REIGNIER Why ring not out the bells aloud throughout
    the town?
Dolphin, command the citizens make bonfires
And feast and banquet in the open streets
To celebrate the joy that God hath given us.

ALENÇON All France will be replete with mirth and joy   15
When they shall hear how we have played the
    men.

DAUPHIN 'Tis Joan, not we, by whom the day is won;

---

39 s.d. **Retreat** signal for withdrawal from battle I.vi.1 **Advance** raise
4 **Astraea's daughter** daughter of the goddess of justice (compare *Deborah*,
I.ii.105) 6 **Adonis'** of the youth loved by Venus (for a description of his garden,
see Edmund Spenser, *The Faerie Queene*, III.vi.29–50) 10 **hap** good fortune
16 **played the men** proved our courage

29

For which I will divide my crown with her,
And all the priests and friars in my realm
20   Shall in procession sing her endless praise.
A statelier pyramis to her I'll rear
Than Rhodope's or Memphis' ever was.
In memory of her when she is dead,
Her ashes, in an urn more precious
25   Than the rich-jeweled coffer of Darius,
Transported shall be at high festivals
Before the kings and queens of France.
No longer on Saint Denis will we cry,
But Joan la Pucelle shall be France's saint.
30   Come in, and let us banquet royally,
After this golden day of victory.   *Flourish. Exeunt.*

---

21 **pyramis** pyramid   22 **Rhodope's** (according to legend, the famous Greek
courtesan Rhodopis built the third pyramid)   25 **coffer of Darius** (the Persian
monarch's jewel chest, said to have been used by Alexander the Great to hold a
copy of Homer)   28 **Saint Denis** patron saint of France

ACT II

Scene I. [*Orleans.*]

*Enter a [French] Sergeant of a band,
with two Sentinels.*

SERGEANT Sirs, take your places and be vigilant;
  If any noise or soldier you perceive
  Near to the walls, by some apparent sign
  Let us have knowledge at the court of guard.

SENTINEL Sergeant, you shall. Thus are poor servi-
    tors,   [*Exit Sergeant.*] 5
  When others sleep upon their quiet beds,
  Constrained to watch in darkness, rain, and cold.

*Enter Talbot, Bedford, and Burgundy, [and forces,] with
scaling-ladders, their drums beating a dead march.*

TALBOT Lord Regent, and redoubted Burgundy,
  By whose approach the regions of Artois,
  Wallon, and Picardy are friends to us,   10

II.i.4 **court of guard** headquarters of the guard   5 **servitors** soldiers
8 **redoubted** distinguished   9 **approach** presence   9-10 **Artois, Wallon, and
Picardy** (provinces in northeastern France, parts of which are now in Belgium)

31

This happy night the Frenchmen are secure,
Having all day caroused and banqueted;
Embrace we then this opportunity
As fitting best to quittance their deceit
15   Contrived by art and baleful sorcery.

BEDFORD Coward of France! how much he wrongs his
        fame,
Despairing of his own arm's fortitude,
To join with witches and the help of hell.

BURGUNDY Traitors have never other company.
20   But what's that Pucelle whom they term so pure?

TALBOT A maid, they say.

BEDFORD   A maid? And be so martial?

BURGUNDY Pray God she prove not masculine ere
        long,
If underneath the standard of the French
She carry armor as she hath begun.

TALBOT Well, let them practice and converse with
25   spirits.
God is our fortress, in whose conquering name
Let us resolve to scale their flinty bulwarks.

BEDFORD Ascend, brave Talbot; we will follow thee.

TALBOT Not all together: better far, I guess,
30   That we do make our entrance several ways;
That, if it chance the one of us do fail,
The other yet may rise against their force.

BEDFORD Agreed; I'll to yond corner.

BURGUNDY   And I to this.

TALBOT And here will Talbot mount, or make his
        grave.

---

11 **secure** careless 13 **Embrace we** let us seize 14 **quittance** repay 15 **art**
(black) magic 15 **baleful** harmful 22 **prove not masculine** (1) does not turn
out to be a man (?) (2) does not become pregnant with a male child 24 **practice**
conjure 27 **flinty** rugged 30 **several** by separate 33 **yond** yonder

Now, Salisbury, for thee, and for the right   35
Of English Henry, shall this might appear
How much in duty I am bound to both.

SENTINEL Arm! arm! the enemy doth make assault!
                    [*The English, scaling the walls,*] *cry "St. George!*
                                        a Talbot!" [*and enter the town*].

The French leap o'er the walls in their shirts. Enter
several ways Bastard, Alençon, Reignier, half ready, and
half unready.

ALENÇON How now, my lords! what, all unready so?

BASTARD Unready? Ay, and glad we 'scaped so well.   40

REIGNIER 'Twas time, I trow, to wake and leave our
            beds,
      Hearing alarums at our chamber doors.

ALENÇON Of all exploits since first I followed arms,
      Ne'er heard I of a warlike enterprise
      More venturous or desperate than this.   45

BASTARD I think this Talbot be a fiend of hell.

REIGNIER If not of hell, the heavens, sure, favor him.

ALENÇON Here cometh Charles; I marvel how he
            sped.

                Enter Charles [*the Dauphin*] *and Joan.*

BASTARD Tut, holy Joan was his defensive guard.

DAUPHIN Is this thy cunning, thou deceitful dame?   50
      Didst thou at first, to flatter us withal,
      Make us partakers of a little gain,
      That now our loss might be ten times so much?

PUCELLE Wherefore is Charles impatient with his
            friend?
      At all times will you have my power alike?   55
      Sleeping or waking must I still prevail,

38 s.d. **ready** dressed   41 **trow** think   48 **marvel how he sped** wonder how he
fared   50 **cunning** craftiness   51 **to flatter us withal** in order to deceive us
56 **still** always

    Or will you blame and lay the fault on me?
    Improvident soldiers! had your watch been good,
    This sudden mischief never could have fall'n.

60 DAUPHIN Duke of Alençon, this was your default,
    That, being captain of the watch tonight,
    Did look no better to that weighty charge.

ALENÇON Had all your quarters been as safely kept
    As that whereof I had the government,
65   We had not been thus shamefully surprised.

BASTARD Mine was secure.

REIGNIER   And so was mine, my lord.

DAUPHIN And, for myself, most part of all this night,
    Within her quarter and mine own precinct
    I was employed in passing to and fro,
70   About relieving of the sentinels.
    Then how or which way should they first break in?

PUCELLE Question, my lords, no further of the case,
    How or which way; 'tis sure they found some place
    But weakly guarded, where the breach was made.
75   And now there rests no other shift but this,
    To gather our soldiers, scattered and dispersed,
    And lay new platforms to endamage them.

*Alarum. Enter an [English] Soldier, crying, "A Talbot!
a Talbot!" They fly, leaving their clothes behind.*

SOLDIER I'll be so bold to take what they have left.
    The cry of Talbot serves me for a sword,
80   For I have loaden me with many spoils,
    Using no other weapon but his name.   *Exit.*

---

58 **Improvident** unwary   60 **default** fault   62 **weighty charge** important
responsibility   64 **government** command   68 **quarter** (1) assigned area for
defense (2) chamber   68 **precinct** area of command   75 **shift** expedient,
stratagem   77 **lay … them** make new plans to harm the English   80 **loaden me**
burdened myself

Scene II. [*Orleans. Within the town.*]

Enter Talbot, Bedford, Burgundy,
[*a Captain, and others*].

BEDFORD The day begins to break, and night is fled,
Whose pitchy mantle over-veiled the earth.
Here sound retreat, and cease our hot pursuit.

Retreat.

TALBOT Bring forth the body of old Salisbury,
And here advance it in the marketplace,   5
The middle center of this cursèd town.
Now have I paid my vow unto his soul;
For every drop of blood was drawn from him
There hath at least five Frenchmen died tonight.
And that hereafter ages may behold   10
What ruin happened in revenge of him,
Within their chiefest temple I'll erect
A tomb, wherein his corpse shall be interred;
Upon the which, that everyone may read,
Shall be engraved the sack of Orleans,   15
The treacherous manner of his mournful death,
And what a terror he had been to France.
But, lords, in all our bloody massacre,
I muse we met not with the Dolphin's grace,
His new-come champion, virtuous Joan of Arc,   20
Nor any of his false confederates.

BEDFORD 'Tis thought, Lord Talbot, when the fight
      began,
Roused on the sudden from their drowsy beds,

II.ii.2 **pitchy** dark   5 **advance it** raise it up   12 **chiefest temple** cathedral
15 **sack** plundering   19 **muse** wonder why   19 **the Dolphin's grace** i.e., his
grace, the Dauphin   21 **confederates** companions

They did amongst the troops of armèd men
25　Leap o'er the walls for refuge in the field.

BURGUNDY Myself, as far as I could well discern
For smoke and dusky vapors of the night,
Am sure I scared the Dolphin and his trull,
When arm in arm they both came swiftly running,
30　Like to a pair of loving turtle-doves
That could not live asunder day or night.
After that things are set in order here,
We'll follow them with all the power we have.

Enter a Messenger.

MESSENGER All hail, my lords! Which of this princely
train
35　Call ye the warlike Talbot, for his acts
So much applauded through the realm of France?

TALBOT Here is the Talbot; who would speak with
him?

MESSENGER The virtuous lady, Countess of Auvergne,
With modesty admiring thy renown,
40　By me entreats, great lord, thou wouldst vouchsafe
To visit her poor castle where she lies,
That she may boast she hath beheld the man
Whose glory fills the world with loud report.

BURGUNDY Is it even so? Nay, then, I see our wars
45　Will turn unto a peaceful comic sport,
When ladies crave to be encountered with.
You may not, my lord, despise her gentle suit.

TALBOT Ne'er trust me then; for when a world of men
Could not prevail with all their oratory,
50　Yet hath a woman's kindness overruled;

---

27 **For** because of　28 **trull** concubine, harlot　34 **princely train** noble
company　37 **the** (used with the surname to designate the head of a family or
clan)　40 **vouchsafe** condescend　41 **lies** resides　46 **encountered** met (for an
amatory interview)　47 **gentle suit** mannerly request　50 **overruled** prevailed

And therefore tell her I return great thanks
And in submission will attend on her.
Will not your honors bear me company?

BEDFORD No, truly, 'tis more than manners will,   55
And I have heard it said, unbidden guests
Are often welcomest when they are gone.

TALBOT Well then, alone, since there's no remedy,
I mean to prove this lady's courtesy.
Come hither, captain. (*Whispers*) You perceive my
    mind?

CAPTAIN I do, my lord, and mean accordingly.   60
                                        Exeunt.

Scene III. [*Auvergne. The Countess' castle.*]

Enter Countess [and her Porter].

COUNTESS Porter, remember what I gave in charge,
And when you have done so, bring the keys to me.

PORTER Madam, I will.   *Exit.*

COUNTESS The plot is laid; if all things fall out right,
I shall as famous be by this exploit   5
As Scythian Tomyris by Cyrus' death.
Great is the rumor of this dreadful knight,
And his achievements of no less account;
Fain would mine eyes be witness with mine ears,
To give their censure of these rare reports.   10

Enter Messenger and Talbot.

52 in submission deferentially 54 will require 55 unbidden uninvited
58 prove ... courtesy try out this lady's hospitality 59 perceive my mind
understand my plan II.iii.1 gave in charge instructed you to do 6 Tomyris
queen of a fierce Central Asian people who slew Cyrus the Great in battle
7 rumor reputation 9 Fain gladly 10 censure judgment

MESSENGER Madam,
    According as your ladyship desired,
    By message craved, so is Lord Talbot come.

COUNTESS And he is welcome. What! is this the man?

MESSENGER Madam, it is.

15 COUNTESS   Is this the scourge of France?
    Is this the Talbot, so much feared abroad
    That with his name the mothers still their babes?
    I see report is fabulous and false.
    I thought I should have seen some Hercules,
20   A second Hector, for his grim aspect
    And large proportion of his strong-knit limbs.
    Alas, this is a child, a silly dwarf!
    It cannot be this weak and writhled shrimp
    Should strike such terror to his enemies.

25 TALBOT Madam, I have been bold to trouble you,
    But since your ladyship is not at leisure,
    I'll sort some other time to visit you.

COUNTESS What means he now? Go ask him whither
    he goes.

MESSENGER Stay, my Lord Talbot, for my lady craves
30   To know the cause of your abrupt departure.

TALBOT Marry, for that she's in a wrong belief,
    I go to certify her Talbot's here.

Enter Porter with keys.

COUNTESS If thou be he, then art thou prisoner.

TALBOT Prisoner! to whom?

COUNTESS   To me, bloodthirsty lord;
35   And for that cause I trained thee to my house.
    Long time thy shadow hath been thrall to me,

13 **craved** invited   17 **still** silence   18 **fabulous** merely fictional   20 **aspect** countenance   21 **strong-knit** well-muscled   22 **silly** feeble   23 **writhled** wrinkled   27 **sort** choose   31 **Marry** why   31 **for that** because   32 **certify** inform   35 **trained** lured

For in my gallery thy picture hangs.
But now the substances shall endure the like,
And I will chain these legs and arms of thine
That hast by tyranny these many years   40
Wasted our country, slain our citizens,
And sent our sons and husbands captivate.

TALBOT Ha, ha, ha!

COUNTESS Laughest thou, wretch? Thy mirth shall turn
    to moan.

TALBOT I laugh to see your ladyship so fond   45
    To think that you have aught but Talbot's shadow
    Wherein to practice your severity.

COUNTESS Why, art not thou the man?

TALBOT   I am indeed.

COUNTESS Then have I substance too.

TALBOT No, no, I am but shadow of myself: 50
    You are deceived, my substance is not here,
    For what you see is but the smallest part
    And least proportion of humanity.
    I tell you, madam, were the whole frame here,
    It is of such a spacious lofty pitch,   55
    Your roof were not sufficient to contain 't.

COUNTESS This is a riddling merchant for the
    nonce;
    He will be here, and yet he is not here.
    How can these contrarieties agree?

TALBOT That will I show you presently.   60
               Winds his horn; drums strike up; a peal
                     of ordnance; enter Soldiers.
    How say you, madam? Are you now persuaded
    That Talbot is but shadow of himself?

37 **picture** (possibly implying that the Countess was trying to practice witchcraft on him) 42 **captivate** captive 45 **fond** foolish 47 **severity** cruelty 54 **frame** structure 55 **pitch** stature 57 **riddling merchant** enigmatic fellow 57 **for the nonce** for the occasion (merely a line-filler) 59 **contrarieties** contradictions 60 s.d. **Winds** blows 60 s.d. **peal of ordnance** salute of guns

39

These are his substance, sinews, arms, and strength,
With which he yoketh your rebellious necks,
65   Razeth your cities and subverts your towns,
And in a moment makes them desolate.

COUNTESS   Victorious Talbot, pardon my abuse;
I find thou art no less than fame hath bruited
And more than may be gathered by thy shape.
70   Let my presumption not provoke thy wrath,
For I am sorry that with reverence
I did not entertain thee as thou art.

TALBOT   Be not dismayed, fair lady, nor misconster
The mind of Talbot, as you did mistake
75   The outward composition of his body.
What you have done hath not offended me,
Nor other satisfaction do I crave,
But only, with your patience, that we may
Taste of your wine and see what cates you have,
80   For soldiers' stomachs always serve them well.

COUNTESS   With all my heart, and think me honorèd
To feast so great a warrior in my house.   *Exeunt.*

Scene IV. [*London. The Temple Garden.*]

*Enter Richard Plantagenet, Warwick, Somerset,
[William de la] Pole [Earl of Suffolk, Vernon, and
another Lawyer].*

PLANTAGENET   Great lords and gentlemen, what means
this silence?
Dare no man answer in a case of truth?

---

64 **yoketh** brings into subjection   65 **subverts** overthrows   68 **bruited** reported
71 **reverence** respect   73 **misconster** misunderstand   75 **composition**
form   79 **cates** choice foods   II.iv. s.d. **Temple Garden** (the Inner and Middle
Temples were residences for students of the common law)

SUFFOLK Within the Temple Hall we were too loud;
   The garden here is more convenient.

PLANTAGENET Then say at once if I maintained the
     truth;   5
   Or else was wrangling Somerset in th' error?

SUFFOLK Faith, I have been a truant in the law,
   And never yet could frame my will to it,
   And therefore frame the law unto my will.

SOMERSET Judge you, my lord of Warwick, then,
     between us.   10

WARWICK Between two hawks, which flies the higher
     pitch;
   Between two dogs, which hath the deeper mouth;
   Between two blades, which bears the better temper;
   Between two horses, which doth bear him best;
   Between two girls, which hath the merriest eye—   15
   I have perhaps some shallow spirit of judgment;
   But in these nice sharp quillets of the law,
   Good faith, I am no wiser than a daw.

PLANTAGENET Tut, tut, here is a mannerly forbearance.
   The truth appears so naked on my side   20
   That any purblind eye may find it out.

SOMERSET And on my side it is so well appareled,
   So clear, so shining, and so evident,
   That it will glimmer through a blind man's eye.

PLANTAGENET Since you are tongue-tied and so loath
     to speak,   25
   In dumb significants proclaim your thoughts:
   Let him that is a true-born gentleman
   And stands upon the honor of his birth,

6 **wrangling** quarrelsome   7 **Faith** in truth   7 **truant** lazy student   8 **frame**
dispose   9 **frame** twist   12 **mouth** bark, bay   14 **bear him** behave
himself   16 **shallow spirit** small amount   17 **nice sharp quillets** precise and
subtle distinctions   18 **daw** simpleton   21 **purblind** nearly blind   22 **appareled** (1) dressed (2) ordered   26 **In dumb significants** by mute signs
28 **stands upon** takes pride in

If he suppose that I have pleaded truth,
30   From off this brier pluck a white rose with me.

SOMERSET   Let him that is no coward nor no flatterer,
     But dare maintain the party of the truth,
     Pluck a red rose from off this thorn with me.

WARWICK   I love no colors; and without all color
35   Of base insinuating flattery
     I pluck this white rose with Plantagenet.

SUFFOLK   I pluck this red rose with young Somerset
     And say withal I think he held the right.

VERNON   Stay, lords and gentlemen, and pluck no more
40   Till you conclude that he upon whose side
     The fewest roses are cropped from the tree
     Shall yield the other in the right opinion.

SOMERSET   Good Master Vernon, it is well objected;
     If I have fewest, I subscribe in silence.

45 PLANTAGENET   And I.

VERNON   Then for the truth and plainness of the case,
     I pluck this pale and maiden blossom here,
     Giving my verdict on the white rose side.

SOMERSET   Prick not your finger as you pluck it off,
50   Lest bleeding you do paint the white rose red
     And fall on my side so against your will.

VERNON   If I, my lord, for my opinion bleed,
     Opinion shall be surgeon to my hurt
     And keep me on the side where still I am.

55 SOMERSET   Well, well, come on, who else?

LAWYER   Unless my study and my books be false,
     The argument you held was wrong in you;
     In sign whereof I pluck a white rose too.

PLANTAGENET   Now, Somerset, where is your argument?

---

34 **colors** (1) pretenses (2) adornments of speech   38 **withal** thereby
41 **cropped** plucked   43 **objected** proposed   47 **maiden** flawless

SOMERSET Here in my scabbard, meditating that   60
  Shall dye your white rose in a bloody red.

PLANTAGENET Meantime your cheeks do counterfeit
    our roses,
  For pale they look with fear, as witnessing
  The truth on our side.

SOMERSET   No, Plantagenet,
  'Tis not for fear, but anger that thy cheeks   65
  Blush for pure shame to counterfeit our roses,
  And yet thy tongue will not confess thy error.

PLANTAGENET Hath not thy rose a canker, Somerset?

SOMERSET Hath not thy rose a thorn, Plantagenet?

PLANTAGENET Ay, sharp and piercing, to maintain his
    truth   70
  Whiles thy consuming canker eats his falsehood.

SOMERSET Well, I'll find friends to wear my bleeding
    roses,
  That shall maintain what I have said is true
  Where false Plantagenet dare not be seen.

PLANTAGENET Now, by this maiden blossom in my
    hand,   75
  I scorn thee and thy fashion, peevish boy.

SUFFOLK Turn not thy scorns this way, Plantagenet.

PLANTAGENET Proud Pole, I will, and scorn both him
    and thee.

SUFFOLK I'll turn my part thereof into thy throat.

SOMERSET Away, away, good William de la Pole!   80
  We grace the yeoman by conversing with him.

WARWICK Now, by God's will, thou wrong'st him,
    Somerset;

60 **meditating** planning 62 **counterfeit** imitate 68 **canker** (1) disease
(2) caterpillar larva 76 **fashion** (1) manner of behavior (2) faction (?) 81 **grace
the yeoman** dignify this commoner

43

His grandfather was Lionel Duke of Clarence,
Third son to the third Edward King of England:
85   Spring crestless yeomen from so deep a root?

PLANTAGENET   He bears him on the place's privilege,
Or durst not, for his craven heart, say thus.

SOMERSET   By him that made me, I'll maintain my
          words
On any plot of ground in Christendom.
90   Was not thy father, Richard Earl of Cambridge,
For treason executed in our late king's days?
And, by his treason, stand'st not thou attainted,
Corrupted, and exempt from ancient gentry?
His trespass yet lives guilty in thy blood,
95   And, till thou be restored, thou art a yeoman.

PLANTAGENET   My father was attachèd, not attainted,
Condemned to die for treason, but no traitor;
And that I'll prove on better men than Somerset,
Were growing time once ripened to my will.
100   For your partaker Pole and you yourself,
I'll note you in my book of memory
To scourge you for this apprehension.
Look to it well and say you are well warned.

SOMERSET   Ah, thou shalt find us ready for thee still,
105   And know us by these colors for thy foes,
For these my friends in spite of thee shall wear.

PLANTAGENET   And, by my soul, this pale and angry
          rose,
As cognizance of my blood-drinking hate,

---

83 **grandfather** i.e., great-great-grandfather   85 **crestless** not having the right to
a coat of arms   86 **privilege** i.e., of sanctuary (since the Temple was founded as a
religious house)   92–93 **attainted ... gentry** (legal penalties by which the heirs
of a person convicted of treason were prevented from inheriting his property and
titles)   94 **trespass** crime   95 **And ... yeoman** (therefore, you shall remain a
commoner until your titles are legally restored)   96 **attachèd** arrested   98 **prove**
establish through trial by combat   99 **Were ... will** i.e., if I should ever be
restored to the nobility   100 **partaker** partisan   102 **apprehension** notion,
display of wit   108 **cognizance** a badge   108 **blood-drinking** bloodthirsty

Will I forever and my faction wear
Until it wither with me to my grave   110
Or flourish to the height of my degree.

SUFFOLK Go forward and be choked with thy ambition!
And so farewell until I meet thee next.   *Exit*.

SOMERSET Have with thee, Pole. Farewell, ambitious Richard.   *Exit*.

PLANTAGENET How I am braved and must perforce
endure it!   115

WARWICK This blot that they object against your house
Shall be whipped out in the next parliament
Called for the truce of Winchester and Gloucester,
And if thou be not then created York,
I will not live to be accounted Warwick.   120
Meantime, in signal of my love to thee,
Against proud Somerset and William Pole,
Will I upon thy party wear this rose.
And here I prophesy: this brawl today,
Grown to this faction in the Temple garden,   125
Shall send, between the red rose and the white,
A thousand souls to death and deadly night.

PLANTAGENET Good Master Vernon, I am bound to
you
That you on my behalf would pluck a flower.

VERNON In your behalf still will I wear the same.   130

LAWYER And so will I.

PLANTAGENET Thanks, gentle [sir].
Come, let us four to dinner: I dare say
This quarrel will drink blood another day. *Exeunt*.

---

111 to ... degree until I regain my high rank 114 Have with thee I'll go with
you 115 braved defied 115 perforce necessarily 117 whipped quickly
stricken 119 York i.e., Duke of York 120 accounted considered 123 upon
thy party in support of you 124 brawl quarrel 134 drink blood result in
bloodshed

Scene V. [*The Tower of London.*]

Enter Mortimer, brought in a chair, and Jailers.

MORTIMER Kind keepers of my weak decaying age,
Let dying Mortimer here rest himself.
Even like a man new halèd from the rack,
So fare my limbs with long imprisonment,
5   And these gray locks, the pursuivants of death,
Nestor-like agèd in an age of care,
Argue the end of Edmund Mortimer.
These eyes, like lamps whose wasting oil is spent,
Wax dim, as drawing to their exigent;
10   Weak shoulders, overborne with burthening grief,
And pithless arms, like to a withered vine
That droops his sapless branches to the ground.
Yet are these feet, whose strengthless stay is
    numb,
Unable to support this lump of clay,
15   Swift-wingèd with desire to get a grave,
As witting I no other comfort have.
But tell me, keeper, will my nephew come?

FIRST JAILER Richard Plantagenet, my lord, will come:
We sent unto the Temple, unto his chamber,
20   And answer was returned that he will come.

MORTIMER Enough; my soul shall then be satisfied.
Poor gentleman! his wrong doth equal mine.
Since Henry Monmouth first began to reign,
Before whose glory I was great in arms,

II.v.3 **new … rack** just released from the torturer's rack 5 **pursuivants**
heralds 6 **Nestor-like** (the Greek king Nestor, in Homer's *Iliad*, is a type of old
age) 7 **Argue** foretell 8 **wasting** consuming 9 **Wax** grow 9 **exigent**
end 10 **burthening** (dissyllabic) burdensome 11 **pithless** strengthless
13 **stay** support 23 **Henry Monmouth** King Henry V

This loathsome sequestration have I had;   25
And even since then hath Richard been obscured,
Deprived of honor and inheritance.
But now the arbitrator of despairs,
Just Death, kind umpire of men's miseries,
With sweet enlargement doth dismiss me hence.   30
I would his troubles likewise were expired,
That so he might recover what was lost.

Enter Richard [Plantagenet].

FIRST JAILER My lord, your loving nephew now is
    come.

MORTIMER Richard Plantagenet, my friend, is he
    come?

PLANTAGENET Ay, noble uncle, thus ignobly used,   35
    Your nephew, late despisèd Richard, comes.

MORTIMER Direct mine arms I may embrace his neck
    And in his bosom spend my latter gasp.
    O, tell me when my lips do touch his cheeks,
    That I may kindly give one fainting kiss.   40
    And now declare, sweet stem from York's great
        stock,
    Why didst thou say, of late thou wert despised?

PLANTAGENET First, lean thine agèd back against mine
        arm,
    And, in that ease, I'll tell thee my disease.
    This day, in argument upon a case,   45
    Some words there grew 'twixt Somerset and me;
    Among which terms he used his lavish tongue
    And did upbraid me with my father's death:
    Which obloquy set bars before my tongue,
    Else with the like I had requited him.   50

25 **sequestration** imprisonment 26 **obscured** degraded 29 **umpire** arbitrator 30 **enlargement** release 31 **his** i.e., Plantagenet's 36 **late despisèd** just insulted 37 **I may** (so that) I may 38 **spend my latter gasp** draw my last breath 41 **stock** trunk (i.e., lineage) 44 **disease** source of my discomfort 47 **lavish** licentious, unrestrained 48 **upbraid** insult 49 **obloquy** reproach 50 **requited** repaid

Therefore, good uncle, for my father's sake,
In honor of a true Plantagenet,
And for alliance' sake, declare the cause
My father, Earl of Cambridge, lost his head.

MORTIMER That cause, fair nephew, that imprisoned
55   me
And hath detained me all my flow'ring youth
Within a loathsome dungeon, there to pine,
Was cursèd instrument of his decease.

PLANTAGENET Discover more at large what cause that
              was,
60   For I am ignorant and cannot guess.

MORTIMER I will, if that my fading breath permit
And death approach not ere my tale be done.
Henry the Fourth, grandfather to this king,
Deposed his nephew Richard, Edward's son,
65   The first-begotten and the lawful heir
Of Edward king, the third of that descent:
During whose reign the Percies of the north,
Finding his usurpation most unjust,
Endeavored my advancement to the throne.
70   The reason moved these warlike lords to this
Was, for that—young Richard thus removed,
Leaving no heir begotten of his body—
I was the next by birth and parentage:
For by my mother I derivèd am
75   From Lionel Duke of Clarence, third son
To King Edward the Third; whereas he
From John of Gaunt doth bring his pedigree,
Being but fourth of that heroic line.
But mark: as in this haughty great attempt

53 **the cause** for what reason   56 **flow'ring** vigorous, flourishing   59 **Discover** explain   64 **nephew** (cousin)   64–66 **Edward's ... descent** i.e., Richard II, son of Edward the Black Prince and grandson of King Edward III   67 **Percies** noble family of Northumberland   70 **moved** that provoked   71 **young** (Richard was actually over thirty at the time of his deposition)   74 **mother** (actually, grandmother)   74 **derivèd** descended   79 **mark** listen attentively   79 **haughty** lofty

They labored to plant the rightful heir,   80
I lost my liberty and they their lives.
Long after this, when Henry the Fifth,
Succeeding his father Bolingbroke, did reign,
Thy father, Earl of Cambridge, then derived
From famous Edmund Langley, Duke of York,   85
Marrying my sister that thy mother was,
Again, in pity of my hard distress,
Levied an army, weening to redeem
And have installed me in the diadem;
But, as the rest, so fell that noble earl   90
And was beheaded. Thus the Mortimers,
In whom the title rested, were suppressed.

PLANTAGENET Of which, my lord, your honor is the
    last.

MORTIMER True; and thou seest that I no issue have
    And that my fainting words do warrant death.   95
    Thou art my heir; the rest I wish thee gather,
    But yet be wary in thy studious care.

PLANTAGENET Thy grave admonishments prevail with
    me,
    But yet, methinks, my father's execution
    Was nothing less than bloody tyranny.   100

MORTIMER With silence, nephew, be thou politic:
    Strong-fixèd is the house of Lancaster,
    And like a mountain, not to be removed.
    But now thy uncle is removing hence,
    As princes do their courts, when they are cloyed   105
    With long continuance in a settled place.

PLANTAGENET O, uncle, would some part of my young
    years

88-89 Levied ... diadem raised an army, with the intention of rescuing me and
having me crowned king   95 warrant give assurance of   96 the rest ... gather
(1) I want you to conclude for yourself (2) I hope that you may gain all that is
rightfully yours   97 But ... care i.e., but always be careful even as you take pains
in this enterprise   105 cloyed satiated

Might but redeem the passage of your age!

MORTIMER Thou dost then wrong me, as that
          slaughterer doth
110   Which giveth many wounds when one will kill.
         Mourn not, except thou sorrow for my good;
         Only give order for my funeral.
         And so farewell, and fair be all thy hopes,
         And prosperous be thy life in peace and war! *Dies.*

PLANTAGENET And peace, no war, befall thy parting
115   soul!
         In prison hast thou spent a pilgrimage
         And like a hermit overpassed thy days.
         Well, I will lock his counsel in my breast,
         And what I do imagine, let that rest.
120   Keepers, convey him hence, and I myself
         Will see his burial better than his life.

                [*Exeunt Jailers with the body of Mortimer.*]

         Here dies the dusky torch of Mortimer,
         Choked with ambition of the meaner sort.
         And for those wrongs, those bitter injuries
125   Which Somerset hath offered to my house,
         I doubt not but with honor to redress.
         And therefore haste I to the parliament,
         Either to be restorèd to my blood,
         Or make my will th'advantage of my good.

                                              Exit.

108 **redeem the passage** buy back the passing 112 **give order** make
arrangements 116 **pilgrimage** full life's journey 117 **overpassed** lived
out 121 **Will ... life** will see that he receives the honor in his funeral that was
denied him during his lifetime 122 **dusky** gloomy 123 **Choked ... sort** stifled
by the ambition of men of inferior birth (i.e., the House of Lancaster)
126 **redress** remedy 129 **will ... good** determination of purpose the means of
achieving my ambition (see Textual Note)

ACT III

Scene I. [*London. The Parliament-house.*]

Flourish. Enter King, Exeter, Gloucester, Winchester,
Warwick, Somerset, Suffolk, Richard Plantagenet.
Gloucester offers to put up a bill; Winchester snatches it,
tears it.

WINCHESTER Com'st thou with deep premeditated
    lines,
  With written pamphlets studiously devised?
  Humphrey of Gloucester, if thou canst accuse
  Or aught intend'st to lay unto my charge,
  Do it without invention, suddenly,   5
  As I with sudden and extemporal speech
  Purpose to answer what thou canst object.

GLOUCESTER Presumptuous priest! this place com-
    mands my patience,
  Or thou shouldst find thou hast dishonored me.
  Think not, although in writing I preferred   10
  The manner of thy vile outrageous crimes,

III.i.s.d. **offers ... bill** attempts to post a statement of accusations 1 **deep premeditated lines** statements carefully thought out in advance 5 **invention** (seeking out the grounds for argument in the manner of a rhetorician or a lawyer trained in oratory) 6 **extemporal** extemporaneous 10 **preferred** set forth

51

That therefore I have forged, or am not able
Verbatim to rehearse the method of my pen.
No, prelate, such is thy audacious wickedness,
15 Thy lewd, pestiferous, and dissentious pranks,
As very infants prattle of thy pride.
Thou art a most pernicious usurer,
Froward by nature, enemy to peace,
Lascivious, wanton, more than well beseems
20 A man of thy profession and degree.
And for thy treachery, what's more manifest?
In that thou laid'st a trap to take my life,
As well at London Bridge as at the Tower.
Beside, I fear me, if thy thoughts were sifted,
25 The king, thy sovereign, is not quite exempt
From envious malice of thy swelling heart.

WINCHESTER Gloucester, I do defy thee. Lords,
     vouchsafe
To give me hearing what I shall reply.
If I were covetous, ambitious, or perverse,
30 As he will have me, how am I so poor?
Or how haps it I seek not to advance
Or raise myself, but keep my wonted calling?
And for dissension, who preferreth peace
More than I do?—except I be provoked.
35 No, my good lords, it is not that offends;
It is not that hath incensed the duke:
It is, because no one should sway but he,
No one but he should be about the king,
And that engenders thunder in his breast
40 And makes him roar these accusations forth.
But he shall know I am as good—

---

12 **forged** fabricated lies   13 **rehearse ... pen** repeat the contents of what I have
written   15 **lewd ... pranks** wicked, mischievous, and quarrelsome offenses
16 **As very** that even   17 **pernicious usurer** (alluding to Winchester's reputation
for gaining riches through extortions and loans made at exorbitant rates of
interest)   18 **Froward** inclined to evil   19 **beseems** is fitting to   24 **sifted**
closely examined   26 **swelling** proud   30 **have me** make me out to be
31 **haps it** does it happen   32 **calling** religious vocation   36 **incensed** enraged
37 **sway** rule

GLOUCESTER   As good?
  Thou bastard of my grandfather!

WINCHESTER Ay, lordly sir; for what are you, I pray,
  But one imperious in another's throne?

GLOUCESTER Am I not Protector, saucy priest?   45

WINCHESTER And am not I a prelate of the church?

GLOUCESTER Yes, as an outlaw in a castle keeps
  And useth it to patronage his theft.

WINCHESTER Unreverent Gloucester!

GLOUCESTER   Thou art reverent
  Touching thy spiritual function, not thy life.   50

WINCHESTER Rome shall remedy this.

WARWICK   Roam thither, then.
  My lord, it were your duty to forbear.

SOMERSET Ay, see the bishop be not overborne.
  Methinks my lord should be religious
  And know the office that belongs to such.   55

WARWICK Methinks his lordship should be humbler;
  It fitteth not a prelate so to plead.

SOMERSET Yes, when his holy state is touched so
    near.

WARWICK State holy or unhallowed, what of that?
  Is not his grace Protector to the king?   60

PLANTAGENET [*Aside*] Plantagenet, I see, must hold
    his tongue,
  Lest it be said, "Speak, sirrah, when you should;

---

42 **bastard** (Winchester was an illegitimate son of John of Gaunt, Duke of
Lancaster) 43 **lordly** haughty 44 **imperious** ruling 48 **patronage**
defend 50 **Touching ... function** only in respect of your high ecclesiastical
office 53 **overborne** prevailed over 54 **lord** i.e., Gloucester 55 **office**
respect 56 **lordship** Winchester 58 **holy ... near** ecclesiastical office is so
directly involved 59 **holy or unhallowed** ecclesiastical or secular 60 **grace**
i.e., Gloucester

> Must your bold verdict enter talk with lords?"
> Else would I have a fling at Winchester.

65 KING Uncles of Gloucester and of Winchester,
     The special watchmen of our English weal,
     I would prevail, if prayers might prevail,
     To join your hearts in love and amity.
     O, what a scandal is it to our crown,
70   That two such noble peers as ye should jar!
     Believe me, lords, my tender years can tell
     Civil dissension is a viperous worm
     That gnaws the bowels of the commonwealth.

A noise within, "Down with the tawny-coats!"

What tumult's this?

WARWICK   An uproar, I dare warrant,
75   Begun through malice of the bishop's men.

A noise again, "Stones! stones!"

Enter Mayor.

MAYOR O my good lords, and virtuous Henry,
     Pity the city of London, pity us!
     The bishop and the Duke of Gloucester's men,
     Forbidden late to carry any weapon,
80   Have filled their pockets full of pebble stones
     And banding themselves in contrary parts
     Do pelt so fast at one another's pate
     That many have their giddy brains knocked out.
     Our windows are broke down in every street,
85   And we for fear compelled to shut our shops.

*Enter [Servingmen of Gloucester and Winchester]
in skirmish, with bloody pates.*

KING We charge you, on allegiance to ourself,
     To hold your slaught'ring hands and keep the
        peace.

63 **bold verdict** presumptuous opinion 64 **have a fling at** reprove 66 **watchmen** guardians 66 **weal** state 72 **worm** serpent 74 **warrant** swear 78
bishop bishop's 79 **late** recently 81 **parts** parties 82 **pate** head 83 **giddy**
foolish

Pray, uncle Gloucester, mitigate this strife.

FIRST SERVINGMAN Nay, if we be forbidden stones,
we'll fall to it with our teeth.   90

SECOND SERVINGMAN Do what ye dare, we are as
resolute.   *Skirmish again.*

GLOUCESTER You of my household, leave this peevish
    broil
And set this unaccustomed fight aside.

THIRD SERVINGMAN My lord, we know your grace to be
    a man   95
Just and upright; and, for your royal birth,
Inferior to none but to his majesty,
And ere that we will suffer such a prince,
So kind a father of the commonweal,
To be disgracèd by an inkhorn mate,   100
We and our wives and children all will fight
And have our bodies slaughtered by thy foes.

FIRST SERVINGMAN Ay, and the very parings of our
    nails
Shall pitch a field when we are dead. *Begin again.*

GLOUCESTER   Stay, stay, I say!
And if you love me, as you say you do,   105
Let me persuade you to forbear awhile.

KING O, how this discord doth afflict my soul!
Can you, my Lord of Winchester, behold
My sighs and tears and will not once relent?
Who should be pitiful, if you be not?   110
Or who should study to prefer a peace,
If holy churchmen take delight in broils?

WARWICK Yield, my Lord Protector; yield, Win-
    chester,

---

88 **mitigate** appease 94 **unaccustomed** indecorous 98 **suffer** permit
100 **inkhorn mate** scribbling fellow (an unlettered person's disparaging allusion
to the literacy of clergymen) 104 **pitch a field** i.e., serve as stakes in a pitched
battlefield 111 **study** make it his aim

Except you mean with obstinate repulse
115   To slay your sovereign and destroy the realm.
You see what mischief and what murder too
Hath been enacted through your enmity;
Then be at peace, except ye thirst for blood.

WINCHESTER He shall submit, or I will never yield.

GLOUCESTER Compassion on the king commands me
120   stoop;
Or I would see his heart out ere the priest
Should ever get that privilege of me.

WARWICK Behold, my Lord of Winchester, the duke
Hath banished moody discontented fury,
125   As by his smoothèd brows it doth appear:
Why look you still so stern and tragical?

GLOUCESTER Here, Winchester, I offer thee my hand.

KING Fie, uncle Beaufort! I have heard you preach
That malice was a great and grievous sin,
130   And will not you maintain the thing you teach,
But prove a chief offender in the same?

WARWICK Sweet king! the bishop hath a kindly gird.
For shame, my Lord of Winchester, relent!
What, shall a child instruct you what to do?

WINCHESTER Well, Duke of Gloucester, I will yield
135   to thee
Love for thy love, and hand for hand I give.

GLOUCESTER [*Aside*] Ay, but, I fear me, with a hollow
      heart.
[*Aloud*] See here, my friends and loving countrymen;
This token serveth for a flag of truce
140   Betwixt ourselves and all our followers.
So help me God, as I dissemble not!

---

114 **Except** unless 114 **repulse** refusal 122 **privilege** advantage yielded
126 **tragical** gloomy 132 **kindly gird** fitting gibe 137 **hollow** insincere
139 **token** i.e., handclasp

WINCHESTER [*Aside*] So help me God, as I intend it
    not!

KING O loving uncle, kind Duke of Gloucester,
    How joyful am I made by this contract!
    Away, my masters! trouble us no more,   145
    But join in friendship, as your lords have done.

FIRST SERVINGMAN Content; I'll to the surgeon's.

SECOND SERVINGMAN   And so will I.

THIRD SERVINGMAN And I will see what physic the
    tavern affords.   *Exeunt*.

WARWICK Accept this scroll, most gracious sovereign,   150
    Which in the right of Richard Plantagenet
    We do exhibit to your majesty.

GLOUCESTER Well urged, my Lord of Warwick: for,
    sweet prince,
    And if your grace mark every circumstance,
    You have great reason to do Richard right,   155
    Especially for those occasions
    At Eltham Place I told your majesty.

KING And those occasions, uncle, were of force.
    Therefore, my loving lords, our pleasure is
    That Richard be restorèd to his blood.   160

WARWICK Let Richard be restorèd to his blood;
    So shall his father's wrongs be recompensed.

WINCHESTER As will the rest, so willeth Winchester.

KING If Richard will be true, not that all alone
    But all the whole inheritance I give   165
    That doth belong unto the house of York,
    From whence you spring by lineal descent.

PLANTAGENET Thy humble servant vows obedience
    And humble service till the point of death.

144 **contract** agreement 148 **physic** remedy 149 **affords** provides
150 **scroll** document 154 **And if** if 154 **mark** take notice of 156 **occasions**
reasons 160 **blood** i.e., title and rights of nobility

170 KING Stoop then and set your knee against my foot,
        And in reguerdon of that duty done,
        I girt thee with the valiant sword of York.
        Rise, Richard, like a true Plantagenet,
        And rise created princely Duke of York.

    PLANTAGENET And so thrive Richard as thy foes may
175   fall!
        And as my duty springs, so perish they
        That grudge one thought against your majesty!

    ALL Welcome, high prince, the mighty Duke of York!

    SOMERSET [Aside] Perish, base prince, ignoble Duke
        of York!

180 GLOUCESTER Now will it best avail your majesty
        To cross the seas and to be crowned in France:
        The presence of a king engenders love
        Amongst his subjects and his loyal friends,
        As it disanimates his enemies.

    KING When Gloucester says the word, King Henry
185   goes,
        For friendly counsel cuts off many foes.

    GLOUCESTER Your ships already are in readiness.

                    Sennet. Flourish. Exeunt. Manet Exeter.

    EXETER Ay, we may march in England or in France,
        Not seeing what is likely to ensue.
190   This late dissension grown betwixt the peers
        Burns under feignèd ashes of forged love
        And will at last break out into a flame;
        As festered members rot but by degree
        Till bones and flesh and sinews fall away,
195   So will this base and envious discord breed.
        And now I fear that fatal prophecy

171 **reguerdon** ample reward   172 **girt** gird   177 **grudge one thought** entertain one grudging thought   184 **disanimates** disheartens   187 s.d. **Sennet**
trumpet signal for the exit of an important personage   187 s.d. **Manet** remains
(Latin)   191 **forged** pretended   193 **members** parts of the body   193 **by
degree** little by little, gradually

Which in the time of Henry named the Fifth
Was in the mouth of every sucking babe,
That Henry born at Monmouth should win all
And Henry born at Windsor should lose all: 200
Which is so plain that Exeter doth wish
His days may finish ere that hapless time.   *Exit.*

Scene II. [*France. Before Rouen.*]

*Enter [La] Pucelle disguised, with four Soldiers
with sacks upon their backs.*

PUCELLE These are the city gates, the gates of Rouen,
Through which our policy must make a breach.
Take heed, be wary how you place your words;
Talk like the vulgar sort of market men
That come to gather money for their corn.   5
If we have entrance, as I hope we shall,
And that we find the slothful watch but weak,
I'll by a sign give notice to our friends
That Charles the Dolphin may encounter them.

SOLDIER Our sacks shall be a mean to sack the city,   10
And we be lords and rulers over Rouen;
Therefore we'll knock.   *Knock.*

WATCHMAN [*Within*] *Qui est là?*

PUCELLE *Paysans là, pauvres gens de France:*
Poor market folks that come to sell their corn.   15

WATCHMAN Enter, go in, the market bell is rung.

PUCELLE Now, Rouen, I'll shake thy bulwarks to the
     ground.   *Exeunt.*

198 **sucking** nursing III.ii.2 **policy** stratagem 4 **vulgar** common 4 **market men** people going to market 5 **corn** grain 9 **encounter** assail 10 **mean** means 13 **Qui est là** who is there? 14 **Paysans ... France** peasants here, poor folk of France

59

Enter Charles [the Dauphin], Bastard, Alençon,
[Reignier, and forces].

DAUPHIN Saint Denis bless this happy stratagem,
And once again we'll sleep secure in Rouen!

20 BASTARD Here entered Pucelle and her practisants.
Now she is there, how will she specify:
Here is the best and safest passage in?

REIGNIER By thrusting out a torch from yonder tower,
Which, once discerned, shows that her meaning is:
25 No way to that, for weakness, which she entered.

Enter [La] Pucelle on the top, thrusting out a
torch burning.

PUCELLE Behold, this is the happy wedding torch
That joineth Rouen unto her countrymen,
But burning fatal to the Talbonites!   [*Exit.*]

BASTARD See, noble Charles, the beacon of our friend,
30 The burning torch, in yonder turret stands.

DAUPHIN Now shine it like a comet of revenge,
A prophet to the fall of all our foes!

REIGNIER Defer no time, delays have dangerous
ends;
Enter and cry, "The Dolphin!" presently,
35 And then do execution on the watch.

Alarum. [Exeunt.]

An alarum. Talbot in an excursion.

TALBOT France, thou shalt rue this treason with thy
tears,
If Talbot but survive thy treachery.
Pucelle, that witch, that damnèd sorceress,
Hath wrought this hellish mischief unawares,
40 That hardly we escaped the pride of France.

Exit.

20 **practisants** companions in the stratagem 25 **to** comparable to 28 **Talbo-**
nites followers of Talbot 31 **shine it** may it shine 33 **Defer** waste
35 s.d. **excursion** sortie 40 **pride** finest warriors

An alarum: excursions. Bedford, brought in sick in a
chair. Enter Talbot and Burgundy without: within [La]
Pucelle, Charles [the Dauphin], Bastard, [Alençon,] and
Reignier on the walls.

PUCELLE Good morrow, gallants! Want ye corn for
    bread?
  I think the Duke of Burgundy will fast
  Before he'll buy again at such a rate.
  'Twas full of darnel; do you like the taste?

BURGUNDY Scoff on, vile fiend and shameless
    courtesan!   45
  I trust ere long to choke thee with thine own
  And make thee curse the harvest of that corn.

DAUPHIN Your grace may starve perhaps before that
    time.

BEDFORD O, let no words, but deeds, revenge this
    treason!

PUCELLE What will you do, good gray-beard? Break
    a lance,   50
  And run a-tilt at death within a chair?

TALBOT Foul fiend of France, and hag of all despite,
  Encompassed with thy lustful paramours!
  Becomes it thee to taunt his valiant age
  And twit with cowardice a man half dead?   55
  Damsel, I'll have a bout with you again,
  Or else let Talbot perish with this shame.

PUCELLE Are ye so hot, sir? Yet, Pucelle, hold thy
    peace;
  If Talbot do but thunder, rain will follow.

    [The English] whisper together in council.

  God speed the parliament! who shall be the
    Speaker?   60

41 **gallants** gentlemen 44 **darnel** weeds 45 **courtesan** prostitute
50–51 **Break ... a-tilt** joust, combat 52 **of all despite** full of malice
53 **Encompassed** surrounded 53 **paramours** lovers 55 **twit** chide 56 **Damsel** girl 58 **hot** angry 60 **Speaker** presiding officer

TALBOT Dare ye come forth and meet us in the field?

PUCELLE Belike your lordship takes us then for fools,
To try if that our own be ours or no.

TALBOT I speak not to that railing Hecate,
65   But unto thee, Alençon, and the rest.
Will ye, like soldiers, come and fight it out?

ALENÇON Signior, no.

TALBOT Signior, hang! base muleters of France!
Like peasant foot-boys do they keep the walls
70   And dare not take up arms like gentlemen.

PUCELLE Away, captains! let's get us from the walls;
For Talbot means no goodness by his looks.
Good-bye, my lord! we came but to tell you
That we are here.   *Exeunt from the walls.*

75   TALBOT And there will we be too, ere it be long,
Or else reproach be Talbot's greatest fame.
Vow, Burgundy, by honor of thy house,
Pricked on by public wrongs sustained in France,
Either to get the town again or die.
80   And I, as sure as English Henry lives
And as his father here was conqueror,
As sure as in this late-betrayèd town
Great Cordelion's heart was burièd,
So sure I swear to get the town or die.

85   BURGUNDY My vows are equal partners with thy vows.

TALBOT But, ere we go, regard this dying prince,
The valiant Duke of Bedford. Come, my lord,
We will bestow you in some better place,
Fitter for sickness and for crazy age.

90   BEDFORD Lord Talbot, do not so dishonor me;
Here will I sit before the walls of Rouen

62 **Belike** perhaps   64 **railing Hecate** abusive witch (after Hecate, goddess of
sorcery)   67 **Signior** sir   68 **muleters** mule-drivers   69 **foot-boys**
boy-servants   78 **Pricked on** provoked   83 **Cordelion's** King Richard the
Lion-Hearted's   84 **get** retake   86 **regard** behold   89 **crazy** infirm, decrepit

And will be partner of your weal or woe.

BURGUNDY Courageous Bedford, let us now persuade
you.

BEDFORD Not to be gone from hence, for once I read
That stout Pendragon in his litter sick   95
Came to the field and vanquishèd his foes.
Methinks I should revive the soldiers' hearts,
Because I ever found them as myself.

TALBOT Undaunted spirit in a dying breast!
Then be it so: heavens keep old Bedford safe!   100
And now no more ado, brave Burgundy,
But gather we our forces out of hand
And set upon our boasting enemy.

      [Exeunt all but Bedford and his Attendants.]

    An alarum: excursions. Enter Sir John Falstaff
            and a Captain.

CAPTAIN Whither away, Sir John Falstaff, in such
haste?

FALSTAFF Whither away? To save myself by flight;   105
We are like to have the overthrow again.

CAPTAIN What! Will you fly, and leave Lord Talbot?

FALSTAFF   Ay,
All the Talbots in the world, to save my life.

                           Exit.

CAPTAIN Cowardly knight, ill fortune follow thee!

                           Exit.

   Retreat. Excursions. [La] Pucelle, Alençon, and
     Charles [the Dauphin enter and] fly.

BEDFORD Now, quiet soul, depart when heaven please,   110

92 **weal or woe** good or bad fortune   95 **Pendragon** Uther Pendragon, father of
King Arthur   95 **litter** stretcher-bed   103 s.d. **excursions** entries and exits of
skirmishing troops   106 **have the overthrow** be defeated

For I have seen our enemies' overthrow.
What is the trust or strength of foolish man?
They that of late were daring with their scoffs
Are glad and fain by flight to save themselves.

Bedford dies and is carried in by two in his chair.

An alarum. Enter Talbot, Burgundy, and the rest
[of their men].

115 TALBOT Lost, and recovered in a day again!
This is a double honor, Burgundy;
Yet heavens have glory for this victory!

BURGUNDY Warlike and martial Talbot, Burgundy
Enshrines thee in his heart and there erects
120   Thy noble deeds as valor's monuments.

TALBOT Thanks, gentle duke. But where is Pucelle
       now?
I think her old familiar is asleep.
Now where's the Bastard's braves, and Charles
       his gleeks?
What, all amort? Rouen hangs her head for grief
125   That such a valiant company are fled.
Now will we take some order in the town,
Placing therein some expert officers,
And then depart to Paris to the king,
For there young Henry with his nobles lie.

130 BURGUNDY What wills Lord Talbot pleaseth Burgundy.

TALBOT But yet, before we go, let's not forget
The noble Duke of Bedford, late deceased,
But see his exequies fulfilled in Rouen.
A braver soldier never couchèd lance,
135   A gentler heart did never sway in court.
But kings and mightiest potentates must die,
For that's the end of human misery.   *Exeunt.*

114 **fain** eager   122 **familiar** servant demon   123 **braves** boasts   123 **gleeks**
jests, scoffs   124 **amort** dejected   126 **take some order** restore order
127 **expert** experienced   129 **lie** reside   133 **exequies** funeral ceremonies
134 **couchèd** leveled for the assault   135 **gentler** nobler   135 **sway** prevail

Scene III. [*The plains near Rouen.*]

*Enter Charles [the Dauphin], Bastard, Alençon, [La]
Pucelle, [and forces].*

PUCELLE Dismay not, princes, at this accident,
  Nor grieve that Rouen is so recoverèd.
  Care is no cure, but rather corrosive,
  For things that are not to be remedied.
  Let frantic Talbot triumph for a while   5
  And like a peacock sweep along his tail;
  We'll pull his plumes and take away his train,
  If Dolphin and the rest will be but ruled.

DAUPHIN We have been guided by thee hitherto
  And of thy cunning had no diffidence;   10
  One sudden foil shall never breed distrust.

BASTARD Search out thy wit for secret policies,
  And we will make thee famous through the world.

ALENÇON We'll set thy statue in some holy place,
  And have thee reverenced like a blessèd saint.   15
  Employ thee then, sweet virgin, for our good.

PUCELLE Then thus it must be; this doth Joan devise:
  By fair persuasions mixed with sugared words
  We will entice the Duke of Burgundy
  To leave the Talbot and to follow us.   20

DAUPHIN Ay, marry, sweeting, if we could do that,
  France were no place for Henry's warriors,

III.iii.3 **corrosive** a caustic drug   5 **frantic** raging   7 **pull** pluck   7 **train**
(1) followers (2) equipment for battle   8 **ruled** guided (by Joan)   10 **diffidence**
lack of confidence   11 **foil** defeat   12 **Search out thy wit** examine your mind
16 **Employ thee** apply your efforts   17 **devise** determine   18 **sugared**
sweet-sounding   21 **sweeting** sweetheart

Nor should that nation boast it so with us,
But be extirpèd from our provinces.

ALENÇON Forever should they be expulsed from
25   France
And not have title of an earldom here.

PUCELLE Your honors shall perceive how I will work
To bring this matter to the wishèd end.

Drum sounds afar off.

Hark! by the sound of drum you may perceive
30   Their powers are marching unto Paris-ward.

Here sound an English march.

There goes the Talbot, with his colors spread,
And all the troops of English after him.

*French march. [Enter the Duke of Burgundy and
forces.]*
Now in the rearward comes the duke and his;
Fortune in favor makes him lag behind.
35   Summon a parley; we will talk with him.

Trumpets sound a parley.

DAUPHIN A parley with the Duke of Burgundy!

BURGUNDY Who craves a parley with the Burgundy?

PUCELLE The princely Charles of France, thy
countryman.

BURGUNDY What say'st thou, Charles? For I am
marching hence.

DAUPHIN Speak, Pucelle, and enchant him with thy
40   words.

PUCELLE Brave Burgundy, undoubted hope of France!
Stay, let thy humble handmaid speak to thee.

BURGUNDY Speak on, but be not over-tedious.

23 **boast it so with** lord it over   24 **extirpèd** rooted out   25 **expulsed** driven
out   26 **title of** claim to   30 **unto Paris-ward** toward Paris   31 **colors spread**
banners unfurled   34 **in favor** to our advantage

PUCELLE Look on thy country, look on fertile France,
  And see the cities and the towns defaced   45
  By wasting ruin of the cruel foe,
  As looks the mother on her lowly babe
  When death doth close his tender-dying eyes.
  See, see the pining malady of France;
  Behold the wounds, the most unnatural wounds,   50
  Which thou thyself hast given her woeful breast.
  O, turn thy edgèd sword another way;
  Strike those that hurt, and hurt not those that help.
  One drop of blood drawn from thy country's bosom
  Should grieve thee more than streams of foreign
      gore.   55
  Return thee therefore with a flood of tears,
  And wash away thy country's stainèd spots.

BURGUNDY Either she hath bewitched me with her
      words,
  Or nature makes me suddenly relent.

PUCELLE Besides, all French and France exclaims on
      thee,   60
  Doubting thy birth and lawful progeny.
  Who join'st thou with, but with a lordly nation
  That will not trust thee but for profit's sake?
  When Talbot hath set footing once in France
  And fashioned thee that instrument of ill,   65
  Who then but English Henry will be lord,
  And thou be thrust out like a fugitive?
  Call we to mind, and mark but this for proof:
  Was not the Duke of Orleans thy foe?
  And was he not in England prisoner?   70
  But when they heard he was thine enemy,
  They set him free without his ransom paid,
  In spite of Burgundy and all his friends.
  See then, thou fight'st against thy countrymen

48 **tender-dying** prematurely dying 49 **pining** consuming 52 **edgèd**
sharp 57 **stainèd** disgraceful 60 **exclaims on** cries out against 61 **lawful
progeny** legitimate parentage 62 **lordly** imperious, disdainful 64 **set footing**
entered 65 **fashioned thee** made you into

67

75   And join'st with them will be thy slaughter-men.
Come, come, return; return, thou wandering lord;
Charles and the rest will take thee in their arms.

BURGUNDY I am vanquishèd; these haughty words of
hers
Have battered me like roaring cannon-shot,
80   And made me almost yield upon my knees.
Forgive me, country, and sweet countrymen,
And, lords, accept this hearty kind embrace.
My forces and my power of men are yours.
So farewell, Talbot; I'll no longer trust thee.

PUCELLE [*Aside*] Done like a Frenchman: turn and
85   turn again!

DAUPHIN Welcome, brave duke! thy friendship makes
us fresh.

BASTARD And doth beget new courage in our breasts.

ALENÇON Pucelle hath bravely played her part in this,
And doth deserve a coronet of gold.

DAUPHIN Now let us on, my lords, and join our
90   powers,
And seek how we may prejudice the foe.   *Exeunt*.

---

75 **slaughter-men** executioners   78 **haughty** loftily brave   82 **kind** (1) friendly
(2) of a kinsman   83 **my power of men** (1) my full complement of troops (?)
(2) command over my troops   85 **turn and turn again** change sides frequently
86 **makes us fresh** renews our spirits   89 **coronet** a small crown worn on state
occasions by members of the nobility   91 **prejudice** damage

Scene IV. [*Paris. The Palace.*]

Enter the King, Gloucester, Winchester, York, Suffolk,
Somerset, Warwick, Exeter, [Vernon, Basset, and
others]. To them, with his Soldiers, Talbot.

TALBOT My gracious prince, and honorable peers,
Hearing of your arrival in this realm,
I have awhile given truce unto my wars
To do my duty to my sovereign.
In sign whereof, this arm, that hath reclaimed   5
To your obedience fifty fortresses,
Twelve cities, and seven wallèd towns of strength,
Beside five hundred prisoners of esteem,
Lets fall his sword before your highness' feet,
And with submissive loyalty of heart   10
Ascribes the glory of his conquest got
First to my God and next unto your grace.

KING Is this the Lord Talbot, uncle Gloucester,
That hath so long been resident in France?

GLOUCESTER Yes, if it please your majesty, my liege.   15

KING Welcome, brave captain and victorious lord!
When I was young (as yet I am not old)
I do remember how my father said
A stouter champion never handled sword.
Long since we were resolvèd of your truth,   20
Your faithful service, and your toil in war;
Yet never have you tasted our reward
Or been reguerdoned with so much as thanks,

III.iv.5 **reclaimed** subdued   8 **esteem** good reputation in battle and high birth
(thus likely to command a profitable ransom)   15 **liege** sovereign lord
18 **remember** (but Henry VI was only nine months old when his father died)
20 **resolvèd of your truth** convinced of your loyalty   23 **reguerdoned** repaid

69

       Because till now we never saw your face.

25   Therefore, stand up, and for these good deserts
       We here create you Earl of Shrewsbury,
       And in our coronation take your place.

Sennet. Flourish, Exeunt. Manet Vernon and Basset.

VERNON Now, sir, to you, that were so hot at sea,
       Disgracing of these colors that I wear
30   In honor of my noble Lord of York—
       Dar'st thou maintain the former words thou
         spak'st?

BASSET Yes, sir, as well as you dare patronage
       The envious barking of your saucy tongue
       Against my lord the Duke of Somerset.

35 VERNON Sirrah, thy lord I honor as he is.

BASSET Why, what is he? As good a man as York.

VERNON Hark ye, not so: in witness, take ye that.

                      Strikes him.

BASSET Villain, thou knowest the law of arms is such
       That whoso draws a sword, 'tis present death,
40   Or else this blow should broach thy dearest blood.
       But I'll unto his majesty and crave
       I may have liberty to venge this wrong.
       When thou shalt see I'll meet thee to thy cost.

VERNON Well, miscreant, I'll be there as soon as
         you,
45   And, after, meet you sooner than you would.

                      Exeunt.

---

27 s.d. **Manet** remains (the Latin singular with a plural subject is common in
Elizabethan stage directions) 28 **hot** passionate 29 **Disgracing of**
disparaging 32 **patronage** (1) maintain (2) defend 37 **in witness** as proof
39 **draws a sword** i.e., in a royal residence 39 **present** immediate 40 **broach**
draw as with a tap 41 **crave** beg 42 **venge** avenge 44 **miscreant** coward

ACT IV

Scene I. [*Paris. A hall of state.*]

Enter King, Gloucester, Winchester, York, Suffolk,
Somerset, Warwick, Talbot, Exeter, Governor [of Paris
and others].

GLOUCESTER Lord bishop, set the crown upon his head.

WINCHESTER God save King Henry, of that name the
   sixth!

GLOUCESTER Now, governor of Paris, take your oath,
   That you elect no other king but him;
   Esteem none friends but such as are his friends,   5
   And none your foes but such as shall pretend
   Malicious practices against his state:
   This shall ye do, so help you righteous God!

Enter Falstaff.

FALSTAFF My gracious sovereign, as I rode from Calais
   To haste unto your coronation,   10
   A letter was delivered to my hands,
   Writ to your grace from th' Duke of Burgundy.

IV.i.6 **pretend** purpose 7 **practices** stratagems

71

TALBOT Shame to the Duke of Burgundy and thee!
　　　I vowed, base knight, when I did meet thee next,
15　　To tear the garter from thy craven's leg,

　　　　　　　　　　　　　　[*Plucking it off.*]

　　　Which I have done, because unworthily
　　　Thou wast installèd in that high degree.
　　　Pardon me, princely Henry, and the rest:
　　　This dastard, at the battle of Poictiers,
20　　When but in all I was six thousand strong
　　　And that the French were almost ten to one,
　　　Before we met or that a stroke was given,
　　　Like to a trusty squire did run away.
　　　In which assault we lost twelve hundred men;
25　　Myself and divers gentlemen beside
　　　Were there surprised and taken prisoners.
　　　Then judge, great lords, if I have done amiss,
　　　Or whether that such cowards ought to wear
　　　This ornament of knighthood, yea or no.

30　GLOUCESTER To say the truth, this fact was infamous
　　　And ill beseeming any common man,
　　　Much more a knight, a captain, and a leader.

TALBOT When first this order was ordained, my lords,
　　　Knights of the Garter were of noble birth,
35　　Valiant and virtuous, full of haughty courage,
　　　Such as were grown to credit by the wars;
　　　Not fearing death, nor shrinking for distress,
　　　But always resolute in most extremes.
　　　He then that is not furnished in this sort
40　　Doth but usurp the sacred name of knight,
　　　Profaning this most honorable order,
　　　And should (if I were worthy to be judge)

---

15 **garter** badge of the Order of the Garter, England's highest degree of
knighthood　15 **craven's** coward's　17 **degree** dignity　19 **Poictiers** i.e., Patay
(1429)　23 **trusty squire** (used contemptuously: a person of inferior
character)　30 **fact** deed　35 **haughty** high　36 **credit** honorable
reputation　37 **distress** adversity　38 **in most extremes** in the most difficult
situations　39 **furnished in this sort** possessed of such qualities

Be quite degraded, like a hedge-born swain
That doth presume to boast of gentle blood.

KING Stain to thy countrymen, thou hear'st
      thy doom!   45
Be packing, therefore, thou that wast a knight:
Henceforth we banish thee on pain of death.

                           [*Exit Falstaff.*]

And now, Lord Protector, view the letter
Sent from our uncle Duke of Burgundy.

GLOUCESTER What means his grace, that he hath
      changed his style?   50
No more but pain and bluntly, "To the king!"
Hath he forgot he is his sovereign?
Or doth this churlish superscription
Pretend some alteration in good will?
What's here? "I have, upon especial cause,   55
Moved with compassion of my country's wrack,
Together with the pitiful complaints
Of such as your oppression feeds upon,
Forsaken your pernicious faction
And joined with Charles, the rightful King of
      France."   60
O monstrous treachery! can this be so,
That in alliance, amity, and oaths,
There should be found such false dissembling
      guile?

KING What! doth my uncle Burgundy revolt?

GLOUCESTER He doth, my lord, and is become your foe.   65

KING Is that the worst this letter doth contain?

GLOUCESTER It is the worst, and all, my lord, he writes.

KING Why, then, Lord Talbot there shall talk with him

43 **hedge-born swain** low peasant 45 **doom** judgment, condemnation 46 **Be packing** begone 50 **style** form of address 54 **Pretend** signify 56 **wrack** misfortune

And give him chastisement for this abuse.
70   How say you, my lord; are you not content?

TALBOT Content, my liege? Yes, but that I am prevented,
I should have begged I might have been employed.

KING Then gather strength, and march unto him straight;
Let him perceive how ill we brook his treason
75   And what offense it is to flout his friends.

TALBOT I go, my lord, in heart desiring still
You may behold confusion of your foes.   [*Exit.*]

Enter Vernon and Basset.

VERNON Grant me the combat, gracious sovereign.

BASSET And me, my lord, grant me the combat too.

80   YORK This is my servant; hear him, noble prince.

SOMERSET And this is mine; sweet Henry, favor him.

KING Be patient, lords, and give them leave to speak.
Say, gentlemen, what makes you thus exclaim,
And wherefore crave you combat? Or with whom?

VERNON With him, my lord, for he hath done me
85   wrong.

BASSET And I with him, for he hath done me wrong.

KING What is that wrong whereof you both complain?
First let me know, and then I'll answer you.

BASSET Crossing the sea from England into France,
90   This fellow here, with envious carping tongue,
Upbraided me about the rose I wear,
Saying, the sanguine color of the leaves

71 **prevented** anticipated   74 **brook** bear with   78 **combat** trial by arms
90 **carping** fault-finding   91 **Upbraided** reproached   92 **sanguine** blood-red

Did represent my master's blushing cheeks,
When stubbornly he did repugn the truth
About a certain question in the law   95
Argued betwixt the Duke of York and him;
With other vile and ignominious terms;
In confutation of which rude reproach
And in defense of my lord's worthiness,
I crave the benefit of law of arms.   100

VERNON And that is my petition, noble lord:
For though he seem with forgèd quaint conceit
To set a gloss upon his bold intent,
Yet know, my lord, I was provoked by him,
And he first took exceptions at this badge,   105
Pronouncing that the paleness of this flower
Bewrayed the faintness of my master's heart.

YORK Will not this malice, Somerset, be left?

SOMERSET Your private grudge, my Lord of York, will
    out,
Though ne'er so cunningly you smother it.   110

KING Good Lord, what madness rules in brain-
    sick men,
When for so slight and frivolous a cause
Such factious emulations shall arise!
Good cousins both, of York and Somerset,
Quiet yourselves, I pray, and be at peace.   115

YORK Let this dissension first be tried by fight,
And then your highness shall command a peace.

SOMERSET The quarrel toucheth none but us alone;
Betwixt ourselves let us decide it then.

YORK There is my pledge; accept it, Somerset.   120

VERNON Nay, let it rest where it began at first.

94 **repugn** resist   100 **benefit ... arms** privilege of trial by combat   102 **forgèd quaint conceit** crafty manner of expression   103 **set a gloss upon** veil in specious language   105 **took exceptions at** disapproved of   107 **Bewrayed** revealed   113 **emulations** contentions   118 **toucheth** concerns   120 **pledge** challenge (made by casting down one's glove)

BASSET Confirm it so, mine honorable lord.

GLOUCESTER Confirm it so? Confounded be your strife!
    And perish ye with your audacious prate!
125   Presumptuous vassals, are you not ashamed
    With this immodest clamorous outrage
    To trouble and disturb the king and us?
    And you, my lords, methinks you do not well
    To bear with their perverse objections,
130   Much less to take occasion from their mouths
    To raise a mutiny betwixt yourselves.
    Let me persuade you take a better course.

EXETER It grieves his highness. Good my lords, be
    friends.

KING Come hither, you that would be com-
    batants:
135   Henceforth I charge you, as you love our favor,
    Quite to forget this quarrel and the cause.
    And you, my lords, remember where we are:
    In France, amongst a fickle wavering nation;
    If they perceive dissension in our looks
140   And that within ourselves we disagree,
    How will their grudging stomachs be provoked
    To willful disobedience, and rebel!
    Beside, what infamy will there arise,
    When foreign princes shall be certified
145   That for a toy, a thing of no regard,
    King Henry's peers and chief nobility
    Destroyed themselves and lost the realm of France!
    O, think upon the conquest of my father,
    My tender years, and let us not forgo
150   That for a trifle that was bought with blood!
    Let me be umpire in this doubtful strife.
    I see no reason, if I wear this rose,

                              [*Putting on a red rose.*]

124 prate chatter   126 immodest arrogant   141 grudging stomachs resentful
dispositions   144 certified informed   145 toy trifle

That anyone should therefore be suspicious
I more incline to Somerset than York;
Both are my kinsmen, and I love them both.   155
As well they may upbraid me with my crown
Because, forsooth, the King of Scots is crowned.
But your discretions better can persuade
Than I am able to instruct or teach,
And therefore, as we hither came in peace,   160
So let us still continue peace and love.
Cousin of York, we institute your grace
To be our Regent in these parts of France;
And, good my Lord of Somerset, unite
Your troops of horsemen with his bands of foot,   165
And, like true subjects, sons of your progenitors,
Go cheerfully together and digest
Your angry choler on your enemies.
Ourself, my Lord Protector, and the rest
After some respite will return to Calais;   170
From thence to England, where I hope ere long
To be presented, by your victories,
With Charles, Alençon, and that traitorous rout.

>   *Flourish. Exeunt. Manet York, Warwick,*
>   *Exeter, Vernon.*

WARWICK My Lord of York, I promise you, the king
Prettily, methought, did play the orator.   175

YORK And so he did, but yet I like it not,
In that he wears the badge of Somerset.

WARWICK Tush, that was but his fancy, blame him
not;
I dare presume, sweet prince, he thought no harm.

YORK And if—I wish—he did. But let it rest;   180
Other affairs must now be managèd.

>   *Exeunt. Manet Exeter.*

157 **forsooth** in truth (used derisively) 158 **discretions** lordships,
judgments 168 **choler** bile (according to earlier physiology, the cause of anger or
hot temper) 173 **rout** crowd

77

EXETER Well didst thou, Richard, to suppress thy
                voice;
            For, had the passions of thy heart burst out,
            I fear we should have seen deciphered there
185   More rancorous spite, more furious raging broils,
            Than yet can be imagined or supposed.
            But howsoe'er, no simple man that sees
            This jarring discord of nobility,
            This shouldering of each other in the court,
190   This factious bandying of their favorites,
            But that it doth presage some ill event.
            'Tis much when scepters are in children's hands,
            But more when envy breeds unkind division;
            There comes the ruin, there begins confusion. *Exit.*

Scene II. [*Before Bordeaux.*]

Enter Talbot, with trump and drum.

TALBOT Go to the gates of Bordeaux, trumpeter;
            Summon their general unto the wall.

                                    [*Trumpet*] *sounds.*

Enter General aloft [*with others*].

            English John Talbot, captains, calls you forth,
            Servant in arms to Harry King of England,
5   And thus he would: open your city gates,
            Be humble to us, call my sovereign yours
            And do him homage as obedient subjects,
            And I'll withdraw me and my bloody power.
            But, if you frown upon this proffered peace,
10   You tempt the fury of my three attendants,

184 **deciphered** revealed   189 **shouldering** jostling   190 **bandying** contention
191 **presage some ill event** predict some evil outcome   192 **much** difficult
193 **unkind division** unnatural disunion

78

Lean Famine, quartering Steel, and climbing Fire,
Who in a moment even with the earth
Shall lay your stately and air-braving towers,
If you forsake the offer of their love.

GENERAL Thou ominous and fearful owl of death,   15
Our nation's terror and their bloody scourge!
The period of thy tyranny approacheth.
On us thou canst not enter but by death,
For, I protest, we are well fortified
And strong enough to issue out and fight.   20
If thou retire, the Dolphin, well appointed,
Stands with the snares of war to tangle thee.
On either hand thee there are squadrons pitched
To wall thee from the liberty of flight,
And no way canst thou turn thee for redress,   25
But death doth front thee with apparent spoil,
And pale destruction meets thee in the face.
Ten thousand French have ta'en the sacrament
To rive their dangerous artillery
Upon no Christian soul but English Talbot.   30
Lo, there thou stand'st, a breathing valiant man,
Of an invincible unconquered spirit!
This is the latest glory of thy praise
That I, thy enemy, due thee withal,
For ere the glass that now begins to run   35
Finish the process of his sandy hour,
These eyes, that see thee now well colorèd,
Shall see thee withered, bloody, pale, and dead.

                              Drum afar off.

Hark! hark! The Dolphin's drum, a warning bell,
Sings heavy music to thy timorous soul,   40

IV.ii.11 **quartering** that cuts men into quarters 12 even level 13 **air-braving** skyscraping 15 **owl of death** (alluding to the owl as a supposed harbinger of death or misfortune) 17 **period** end 21 **appointed** equipped 23 **hand** side of 25 **redress** relief 26 **front** confront 26 **apparent spoil** obvious destruction 28 **ta'en the sacrament** confirmed their oaths by receiving holy communion 29 **rive** burst 33 **latest** final 34 **due** endue 37 **well colorèd** of healthy complexion 40 **heavy** doleful

And mine shall ring thy dire departure out.

Exit [with his followers].

TALBOT He fables not, I hear the enemy;
Out, some light horsemen, and peruse their wings.
O, negligent and heedless discipline!
45 How are we parked and bounded in a pale,
A little herd of England's timorous deer,
Mazed with a yelping kennel of French curs!
If we be English deer, be then in blood,
Not rascal-like to fall down with a pinch,
50 But rather moody-mad; and, desperate stags,
Turn on the bloody hounds with heads of steel
And make the cowards stand aloof at bay.
Sell every man his life as dear as mine,
And they shall find dear deer of us, my friends.
55 God and Saint George, Talbot and England's right,
Prosper our colors in this dangerous fight! [*Exeunt*.]

Scene III. [*Plains in Gascony*.]

*Enter a Messenger that meets York. Enter York with
trumpet and many Soldiers.*

YORK Are not the speedy scouts returned again
That dogged the mighty army of the Dolphin?

MESSENGER They are returned, my lord, and give it
out
That he is marched to Bordeaux with his power
5 To fight with Talbot. As he marched along,
By your espials were discoverèd

---

42 **fables not** does not speak falsely   43 **light** lightly armed   43 **peruse their wings** scout their flanks   45 **parked ... pale** surrounded and hemmed in by a fence   47 **Mazed with** terrified by   48 **in blood** (1) in full vigor (2) in temper   49 **rascal-like** like inferior deer   49 **pinch** nip   50 **moody-mad** furious in mood   51 **bloody** bloodthirsty   54 **dear** costly   IV.iii.2 **dogged** tracked, closely pursued   3 **give it out** report   6 **espials** spies

Two mightier troops than that the Dolphin led,
Which joined with him and made their march for
   Bordeaux.

YORK A plague upon that villain Somerset,
  That thus delays my promisèd supply   10
  Of horsemen that were levied for this siege!
  Renownèd Talbot doth expect my aid,
  And I am louted by a traitor villain
  And cannot help the noble chevalier.
  God comfort him in this necessity!   15
  If he miscarry, farewell wars in France.

Enter another Messenger: [Sir William Lucy.]

LUCY Thou princely leader of our English strength,
  Never so needful on the earth of France,
  Spur to the rescue of the noble Talbot,
  Who now is girdled with a waist of iron   20
  And hemmed about with grim destruction.
  To Bordeaux, warlike duke! to Bordeaux, York!
  Else, farewell Talbot, France, and England's honor.

YORK O God, that Somerset, who in proud heart
  Doth stop my cornets, were in Talbot's place!   25
  So should we save a valiant gentleman
  By forfeiting a traitor and a coward.
  Mad ire and wrathful fury makes me weep,
  That thus we die, while remiss traitors sleep.

LUCY O, send some succor to the distressed lord!   30

YORK He dies, we lose; I break my warlike word;
  We mourn, France smiles; we lose, they daily get;
  All long of this vile traitor Somerset.

LUCY Then God take mercy on brave Talbot's soul,
  And on his son young John, who two hours since 35
  I met in travel toward his warlike father!
  This seven years did not Talbot see his son,
  And now they meet where both their lives are done.

12 **expect** await 13 **louted** mocked 14 **chevalier** knight 16 **miscarry** be
destroyed 25 **stop my cornets** withhold my squadrons of cavalry 33 **long** on
account

YORK Alas, what joy shall noble Talbot have
40   To bid his young son welcome to his grave?
      Away! vexation almost stops my breath,
      That sundered friends greet in the hour of death.
      Lucy, farewell, no more my fortune can
      But curse the cause I cannot aid the man.
45   Maine, Blois, Poictiers, and Tours are won away,
      Long all of Somerset and his delay.
                              Exit [with his Soldiers].

LUCY Thus, while the vulture of sedition
      Feeds in the bosom of such great commanders,
      Sleeping neglection doth betray to loss
50   The conquest of our scarce-cold conqueror,
      That ever living man of memory,
      Henry the Fifth. Whiles they each other cross,
      Lives, honors, lands, and all hurry to loss.

                Scene IV. [*Other plains in Gascony.*]

                Enter Somerset with his army,
                [a Captain of Talbot's with him].

SOMERSET It is too late, I cannot send them now;
      This expedition was by York and Talbot
      Too rashly plotted. All our general force
      Might with a sally of the very town
5   Be buckled with. The over-daring Talbot
      Hath sullied all his gloss of former honor
      By this unheedful, desperate, wild adventure;
      York set him on to fight and die in shame,
      That, Talbot dead, great York might bear the name.

42 **sundered** separated 43 **fortune can** circumstances enable me to do
44 **cause** reason why 49 **neglection** negligence 50 **scarce-cold** barely
dead IV.iv.3 **general** whole 4 **sally** sudden outrush 4 **very** itself 6 **gloss**
luster

CAPTAIN Here is Sir William Lucy, who with me   10
    Set from our o'er-matched forces forth for aid.

SOMERSET How now, Sir William! whither were you
    sent?

LUCY Whither, my lord? from bought and sold Lord
    Talbot;
    Who, ringed about with bold adversity,
    Cries out for noble York and Somerset   15
    To beat assailing death from his weak regions;
    And whiles the honorable captain there
    Drops bloody sweat from his war-wearied limbs,
    And in advantage ling'ring looks for rescue,
    You, his false hopes, the trust of England's honor,   20
    Keep off aloof with worthless emulation.
    Let not your private discord keep away
    The levied succors that should lend him aid
    While he, renownèd noble gentleman,
    Yield up his life unto a world of odds: 25
    Orleans the Bastard, Charles, Burgundy,
    Alençon, Reignier compass him about,
    And Talbot perisheth by your default.

SOMERSET York set him on, York should have sent
    him aid.

LUCY And York as fast upon your grace exclaims,   30
    Swearing that you withhold his levied host,
    Collected for this expedition.

SOMERSET York lies; he might have sent and had the
    horse!
    I owe him little duty, and less love,
    And take foul scorn to fawn on him by sending.   35

LUCY The fraud of England, not the force of France,
    Hath now entrapped the noble-minded Talbot;

11 **o'er-matched** outnumbered   14 **bold adversity** confident opponents
16 **regions** places   19 **in advantage ling'ring** (1) desperately clinging to every
advantage (?) (2) while holding out on advantageous ground (?)   21 **emulation**
rivalry   23 **succors** reinforcements   35 **take** submit to

Never to England shall he bear his life,
But dies betrayed to fortune by your strife.

SOMERSET Come, go; I will dispatch the horsemen
40   straight;
Within six hours they will be at his aid.

LUCY Too late comes rescue, he is ta'en or slain,
For fly he could not, if he would have fled,
And fly would Talbot never though he might.

45 SOMERSET If he be dead, brave Talbot, then adieu!

LUCY His fame lives in the world, his shame in you.
                                           Exeunt.

Scene V. [*The English camp near Bordeaux*.]

Enter Talbot and his son.

TALBOT O young John Talbot! I did send for thee
To tutor thee in stratagems of war,
That Talbot's name might be in thee revived
When sapless age and weak unable limbs
5   Should bring thy father to his drooping chair.
But, O malignant and ill-boding stars!
Now thou art come unto a feast of death,
A terrible and unavoided danger:
Therefore, dear boy, mount on my swiftest horse,
10   And I'll direct thee how thou shalt escape
By sudden flight. Come, dally not, be gone.

JOHN Is my name Talbot? And am I your son?
And shall I fly? O, if you love my mother,
Dishonor not her honorable name,
15   To make a bastard and a slave of me.

IV.v.4 **sapless** withered   4 **unable** powerless   5 **drooping chair** decline from
vigor   8 **unavoided** unavoidable

The world will say, he is not Talbot's blood,
That basely fled when noble Talbot stood.

TALBOT Fly, to revenge my death, if I be slain.

JOHN He that flies so will ne'er return again.

TALBOT If we both stay, we both are sure to die.   20

JOHN Then let me stay, and, father, do you fly:
Your loss is great, so your regard should be;
My worth unknown, no loss is known in me.
Upon my death the French can little boast;
In yours they will, in you all hopes are lost.   25
Flight cannot stain the honor you have won,
But mine it will, that no exploit have done;
You fled for vantage, everyone will swear,
But, if I bow, they'll say it was for fear.
There is no hope that ever I will stay   30
If the first hour I shrink and run away.
Here on my knee I beg mortality,
Rather than life preserved with infamy.

TALBOT Shall all thy mother's hopes lie in one tomb?

JOHN Ay, rather than I'll shame my mother's womb.   35

TALBOT Upon my blessing, I command thee go.

JOHN To fight I will, but not to fly the foe.

TALBOT Part of thy father may be saved in thee.

JOHN No part of him but will be shame in me.

TALBOT Thou never hadst renown, nor canst not lose
it.   40

JOHN Yes, your renownèd name: shall flight abuse it?

TALBOT Thy father's charge shall clear thee from that
stain.

JOHN You cannot witness for me, being slain.
If death be so apparent, then both fly.

28 **for vantage** to gain a tactical advantage   29 **bow** flee   32 **mortality**
death   42 **charge** attack

85

45   TALBOT And leave my followers here to fight and die?
           My age was never tainted with such shame.

     JOHN And shall my youth be guilty of such blame?
           No more can I be severed from your side
           Than can yourself yourself in twain divide.
50   Stay, go, do what you will, the like do I;
           For live I will not, if my father die.

     TALBOT Then here I take my leave of thee, fair son,
           Born to eclipse thy life this afternoon.
           Come, side by side together live and die;
55   And soul with soul from France to heaven fly.
                                          Exit [with Son].

                  Scene VI. [*A field of battle.*]

           *Alarum: excursions, wherein Talbot's Son is hemmed
                 about, and Talbot rescues him.*

     TALBOT Saint George and victory! fight, soldiers, fight!
           The Regent hath with Talbot broke his word
           And left us to the rage of France his sword.
           Where is John Talbot? Pause, and take thy breath;
5   I gave thee life and rescued thee from death.

     JOHN O, twice my father, twice am I thy son!
           The life thou gav'st me first was lost and done,
           Till with thy warlike sword, despite of fate,
           To my determined time thou gav'st new date.

     TALBOT When from the Dolphin's crest thy sword
10   struck fire,
           It warmed thy father's heart with proud desire
           Of bold-faced victory. Then leaden age,
           Quickened with youthful spleen and warlike rage,

---

49 twain two   53 eclipse end   IV.vi.8 despite of in spite of   9 determined
predestined, fated   12 leaden spiritless   13 Quickened animated   13 spleen
high spirits, courage

Beat down Alençon, Orleans, Burgundy,
And from the pride of Gallia rescued thee.   15
The ireful bastard Orleans, that drew blood
From thee, my boy, and had the maidenhood
Of thy first fight, I soon encounterèd,
And interchanging blows I quickly shed
Some of his bastard blood; and in disgrace   20
Bespoke him thus: "Contaminated, base,
And misbegotten blood I spill of thine,
Mean and right poor, for that pure blood of mine
Which thou didst force from Talbot, my brave boy."
Here, purposing the Bastard to destroy,   25
Came in strong rescue. Speak, thy father's care,
Art thou not weary, John? How dost thou fare?
Wilt thou yet leave the battle, boy, and fly,
Now thou art sealed the son of chivalry?
Fly, to revenge my death when I am dead;   30
The help of one stands me in little stead.
O, too much folly is it, well I wot,
To hazard all our lives in one small boat!
If I today die not with Frenchmen's rage,
Tomorrow I shall die with mickle age.   35
By me they nothing gain and if I stay;
'Tis but the short'ning of my life one day.
In thee thy mother dies, our household's name,
My death's revenge, thy youth, and England's fame:
All these and more we hazard by thy stay;   40
All these are saved if thou wilt fly away.

JOHN The sword of Orleans hath not made me smart;
    These words of yours draw life-blood from my
       heart.
    On that advantage, bought with such a shame,
    To save a paltry life and slay bright fame,   45
    Before young Talbot from old Talbot fly,
    The coward horse that bears me fall and die!
    And like me to the peasant boys of France,

15 **Gallia** France 25 **Here** i.e., here I 29 **sealed** authenticated (by his deeds) 32 **wot** know 33 **hazard** gamble 35 **mickle** much, advanced 48 **like** compare

To be shame's scorn and subject of mischance!
50   Surely, by all the glory you have won,
And if I fly, I am not Talbot's son.
Then talk no more of flight, it is no boot;
If son to Talbot, die at Talbot's foot.

TALBOT Then follow thou thy desperate sire of Crete,
55   Thou Icarus; thy life to me is sweet;
If thou wilt fight, fight by thy father's side;
And, commendable proved, let's die in pride.

Exit [with Son].

Scene VII. [*Another part of the field.*]

*Alarum: excursions. Enter old Talbot, led [by
a Servant].*

TALBOT Where is my other life? Mine own is gone.
O, where's young Talbot? Where is valiant John?
Triumphant death, smeared with captivity,
Young Talbot's valor makes me smile at thee.
5   When he perceived me shrink and on my knee,
His bloody sword he brandished over me,
And like a hungry lion did commence
Rough deeds of rage and stern impatience,
But when my angry guardant stood alone,
10   Tend'ring my ruin and assailed of none,
Dizzy-eyed fury and great rage of heart
Suddenly made him from my side to start
Into the clust'ring battle of the French,
And in that sea of blood my boy did drench

---

49 **subject of mischance** an example of unhappy fate   52 **boot** use   54 **sire of
Crete** Daedalus (who made wings of feathers and wax on which he and his son
Icarus attempted to escape from King Minos of Crete)   57 **pride** glory
IV.vii.3 **captivity** the blood of your captives (?)   5 **shrink** give way   9 **guardant**
protector   10 **Tend'ring** tenderly caring for me in   10 **of** by   11 **Dizzy-eyed**
giddy   13 **clust'ring battle** close-grouped battle formation

His over-mounting spirit and there died,   15
My Icarus, my blossom, in his pride.

Enter [Soldiers,] with John Talbot, borne.

SERVANT O my dear lord, lo, where your son is
    borne!

TALBOT Thou antic death, which laugh'st us here to
    scorn,
    Anon, from thy insulting tyranny,
    Coupled in bonds of perpetuity,   20
    Two Talbots, wingèd through the lither sky,
    In thy despite shall 'scape mortality.
    O thou, whose wounds become hard-favored
    death,
    Speak to thy father ere thou yield thy breath!
    Brave Death by speaking, whether he will or no;   25
    Imagine him a Frenchman and thy foe.
    Poor boy! he smiles, methinks, as who should say,
    "Had Death been French, then Death had died
    today."
    Come, come and lay him in his father's arms;
    My spirit can no longer bear these harms.   30
    Soldiers, adieu! I have what I would have,
    Now my old arms are young John Talbot's grave.
Dies.

Enter Charles [the Dauphin], Alençon, Burgundy,
Bastard, and [La] Pucelle, [with forces].

DAUPHIN Had York and Somerset brought rescue in,
    We should have found a bloody day of this.

BASTARD How the young whelp of Talbot's, raging
    wood,   35
    Did flesh his puny-sword in Frenchmen's blood!

PUCELLE Once I encountered him, and thus I said:

15 **over-mounting** too highly aspiring 18 **antic** (1) grinning (2) buffoon
19 **Anon** immediately 20 **of perpetuity** eternal 21 **lither** yielding, pliant
23 **hard-favored** ugly-looking 35 **wood** mad 36 **flesh his puny-sword**
initiate his untried sword in battle

"Thou maiden youth, be vanquished by a maid."
But, with a proud majestical high scorn,
40   He answered thus: "Young Talbot was not born
To be the pillage of a giglot wench."
So, rushing in the bowels of the French,
He left me proudly, as unworthy fight.

BURGUNDY Doubtless he would have made a noble
    knight.
45   See, where he lies inhearsèd in the arms
Of the most bloody nurser of his harms!

BASTARD Hew them to pieces, hack their bones
    asunder,
Whose life was England's glory, Gallia's wonder.

DAUPHIN O no, forbear! for that which we have fled
50   During the life, let us not wrong it dead.

Enter Lucy, [attended by a French Herald].

LUCY Herald, conduct me to the Dolphin's tent,
To know who hath obtained the glory of the day.

DAUPHIN On what submissive message art thou sent?

LUCY Submission, Dolphin! 'Tis a mere French word;
55   We English warriors wot not what it means.
I come to know what prisoners thou hast ta'en
And to survey the bodies of the dead.

DAUPHIN For prisoners ask'st thou? Hell our prison
    is.
But tell me whom thou seek'st.

60   LUCY But where's the great Alcides of the field,
Valiant Lord Talbot, Earl of Shrewsbury,
Created, for his rare success in arms,
Great Earl of Washford, Waterford, and Valence,
Lord Talbot of Goodrig and Urchinfield,
65   Lord Strange of Blackmere, Lord Verdun of Alton,

41 **pillage** plunder 41 **giglot** wanton 42 **bowels** midst 43 **unworthy fight** not worthy of fighting with 45 **inhearsèd** enclosed as in a hearse 46 **nurser** fosterer 58 **Hell our prison is** i.e., we kill all our enemies 60 **Alcides** Hercules

Lord Cromwell of Wingfield, Lord Furnival of
   Sheffield,
The thrice-victorious Lord of Falconbridge,
Knight of the noble order of Saint George,
Worthy Saint Michael, and the Golden Fleece,
Great Marshal to Henry the Sixth   70
Of all his wars within the realm of France?

PUCELLE Here's a silly stately style indeed!
The Turk, that two and fifty kingdoms hath,
Writes not so tedious a style as this.
Him that thou magnifi'st with all these titles   75
Stinking and fly-blown lies here at our feet.

LUCY Is Talbot slain, the Frenchmen's only scourge,
Your kingdom's terror and black Nemesis?
O, were mine eyeballs into bullets turned,
That I in rage might shoot them at your faces!   80
O, that I could but call these dead to life,
It were enough to fright the realm of France!
Were but his picture left amongst you here,
It would amaze the proudest of you all.
Give me their bodies, that I may bear them hence   85
And give them burial as beseems their worth.

PUCELLE I think this upstart is old Talbot's ghost,
He speaks with such a proud commanding spirit.
For God's sake, let him have him; to keep them
   here,
They would but stink and putrefy the air.   90

DAUPHIN Go, take their bodies hence.

LUCY I'll bear them hence, but from their ashes shall
   be reared
A phoenix that shall make all France afeard.

68-70 **Saint George ... Saint Michael ... the Golden Fleece** chivalric orders
of England, France, and the Holy Roman Empire respectively   72 **stately style**
imposing title   73 **the Turk** the Sultan   84 **amaze** stupefy, terrify   93 **phoenix**
in mythology, an Arabian bird that is resurrected from the ashes of its own funeral
pyre   93 **afeard** afraid

DAUPHIN So we be rid of them, do with him what
       thou wilt.
95   And now to Paris, in this conquering vein:
       All will be ours, now bloody Talbot's slain.

                                        Exeunt.

95 vein mood

ACT V

Scene I. [*London. The palace.*]

Sennet. Enter King, Gloucester, and Exeter.

KING Have you perused the letters from the pope,
　The emperor, and the Earl of Armagnac?

GLOUCESTER I have, my lord, and their intent is this:
　They humbly sue unto your excellence
　To have a godly peace concluded of　　　　　　　　　5
　Between the realms of England and of France.

KING How doth your grace affect their motion?

GLOUCESTER Well, my good lord, and as the only
　　means
　To stop effusion of our Christian blood
　And stablish quietness on every side.　　　　　　　10

KING Ay, marry, uncle, for I always thought
　It was both impious and unnatural
　That such immanity and bloody strife
　Should reign among professors of one faith.

GLOUCESTER Beside, my lord, the sooner to effect　　15
　And surer bind this knot of amity,
　The Earl of Armagnac, near knit to Charles,
　A man of great authority in France,

V.i.7 **affect** like　10 **stablish** establish　13 **immanity** monstrous cruelty
14 **professors of** believers in　17 **near knit** closely bound by blood relationship

Proffers his only daughter to your grace
20   In marriage, with a large and sumptuous dowry.

KING Marriage, uncle! alas, my years are young,
        And fitter is my study and my books
        Than wanton dalliance with a paramour.
        Yet call th' ambassadors, and, as you please,
25   So let them have their answers every one:
        I shall be well content with any choice
        Tends to God's glory and my country's weal.

        *Enter Winchester [in Cardinal's habit],
        and three Ambassadors, [one of them a Legate].*

EXETER What! is my Lord of Winchester installed,
        And called unto a cardinal's degree?
30   Then I perceive that will be verified
        Henry the Fifth did sometime prophesy:
        "If once he come to be a cardinal,
        He'll make his cap co-equal with the crown."

KING My lords ambassadors, your several suits
35   Have been considered and debated on.
        Your purpose is both good and reasonable,
        And therefore are we certainly resolved
        To draw conditions of a friendly peace,
        Which by my Lord of Winchester we mean
40   Shall be transported presently to France.

GLOUCESTER And for the proffer of my lord your mas-
                ter,
        I have informed his highness so at large
        As, liking of the lady's virtuous gifts,
        Her beauty and the value of her dower,
45   He doth intend she shall be England's queen.

KING In argument and proof of which contract,
        Bear her this jewel, pledge of my affection.

---

23 wanton ... paramour lascivious sport with a mistress 27 s.d. **Legate**
representative of the Pope 31 **sometime** once 33 **cap** red cardinal's
skullcap 34 **several suits** individual requests 41 **master** i.e., the Count of
Armagnac 43 **As** that 44 **dower** marriage settlement

And so, my Lord Protector, see them guarded
And safely brought to Dover, wherein shipped,
Commit them to the fortune of the sea.   50
     Exeunt [all but Winchester and the Legate].

WINCHESTER Stay, my Lord Legate; you shall first
  receive
The sum of money which I promisèd
Should be delivered to his Holiness
For clothing me in these grave ornaments.

LEGATE I will attend upon your lordship's leisure.   55

WINCHESTER [*Aside*] Now Winchester will not submit,
  I trow,
Or be inferior to the proudest peer.
Humphrey of Gloucester, thou shalt well perceive
That, neither in birth or for authority,
The bishop will be overborne by thee.   60
I'll either make thee stoop and bend thy knee,
Or sack this country with a mutiny.   *Exeunt.*

    Scene II. [*France. Plains in Anjou*].

 Enter Charles [the Dauphin], Burgundy, Alençon,
 Bastard, Reignier, and Joan [la Pucelle, with forces].

DAUPHIN These news, my lords, may cheer our droop-
  ing spirits:
'Tis said the stout Parisians do revolt
And turn again unto the warlike French.

ALENÇON Then march to Paris, royal Charles of
  France.
And keep not back your powers in dalliance.   5

49 **shipped** embarked 54 **grave ornaments** symbols of high rank 62 **mutiny**
rebellion V.ii.5 **dalliance** idleness

PUCELLE Peace be amongst them, if they turn to us;
　　Else, ruin combat with their palaces!

Enter Scout.

SCOUT Success unto our valiant general,
　　And happiness to his accomplices!

DAUPHIN What tidings send our scouts? I prithee,
10　　speak.

SCOUT The English army, that divided was
　　Into two parties, is now conjoined in one,
　　And means to give you battle presently.

DAUPHIN Somewhat too sudden, sirs, the warning is,
15　　But we will presently provide for them.

BURGUNDY I trust the ghost of Talbot is not there;
　　Now he is gone, my lord, you need not fear.

PUCELLE Of all base passions, fear is most accursed.
　　Command the conquest, Charles, it shall be thine;
20　　Let Henry fret and all the world repine.

DAUPHIN Then on, my lords, and France be fortunate!
　　　　　　　　　　　　　　　　　　Exeunt.

Scene III. [*Before Angiers.*]

Alarum. Excursions. Enter Joan la Pucelle.

PUCELLE The Regent conquers, and the Frenchmen
　　fly.
　　Now help, ye charming spells and periapts,
　　And ye choice spirits that admonish me
　　And give me signs of future accidents.　　*Thunder.*

---

12 **conjoined** united 20 **repine** complain V.iii.1 **Regent** i.e., York
2 **charming** exercising magic power 2 **periapts** amulets 3 **choice** excellent
3 **admonish** inform 4 **accidents** events

You speedy helpers, that are substitutes   5
Under the lordly monarch of the north,
Appear and aid me in this enterprise.

                    Enter Fiends.

This speedy and quick appearance argues proof
Of your accustomed diligence to me.
Now, ye familiar spirits, that are culled   10
Out of the powerful regions under earth,
Help me this once, that France may get the field.
                              They walk, and speak not.
O, hold me not with silence over-long!
Where I was wont to feed you with my blood,
I'll lop a member off and give it you   15
In earnest of a further benefit,
So you do condescend to help me now.
                              They hang their heads.
No hope to have redress? My body shall
Pay recompense, if you will grant my suit.
                              They shake their heads.
Cannot my body nor blood-sacrifice   20
Entreat you to your wonted furtherance?
Then take my soul; my body, soul, and all,
Before that England give the French the foil.
                              They depart.
See, they forsake me! Now the time is come
That France must vail her lofty plumèd crest   25
And let her hand fall into England's lap.
My ancient incantations are too weak,
And hell too strong for me to buckle with.
Now, France, thy glory droopeth to the dust.   *Exit.*

Excursions. Burgundy and York fight hand to hand.
French fly, [*pursued. York returns with La Pucelle*
captive].

---

6 **monarch of the north** the devil (evil spirits were traditionally thought to dwell
in the regions of the north)   10 **culled** gathered   12 **get** win   15 **member** part
of the body   16 **earnest** pledge   21 **furtherance** assistance   23 **the foil** defeat,
repulse   25 **vail** lower or take off in token of submission   27 **ancient** former

30 YORK Damsel of France, I think I have you fast;
            Unchain your spirits now with spelling charms
            And try if they can gain your liberty.
            A goodly prize, fit for the devil's grace!
            See, how the ugly witch doth bend her brows,
35   As if, with Circe, she would change my shape!

    PUCELLE Changed to a worser shape thou canst not be.

    YORK O, Charles the Dolphin is a proper man;
          No shape but his can please your dainty eye.

    PUCELLE A plaguing mischief light on Charles and
                thee!
40   And may ye both be suddenly surprised
            By bloody hands, in sleeping on your beds!

    YORK Fell banning hag, enchantress, hold thy
          tongue!

    PUCELLE I prithee, give me leave to curse awhile.

    YORK Curse, miscreant, when thou comest to the
          stake.   *Exeunt.*

        Alarum. Enter Suffolk, with Margaret in his hand.

45 SUFFOLK Be what thou wilt, thou art my prisoner.
                                            Gazes on her.
            O fairest beauty, do not fear nor fly!
            For I will touch thee but with reverent hands;
            I kiss these fingers for eternal peace
            And lay them gently on thy tender side.
50   Who art thou? Say, that I may honor thee.

    MARGARET Margaret my name, and daughter to a
                king,
              The King of Naples, whosoe'er thou art.

    SUFFOLK An earl I am, and Suffolk am I called.
            Be not offended, nature's miracle,

31 **spelling** spell-casting 35 **with Circe** like Circe (the sorceress in the *Odyssey* who transformed men into beasts) 38 **dainty** fastidious 39 **plaguing** tormenting 42 **Fell banning** evil cursing 47 **reverent** respectful

Thou art allotted to be ta'en by me: 55
So doth the swan her downy cygnets save,
Keeping them prisoner underneath her wings.
Yet if this servile usage once offend,
Go and be free again as Suffolk's friend.

                                  She is going.

O, stay! [*Aside*] I have no power to let her pass;   60
My hand would free her, but my heart says no.
As plays the sun upon the glassy streams,
Twinkling another counterfeited beam,
So seems this gorgeous beauty to mine eyes.
Fain would I woo her, yet I dare not speak;   65
I'll call for pen and ink, and write my mind.
Fie, De la Pole! disable not thyself.
Hast not a tongue? Is she not here?
Wilt thou be daunted at a woman's sight?
Ay, beauty's princely majesty is such,   70
Confounds the tongue and makes the senses
    rough.

MARGARET Say, Earl of Suffolk, if thy name be so,
What ransom must I pay before I pass?
For I perceive I am thy prisoner.

SUFFOLK [*Aside*] How canst thou tell she will deny thy
    suit,   75
Before thou make a trial of her love?

MARGARET Why speak'st thou not? What ransom must
    I pay?

SUFFOLK [*Aside*] She's beautiful and therefore to be
    wooed;
She is a woman, therefore to be won.

MARGARET Wilt thou accept of ransom, yea or no?   80

SUFFOLK [*Aside*] Fond man, remember that thou hast
    a wife;
Then how can Margaret be thy paramour?

55 **allotted** fated   58 **servile usage** unworthy treatment   62 **glassy** smooth
63 **counterfeited** reflected   67 **disable** disparage   71 **rough** dull

MARGARET I were best to leave him, for he will not
 hear.

SUFFOLK [*Aside*] There all is marred; there lies a
 cooling card.

85 MARGARET He talks at random; sure, the man is mad.

SUFFOLK [*Still aside, but more loudly*] And yet a
 dispensation may be had.

MARGARET And yet I would that you would answer
 me.

SUFFOLK [*Aside*] I'll win this Lady Margaret. For
 whom?
 Why, for my king. [*Somewhat more loudly*] Tush,
 that's a wooden thing!

90 MARGARET He talks of wood: it is some carpenter.

SUFFOLK [*Aside*] Yet so my fancy may be satisfied
 And peace establishèd between these realms.
 But there remains a scruple in that too:
 For though her father be the King of Naples,
95 Duke of Anjou and Maine, yet is he poor,
 And our nobility will scorn the match.

MARGARET Hear ye, captain, are you not at leisure?

SUFFOLK [*Aside*] It shall be so, disdain they ne'er so
 much:
 Henry is youthful and will quickly yield.
100 [*Aloud*] Madam, I have a secret to reveal.

MARGARET [*Aside*] What though I be enthralled? he
 seems a knight,
 And will not any way dishonor me.

SUFFOLK Lady, vouchsafe to listen what I say.

MARGARET [*Aside*] Perhaps I shall be rescued by the
 French,

84 **cooling card** something to cool my ardor   86 **dispensation** i.e., annulment of
a previous marriage 89 **wooden** dull 90 **it** he 93 **scruple** difficulty
101 **enthralled** captured

And then I need not crave his courtesy.   105

SUFFOLK Sweet madam, give me hearing in a cause.

MARGARET [*Aside*] Tush, women have been captivate
    ere now.

SUFFOLK Lady, wherefore talk you so?

MARGARET I cry you mercy, 'tis but *quid* for *quo*.

SUFFOLK Say, gentle princess, would you not suppose   110
    Your bondage happy, to be made a queen?

MARGARET To be a queen in bondage is more vile
    Than is a slave in base servility,
    For princes should be free.

SUFFOLK   And so shall you,
    If happy England's royal king be free.   115

MARGARET Why, what concerns his freedom unto me?

SUFFOLK I'll undertake to make thee Henry's queen,
    To put a golden scepter in thy hand
    And set a precious crown upon thy head,
    If thou wilt condescend to be my—

MARGARET   What?   120

SUFFOLK His love.

MARGARET I am unworthy to be Henry's wife.

SUFFOLK No, gentle madam, I unworthy am
    To woo so fair a dame to be his wife,
    And have no portion in the choice myself.   125
    How say you, madam, are ye so content?

MARGARET And if my father please, I am content.

SUFFOLK Then call our captains and our colors forth.
    And, madam, at your father's castle walls
    We'll crave a parley, to confer with him.   130

---

109 **cry you mercy** beg your pardon   109 **quid for quo** even exchange, tit for
tat   125 **no portion in** (1) no share in (2) nothing to gain by

Sound [a parley.] Enter Reignier on the walls.

See, Reignier, see, thy daughter prisoner!

REIGNIER To whom?

SUFFOLK   To me.

REIGNIER   Suffolk, what remedy?
I am a soldier and unapt to weep
Or to exclaim on fortune's fickleness.

135 SUFFOLK Yes, there is remedy enough, my lord:
Consent, and for thy honor give consent,
Thy daughter shall be wedded to my king,
Whom I with pain have wooed and won thereto,
And this her easy-held imprisonment
140   Hath gained thy daughter princely liberty.

REIGNIER Speaks Suffolk as he thinks?

SUFFOLK   Fair Margaret knows
That Suffolk doth not flatter, face, or feign.

REIGNIER Upon thy princely warrant, I descend
To give thee answer of thy just demand.

                                        [Exit.]

145 SUFFOLK And here I will expect thy coming.

                Trumpets sound. Enter Reignier.

REIGNIER Welcome, brave earl, into our territories;
Command in Anjou what your honor pleases.

SUFFOLK Thanks, Reignier, happy for so sweet a
          child,
Fit to be made companion with a king.
150   What answer makes your grace unto my suit?

REIGNIER Since thou dost deign to woo her little
          worth
To be the princely bride of such a lord,
Upon condition I may quietly

---

133 **unapt** not ready 138 **Whom** i.e., Margaret 138 **pain** much effort
142 **face** deceive 145 **expect** await 148 **for** in having 151 **her little worth** a
lady of such modest rank and fortune

Enjoy mine own, the country Maine and Anjou,
Free from oppression or the stroke of war,   165
My daughter shall be Henry's, if he please.

SUFFOLK That is her ransom; I deliver her,
And those two counties I will undertake
Your grace shall well and quietly enjoy.

REIGNIER And I again, in Henry's royal name,   160
As deputy unto that gracious king,
Give thee her hand, for sign of plighted faith.

SUFFOLK Reignier of France, I give thee kingly thanks
Because this is in traffic of a king.
[*Aside*] And yet, methinks, I could be well content   165
To be mine own attorney in this case.
[*Aloud*] I'll over then to England with this news,
And make this marriage to be solemnized.
So farewell, Reignier; set this diamond safe
In golden palaces, as it becomes.   170

REIGNIER I do embrace thee, as I would embrace
The Christian prince, King Henry, were he here.

MARGARET Farewell, my lord; good wishes, praise, and
    prayers
Shall Suffolk ever have of Margaret.   *She is going.*

SUFFOLK Farewell, sweet madam; but hark you,
    Margaret: 175
No princely commendations to my king?

MARGARET Such commendations as becomes a maid,
A virgin, and his servant, say to him.

SUFFOLK Words sweetly placed and modestly di-
    rected.
But, madam, I must trouble you again: 180
No loving token to his majesty?

MARGARET Yes, my good lord, a pure unspotted heart,
Never yet taint with love, I send the king.

161 **deputy** i.e., Suffolk   162 **plighted faith** promise to marry   164 **in traffic**
in negotiation   166 **attorney** pleader   179 **directed** uttered   183 **taint with
love** tinged with immodest desire

SUFFOLK And this withal.   *Kisses her.*

185 MARGARET That for thyself; I will not so presume
To send such peevish tokens to a king.

[*Exeunt Reignier and Margaret.*]

SUFFOLK O, wert thou for myself! But, Suffolk, stay;
Thou mayst not wander in that labyrinth;
There Minotaurs and ugly treasons lurk.
190 Solicit Henry with her wondrous praise;
Bethink thee on her virtues that surmount,
And natural graces that extinguish art;
Repeat their semblance often on the seas,
That, when thou com'st to kneel at Henry's feet,
195 Thou mayst bereave him of his wits with wonder.

Exit.

Scene IV. [*Camp of the Duke of York in Anjou.*]

Enter York, Warwick, [and others].

YORK Bring forth that sorceress condemned to burn.

[*Enter La Pucelle, guarded, and a Shepherd.*]

SHEPHERD Ah, Joan, this kills thy father's heart out-
right!
Have I sought every country far and near,
And now it is my chance to find thee out,
5 Must I behold thy timeless cruel death?
Ah, Joan, sweet daughter Joan, I'll die with thee!

186 **peevish tokens** foolish signs of affection   189 **Minotaurs** (alluding to the
mythological monster of Crete, half-bull and half-man, who was slain by
Theseus) 190 **Solicit** allure 192 **extinguish** obscure by greater
brilliancy 193 **Repeat their semblance** remind yourself of their
appearance 195 **bereave** dispossess V.iv.3 **sought** searched 4 **now** now
that 5 **timeless** untimely

PUCELLE Decrepit miser! base ignoble wretch!
  I am descended of a greater blood.
  Thou art no father nor no friend of mine.

SHEPHERD Out, out! My lords, and please you, 'tis
    not so.   10
  I did beget her, all the parish knows;
  Her mother liveth yet, can testify
  She was the first fruit of my bachelorship.

WARWICK Graceless! wilt thou deny thy parentage?

YORK This argues what her kind of life hath been, 15
  Wicked and vile, and so her death concludes.

SHEPHERD Fie, Joan, that thou wilt be so obstacle!
  God knows thou art a collop of my flesh,
  And for thy sake have I shed many a tear.
  Deny me not, I prithee, gentle Joan.   20

PUCELLE Peasant, avaunt! You have suborned this
    man
  Of purpose to obscure my noble birth.

SHEPHERD 'Tis true, I gave a noble to the priest
  The morn that I was wedded to her mother.
  Kneel down and take my blessing, good my girl. 25
  Wilt thou not stoop? Now cursèd be the time
  Of thy nativity! I would the milk
  Thy mother gave thee when thou suck'dst her
    breast
  Had been a little ratsbane for thy sake!
  Or else, when thou didst keep my lambs a-field, 30
  I wish some ravenous wolf had eaten thee!
  Dost thou deny thy father, cursèd drab?
  O, burn her, burn her! hanging is too good.   *Exit.*

---

7 **miser** old wretch 10 **Out, out** alas 10 **and** if it 13 **first ... bachelorship** i.e., begotten out of wedlock (but the shepherd apparently is confused about the meaning of *bachelorship*) 17 **obstacle** obstinate (a malapropism) 18 **collop** piece 21 **avaunt** begone 21 **suborned** bribed 22 **obscure** conceal 23 **noble** gold coin worth about ten shillings 29 **ratsbane** rat poison 32 **drab** prostitute

YORK Take her away, for she hath lived too long,
35   To fill the world with vicious qualities.

PUCELLE First, let me tell you whom you have con-
          demned:
        Not me begotten of a shepherd swain
        But issued from the progeny of kings;
        Virtuous and holy, chosen from above,
40   By inspiration of celestial grace,
        To work exceeding miracles on earth.
        I never had to do with wicked spirits,
        But you, that are polluted with your lusts,
        Stained with the guiltless blood of innocents,
45   Corrupt and tainted with a thousand vices,
        Because you want the grace that others have,
        You judge it straight a thing impossible
        To compass wonders but by help of devils.
        No, misconceived! Joan of Arc hath been
50   A virgin from her tender infancy,
        Chaste and immaculate in very thought,
        Whose maiden blood, thus rigorously effused,
        Will cry for vengeance at the gates of heaven.

YORK Ay, ay; away with her to execution!

55 WARWICK And hark ye, sirs: because she is a maid,
        Spare for no faggots, let there be enow;
        Place barrels of pitch upon the fatal stake,
        That so her torture may be shortenèd.

PUCELLE Will nothing turn your unrelenting hearts?
60   Then, Joan, discover thine infirmity,
        That warranteth by law to be thy privilege.
        I am with child, ye bloody homicides;
        Murder not then the fruit within my womb,
        Although ye hale me to a violent death.

YORK Now heaven forfend! the holy maid with
65   child!

48 **compass** accomplish 49 **misconceivèd** deceived person 52 **rigorously
effused** cruelly shed 56 **Spare for no** do not spare 56 **enow** enough
60 **discover thine infirmity** reveal your bodily unfitness 64 **hale** drag 65
forfend forbid

WARWICK The greatest miracle that e'er ye wrought.
Is all your strict preciseness come to this?

YORK She and the Dolphin have been juggling;
I did imagine what would be her refuge.

WARWICK Well, go to; we'll have no bastards live,   70
Especially since Charles must father it.

PUCELLE You are deceived, my child is none of his,
It was Alençon that enjoyed my love.

YORK Alençon! that notorious Machiavel!
It dies, and if it had a thousand lives.   75

PUCELLE O, give me leave, I have deluded you:
'Twas neither Charles nor yet the duke I named,
But Reignier, king of Naples, that prevailed.

WARWICK A married man! that's most intolerable.

YORK Why, here's a girl! I think she knows not well,   80
There were so many, whom she may accuse.

WARWICK It's sign she hath been liberal and free.

YORK And yet, forsooth, she is a virgin pure.
Strumpet, thy words condemn thy brat and thee.
Use no entreaty, for it is in vain.   85

PUCELLE Then lead me hence; with whom I leave my
curse:
May never glorious sun reflex his beams
Upon the country where you make abode,
But darkness and the gloomy shade of death
Environ you, till mischief and despair   90
Drive you to break your necks or hang yourselves!
Exit, [guarded].

---

67 **preciseness** pretense of scrupulousness 68 **juggling** playing tricks
69 **imagine** wonder 69 **refuge** excuse 70 **go to** come, come 74 **Machiavel**
intriguer (after Niccolò Machiavelli, author of *The Prince*) 78 **prevailed** i.e.,
gained her love 80 **girl** wench 82 **liberal and free** (used ironically, since a lady
was supposed to have these qualities, without Joan's implied wantonness)
83 **forsooth** in truth 87 **reflex** reflect

YORK Break thou in pieces and consume to ashes,
    Thou foul accursèd minister of hell.

Enter Cardinal [Beaufort, Bishop of Winchester].

WINCHESTER Lord Regent, I do greet your excellence
95   With letters of commission from the king.
    For know, my lords, the states of Christendom,
    Moved with remorse of these outrageous broils,
    Have earnestly implored a general peace
    Betwixt our nation and the aspiring French,
100   And here at hand the Dolphin and his train
    Approacheth, to confer about some matter.

YORK Is all our travail turned to this effect?
    After the slaughter of so many peers,
    So many captains, gentlemen, and soldiers,
105   That in this quarrel have been overthrown
    And sold their bodies for their country's benefit,
    Shall we at last conclude effeminate peace?
    Have we not lost most part of all the towns,
    By treason, falsehood, and by treachery,
110   Our great progenitors had conquerèd?
    O, Warwick, Warwick! I foresee with grief
    The utter loss of all the realm of France.

WARWICK Be patient, York; if we conclude a peace,
    It shall be with such strict and severe covenants
115   As little shall the Frenchmen gain thereby.

Enter Charles [Dauphin], Alençon, Bastard, Reignier,
    [and others].

DAUPHIN Since, lords of England, it is thus agreed
    That peaceful truce shall be proclaimed in France,
    We come to be informèd by yourselves
    What the conditions of that league must be.

120 YORK Speak, Winchester, for boiling choler chokes
    The hollow passage of my poisoned voice
    By sight of these our baleful enemies.

93 **minister** agent 97 **remorse of** sorrow at 100 **train** retinue 102 **travail**
labor, trouble 114 **covenants** conditions 121 **poisoned** sickened as though
with poison

WINCHESTER Charles, and the rest, it is enacted thus:
  That, in regard King Henry gives consent,
  Of mere compassion and of lenity,   125
  To ease your country of distressful war
  And suffer you to breathe in fruitful peace,
  You shall become true liegemen to his crown.
  And, Charles, upon condition thou wilt swear
  To pay him tribute, and submit thyself,   130
  Thou shalt be placed as viceroy under him,
  And still enjoy thy regal dignity.

ALENÇON Must he be then as shadow of himself?
  Adorn his temples with a coronet,
  And yet, in substance and authority,   135
  Retain but privilege of a private man?
  This proffer is absurd and reasonless.

DAUPHIN 'Tis known already that I am possessed
  With more than half the Gallian territories,
  And therein reverenced for their lawful king: 140
  Shall I, for lucre of the rest unvanquished,
  Detract so much from that prerogative
  As to be called but viceroy of the whole?
  No, lord ambassador, I'll rather keep
  That which I have than, coveting for more,   145
  Be cast from possibility of all.

YORK Insulting Charles! hast thou by secret means
  Used intercession to obtain a league,
  And, now the matter grows to compromise,
  Stand'st thou aloof upon comparison?   150
  Either accept the title thou usurp'st,
  Of benefit proceeding from our king
  And not of any challenge of desert,
  Or we will plague thee with incessant wars.

REIGNIER My lord, you do not well in obstinacy   155

125 Of out of 128 liegemen vassals 140 reverenced for honored as
141 lucre gain 142 prerogative preeminence (as king) 146 cast driven
148 league alliance 150 upon comparison weighing the odds 152 Of
through 153 challenge of desert claim that it is yours by right

To cavil in the course of this contract:
If once it be neglected, ten to one
We shall not find like opportunity.

ALENÇON To say the truth, it is your policy
160   To save your subjects from such massacre
And ruthless slaughters as are daily seen
By our proceeding in hostility;
And therefore take this compact of a truce—
[*Aside*] Although you break it when your pleasure
    serves.

WARWICK How say'st thou, Charles? shall our condi-
165   tion stand?

DAUPHIN It shall;
Only reserved, you claim no interest
In any of our towns of garrison.

YORK Then swear allegiance to his majesty,
170   As thou art knight, never to disobey
Nor be rebellious to the crown of England,
Thou, nor thy nobles, to the crown of England.

[*The Dauphin and French nobles give signs of fealty.*]

So, now dismiss your army when ye please;
Hang up your ensigns, let your drums be still,
175   For here we entertain a solemn peace.
                                        Exeunt.

---

156 cavil find fault without good reason   163 **compact of** mutual agreement
for   174 **ensigns** banners   175 **entertain** accept

Scene V. [*London. The royal palace.*]

Enter Suffolk in conference with the King, Gloucester,
and Exeter.

KING Your wondrous rare description, noble earl,
Of beauteous Margaret hath astonished me.
Her virtues, gracèd with external gifts,
Do breed love's settled passions in my heart,
And like as rigor of tempestuous gusts   5
Provokes the mightiest hulk against the tide,
So am I driven by breath of her renown
Either to suffer shipwreck or arrive
Where I may have fruition of her love.

SUFFOLK Tush, my good lord, this superficial tale   10
Is but a preface of her worthy praise.
The chief perfections of that lovely dame,
Had I sufficient skill to utter them,
Would make a volume of enticing lines,
Able to ravish any dull conceit;   15
And, which is more, she is not so divine,
So full replete with choice of all delights,
But with as humble lowliness of mind
She is content to be at your command;
Command, I mean, of virtuous chaste intents,   20
To love and honor Henry as her lord.

KING And otherwise will Henry ne'er presume.
Therefore, my Lord Protector, give consent
That Margaret may be England's royal queen.

V.v.5 **rigor** violence 6 **Provokes** drives on 6 **hulk** ship 7 **breath**
utterance 10 **superficial** touching only the surface 15 **ravish ... conceit** i.e.,
enchant even the dullest imagination 20 **intents** intentions

25 GLOUCESTER So should I give consent to flatter sin.
          You know, my lord, your highness is betrothed
          Unto another lady of esteem.
          How shall we then dispense with that contract,
          And not deface your honor with reproach?

30 SUFFOLK As doth a ruler with unlawful oaths,
          Or one that, at a triumph having vowed
          To try his strength, forsaketh yet the lists
          By reason of his adversary's odds.
          A poor earl's daughter is unequal odds,
35   And therefore may be broke without offense.

    GLOUCESTER Why, what, I pray, is Margaret more than
              that?
          Her father is no better than an earl,
          Although in glorious titles he excel.

    SUFFOLK Yes, my lord, her father is a king,
40   The King of Naples and Jerusalem,
          And of such great authority in France
          As his alliance will confirm our peace
          And keep the Frenchmen in allegiance.

    GLOUCESTER And so the Earl of Armagnac may do
45   Because he is near kinsman unto Charles.

    EXETER Beside, his wealth doth warrant a liberal
              dower,
          Where Reignier sooner will receive than give.

    SUFFOLK A dower, my lords! disgrace not so your king,
          That he should be so abject, base, and poor,
50   To choose for wealth and not for perfect love.
          Henry is able to enrich his queen
          And not to seek a queen to make him rich.
          So worthless peasants bargain for their wives,
          As market men for oxen, sheep, or horse.
55   Marriage is a matter of more worth

25 **flatter** condone 27 **another lady** i.e., the daughter of the Earl of
Armagnac 31 **triumph** tournament 32 **lists** tournament ground 33 **odds**
inferiority 35 **broke** i.e., the pledge of marriage may be broken

Than to be dealt in by attorneyship;
Not whom we will, but whom his grace affects,
Must be companion of his nuptial bed.
And therefore, lords, since he affects her most,
Most of all these reasons bindeth us,   60
In our opinions she should be preferred.
For what is wedlock forcèd but a hell,
An age of discord and continual strife?
Whereas the contrary bringeth bliss,
And is a pattern of celestial peace.   65
Whom should we match with Henry, being a king,
But Margaret, that is daughter to a king?
Her peerless feature, joinèd with her birth,
Approves her fit for none but for a king.
Her valiant courage and undaunted spirit,   70
More than in women commonly is seen,
Will answer our hope in issue of a king;
For Henry, son unto a conqueror,
Is likely to beget more conquerors,
If with a lady of so high resolve   75
As is fair Margaret he be linked in love.
Then yield, my lords, and here conclude with me
That Margaret shall be queen, and none but she.

KING Whether it be through force of your report,
     My noble Lord of Suffolk, or for that   80
     My tender youth was never yet attaint
     With any passion of inflaming love,
     I cannot tell; but this I am assured,
     I feel such sharp dissension in my breast,
     Such fierce alarums both of hope and fear,   85
     As I am sick with working of my thoughts.
     Take, therefore, shipping; post, my lord, to France;
     Agree to any convenants, and procure
     That Lady Margaret do vouchsafe to come
     To cross the seas to England and be crowned   90
     King Henry's faithful and anointed queen.

56 **attorneyship** proxy 59 **since** the fact that 68 **feature** comeliness
69 **Approves** proves 81 attaint stained

113

For your expenses and sufficient charge,
Among the people gather up a tenth.
Be gone, I say, for, till you do return,
95   I rest perplexèd with a thousand cares.
And you, good uncle, banish all offense;
If you do censure me by what you were,
Not what you are, I know it will excuse
This sudden execution of my will.
100 And so, conduct me where, from company,
I may revolve and ruminate my grief.   *Exit.*

GLOUCESTER Ay, grief, I fear me, both at first and last.

Exit Gloucester [with Exeter].

SUFFOLK Thus Suffolk hath prevailed, and thus he
goes,
As did the youthful Paris once to Greece,
105 With hope to find the like event in love,
But prosper better than the Trojan did.
Margaret shall now be queen, and rule the king;
But I will rule both her, her king, and realm.   *Exit.*

FINIS

92 **sufficient charge** adequate money to meet costs   93 **tenth** (a levy of a tenth of the value of personal property, collected to meet unusual expenses such as a royal marriage)   95 **rest** remain   97 **censure** judge   99 **execution** carrying into effect   101 **revolve and ruminate** consider and meditate upon   105 **event** result

Textual Note

The First Part of Henry the Sixth is preserved only in the Folio of 1623, the basis of the present edition. Though acted infrequently after Shakespeare's lifetime, apparently the drama was originally well received. In the epilogue to Shakespeare's *Henry V*, the Chorus asks the spectators to applaud this more recent work by reminding them of the company's earlier dramatizations of the reign of Henry VI:

> Which oft our stage hath shown; and for their sake,
> In your fair minds let this acceptance take.

It is even likely that in its earliest production *1 Henry VI* was the theatrical hit of the year. On March 3, 1592, the producer Philip Henslowe recorded in his diary that the first performance of a new (or refurbished) play called "harey the vj." had grossed £3.16s.8d., a sum indicating an exceptionally profitable opening. Over the next ten months this work was acted at least fourteen, perhaps fifteen, additional times. It may be that the patriotic theme appealed strongly to a London audience still exulting over the debacle of the Spanish Armada; for the heroic death of Lord Talbot in the fourth act, as Thomas Nashe wrote during the same year in *Pierce Penniless*, had been found deeply moving by "ten thousand spectators at least (at several times), who, in the tragedian that represents his person, imagine they behold him fresh bleeding."

The entry in Henslowe's diary and Nashe's allusion in his pamphlet to "Talbot (the terror of the French)" suggest that the play in question may have been *1 Henry VI*. Still, some doubt must remain whether this particular version was the same as that printed in the Folio, and whether Shakespeare had participated in its composition. With few exceptions, however, modern Shakespearian critics have assumed that *1 Henry VI* as we know it does come, along with the second and third parts of the trilogy, from Shakespeare's apprentice years as a playwright. In the absence of any positive evidence to the contrary, it thus seems reasonable to declare for late 1591 or early 1592 as the likeliest date of original composition for the play printed in the Folio and to presume that it is substantially, perhaps entirely, from the hand of Shakespeare.

The Folio is the only authority and affords a remarkably clear text, apart from a few baffling words and some apparently mangled lines of verse. In the present edition, therefore, the temptation to emend the original has been resisted as much as possible. Only two words to fill apparent lacunae have been supplied from consultation with the later Folios. These are *Nero* (I.iv.95) and *sir* (II.iv. 132). Both of these are bracketed in the text and their sources given in the notes below. Without editorial comment, punctuation and spelling have been modernized (though "Dolphin" is retained in the dialogue), names prefixed to speeches and appearing in stage directions expanded and regularized, act and scene divisions translated where the Folio gives them in Latin, and obvious typographical errors corrected.

In the few instances where lines of verse are improperly divided in the Folio, they have been rearranged; all such corrections are noted in the table below. Occasionally when the printers of the Folio may seem to have divided a single line into two verses, it is quite clear that the line was too long for the space available, and was simply broken at a clause, rather than at the end of the column. Because the stage directions in the original are on the whole clear and amply descriptive, they have been reproduced with a minimum of emendations and additions; wherever changes have been made, they are enclosed in square brackets. In dividing acts and scenes the Folio is deficient: no scene divisions are given for Acts I and II; Act III is correctly divided into four scenes; Act IV is not only too long—since nothing but the final scene is left for Act V—but within it the scenes are also inaccurately divided. The act and scene divisions of the present edition are therefore those of the Globe text; wherever they differ from those of the Folio, they are enclosed in square brackets. The table that follows includes emendations and corrections of the Folio text. The altered reading appears first, in bold; the original follows, in roman. Where a Folio reading is retained, but seems extremely dubious, the word is given in roman, and commentary or suggested emendation is placed within square brackets.

I.i.94 **Reignier** Reynold   96 **crownèd** crown'd   132 **vanward** Vauward

I.ii.30 **bred** breed   99 fine [so F, but later editors, following mention in Holinshed's *Chronicles* of a pattern of "five" fleurs-de-lis on the sword, emend to five; conceivably the *n* in F is a mistakenly inverted *u* (i.e., for *v*)]   103 s.d. **la** de   113 **rites** rights   132 **enterèd** entred

I.iii.29 **Humphrey** Vmpheir

I.iv.10 Went [so F, but Tyrwhitt's conjecture **Wont** is accepted by some modern editors]   16-18 [two lines in F, but perhaps should be printed as three, divided after **watched, them,** and **longer**]   29 **ransomèd** ransom'd   69 s.d. **fall** falls   95 **Nero** [not in F; conjectured by Malone from the Second Folio reading "and *Nero* like will" for "and like thee"]   101 **la** de

I.v.s.d. **la** de

I.vi.3 **la** de   6 garden [so F, but *were* in line 7 suggests that the intended reading may have been **gardens**]   29 **la** de

II.i.7 s.d. drums ... march [so F, but sounding drums seems a most peculiar way of beginning a surprise attack]   29 **all together** altogether   77 [F reads **Exeunt** here, but the following stage direction renders the word superfluous]   77 s.d. **an** a

II.ii.6 **center** Centure   20 **Arc** Acre   59 **Whispers** [printed at end of line in F]

II.iii.11-12 [printed as one line in F]

II.iv.s.d. **Vernon, and another Lawyer** and others   117 whipped [so F, but second Folio and all subsequent editions read **wiped**]   132 **sir** [not in F; supplied by Second Folio]

II.v.121 s.d. **Exeunt ... Mortimer** Exit   129 will [so F, though modern editors, following Theobald, conjecture **ill** (i.e., turn my injuries to my benefit)]

III.i.52-53 [most modern editions reassign line 52 to Somerset and line 53 to Warwick]   164 all [so F, but the word is superfluous for both sense and meter]   200 **lose** loose

III.ii.50-51 [printed as three (metrically defective) lines in F, divided after **graybeard, death,** and **chair**]   59 s.d. **The English** They   103 s.d. **Exeunt ... Attendants** Exit   123 **gleeks** glikes

IV.i.s.d. **Exeter ... Paris and Gouernor** Exeter   173 s.d. **Flourish** [apparently misplaced in F in s.d. that follows line 181]

TEXTUAL NOTE

IV.ii. **Before Bordeaux** [supplied by s.d. in F]   3 **calls** call   34 **due** dew   50 **moody-mad** moodie mad

IV.iii.20 **waist** waste

IV.iv.16 **regions** [so F, but most modern editors emend to **legions**]

IV.vi.18 **encounterèd** encountred

IV.vii.96 s.d. **Exeunt** Exit

V.i. **Scene I** Scena secunda

V.ii. **Scene II** Scena Tertia

V.iii. s.d. **la** de   44 **comest** comst   57 **her** his   179 **modestly** modestie   184 s.d. **Kisses** Kisse   188, 195 **mayst** mayest   190 **wondrous** wonderous   192 **And Mad**

V.iv. s.d. **and others** Shepheard, Pucell [who obviously enter after line 1]   49 **Arc** Aire   58 **shortenèd** shortned   60 **discover** discouet   93 s.d. [placed in F after line 91]

V.v. **Scene V** Actus Quintus

WILLIAM SHAKESPEARE

THE SECOND PART OF HENRY THE SIXTH

WITH THE DEATH OF THE GOOD DUKE HUMPHREY

Edited by Arthur Freeman

KING HENRY THE SIXTH

HUMPHREY, Duke of Gloucester, uncle to the King, and Protector

CARDINAL BEAUFORT, Bishop of Winchester, great-uncle to the King

RICHARD PLANTAGENET, Duke of York

EDWARD
RICHARD, afterwards Richard III } his sons

DUKE OF SOMERSET

HUMPHREY, Duke of Buckingham

WILLIAM DE LA POLE, Marquess (afterwards Duke) of Suffolk

EARL OF SALISBURY

RICHARD, Earl of Warwick, his son

LORD CLIFFORD

YOUNG CLIFFORD, his son

LORD SAY

LORD SCALES

SIR HUMPHREY STAFFORD

SIR WILLIAM STAFFORD, his brother

SIR JOHN STANLEY

SIR MATTHEW GOFFE

VAUX

LIEUTENANT, MASTER, and MASTER'S-MATE, WALTER WHITMORE, and two GENTLEMEN, prisoners with Suffolk

JOHN HUM and JOHN SOUTHWELL, PRIESTS, ROGER BOLINGBROKE, a CONJUROR, and a SPIRIT

THOMAS HORNER, an armorer, and PETER THUMP, his apprentice

MAYOR OF SAINT ALBANS

CLERK OF CHATHAM

ALEXANDER IDEN, a Kentish landowner

SAUNDER SIMPCOX, an impostor

JACK CADE

GEORGE BEVIS, JOHN HOLLAND, DICK THE BUTCHER, SMITH THE WEAVER, MICHAEL, all followers of Cade

TWO MURDERERS

QUEEN MARGARET
ELEANOR, Duchess of Gloucester
MARGERY JOURDAIN, a witch
WIFE OF SIMPCOX

Two PETITIONERS, BEADLE, HERALD, SHERIFF, ALDERMEN,
three NEIGHBORS OF HORNER, three PRENTICES;
FALCONERS, CITIZENS, GUARDS, SOLDIERS, MESSENGERS,
ATTENDANTS

Scene: England]

THE SECOND PART OF
HENRY THE SIXTH
WITH THE DEATH OF THE
GOOD DUKE HUMPHREY

ACT I

Scene I. [*London. The Palace.*]

Flourish of trumpets: then hautboys. Enter at one door
King Henry the Sixth, and Humphrey, Duke of
Gloucester, the Duke of Somerset, the Duke of
Buckingham, Cardinal Beaufort, and others. Enter at the
other door the Duke of York, and the Marquess of
Suffolk, and Queen Margaret, and the Earl of Salisbury
and Warwick.

SUFFOLK As by your high imperial Majesty
I had in charge at my depart for France,
As procurator to your Excellence,
To marry Princess Margaret for your Grace,
So in the famous ancient city, Tours,   5

Text references are printed in **boldface** type; the annotation follows in roman
type.
I.i. s.d. **Flourish** fanfare   s.d. **hautboys** oboes   3 **procurator** deputy

In presence of the Kings of France and Sicil,
The Dukes of Orleans, Calaber, Bretagne and
    Alençon,
Seven earls, twelve barons, and twenty reverend
    bishops,
I have performed my task and was espoused,
And humbly now upon my bended knee,
In sight of England and her lordly peers,
Deliver up my title in the Queen
To your most gracious hands, that are the
    substance
Of that great shadow I did represent—
The happiest gift that ever marquess gave,
The fairest queen that ever king received.

KING Suffolk, arise. Welcome, Queen Margaret:
I can express no kinder sign of love
Than this kind kiss. O Lord, that lends me life,
Lend me a heart replete with thankfulness!
For Thou hast given me in this beauteous face
A world of earthly blessings to my soul,
If sympathy of love unite our thoughts.

QUEEN Great King of England and my gracious lord,
The mutual conference that my mind hath had,
By day, by night, waking, and in my dreams,
In courtly company or at my beads,
With you mine alderliefest sovereign,
Makes me the bolder to salute my king
With ruder terms, such as my wit affords
And overjoy of heart doth minister.

KING Her sight did ravish, but her grace in speech,
Her words yclad with wisdom's majesty,
Makes me from wond'ring fall to weeping joys,
Such is the fullness of my heart's content.
Lords, with one cheerful voice welcome my love,

---

7 **Calaber** location uncertain, but evidently *not* Calabria   15 **happiest** most fortunate   18-19 **kinder ... kind** more natural ... affectionate   25 **mutual conference** intimate conversation   28 **alderliefest** dearest of all   30 **wit** intelligence, understanding   31 **minister** provide   33 **yclad** clad (archaic)

All kneel Long live Queen Margaret, England's hap-
     piness!

QUEEN We thank you all.   *Flourish.*

SUFFOLK My Lord Protector, so it please your Grace,
     Here are the articles of contracted peace   40
     Between our sovereign and the French King
          Charles,
     For eighteen months concluded by consent.

GLOUCESTER *(Reads.)* "*Imprimis*, It is agreed be-
     tween the French King Charles, and William de la
     Pole, Marquess of Suffolk, ambassador for Henry   45
     King of England, that the said Henry shall espouse
     the Lady Margaret, daughter unto Reignier King
     of Naples, Sicilia and Jerusalem, and crown her
     Queen of England ere the thirtieth of May next
     ensuing. *Item*, That the duchy of Anjou and the   50
     county of Maine shall be released and delivered to
     the king her father"—   *Gloucester lets it fall.*

KING Uncle, how now?

GLOUCESTER   Pardon me, gracious lord;
     Some sudden qualm hath struck me at the heart,
     And dimmed mine eyes, that I can read no further.   55

KING Uncle of Winchester, I pray read on.

CARDINAL [*Reads*] "Item, It is further agreed between
     them, that the duchies of Anjou and Maine shall
     be released and delivered over to the King her
     father, and she sent over of the King of England's   60
     own proper cost and charges, without having any
     dowry."

KING They please us well.
     Lord Marquess, kneel down: we here create thee
     First Duke of Suffolk, and girt thee with the sword.   65
     Cousin of York, we here discharge your Grace
     From being regent i' th' parts of France,

43 Imprimis in the first place   61 **proper** personal

Till term of eighteen months be full expired.
Thanks, uncle Winchester, Gloucester, York,
70 Buckingham, Somerset, Salisbury, and Warwick;
We thank you all for this great favor done,
In entertainment to my princely queen.
Come, let us in, and with all speed provide
To see her coronation be performed.

Exit King, Queen, and Suffolk; and
Gloucester stays all the rest.

GLOUCESTER Brave peers of England, pillars of the
75 state,
To you Duke Humphrey must unload his grief—
Your grief, the common grief of all the land.
What! Did my brother Henry spend his youth,
His valor, coin, and people, in the wars?
80 Did he so often lodge in open field,
In winter's cold, and summer's parching heat,
To conquer France, his true inheritance?
And did my brother Bedford toil his wits,
To keep by policy what Henry got?
85 Have you yourselves, Somerset, Buckingham,
Brave York, Salisbury, and victorious Warwick,
Received deep scars in France and Normandy?
Or hath mine uncle Beaufort and myself,
With all the learnèd council of the realm,
90 Studied so long, sat in the council house
Early and late, debating to and fro
How France and Frenchmen might be kept in awe,
And had his Highness in his infancy
Crownèd in Paris in despite of foes?
95 And shall these labors and these honors die?
Shall Henry's conquest, Bedford's vigilance,
Your deeds of war and all our counsel die?
O peers of England, shameful is this league!
Fatal this marriage, canceling your fame,

---

72 **entertainment** welcome   82 **inheritance** i.e., by his marriage with Katherine
of Valois (see *Henry V*, V.ii.333)   83 **Bedford** John, Duke of Bedford, the second
of Henry IV's three sons   84 **policy** political craft, statesmanship   89 **council**
the privy council

Blotting your names from books of memory,   100
Razing the characters of your renown,
Defacing monuments of conquered France,
Undoing all, as all had never been.

CARDINAL Nephew, what means this passionate dis-
      course,
This peroration with such circumstance?   105
For France, 'tis ours; and we will keep it still.

GLOUCESTER Ay, uncle, we will keep it, if we can;
But now it is impossible we should.
Suffolk, the new-made duke that rules the roast,
Hath given the duchy of Anjou and Maine   110
Unto the poor King Reignier, whose large style
Agrees not with the leanness of his purse.

SALISBURY Now, by the death of Him that died for all,
These counties were the keys of Normandy!
But wherefore weeps Warwick, my valiant son?   115

WARWICK For grief that they are past recovery:
For, were there hope to conquer them again,
My sword should shed hot blood, mine eyes no
      tears.
Anjou and Maine! myself did win them both;
Those provinces these arms of mine did conquer: 120
And are the cities that I got with wounds
Delivered up again with peaceful words?
Mort Dieu!

YORK For Suffolk's duke, may he be suffocate
That dims the honor of this warlike isle!   125
France should have torn and rent my very heart
Before I would have yielded to this league.
I never read but England's kings have had
Large sums of gold and dowries with their wives;

---

101 **Razing the characters** effacing the written letters   105 **peroration with such circumstance** rhetorical discourse with so many details or illustrations   109 **rules the roast** domineers (from the proverbial expression "to rule the roast after one's own diet")   112 **Agrees** accords   123 **Mort Dieu** by God's death

130   And our King Henry gives away his own,
        To match with her that brings no vantages.

        GLOUCESTER A proper jest, and never heard before,
        That Suffolk should demand a whole fifteenth
        For costs and charges in transporting her!
        She should have stayed in France, and sterved in
135   France,
        Before—

        CARDINAL My lord of Gloucester, now ye grow too
              hot:
        It was the pleasure of my lord the King.

        GLOUCESTER My lord of Winchester, I know your
              mind;
140   'Tis not my speeches that you do mislike,
        But 'tis my presence that doth trouble ye.
        Rancor will out: proud prelate, in thy face
        I see thy fury. If I longer stay,
        We shall begin our ancient bickerings.
145   Lordings, farewell, and say, when I am gone,
        I prophesied France will be lost ere long.
                                        Exit Gloucester.

        CARDINAL So, there goes our Protector in a rage.
        'Tis known to you he is mine enemy.—
        Nay more, an enemy unto you all,
150   And no great friend, I fear me, to the King.
        Consider, lords, he is the next of blood,
        And heir apparent to the English crown:
        Had Henry got an empire by his marriage,
        And all the wealthy kingdoms of the west,
155   There's reason he should be displeased at it.
        Look to it, lords: let not his smoothing words
        Bewitch your hearts, be wise and circumspect.
        What though the common people favor him,
        Calling him "Humphrey, the good Duke of
              Gloucester,"
160   Clapping their hands, and crying with loud voice,

131 **vantages** profit   133 **fifteenth** tax of one-fifteenth part levied on
property   135 **sterved** (1) died (2) starved

128

"Jesu maintain your royal excellence!"
With "God preserve the good Duke Humphrey!"
I fear me, lords, for all this flattering gloss,
He will be found a dangerous Protector.

BUCKINGHAM Why should he then protect our
        sovereign,   165
He being of age to govern of himself?
Cousin of Somerset, join you with me,
And altogether with the Duke of Suffolk,
We'll quickly hoise Duke Humphrey from his
        seat.

CARDINAL This weighty business will not brook
        delay;   170
I'll to the Duke of Suffolk presently.
                              Exit Cardinal.

SOMERSET Cousin of Buckingham, though
        Humphrey's pride
And greatness of his place be grief to us,
Yet let us watch the haughty Cardinal.
His insolence is more intolerable   175
Than all the princes' in the land beside.
If Gloucester be displaced, he'll be Protector.

BUCKINGHAM Or thou or I, Somerset, will be
        Protector,
Despite Duke Humphrey or the Cardinal.
                    Exit Buckingham and Somerset.

SALISBURY Pride went before, Ambition follows him.   180
While these do labor for their own preferment,
Behoves it us to labor for the realm.
I never saw but Humphrey Duke of Gloucester
Did bear him like a noble gentleman.
Oft have I seen the haughty Cardinal,   185
More like a soldier than a man o' th' church,
As stout and proud as he were lord of all,

169 **hoise** hoist   170 **brook** tolerate   171 **presently** immediately   173 **place** position   178 **Or ... or** either ... or   182 **Behoves** behooves   187 **stout** fierce, arrogant

129

            Swear like a ruffian and demean himself
            Unlike the ruler of a commonweal.
190   Warwick, my son, the comfort of my age,
            Thy deeds, thy plainness, and thy housekeeping,
            Hath won the greatest favor of the commons,
            Excepting none but good Duke Humphrey:
            And, brother York, thy acts in Ireland,
195   In bringing them to civil discipline,
            Thy late exploits done in the heart of France,
            When thou wert regent for our sovereign,
            Have made thee feared and honored of the people:
            Join we together for the public good,
200   In what we can, to bridle and suppress
            The pride of Suffolk and the Cardinal,
            With Somerset's and Buckingham's ambition;
            And, as we may, cherish Duke Humphrey's deeds,
            While they do tend the profit of the land.

205 WARWICK So God help Warwick, as he loves the land,
            And common profit of his country!

     YORK And so says York—[aside] for he hath greatest
            cause.

     SALISBURY Then let's make haste away, and look unto
            the main.

     WARWICK Unto the main! O father, Maine is lost,
210   That Maine which by main force Warwick did win,
            And would have kept so long as breath did last!
            Main chance, father, you meant, but I meant Maine,
            Which I will win from France, or else be slain.
                        Exit Warwick and Salisbury; manet York.

     YORK Anjou and Maine are given to the French;
215   Paris is lost; the state of Normandy
            Stands on a tickle point now they are gone:
            Suffolk concluded on the articles,
            The peers agreed, and Henry was well pleased

191 housekeeping hospitality   204 tend foster   208 main i.e., main chance, a
gambling term for the most important thing at stake   213 s.d. manet remains
(Latin)   216 on a tickle point in an unstable position   216 now now that

To change two dukedoms for a duke's fair daughter.
I cannot blame them all—what is't to them?   220
'Tis thine they give away, and not their own.
Pirates may make cheap pennyworths of their
     pillage,
And purchase friends, and give to courtesans,
Still reveling like lords till all be gone;
While as the silly owner of the goods   225
Weeps over them and wrings his hapless hands,
And shakes his head and trembling stands aloof,
While all is shared and all is borne away,
Ready to sterve and dare not touch his own:
So York must sit, and fret, and bite his tongue,   230
While his own lands are bargained for and sold.
Methinks the realms of England, France, and Ire-
     land
Bear that proportion to my flesh and blood
As did the fatal brand Althaea burned
Unto the Prince's heart of Calydon.   235
Anjou and Maine both given unto the French?
Cold news for me, for I had hope of France,
Even as I have of fertile England's soil.
A day will come when York shall claim his own;
And therefore I will take the Nevils' parts   240
And make a show of love to proud Duke Hum-
     phrey,
And, when I spy advantage, claim the crown,
For that's the golden mark I seek to hit.
Nor shall proud Lancaster usurp my right,
Nor hold the scepter in his childish fist,   245
Nor wear the diadem upon his head,
Whose church-like humors fits not for a crown.
Then, York, be still awhile, till time do serve:
Watch thou and wake, when others be asleep,
To pry into the secrets of the state;   250

222 **make ... pillage** squander recklessly what they steal   225 **silly** pitiful
234 **Althaea** Althaea caused the death of her son, Meleager, Prince of Calydon, by
temperamentally burning a brand (log) upon which the Fates had told her his life
would depend   235 **Prince's ... Calydon** the Prince of Calydon's heart
244 **Lancaster** i.e., Henry VI   247 **humors** temperament

Till Henry surfeit in the joys of love,
With his new bride and England's dear-bought
    queen,
And Humphrey with the peers be fall'n at jars:
Then will I raise aloft the milk-white rose,
255   With whose sweet smell the air shall be perfumed,
And in my standard bear the arms of York,
To grapple with the house of Lancaster;
And, force perforce, I'll make him yield the
    crown,
Whose bookish rule hath pulled fair England
    down.   *Exit York.*

Scene II. [*The Duke of Gloucester's house.*]

Enter Gloucester and his wife Eleanor.

DUCHESS Why droops my lord, like over-ripened corn
Hanging the head at Ceres' plenteous load?
Why doth the great Duke Humphrey knit his
    brows,
As frowning at the favors of the world?
5   Why are thine eyes fixed to the sullen earth,
Gazing on that which seems to dim thy sight?
What seest thou there? King Henry's diadem,
Enchased with all the honors of the world?
If so, gaze on, and grovel on thy face,
10   Until thy head be circled with the same.
Put forth thy hand, reach at the glorious gold.
What, is't too short? I'll lengthen it with mine;
And, having both together heaved it up,
We'll both together lift our heads to heaven,
15   And never more abase our sight so low
As to vouchsafe one glance unto the ground.

253 **at jars** to quarreling   258 **force perforce** willy-nilly   259 **bookish** scho-
larly, i.e., inactive   I.11.2 **Ceres** the goddess of the harvest   5 **sullen** dull
8 **Enchased** adorned

GLOUCESTER O Nell, sweet Nell, if thou dost love thy
    lord,
    Banish the canker of ambitious thoughts:
    And may that thought, when I imagine ill
    Against my King and nephew, virtuous Henry,   20
    Be my last breathing in this mortal world!
    My troublous dreams this night doth make me
    sad.

DUCHESS What dreamed my lord? Tell me, and I'll
    requite it
    With sweet rehearsal of my morning's dream.

GLOUCESTER Methought this staff, mine office-badge in
    court,   25
    Was broke in twain: by whom, I have forgot,
    But as I think, it was by th' Cardinal;
    And on the pieces of the broken wand
    Were placed the heads of Edmund Duke of Somerset,
    And William de la Pole, first Duke of Suffolk.   30
    This was my dream: what it doth bode, God
    knows.

DUCHESS Tut, this was nothing but an argument
    That he that breaks a stick of Gloucester's grove
    Shall lose his head for his presumption.
    But list to me, my Humphrey, my sweet Duke: 35
    Methought I sat in seat of majesty
    In the cathedral church of Westminster,
    And in that chair where kings and queens were
    crowned;
    Where Henry and Dame Margaret kneeled to me,
    And on my head did set the diadem.   40

GLOUCESTER Nay, Eleanor, then must I chide outright:
    Presumptuous dame, ill-nurtured Eleanor,
    Art thou not second woman in the realm,
    And the Protector's wife, beloved of him?
    Hast thou not worldly pleasure at command   45

22 **this night** last night   24 **morning's dream** morning dreams were reputed
true

Above the reach or compass of thy thought?
And wilt thou still be hammering treachery,
To tumble down thy husband and thyself
From top of honor to disgrace's feet?
50   Away from me, and let me hear no more!

DUCHESS What, what, my lord! Are you so choleric
With Eleanor, for telling but her dream?
Next time I'll keep my dreams unto myself,
And not be checked.

55   GLOUCESTER Nay, be not angry; I am pleased again.

Enter Messenger.

MESSENGER My Lord Protector, 'tis his Highness'
    pleasure
You do prepare to ride unto Saint Albans,
Where as the King and Queen do mean to hawk.

GLOUCESTER I go. Come, Nell, thou wilt ride with us?

60   DUCHESS Yes, my good lord, I'll follow presently.
                          Exit Gloucester [and Messenger].
Follow I must; I cannot go before,
While Gloucester bears this base and humble mind.
Were I a man, a duke, and next of blood,
I would remove these tedious stumbling-blocks
65   And smooth my way upon their headless necks;
And, being a woman, I will not be slack
To play my part in Fortune's pageant.
Where are you there, Sir John? Nay, fear not, man,
We are alone; here's none but thee and I.

Enter Hum.

70   HUM Jesus preserve your royal Majesty!

DUCHESS What say'st thou, "majesty"? I am but Grace.

47 **hammering** devising   51 **choleric** angry   58 **Where as** where   58 **hawk**
hunt with hawks   60 **presently** immediately   63 **next of blood** i.e., the successor to the crown, if Henry VI dies without issue

HUM But, by the grace of God, and Hum's advice,
   Your Grace's title shall be multiplied.

DUCHESS What say'st thou, man? Hast thou as yet
      conferred
   With Margery Jourdain, the cunning witch,   75
   With Roger Bolingbroke, the conjuror?
   And will they undertake to do me good?

HUM This they have promisèd, to show your Highness
   A spirit raised from depth of underground,
   That shall make answer to such questions   80
   As by your Grace shall be propounded him.

DUCHESS It is enough: I'll think upon the questions.
   When from Saint Albans we do make return,
   We'll see these things effected to the full.
   Here, Hum, take this reward; make merry, man,   85
   With thy confederates in this weighty cause.

                                   Exit Eleanor.

HUM Hum must make merry with the Duchess' gold;
   Marry, and shall. But, how now, Sir John Hum!
   Seal up your lips, and give no words but mum:
   The business asketh silent secrecy.   90
   Dame Eleanor gives gold to bring the witch:
   Gold cannot come amiss, were she a devil.
   Yet have I gold flies from another coast—
   I dare not say, from the rich Cardinal
   And from the great and new-made Duke of Suffolk.   95
   Yet I do find it so—for, to be plain,
   They, knowing Dame Eleanor's aspiring humor,
   Have hirèd me to undermine the Duchess
   And buzz these conjurations in her brain.
   They say "A crafty knave does need no broker";   100
   Yet am I Suffolk and the Cardinal's broker.
   Hum, if you take not heed, you shall go near

73 **Your ... multiplied** a play on I Peter, i.2: "Grace and peace be multiplied unto you" 88 **Marry** a mild oath, from "By the Virgin Mary" 90 **asketh** requires 93 **coast** quarter 97 **humor** temperament 99 **conjurations** incantations 101 **broker** agent, go-between

To call them both a pair of crafty knaves.
Well, so it stands; and thus, I fear, at last
105 Hum's knavery will be the Duchess' wrack,
And her attainture will be Humphrey's fall.
Sort how it will, I shall have gold for all.   *Exit.*

Scene III. [*The palace.*]

*Enter three or four Petitioners; [Peter Thump],
the Armorer's man, being one.*

FIRST PETITIONER My masters, let's stand close: my
Lord Protector will come this way by and by, and
then we may deliver our supplications in the quill.

SECOND PETITIONER Marry, the Lord protect him, for
5   he's a good man, Jesu bless him!

Enter Suffolk and Queen.

PETER Here 'a comes, methinks, and the Queen with
him. I'll be the first, sure.

SECOND PETITIONER Come back, fool! this is the Duke
of Suffolk, and not my Lord Protector.

10 SUFFOLK How now, fellow! wouldst anything with me?

FIRST PETITIONER I pray, my lord, pardon me: I took
ye for my Lord Protector.

QUEEN For my Lord Protector! Are your supplications to his lordship? Let me see them: what is
15   thine?

FIRST PETITIONER Mine is, and't please your Grace,
against John Goodman, my Lord Cardinal's man,
for keeping my house, and lands, and wife and all,
from me.

105 **wrack** ruin 106 **attainture** incrimination I.iii.3 **in the quill** in
succession (?) 6 **'a** he 17 **man** agent, protégé

SUFFOLK Thy wife too! that's some wrong, indeed.   20
What's yours? What's here? [*Reads*] "Against the
Duke of Suffolk, for enclosing the commons of
Melford." How now, sir knave!

SECOND PETITIONER Alas, sir, I am but a poor petitioner of our whole township.   25

PETER [*Giving his petition*] Against my master,
Thomas Horner, for saying that the Duke of York
was rightful heir to the crown.

QUEEN What say'st thou? did the Duke of York say
he was rightful heir to the crown?   30

PETER That my master was? No, forsooth: my master
said that he was, and that the King was an usurer.

QUEEN An usurper, thou wouldst say.

PETER Ay, forsooth, an usurper.

SUFFOLK Who is there? (*Enter Servant.*) Take this fel-   35
low in, and send for his master with a pursuivant
presently. We'll hear more of your matter before
the King.   *Exit* [*Servant with Peter*].

QUEEN And as for you, that love to be protected
Under the wings of our Protector's grace,   40
Begin your suits anew, and sue to him.
                          Tear[*s*] *the supplication.*
Away, base cullions! Suffolk, let them go.

ALL Come, let's be gone.   *Exit.*

QUEEN My Lord of Suffolk, say, is this the guise,
Is this the fashions in the court of England?   45
Is this the government of Britain's isle,
And this the royalty of Albion's King?
What! Shall King Henry be a pupil still
Under the surly Gloucester's governance?
Am I a queen in title and in style,   50

22 **enclosing the commons** fencing off the public pasture   36 **pursuivant**
warrant officer   42 **cullions** rascals   44 **guise** custom   47 **Albion's**
England's   50 **style** name

And must be made a subject to a duke?
I tell thee, Pole, when in the city Tours
Thou ran'st a tilt in honor of my love
And stol'st away the ladies' hearts of France,
55   I thought King Henry had resembled thee
In courage, courtship, and proportion:
But all his mind is bent to holiness,
To number Ave-Maries on his beads;
His champions are the prophets and apostles,
60   His weapons holy saws of sacred writ,
His study is his tilt-yard, and his loves
Are brazen images of canonized saints.
I would the College of the Cardinals
Would choose him Pope and carry him to Rome,
65   And set the triple crown upon his head:
That were a state fit for his Holiness.

SUFFOLK Madam, be patient: as I was cause
Your Highness came to England, so will I
In England work your Grace's full content.

QUEEN Beside the haughty Protector, have we
70   Beaufort
The imperious churchman, Somerset, Buckingham,
And grumbling York; and not the least of these
But can do more in England than the King.

SUFFOLK And he of these that can do most of all
75   Cannot do more in England than the Nevils:
Salisbury and Warwick are no simple peers.

QUEEN Not all these lords do vex me half so much
As that proud dame, the Lord Protector's wife:
She sweeps it through the court with troops of
        ladies,
80   More like an empress than Duke Humphrey's wife.
Strangers in court do take her for the Queen:

53 ran'st a tilt competed in a tourney 56 proportion shape 58 number ...
beads say Rosaries 59 champions warriors chosen to represent him (chivalric
term) 60 saws maxims, platitudes 65 triple crown the papal tiara 81
Strangers foreigners

She bears a duke's revenues on her back,
And in her heart she scorns our poverty.
Shall I not live to be avenged on her?
Contemptuous base-born callet as she is,   85
She vaunted 'mongst her minions t'other day,
The very train of her worst wearing gown
Was better worth than all my father's lands,
Till Suffolk gave two dukedoms for his daughter.

SUFFOLK Madam, myself have limed a bush for her,   90
And placed a quire of such enticing birds
That she will light to listen to the lays,
And never mount to trouble you again.
So let her rest: and, madam, list to me,
For I am bold to counsel you in this: 95
Although we fancy not the Cardinal,
Yet must we join with him and with the lords,
Till we have brought Duke Humphrey in disgrace.
As for the Duke of York, this late complaint
Will make but little for his benefit.   100
So, one by one, we'll weed them all at last,
And you yourself shall steer the happy helm.

*Sound a sennet. Enter King Henry, and the Duke of
York and the Duke of Somerset on both sides of the
King, whispering with him; and enter Gloucester, Dame
Eleanor, the Duke of Buckingham, Salisbury, the Earl of
Warwick, and the Cardinal of Winchester.*

KING For my part, noble lords, I care not which:
Or Somerset or York, all's one to me.

YORK If York have ill demeaned himself in France,   105
Then let him be denayed the regentship.

---

85 **Contemptuous** contemptible   85 **callet** trull   86 **minions** effeminate or
female retainers (contemptuous)   90 **limed a bush** small birds were trapped by
smearing bird-lime (a sticky preparation of holly-bark) over the twigs of
bushes   91 **quire** (1) group (2) choir   92 **lays** songs   99 **this late complaint**
i.e., Peter's   102 **happy** fortunate   102 s.d. **sennet** phrase on the trumpet
106 **denayed** old form of "denied"

SOMERSET If Somerset be unworthy of the place,
    Let York be regent; I will yield to him.

WARWICK Whether your Grace be worthy, yea or no,
110   Dispute not that: York is the worthier.

CARDINAL Ambitious Warwick, let thy betters speak.

WARWICK The Cardinal's not my better in the field.

BUCKINGHAM All in this presence are thy betters,
    Warwick.

WARWICK Warwick may live to be the best of all.

SALISBURY Peace, son; and show some reason, Buck-
115   ingham,
    Why Somerset should be preferred in this.

QUEEN Because the King, forsooth, will have it so.

GLOUCESTER Madam, the King is old enough himself
    To give his censure. These are no women's
    matters.

120 QUEEN If he be old enough, what needs your Grace
    To be Protector of his Excellence?

GLOUCESTER Madam, I am Protector of the realm,
    And at his pleasure will resign my place.

SUFFOLK Resign it then and leave thine insolence.
125   Since thou wert King—as who is King but thou?—
    The commonwealth hath daily run to wrack,
    The Dolphin hath prevailed beyond the seas,
    And all the peers and nobles of the realm
    Have been as bondmen to thy sovereignty.

CARDINAL The commons hast thou racked; the clergy's
130   bags
    Are lank and lean with thy extortions.

---

113 **betters** superiors in rank 116 **preferred in this** promoted to this
position 119 **censure** opinion, judgment 127 **Dolphin** Dauphin, eldest son of
the King of France 129 **bondmen** slaves, serfs

SOMERSET Thy sumptuous buildings and thy wife's
    attire
Have cost a mass of public treasury.

BUCKINGHAM Thy cruelty in execution
Upon offenders hath exceeded law,   135
And left thee to the mercy of the law.

QUEEN Thy sale of offices and towns in France,
If they were known, as the suspect is great,
Would make thee quickly hop without thy head.
        Exit Gloucester. [The Queen drops her fan.]
Give me my fan! What, minion, can ye not?   140
        She gives the Duchess a box on the ear.
I cry you mercy, madam; was it you?

DUCHESS Was't I! Yea, I it was, proud Frenchwoman:
Could I come near your beauty with my nails,
I'd set my ten commandments in your face.

KING Sweet aunt, be quiet; 'twas against her will.   145

DUCHESS Against her will, good King? Look to't, in
    time
She'll hamper thee, and dandle thee like a baby.
Though in this place most master wear no breeches,
She shall not strike Dame Eleanor unrevenged.
        Exit Eleanor.

BUCKINGHAM Lord Cardinal, I will follow Eleanor,   150
And listen after Humphrey, how he proceeds.
She's tickled now; her fury needs no spurs,
She'll gallop far enough to her destruction.
        Exit Buckingham.

        Enter Gloucester

GLOUCESTER Now, lords, my choler being over-blown
With walking once about the quadrangle,   155

138 **suspect** suspicion   141 **cry you mercy** beg your pardon   144 **set ... face**
mark with fingernails   145 **quiet** calm   145 **against her will** unwittingly
148 **most master** the greatest master; i.e., here the wife rules the house
152 **tickled** provoked, touched

I come to talk of commonwealth affairs.
As for your spiteful false objections,
Prove them, and I lie open to the law:
But God in mercy so deal with my soul,
160   As I in duty love my king and country!
But to the matter that we have in hand:
I say, my Sovereign, York is meetest man
To be your regent in the realm of France.

SUFFOLK Before we make election, give me leave
165   To show some reason, of no little force,
That York is most unmeet of any man.

YORK I'll tell thee, Suffolk, why I am unmeet:
First, for I cannot flatter thee in pride;
Next, if I be appointed for the place,
170   My Lord of Somerset will keep me here,
Without discharge, money, or furniture,
Till France be won into the Dolphin's hands.
Last time, I danced attendance on his will
Till Paris was besieged, famished, and lost.

175 WARWICK That can I witness; and a fouler fact
Did never traitor in the land commit.

SUFFOLK Peace, headstrong Warwick!

WARWICK Image of pride, why should I hold my
      peace?
            Enter [Horner, the] Armorer, and [Peter], his
                  man, [both guarded].

SUFFOLK Because here is a man accused of treason.
180   Pray God the Duke of York excuse himself!

YORK Doth anyone accuse York for a traitor?

KING What mean'st thou, Suffolk? Tell me, what are
      these?

157 **objections** accusations   162 **meetest** most suitable   168 **for ... pride**
because I cannot entertain you sumptuously   171 **discharge** payment of what he
owes   171 **furniture** equipment (for war)   175 **fact** evil deed   178 **Image**
embodiment, epitome   181 **for** as

SUFFOLK Please it your Majesty, this is the man
     That doth accuse his master of high treason.
     His words were these: that Richard Duke of York   185
     Was rightful heir unto the English crown,
     And that your Majesty was an usurper.

KING Say, man, were these thy words?

HORNER And't shall please your Majesty, I never said
     nor thought any such matter! God is my witness,   190
     I am falsely accused by the villain.

PETER By these ten bones, my lords, he did speak
     them to me in the garret one night, as we were
     scouring my Lord of York's armor.

YORK Base dunghill villain and mechanical,   195
     I'll have thy head for this thy traitor's speech!
     I do beseech your royal Majesty,
     Let him have all the rigor of the law.

HORNER Alas, my lord, hang me if ever I spake the
     words! My accuser is my prentice; and when I did   200
     correct him for his fault the other day, he did vow
     upon his knees he would be even with me: I have
     good witness of this; therefore I beseech your
     Majesty, do not cast away an honest man for a
     villain's accusation.   205

KING Uncle, what shall we say to this in law?

GLOUCESTER This doom, my lord, if I may judge:
     Let Somerset be regent o'er the French,
     Because in York this breeds suspicion.
     And let these have a day appointed them   210
     For single combat, in convenient place,
     For he hath witness of his servant's malice.
     This is the law, and this Duke Humphrey's doom.

SOMERSET I humbly thank your royal Majesty.

192 **ten bones** i.e., fingers 195 **mechanical** manual laborer, i.e., drudge
200 **prentice** apprentice 201 **fault** mistake 207 **doom** sentence 209 **breeds
suspicion** suggests doubt (of his loyalty) 211 **single combat** a duel
211 **convenient** appropriate

215 HORNER And I accept the combat willingly.

PETER Alas, my lord, I cannot fight; for God's sake,
pity my case! The spite of man prevaileth against
me. O Lord, have mercy upon me! I shall never be
able to fight a blow. O Lord, my heart!

GLOUCESTER Sirrah, or you must fight, or else be
220   hanged.

KING Away with them to prison; and the day of combat shall be the last of the next month. Come,
Somerset, we'll see thee sent away.

Flourish; exeunt.

Scene IV. [*A garden outside Gloucester's house,*
before a tower.]

Enter the witch [Margaret Jourdain], the two priests
[Hum and Southwell,] and Bolingbroke [the conjuror].

HUM Come, my masters; the Duchess, I tell you, ex-
pects performance of your promises.

BOLINGBROKE Master Hum, we are therefore provided: will her ladyship behold and hear our
5   exorcisms?

HUM Ay, what else? Fear you not her courage.

BOLINGBROKE I have heard her reported to be a
woman of an invincible spirit: but it shall be convenient, Master Hum, that you be by her aloft,
10   while we be busy below; and so, I pray you, go,
in God's name, and leave us. (*Exit Hum.*) Mother
Jourdain, be you prostrate and grovel on the earth;
John Southwell, read you; and let us to our work.

---

220 **Sirrah** contemptuous term of address   I.iv.3-4 **therefore provided**
equipped for that   5 **exorcisms** ceremonies for expelling the Devil (but here a
malapropism for *raising* the Devil)   6 **Fear** doubt

Enter Duchess aloft, [Hum following].

DUCHESS Well said, my masters; and welcome all. To
   this gear, the sooner the better.   15

BOLINGBROKE Patience, good lady; wizards know their
      times.
   Deep night, dark night, the silent of the night,
   The time of night when Troy was set on fire,
   The time when screech-owls cry, and ban-dogs
      howl
   And spirits walk, and ghosts break up their graves—   20
   That time best fits the work we have in hand.
   Madam, sit you, and fear not: whom we raise
   We will make fast within a hallowed verge.
   *Here [they] do the ceremonies belonging, and make the
   circle; Bolingbroke or Southwell reads, "Conjuro te, etc."
   It thunders and lightens terribly; then the Spirit riseth.*

SPIRIT *Adsum.*

MARGERY JOURDAIN Asnath,   25
   By the eternal God, whose name and power
   Thou tremblest at, answer that I shall ask:
   For till thou speak, thou shalt not pass from hence.

SPIRIT Ask what thou wilt. That I had said and done!

BOLINGBROKE [*Consulting a paper*] First of the King:
   what shall of him become?   30

SPIRIT The Duke yet lives that Henry shall depose,
   But him outlive, and die a violent death.
                         [*Southwell writes out the questions
                                        and answers.*]

BOLINGBROKE What fates await the Duke of Suffolk?

---

15 **gear** business 17 **silent** silent time 19 **ban-dogs** fierce dogs chained
up 23 **hallowed verge** charmed circle 23 s.d. **Conjuro te, etc.** beginning of
the incantation: "I conjure you … " 23 s.d. **lightens** makes lightning
24 **Adsum** here I am 25 **Asnath** obscure; possibly an anagram for
"Sathan" 31-32 **The Duke … death** a typically cryptic and ambiguous
prophecy: either "The duke who will depose Henry is now living," or "the duke
Henry will depose is now living." See lines 62-63

SPIRIT By water shall he die, and take his end.

35 BOLINGBROKE What shall befall the Duke of Somerset?

SPIRIT Let him shun castles:
    Safer shall he be upon sandy plains
    Than where castles mounted stand.
    Have done, for more I hardly can endure.

BOLINGBROKE Descend to darkness and the burning
40   lake!
    False fiend, avoid!
               Thunder and lightning; he sinks down again.

       Enter the Duke of York and the Duke of Buck-
         ingham with their guard and break in.

YORK Lay hands upon these traitors and their trash.
    Beldam, I think we watched you at an inch.
    What, madam, are you there? The King and
      commonweal
45 Are deeply indebted for this piece of pains.
    My Lord Protector will, I doubt it not,
    See you well guerdoned for these good deserts.

DUCHESS Not half so bad as thine to England's King,
    Injurious Duke, that threatest where's no cause.

BUCKINGHAM True, madam, none at all: what call you
50   this?
    Away with them! Let them be clapped up close,
    And kept asunder. You, madam, shall with us.
    Stafford, take her to thee.
               Exit Duchess above [*and Hum, guarded*].
    We'll see your trinkets here all forthcoming.
55 All, away!
            Exit [*Margery Jourdain, Southwell, and*
            Bolingbroke, with the rest of the guard].

---

41 **avoid** go hence 43 **at an inch** closely (enough) 45 **piece of pains**
masterpiece of service (ironic) 47 **guerdoned** rewarded 49 **Injurious** abusive
54 **trinkets** i.e., the conjuring apparatus, including Southwell's written record

YORK Lord Buckingham, methinks you watched her
    well:
  A pretty plot, well chosen to build upon!
  Now, pray, my lord, let's see the devil's writ.
  What have we here?   *Reads.*
  "The Duke yet lives that Henry shall depose;   60
  But him outlive, and die a violent death."
  Why, this is just *"Aio te, Acacida,*
  Romanos vincere posse." Well, to the rest:
  "Tell me what fate awaits the Duke of Suffolk?
  By water shall he die, and take his end.   65
  What shall betide the Duke of Somerset?
  Let him shun castles;
  Safer shall he be upon the sandy plains
  Than where castles mounted stand."
  Come, come, my lords, these oracles are hard,   70
  Hardly attained, and hardly understood.
  The King is now in progress towards Saint Albans;
  With him, the husband of this lovely lady.
  Thither goes these news, as fast as horse can carry
    them—
  A sorry breakfast for my Lord Protector.   75

BUCKINGHAM Your Grace shall give me leave, my lord
  of York,
  To be the post, in hope of his reward.

YORK At your pleasure, my good lord. Who's within
  there, ho!

Enter a Servingman.

Invite my Lords of Salisbury and Warwick
To sup with me tomorrow night. Away!   *Exeunt.*   80

62-63 **Aio ... posse** from Ennius, the ambiguous response of the Pythian oracle
Apollo to King Pyrrhus, when Pyrrhus asked if he would conquer Rome: either "I
affirm that you, descendant of Aeacus, can conquer the Romans," or "I affirm that
the Romans can conquer you, etc." 70-71 **hard ... Hardly ... hardly** obscure ...
with difficulty ... scarcely to be 73 **lovely** lovable 77 **post** messenger

ACT II

Scene I. [*Saint Albans.*]

*Enter the King, Queen, with a hawk on her fist, Gloucester,
Cardinal, and Suffolk, with falconers hallooing.*

QUEEN Believe me, lords, for flying at the brook,
  I saw not better sport these seven years' day:
  Yet, by your leave, the wind was very high;
  And, ten to one, old Joan had not gone out.

5 KING But what a point, my lord, your falcon made,
  And what a pitch she flew above the rest!
  To see how God in all his creatures works!
  Yea, man and birds are fain of climbing high.

SUFFOLK No marvel, and it like your Majesty,
10 My Lord Protector's hawks do tow'r so well:
  They know their master loves to be aloft,
  And bears his thoughts above his falcon's pitch.

GLOUCESTER My lord, 'tis but a base ignoble mind
  That mounts no higher than a bird can soar.

CARDINAL I thought as much: he would be above the
15 clouds.

II.i.1 **at the brook** i.e., at waterfowl **4 ten ... out** the odds were against this
hawk (the Queen's?) flying **5 point** position from which to swoop **6 pitch**
altitude

GLOUCESTER Ay, my lord Cardinal, how think you by
    that?
  Were it not good your Grace could fly to heaven?

KING The treasury of everlasting joy.

CARDINAL Thy heaven is on earth; thine eyes and
    thoughts
  Beat on a crown, the treasure of thy heart.   20
  Pernicious Protector, dangerous peer,
  That smooth'st it so with King and commonweal!

GLOUCESTER What, Cardinal, is your priesthood grown
    peremptory?
  Tantaene animis coelestibus irae?
  Churchmen so hot? Good uncle, can you dote,   25
  To hide such malice with such holiness?

SUFFOLK No malice, sir; no more than well becomes
  So good a quarrel and so bad a peer.

GLOUCESTER As who, my lord?

SUFFOLK   Why, as you, my lord,
  An't like your lordly Lord-Protectorship.   30

GLOUCESTER Why, Suffolk, England knows thine
    insolence.

QUEEN And thy ambition, Gloucester.

KING I prithee peace,
  Good Queen, and whet not on these furious peers,
  For blessèd are the peacemakers on earth.   35

CARDINAL Let me be blessèd for the peace I make,
  Against this proud Protector, with my sword!

GLOUCESTER [*Aside*] Faith, holy uncle, would 'twere
    come to that!

CARDINAL [*Aside*] Marry, when thou dar'st.

---

20 **Beat on** harp on 22 **smooth'st it** flatters 23 **peremptory** overbearing
24 **Tantaene ... irae** *Aeneid*, I,11: "So much anger in heavenly souls?" 25 **can
you dote?** are you so much a fool (as to attempt)

GLOUCESTER [*Aside*] Make up no factious numbers for
   the matter;
   In thine own person answer thy abuse.

CARDINAL [*Aside*] Ay, where thou dar'st not peep:
   and if thou dar'st,
   This evening, on the east side of the grove.

KING How now, my lords!

CARDINAL   Believe me, cousin Gloucester,
   Had not your man put up the fowl so suddenly,
   We had had more sport. [*Aside*] Come with thy
   two-hand sword.

GLOUCESTER True, uncle.

CARDINAL [*Aside*] Are ye advised? The east side of
   the grove?

GLOUCESTER [*Aside*] Cardinal, I am with you.

KING   Why, how now, uncle Gloucester!

GLOUCESTER Talking of hawking; nothing else, my
   lord.
   [*Aside*] Now, by God's mother, priest, I'll shave
   your crown for this.
   Or all my fence shall fail.

CARDINAL [*Aside*] *Medice, teipsum*—
   Protector, see to't well, protect yourself.

KING The winds grow high, so do your stomachs,
   lords.
   How irksome is this music to my heart!
   When such strings jar, what hope of harmony?
   I pray, my lords, let me compound this strife.

40 **Make … matter** bring none of your own faction into the quarrel   **42 and if**
if   **45 put up the fowl** flushed the game ("your man" disrespectfully suggests
King Henry)   **48 advised** agreed   **52 fence** skill at swordplay   **53 Medice,
teipsum** "physician, [cure] thyself"   **55 stomachs** tempers   **58 compound**
compose

Enter one, crying "A miracle!"

GLOUCESTER What means this noise?
  Fellow, what miracle dost thou proclaim?   60

ONE A miracle! a miracle!

SUFFOLK Come to the King and tell him what miracle.

ONE Forsooth, a blind man at Saint Alban's shrine,
  Within this half hour hath received his sight—
  A man that ne'er saw in his life before.   65

KING Now, God be praised, that to believing souls
  Gives light in darkness, comfort in despair!

*Enter the Mayor of Saint Albans and his brethren,
bearing the man [Saunder Simpcox] between two in a
chair, [Simpcox's Wife following].*

CARDINAL Here comes the townsmen, on procession,
  To present your Highness with the man.

KING Great is his comfort in this earthly vale,   70
  Although by sight his sin be multiplied.

GLOUCESTER Stand by, my masters: bring him near the
    King:
  His Highness' pleasure is to talk with him.

KING Good fellow, tell us here the circumstance,
  That we for thee may glorify the Lord.   75
  What, hast thou been long blind, and now restored?

SIMPCOX Born blind, and't please your Grace.

WIFE Ay, indeed, was he.

SUFFOLK What woman is this?

WIFE His wife, and't like your Worship.   80

GLOUCESTER Hadst thou been his mother, thou couldst
  have better told.

---

68 on in 71 **Although … multiplied** c.f. John, ix.41: "If ye were blind, ye
would have no sin, but now ye say, We see: therefore your sin remaineth"

KING Where wert thou born?

SIMPCOX At Berwick in the north, and't like your
  Grace.

KING Poor soul, God's goodness hath been great to
  thee:
85 Let never day nor night unhallowed pass,
  But still remember what the Lord hath done.

QUEEN Tell me, good fellow, cam'st thou here by
  chance,
  Or of devotion, to this holy shrine?

SIMPCOX God knows, of pure devotion, being called
90 A hundred times and oftener, in my sleep,
  By good Saint Alban; who said, "Simpcox, come,
  Come, offer at my shrine, and I will help thee."

WIFE Most true, forsooth; and many time and oft
  Myself have heard a voice to call him so.

CARDINAL What, art thou lame?

95 SIMPCOX   Ay, God Almighty help me.

SUFFOLK How cam'st thou so?

SIMPCOX   A fall off of a tree.

WIFE A plum tree, master.

GLOUCESTER   How long hast thou been blind?

SIMPCOX O, born so, master.

GLOUCESTER   What, and wouldst climb a tree?

SIMPCOX But that in all my life, when I was a youth.

100 WIFE Too true, and bought his climbing very dear.

GLOUCESTER 'Mass, thou lov'dst plums well, that
  wouldst venture so.

86 still always   99 But that only once   101 'Mass by the mass

152

SIMPCOX Alas, good master, my wife desired some
    damsons,
And made me climb, with danger of my life.

GLOUCESTER [*Aside*] A subtle knave! But yet it shall
    not serve.
Let me see thine eyes: wink now: now open them.   105
In my opinion yet thou see'st not well.

SIMPCOX Yes, master, clear as day, I thank God and
    Saint Alban.

GLOUCESTER Say'st thou me so? What color is this
    cloak of?

SIMPCOX Red, master; red as blood.

GLOUCESTER Why, that's well said. What color is my
    gown off?   110

SIMPCOX Black, forsooth, coal-black, as jet.

KING Why, then, thou know'st what color jet is of?

SUFFOLK And yet, I think, jet did he never see.

GLOUCESTER But cloaks and gowns, before this day, a
    many.

WIFE Never, before this day, in all his life!   115

GLOUCESTER Tell me, sirrah, what's my name?

SIMPCOX Alas, master, I know not.

GLOUCESTER What's his name?

SIMPCOX I know not.

GLOUCESTER Nor his?   120

SIMPCOX No, indeed, master.

GLOUCESTER What's thine own name?

SIMPCOX Saunder Simpcox, and if it please you,
    master.

105 wink close them

153

125 GLOUCESTER Then, Saunder, sit there, the lying'st knave
       in Christendom. If thou hadst been born blind, thou
       might'st as well have known all our names as thus
       to name the several colors we do wear. Sight may
       distinguish of colors, but suddenly to nominate
130   them all, it is impossible. My lords, Saint Alban
       here hath done a miracle—and would ye not think
       his cunning to be great that could restore this
       cripple to his legs again?

SIMPCOX O master, that you could!

135 GLOUCESTER My masters of Saint Albans,
       Have you not beadles in your town,
       And things called whips?

MAYOR Yes, my lord, if it please your Grace.

GLOUCESTER Then send for one presently.

140 MAYOR Sirrah, go fetch the beadle hither straight.
                                    Exit [an Attendant].

GLOUCESTER Now fetch me a stool hither by and by.
       [*They bring one.*] Now, sirrah, if you mean to save
       yourself from whipping, leap me over this stool
       and run away.

145 SIMPCOX Alas, master, I am not able to stand alone:
       You go about to torture me in vain.

                    Enter a Beadle with whips.

GLOUCESTER Well, sir, we must have you find your legs.
       Sirrah beadle, whip him till he leap over that same
       stool.

150 BEADLE I will, my lord. Come on, sirrah: off with your
       doublet quickly.

---

129 **nominate** give them names   136 **beadles** minor parish officials, entrusted
with keeping order in church, and punishing petty offenders   143 **leap me** leap
for me

SIMPCOX Alas, master, what shall I do? I am not able
to stand.

> *After the Beadle hath hit him once, he*
> *leaps over the stool and runs away; and*
> *they follow and cry, "A miracle!"*

KING O God, seest Thou this, and bearest so long?

QUEEN It made me laugh to see the villain run.   155

GLOUCESTER Follow the knave, and take this drab
away.

WIFE Alas, sir, we did it for pure need.

GLOUCESTER Let them be whipped through every
market-town
Till they come to Berwick, from whence they came.
> *Exit [Mayor, Beadle, Wife, etc.].*

CARDINAL Duke Humphrey has done a miracle today.   160

SUFFOLK True—made the lame to leap and fly away.

GLOUCESTER But you have done more miracles than I:
You made in a day, my lord, whole towns to fly.

> *Enter Buckingham.*

KING What tidings with our cousin Buckingham?

BUCKINGHAM Such as my heart doth tremble to un-
fold: 165
A sort of naughty persons, lewdly bent,
Under the countenance and confederacy
Of Lady Eleanor, the Protector's wife,
The ringleader and head of all this rout,
Have practiced dangerously against your state,   170
Dealing with witches and with conjurors,
Whom we have apprehended in the fact,
Raising up wicked spirits from under ground,

156 drab whore   163 You ... fly i.e., by presenting them to the King of
France 166 sort ... bent group of worthless persons, wickedly inclined
167 countenance and confederacy patronage and participation 172 in the
fact in the act

Demanding of King Henry's life and death,
175   And other of your Highness' Privy Council,
As more at large your Grace shall understand.

CARDINAL [*Aside*] And so, my Lord Protector, by this
    means
Your lady is forthcoming yet at London.
This news, I think, hath turned your weapon's edge;
180   'Tis like, my lord, you will not keep your hour.

GLOUCESTER [*Aside*] Ambitious churchman, leave to
    afflict my heart:
Sorrow and grief have vanquished all my powers;
And, vanquished as I am, I yield to thee,
Or to the meanest groom.

185   KING O God, what mischiefs work the wicked ones,
Heaping confusion on their own heads thereby!

QUEEN Gloucester, see here the tainture of thy nest.
And look thyself be faultless, thou wert best.

GLOUCESTER Madam, for myself, to heaven I do appeal,
190   How I have loved my King and commonweal!
And for my wife, I know not how it stands.
Sorry I am to hear what I have heard;
Noble she is; but if she have forgot
Honor and virtue and conversed with such
195   As, like to pitch, defile nobility,
I banish her my bed and company,
And give her as a prey to law and shame,
That hath dishonored Gloucester's honest name.

KING Well, for this night we will repose us here:
200   Tomorrow toward London back again,
To look into this business thoroughly,
And call these foul offenders to their answers;
And poise the cause in Justice' equal scales,
Whose beam stands sure, whose rightful
    cause prevails.   *Flourish. Exeunt.*

174 **Demanding** of inquiring about   178 **forthcoming** due for trial   180 **hour**
appointment   187 **tainture** defilement   203-4 **poise ... prevails** balance the
testimony in the scales of justice to see which weighs more

Scene II. [*London. The Duke of York's garden.*]

Enter York, Salisbury, and Warwick.

YORK Now, my good Lords of Salisbury and Warwick,
Our simple supper ended, give me leave,
In this close walk, to satisfy myself
In craving your opinion of my title,
Which is infallible, to England's crown.   5

SALISBURY My lord, I long to hear it at full.

WARWICK Sweet York, begin: and if thy claim be good,
The Nevils are thy subjects to command.

YORK Then thus:
Edward the Third, my lords, had seven sons: 10
The first, Edward the Black Prince, Prince of Wales;
The second, William of Hatfield; and the third,
Lionel Duke of Clarence; next to whom
Was John of Gaunt, the Duke of Lancaster;
The fifth was Edmund Langley, Duke of York;   15
The sixth was Thomas of Woodstock, Duke of
     Gloucester;
William of Windsor was the seventh and last.
Edward the Black Prince died before his father,
And left behind him Richard, his only son,
Who after Edward the Third's death reigned as King; 20
Till Henry Bolingbroke, Duke of Lancaster,
The eldest son and heir of John of Gaunt,
Crowned by the name of Henry the Fourth,
Seized on the realm, deposed the rightful king,
Sent his poor queen to France, from whence she
     came,   25
And him to Pomfret; where, as all you know,
Harmless Richard was murdered traitorously.

II.ii.3 **close walk** private or concealed pathway

WARWICK Father, the Duke hath told the truth;
　　Thus got the house of Lancaster the crown.

30 YORK Which now they hold by force and not by right:
　　For Richard, the first son's heir, being dead,
　　The issue of the next son should have reigned.

SALISBURY But William of Hatfield died without an
　　　　heir.

YORK The third son, Duke of Clarence, from whose
　　　　line
35 　　I claim the crown, had issue, Philippa, a daughter,
　　Who married Edmund Mortimer, Earl of March;
　　Edmund had issue, Roger Earl of March;
　　Roger had issue, Edmund, Anne and Eleanor.

SALISBURY This Edmund, in the reign of Bolingbroke,
40 　　As I have read, laid claim unto the crown;
　　And, but for Owen Glendower, had been King,
　　Who kept him in captivity till he died.
　　But to the rest.

YORK　　　　　　　His eldest sister, Anne,
　　My mother, being heir unto the crown,
45 　　Married Richard, Earl of Cambridge,
　　Who was to Edmund Langley,
　　Edward the Third's fifth son, the son.
　　By her I claim the kingdom: she was heir
　　To Roger Earl of March, who was the son
50 　　Of Edmund Mortimer, who married Philippa,
　　Sole daughter unto Lionel, Duke of Clarence:
　　So, if the issue of the elder son
　　Succeed before the younger, I am King.

WARWICK What plain proceedings is more plain than
　　　　this?
55 　　Henry doth claim the crown from John of Gaunt,
　　The fourth son; York claims it from the third.
　　Till Lionel's issue fails, his should not reign:
　　It fails not yet, but flourishes in thee,

54 **proceedings** order of events (in the pedigree)

And in thy sons, fair slips of such a stock.
Then, father Salisbury, kneel we together,   60
And in this private plot be we the first
That shall salute our rightful sovereign
With honor of his birthright to the crown.

BOTH [*Kneeling*] Long live our sovereign Richard,
    England's King!

YORK We thank you, lords. But I am not your king   65
    Till I be crowned and that my sword be stained
    With heart-blood of the house of Lancaster;
    And that's not suddenly to be performed,
    But with advice and silent secrecy.
    Do you as I do in these dangerous days: 70
    Wink at the Duke of Suffolk's insolence,
    At Beaufort's pride, at Somerset's ambition,
    At Buckingham and all the crew of them,
    Till they have snared the shepherd of the flock,
    That virtuous prince, the good Duke Humphrey: 75
    'Tis that they seek, and they in seeking that
    Shall find their deaths, if York can prophesy.

SALISBURY My lord, break we off; we know your mind
    at full.

WARWICK My heart assures me that the Earl of War-
    wick
    Shall one day make the Duke of York a king.   80

YORK And, Nevil, this I do assure myself:
    Richard shall live to make the Earl of Warwick
    The greatest man in England but the King. *Exeunt*.

59 **slips** shoots, cuttings   69 **advice** deliberation   71 **Wink at** close your eyes to

Scene III. [*A hall of justice.*]

Sound trumpets. Enter King Henry, and the Queen,
Gloucester, the Duke of Suffolk, and the Duke of
Buckingham, the Cardinal, and the Duchess of
Gloucester, led with the Officers; and then enter to
them the Duke of York, and the Earls of Salisbury
and Warwick.

KING Stand forth, Dame Eleanor Cobham,
   Gloucester's wife.
In sight of God and us, your guilt is great:
Receive the sentence of the law for sins
Such as by God's book are adjudged to death.
5 You four, from hence to prison back again;
From thence unto the place of execution:
The witch in Smithfield shall be burnt to ashes,
And you three shall be strangled on the gallows.
You, madam, for you are more nobly born,
10 Despoilèd of your honor in your life,
Shall, after three days' open penance done,
Live in your country here in banishment,
With Sir John Stanley, in the Isle of Man.

DUCHESS Welcome is banishment, welcome were my
   death.

GLOUCESTER Eleanor, the law thou seest hath judgèd
15   thee:
I cannot justify whom the law condemns.
              [*Exeunt the Duchess and the*
                other prisoners, guarded.]
Mine eyes are full of tears, my heart of grief.
Ah, Humphrey, this dishonor in thine age

II.iii.4 **God's ... death** Exodus, xxii.18: "Thou shalt not suffer a witch to
live" 7 **Smithfield** a place of public execution in east-central London, now the
site of the wholesale meat markets

Will bring thy head with sorrow to the ground!
I beseech your Majesty, give me leave to go;   20
Sorrow would solace, and mine age would ease.

KING Stay, Humphrey Duke of Gloucester: ere thou go,
Give up thy staff: Henry will to himself
Protector be; and God shall be my hope,
My stay, my guide and lanthorn to my feet.   25
And go in peace, Humphrey, no less beloved
Than when thou wert Protector to thy King.

QUEEN I see no reason why a king of years
Should be to be protected like a child.
God and King Henry govern England's realm!   30
Give up your staff, sir, and the King his realm.

GLOUCESTER My staff? Here, noble Henry, is my staff:
As willingly do I the same resign
As e'er thy father Henry made it mine;
And even as willingly at thy feet I leave it   35
As others would ambitiously receive it.
Farewell, good King: when I am dead and gone,
May honorable peace attend thy throne.
                                              Exit Gloucester.

QUEEN Why, now is Henry King, and Margaret Queen;
And Humphrey Duke of Gloucester scarce himself,   40
That bears so shrewd a maim: two pulls at once:
His lady banished, and a limb lopped off.
This staff of honor raught, there let it stand
Where it best fits to be, in Henry's hand.

SUFFOLK Thus droops this lofty pine and hangs his
          sprays;   45
Thus Eleanor's pride dies in her youngest days.

YORK Lords, let him go. Please it your Majesty,
This is the day appointed for the combat,
And ready are the appellant and defendant,

21 would desires 25 lanthorn lantern (old form) 28-29 king ... be a king
should be of age 41 shrewd a maim sharp or painful a mutilation 41 pulls
pluckings (as of fruit, or a branch) 43 raught reached, attained (by us)

50   The armorer and his man, to enter the lists,
        So please your Highness to behold the fight.

        QUEEN Ay, good my lord: for purposely therefore
        Left I the court, to see this quarrel tried.

        KING A God's name, see the lists and all things fit:
55   Here let them end it; and God defend the right!

        YORK I never saw a fellow worse bested,
        Or more afraid to fight, than is the appellant,
        The servant of this armorer, my lords.

        *Enter at one door [Thomas Horner] the Armorer, and
        his neighbors, drinking to him so much that he is drunk;
        and he enters with a drum before him and his staff with
        a sand-bag fastened to it; and at the other door his man,
        with a drum and sand-bag, and Prentices drinking
        to him.*

        FIRST NEIGHBOR Here, neighbor Horner, I drink to you
60   in a cup of sack: and fear not, neighbor, you
        shall do well enough.

        SECOND NEIGHBOR And here, neighbor, here's a cup of
        charneco.

        THIRD NEIGHBOR And here's a pot of good double
65   beer, neighbor: drink, and fear not your man.

        HORNER Let it come; i'faith I'll pledge you all, and a
        fig for Peter!

        FIRST PRENTICE Here, Peter, I drink to thee: and be not
        afeared.

70   SECOND PRENTICE Here, Peter, here's a pint of claret
        wine for thee.

        THIRD PRENTICE And here's a quart for me; be merry,
        Peter, and fear not thy master: fight for credit of
        the prentices.

---

56 **worse bested** in worse circumstances 58 s.d. **staff with a sand-bag
fastened to it** a mock-weapon used in sporting combat 60 **in** with 60 **sack**
sweet sherry 63 **charneco** a kind of port wine 64 **double** extra strong

PETER I thank you all, but I'll drink no more. Here,   75
    Robin, and if I die, here I give thee my hammer;
    and Will, thou shalt have my apron; and here,
    Tom, take all the money that I have. O Lord bless
    me, I pray God, for I am never able to deal with
    my master, he hath learnt so much fence already.   80

SALISBURY Come, leave your drinking, and fall to
    blows. Sirrah, what's thy name?

PETER Peter, forsooth.

SALISBURY Peter? What more?

PETER Thump.   85

SALISBURY Thump! then see thou thump thy master well.

HORNER Here's to thee, neighbor; fill all the pots again,
    for before we fight, look you, I will tell you my
    mind: for I am come hither, as it were, of my man's
    instigation, to prove myself an honest man, and Peter   90
    a knave: and so have at you, Peter, with downright
    blows, as Bevis of Southampton fell upon Ascapart.

YORK Dispatch; this knave's tongue begins to double.
    Sound trumpets; alarum to the combatants!
          They fight, and Peter strikes him down.

HORNER Hold, Peter, hold! I confess, I confess treason.   95
                      He dies.

YORK Take away his weapon. Fellow, thank God, and
    the good wine in thy master's way.

PETER O God, have I overcome mine enemies in this
    presence? O Peter, thou hast prevailed in right!

KING Go, take hence that traitor from our sight;   100
    For by his death we do perceive his guilt:
    And God in justice hath revealed to us

92 **Bevis ... Ascapart** a legendary English knight and his adversary, a giant thirty
feet high; a pun may have been intended on the name of an actor, Bevis, playing
the part of Horner   93 **double** stutter   94 **Sound ... combatants** given as
York's line in F (Q omits) but possibly intended as a stage direction   99 **presence**
i.e., of the King

The truth and innocence of this poor fellow,
Which he had thought to have murdered wrongfully.
105   Come, fellow, follow us for thy reward.
                              Sound a flourish; exeunt.

Scene IV. [*A street.*]

*Enter Gloucester and his men,
in mourning cloaks.*

GLOUCESTER Thus sometimes hath the brightest day a
         cloud;
     And after summer evermore succeeds
     Barren winter with his wrathful nipping cold:
     So cares and joys abound, as seasons fleet.
     Sirs, what's o'clock?

5   SERVANT   Ten, my lord.

GLOUCESTER Ten is the hour that was appointed me
     To watch the coming of my punished duchess:
     Uneath may she endure the flinty streets,
     To tread them with her tender-feeling feet.
10   Sweet Nell, ill can thy noble mind abrook
     The abject people gazing on thy face
     With envious looks, laughing at thy shame,
     That erst did follow thy proud chariot-wheels
     When thou didst ride in triumph through the streets.
15   But, soft! I think she comes, and I'll prepare
     My tear-stained eyes to see her miseries.

II.iv.8 **Uneath** with difficulty   10 **abrook** tolerate   11 **abject** despicable
12 **envious** malicious   13 **erst** formerly   15 **soft** stay, hold (exclamation)

Enter Duchess of Gloucester barefoot, and a white sheet
about her, with a wax candle in her hand, and verses
written on her back and pinned on; and accompanied
with the Sheriffs of London and Sir John Stanley, and
Officers, with bill and halberds.

SERVANT So please your Grace, we'll take her from the
    sheriff.

GLOUCESTER No, stir not, for your lives; let her pass by.

DUCHESS Come you, my lord, to see my open shame?
    Now thou dost penance too. Look how they gaze!   20
    See how the giddy multitude do point,
    And nod their heads, and throw their eyes on thee!
    Ah, Gloucester, hide thee from their hateful looks,
    And, in thy closet pent up, rue my shame,
    And ban thine enemies, both mine and thine.   25

GLOUCESTER Be patient, gentle Nell; forget this grief.

DUCHESS Ah, Gloucester, teach me to forget myself!
    For whilst I think I am thy married wife
    And thou a prince, Protector of this land,
    Methinks I should not thus be led along,   30
    Mailed up in shame, with papers on my back,
    And followed with a rabble that rejoice
    To see my tears and hear my deep-fet groans.
    The ruthless flint doth cut my tender feet,
    And when I start, the envious people laugh   35
    And bid me be advisèd how I tread.
    Ah, Humphrey, can I bear this shameful yoke?
    Trowest thou that e'er I'll look upon the world
    Or count them happy that enjoys the sun?
    No; dark shall be my light and night my day;   40
    To think upon my pomp shall be my hell.
    Sometime I'll say, I am Duke Humphrey's wife,

16 s.d. **bills and halberds** long, ax-headed weapons   25 ban curse   31 **Mailed**
wrapped (hawking term)   33 **deep-fet** deep-fetched, profound   35 **envious**
malicious

And he a prince, and ruler of the land:
Yet so he ruled and such a prince he was
45 As he stood by whilst I, his forlorn duchess,
Was made a wonder and a pointing-stock
To every idle rascal follower.
But be thou mild and blush not at my shame,
Nor stir at nothing, till the ax of death
50 Hang over thee, as, sure, it shortly will;
For Suffolk—he that can do all in all
With her that hateth thee and hates us all—
And York, and impious Beaufort, that false priest,
Have all limed bushes to betray thy wings;
55 And fly thou how thou canst, they'll tangle thee.
But fear not thou, until thy foot be snared,
Nor never seek prevention of thy foes.

GLOUCESTER Ah, Nell, forbear! Thou aimest all awry.
I must offend before I be attainted;
60 And had I twenty times so many foes,
And each of them had twenty times their power,
All these could not procure me any scathe,
So long as I am loyal, true and crimeless.
Wouldst have me rescue thee from this reproach?
65 Why, yet thy scandal were not wiped away,
But I in danger for the breach of law.
Thy greatest help is quiet, gentle Nell:
I pray thee, sort thy heart to patience;
These few days' wonder will be quickly worn.

Enter a Herald.

HERALD I summon your Grace to his Majesty's Parlia-
70   ment,
Holden at Bury the first of this next month.

GLOUCESTER And my consent ne'er asked herein before?
This is close dealing. Well, I will be there.
                                         Exit Herald.

54 **limed bushes** smeared with a sticky substance (a means of catching
birds) 57 **prevention** remedy by anticipation 59 **attainted** condemned
62 **scathe** damage 68 **sort** adapt 69 **few days' wonder** spectacle, sensation
73 **close** secret

My Nell, I take my leave: and, master sheriff,
Let not her penance exceed the King's commission.   75

SHERIFF And't please your Grace, here my commission
       stays,
And Sir John Stanley is appointed now
To take her with him to the Isle of Man.

GLOUCESTER Must you, Sir John, protect my lady here?

STANLEY So am I given in charge, may't please your
       Grace.   80

GLOUCESTER Entreat her not the worse in that I pray
You use her well. The world may laugh again;
And I may live to do you kindness if
You do it her: and so, Sir John, farewell.

DUCHESS What, gone, my lord, and bid me not fare-
       well?   85

GLOUCESTER Witness my tears, I cannot stay to speak.
                         Exit Gloucester [and Serving-men].

DUCHESS Art thou gone too? All comfort go with thee!
For none abides with me: my joy is death—
Death, at whose name I oft have been afeared,
Because I wished this world's eternity.   90
Stanley, I prithee go, and take me hence;
I care not whither, for I beg no favor;
Only convey me where thou art commanded.

STANLEY Why, madam, that is to the Isle of Man,
There to be used according to your state.   95

DUCHESS That's bad enough, for I am but reproach:
And shall I then be used reproachfully?

STANLEY Like to a duchess, and Duke Humphrey's
       lady:
According to that state you shall be used.

99 **state** dignity

167

100 DUCHESS Sheriff farewell, and better than I fare,
Although thou hast been conduct of my shame.

SHERIFF It is my office; and madam, pardon me.

DUCHESS Ay, ay, farewell; thy office is discharged.
Come, Stanley, shall we go?

STANLEY Madam, your penance done, throw off this
105   sheet,
And go we to attire you for our journey.

DUCHESS My shame will not be shifted with my sheet:
No, it will hang upon my richest robes,
And show itself, attire me how I can.
110 Go, lead the way; I long to see my prison.

Exeunt.

---

100 **better than I fare** fare better than I   101 **conduct** guide   107 **shifted** play
on "shift," i.e., smock, what Eleanor is wearing

ACT III

Scene I. [*The Abbey at Bury St. Edmunds.*]

Sound a Sennet. Enter King, Queen, Cardinal, Suffolk,
York, Buckingham, Salisbury and Warwick [and
Attendants] to the Parliament.

KING I muse my Lord of Gloucester is not come:
    'Tis not his wont to be the hindmost man,
    Whate'er occasion keeps him from us now.

QUEEN Can you not see? Or will ye not observe
    The strangeness of his altered countenance?   5
    With what a majesty he bears himself,
    How insolent of late he is become,
    How proud, how peremptory, and unlike himself?
    We know the time since he was mild and affable,
    And if we did but glance a far-off look,   10
    Immediately he was upon his knee,
    That all the court admired him for submission.
    But meet him now, and, be it in the morn,
    When everyone will give the time of day,
    He knits his brow and shows an angry eye   15
    And passeth by with stiff unbowèd knee,
    Disdaining duty that to us belongs.
    Small curs are not regarded when they grin,
    But great men tremble when the lion roars;
    And Humphrey is no little man in England.   20
    First note that he is near you in descent,

III.i.18 **grin** bare their teeth

169

And should you fall, he is the next will mount.
Me seemeth then it is no policy,
Respecting what a rancorous mind he bears,
25   And his advantage following your decease,
That he should come about your royal person
Or be admitted to your Highness' Council.
By flattery hath he won the commons' hearts,
And when he please to make commotion,
30   'Tis to be feared they all will follow him.
Now 'tis the spring, and weeds are shallow-rooted;
Suffer them now, and they'll o'ergrow the garden,
And choke the herbs for want of husbandry.
The reverent care I bear unto my lord
35   Made me collect these dangers in the Duke.
If it be fond, call it a woman's fear—
Which fear if better reasons can supplant,
I will subscribe, and say I wronged the Duke.
My Lord of Suffolk, Buckingham, and York,
40   Reprove my allegation, if you can,
Or else conclude my words effectual.

SUFFOLK Well hath your Highness seen into this duke;
And had I first been put to speak my mind,
I think I should have told your Grace's tale.
45   The Duchess by his subornation,
Upon my life, began her devilish practices:
Or if he were not privy to those faults,
Yet, by reputing of his high descent,
As next the King he was successive heir,
50   And such high vaunts of his nobility,
Did instigate the bedlam brain-sick Duchess
By wicked means to frame our sovereign's fall.
Smooth runs the water where the brook is deep,
And in his simple show he harbors treason.
55   The fox barks not when he would steal the lamb.
No, no, my sovereign; Gloucester is a man
Unsounded yet, and full of deep deceit.

23–24 no policy,/ Respecting unwise, considering   35 collect i.e., as if by
weeding 36 fond foolish 38 subscribe agree 40 Reprove disprove
41 effectual pertinent, conclusive 47 privy to acquainted with 51 bedlam crazy

CARDINAL Did he not, contrary to form of law,
   Devise strange deaths for small offenses done?

YORK And did he not, in his Protectorship,   60
   Levy great sums of money through the realm
   For soldiers' pay in France, and never sent it?
   By means whereof the towns each day revolted.

BUCKINGHAM Tut, these are petty faults to faults un-
      known,
   Which time will bring to light in smooth Duke
      Humphrey.   65

KING My lords, at once: the care you have of us,
   To mow down thorns that would annoy our foot,
   Is worthy praise: but, shall I speak my conscience,
   Our kinsman Gloucester is as innocent
   From meaning treason to our royal person   70
   As is the sucking lamb or harmless dove.
   The Duke is virtuous, mild, and too well given
   To dream on evil, or to work my downfall.

QUEEN Ah, what's more dangerous than this fond
      affiance!
   Seems he a dove? His feathers are but borrowed,   75
   For he's disposèd as the hateful raven.
   Is he a lamb? His skin is surely lent him,
   For he's inclined as is the ravenous wolves.
   Who cannot steal a shape, that means deceit?
   Take heed, my lord: the welfare of us all   80
   Hangs on the cutting short that fraudful man.

                      Enter Somerset.

SOMERSET All health unto my gracious sovereign!

KING Welcome, Lord Somerset. What news from
      France?

SOMERSET That all your interest in those territories
   Is utterly bereft you: all is lost.   85

74 **fond affiance** foolish trust

KING Cold news, Lord Somerset: but God's will be
      done!

YORK [*Aside*] Cold news for me; for I had hope of
      France
      As firmly as I hope for fertile England.
      Thus are my blossoms blasted in the bud,
90   And caterpillars eat my leaves away;
      But I will remedy this gear ere long,
      Or sell my title for a glorious grave.

                    Enter Gloucester.

GLOUCESTER All happiness unto my lord the King!
      Pardon, my liege, that I have stayed so long.

SUFFOLK Nay, Gloucester, know that thou art come
95   too soon,
      Unless thou wert more loyal than thou art:
      I do arrest thee of high treason here.

GLOUCESTER Well, Suffolk, thou shalt not see me
      blush,
      Nor change my countenance for this arrest:
100   A heart unspotted is not easily daunted.
      The purest spring is not so free from mud
      As I am clear from treason to my sovereign.
      Who can accuse me? Wherein am I guilty?

YORK 'Tis thought, my lord, that you took bribes of
      France,
105   And, being Protector, stayed the soldiers' pay;
      By means whereof his Highness hath lost France.

GLOUCESTER Is it but thought so? What are they that
      think it?
      I never robbed the soldiers of their pay,
      Nor ever had one penny bribe from France.
110   So help me God, as I have watched the night,
      Ay, night by night, in studying good for England!

87–88 **Cold … England** almost a literal repetition of I.i.238-39   91 **gear**
business   94 **stayed** delayed   104 **France** the King of France

172

That doit that e'er I wrested from the King,
Or any groat I hoarded to my use,
Be brought against me at my trial-day!
No; many a pound of mine own proper store,   115
Because I would not tax the needy commons,
Have I dispursèd to the garrisons,
And never asked for restitution.

CARDINAL It serves you well, my lord, to say so much.

GLOUCESTER I say no more than truth, so help me God! 120

YORK In your Protectorship you did devise
Strange tortures for offenders, never heard of,
That England was defamed by tyranny.

GLOUCESTER Why, 'tis well known that whiles I was
    Protector
Pity was all the fault that was in me: 125
For I should melt at an offender's tears,
And lowly words were ransom for their fault.
Unless it were a bloody murderer,
Or foul felonious thief that fleeced poor
    passengers,
I never gave them condign punishment.   130
Murder indeed, that bloody sin, I tortured
Above the felon or what trespass else.

SUFFOLK My lord, these faults are easy, quickly
    answered;
But mightier crimes are laid unto your charge,
Whereof you cannot easily purge yourself.   135
I do arrest you in his Highness' name,
And here commit you to my Lord Cardinal
To keep, until your further time of trial.

KING My lord of Gloucester, 'tis my special hope
That you will clear yourself from all suspense.   140
My conscience tells me you are innocent.

112 **doit** Dutch coin of minimal value 115 **proper store** personal possession
117 **dispursèd** disbursed 123 **That** so that 129 **passengers** travelers 130
condign deserved 132 **What** whatever 140 **suspense** suspicion

GLOUCESTER Ah, gracious lord, these days are danger-
       ous:
       Virtue is choked with foul ambition,
       And charity chased hence by rancor's hand;
145   Foul subornation is predominant,
       And equity exiled your Highness' land.
       I know their complot is to have my life,
       And if my death might make this island happy,
       And prove the period of their tyranny,
150   I would expend it with all willingness.
       But mine is made the prologue to their play:
       For thousands more, that yet suspect no peril,
       Will not conclude their plotted tragedy.
       Beaufort's red sparkling eyes blab his heart's malice,
155   And Suffolk's cloudy brow his stormy hate;
       Sharp Buckingham unburthens with his tongue
       The envious load that lies upon his heart;
       And doggèd York, that reaches at the moon,
       Whose overweening arm I have plucked back,
160   By false accuse doth level at my life.
       And you, my sovereign lady, with the rest,
       Causeless have laid disgraces on my head,
       And with your best endeavor have stirred up
       My liefest liege to be mine enemy.
165   Ay, all of you have laid your heads together—
       Myself had notice of your conventicles—
       And all to make away my guiltless life.
       I shall not want false witness to condemn me,
       Nor store of treasons to augment my guilt;
170   The ancient proverb will be well effected:
       "A staff is quickly found to beat a dog."

CARDINAL My liege, his railing is intolerable.
       If those that care to keep your royal person
       From treason's secret knife and traitor's rage
175   Be thus upbraided, chid, and rated at,

---

147 complot plot   149 period end, limit   160 level at   aim at   164 liefest
dearest   166 conventicles meetings   168 want lack   175 rated at inveighed
against

And the offender granted scope of speech,
'Twill make them cool in zeal unto your Grace.

SUFFOLK Hath he not twit our sovereign lady here
With ignominious words, though clerkly couched,
As if she had suborNèd some to swear   180
False allegations to o'erthrow his state?

QUEEN But I can give the loser leave to chide.

GLOUCESTER Far truer spoke than meant: I lose indeed;
Beshrew the winners, for they played me false!
And well such losers may have leave to speak.   185

BUCKINGHAM He'll wrest the sense and hold us here
all day.
Lord Cardinal, he is your prisoner.

CARDINAL Sirs, take away the Duke, and guard him
sure.

GLOUCESTER Ah, thus King Henry throws away his
crutch
Before his legs be firm to bear his body.   190
Thus is the shepherd beaten from thy side,
And wolves are gnarling who shall gnaw thee first.
Ah, that my fear were false! Ah, that it were!
For, good King Henry, thy decay I fear.
                              Exit Gloucester [*guarded*].

KING My lords, what to your wisdom seemeth best,   195
Do or undo, as if ourself were here.

QUEEN What, will your Highness leave the Parliament?

KING Ay, Margaret; my heart is drowned with grief,
Whose flood begins to flow within mine eyes,
My body round engirt with misery: 200
For what's more miserable than discontent?
Ah, uncle Humphrey, in thy face I see
The map of honor, truth, and loyalty;

179 **ignominious ... couched** infamous words, although learnedly (i.e., cleverly)
phrased 186 **wrest the sense** distort the meaning (of what we say)
192 **gnarling** snarling 194 **decay** downfall

175

And yet, good Humphrey, is the hour to come
205   That e'er I proved thee false or feared thy faith?
What louring star now envies thy estate,
That these great lords, and Margaret our Queen
Do seek subversion of thy harmless life?
Thou never didst them wrong, nor no man wrong:
210   And as the butcher takes away the calf,
And binds the wretch, and beats it when it strays,
Bearing it to the bloody slaughter-house,
Even so remorseless have they borne him hence;
And as the dam runs lowing up and down,
215   Looking the way her harmless young one went,
And can do nought but wail her darling's loss,
Even so myself bewails good Gloucester's case
With sad unhelpful tears, and with dimmed eyes
Look after him and cannot do him good,
220   So mighty are his vowèd enemies.
His fortunes I will weep, and 'twixt each groan
Say "Who's a traitor? Gloucester he is none."

Exit King, Salisbury, and Warwick.

QUEEN Free lords, cold snow melts with the sun's hot
     beams.
Henry my lord is cold in great affairs,
225   Too full of foolish pity; and Gloucester's show
Beguiles him as the mournful crocodile
With sorrow snares relenting passengers,
Or as the snake, rolled in a flow'ring bank,
With shining checkered slough, doth sting a child
230   That for the beauty thinks it excellent.
Believe me, lords, were none more wise than I—
And yet herein I judge mine own wit good—
This Gloucester should be quickly rid the world,
To rid us from the fear we have of him.

235 CARDINAL That he should die is worthy policy,

---

208 **subversion** overthrow   223 **Free** noble, magnanimous   225 **show** outward
appearance   227 **passengers** travelers   235 **is worthy policy** deserves shrewd
planning

But yet we want a color for his death:
'Tis meet he be condemned by course of law.

SUFFOLK But in my mind that were no policy:
The King will labor still to save his life,
The commons haply rise, to save his life;   240
And yet we have but trivial argument,
More than mistrust, that shows him worthy death.

YORK So that, by this, you would not have him die.

SUFFOLK Ah, York, no man alive so fain as I!

YORK [Aside] 'Tis York that hath more reason for his
        death.   245
    [Aloud] But my Lord Cardinal, and you, my Lord
        of Suffolk,
Say as you think, and speak it from your souls:
Were't not all one, an empty eagle were set
To guard the chicken from a hungry kite,
As place Duke Humphrey for the King's Protector?   250

QUEEN So, the poor chicken should be sure of death.

SUFFOLK Madam, 'tis true; and were't not madness,
        then,
To make the fox surveyor of the fold?
Who being accused a crafty murderer,
His guilt should be but idly posted over,   255
Because his purpose is not executed.
No: let him die, in that he is a fox,
By nature proved an enemy to the flock,
Before his chaps be stained with crimson blood,
As Humphrey proved by reasons to my liege.   260
And do not stand on quillets how to slay him:
Be it by gins, by snares, by subtlety,
Sleeping or waking, 'tis no matter how,

236 color pretext (perhaps punning on "collar," i.e., hangman's noose)
237 meet appropriate 244 fain willingly 249 kite bird of prey 251 So if
so 253 surveyor overseer 254 Who being whoever has been 255 posted
over hurried past 256 executed accomplished 259 chaps jaws 260 As ...
liege i.e., above, lines 191–94 261 quillets fine distinctions, quibbles 262 gins
traps

So he be dead; for that is good deceit
265 Which mates him first that first intends deceit.

QUEEN Thrice-noble Suffolk, 'tis resolutely spoke.

SUFFOLK Not resolute, except so much were done;
For things are often spoke and seldom meant:
But that my heart accordeth with my tongue,
270 Seeing the deed is meritorious,
And to preserve my sovereign from his foe,
Say but the word, and I will be his priest.

CARDINAL But I would have him dead, my Lord of
Suffolk,
Ere you can take due orders for a priest:
275 Say you consent and censure well the deed,
And I'll provide his executioner;
I tender so the safety of my liege.

SUFFOLK Here is my hand, the deed is worthy doing.

QUEEN And so say I.

280 YORK And I: and now we three have spoke it,
It skills not greatly who impugns our doom.

Enter a Post.

POST Great lords, from Ireland am I come amain,
To signify that rebels there are up,
And put the Englishmen unto the sword.
285 Send succors, lords, and stop the rage betime,
Before the wound do grow uncurable;
For, being green, there is great hope of help.

CARDINAL A breach that craves a quick expedient stop!
What counsel give you in this weighty cause?

290 YORK That Somerset be sent as regent thither.

---

265 **mates** checkmates, suppresses 267 **except so much** unless as much
270 **meritorious** worthy reward (esp. in a religious sense, from God) 272 **be his
priest** i.e., kill him 275 **censure well** approve of 277 **I tender so** I am so
solicitous of 281 **It … doom** it matters little who disapproves of our
decision 282 **amain** in haste 283 **up** up in arms 285 **betime** in time,
rapidly 287 **green** fresh

'Tis meet that lucky ruler be employed;
Witness the fortune he hath had in France.

SOMERSET If York, with all his far-fet policy,
Had been the regent there instead of me,
He never would have stayed in France so long.   295

YORK No, not to lose it all, as thou hast done.
I rather would have lost my life betimes
Than bring a burden of dishonor home
By staying there so long till all were lost.
Show me one scar charactered on thy skin: 300
Men's flesh preserved so whole do seldom win.

QUEEN Nay then, this spark will prove a raging fire,
If wind and fuel be brought to feed it with!
No more, good York; sweet Somerset, be still:
Thy fortune, York, hadst thou been regent there,   305
Might happily have proved far worse than his.

YORK What, worse than nought? Nay, then a shame
take all!

SOMERSET And in the number thee, that wishest shame!

CARDINAL My Lord of York, try what your fortune is.
Th' uncivil kerns of Ireland are in arms   310
And temper clay with blood of Englishmen.
To Ireland will you lead a band of men,
Collected choicely, from each county some,
And try your hap against the Irishmen?

YORK I will, my lord, so please his Majesty.   315

SUFFOLK Why, our authority is his consent,
And what we do establish he confirms:
Then, noble York, take thou this task in hand.

YORK I am content: provide me soldiers, lords,
Whiles I take order for mine own affairs.   320

293 **far-fet** far-fetched, i.e., deep   297 **betimes** early   299 **staying ... till**
delaying or temporizing there until   300 **charactered** inscribed   306 **happily** by
chance   310 **kerns** light-armed Irish foot-soldiers   311 **temper** moisten (as with
mortar)

SUFFOLK A charge, Lord York, that I will see performed.
But now return we to the false Duke Humphrey.

CARDINAL No more of him; for I will deal with him
That henceforth he shall trouble us no more.
325　　And so break off: the day is almost spent;
Lord Suffolk, you and I must talk of that event.

YORK My Lord of Suffolk, within fourteen days
At Bristow I expect my soldiers;
For there I'll ship them all for Ireland.

330 SUFFOLK I'll see it truely done, my Lord of York.
Exeunt. Manet York [alone].

YORK Now, York, or never, steel thy fearful thoughts,
And change misdoubt to resolution:
Be that thou hop'st to be, or what thou art
Resign to death; it is not worth th' enjoying.
335　　Let pale-faced fear keep with the mean-born man,
And find no harbor in a royal heart.
Faster than spring-time show'rs comes thought on
　　thought,
And not a thought but thinks on dignity.
My brain more busy than the laboring spider
340　　Weaves tedious snares to trap mine enemies.
Well, nobles, well: 'tis politicly done,
To send me packing with an host of men:
I fear me you but warm the starvèd snake,
Who, cherished in your breasts, will sting your hearts.
345　　'Twas men I lacked, and you will give them me:
I take it kindly; yet be well assured
You put sharp weapons in a madman's hands.
Whiles I in Ireland nourish a mighty band,
I will stir up in England some black storm
350　　Shall blow ten thousand souls to heaven or hell;
And this fell tempest shall not cease to rage
Until the golden circuit on my head,
Like to the glorious sun's transparent beams,

328 **Bristow** Bristol　338 **dignity** rank　340 **tedious** laborious, intricate
351 **fell** evil　352 **circuit** circle (crown)

Do calm the fury of this mad-bred flaw.
And, for a minister of my intent,   355
I have seduced a headstrong Kentishman,
John Cade of Ashford,
To make commotion, as full well he can,
Under the title of John Mortimer.
In Ireland have I seen this stubborn Cade   360
Oppose himself against a troop of kerns,
And fought so long, till that his thighs with darts
Were almost like a sharp-quilled porpentine;
And, in the end being rescued, I have seen
Him caper upright like a wild Morisco,   365
Shaking the bloody darts as he his bells.
Full often, like a shag-haired crafty kern,
Hath he conversèd with the enemy,
And undiscovered come to me again
And given me notice of their villainies.   370
This devil here shall be my substitute;
For that John Mortimer, which now is dead,
In face, in gait, in speech, he doth resemble:
By this I shall perceive the commons' mind,
How they affect the house and claim of York.   375
Say he be taken, racked, and torturèd:
I know no pain they can inflict upon him
Will make him say I moved him to those arms.
Say that he thrive, as 'tis great like he will:
Why, then from Ireland come I with my strength   380
And reap the harvest which that rascal sowed.
For Humphrey being dead, as he shall be,
And Henry put apart, the next for me.   *Exit*.

354 **flaw** squall of wind 363 **porpentine** porcupine 365 **Morisco** Moorish, or morris-dancer; the dance is performed in grotesque attire with bells attached to the legs 366 **he** i.e., the dancer 375 **affect** favor, approve

Scene II. [*Bury St. Edmunds. A room of state.*]

*Enter two or three running over the stage, from
the murder of Gloucester.*

FIRST MURDERER Run to my Lord of Suffolk; let him
know
We have dispatched the Duke, as he commanded.

SECOND MURDERER O that it were to do! What have we
done?
Didst ever hear a man so penitent?

Enter Suffolk.

5   FIRST MURDERER Here comes my lord.

SUFFOLK Now, sirs, have you dispatched this thing?

FIRST MURDERER Ay, my good lord, he's dead.

SUFFOLK Why, that's well said. Go, get you to my house;
I will reward you for this venturous deed.
10   The King and all the peers are here at hand.
Have you laid fair the bed? Is all things well,
According as I gave directions?

FIRST MURDERER 'Tis, my good lord.

SUFFOLK Away, be gone.   *Exeunt* [*Murderers*].

*Sound trumpets. Enter the King, the Queen,
Cardinal, Buckingham, Somerset,
with Attendants.*

15   KING Go, call our uncle to our presence straight;
Say we intend to try his Grace today,
If he be guilty, as 'tis publishèd.

SUFFOLK I'll call him presently, my noble lord.   *Exit.*

KING Lords, take your places; and I pray you all,
   Proceed no straiter 'gainst our uncle Gloucester   20
   Than from true evidence of good esteem,
   He be approved in practice culpable.

QUEEN God forbid any malice should prevail,
   That faultless may condemn a nobleman!
   Pray God he may acquit him of suspicion!   25

KING I thank thee, Meg; these words content me much.

                    Enter Suffolk.

   How now! Why look'st thou pale? Why tremblest
      thou?
   Where is our uncle? What's the matter, Suffolk?

SUFFOLK Dead in his bed, my lord; Gloucester is dead.

QUEEN Marry, God forfend!   30

CARDINAL God's secret judgment: I did dream tonight
   The Duke was dumb and could not speak a word.
                              King sounds.

QUEEN How fares my lord? Help, lords, the King is
      dead!

SOMERSET Rear up his body; wring him by the nose.

QUEEN Run, go, help, help! O Henry, ope thine eyes!   35

SUFFOLK He doth revive again; madam, be patient.

KING O heavenly God!

QUEEN   How fares my gracious lord?

SUFFOLK Comfort, my sovereign; gracious Henry, com-
      fort.

KING What, doth my Lord of Suffolk comfort me?
   Came he right now to sing a raven's note,   40
   Whose dismal tune bereft my vital pow'rs,

III.ii.20 **straiter** more strictly 22 **approved** proven 30 **forfend** forbid
32 s.d. **sounds** swoons 34 **wring** squeeze (a method of restoring circulation)

183

And thinks he that the chirping of a wren,
By crying comfort from a hollow breast,
Can chase away the first-conceivèd sound?
45   Hide not thy poison with such sugared words;
Lay not thy hands on me; forbear, I say!
Their touch affrights me as a serpent's sting.
Thou baleful messenger, out of my sight!
Upon thy eyeballs murderous tyranny
50   Sits in grim majesty to fright the world.
Look not upon me, for thine eyes are wounding.
Yet do not go away; come, basilisk,
And kill the innocent gazer with thy sight:
For in the shade of death I shall find joy,
55   In life but double death, now Gloucester's dead.

QUEEN Why do you rate my Lord of Suffolk thus?
Although the Duke was enemy to him,
Yet he most Christian-like laments his death:
And for myself, foe as he was to me,
60   Might liquid tears or heart-offending groans
Or blood-consuming sighs recall his life,
I would be blind with weeping, sick with groans,
Look pale as primrose with blood-drinking sighs,
And all to have the noble Duke alive.
65   What know I how the world may deem of me?
For it is known we were but hollow friends:
It may be judged I made the Duke away;
So shall my name with slander's tongue be wounded,
And princes' courts be filled with my reproach.
70   This get I by his death: ay me, unhappy!
To be a queen, and crowned with infamy!

KING Ay, woe is me for Gloucester, wretched man!

QUEEN Be woe for me, more wretched than he is.
What, dost thou turn away and hide thy face?
75   I am no loathsome leper; look on me.
What! Art thou, like the adder, waxen deaf?
Be poisonous too, and kill thy forlorn Queen.

52 **basilisk** a mythical reptile, supposedly able to kill with its eyes   56 **rate**
berate   76 **waxen** grown

Is all thy comfort shut in Gloucester's tomb?
Why, then, Dame Margaret was ne'er thy joy.
Erect his statuë and worship it,   80
And make my image but an alehouse sign.
Was I for this nigh wracked upon the sea
And twice by awkward wind from England's bank
Drove back again unto my native clime?
What boded this, but well forewarning wind   85
Did seem to say "Seek not a scorpion's nest,
Nor set no footing on this unkind shore?"
What did I then, but cursed the gentle gusts
And he that loosed them forth their brazen caves,
And bid them blow towards England's blessèd shore,   90
Or turn our stern upon a dreadful rock?
Yet Aeolus would not be a murderer,
But left that hateful office unto thee.
The pretty vaulting sea refused to drown me,
Knowing that thou wouldst have me drowned on
    shore   95
With tears as salt as sea, through thy unkindness;
The splitting rocks cow'red in the sinking sands,
And would not dash me with their ragged sides,
Because thy flinty heart, more hard than they,
Might in thy palace perish Margaret.   100
As far as I could ken thy chalky cliffs,
When from thy shore the tempest beat us back,
I stood upon the hatches in the storm,
And when the dusky sky began to rob
My earnest-gaping sight of thy land's view,   105
I took a costly jewel from my neck—
A heart it was, bound in with diamonds—
And threw it towards thy land: the sea received it,
And so I wished thy body might my heart:
And even with this I lost fair England's view,   110
And bid mine eyes be packing with my heart,
And called them blind and dusky spectacles,

83 **awkward** adverse   89 **brazen** extremely strong   92 **Aeolus** god of
winds   94 **vaulting** bounding   101 **ken** discern   107 **heart** heart-shaped
gemstone   112 **spectacles** organs of sight or instruments, like spyglasses

185

For losing ken of Albion's wishèd coast.
How often have I tempted Suffolk's tongue,
115   The agent of thy foul inconstancy,
To sit and witch me, as Ascanius did
When he to madding Dido would unfold
His father's acts, commenced in burning Troy!
Am I not witched like her? Or thou not false like
    him?
120   Ay me, I can no more! Die, Margaret,
For Henry weeps that thou dost live so long.

*Noise within. Enter Warwick, Salisbury and
many Commons.*

WARWICK It is reported, mighty sovereign,
That good Duke Humphrey traitorously is murdered
By Suffolk and the Cardinal Beaufort's means.
125   The commons, like an angry hive of bees
That want their leader, scatter up and down,
And care not who they sting in his revenge.
Myself have calmed their spleenful mutiny,
Until they hear the order of his death.

130   KING That he is dead, good Warwick, 'tis too true;
But how he died God knows, not Henry.
Enter his chamber, view his breathless corpse,
And comment then upon his sudden death.

WARWICK That shall I do, my liege. Stay, Salisbury,
135   With the rude multitude till I return.
                *[Exeunt Warwick to the inner chamber,
                and Salisbury with the Commons.]*

KING O Thou that judgest all things, stay my thoughts,
My thoughts, that labor to persuade my soul
Some violent hands were laid on Humphrey's life!
If my suspect be false, forgive me, God,
140   For judgment only doth belong to Thee.
Fain would I go to chafe his paly lips

116 **witch** bewitch   117 **madding** becoming mad   120 **can** am capable of
128 **spleenful** eager, angry   135 s.d. **inner chamber** see textual note to III.ii
139 **suspect** suspicion   141 **paly** pale

With twenty thousand kisses, and to drain
Upon his face an ocean of salt tears,
To tell my love unto his dumb deaf trunk,
And with my fingers feel his hand unfeeling: 145
But all in vain are these mean obsequies;
And to survey his dead and earthy image,
What were it but to make my sorrow greater?

> *Warwick [from within] draws the curtains and*
> *shows Gloucester in his bed.*

WARWICK Come hither, gracious sovereign, view this
    body.

KING That is to see how deep my grave is made;   150
    For with his soul fled all my worldly solace,
    For, seeing him, I see my life in death.

WARWICK As surely as my soul intends to live
    With that dread King that took our state upon him
    To free us from His Father's wrathful curse,   155
    I do believe that violent hands were laid
    Upon the life of this thrice-famèd Duke.

SUFFOLK A dreadful oath, sworn with a solemn tongue!
    What instance gives Lord Warwick for his vow?

WARWICK See how the blood is settled in his face.   160
    Oft have I seen a timely-parted ghost,
    Of ashy semblance, meager, pale, and bloodless,
    Being all descended to the laboring heart,
    Who, in the conflict that it holds with death,
    Attracts the same for aidance 'gainst the enemy;   165
    Which with the heart there cools, and ne'er
        returneth
    To blush and beautify the cheek again.
    But see, his face is black and full of blood,
    His eyeballs further out than when he lived,
    Staring full ghastly like a strangled man;   170

---

161 **timely-parted ghost** dead man who died naturally   162 **meager** thin
163 **Being** i.e., the blood being   164 **Who** i.e., the heart   165 **the same** i.e., the
blood   166 **Which** i.e., the blood

His hair upreared, his nostrils stretched with
    struggling;
His hands abroad displayed, as one that grasped
And tugged for life, and was by strength subdued.
Look, on the sheets his hair, you see, is sticking;
175   His well-proportioned beard made rough and rugged,
Like to the summer's corn by tempest lodged.
It cannot be but he was murdered here:
The least of all these signs were probable.

SUFFOLK Why, Warwick, who should do the Duke to
    death?
180   Myself and Beaufort had him in protection:
And we, I hope, sir, are no murderers.

WARWICK But both of you were vowed Duke Hum-
    phrey's foes,
And you, forsooth, had the good Duke to keep:
'Tis like you would not feast him like a friend,
185   And 'tis well seen he found an enemy.

QUEEN Then you, belike, suspect these noblemen
As guilty of Duke Humphrey's timeless death?

WARWICK Who finds the heifer dead, and bleeding fresh,
And sees fast by a butcher with an ax,
190   But will suspect 'twas he that made the slaughter?
Who finds the partridge in the puttock's nest,
But may imagine how the bird was dead,
Although the kite soar with unbloodied beak?
Even so suspicious is this tragedy.

QUEEN Are you the butcher, Suffolk? Where's your
195   knife?
Is Beaufort termed a kite? Where are his talons?

SUFFOLK I wear no knife to slaughter sleeping men;
But here's a vengeful sword, rusted with ease,
That shall be scourèd in his rancorous heart
200   That slanders me with murder's crimson badge.

176 **lodged** beaten flat 178 **probable** indicative (of murder) 187 **timeless** untimely 191 **puttock's** kite's

Say, if thou dar'st, proud Lord of Warwickshire,
That I am faulty in Duke Humphrey's death.
                            Exit Cardinal [and others].

WARWICK What dares not Warwick, if false Suffolk
    dare him?

QUEEN He dares not calm his contumelious spirit
    Nor cease to be an arrogant controller,   205
    Though Suffolk dare him twenty thousand times.

WARWICK Madam, be still—with reverence may I say—
    For every word you speak in his behalf
    Is slander to your royal dignity.

SUFFOLK Blunt-witted lord, ignoble in demeanor!   210
    If ever lady wronged her lord so much,
    Thy mother took into her blameful bed
    Some stern untutored churl; and noble stock
    Was graft with crab-tree slip, whose fruit thou art,
    And never of the Nevils' noble race.   215

WARWICK But that the guilt of murder bucklers thee,
    And I should rob the deathsman of his fee,
    Quitting thee thereby of ten thousand shames,
    And that my sovereign's presence makes me mild,
    I would, false murd'rous coward, on thy knee   220
    Make thee beg pardon for thy passèd speech,
    And say it was thy mother that thou meant'st,
    That thou thyself wast born in bastardy;
    And after all this fearful homage done,
    Give thee thy hire and send thy soul to hell,   225
    Pernicious blood-sucker of sleeping men!

SUFFOLK Thou shalt be waking while I shed thy blood,
    If from this presence thou dar'st go with me.

WARWICK Away even now, or I will drag thee hence:
    Unworthy though thou art, I'll cope with thee,   230
    And do some service to Duke Humphrey's ghost.
                            Exeunt [Suffolk and Warwick].

204 **contumelious** slanderous   205 **controller** censorious critic, detractor
213 **stern** rough   216 **bucklers** shields

189

KING What stronger breastplate than a heart untainted!
　　　Thrice is he armed that hath his quarrel just,
　　　And he but naked, though locked up in steel,
235　　Whose conscience with injustice is corrupted.
　　　　　　　　　　　　　　　A noise within.

QUEEN What noise is this?

　　　　　Enter Suffolk and Warwick,
　　　　　with their weapons drawn.

KING Why, how now, lord! Your wrathful weapons
　　　drawn
　　　Here in our presence? Dare you be so bold?
　　　Why, what tumultuous clamor have we here?

240　SUFFOLK The trait'rous Warwick, with the men of Bury,
　　　Set all upon me, mighty sovereign.

　　　　　　　Enter Salisbury.

SALISBURY [*To the Commons without*] Sirs, stand apart:
　　　the King shall know your mind.
　　　Dread Lord, the commons send you word by me,
　　　Unless Lord Suffolk straight be done to death,
245　　Or banishèd fair England's territories,
　　　They will by violence tear him from your palace,
　　　And torture him with grievous ling'ring death.
　　　They say, by him the good Duke Humphrey died;
　　　They say, in him they fear your Highness' death;
250　　And mere instinct of love and loyalty,
　　　Free from a stubborn opposite intent,
　　　As being thought to contradict your liking,
　　　Makes them thus forward in his banishment.
　　　They say, in care of your most royal person,
255　　That if your Highness should intend to sleep,
　　　And charge that no man should disturb your rest
　　　In pain of your dislike, or pain of death,
　　　Yet, notwithstanding such a strait edict,
　　　Were there a serpent seen, with forkèd tongue,
260　　That slyly glided towards your Majesty,

250 **mere** pure　251 **opposite** antagonistic　258 **strait** strict

It were but necessary you were waked;
Lest, being suffered in that harmful slumber,
The mortal worm might make the sleep eternal.
And therefore do they cry, though you forbid,
That they will guard you, whe'r you will or no,   265
From such fell serpents as false Suffolk is;
With whose envenomèd and fatal sting
Your loving uncle, twenty times his worth,
They say, is shamefully bereft of life.

COMMONS *within* An answer from the King, my Lord
  of Salisbury!   270

SUFFOLK 'Tis like the commons, rude unpolished
    hinds,
  Could send such message to their sovereign:
  But you, my lord, were glad to be employed,
  To show how quaint an orator you are.
  But all the honor Salisbury hath won   275
  Is, that he was the Lord Ambassador
  Sent from a sort of tinkers to the King.

[COMMONS] *within* An answer from the King, or we
    will all break in!

KING Go, Salisbury, and tell them all from me,
  I thank them for their tender loving care;   280
  And had I not been cited so by them,
  Yet did I purpose as they do entreat;
  For sure, my thoughts do hourly prophesy
  Mischance unto my state by Suffolk's means.
  And therefore, by His Majesty I swear,   285
  Whose far unworthy deputy I am,
  He shall not breathe infection in this air
  But three days longer, on the pain of death.
                              Exit Salisbury.

QUEEN O Henry, let me plead for gentle Suffolk!

262 **suffered** allowed to continue   263 **mortal worm** deadly snake   265 **whe'r**
whether   266 **fell** cruel   271 **like** likely   271 **hinds** boors   274 **quaint** clever,
fine   277 **sort** group   281 **cited** incited, urged   289 **gentle** noble

290   KING Ungentle queen, to call him gentle Suffolk!
            No more, I say: if thou dost plead for him,
            Thou wilt but add increase unto my wrath.
            Had I but said, I would have kept my word;
            But when I swear, it is irrevocable.
            [To Suffolk] If after three days' space thou here be'st
295   found
            On any ground that I am ruler of,
            The world shall not be ransom for thy life.
            Come, Warwick, come, good Warwick, go with me;
            I have great matters to impart to thee.
                                    Exit King and Warwick.
                                    Manet Queen and Suffolk.

300   QUEEN Mischance and sorrow go along with you!
            Heart's discontent and sour affliction
            Be playfellows to keep you company!
            There's two of you; the Devil make a third!
            And threefold vengeance tend upon your steps!

305   SUFFOLK Cease, gentle Queen, these execrations,
            And let thy Suffolk take his heavy leave.

      QUEEN Fie, coward woman and soft-hearted wretch!
            Hast thou not spirit to curse thine enemy?

      SUFFOLK A plague upon them! wherefore should I curse
            them?
310   Would curses kill, as doth the mandrake's groan,
            I would invent as bitter searching terms,
            As curst, as harsh, and horrible to hear,
            Delivered strongly through my fixèd teeth,
            With full as many signs of deadly hate,
315   As lean-faced Envy in her loathsome cave.
            My tongue should stumble in mine earnest words;
            Mine eyes should sparkle like the beaten flint;
            Mine hair be fixed an end, as one distract;

290 Ungentle unkind, harsh   310 mandrake's groan the mandrake is a
poisonous plant, its forked root shaped like two human legs; when uprooted it
supposedly groaned like a human, the sound being fatal to any hearer
311 searching cutting, lancing (as in surgery)   318 an on   318 distract dis-
tracted, mad

Ay, every joint should seem to curse and ban:
And even now my burdened heart would break,   320
Should I not curse them. Poison be their drink!
Gall, worse than gall, the daintiest that they taste!
Their sweetest shade a grove of cypress trees!
Their chiefest prospect murd'ring basilisks!
Their softest touch as smart as lizards' stings!   325
Their music frightful as the serpent's hiss,
And boding screech-owls make the consort full!
All the foul terrors in dark-seated hell—

QUEEN Enough, sweet Suffolk; thou torment'st thyself;
And these dread curses, like the sun 'gainst glass,   330
Or like an overchargèd gun, recoil,
And turns the force of them upon thyself.

SUFFOLK You bade me ban, and will you bid me leave?
Now, by the ground that I am banished from,
Well could I curse away a winter's night,   335
Though standing naked on a mountain top,
Where biting cold would never let grass grow,
And think it but a minute spent in sport.

QUEEN O, let me entreat thee cease. Give me thy hand,
That I may dew it with my mournful tears;   340
Nor let the rain of heaven wet this place,
To wash away my woeful monuments.
O, could this kiss be printed in thy hand,
That thou mightst think upon these by the seal,
Through whom a thousand sighs are breathed for
        thee!   345
So, get thee gone, that I may know my grief;
'Tis but surmised whiles thou art standing by,
As one that surfeits thinking on a want.
I will repeal thee, or, be well assured,
Adventure to be banishèd myself: 350
And banishèd I am, if but from thee.
Go, speak not to me; even now be gone.

319 **curse and ban** formally excommunicate 323 **cypress** traditionally grown in
graveyards 324 **basilisks** mythical reptiles thought to kill by a glance
327 **consort** group of musicians 334 **these** i.e., these lips 350 **Adventure**
venture

O, go not yet! Even thus two friends condemned
Embrace and kiss and take ten thousand leaves,
355   Loather a hundred times to part than die.
Yet now farewell, and farewell life with thee!

SUFFOLK Thus is poor Suffolk ten times banishèd;
Once by the King, and three times thrice by thee.
'Tis not the land I care for, wert thou thence;
360   A wilderness is populous enough,
So Suffolk had thy heavenly company:
For where thou art, there is the world itself,
With every several pleasure in the world,
And where thou art not, desolation.
365   I can no more: live thou to joy thy life;
Myself to joy in nought but that thou liv'st.

                    Enter Vaux.

QUEEN Whither goes Vaux so fast? What news, I
    prithee?

VAUX To signify unto his Majesty
That Cardinal Beaufort is at point of death;
370   For suddenly a grievous sickness took him,
That makes him gasp, and stare, and catch the air,
Blaspheming God, and cursing men on earth.
Sometime he talks as if Duke Humphrey's ghost
Were by his side; sometime he calls the King,
375   And whispers to his pillow, as to him,
The secrets of his overchargèd soul:
And I am sent to tell his Majesty
That even now he cries aloud for him.

QUEEN Go tell this heavy message to the King.
                            Exit [Vaux].
380   Ay, me! What is this world! What news are these!
But wherefore grieve I at an hour's poor loss,
Omitting Suffolk's exile, my soul's treasure?
Why only, Suffolk, mourn I not for thee,
And with the southern clouds contend in tears,

363 **several** single

Theirs for the earth's increase, mine for my
    sorrows?   385
Now get thee hence: the King, thou know'st, is
    coming;
If thou be found by me, thou art but dead.

SUFFOLK If I depart from thee I cannot live;
    And in thy sight to die, what were it else
    But like a pleasant slumber in thy lap?   390
    Here could I breathe my soul into the air,
    As mild and gentle as the cradle-babe
    Dying with mother's dug between its lips;
    Where, from thy sight, I should be raging mad,
    And cry out for thee to close up mine eyes,   395
    To have thee with thy lips to stop my mouth:
    So shouldst thou either turn my flying soul,
    Or I should breathe it so into thy body,
    And then it lived in sweet Elysium.
    To die by thee were but to die in jest;   400
    From thee to die were torture more than death:
    O, let me stay, befall what may befall!

QUEEN Away! Though parting be a fretful corrosive,
    It is applièd to a deathful wound.
    To France, sweet Suffolk: let me hear from thee;   405
    For wheresoe'er thou art in this world's globe,
    I'll have an Iris that shall find thee out.

SUFFOLK I go.

QUEEN And take my heart with thee. *She kisseth him.*

SUFFOLK A jewel, locked into the wofull'st cask   410
    That ever did contain a thing of worth.
    Even as a splitted bark, so sunder we:
    This way fall I to death.   *Exit Suffolk*

QUEEN   This way for me.
                       Exit Queen.

---

385 **increase** fruition 403 **corrosive** caustic remedy 407 **Iris** Juno's messenger, and goddess of the rainbow

Scene III. [*A bedchamber.*]

*Enter the King, Salisbury, and Warwick; and then the
curtains be drawn, and the Cardinal is discovered in his
bed, raving and staring as if he were mad.*

KING How fares my lord? Speak, Beaufort, to thy
      sovereign.

CARDINAL If thou be'st Death, I'll give thee England's
      treasure,
      Enough to purchase such another island,
      So thou wilt let me live, and feel no pain.

5   KING Ah, what a sign it is of evil life,
      Where death's approach is seen so terrible!

WARWICK Beaufort, it is thy sovereign speaks to thee.

CARDINAL Bring me unto my trial when you will.
      Died he not in his bed? Where should he die?
10   Can I make men live, whe'r they will or no?
      O, torture me no more! I will confess.
      Alive again? Then show me where he is:
      I'll give a thousand pound to look upon him.
      He hath no eyes, the dust hath blinded them.
15   Comb down his hair; look, look! It stands upright,
      Like lime-twigs set to catch my wingèd soul.
      Give me some drink, and bid the apothecary
      Bring the strong poison that I bought of him.

   KING O thou eternal Mover of the heavens,
20   Look with a gentle eye upon this wretch!
      O, beat away the busy meddling fiend

III.iii.16 **lime-twigs** twigs smeared with bird-lime

That lays strong siege unto this wretch's soul
And from his bosom purge this black despair!

WARWICK See how the pangs of death do make him
  grin.

SALISBURY Disturb him not, let him pass peaceably.   25

KING Peace to his soul, if God's good pleasure be.
  Lord Cardinal, if thou think'st on heaven's bliss,
  Hold up thy hand, make signal of thy hope.
                              The Cardinal dies.
  He dies, and makes no sign. O God, forgive him!

WARWICK So bad a death argues a monstrous life.   30

KING Forbear to judge, for we are sinners all.
  Close up his eyes and draw the curtain close;
  And let us all to meditation.   *Exeunt.*

---

24 **grin** bare his teeth, grimace   30 **argues** suggests, betokens

ACT IV

Scene I. [*The Coast of Kent.*]

*Alarum. Fight at sea. Ordnance goes off. And then enter
the Lieutenant of the ship, and the Master, and the
Master's Mate, and the Duke of Suffolk, disguised, and
others with him, and Walter Whitmore.*

LIEUTENANT The gaudy, blabbing and remorseful day
Is crept into bosom of the sea,
And now loud-howling wolves arouse the jades
That drag the tragic melancholy night;
5 Who, with their drowsy, slow, and flagging wings
Clip dead men's graves, and from their misty jaws
Breathe foul contagious darkness in the air.
Therefore bring forth the soldiers of our prize,
For whilst our pinnace anchors in the Downs
10 Here shall they make their ransom on the sand,
Or with their blood stain this discolored shore.
Master, this prisoner freely give I thee;
And thou that art his mate, make boot of this;
The other, Walter Whitmore, is thy share.

FIRST GENTLEMAN What is my ransom, master? Let me
15   know.

IV.i.1 **Lieutenant** "Captain" in Q: i.e., the military commander of the pirate
ship   3 **jades** horses (contemptuous)   6 **Clip** embrace, hover over   9 **Downs**
bay area off the Kentish coast   13 **make boot of** profit by

198

MASTER A thousand crowns, or else lay down your head.

MATE And so much shall you give, or off goes yours.
                    [The prisoners react adversely.]

LIEUTENANT What! Think you much to pay two thou-
    sand crowns,
    And bear the name and port of gentlemen?
    Cut both the villains' throats; for die you shall: 20
    The lives of those which we have lost in fight
    Be counterpoised with such a petty sum!

FIRST GENTLEMAN I'll give it, sir; and therefore spare my
    life.

SECOND GENTLEMAN And so will I, and write home for
    it straight.

WHITMORE [*To Suffolk*] I lost mine eye in laying the
    prize aboard,   25
    And therefore to revenge it shalt thou die;
    And so should these, if I might have my will.

LIEUTENANT Be not so rash: take ransom, let him live.

SUFFOLK Look on my George; I am a gentleman.
    Rate me at what thou wilt, thou shalt be paid.   30

WHITMORE And so am I: my name is Walter Whitmore.
    How now! Why starts thou? What, doth death
    affright?

SUFFOLK Thy name affrights me, in whose sound is
    death.
    A cunning man did calculate my birth,
    And told me that by "water" I should die: 35
    Yet let not this make thee be bloody-minded;
    Thy name is Gaultier, being rightly sounded.

WHITMORE Gaultier or Walter, which it is I care not.
    Never yet did base dishonor blur our name,
    But with our sword we wiped away the blot.   40

19 **port** style, stature   29 **George** insignia or badge of the Order of the Garter, showing Saint George on horseback   34 **calculate my birth** cast my horoscope   35 **water** "Walter" is pronounced "water," and occasionally so spelled in Q and F

Therefore, when merchant-like I sell revenge,
Broke be my sword, my arms torn and defaced,
And I proclaimed a coward through the world!

SUFFOLK Stay, Whitmore, for thy prisoner is a prince,
45   The Duke of Suffolk, William de la Pole.

WHITMORE The Duke of Suffolk, muffled up in rags?

SUFFOLK Ay, but these rags are no part of the Duke:
Jove sometime went disguised, and why not I?

LIEUTENANT But Jove was never slain, as thou shalt be.

50   SUFFOLK Obscure and lousy swain, King Henry's blood,
The honorable blood of Lancaster,
Must not be shed by such a jaded groom.
Hast thou not kissed thy hand and held my stirrup?
Bare-headed plodded by my foot-cloth mule,
55   And thought thee happy when I shook my head?
How often has thou waited at my cup,
Fed from my trencher, kneeled down at the board,
When I have feasted with Queen Margaret?
Remember it, and let it make thee crest-fall'n,
60   Ay, and allay this thy abortive pride:
How in our voiding lobby hast thou stood
And duly waited for my coming forth.
This hand of mine hath writ in thy behalf,
And therefore shall it charm thy riotous tongue.

WHITMORE Speak, Captain, shall I stab the forlorn
65   swain?

LIEUTENANT First let my words stab him, as he hath me.

SUFFOLK Base slave, thy words are blunt, and so art
thou.

LIEUTENANT Convey him hence and on our long-boat's
side
Strike off his head.

52 **groom** low, ignoble fellow   54 **foot-cloth** ornamented with elaborate hangings, as in processions and tourneys   60 **abortive** monstrous, untimely
61 **voiding lobby** waiting-room   65 **forlorn swain** wretched (a) fellow (b) lover
(of the Queen)

SUFFOLK   Thou dar'st not, for thy own.

LIEUTENANT Yes, Poole!

SUFFOLK   Poole?   70

LIEUTENANT Ay, kennel, puddle, sink, whose filth
      and dirt
    Troubles the silver spring where England drinks.
    Now will I dam up this thy yawning mouth
    For swallowing the treasure of the realm;
    Thy lips, that kissed the Queen, shall sweep the
      ground;   75
    And thou that smil'dst at good Duke Humphrey's
      death
    Against the senseless winds shalt grin in vain,
    Who in contempt shall hiss at thee again.
    And wedded be thou to the hags of hell,
    For daring to affy a mighty lord   80
    Unto the daughter of a worthless king,
    Having neither subject, wealth, nor diadem.
    By devilish policy art thou grown great
    And like ambitious Sylla overgorged
    With gobbets of thy mother's bleeding heart.   85
    By thee Anjou and Maine were sold to France,
    The false revolting Normans thorough thee
    Disdain to call us lord, and Picardy
    Hath slain their governors, surprised our forts,
    And sent the ragged soldiers wounded home.   90
    The princely Warwick, and the Nevils all,
    Whose dreadful swords were never drawn in vain,
    As hating thee, are rising up in arms;
    And now the house of York, thrust from the crown
    By shameful murder of a guiltless king   95
    And lofty proud encroaching tyranny,
    Burns with revenging fire, whose hopeful colors

70 **Poole ... Poole** puns on "to poll" (shave the head, as for execution), "pool"
(cesspool), and "Pole" (de la Pole)   71 **kennel** gutter   80 **affy** betroth   84 **Sylla**
i.e., Sulla, dictator of Rome, who proscribed and persecuted followers of his rival
Marius. Rome (and for Suffolk, England) is represented as the "mother," and the
victims (e.g., Gloucester) as "gobbets"   87 **thorough** through (old form)

Advance our half-faced sun, striving to shine,
Under the which is writ *Invitis nubibus*.
100   The commons here in Kent are up in arms;
And, to conclude, reproach and beggary
Is crept into the palace of our King,
And all by thee. Away! Convey him hence.

SUFFOLK   O that I were a god, to shoot forth thunder
105   Upon these paltry, servile, abject drudges!
Small things make base men proud: this villain here,
Being captain of a pinnace, threatens more
Than Bargulus the strong Illyrian pirate.
Drones suck not eagles' blood, but rob bee-hives:
110   It is impossible that I should die
By such a lowly vassal as thyself.
Thy words move rage and not remorse in me.

LIEUTENANT   Ay, but my deeds shall stay thy fury soon.

SUFFOLK   I go of message from the Queen to France;
115   I charge thee waft me safely cross the Channel.

WHITMORE   Come, Suffolk, I must waft thee to thy
death.

SUFFOLK   *Pene gelidus timor occupat artus:* it is thee I
fear.

WHITMORE   Thou shalt have cause to fear before I leave
thee.
What, are ye daunted now? Now will ye stoop?

120   FIRST GENTLEMAN   My gracious lord, entreat him, speak
him fair.

SUFFOLK   Suffolk's imperial tongue is stern and rough,
Used to command, untaught to plead for favor.
Far be it we should honor such as these

98 **Advance our half-faced sun** raise high our insignia, the sun emerging from clouds (Edward III's personal badge)   99 **Invitis nubibus** "in spite of the clouds"   108 **Bargulus ... pirate** Bargalus or Bardulis, a pirate in Greek waters mentioned by Cicero   114 **France** i.e., the king of France   117 **Pene ... artus** "chill fear almost seizes my limbs": source unidentified, possibly a corrupt recollection of *Aeneid*, VII, 446

With humble suit: no, rather let my head
Stoop to the block than these knees bow to any,   125
Save to the God of heaven, and to my King;
And sooner dance upon a bloody pole
Than stand uncovered to the vulgar groom.
True nobility is exempt from fear:
More can I bear than you dare execute.   130

LIEUTENANT Hale him away, and let him talk no more.

SUFFOLK Come, soldiers, show what cruelty ye can,
That this my death may never be forgot.
Great men oft die by vile besonians:
A Roman sworder and banditto slave   135
Murdered sweet Tully; Brutus' bastard hand
Stabbed Julius Caesar; savage islanders
Pompey the Great; and Suffolk dies by pirates.
                    Exit Walter with Suffolk.

LIEUTENANT And as for these whose ransom we have set,
It is our pleasure one of them depart: 140
Therefore come you with us and let him go.
                    *Exit Lieutenant, and the rest;
                    manet the First Gentleman.*

              *Enter Walter [Whitmore] with the body
              [of Suffolk].*

WHITMORE There let his head and lifeless body lie,
Until the Queen his mistress bury it.   *Exit Walter.*

FIRST GENTLEMAN O barbarous and bloody spectacle!
His body will I bear unto the King: 145
If he revenge it not, yet will his friends;
So will the Queen, that living held him dear.
                    [Exit, with Suffolk's body.]

---

134 besonians base fellows, wretches   135 sworder gladiator   136 Tully
Cicero   136 Brutus' bastard hand a false tradition held that Brutus was Caesar's
bastard son

Scene II. [*Blackheath.*]

Enter Bevis and John Holland.

BEVIS Come, and get thee a sword, though made of a
lath: they have been up these two days.

HOLLAND They have the more need to sleep now, then.

BEVIS I tell thee, Jack Cade the clothier means to
5 dress the commonwealth, and turn it, and set a new
nap upon it.

HOLLAND So he had need, for 'tis threadbare. Well, I
say, it was never merry world in England since
gentlemen came up.

10 BEVIS O miserable age! virtue is not regarded in han-
dicraftsmen.

HOLLAND The nobility think scorn to go in leather
aprons.

BEVIS Nay, more, the King's Council are no good work-
15 men.

HOLLAN True: and yet it is said, "Labor in thy vocation"; which is as much to say as, "Let the magistrates be laboring men"; and therefore should we
be magistrates.

20 BEVIS Thou hast hit it: for there's no better sign of a
brave mind than a hard hand.

HOLLAND I see them! I see them! There's Best's son,
the tanner of Wingham.

IV.ii. s.d. Bevis and John Holland actors in the company: see note to
II.iii.92 **1–2 sword … lath** a mock-weapon, as employed by soldier-clowns in
the early Tudor plays **2 up** i.e., up in arms **9 came up** came into fashion
17–18 magistrates rulers, administrators

BEVIS He shall have the skins of our enemies, to make
dog's-leather of.   25

HOLLAND And Dick the butcher.

BEVIS Then is sin struck down like an ox, and iniquity's throat cut like a calf.

HOLLAND And Smith the weaver.

BEVIS *Argo*, their thread of life is spun.   30

HOLLAND Come, come, let's fall in with them.

*Drum. Enter Cade, Dick [the] Butcher, Smith the Weaver,
and a Sawyer, with infinite numbers.*

CADE We John Cade, so termed of our supposed
father—

DICK [*Aside*] Or rather, of stealing a cade of herrings.

CADE For our enemies shall fall before us, inspired   35
with the spirit of putting down kings and princes
... Command silence.

DICK Silence!

CADE My father was a Mortimer—

DICK [*Aside*] He was an honest man, and a good brick-   40
layer.

CADE My mother a Plantagenet—

DICK [*Aside*] I knew her well; she was a midwife.

CADE My wife descended of the Lacies—

DICK [*Aside*] She was indeed a pedlar's daughter, and   45
sold many laces.

SMITH [*Aside*] But now of late, not able to travel with
her furred pack, she washes bucks here at home.

---

25 **dog's-leather** leather for gloves   30 **Argo** corruption of Latin *ergo* =
therefore   34 **cade** barrel of five hundred   35 **fall** pun on Latin sense of "Cade"
(*cadere*, to fall)   47–48 **travel with her furred pack** (1) travel with a fur
knapsack, as a pedlar (2) labor as a prostitute   48 **washes bucks** (1) does rough
laundry (2) absolves cuckolds (by making them "even" with their wives)

CADE Therefore am I of an honorable house.

50 DICK [*Aside*] Ay, by my faith, the field is honorable; and there was he born, under a hedge: for his father had never a house but the cage.

CADE Valiant I am.

SMITH [*Aside*] 'A must needs, for beggary is valiant.

55 CADE I am able to endure much.

DICK [*Aside*] No question of that; for I have seen him whipped three market-days together.

CADE I fear neither sword nor fire.

SMITH [*Aside*] He need not fear the sword, for his
60 coat is of proof.

DICK [*Aside*] But methinks he should stand in fear of fire, being burnt i' th' hand for stealing of sheep.

CADE Be brave, then; for your captain is brave, and vows reformation. There shall be in England seven
65 halfpenny loaves sold for a penny; the three-hooped pot shall have ten hoops; and I will make it felony to drink small beer. All the realm shall be in common, and in Cheapside shall my palfry go to grass; and when I am King, as King I will be—

70 ALL God save your Majesty!

CADE I thank you, good people—there shall be no money; all shall eat and drink on my score; and I will apparel them all in one livery, that they may agree like brothers, and worship me their lord.

75 DICK The first thing we do, let's kill all the lawyers.

CADE Nay, that I mean to do. Is not this a lamentable

52 **cage** a temporary prison for vagabonds and harlots, commonly set up in marketplaces 60 **of proof** (1) reliable (2) wellworn 62 **burnt i' th' hand** with the letter "T," for "thief" 65-66 **three-hooped ... hoops** i.e., the quart measure will contain three quarts 67-68 **in common** held communally 68 **Cheapside** elegant commercial district of London 72 **on my score** at my expense

thing, that of the skin of an innocent lamb should
be made parchment? That parchment, being scribbled o'er, should undo a man? Some say the bee
stings; but I say, 'tis the bee's wax: for I did but   80
seal once to a thing, and I was never mine own
man since. How now! who's there?

Enter a Clerk, [led by others].

SMITH The clerk of Chatham: he can write and read,
and cast accompt.

CADE O monstrous!   85

SMITH We took him setting of boys' copies.

CADE Here's a villain!

SMITH H'as a book in his pocket with red letters in't.

CADE Nay, then, he is a conjurer.

DICK Nay, he can make obligations, and write court-   90
hand.

CADE I am sorry for't: the man is a proper man, of
mine honor; unless I find him guilty, he shall not
die. Come hither, sirrah, I must examine thee: what
is thy name?   95

CLERK Emmanuel.

DICK They use to write it on the top of letters: 'twill
go hard with you.

CADE Let me alone. Dost thou use to write thy name?
Or hast thou a mark to thyself, like an honest   100
plain-dealing man?

CLERK Sir, I thank God, I have been so well brought
up that I can write my name.

81-82 **mine own man** my own master   84 **accompt** account   86 **setting of
boys' copies** teaching schoolchildren to write   90 **obligations** bonds
90-91 **court-hand** formal legal script   97 **They ... letters** "Emmanuel" ("God
with us") was often prefixed to formal letters, deeds, etc.   100 **mark** i.e., an "X"

ALL He hath confessed: away with him! He's a villain
105   and a traitor.

CADE Away with him, I say! Hang him with his pen
and ink-horn about his neck.

Exit one with the Clerk.

Enter Michael.

MICHAEL Where's our general?

CADE Here I am, thou particular fellow.

110 MICHAEL Fly, fly, fly! Sir Humphrey Stafford and his
brother are hard by, with the King's forces.

CADE Stand, villain, stand, or I'll fell thee down. He
shall be encountered with a man as good as himself:
he is but a knight, is 'a?

115 MICHAEL No.

CADE To equal him, I will make myself a knight presently. [*Kneels.*] Rise up Sir John Mortimer. [*Rises.*]
Now have at him!

*Enter Sir Humphrey Stafford and his Brother,
with [a Herald], drum and Soldiers.*

STAFFORD Rebellious hinds, the filth and scum of Kent,
120   Marked for the gallows: lay your weapons down.
Home to your cottages, forsake this groom!
The King is merciful, if you revolt.

BROTHER But angry, wrathful, and inclined to blood,
If you go forward: therefore yield, or die.

125 CADE As for these silken-coated slaves, I pass not.
It is to you, good people, that I speak,
Over whom, in time to come, I hope to reign:
For I am rightful heir unto the crown.

STAFFORD Villain, thy father was a plasterer,
130   And thou thyself a shearman, art thou not?

109 **particular** private (pun on "general")   122 **revolt** turn (against Cade)
125 **pass** care   130 **shearman** worker with cloth

CADE And Adam was a gardener.

BROTHER And what of that?

CADE Marry, this: Edmund Mortimer, Earl of March,
  Married the Duke of Clarence' daughter, did he not?

STAFFORD Ay, sir.   135

CADE By her he had two children at one birth.

BROTHER That's false.

CADE Ay, there's the question; but I say, 'tis true:
  The elder of them, being put to nurse,
  Was by a beggar-woman stol'n away,   140
  And, ignorant of his birth and parentage,
  Became a bricklayer when he came to age:
  His son am I; deny it, if you can.

DICK Nay, 'tis too true; therefore he shall be king.

SMITH Sir, he made a chimney in my father's house,   145
  and the bricks are alive at this day to testify it; therefore deny it not.

STAFFORD And will you credit this base drudge's words,
  That speaks he knows not what?

ALL Ay, marry, will we; therefore get ye gone.   150

BROTHER Jack Cade, the Duke of York hath taught you
  this.

CADE [*Aside*] He lies, for I invented it myself.—Go
  to, sirrah, tell the King from me, that, for his father's
  sake, Henry the Fifth, in whose time boys went to   155
  span-counter for French crowns, I am content he
  shall reign; but I'll be Protector over him.

DICK And furthermore, we'll have the Lord Say's head
  for selling the Dukedom of Maine.

CADE And good reason: for thereby is England   160

156 **span-counter** a game played with marbles close up to the opponents;
figuratively close combat

mained, and fain to go with a staff, but that my
puissance holds it up. Fellow kings, I tell you that
that Lord Say hath gelded the commonwealth, and
made it an eunuch: and more than that, he can
165   speak French; and therefore he is a traitor.

STAFFORD O gross and miserable ignorance!

CADE Nay, answer, if you can: the Frenchmen are our
enemies; go to, then, I ask but this: can he that
speaks with the tongue of an enemy be a good
170   counselor, or no?

ALL No, no, and therefore we'll have his head.

BROTHER Well, seeing gentle words will not prevail,
Assail them with the army of the King.

STAFFORD Herald, away; and throughout every town
175   Proclaim them traitors that are up with Cade;
That those which fly before the battle ends
May, even in their wives' and children's sight,
Be hanged up for example at their doors:
And you that be the King's friends, follow me.
                    Exit [Staffords and their forces].

180   CADE And you that love the commons, follow me.
Now show yourselves men; 'tis for liberty.
We will not leave one lord, one gentleman:
Spare none but such as go in clouted shoon;
For they are thrifty honest men and such
185   As would, but that they dare not, take our parts.

DICK They are all in order and march towards us.

CADE But then are we in order when we are most out
of order. Come, march forward.   [Exeunt.]

---

161 **mained** maimed (variant spelling)   183 **clouted shoon** hobnailed boots

Scene III. [*Another part of Blackheath.*]

*Alarums to the fight, wherein both the Staffords
are slain. Enter Cade and the rest.*

CADE Where's Dick, the butcher of Ashford?

DICK Here, sir.

CADE They fell before thee like sheep and oxen, and
thou behav'dst thyself as if thou hadst been in thine
own slaughter-house: therefore thus will I reward   5
thee, the Lent shall be as long again as it is; and
thou shalt have a license to kill for a hundred
lacking one.

DICK I desire no more.

CADE And, to speak truth, thou deserv'st no less. [*He*   10
puts on Sir Humphrey's armor.] This monument
of the victory will I bear; and the bodies shall be
dragged at my horse heels till I do come to London,
where we will have the Mayor's sword borne before us.   15

DICK If we mean to thrive and do good, break open
the jails and let out the prisoners.

CADE Fear not that, I warrant thee. Come, let's march
towards London.   *Exeunt.*

IV.iii.7 **license to kill** only infirm persons were permitted to eat meat during
Lent, and favored butchers specially licensed to kill for them 7-8 **hundred
lacking one** i.e., ninety-nine years, the usual term of a lease

Scene IV. [*London. The Palace.*]

Enter the King with a supplication, and the Queen with
Suffolk's head, the Duke of Buckingham and the Lord
Say.

QUEEN [*Aside*] Oft have I heard that grief softens the
     mind
   And makes it fearful and degenerate:
   Think therefore on revenge, and cease to weep.
   But who can cease to weep and look on this?
5 Here may his head lie on my throbbing breast;
   But where's the body that I should embrace?

BUCKINGHAM What answer makes your Grace to the
   rebels' supplication?

KING I'll send some holy bishop to entreat;
10 For God forbid so many simple souls
   Should perish by the sword! And I myself,
   Rather than bloody war shall cut them short,
   Will parley with Jack Cade their General.
   But stay, I'll read it over once again.

QUEEN [*Aside*] Ah, barbarous villains! Hath this lovely
15   face
   Ruled, like a wandering planet over me,
   And could it not enforce them to relent,
   That were unworthy to behold the same?

KING Lord Say, Jack Cade hath sworn to have thy
   head.

20 SAY Ay, but I hope your Highness shall have his.

KING How now, madam!

IV.iv.16 **wandering planet** i.e., the star under which one is born,
astrologically

Still lamenting and mourning for Suffolk's death?
I fear me, love, if that I had been dead,
Thou wouldest not have mourned so much for me.

QUEEN No, my love, I should not mourn, but die for
    thee.   25

Enter a Messenger.

KING How now! What news? Why com'st thou in
    such haste?

MESSENGER The rebels are in Southwark: fly, my
    lord!
Jack Cade proclaims himself Lord Mortimer,
Descended from the Duke of Clarence' house,
And calls your Grace usurper openly,   30
And vows to crown himself in Westminster.
His army is a ragged multitude
Of hinds and presents, rude and merciless:
Sir Humphrey Stafford and his brother's death
Hath given them heart and courage to proceed.   35
All scholars, lawyers, courtiers, gentlemen,
They call false caterpillars and intend their death.

KING O graceless men! They know not what they do.

BUCKINGHAM My gracious lord, retire to Killing-
    worth,
Until a power be raised to put them down.   40

QUEEN Ah, were the Duke of Suffolk now alive,
These Kentish rebels would be soon appeased!

KING Lord Say, the traitors hateth thee;
Therefore away with us to Killingworth.

SAY So might your Grace's person be in danger.   45
The sight of me is odious in their eyes:
And therefore in this city will I stay,
And live alone as secret as I may.

---

37 **caterpillars** parasites (a common figure for capitalistic oppressors)   39 **Killingworth** Kenilworth Castle

Enter another Messenger.

SECOND MESSENGER Jack Cade hath gotten London
        Bridge!
50   The citizens fly and forsake their houses;
        The rascal people, thirsting after prey,
        Join with the traitor, and they jointly swear
        To spoil the city and your royal court.

BUCKINGHAM Then linger not, my lord; away, take
        horse.

KING Come, Margaret: God, our hope, will succor
55   us.

QUEEN My hope is gone, now Suffolk is deceased.

KING Farewell, my lord: trust not the Kentish rebels.

BUCKINGHAM Trust nobody, for fear you be betrayed.

SAY The trust I have is in mine innocence,
60   And therefore am I bold and resolute.   *Exeunt.*

Scene V. [*London, The Tower.*]

Enter Lord Scales upon the Tower, walking.
Then enters two or three Citizens below.

SCALES How now! Is Jack Cade slain?

FIRST CITIZEN No, my lord, nor likely to be slain; for
        they have won the Bridge, killing all those that
        withstand them: the Lord Mayor craves aid of your
5   honor from the Tower to defend the city from the
        rebels.

SCALES Such aid as I can spare you shall command,
        But I am troubled here with them myself:

_____

53 **spoil** despoil   56 **My ... deceased** (a possible "aside")

The rebels have assayed to win the Tower.
But get you to Smithfield, and gather head,   10
And thither I will send you Matthew Goffe.
Fight for your King, your country and your lives;
And so farewell, for I must hence again.

Exeunt.

Scene VI. [*London. Cannon Street.*]

*Enter Jack Cade and the rest, and strikes his
sword on London Stone.*

CADE Now is Mortimer lord of this city. And here,
sitting upon London Stone, I charge and command
that, of the city's cost, the pissing-conduit run
nothing but claret wine this first year of our reign.
And now henceforward it shall be treason for any   5
that calls me other than Lord Mortimer.

Enter a Soldier, running.

SOLDIER Jack Cade! Jack Cade!

CADE Knock him down there.   *They kill him.*

SMITH If this fellow be wise, he'll never call ye Jack
Cade more: I think he hath a very fair warning.   10

DICK My lord, there's an army gathered together in
Smithfield.

CADE Come, then, let's go fight with them: but first,
go and set London Bridge on fire; and if you can,
burn down the Tower too. Come, let's away.   15

Exeunt Omnes.

IV.vi.3 **pissing-conduit** an open gutter of drinking-water in London, derisively so
termed

Scene VII. [*London. Smithfield.*]

Alarums. Matthew Goffe is slain, and all the rest.
Then enter Jack Cade, with his company.

CADE So, sirs: now go some and pull down the
Savoy; others to th' Inns of Court; down with them
all.

DICK I have a suit unto your lordship.

5 CADE Be it a lordship, thou shalt have it for that
word.

DICK Only that the laws of England may come out
of your mouth.

HOLLAND [*Aside*] Mass, 'twill be sore law, then; for he
10 was trust in the mouth with a spear, and 'tis not
whole yet.

SMITH [*Aside*] Nay, John, it will be stinking law; for
his breath stinks with eating toasted cheese.

CADE I have thought upon it; it shall be so. Away,
15 burn all the records of the realm: my mouth shall
be the parliament of England.

HOLLAND [*Aside*] Then we are like to have biting
statutes, unless his teeth be pulled out.

CADE And henceforward all things shall be in com-
20 mon.

Enter a Messenger.

MESSENGER My lord, a prize, a prize! Here's the Lord
Say, which sold the towns in France; he that made

IV.vii.17 **biting** severe

us pay one and twenty fifteens, and one shilling
to the pound, the last subsidy.

Enter George, with the Lord Say.

CADE Well, he shall be beheaded for it ten times. Ah,   25
thou say, thou serge, nay, thou buckram lord, now
art thou within point-blank of our jurisdiction
regal! What canst thou answer to my Majesty
for giving up of Normandy unto Mounsieur
Basimecu, the Dolphin of France? Be it known   30
unto thee by these presence, even the presence of
Lord Mortimer, that I am the besom that must
sweep the court clean of such filth as thou art.
Thou hast most traitorously corrupted the youth
of the realm in erecting a grammar school: and   35
whereas before, our forefathers had no other books
but the score and the tally, thou hast caused printing to be used, and contrary to the King, his crown
and dignity, thou hast built a paper-mill. It will
be proved to thy face that thou hast men about   40
thee that usually talk of a noun and a verb, and
such abhominable words as no Christian ear can
endure to hear. Thou hast appointed justices of
peace, to call poor men before them about matters
they were not able to answer. Moreover, thou hast   45
put them in prison, and because they could not
read thou hast hanged them, when, indeed, only
for that cause they have been most worthy to live.
Thou dost ride on a foot-cloth, dost thou not?

23 one and twenty fifteens taxes (a gross exaggeration)   26 say ... serge ...
buckram puns on Lord Say's name: say is a silk cloth, resembling serge; serge a
serviceable but less elegant material; and buckram a coarse linen stiffened with
glue, commonly used in making theatrical properties   30 Basimecu pseudo-
French pun on *baise mon cul* = "kiss my backside"   30–31 Be ... presence play
on the formal beginning of documents, *Noverint universi per praesentes* ("Be it
known unto all by these presents")   32 besom broom   37–39 printing ...
paper-mill (fragrant anachronisms, perhaps intentionally humorous)   42 abhominable possibly a pun on *"ad hominem"*   46–47 because they could not read
refers to the legal exemption from hanging and other penalties ("benefit of clergy")
which Latin-reading offenders could claim   49 foot-cloth horse or mule decorated for a procession

50   SAY What of that?

CADE Marry, thou ought'st not let thy horse wear
a cloak, when honester men than thou go in their
hose and doublets.

DICK And work in their shirt too as myself, for ex-
55   ample, that am a butcher.

SAY You men of Kent—

DICK What say you of Kent?

SAY Nothing but this: 'tis *bona terra, mala gens.*

CADE Away with him, away with him! He speaks
60   Latin.

SAY Hear me but speak, and bear me where you will.
Kent, in the *Commentaries* Caesar writ,
Is termed the civil'st place of all this isle:
Sweet is the country, because full of riches;
65   The people liberal, valiant, active, wealthy;
Which makes me hope you are not void of pity.
I sold not Maine, I lost not Normandy,
Yet to recover them would lose my life.
Justice with favor have I always done;
Prayers and tears have moved me, gifts could
70   never.
When have I aught exacted at your hands,
But to maintain the King, the realm, and you?
Large gifts have I bestowed on learnèd clerks,
Because my book preferred me to the King,
75   And seeing ignorance is the curse of God,
Knowledge the wing wherewith we fly to heaven,
Unless you be possessed with devilish spirits,
You cannot but forbear to murder me:
This tongue hath parleyed unto foreign kings
80   For your behoof—

CADE Tut, when struck'st thou one blow in the field?

58 **bona terra, mala gens** good land, bad inhabitants 73 **clerks** scholars
74 **book** learning 80 **behoof** behalf

SAY Great men have reaching hands: oft have I
    struck
  Those that I never saw, and struck them dead.

GEORGE O monstrous coward! What, to come behind
  folks?   85

SAY These cheeks are pale for watching for your
  good.

CADE Give him a box o' th' ear and that will make
  'em red again.

SAY Long sitting to determine poor men's causes
  Hath made me full of sickness and diseases.   90

CADE Ye shall have a hempen caudle then and the
  help of hatchet.

DICK Why dost thou quiver, man?

SAY The palsy, and not fear, provokes me.

CADE Nay, he nods at us, as who should say, "I'll be   95
  even with you." I'll see if his head will stand
  steadier on a pole, or no: take him away, and be-
  head him.

SAY Tell me: wherein have I offended most?
  Have I affected wealth or honor? Speak!   100
  Are my chests filled up with extorted gold?
  Is my apparel sumptuous to behold?
  Whom have I injured, that ye seek my death?
  These hands are free from guiltless blood-shedding,
  This breast from harboring foul deceitful thoughts. 105
  O, let me live!

CADE [*Aside*] I feel remorse in myself with his
  words; but I'll bridle it: he shall die, and it be but

91-92 Ye ... hatchet you will be first hanged (a "caudle" is a curative gruel, a
"hempen caudle" a euphemism for hanging) and then beheaded   104 **guiltless
blood-shedding** shedding guiltless blood

for pleading so well for his life.—Away with him!
110   He has a familiar under his tongue; he speaks not
a God's name. Go, take him away, I say, and
strike off his head presently; and then break into
his son-in-law's house, Sir James Cromer, and
strike off his head, and bring them both upon two
115   poles hither.

ALL It shall be done.

SAY Ah, countrymen! If when you make your
prayers,
God should be so obdurate as yourselves,
How would it fare with your departed souls?
120   And therefore yet relent, and save my life.

CADE Away with him! And do as I command ye.
                                      [*Say is led away.*]
The proudest peer in the realm shall not wear a
head on his shoulders, unless he pay me tribute;
there shall not a maid be married, but she shall pay
125   to me her maidenhead ere they have it: men shall
hold of me *in capite;* and we charge and command that their wives be as free as heart can wish
or tongue can tell.

DICK My lord, when shall we go to Cheapside and
130   take up commodities upon our bills?

CADE Marry, presently.

ALL O, brave!

                    Enter one with the heads.

CADE But is not this braver? Let them kiss one another, for they loved well when they were alive.
135   Now part them again, lest they consult about the
giving up of some more towns in France. Soldiers,
defer the spoil of the city until night: for with these

110 **familiar** demonic attendant of a witch   111 **a** in   126 **in capite** in chief, the
legal term for holding property direct from the King, at the "head" of the
state   130 **take ... bills** (1) borrow money from usurers with promissory notes
(2) pillage property with our weapons

borne before us, instead of maces, will we ride
through the streets; and at every corner have them
kiss. Away!   *Exit* [*all*].   140

Scene VIII. [*Southwark*.]

Alarum and retreat.
Enter again Cade and all his rabblement.

CADE Up Fish Street! Down Saint Magnus' Corner!
Kill and knock down! Throw them into Thames!
(*Sound a parley*.) What noise is this I hear? Dare
any be so bold to sound retreat or parley, when I
command them kill?   5

Enter Buckingham and old Clifford.

BUCKINGHAM Ay, here they be that dare and will
   disturb thee:
Know, Cade, we come ambassadors from the King
Unto the commons whom thou hast misled,
And here pronounce free pardon to them all
That will forsake thee and go home in peace.   10

CLIFFORD What say ye, countrymen? Will ye relent,
And yield to mercy whilst 'tis offered you,
Or let a rebel lead you to your deaths?
Who loves the King and will embrace his pardon,
Fling up his cap, and say "God save his Majesty!"   15
Who hateth him and honors not his father,
Henry the Fifth, that made all France to quake,
Shake he his weapon at us and pass by.

ALL God save the King! God save the King!

CADE What, Buckingham and Clifford, are ye so   20
brave? And you, base peasants, do ye believe him?
Will you needs be hanged with your pardons about
your necks? Hath my sword therefore broke

221

through London gates, that you should leave me
25   at the White Hart in Southwark? I thought ye
would never have given out these arms till you had
recovered your ancient freedom: but you are all
recreants and dastards, and delight to live in slavery
to the nobility. Let them break your backs with
30   burdens, take your houses over your heads, ravish
your wives and daughters before your faces. For
me, I will make shift for one; and so, God's curse
light upon you all!

ALL We'll follow Cade, we'll follow Cade!

35   CLIFFORD Is Cade the son of Henry the Fifth,
That thus you do exclaim you'll go with him?
Will he conduct you through the heart of France,
And make the meanest of you earls and dukes?
Alas, he hath no home, no place to fly to;
40   Nor knows he how to live but by the spoil,
Unless by robbing of your friends and us.
Were't not a shame, that whilst you live at jar,
The fearful French, whom you late vanquishèd,
Should make a start o'er seas and vanquish you?
45   Methinks already in this civil broil
I see them lording it in London streets,
Crying "*Villiago!*" unto all they meet.
Better ten thousand base-born Cades miscarry
Than you should stoop unto a Frenchman's mercy.
50   To France, to France! and get what you have lost:
Spare England, for it is your native coast.
Henry hath money, you are strong and manly;
God on our side, doubt not of victory.

ALL A Clifford! A Clifford! We'll follow the King and
55   Clifford.

CADE Was ever feather so lightly blown to and fro as
this multitude? The name of Henry the Fifth hales
them to an hundred mischiefs and makes them

IV.viii.25 **White Hart in Southwark** inn where Cade lodged ("White Hart" puns
on pale, or cowardly, heart)   42 **at jar** quarreling   47 **Villiago** villain, coward
(Spanish or Italian)

leave me desolate. I see them lay their heads together to surprise me. My sword make way for me,   60
for here is no staying: in despite of the devils and
hell, have through the very middest of you! And
heavens and honor be witness that no want of resolution in me, but only my followers' base and
ignominious treasons, makes me betake me to my   65
heels.

He runs through them with his staff,
and flies away.

BUCKINGHAM What, is he fled? Go some, and follow
    him;
And he that brings his head unto the King
Shall have a thousand crowns for his reward.
                    Exeunt some of them.
Follow me, soldiers: we'll devise a mean   70
To reconcile you all unto the King.
                    Exeunt omnes.

Scene IX. [*Kenilworth Castle.*]

Sound trumpets. Enter King, Queen, and
Somerset, on the terrace.

KING Was ever king that joyed an earthly throne,
And could command no more content than I?
No sooner was I crept out of my cradle
But I was made a king, at nine months old.
Was never subject longed to be a king   5
As I do long and wish to be a subject.

Enter Buckingham and [old] Clifford.

BUCKINGHAM Health and glad tidings to your
    Majesty!

KING Why, Buckingham, is the traitor Cade sur-
    prised?
Or is he but retired to make him strong?

Enter multitudes, with halters about their necks.

CLIFFORD He is fled, my lord, and all his powers do
10   yield,
          And humbly thus, with halters on their necks,
          Expect your Highness' doom, of life or death.

KING Then, heaven, set ope thy everlasting gates,
      To entertain my vows of thanks and praise!
15   Soldiers, this day have you redeemed your lives
      And showed how well you love your Prince and
          country:
      Continue still in this so good a mind,
      And Henry, though he be infortunate,
      Assure yourselves, will never be unkind:
20   And so, with thanks and pardon to you all,
      I do dismiss you to your several countries.

ALL God save the King! God save the King!

Enter a Messenger.

MESSENGER Please it your Grace to be advertisèd
      The Duke of York is newly come from Ireland,
25   And with a puissant and a mighty power
      Of gallowglasses and stout kerns
      Is marching hitherward in proud array,
      And still proclaimeth, as he comes along,
      His arms are only to remove from thee
30   The Duke of Somerset, whom he terms a traitor.

KING Thus stands my state, 'twixt Cade and York
          distressed,
      Like to a ship, that having 'scaped a tempest,
      Is straightway calmed, and boarded with a pirate.
      But now is Cade driven back, his men dispersed;
35   And now is York in arms to second him.
      I pray thee, Buckingham, go and meet him,

IV.ix.11 **halters** nooses (a symbol of complete submission) 14 **entertain**
receive 21 **countries** counties, areas 23 **advertised** informed 26 **gallow-
glasses** heavily armed Irish footsoldiers 26 **kerns** light-armed troops 33 **with**
by

And ask him what's the reason of these arms.
Tell him I'll send Duke Edmund to the Tower,
And, Somerset, we will commit thee thither,
Until his army be dismissed from him.   40

SOMERSET My lord,
  I'll yield myself to prison willingly,
  Or unto death, to do my country good.

KING In any case, be not too rough in terms,
  For he is fierce, and cannot brook hard language.   45

BUCKINGHAM I will, my lord; and doubt not so to deal
  As all things shall redound unto your good.

KING Come, wife, let's in, and learn to govern better;
  For yet may England curse my wretched reign.
                                    Flourish. Exeunt.

Scene X. [*Kent. Iden's garden.*]

Enter Cade.

CADE Fie on ambitions! Fie on myself, that have a
  sword, and yet am ready to famish! These five days
  have I hid me in these woods and durst not peep
  out, for all the country is laid for me; but now
  am I so hungry that if I might have a lease of my   5
  life for a thousand years I could stay no longer.
  Wherefore, on a brick wall have I climbed into this
  garden, to see if I can eat grass, or pick a sallet
  another while, which is not amiss to cool a man's
  stomach this hot weather. And I think this word   10
  "sallet" was born to do me good: for many a time,
  but for a sallet, my brainpan had been cleft with

IV.x.4 laid set with traps 8 sallet (1) salad (2) iron helmet 9-10 cool a man's
stomach (1) satisfy a man's hunger and thirst (2) pacify a man's anger 10 word
pun on "wort," i.e. medicinal or edible herb

a brown bill; and many a time, when I have been
dry and bravely marching, it hath served me in-
15   stead of a quart pot to drink in; and now the word
"sallet" must serve me to feed on.

Enter [Alexander] Iden.

IDEN Lord, who would live turmoilèd in the court,
And may enjoy such quiet walks as these?
This small inheritance my father left me
20   Contenteth me, and worth a monarchy.
I seek not to wax great by others' waning,
Or gather wealth, I care not with what envy:
Sufficeth that I have maintains my state,
And sends the poor well pleasèd from my gate.

25   CADE Here's the lord of the soil come to seize me for
a stray, for entering his fee-simple without leave.
Ah, villain, thou wilt betray me, and get a thousand
crowns of the King by carrying my head to him:
but I'll make thee eat iron like an ostrich, and
30   swallow my sword like a great pin, ere thou and
I part.

IDEN Why, rude companion, whatsoe'er thou be,
I know thee not; why then should I betray thee?
Is't not enough to break into my garden,
35   And like a thief to come to rob my grounds,
Climbing my walls in spite of me the owner,
But thou wilt brave me with these saucy terms?

CADE Brave thee! Ay, by the best blood that ever
was broached, and beard thee too. Look on me
40   well: I have eat no meat these five days; yet, come
thou and thy five men, and if I do not leave you
all as dead as a doornail, I pray God I may never
eat grass more.

13 **brown bill** halberd used by constables   20 **worth** is worth   25-26 **Here's ...
leave** the absolute owner ("lord of the soil") of an estate ("fee-simple") was
entitled to impound any stray animal which wandered accidentally over the bounds
of the property   32 **companion** fellow (derogatory)   37 **brave** challenge
39 **beard thee** defy you to your face

IDEN Nay, it shall ne'er be said, while England
    stands,
  That Alexander Iden, an esquire of Kent,   45
  Took odds to combat a poor famished man.
  Oppose thy steadfast-gazing eyes to mine,
  See if thou canst outface me with thy looks;
  Set limb to limb, and thou art far the lesser:
  Thy hand is but a finger to my fist,   50
  Thy leg a stick comparèd with this truncheon;
  My foot shall fight with all the strength thou hast;
  And if mine arm be heavèd in the air,
  Thy grave is digged already in the earth.
  As for words, whose greatness answers words,   55
  Let this my sword report what speech forbears.

CADE By my valor, the most complete champion that
  ever I heard! Steel, if thou turn the edge, or cut
  not out the burly-boned clown in chines of beef
  ere thou sleep in thy sheath, I beseech God on my   60
  knees thou mayst be turned to hobnails.
              They fight, and Cade falls down.
  O, I am slain! Famine and no other hath slain
  me: let ten thousand devils come against me, and
  give me but the ten meals I have lost, and I'd defy
  them all. Wither, garden, and be henceforth a   65
  burying-place to all that do dwell in this house,
  because the unconquered soul of Cade is fled.

IDEN Is't Cade that I have slain, that monstrous
    traitor?
  Sword, I will hallow thee for this thy deed,
  And hang thee o'er my tomb when I am dead: 70
  Ne'er shall this blood be wipèd from thy point,
  But thou shalt wear it as a herald's coat,
  To emblaze the honor that thy master got.

CADE Iden, farewell, and be proud of thy victory.
  Tell Kent from me, she hath lost her best man,   75

46 **Took odds** relied on help   59 **chines** portion of flesh surrounding the
backbone   73 **emblaze** emblazon, set forth (as in a coat of arms)

and exhort all the world to be cowards: for I, that
never feared any, am vanquished by famine, not
by valor.   *Dies.*

IDEN How much thou wrong'st me, heaven be my
judge.
Die, damnèd wretch, the curse of her that bare
80   thee:
And as I thrust thy body in with my sword,
So wish I I might thrust thy soul to hell.
Hence will I drag thee headlong by the heels
Unto a dunghill which shall be thy grave,
85   And there cut off thy most ungracious head,
Which I will bear in triumph to the King,
Leaving thy trunk for crows to feed upon.

Exit.

83 **headlong** head downwards

ACT V

Scene I. [*Fields between London and Saint Albans.*]

*Enter York, and his army of Irish, with
drum and colors.*

YORK From Ireland thus comes York to claim his
    right,
And pluck the crown from feeble Henry's head.
Ring, bells, aloud; burn, bonfires, clear and bright,
To entertain great England's lawful king.
Ah, *sancta majestas!* Who would not buy thee
    dear?   5
Let them obey that knows not how to rule;
This hand was made to handle nought but gold.
I cannot give due action to my words,
Except a sword or scepter balance it:
A scepter shall it have, have I a soul,   10
On which I'll toss the fleur-de-luce of France.

Enter Buckingham.

Whom have we here? Buckingham, to disturb me?
The King hath sent him, sure: I must dissemble.

BUCKINGHAM York, if thou meanest well, I greet thee
    well.

V.i.5 **sancta majestas** holy majesty (Ovid)   11 **fleur-de-luce** fleur-de-lys, the
heraldic emblem of French kings

YORK Humphrey of Buckingham, I accept thy greet-
15   ing.
          Art thou a messenger, or come of pleasure?

BUCKINGHAM A messenger from Henry, our dread
          liege,
          To know the reason of these arms in peace;
          Or why thou, being a subject as I am,
20   Against thy oath and true allegiance sworn,
          Should raise so great a power without his leave,
          Or dare to bring thy force so near the court.

YORK [*Aside*] Scarce can I speak, my choler is so
          great.
          O, I could hew up rocks and fight with flint,
25   I am so angry at these abject terms;
          And now, like Ajax Telamonius,
          On sleep or oxen could I spend my fury.
          I am far better born than is the King,
          More like a king, more kingly in my thoughts:
30   But I must make fair weather yet awhile,
          Till Henry be more weak and I more strong.
          [*Aloud*] Buckingham, I prithee, pardon me,
          That I have given no answer all this while;
          My mind was troubled with deep melancholy.
35   The cause why I have brought this army hither
          Is to remove proud Somerset from the King,
          Seditious to his Grace, and to the state.

BUCKINGHAM That is too much presumption on thy
          part:
          But if thy arms be to no other end,
40   The King hath yielded unto thy demand:
          The Duke of Somerset is in the Tower.

YORK Upon thine honor, is he prisoner?

BUCKINGHAM Upon mine honor, he is prisoner.

YORK Then, Buckingham, I do dismiss my pow'rs.

25 **abject** degrading 26–27 **like Ajax … fury** Ajax, son of Telamon, in a mad
rage over being denied an honor, slaughtered a flock of sheep and then killed
himself

Soldiers, I thank you all; disperse yourselves;   45
Meet me tomorrow in Saint George's Field,
You shall have pay and everything you wish.
And let my sovereign, virtuous Henry,
Command my eldest son, nay, all my sons,
As pledges of my fealty and love;   50
I'll send them all as willing as I live:
Lands, goods, horse, armor, anything I have,
Is his to use, so Somerset may die.

BUCKINGHAM York, I commend this kind submission:
We twain will go into his Highness' tent.   55

Enter King and Attendants.

KING Buckingham, doth York intend no harm to us,
That thus he marcheth with thee arm in arm?

YORK In all submission and humility
York doth present himself unto your Highness.

KING Then what intends these forces thou dost bring?   60

YORK To heave the traitor Somerset from hence,
And fight against that monstrous rebel Cade,
Who since I heard to be discomfited.

Enter Iden, with Cade's head.

IDEN If one so rude and of so mean condition
May pass into the presence of a king,   65
Lo, I present your Grace a traitor's head,
The head of Cade, whom I in combat slew.

KING The head of Cade! Great God, how just art
Thou!
O, let me view his visage, being dead,
That living wrought me such exceeding trouble.   70
Tell me, my friend, art thou the man that slew him?

IDEN I was, an't like your Majesty.

KING How art thou called? And what is thy degree?

53 so provided that 54 kind natural, proper

IDEN Alexander Iden, that's my name;
75   A poor esquire of Kent, that loves his King.

BUCKINGHAM So please it you, my lord, 'twere not
          amiss
          He were created knight for his good service.

KING Iden, kneel down. [*He kneels.*] Rise up a knight.
        We give thee for reward a thousand marks,
80   And will that thou henceforth attend on us.

IDEN May Iden live to merit such a bounty,
        And never live but true unto his liege!

Enter Queen and Somerset.

KING See, Buckingham, Somerset comes with th'
          Queen:
        Go, bid her hide him quickly from the Duke.

85 QUEEN For thousand Yorks he shall not hide his head,
        But boldly stand and front him to his face.

YORK How now! Is Somerset at liberty?
        Then, York, unloose thy long-imprisoned thoughts,
        And let thy tongue be equal with thy heart.
90   Shall I endure the sight of Somerset?
        False King, why hast thou broken faith with me,
        Knowing how hardly I can brook abuse?
        King did I call thee? No, thou art not King,
        Not fit to govern and rule multitudes,
95   Which dar'st not, no, nor canst not rule a traitor.
        That head of thine doth not become a crown;
        Thy hand is made to grasp a palmer's staff,
        And not to grace an awful princely scepter.
        That gold must round engirt these brows of mine,
100   Whose smile and frown, like to Achilles' spear,
        Is able with the change to kill and cure.
        Here is a hand to hold a scepter up

86 **front** confront 92 **how hardly** with what difficulty 97 **palmer's staff**
insignia of the returned pilgrim, hence emblem of piety 100–1 **like ... cure**
Telephus, wounded by Achilles' spear, was supposedly cured by the application of
its rust

And with the same to act controlling laws.
Give place: by heaven, thou shalt rule no more
O'er him whom heaven created for thy ruler.   105

SOMERSET O monstrous traitor! I arrest thee, York,
    Of capital treason 'gainst the King and crown:
    Obey, audacious traitor; kneel for grace.

YORK Wouldst have me kneel? First let me ask of
    these,
    If they can brook I bow a knee to man.   110
    Sirrah, call in my sons to be my bail:
                      [*Exit Attendant*.]
    I know ere they will have me go to ward,
    They'll pawn their swords for my enfranchisement.

QUEEN Call hither Clifford; bid him come amain,
    To say if that the bastard boys of York   115
    Shall be the surety for their traitor father.
                      [*Exit Attendant*.]

YORK O blood-bespotted Neapolitan,
    Outcast of Naples, England's bloody scourge!
    The sons of York, thy betters in their birth,
    Shall be their father's bail; and bane to those   120
    That for my surety will refuse the boys!

        Enter Edward and Richard.

See where they come: I'll warrant they'll make it
    good.

        Enter Clifford and his Son.

QUEEN And here comes Clifford to deny their bail.

CLIFFORD (*Kneels to Henry*) Health and all happiness
    to my lord the King!

YORK I thank thee, Clifford: say, what news with thee?   125

---

109 **these** i.e., the troops   112 **to ward** into custody   117 **Neapolitan** traditionally murderous and fond of intrigue. Although Margaret was French, her father
claimed the throne of Naples (cf. I.i.47–48)

Nay, do not fright us with an angry look:
We are thy sovereign, Clifford, kneel again;
For thy mistaking so, we pardon thee.

CLIFFORD This is my King, York, I do not mistake;
130   But thou mistakes me much to think I do.
To Bedlam with him! Is the man grown mad?

KING Ay, Clifford; a bedlam and ambitious humor
Makes him oppose himself against his King.

CLIFFORD He is a traitor; let him to the Tower,
135   And chop away that factious pate of his.

QUEEN He is arrested, but will not obey;
His sons, he says, shall give their words for him.

YORK Will you not, sons?

EDWARD Ay, noble father, if our words will serve.

140   RICHARD And if words will not, then our weapons shall.

CLIFFORD Why, what a brood of traitors have we here!

YORK Look in a glass, and call thy image so.
I am thy King, and thou a false-heart traitor.
Call hither to the stake my two brave bears,
145   That with the very shaking of their chains
They may astonish these fell-lurking curs:
Bid Salisbury and Warwick come to me.

Enter the Earls of Warwick and Salisbury.

CLIFFORD Are these thy bears? We'll bait thy bears to
    death,
And manacle the bear'ard in their chains,
150   If thou dar'st bring them to the baiting place.

RICHARD Oft have I seen a hot o'erweening cur
Run back and bite, because he was withheld;
Who, being suffered, with the bear's fell paw

131 **Bedlam** Bethlehem Hospital in London, where insane persons were confined   132 **bedlam** crazy   146 **astonish** terrify   146 **fell-lurking** balefully skulking   149 **bear'ard** bear-ward, the keeper of bears intended for baiting in the ring   153 **suffered** loosed   153 **with** i.e., struck with

234

Hath clapped his tail between his legs and cried:
And such a piece of service will you do,   155
If you oppose yourselves to match Lord Warwick.

CLIFFORD Hence, heap of wrath, foul indigested lump,
    As crooked in thy manners as thy shape!

YORK Nay, we shall heat you thoroughly anon.

CLIFFORD Take heed, lest by your heat you burn your-
    selves.   160

KING Why, Warwick, hath thy knee forgot to bow?
    Old Salisbury, shame to thy silver hair,
    Thou mad misleader of thy brain-sick son!
    What, wilt thou on thy death-bed play the ruffian,
    And seek for sorrow with thy spectacles?   165
    O, where is faith? O, where is loyalty?
    If it be banished from the frosty head,
    Where shall it find a harbor in the earth?
    Wilt thou go dig a grave to find out war,
    And shame thine honorable age with blood?   170
    Why art thou old, and want'st experience?
    Or wherefore dost abuse it, if thou hast it?
    For shame! In duty bend thy knee to me,
    That bows unto the grave with mickle age.

SALISBURY My lord, I have considered with myself   175
    The title of this most renownèd duke,
    And in my conscience do repute his Grace
    The rightful heir to England's royal seat.

KING Hast thou not sworn allegiance unto me?

SALISBURY I have.   180

KING Canst thou dispense with heaven for such an
    oath?

SALISBURY It is great sin to swear unto a sin,
    But greater sin to keep a sinful oath.

157 **indigested** shapeless 165 **spectacles** organs of sight 171 **want'st**
lack 172 **abuse** misuse 174 **mickle** much, great 181 **dispense with** come to
terms with

Who can be bound by any solemn vow
185   To do a murd'rous deed, to rob a man,
To force a spotless virgin's chastity,
To reave the orphan of his patrimony,
To wring the widow from her customed right,
And have no other reason for this wrong
190   But that he was bound by a solemn oath?

QUEEN A subtle traitor needs no sophister.

KING Call Buckingham, and bid him arm himself.

YORK Call Buckingham, and all the friends thou hast,
I am resolved for death or dignity.

195   CLIFFORD The first I warrant thee, if dreams prove true.

WARWICK You were best to go to bed and dream again,
To keep thee from the tempest of the field.

CLIFFORD I am resolved to bear a greater storm
Than any thou canst conjure up today;
200   And that I'll write upon thy burgonet,
Might I but know thee by thy housèd badge.

WARWICK Now, by my father's badge, old Nevil's crest,
The rampant bear chained to the ragged staff,
This day I'll wear aloft my burgonet,
205   As on a mountain top the cedar shows
That keeps his leaves in spite of any storm,
Even to affright thee with the view thereof.

CLIFFORD And from thy burgonet I'll rend thy bear
And tread it under foot with all contempt,
210   Despite the bear'ard that protects the bear.

YOUNG CLIFFORD And so to arms, victorious father,
To quell the rebels and their complices.

RICHARD Fie! Charity, for shame! Speak not in spite,
For you shall sup with Jesu Christ tonight.

---

187 **reave** bereave, rob 188 **customed right** i.e., of part of her husband's estate
for life 191 **sophister** cunning spokesman 200 **burgonet** helmet
201 **housèd badge** emblem of the family

YOUNG CLIFFORD Foul stigmatic, that's more than thou
    canst tell.   215

RICHARD If not in heaven, you'll surely sup in hell.
                                       Exeunt.

Scene II. [*Saint Albans.*]

Enter Warwick.

WARWICK Clifford of Cumberland, 'tis Warwick calls:
    And if thou dost not hide thee from the bear,
    Now, when the angry trumpet sounds alarum,
    And dead men's cries do fill the empty air,
    Clifford, I say, come forth and fight with me!   5
    Proud northern lord, Clifford of Cumberland,
    Warwick is hoarse with calling thee to arms.

Enter York.

How now, my noble lord! What, all afoot?

YORK The deadly-handed Clifford slew my steed,
    But match to match I have encountered him,   10
    And made a prey for carrion kites and crows
    Even of the bonny beast he loved so well.

Enter Clifford.

WARWICK Of one or both of us the time is come.

YORK Hold, Warwick, seek thee out some other chase,
    For I myself must hunt this deer to death.   15

WARWICK Then, nobly, York; 'tis for a crown thou
    fight'st.
    As I intend, Clifford, to thrive today,
    It grieves my soul to leave thee unassailed.
                                     Exit Warwick.

215 **stigmatic** branded criminal, hence a deformed person (branded by God, as if
in punishment)   V.ii.14 **chase** game

CLIFFORD What seest thou in me, York? Why dost thou
    pause?

20 YORK With thy brave bearing should I be in love,
    But that thou art so fast mine enemy.

CLIFFORD Nor should thy prowess want praise and
    esteem,
    But that 'tis shown ignobly, and in treason.

YORK So let it help me now against thy sword,
25   As I in justice and true right express it.

CLIFFORD My soul and body on the action both!

YORK A dreadful lay! Address thee instantly.
                Alarums, and they fight, and
                York kills Clifford.

CLIFFORD *La fin couronne les œuvres.*   [*Dies.*]

YORK Thus war hath given thee peace, for thou art
    still.
30   Peace with his soul, heaven, if it be thy will!
                            Exit York.

Enter Young Clifford.

YOUNG CLIFFORD Shame and confusion! All is on the
    rout;
    Fear frames disorder, and disorder wounds
    Where it should guard. O war, thou son of hell,
    Whom angry heavens do make their minister,
35   Throw in the frozen bosoms of our part
    Hot coals of vengeance! Let no soldier fly.
    He that is truly dedicate to war
    Hath no self-love; nor he that loves himself
    Hath not essentially, but by circumstance,
    The name of valor. [*Sees his dead father.*] O, let the
40   vile world end,
    And the premisèd flames of the last day

27 **lay** wager 27 **Address** prepare 28 **La ... œuvres** "the end crowns the
work" 39 **not ... circumstance** not by nature, but by accident 41 **premisèd**
predestined

238

Knit earth and heaven together!
Now let the general trumpet blow his blast,
Particularities and petty sounds
To cease! Wast thou ordained, dear father,   45
To lose thy youth in peace, and to achieve
The silver livery of advisèd age,
And, in thy reverence and thy chair-days, thus
To die in ruffian battle? Even at this sight
My heart is turned to stone: and while 'tis mine,   50
It shall be stony. York not our old men spares;
No more will I their babes: tears virginal
Shall be to me even as the dew to fire,
And beauty, that the tyrant oft reclaims,
Shall to my flaming wrath be oil and flax.   55
Henceforth I will not have to do with pity:
Meet I an infant of the house of York,
Into as many gobbets will I cut it
As wild Medea young Absyrtus did:
In cruelty will I seek out my fame.   60
Come, thou new ruin of old Clifford's house:
As did Aeneas old Anchises bear,
So bear I thee upon my manly shoulders;
But then Aeneas bare a living load,
Nothing so heavy as these woes of mine.   65
                    Exit Young Clifford with his father.

*Enter the Duke of Somerset and Richard fighting, and
Richard kills him under the sign of the Castle, in Saint
Albans.*

RICHARD So, lie thou there;
For underneath an alehouse' paltry sign,
The Castle in Saint Albans, Somerset
Hath made the wizard famous in his death.
Sword, hold thy temper; heart, be wrathful still: 70
Priests pray for enemies, but princes kill.   *Exit.*

---

44 **Particularities** trifles 59 **As ... did** Medea, fleeing with Jason from Colchis,
murdered her brother Absyrtus and cut the body into pieces, so that her father
would be delayed in his pursuit

Fight. Excursions. Enter King, Queen,
and others.

QUEEN Away, my lord! You are slow; for shame,
    away!

KING Can we outrun the heavens? Good Margaret,
    stay.

QUEEN What are you made of? You'll nor fight nor
    fly:
75   Now is it manhood, wisdom, and defense,
    To give the enemy way, and to secure us
    By what we can, which can no more but fly.
                            Alarum afar off.
    If you be ta'en, we then should see the bottom
    Of all our fortunes: but if we haply scape—
80   As well we may, if not through your neglect—
    We shall to London get, where you are loved
    And where this breach now in our fortunes made
    May readily be stopped.

Enter [Young] Clifford.

YOUNG CLIFFORD But that my heart's on future mischief
    set,
85   I would speak blasphemy ere bid you fly:
    But fly you must; uncurable discomfit
    Reigns in the hearts of all our present parts.
    Away, for your relief, and we will live
    To see their day and them our fortune give.
90   Away, my lord, away!   *Exeunt.*

---

71 s.d. **Excursions** turbulent action   86 **discomfit** defeat

Scene III. [*Fields near Saint Albans.*]

*Alarum. Retreat. Enter York, Richard, Warwick,
and Soldiers, with drum and colors.*

YORK Of Salisbury, who can report of him,
That winter lion, who in rage forgets
Agèd contusions and all brush of time,
And, like a gallant in the brow of youth,
Repairs him with occasion? This happy day   5
Is not itself, nor have we won one foot,
If Salisbury be lost.

RICHARD   My noble father,
Three times today I holp him to his horse,
Three times bestrid him; thrice I led him off,
Persuaded him from any further act: 10
But still, where danger was, still there I met him;
And like rich hangings in a homely house,
So was his will in his old feeble body.
But, noble as he is, look where he comes.

Enter Salisbury.

Now, by my sword, well hast thou fought today.   15

SALISBURY By th' mass, so did we all. I thank you,
    Richard:
God knows how long it is I have to live,
And it hath pleased Him that three times today
You have defended me from imminent death.
Well, lords, we have not got that which we have: 20
'Tis not enough our foes are this time fled,
Being opposites of such repairing nature.

V.iii.5 **Repairs him with occasion** revives with opportunity   8 **holp** helped
9 **bestrid** straddled (to defend)   20 **we have not got that which we have** we
have not secured what we have acquired   22 **repairing nature** powers of
recovery

YORK I know our safety is to follow them;
        For, as I hear, the King is fled to London,
25   To call a present court of Parliament.
        Let us pursue him ere the writs go forth.
        What says Lord Warwick? Shall we after them?

WARWICK After them! Nay, before them, if we can.
        Now, by my hand, lords, 'twas a glorious day:
30   Saint Albans battle won by famous York
        Shall be eternized in all age to come.
        Sound drum and trumpets, and to London all:
        And more such days as these to us befall!   *Exeunt.*

FINIS

Textual Note

In 1594 appeared an anonymous quarto (Q) entitled
"THE/First part of the Con-/tention betwixt the two
famous Houses of Yorke/ and Lancaster, with the death
of the good/Duke Humphrey:/And the banishment and
death of the Duke of/*Suffolke*, and the Tragicall end of
the proud Cardinall/of *Winchester*, with the notable Rebel-
lion/of *Iacke Cade:/And the Duke of Yorkes first claime
unto the/Crowne*," consisting of some 2200 lines which
parallel closely and occasionally match the 1623 Folio
(F) text of *2 Henry VI*. Considered as an independent
play, Q is shorter, cruder, and vastly inferior in language
and characterization to F, but its relationship to the "finished" work offers an interesting problem. As early as
1734 it was theorized, by Lewis Theobald, that Q represents a primitive version of the play later revised by
Shakespeare and published. In 1787 Edmond Malone,
taking Greene's famous slur on the "upstart crow" to
imply plagiarism on Shakespeare's part, suggested that
Greene, and Peele, or possibly (1821) Marlowe, were the
original authors of *The Contention* and its companion
piece, *The True Tragedie of Richard Duke of Yorke* (1595),
which bears a similar relation to *3 Henry VI*.

In the late 1920s, however, with the studies of Peter
Alexander (*Shakespeare's Henry VI and Richard III*,
1929) and Madeleine Doran (*Henry VI*, 1928), a different explanation was advanced: that Q is actually a
mutilated and wholly derivative "bad" version of the
"good" text preserved in the Folio; that it derives, like
many other unauthorized Elizabethan quartos, from a
memorial reconstruction of the acted play—possibly by
the bit-player who took the parts of the Armorer, the
Spirit, the Mayor, Vaux, and Scales. In support of this
explanation it has been shown that Q contains frequent
echoes of unrelated contemporary plays such as Marlowe's

Edward II, and *Arden of Feversham*, as if the "reporter" who furnished the copy to the typesetter were fleshing out what he had memorized imperfectly with scraps of the rest of his repertory. The F text is relatively free of such contaminations.

Some modern scholars (Feuillerat, Prouty, J. D. Wilson) argue for a return to the "revision" theory, but the consensus opposes them. Good summaries of the conflicting evidence, and a discussion of the complications compounded by the third quarto (1619) of *The Contention*, may be found in G. B. Evans' review of Prouty's *The Contention and Shakespeare's '2 Henry VI'* (*JEGP*, LIII [1954], 628–37) and J. G. McManaway, "*The Contention* and *2 Henry VI*," *Wiener Beiträge zur Englischen Philologie*, LXV (1957), 143–154.

As a "bad" quarto, the textual utility of Q is slight, except in its stage directions, which are frequently fuller than those of F (e.g., I. i. 52 s.d., which occurs only in Q). In some passages, however (e.g., II. i. 125 ff., II. iii. 58 s.d. ff.) the F editors appear to have used slices of Q as printer's copy, possibly when the holograph script they employed primarily was defective or illegible; and in such instances the F text is likely to be mediocre, or misaligned (I. i. 64–65), and Q readings may be preferable. Basically the copy for F seems to have been an author's manuscript or "foul papers," but there is evidence as well of a theatrical bookkeeper's interpolations and cuts.

This edition follows F except where indicated in the following; stage directions derived from Q are so designated. Editorial additions are set off in square brackets; spelling, punctuation, and capitalization have been modernized; and names in speech prefixes and stage directions (e.g., Duke Humphrey *alias* Gloucester, Winchester *alias* Beaufort *alias* Cardinal) regularized. In a few instances verse has been slightly rearranged. The following list of significant departures from F gives the reading of the present text in bold, followed by a bracketed [Q] if the quarto provides the reading, and the F text, *literatim*, in roman.

TEXTUAL NOTE

I.i. s.d. **Enter ... Warwick** [Q] Enter King, Duke Humfrey, Salisbury, Warwicke, and Beauford on the one side. The Queene, Suffolke, Yorke, Somerset, and Buckingham, on the other 52 s.d. [Q] F omits   58 duchies [Q gives "Duches"] Dutchesse 64-65 **create thee/First** [Q] create thee the first   74 s.d. **Gloucester ... rest** [Q] Manet the rest   93 **had** hath   178 **Protector** [Q] Protectors 251 **surfeit in the** surfetting in   256 **in** [Q] in in

I.ii.60 s.d. follows line 59 [F, Q]   69 s.d. **Hum** [Q and chronicles] Hume

I.iii.13 **For** To   31 **That my master was?** That my Mistresse was?   32 **usurer** Vsurper   33-34 [Q] F omits   102 s.d. **sound** Exit. Sound   102 s.d. **Enter ... Winchester** [Q] Enter the King, Duke Humfrey, Cardinall, Buckingham, Yorke, Salisbury, Warwicke, and the Duchesse   144 **I'd** [Q] I could   152 **fury** Fume

I.iv.25 **Asnath** Asmath   36-38 Q prints as prose; probably a corruption of original octosyllabic couplets   41 s.d. **He sinks down again** [Q] Exit Spirit   53 s.d. [Q] F omits   62-63 **Aio ... posse** Aio Aeacida Romanos vincere posso   70-71 **hard ... understood** [Hibbard conj.] hardly attain'd,/ And hardly vnderstood

II.i. s.d. **with a hawk on her fist** [Q] F omits   25-26 **Good uncle, can you dote,/ To hide such malice with such holiness?** [Cairncross conj.] Good Vnkle hide such mallice:/ With such Holynesse can you doe it?   30 **Lord-Protectorship** Lords Protectorship   39-40 between these lines Q inserts the following: "**Humphrey.** Dare. I tell thee Priest, Plantagenets could neuer brooke the dare./**Card.** I am Plantagenet as well as thou, and sonne to Iohn of Gaunt./ **Humph.** In Bastardie./**Cardin.** I scorne thy words"   46-48 F gives all these lines to Gloucester   71 **by sight** by his sight   91 **Simpcox** Symon   107 **Alban** Albones   125-33 Q gives as prose; F, following the text of Q, aligns haphazardly as verse   132 **his** [Q] it   140-51 here F again follows the Q copy, which is aligned roughly as verse, yet prints these lines as prose. Probably they were verse originally, but so corrupt now that no plausible restoration of arrangement can be attempted

II.ii.35 **Philippa** Philip   47 **son, the son** Sonnes sonne   50 **Philippa** Phillip

II.iii. s.d. **Enter ... Warwick** [Q] Enter the King and State, with Guard, to banish the Duchesse   3 **sins** sinne   66 **i' faith I'll** [Q] yfaith, and Ile   69 **afeared** [Q] afraid   70-72 **Second Prentice ... a quart for me** [Q] F omits; and as F provides only two prentices, Second Prentice speaks the line here given to Third Prentice   75-77 **I thank ... my apron** [Q] I thanke you all: drinke, and pray for me, I pray you, for I thinke I haue taken my last Draught in this World. Here *Robin*, and if I dye, I giue thee my Aporne; and *Will*, thou shalt haue my Hammer   87-92 **Here's ... Ascapart** [Q] Masters, I am come hither as it were vpon my Mans instigation, to proue him a Knaue, and my selfe an honest man: and touching the Duke of Yorke, I will take my death, I neuer meant him any ill, nor the King, nor the Queene: and therefore **Peter** haue at thee with a downe-right blow   95 s.d. [Q] F omits

II.iv.16 s.d. **Enter ... halberds** [Q] Enter the Duchesse in a white Sheet, and a Taper burning in her hand, with the Sherife and officers 73 s.d. [Q] F omits

III.i.222 s.d. **Exit ... Warwick** [Q] Exit

245

TEXTUAL NOTE

III.ii. s.d. **Enter … Gloucester** [F] Here Q actually stages the murder on the inner stage, where Gloucester's body, concealed by curtains, remains throughout the scene: "Then the Curtaines being drawne, Duke **Humphrey** is discoured in his bed, and two men lying on his brest and smothering him in his bed. And then enter the Duke of **Suffolke** to them." But the F stage directions here, and at III.ii. 148 below, appear to intend eliminating this use of the inner stage: thus "Bed put forth" rather than "**Warwicke** drawes the curtaines and showes Duke **Humphrey** in his bed," and the lines of explanatory dialogue (III.ii.1–4) not found in Q. The Q staging, however, seems more efficient and theatrical, and has been partially retained in this text 14 s.d. **Buckingham** [Q] Suffolke 26 **Meg** Nell 79 **Margaret** Elianor 100 **Margaret** Elianor 116 **witch** watch 120 **Margaret** Elinor 121 s.d. **Salisbury** [Q] F omits 148 s.d. **Warwick … bed** [Q] Bed put forth [following line 146 in F] 202 s.d. **Exit Cardinal** [Q] F omits 265 **whe'r** where 288 s.d. **Exit Salisbury** [Q] F omits 299 **Exit … Suffolk** [Q] Exit 366 **to** no 409 s.d. **She kisseth him** [Q] F omits 413 s.d. **Exit Suffolk … Exit Queen** [Q] Exeunt [follows 413 in F]

III.iii. s.d. **and then … mad** [Q] to the Cardinal in bed [for the discrepancy compare III.ii. s.d. above] 10 **whe'r** [Q whether] where 28 s.d. **The Cardinal dies** [Q] F omits

IV.i. s.d. **And then … Whitmore** [Q with emendation from "Captaine" to "Lieutenant"] Enter Lieutenant, Suffolke and others 6 **Clip** Cleape 48 **Jove … I** [Q] F omits 50 **Obscure … blood** F assigns this line to the Lieutenant; Q to Suffolk 70 **Poole … Poole** [Q] Lieu[tenant]. Poole, Sir Poole? Lord 77 **shalt** shall 86 **mother's bleeding** Mother-bleeding 94 **are** and 114 **Ay … soon** [Q] F omits 117 **Whitmore** Lieu. Water: W 118 **Pene** Pine 133 **Come … can** F assigns to the Lieutenant

IV.ii.35 **fall** faile 83 **Chatham** [Q Chattam] Chartam 100 **an** a

IV.iv.24 **wouldest** would'st 58 **be betrayed** betraid

IV.v.2–6 **No … rebels** F and Q print as verse

IV.vi. s.d. **sword** [Q] staffe 9 **Smith** But[cher] [i.e., Dick]

IV.vii. 26 **serge** Surge 49 **on** [Q] in 72 **But** Kent 91 **caudle** Candle

IV.viii.13 **rebel** rabble 66 s.d. **He … away** [Q] Exit

IV.ix.33 **calmed** calme

IV.x.21 **waning** warning 27 **Ah** a 60 **God** [Q] Ioue 61 s.d. **They … down** [Q] Heere they Fight

V.i.109 **these** thee 111 **sons** sonne 113 **for** of 122 s.d. **and his son** [Q] F omits 124 s.d. **(Kneels to Henry.)** [Q] F omits 194 **or** and

V.ii.27 s.d. **Alarums … Clifford** [Q] F omits 28 **œuvres** eumenes 30 s.d. **Exit York** [Q] F omits 65 s.d. **Exit … father** [Q] F omits 65 s.d. **Enter Somerset … Albans** [Q] Enter Richard, and Somerset to fight 71 s.d. **Exit** [Q] F omits

V.iii.15 **Now … today** F assigns to Salisbury

WILLIAM SHAKESPEARE

THE THIRD PART OF HENRY THE SIXTH

WITH THE DEATH OF THE DUKE OF YORK

Edited by Milton Crane

KING HENRY THE SIXTH
EDWARD, Prince of Wales, his son
LEWIS XI, King of France
DUKE OF SOMERSET
DUKE OF EXETER
EARL OF OXFORD
EARL OF NORTHUMBERLAND
EARL OF WESTMORELAND
LORD CLIFFORD
RICHARD PLANTAGENET, Duke of York
EDWARD, Earl of March, afterwards King
   Edward IV
EDMUND, Earl of Rutland
} his sons
GEORGE, afterwards Duke of Clarence
RICHARD, afterwards Duke of Gloucester
DUKE OF NORFOLK
EARL OF WARWICK
MARQUESS OF MONTAGUE
EARL OF PEMBROKE
LORD HASTINGS
LORD STAFFORD
SIR JOHN MORTIMER
SIR HUGH MORTIMER
} uncles to the Duke of York
HENRY, Earl of Richmond, a youth
LORD RIVERS, brother to Lady Grey
SIR WILLIAM STANLEY
SIR JOHN MONTGOMERY
SIR JOHN SOMERVILLE
TUTOR TO RUTLAND

MAYOR OF YORK and ALDERMEN
MAYOR OF COVENTRY
LIEUTENANT OF THE TOWER
A NOBLEMAN
TWO KEEPERS
A HUNTSMAN
A SON THAT HAS KILLED HIS FATHER
A FATHER THAT HAS KILLED HIS SON
THE FRENCH ADMIRAL
QUEEN MARGARET
LADY ELIZABETH GREY, afterwards Queen to Edward IV
BONA, sister to the French Queen

SOLDIERS, ATTENDANTS, MESSENGERS, WATCHMEN, etc.
Scene: England and France]

THE THIRD PART OF
HENRY THE SIXTH
WITH THE DEATH OF
THE DUKE OF YORK

ACT I

Scene I. [*London. The Parliament House.*]

Alarum. Enter Plantagenet [the Duke of York], Edward,
Richard, Norfolk, Montague, Warwick, and Soldiers.

WARWICK I wonder how the King escaped our hands?

YORK While we pursued the horsemen of the North,
He slily stole away, and left his men;
Whereat the great Lord of Northumberland,
Whose warlike ears could never brook retreat,   5
Cheered up the drooping army; and himself,
Lord Clifford, and Lord Stafford all abreast
Charged our main battle's front, and, breaking in,
Were by the swords of common soldiers slain.

EDWARD Lord Stafford's father, Duke of Buckingham,   10
Is either slain or wounded dangerous.

Text references are printed in **boldface** type; the annotation follows in roman
type.
I.i. s.d. **Alarum** trumpet call to arms   5 **brook** endure   8 **battle's** army's
11 **dangerous** dangerously

I cleft his beaver with a downright blow;
That this is true, father, behold his blood.

[Shows his bloody sword.]

MONTAGUE And, brother, here's the Earl of Wiltshire's
blood,

15   Whom I encountered as the battles joined.

RICHARD Speak thou for me, and tell them what I did.

[Throws down the Duke of Somerset's head.]

YORK Richard hath best deserved of all my sons.
But is your Grace dead, my Lord of Somerset?

NORFOLK Such hope have all the line of John of
Gaunt!

20   RICHARD Thus do I hope to shake King Henry's head.

WARWICK And so do I, victorious Prince of York.
Before I see thee seated in that throne
Which now the house of Lancaster usurps,
I vow by heaven these eyes shall never close.

25   This is the palace of the fearful King,
And this the regal seat. Possess it, York;
For this is thine and not King Henry's heirs'.

YORK Assist me, then, sweet Warwick, and I will;
For hither we have broken in by force.

30   NORFOLK We'll all assist you. He that flies shall die.

YORK Thanks, gentle Norfolk; stay by me, my lords;
And, soldiers, stay and lodge by me this night.

They go up.

WARWICK And when the King comes, offer him no
violence,
Unless he seek to thrust you out perforce.

35   YORK The Queen this day here holds her parliament,

12 **beaver** visor 19 **Such … Gaunt!** may all of the line of John of Gaunt have such hope (ironical; though emendation of *hope* to *hap* [fate] is plausible) 25 **fearful** timorous 32 s.d. **go up** i.e., to the chair of state, presumably toward the rear of the stage

But little thinks we shall be of her council.
By words or blows here let us win our right.

RICHARD Armed as we are, let's stay within this house.

WARWICK The bloody parliament shall this be called,
Unless Plantagenet, Duke of York, be King,   40
And bashful Henry deposed, whose cowardice
Hath made us by-words to our enemies.

YORK Then leave me not, my lords. Be resolute;
I mean to take possession of my right.

WARWICK Neither the King, nor he that loves him best,   45
The proudest he that holds up Lancaster,
Dares stir a wing, if Warwick shake his bells.
I'll plant Plantagenet, root him up who dares.
Resolve thee, Richard; claim the English crown.
                    [*York seats himself in the throne.*]

*Flourish. Enter King Henry, Clifford, Northumber-
    land, Westmoreland, Exeter, and the rest.*

KING HENRY My lords, look where the sturdy rebel
    sits,   50
Even in the chair of state. Belike he means,
Backed by the power of Warwick, that false peer,
To aspire unto the crown and reign as king.
Earl of Northumberland, he slew thy father,
And thine, Lord Clifford; and you both have vowed
    revenge   55
On him, his sons, his favorites, and his friends.

NORTHUMBERLAND If I be not, heavens be revenged on
    me!

CLIFFORD The hope thereof makes Clifford mourn in
    steel.

WESTMORELAND What, shall we suffer this? let's pluck
    him down.
My heart for anger burns; I cannot brook it.   60

46 **holds up** supports 47 **bells** falcon's bells 49 s.d. **Flourish** trumpet
fanfare 51 **Belike** apparently 58 **steel** armor 59 **suffer** allow 60 **brook**
endure

KING HENRY Be patient, gentle Earl of Westmoreland.

CLIFFORD Patience is for poltroons, such as he.
    He durst not sit there, had your father lived.
    My gracious lord, here in the parliament
65 Let us assail the family of York.

NORTHUMBERLAND Well hast thou spoken, cousin.
    Be it so.

KING HENRY Ah, know you not the city favors them,
    And they have troops of soldiers at their beck?

EXETER But when the Duke is slain, they'll quickly fly.

KING HENRY Far be the thought of this from Henry's
70   heart,
    To make a shambles of the Parliament House!
    Cousin of Exeter, frowns, words, and threats
    Shall be the war that Henry means to use.
    Thou factious Duke of York, descend my throne,
75 And kneel for grace and mercy at my feet.
    I am thy sovereign.

YORK   I am thine.

EXETER For shame, come down; he made thee Duke
    of York.

YORK It was my inheritance, as the earldom was.

EXETER Thy father was a traitor to the crown.

80 WARWICK Exeter, thou art a traitor to the crown
    In following this usurping Henry.

CLIFFORD Whom should he follow but his natural king?

WARWICK True, Clifford; that's Richard Duke of
    York.

KING HENRY And shall I stand, and thou sit in my
    throne?

85 YORK It must and shall be so: content thyself.

---

61 **gentle** noble 62 **poltroons** cowards 66 **cousin** kinsman 71 **shambles**
slaughterhouse 74 **factious** rebellious

WARWICK Be Duke of Lancaster; let him be King.

WESTMORELAND He is both King and Duke of Lan-
      caster;
And that the Lord of Westmoreland shall maintain.

WARWICK And Warwick shall disprove it. You forget
That we are those which chased you from the field   90
And slew your fathers, and with colors spread
Marched through the city to the palace gates.

NORTHUMBERLAND Yes, Warwick, I remember it to my
      grief,
And, by his soul, thou and thy house shall rue it.

WESTMORELAND Plantagenet, of thee and these thy
      sons,   95
Thy kinsmen and thy friends, I'll have more lives
Than drops of blood were in my father's veins.

CLIFFORD Urge it no more, lest that, instead of words,
I send thee, Warwick, such a messenger
As shall revenge his death before I stir.   100

WARWICK Poor Clifford; how I scorn his worthless
      threats!

YORK Will you we show our title to the crown?
If not, our swords shall plead it in the field.

KING HENRY What title has thou, traitor, to the
      crown?
Thy father was, as thou art, Duke of York;   105
Thy grandfather, Roger Mortimer, Earl of March.
I am the son of Henry the Fifth,
Who made the Dolphin and the French to stoop
And seized upon their towns and provinces.

WARWICK Talk not of France, sith thou hast lost it
      all.   110

91 **colors** flags   100 **his** i.e., my father's   102 **title** legal right   103 **plead**
defend   108 **Dolphin** Dauphin   108 **stoop** yield   110 **sith** since

KING HENRY The Lord Protector lost it, and not I.
When I was crowned I was but nine months old.

RICHARD You are old enough now, and yet methinks
you lose.
Father, tear the crown from the usurper's head.

115 EDWARD Sweet father, do so; set it on your head.

MONTAGUE Good brother, as thou lov'st and honorest
arms,
Let's fight it out and not stand caviling thus.

RICHARD Sound drums and trumpets, and the King
will fly.

YORK Sons, peace!

KING HENRY Peace, thou! and give King Henry leave
120   to speak.

WARWICK Plantagenet shall speak first. Hear him,
lords;
And be you silent and attentive too,
For he that interrupts him shall not live.

KING HENRY Think'st thou that I will leave my kingly
throne,
125   Wherein my grandsire and my father sat?
No: first shall war unpeople this my realm;
Ay, and their colors, often borne in France,
And now in England to our heart's great sorrow,
Shall be my winding-sheet. Why faint you, lords?
130   My title's good, and better far than his.

WARWICK Prove it, Henry, and thou shalt be King.

KING HENRY Henry the Fourth by conquest got the
crown.

YORK 'Twas by rebellion against his king.

---

111 **Lord Protector** Humphrey, Duke of Gloucester   113 **yet** even now
117 **stand** waste time   129 **faint** lose heart

KING HENRY [*Aside*] I know not what to say; my title's
    weak.—
  Tell me, may not a king adopt an heir?   135

YORK What then?

KING HENRY And if he may, then am I lawful king;
  For Richard, in the view of many lords,
  Resigned the crown to Henry the Fourth,
  Whose heir my father was, and I am his.   140

YORK He rose against him, being his sovereign,
  And made him to resign his crown perforce.

WARWICK Suppose, my lords, he did it unconstrained,
  Think you 'twere prejudicial to his crown?

EXETER No; for he could not so resign his crown   145
  But that the next heir should succeed and reign.

KING HENRY Art thou against us, Duke of Exeter?

EXETER His is the right, and therefore pardon me.

YORK Why whisper you, my lords, and answer not?

EXETER My conscience tells me he is lawful king.   150

KING HENRY [*Aside*] All will revolt from me, and turn
    to him.

NORTHUMBERLAND Plantagenet, for all the claim thou
    lay'st,
  Think not that Henry shall be so deposed.

WARWICK Deposed he shall be, in despite of all.

NORTHUMBERLAND Thou art deceived. 'Tis not thy
    Southern power,   155
  Of Essex, Norfolk, Suffolk, nor of Kent,
  Which makes thee thus presumptuous and proud,
  Can set the Duke up in despite of me.

CLIFFORD King Henry, be thy title right or wrong,

137 **And if it**   155 **power army**

160   Lord Clifford vows to fight in thy defense:
    May that ground gape and swallow me alive,
    Where I shall kneel to him that slew my father!

KING HENRY O Clifford, how thy words revive my
    heart!

YORK Henry of Lancaster, resign thy crown.
165   What mutter you, or what conspire you, lords?

WARWICK Do right unto this princely Duke of York,
    Or I will fill the house with armèd men,
    And over the chair of state, where now he sits,
    Write up his title with usurping blood.
            He stamps with his foot, and the Soldiers show
                                themselves.

KING HENRY My Lord of Warwick, hear me but one
170   word:
    Let me for this my lifetime reign as king.

YORK Confirm the crown to me and to mine heirs,
    And thou shalt reign in quiet while thou liv'st.

KING HENRY I am content. Richard Plantagenet,
175   Enjoy the kingdom after my decease.

CLIFFORD What wrong is this unto the Prince your son?

WARWICK What good is this to England and himself!

WESTMORELAND Base, fearful, and despairing Henry!

CLIFFORD How hast thou injured both thyself and us!

180 WESTMORELAND I cannot stay to hear these articles.

NORTHUMBERLAND Nor I.

CLIFFORD Come, cousin, let us tell the Queen these
    news.

WESTMORELAND Farewell, faint-hearted and degenerate
    king,
    In whose cold blood no spark of honor bides.

180 **articles** terms of agreement

NORTHUMBERLAND Be thou a prey unto the house of
   York,   185
And die in bands for this unmanly deed!

CLIFFORD In dreadful war mayst thou be overcome,
Or live in peace abandoned and despised!
                    [*Exeunt Northumberland, Clifford and
                                        Westmoreland.*]

WARWICK Turn this way, Henry, and regard them not.

EXETER They seek revenge, and therefore will not
   yield.   190

KING HENRY Ah, Exeter!

WARWICK   Why should you sigh, my lord?

KING HENRY Not for myself, Lord Warwick, but my
   son,
Whom I unnaturally shall disinherit.
But be it as it may. [*To York*] I here entail   195
The crown to thee and to thine heirs for ever;
Conditionally, that here thou take an oath
To cease this civil war; and, whilst I live,
To honor me as thy king and sovereign;
And neither by treason nor hostility
To seek to put me down and reign thyself.   200

YORK This oath I willingly take and will perform.
                        [*Comes from the throne.*]

WARWICK Long live King Henry! Plantagenet,
   embrace him.

KING HENRY And long live thou and these thy
   forward sons!

YORK Now York and Lancaster are reconciled.

EXETER Accursed be he that seeks to make them foes!   205
             Sennet. Here they come down.

186 **bands** bonds 195 **entail** settle, bestow (as property) 203 **forward**
eager 205 s.d. **Sennet** trumpet call signaling the approach or departure of
processions

YORK Farewell, my gracious lord; I'll to my castle.

WARWICK And I'll keep London with my soldiers.

NORFOLK And I to Norfolk with my followers.

MONTAGUE And I unto the sea from whence I came.

[*Exeunt York and his sons, Warwick, Norfolk, and Montague, with their Soldiers, and Attendants.*]

210 KING HENRY And I with grief and sorrow to the court.

Enter the Queen [Margaret, and Edward the Prince of Wales].

EXETER Here comes the Queen, whose looks bewray
    her anger.
    I'll steal away.

KING HENRY   Exeter, so will I.

QUEEN MARGARET Nay, go not from me. I will follow
    thee.

KING HENRY Be patient, gentle Queen, and I will stay.

QUEEN MARGARET Who can be patient in such ex-
215   tremes?
    Ah, wretched man! Would I had died a maid,
    And never seen thee, never borne thee son,
    Seeing thou hast proved so unnatural a father!
    Hath he deserved to lose his birthright thus?
220 Hadst thou but loved him half so well as I,
    Or felt that pain which I did for him once,
    Or nourished him as I did with my blood,
    Thou wouldst have left thy dearest heart-blood
        there,
    Rather than have made that savage duke thine heir
225 And disinherited thine only son.

PRINCE Father, you cannot disinherit me.
    If you be King, why should not I succeed?

211 **bewray** reveal

KING HENRY Pardon me, Margaret. Pardon me, sweet
 son.
 The Earl of Warwick and the Duke enforced me.

QUEEN MARGARET Enforced thee? Art thou King, and
 wilt be forced?   230
 I shame to hear thee speak. Ah, timorous wretch!
 Thou hast undone thyself, thy son, and me;
 And giv'n unto the house of York such head
 As thou shalt reign but by their sufferance.
 To entail him and his heirs unto the crown,   235
 What is it, but to make thy sepulcher,
 And creep into it far before thy time?
 Warwick is Chancellor and the lord of Calais;
 Stern Falconbridge commands the Narrow Seas;
 The Duke is made Protector of the realm;   240
 And yet shalt thou be safe? Such safety finds
 The trembling lamb environèd with wolves.
 Had I been there, which am a silly woman,
 The soldiers should have tossed me on their pikes
 Before I would have granted to that act.   245
 But thou preferr'st thy life before thine honor:
 And seeing thou dost, I here divorce myself
 Both from thy table, Henry, and thy bed,
 Until that act of parliament be repealed
 Whereby my son is disinherited.   250
 The Northern lords, that have forsworn thy colors,
 Will follow mine, if once they see them spread;
 And spread they shall be, to thy foul disgrace
 And utter ruin of the house of York.
 Thus do I leave thee. Come, son, let's away.   255
 Our army is ready; come, we'll after them.

KING HENRY Stay, gentle Margaret, and hear me
 speak.

QUEEN MARGARET Thou hast spoke too much already;
 get thee gone.

233 **head** advantage 234 **sufferance** permission 239 **Narrow Seas** English
Channel 243 **silly** helpless 245 **granted** assented

KING HENRY Gentle son Edward, thou wilt stay with
    me?

260 QUEEN MARGARET Ay, to be murdered by his enemies.

PRINCE When I return with victory from the field,
    I'll see your Grace: till then I'll follow her.

QUEEN MARGARET Come, son, away; we may not linger
    thus. [*Exeunt Queen Margaret and the Prince.*]

KING HENRY Poor Queen! how love to me and to her
    son
265 Hath made her break out into terms of rage!
Revenged may she be on that hateful Duke,
Whose haughty spirit, wingèd with desire,
Will cost my crown, and like an empty eagle
Tire on the flesh of me and of my son!
270 The loss of those three lords torments my heart.
I'll write unto them and entreat them fair.
Come, cousin, you shall be the messenger.

EXETER And I, I hope, shall reconcile them all.

                            Exeunt.

Scene II. [*Sandal Castle, near Wakefield,
in Yorkshire.*]

Flourish. Enter Richard, Edward, and Montague.

RICHARD Brother, though I be youngest, give me leave.

EDWARD No, I can better play the orator.

MONTAGUE But I have reasons strong and forcible.

---

268 cost (with pun on *coast* = attack) 269 Tire prey or feed ravenously
upon 271 entreat them fair treat them courteously

Enter the Duke of York.

YORK Why, how now, sons and brother! at a strife?
  What is your quarrel? How began it first?   5

EDWARD No quarrel, but a slight contention.

YORK About what?

RICHARD About that which concerns your Grace and
    us—
  The crown of England, father, which is yours.

YORK Mine, boy? Not till King Henry be dead.   10

RICHARD Your right depends not on his life or death.

EDWARD Now you are heir; therefore enjoy it now.
  By giving the house of Lancaster leave to breathe,
  It will outrun you, father, in the end.

YORK I took an oath that he should quietly reign.   15

EDWARD But for a kingdom any oath may be broken.
  I would break a thousand oaths to reign one year.

RICHARD No; God forbid your Grace should be
    forsworn.

YORK I shall be, if I claim by open war.

RICHARD I'll prove the contrary, if you'll hear me
    speak.   20

YORK Thou canst not, son; it is impossible.

RICHARD An oath is of no moment, being not took
  Before a true and lawful magistrate,
  That hath authority over him that swears:
  Henry had none, but did usurp the place;   25
  Then, seeing 'twas he that made you to depose,
  Your oath, my lord, is vain and frivolous.
  Therefore, to arms! And, father, do but think
  How sweet a thing it is to wear a crown,
  Within whose circuit is Elysium   30

I.ii.6 **contention** dispute 18 **forsworn** perjured 26 **depose** take an oath
27 **vain and frivolous** worthless and insufficient

And all that poets feign of bliss and joy.
Why do we linger thus? I cannot rest
Until the white rose that I wear be dyed
Even in the lukewarm blood of Henry's heart.

35 YORK   Richard, enough; I will be King, or die.
Brother, thou shalt to London presently,
And whet on Warwick to this enterprise.
Thou, Richard, shalt to the Duke of Norfolk,
And tell him privily of our intent.
40   You, Edward, shall unto my Lord Cobham,
With whom the Kentishmen will willingly rise.
In them I trust; for they are soldiers,
Witty, courteous, liberal, full of spirit.
While you are thus employed, what resteth more,
45   But that I seek occasion how to rise,
And yet the King not privy to my drift,
Nor any of the house of Lancaster?

Enter [a Messenger] Gabriel.

But stay! What news? Why com'st thou in such
   post?

MESSENGER   The Queen with all the Northern earls
   and lords
50   Intend here to besiege you in your castle:
She is hard by with twenty thousand men;
And therefore fortify your hold, my lord.

YORK   Ay, with my sword. What! think'st thou that
   we fear them?
Edward and Richard, you shall stay with me;
55   My brother Montague shall post to London.
Let noble Warwick, Cobham, and the rest,
Whom we have left protectors of the King,
With pow'rful policy strengthen themselves,
And trust not simple Henry nor his oaths.

---

31 **feign** relate in fiction   36 **presently** at once   43 **Witty** wise   43 **liberal**
generous, gentlemanly   44 **resteth** remains   46 **drift** aim   47 s.d. **Gabriel**
(probably not the name of the messenger, but of Gabriel Spencer, the actor who
played the part)   48 **post** haste   52 **hold** stronghold   58 **policy** secret plans

MONTAGUE Brother, I go. I'll win them, fear it not: 60
   And thus most humbly I do take my leave.
                             Exit Montague.

   Enter [Sir John] Mortimer and [Sir Hugh]
             his Brother.

YORK Sir John and Sir Hugh Mortimer, mine uncles,
   You are come to Sandal in a happy hour;
   The army of the Queen mean to besiege us.

SIR JOHN She shall not need, we'll meet her in the field.   65

YORK What, with five thousand men?

RICHARD Ay, with five hundred, father, for a need.
   A woman's general. What should we fear?
                           A march afar off.

EDWARD I hear their drums: let's set our men in order,
   And issue forth and bid them battle straight.   70

YORK Five men to twenty! Though the odds be great,
   I doubt not, uncle, of our victory.
   Many a battle have I won in France,
   When as the enemy hath been ten to one.
   Why should I not now have the like success?   75
                      Alarum. Exeunt.

    Scene III. [*Field of battle between Sandal Castle*
            and Wakefield.]

     Enter Rutland and his Tutor.

RUTLAND Ah, whither shall I fly to 'scape their hands?
   Ah, tutor, look where bloody Clifford comes!

     Enter Clifford [and Soldiers].

CLIFFORD Chaplain, away! thy priesthood saves thy life.

60 **fear** doubt   63 **happy** fortunate   67 **for a need** if necessary, i.e., if so many
are needed   70 **straight** at once

As for the brat of this accursèd duke,
5   Whose father slew my father, he shall die.

TUTOR And I, my lord, will bear him company.

CLIFFORD Soldiers, away with him!

TUTOR Ah, Clifford, murder not this innocent child,
Lest thou be hated both of God and man!
Exit [dragged off by Soldiers].

10   CLIFFORD How now! Is he dead already? Or is it fear
That makes him close his eyes? I'll open them.

RUTLAND So looks the pent-up lion o'er the wretch
That trembles under his devouring paws;
And so he walks, insulting o'er his prey,
15   And so he comes, to rend his limbs asunder.
Ah, gentle Clifford, kill me with thy sword
And not with such a cruel threat'ning look.
Sweet Clifford, hear me speak before I die.
I am too mean a subject for thy wrath;
20   Be thou revenged on me, and let me live.

CLIFFORD In vain thou speak'st, poor boy; my father's
blood
Hath stopped the passage where thy words should
enter.

RUTLAND Then let my father's blood open it again.
He is a man, and, Clifford, cope with him.

25   CLIFFORD Had I thy brethren here, their lives and thine
Were not revenge sufficient for me;
No, if I digged up thy forefathers' graves
And hung their rotten coffins up in chains,
It could not slake mine ire, nor ease my heart.
30   The sight of any of the house of York
Is as a Fury to torment my soul;
And till I root out their accursèd line
And leave not one alive, I live in hell.
Therefore—

I.iii.14 **insulting** exulting 19 **mean** unworthy 26 **sufficient** (as often in
Shakespeare, *-ient* is here disyllabic)

RUTLAND O, let me pray before I take my death!
　　To thee I pray. Sweet Clifford, pity me!   35

CLIFFORD Such pity as my rapier's point affords.

RUTLAND I never did thee harm. Why wilt thou slay
　　me?

CLIFFORD Thy father hath.

RUTLAND　　　　　　　　But 'twas ere I was born.
　　Thou hast one son. For his sake pity me,   40
　　Lest in revenge thereof, sith God is just,
　　He be as miserably slain as I.
　　Ah, let me live in prison all my days;
　　And when I give occasion of offense,
　　Then let me die, for now thou hast no cause.   45

CLIFFORD No cause?
　　Thy father slew my father. Therefore die.
　　　　　　　　　　　　　　　　　　　[Stabs him.]

RUTLAND *Di faciant laudis summa sit ista tuae!*
　　　　　　　　　　　　　　　　　　　　[Dies.]

CLIFFORD Plantagenet! I come, Plantagenet!
　　And this thy son's blood cleaving to my blade   50
　　Shall rust upon my weapon, till thy blood,
　　Congealed with this, do make me wipe off both.
　　　　　　　　　　　　　　　　　　　　Exit.

41 **sith** since　　48 **Di … tuae!** Ovid, *Heroides* ii.66 (Phyllis to Demophoon): The gods grant that this may be the peak of thy glory!

Scene IV. [*Another part of the field.*]

Alarum. Enter Richard, Duke of York.

YORK The army of the Queen hath got the field:
My uncles both are slain in rescuing me;
And all my followers to the eager foe
Turn back and fly, like ships before the wind
5   Or lambs pursued by hunger-starvèd wolves.
My sons, God knows what hath bechancèd them:
But this I know, they have demeaned themselves
Like men born to renown by life or death.
Three times did Richard make a lane to me,
10 And thrice cried "Courage, father! fight it out!"
And full as oft came Edward to my side,
With purple falchion, painted to the hilt
In blood of those that had encountered him:
And when the hardiest warriors did retire,
Richard cried, "Charge! and give no foot of
15   ground!"
And cried, "A crown, or else a glorious tomb!
A scepter, or an earthly sepulcher!"
With this, we charged again: but out, alas!
We budged again, as I have seen a swan
20 With bootless labor swim against the tide
And spend her strength with overmatching waves.
                              A short alarum within.
Ah, hark! The fatal followers do pursue,
And I am faint, and cannot fly their fury.
And were I strong, I would not shun their fury.

I.iv.1 **got** won   4 **Turn back** turn their backs   6 **bechancèd** happened to
7 **demeaned** behaved   12 **purple** red, i.e., with blood   12 **falchion** curved
sword   18 **out** (interjection expressing regret)   19 **budged** flinched   20 **bootless** unavailing   22 **fatal** destined   24 **And were I** if I were

The sands are numbered that makes up my life.   25
Here must I stay, and here my life must end.

Enter the Queen [Margaret], Clifford, Northumberland,
the young Prince [of Wales], and Soldiers.

Come, bloody Clifford, rough Northumberland,
I dare your quenchless fury to more rage.
I am your butt, and I abide your shot.

NORTHUMBERLAND Yield to our mercy, proud
      Plantagenet.   30

CLIFFORD Ay, to such mercy as his ruthless arm,
With downright payment showed unto my father.
Now Phaëthon hath tumbled from his car,
And made an evening at the noontide prick.

YORK My ashes, as the phoenix, may bring forth   35
A bird that will revenge upon you all;
And in that hope I throw mine eyes to heaven,
Scorning whate'er you can afflict me with.
Why come you not? what? multitudes, and fear?

CLIFFORD So cowards fight when they can fly no
      further;   40
So doves do peck the falcon's piercing talons;
So desperate thieves, all hopeless of their lives,
Breathe out invectives 'gainst the officers.

YORK O Clifford, but bethink thee once again,
And in thy thought o'errun my former time;   45
And, if thou canst for blushing, view this face,
And bite thy tongue, that slanders him with
      cowardice
Whose frown hath made thee faint and fly ere this!

---

25 **makes** (the singular form of the verb is often used with a plural subject)
29 **butt** a mark set up for archers to shoot at   29 **abide** endure   33 **Phaëthon**
... **car** (the son of Phoebus Apollo was killed while trying to drive his father's
chariot)   34 **noontide prick** mark on a sundial face indicating noon   45 **o'errun**
review   47 **bite thy tongue** keep silent

CLIFFORD I will not bandy with thee word for word,
50   But buckler with thee blows, twice two for one.

QUEEN MARGARET Hold, valiant Clifford! For a thou-
        sand causes
     I would prolong awhile the traitor's life.
     Wrath makes him deaf: speak thou, Northumber-
        land.

NORTHUMBERLAND Hold, Clifford! Do not honor him
        so much
55   To prick thy finger, though to wound his heart.
     What valor were it, when a cur doth grin,
     For one to thrust his hand between his teeth,
     When he might spurn him with his foot away?
     It is war's prize to take all vantages;
60   And ten to one is no impeach of valor.
                    [*They lay hands on York, who struggles.*]

CLIFFORD Ay, ay, so strives the woodcock with the gin.

NORTHUMBERLAND So doth the cony struggle in the
        net.

YORK So triumph thieves upon their conquered
        booty;
     So true men yield, with robbers so o'er-matched.

NORTHUMBERLAND What would your Grace have done
65   unto him now?

QUEEN MARGARET Brave warriors, Clifford and North-
        umberland,
     Come, make him stand upon this molehill here
     That raught at mountains with outstretchèd arms,
     Yet parted but the shadow with his hand.
70   What, was it you that would be England's king?
     Was't you that reveled in our parliament,
     And made a preachment of your high descent?
     Where are your mess of sons to back you now?

50 **buckler** grapple in combat 56 **grin** show his teeth 58 **spurn** kick
59 **vantages** opportunities 60 **impeach of** detraction from 61 **gin** trap
62 **cony** rabbit (metaphorically, a gull or dupe) 63 **triumph** exult 68 **raught**
reached 73 **mess** set of four

The wanton Edward, and the lusty George?
And where's that valiant crookback prodigy,   75
Dicky your boy, that with his grumbling voice
Was wont to cheer his dad in mutinies?
Or, with the rest, where is your darling, Rutland?
Look, York, I stained this napkin with the blood
That valiant Clifford, with his rapier's point,   80
Made issue from the bosom of the boy;
And if thine eyes can water for his death,
I give thee this to dry thy cheeks withal.
Alas, poor York! but that I hate thee deadly,
I should lament thy miserable state.   85
I prithee grieve, to make me merry, York.
What, hath thy fiery heart so parched thine entrails
That not a tear can fall for Rutland's death?
Why art thou patient, man? Thou shouldst be mad;
And I, to make thee mad, do mock thee thus.   90
Stamp, rave, and fret, that I may sing and dance.
Thou wouldst be fee'd, I see, to make me sport.
York cannot speak, unless he wear a crown.
A crown for York! and, lords, bow low to him.
Hold you his hands whilst I do set it on.   95
                 [*Puts a paper crown on his head.*]
Ay, marry, sir, now looks he like a king!
Ay, this is he that took King Henry's chair
And this is he was his adopted heir.
But how is it that great Plantagenet
Is crowned so soon, and broke his solemn oath?   100
As I bethink me, you should not be King
Till our King Henry had shook hands with death.
And will you pale your head in Henry's glory,
And rob his temples of the diadem,
Now in his life, against your holy oath?   105
O, 'tis a fault too too unpardonable!
Off with the crown, and with the crown his head!
And whilst we breathe, take time to do him dead.

75 **prodigy** monster   79 **napkin** handkerchief   87 **entrails** (thought of as the
seat of sympathy)   92 **fee'd** paid   96 **marry** (a mild oath, from "By the Virgin
Mary")   103 **pale** enclose, encircle

CLIFFORD That is my office, for my father's sake.

QUEEN MARGARET Nay, stay. Let's hear the orisons he
110   makes.
YORK She-wolf of France, but worse than wolves of
          France,
      Whose tongue more poisons than the adder's tooth!
      How ill-beseeming is it in thy sex
      To triumph like an Amazonian trull
115   Upon their woes whom fortune captivates!
      But that thy face is vizard-like, unchanging,
      Made impudent with use of evil deeds,
      I would assay, proud queen, to make thee blush.
      To tell thee whence thou cam'st, of whom derived,
      Were shame enough to shame thee, wert thou not
120   shameless.
      Thy father bears the type of King of Naples,
      Of both the Sicils and Jerusalem,
      Yet not so wealthy as an English yeoman.
      Hath that poor monarch taught thee to insult?
125   It needs not, nor it boots thee not, proud queen,
      Unless the adage must be verified,
      That beggars mounted run their horse to death.
      'Tis beauty that doth oft make women proud;
      But God he knows thy share thereof is small.
130   'Tis virtue that doth make them most admired;
      The contrary doth make thee wondered at.
      'Tis government that makes them seem divine;
      The want thereof makes thee abominable.
      Thou art as opposite to every good
135   As the Antipodes are unto us,
      Or as the South to the Septentrion.
      O tiger's heart wrapped in a woman's hide!
      How couldst thou drain the lifeblood of the child,
      To bid the father wipe his eyes withal,
140   And yet be seen to bear a woman's face?

114 **trull** prostitute 116 **vizard-like** masklike 121 **type** title 122 **both the
Sicils** Naples and Sicily 125 **boots** avails 132 **government** self-control
136 **Septentrion** North 137 **O ... hide!** (parodied by Robert Greene in *A
Groatsworth of Wit* [1592])

Women are soft, mild, pitiful, and flexible;
Thou stern, obdurate, flinty, rough, remorseless.
Bid'st thou me rage? Why, now thou hast thy wish.
Wouldst have me weep? Why, now thou hast thy
    will.
For raging wind blows up incessant showers,   145
And when the rage allays the rain begins.
These tears are my sweet Rutland's obsequies,
And every drop cries vengeance for his death,
'Gainst thee, fell Clifford, and thee, false French-
    woman.

NORTHUMBERLAND Beshrew me, but his passions
    moves me so   150
That hardly can I check my eyes from tears.

YORK That face of his the hungry cannibals
Would not have touched, would not have stained
    with blood;
But you are more inhuman, more inexorable,
O, ten times more, than tigers of Hyrcania.   155
See, ruthless queen, a hapless father's tears:
This cloth thou dipp'd'st in blood of my sweet boy,
And I with tears do wash the blood away.
Keep thou the napkin, and go boast of this;
And if thou tell'st the heavy story right,   160
Upon my soul, the hearers will shed tears;
Yea, even my foes will shed fast-falling tears
And say "Alas, it was a piteous deed!"
There, take the crown, and, with the crown, my
    curse;
And in thy need such comfort come to thee   165
As now I reap at thy too cruel hand!
Hard-hearted Clifford, take me from the world.
My soul to heaven, my blood upon your heads!

NORTHUMBERLAND Had he been slaughterman to all
    my kin,

149 **fell** fierce, savage   150 **Beshrew** curse   155 **Hyrcania** region of the Caspian
Sea

170   I should not for my life but weep with him
           To see how inly sorrow gripes his soul.

           QUEEN MARGARET What! weeping-ripe, my Lord
               Northumberland?
           Think but upon the wrong he did us all,
           And that will quickly dry thy melting tears.

           CLIFFORD Here's for my oath! here's for my father's
175   death!   [Stabs him.]

           QUEEN MARGARET And here's to right our gentlehearted
               king!   [Stabs him.]

           YORK Open Thy gate of mercy, gracious God!
           My soul flies through these wounds to seek out
               Thee.   [Dies.]

           QUEEN MARGARET Off with his head, and set it on York
               gates,
180   So York may overlook the town of York.
                                              Flourish. Exeunt.

171 inly inwardly   171 gripes grieves   172 weeping-ripe ready to weep

ACT II

Scene I. [*A plain near Mortimer's Cross in Herefordshire.*]

A march. Enter Edward, Richard, and their Power.

EDWARD I wonder how our princely father 'scaped,
    Or whether he be 'scaped away or no
    From Clifford's and Northumberland's pursuit.
    Had he been ta'en, we should have heard the news;
    Had he been slain, we should have heard the news;   5
    Or had he 'scaped, methinks we should have heard
    The happy tidings of his good escape.
    How fares my brother? Why is he so sad?

RICHARD I cannot joy, until I be resolved
    Where our right valiant father is become.   10
    I saw him in the battle range about
    And watched him how he singled Clifford forth.
    Methought he bore him in the thickest troop
    As doth a lion in a herd of neat,
    Or as a bear, encompassed round with dogs,   15
    Who having pinched a few and made them cry,
    The rest stand all aloof, and bark at him.
    So fared our father with his enemies;

II.i.s.d. **Power** army   8 **sad** serious   9 **resolved** freed from doubt   10 **Where ... is become** where ... has gone   12 **singled ... forth** selected (for hunting)   13 **Methought** it seemed to me   14 **neat** cattle   16 **pinched** nipped

So fled his enemies my warlike father:
20   Methinks 'tis prize enough to be his son.
See how the morning opes her golden gates,
And takes her farewell of the glorious sun!
How well resembles it the prime of youth,
Trimmed like a younker prancing to his love!

25   EDWARD   Dazzle mine eyes, or do I see three suns?

RICHARD   Three glorious suns, each one a perfect sun;
Not separated with the racking clouds,
But severed in a pale clear-shining sky.
See, see! they join, embrace, and seem to kiss,
30   As if they vowed some league inviolable:
Now are they but one lamp, one light, one sun.
In this the heaven figures some event.

EDWARD   'Twas wondrous strange, the like yet never
heard of.
I think it cites us, brother, to the field,
35   That we, the sons of brave Plantagenet,
Each one already blazing by our meeds,
Should notwithstanding join our lights together
And overshine the earth as this the world.
Whate'er it bodes, henceforward will I bear
40   Upon my target three fair-shining suns.

RICHARD   Nay, bear three daughters. By your leave I
speak it,
You love the breeder better than the male.

Enter one blowing [a horn].

But what art thou, whose heavy looks foretell
Some dreadful story hanging on thy tongue?

45   MESSENGER   Ah, one that was a woeful looker-on
Whenas the noble Duke of York was slain,
Your princely father and my loving lord!

24 **younker** young man   25 **Dazzle mine eyes** are my eyes dazzled
27 **racking** driving   32 **figures** prefigures   34 **cites** calls   36 **meeds** merits
40 **target** shield   40 **suns** (pun on "sons")   42 **breeder** childbearer

EDWARD O, speak no more, for I have heard too
    much.

RICHARD Say how he died, for I will hear it all.

MESSENGER Environèd he was with many foes,   50
    And stood against them, as the hope of Troy
    Against the Greeks that would have entered Troy.
    But Hercules himself must yield to odds;
    And many strokes, though with a little ax,
    Hews down and fells the hardest-timbered oak.   55
    By many hands your father was subdued;
    But only slaughtered by the ireful arm
    Of unrelenting Clifford and the Queen,
    Who crowned the gracious Duke in high despite,
    Laughed in his face, and when with grief he wept,   60
    The ruthless Queen gave him, to dry his cheeks,
    A napkin steepèd in the harmless blood
    Of sweet young Rutland, by rough Clifford slain;
    And after many scorns, many foul taunts,
    They took his head, and on the gates of York   65
    They set the same; and there it doth remain,
    The saddest spectacle that e'er I viewed.

EDWARD Sweet Duke of York, our prop to lean upon,
    Now thou art gone, we have no staff, no stay.
    O Clifford, boist'rous Clifford! thou hast slain   70
    The flow'r of Europe for his chivalry;
    And treacherously hast thou vanquished him,
    For hand to hand he would have vanquished thee.
    Now my soul's palace is become a prison.
    Ah, would she break from hence, that this my body   75
    Might in the ground be closèd up in rest!
    For never henceforth shall I joy again;
    Never, O never, shall I see more joy.

RICHARD I cannot weep; for all my body's moisture
    Scarce serves to quench my furnace-burning heart;   80
    Nor can my tongue unload my heart's great burden,
    For selfsame wind that I should speak withal

51 **the hope of Troy** i.e., Hector   59 **high despite** haughty contempt   69 **stay**
support   70 **boist'rous** savage   82 **wind** breath

        Is kindling coals that fires all my breast,
        And burns me up with flames that tears would
            quench.
85   To weep is to make less the depth of grief.
        Tears, then, for babes; blows and revenge for me!
        Richard, I bear thy name; I'll venge thy death,
        Or die renownèd by attempting it.

EDWARD His name that valiant duke hath left with
            thee;
90   His dukedom and his chair with me is left.

RICHARD Nay, if thou be that princely eagle's bird,
        Show thy descent by gazing 'gainst the sun:
        For chair and dukedom, throne and kingdom say;
        Either that is thine, or else thou wert not his.

        March. Enter Warwick, Marquess Montague,
                    and their Army.

WARWICK How now, fair lords! What fare? What
95   news abroad?

RICHARD Great Lord of Warwick, if we should
            recompt
        Our baleful news, and at each word's deliverance
        Stab poniards in our flesh till all were told,
        The words would add more anguish than the
            wounds.
100   O valiant lord, the Duke of York is slain!

EDWARD O, Warwick, Warwick! that Plantagenet
        Which held thee dearly as his soul's redemption,
        Is by the stern Lord Clifford done to death.

WARWICK Ten days ago I drowned these news in tears,
105   And now, to add more measure to your woes,
        I come to tell you things sith then befall'n.
        After the bloody fray at Wakefield fought,
        Where your brave father breathed his latest gasp,
        Tidings, as swiftly as the posts could run,

91 **bird** child (the eagle, king of birds, was said to gaze at the sun) 95 **What fare?** what cheer? 95 **abroad** in the world 96 **recompt** recount 105 **measure** quantity 106 **sith** since 109 **posts** messengers

Were brought me of your loss and his depart.   110
I, then in London, keeper of the King,
Mustered my soldiers, gathered flocks of friends,
And very well appointed, as I thought,
Marched toward Saint Albans to intercept the
    Queen,
Bearing the King in my behalf along;   115
For by my scouts I was advertisèd
That she was coming with a full intent
To dash our late decree in parliament
Touching King Henry's oath and your succession.
Short tale to make, we at Saint Albans met,   120
Our battles joined, and both sides fiercely fought:
But whether 'twas the coldness of the King,
Who looked full gently on his warlike Queen,
That robbed my soldiers of their heated spleen;
Or whether 'twas report of her success;   125
Or more than common fear of Clifford's rigor,
Who thunders to his captives blood and death,
I cannot judge: but, to conclude with truth,
Their weapons like to lightning came and went;
Our soldiers', like the night-owl's lazy flight,   130
Or like an idle thresher with a flail,
Fell gently down, as if they struck their friends.
I cheered them up with justice of our cause,
With promise of high pay and great rewards;
But all in vain; they had no heart to fight,   135
And we in them no hope to win the day;
So that we fled; the King unto the Queen;
Lord George your brother, Norfolk and myself,
In haste, post-haste, are come to join with you;
For in the marches here we heard you were,   140
Making another head to fight again.

EDWARD Where is the Duke of Norfolk, gentle
    Warwick?

113 **appointed** equipped   115 **in my behalf** for my advantage   115 **along**
stretched out   116 **advertisèd** informed   118 **dash** frustrate   121 **battles** main
forces   124 **spleen** passion   126 **rigor** cruelty   140 **marches** borderlands (of
Wales)   141 **Making another head** gathering another force

And when came George from Burgundy to Eng-
    land?

WARWICK Some six miles off the Duke is with the
    soldiers;

145   And for your brother, he was lately sent
From your kind aunt, Duchess of Burgundy,
With aid of soldiers to this needful war.

RICHARD 'Twas odds, belike, when valiant Warwick
    fled.
Oft have I heard his praises in pursuit,

150   But ne'er till now his scandal of retire.

WARWICK Nor now my scandal, Richard, dost thou
    hear;
For thou shalt know this strong right hand of mine
Can pluck the diadem from faint Henry's head,
And wring the awful scepter from his fist,

155   Were he as famous and as bold in war
As he is famed for mildness, peace, and prayer.

RICHARD I know it well, Lord Warwick. Blame me
    not.
'Tis love I bear thy glories makes me speak.
But in this troublous time what's to be done?

160   Shall we go throw away our coats of steel,
And wrap our bodies in black mourning gowns,
Numb'ring our Ave-Maries with our beads?
Or shall we on the helmets of our foes
Tell our devotion with revengeful arms?

165   If for the last, say ay, and to it, lords.

WARWICK Why, therefore Warwick came to seek you
    out,
And therefore comes my brother Montague.
Attend me, lords. The proud insulting Queen,
With Clifford and the haught Northumberland,

170   And of their feather many moe proud birds,

148 **odds** inequality (of forces)   150 **scandal of retire** disgraceful imputation of
retreat   154 **awful** awe-inspiring   162 **Ave-Maries** prayers   164 **Tell**
count   168 **Attend** hear   169 **haught** haughty   170 **mor** more (old form)

Have wrought the easy-melting King like wax.
He swore consent to your succession,
His oath enrollèd in the parliament;
And now to London all the crew are gone,
To frustrate both his oath and what beside   175
May make against the house of Lancaster.
Their power, I think, is thirty thousand strong.
Now, if the help of Norfolk and myself,
With all the friends that thou, brave Earl of March,
Amongst the loving Welshmen canst procure,   180
Will but amount to five and twenty thousand,
Why, via! to London will we march amain,
And once again bestride our foaming steeds,
And once again cry "Charge!" upon our foes,
But never once again turn back and fly.   185

RICHARD Ay, now methinks I hear great Warwick
    speak.
Ne'er may he live to see a sunshine day
That cries "Retire," if Warwick bid him stay.

EDWARD Lord Warwick, on thy shoulder will I lean,
And when thou fail'st—as God forbid the hour!—   190
Must Edward fall, which peril heaven forfend!

WARWICK No longer Earl of March, but Duke of
    York.
The next degree is England's royal throne;
For King of England shalt thou be proclaimed
In every borough as we pass along;   195
And he that throws not up his cap for joy
Shall for the fault make forfeit of his head.
King Edward, valiant Richard, Montague,
Stay we no longer, dreaming of renown,
But sound the trumpets, and about our task.   200

RICHARD Then, Clifford, were thy heart as hard as
    steel,
As thou hast shown it flinty by thy deeds,
I come to pierce it, or to give thee mine.

173 **enrollèd** recorded on a parchment roll   182 **via!** away!   191 **forfend** forbid   193 **degree** step   197 **fault** offense

EDWARD Then strike up, drums! God and Saint George
for us!

Enter a Messenger.

205 WARWICK How now? What news?

MESSENGER The Duke of Norfolk sends you word by
me,
The Queen is coming with a puissant host;
And craves your company for speedy counsel.

WARWICK Why then it sorts. Brave warriors, let's
away.   *Exeunt onmes.*

Scene II. [*Before York.*]

*Flourish. Enter the King, the Queen, Clifford,
Northumberland, and [the] Young Prince [of Wales],
with Drum and Trumpets.*

QUEEN MARGARET Welcome, my lord, to this brave
town of York.
Yonder's the head of that arch-enemy
That sought to be encompassed with your crown.
Doth not the object cheer your heart, my lord?

KING HENRY Ay, as the rocks cheer them that fear
5   their wrack.
To see this sight, it irks my very soul.
Withhold revenge, dear God! 'Tis not my fault,
Nor wittingly have I infringed my vow.

CLIFFORD My gracious liege, this too much lenity
10   And harmful pity must be laid aside.
To whom do lions cast their gentle looks?
Not to the beast that would usurp their den.

207 **puissant** powerful   209 **it sorts** it is fitting   209 **omnes** all (Latin)
II.ii.1 **brave** splendid   4 **object** sight   5 **wrack** shipwreck

Whose hand is that the forest bear doth lick?
Not his that spoils her young before her face.
Who 'scapes the lurking serpent's mortal sting?   15
Not he that sets his foot upon her back.
The smallest worm will turn, being trodden on.
And doves will peck in safeguard of their brood.
Ambitious York did level at thy crown,
Thou smiling while he knit his angry brows: 20
He, but a duke, would have his son a king,
And raise his issue like a loving sire;
Thou, being a king, blest with a goodly son,
Didst yield consent to disinherit him,
Which argued thee a most unloving father.   25
Unreasonable creatures feed their young;
And though man's face be fearful to their eyes,
Yet, in protection of their tender ones,
Who hath not seen them, even with those wings
Which sometime they have used with fearful flight,   30
Make war with him that climbed unto their nest,
Offering their own lives in their young's defense?
For shame, my liege! Make them your precedent!
Were it not pity that this goodly boy
Should lose his birthright by his father's fault,   35
And long hereafter say unto his child,
"What my great-grandfather and grandsire got
My careless father fondly gave away"?
Ah, what a shame were this! Look on the boy;
And let his manly face, which promiseth   40
Successful fortune, steel thy melting heart
To hold thine own and leave thine own with him.

KING HENRY Full well hath Clifford played the orator,
Inferring arguments of mighty force.
But, Clifford, tell me, didst thou never hear   45
That things ill got had ever bad success?
And happy always was it for that son
Whose father for his hoarding went to hell?

14 **spoils** carries off   19 **level** aim   25 **argued** proved   26 **Unreasonable** not
endowed with reason   28 **tender** young, beloved   38 **fondly** foolishly
44 **Inferring** adducing   46 **success** outcome

I'll leave my son my virtuous deeds behind;
50   And would my father had left me no more!
For all the rest is held at such a rate
As brings a thousand-fold more care to keep
Than in possession any jot of pleasure.
Ah, cousin York, would thy best friends did know
55   How it doth grieve me that thy head is here!

QUEEN MARGARET My lord, cheer up your spirits; our foes
    are nigh,
And this soft courage makes your followers faint.
You promised knighthood to our forward son.
Unsheathe your sword, and dub him presently.
60   Edward, kneel down.

KING HENRY Edward Plantagenet, arise a knight;
And learn this lesson: Draw thy sword in right.

PRINCE My gracious father, by your kingly leave,
I'll draw it as apparent to the crown,
65   And in that quarrel use it to the death.

CLIFFORD Why, that is spoken like a toward prince.

Enter a Messenger.

MESSENGER Royal commanders, be in readiness;
For with a band of thirty thousand men
Comes Warwick, backing of the Duke of York,
70   And in the towns, as they do march along,
Proclaims him king, and many fly to him.
Darraign your battle, for they are at hand.

CLIFFORD I would your Highness would depart the
    field.
The Queen hath best success when you are absent.

QUEEN MARGARET Ay, good my lord, and leave us to
75   our fortune.

KING HENRY Why, that's my fortune too; therefore I'll
    stay.

57 **soft courage** faint-heartedness   59 **presently** immediately   64 **apparent**
heir apparent   66 **toward** bold   72 **Darraign** set in order

NORTHUMBERLAND Be it with resolution, then, to fight.

PRINCE My royal father, cheer these noble lords
And hearten those that fight in your defense:
Unsheathe your sword, good father; cry "Saint
George!"   80

*March. Enter Edward, Warwick, Richard, Clarence,
Norfolk, Montague, and Soldiers.*

EDWARD Now, perjured Henry, wilt thou kneel for
grace,
And set thy diadem upon my head,
Or bide the mortal fortune of the field?

QUEEN MARGARET Go rate thy minions, proud insult-
ing boy!
Becomes it thee to be thus bold in terms   85
Before thy sovereign and thy lawful king?

EDWARD I am his king, and he should bow his knee.
I was adopted heir by his consent;
Since when, his oath is broke; for, as I hear,
You, that are King, though he do wear the crown,   90
Have caused him, by new act of parliament,
To blot out me, and put his own son in.

CLIFFORD And reason too!
Who should succeed the father but the son?

RICHARD Are you there, butcher? O, I cannot speak!   95

CLIFFORD Ay, Crookback, here I stand to answer thee,
Or any he the proudest of thy sort.

RICHARD 'Twas you that killed young Rutland, was it
not?

CLIFFORD Ay, and old York, and yet not satisfied.

RICHARD For God's sake, lords, give signal to the fight. 100

WARWICK What say'st thou, Henry? Wilt thou yield
the crown?

80 s.d. (thus the Folio; in fact, George is not created Duke of Clarence until II, vi,
104)   84 rate drive away by chiding

QUEEN MARGARET　Why, how now, long-tongued
　　Warwick! Dare you speak?
　　When you and I met at Saint Albans last,
　　Your legs did better service than your hands.

WARWICK　Then 'twas my turn to fly, and now
105　　'tis thine.

CLIFFORD　You said so much before, and yet you fled.

WARWICK　'Twas not your valor, Clifford, drove me
　　thence.

NORTHUMBERLAND　No, nor your manhood that durst
　　make you stay.

RICHARD　Northumberland, I hold thee reverently.
110　　Break off the parley; for scarce I can refrain
　　The execution of my big-swol'n heart
　　Upon that Clifford, that cruel child-killer.

CLIFFORD　I slew thy father. Call'st thou him a child?

RICHARD　Ay, like a dastard and a treacherous coward,
115　　As thou didst kill our tender brother Rutland;
　　But ere sun set I'll make thee curse the deed.

KING HENRY　Have done with words, my lords, and
　　hear me speak.

QUEEN MARGARET　Defy them then, or else hold close
　　thy lips.

KING HENRY　I prithee, give no limits to my tongue:
120　　I am a king, and privileged to speak.

CLIFFORD　My liege, the wound that bred this meeting
　　here
　　Cannot be cured by words. Therefore be still.

RICHARD　Then, executioner, unsheathe thy sword.
　　By Him that made us all, I am resolved
125　　That Clifford's manhood lies upon his tongue.

EDWARD　Say, Henry, shall I have my right, or no?

124 **resolved** convinced

A thousand men have broke their fasts today
That ne'er shall dine unless thou yield the crown.

WARWICK If thou deny, their blood upon thy head!
For York in justice puts his armor on.   130

PRINCE If that be right which Warwick says is right,
There is no wrong, but everything is right.

RICHARD Whoever got thee, there thy mother stands;
For well I wot thou hast thy mother's tongue.

QUEEN MARGARET But thou art neither like thy sire nor
dam,   135
But like a foul misshapen stigmatic,
Marked by the Destinies to be avoided,
As venom toads, or lizards' dreadful stings.

RICHARD Iron of Naples, hid with English gilt,
Whose father bears the title of a king—   140
As if a channel should be called the sea—
Sham'st thou not, knowing whence thou art
extraught,
To let thy tongue detect thy base-born heart?

EDWARD A wisp of straw were worth a thousand
crowns,
To make this shameless callet know herself.   145
Helen of Greece was fairer far than thou,
Although thy husband may be Menelaus;
And ne'er was Agamemnon's brother wronged
By that false woman as this King by thee.
His father reveled in the heart of France,   150
And tamed the King, and made the Dolphin
stoop;
And had he matched according to his state,
He might have kept that glory to this day;
But when he took a beggar to his bed,
And graced thy poor sire with his bridal-day,   155
Even then that sunshine brewed a show'r for him,

133 **got** begot 136 **stigmatic** deformed one 141 **channel** gutter
142 **extraught** descended 143 **detect** reveal 145 **callet** scold, trull
151 **Dolphin** Dauphin 151 **stoop** yield

That washed his father's fortunes forth of France,
And heaped sedition on his crown at home.
For what hath broached this tumult but thy pride?
160 Hadst thou been meek, our title still had slept;
And we, in pity of the gentle King,
Had slipped our claim until another age.

CLARENCE But when we saw our sunshine made thy
          spring,
And that thy summer bred us no increase,
165 We set the ax to thy usurping root;
And though the edge hath something hit ourselves,
Yet, know thou, since we have begun to strike,
We'll never leave till we have hewn thee down,
Or bathed thy growing with our heated bloods.

170 EDWARD And, in this resolution, I defy thee;
Not willing any longer conference,
Since thou deniest the gentle King to speak.
Sound trumpets! Let our bloody colors wave!
And either victory, or else a grave.

175 QUEEN MARGARET Stay, Edward.

EDWARD No, wrangling woman, we'll no longer stay.
These words will cost ten thousand lives this day.
                                    Exeunt omnes.

---

157 **forth of** out of   159 **broached** started   160 **still** always   162 **slipped** not
asserted   171 **longer conference** further discussion

Scene III. [*A field of battle between Towton and
Saxton, in Yorkshire.*]

Alarum. Excusions. Enter Warwick.

WARWICK Forspent with toil, as runners with a race,
I lay me down a little while to breathe;
For strokes received, and many blows repaid,
Have robbed my strong-knit sinews of their
     strength,
And spite of spite needs must I rest awhile.   5

Enter Edward, running.

EDWARD Smile, gentle heaven! or strike, ungentle
     death!
For this world frowns, and Edward's sun is clouded.

WARWICK How now, my lord! What hap? What hope
     of good?

Enter Clarence.

CLARENCE Our hap is loss, our hope but sad despair;
Our ranks are broke, and ruin follows us.   10
What counsel give you? Whither shall we fly?

EDWARD Bootless is flight. They follow us with wings,
And weak we are and cannot shun pursuit.

Enter Richard.

RICHARD Ah, Warwick, why hast thou withdrawn
     thyself?
Thy brother's blood the thirsty earth hath drunk,   15
Broached with the steely point of Clifford's lance;
And in the very pangs of death he cried,

II.iii.1 **Forspent** exhausted 2 **breathe** rest 5 **spite of spite** come what
may 6 **ungentle** ignoble 9 **hap** (1) fortune (2) hope 12 **Bootless** useless
16 **Broached** pierced

289

Like to a dismal clangor heard from far,
"Warwick, revenge! Brother, revenge my death!"
20   So, underneath the belly of their steeds,
That stained their fetlocks in his smoking blood,
The noble gentleman gave up the ghost.

WARWICK Then let the earth be drunken with our
        blood!
I'll kill my horse, because I will not fly.
25   Why stand we like soft-hearted women here,
Wailing our losses, whiles the foe doth rage,
And look upon, as if the tragedy
Were played in jest by counterfeiting actors?
Here on my knee I vow to God above,
30   I'll never pause again, never stand still,
Till either death hath closed these eyes of mine
Or fortune given me measure of revenge.

EDWARD O Warwick, I do bend my knee with thine
And in this vow do chain my soul to thine!
35   And ere my knee rise from the earth's cold face,
I throw my hands, mine eyes, my heart to thee,
Thou setter up and plucker down of kings,
Beseeching thee (if with thy will it stands)
That to my foes this body must be prey,
40   Yet that thy brazen gates of heaven may ope,
And give sweet passage to my sinful soul!
Now, lords, take leave until we meet again,
Where'er it be, in heaven or in earth.

RICHARD Brother, give me thy hand; and, gentle
        Warwick,
45   Let me embrace thee in my weary arms.
I, that did never weep, now melt with woe
That winter should cut off our springtime so.

WARWICK Away, away! Once more, sweet lords,
        farewell.

18 **dismal** boding disaster 21 **smoking** steaming 27 **look upon** look on
38 **stands** agrees

CLARENCE Yet let us all together to our troops,
And give them leave to fly that will not stay,   50
And call them pillars that will stand to us;
And, if we thrive, promise them such rewards
As victors wear at the Olympian games:
This may plant courage in their quailing breasts;
For yet is hope of life and victory.   55
Forslow no longer! Make we hence amain!

Exeunt.

Scene IV. [*Another part of the field.*]

Excursions. Enter Richard and Clifford.

RICHARD Now, Clifford, I have singled thee alone.
Suppose this arm is for the Duke of York,
And this for Rutland, both bound to revenge
Wert thou environed with a brazen wall.

CLIFFORD Now, Richard, I am with thee here alone.   5
This is the hand that stabbed thy father York,
And this the hand that slew thy brother Rutland;
And here's the heart that triumphs in their death
And cheers these hands that slew thy sire and
    brother
To execute the like upon thyself;   10
And so have at thee!

They fight. Warwick comes. Clifford flies.

RICHARD Nay, Warwick, single out some other chase.
For I myself will hunt this wolf to death.

Exeunt.

56 **Forslow** delay   11.iv.8 **triumphs** exults   11 **have at thee** defend yourself

Scene V. [*Another part of the field.*]

Alarum. Enter King Henry alone.

KING HENRY This battle fares like to the morning's
    war,
    When dying clouds contend with growing light,
    What time the shepherd, blowing of his nails,
    Can neither call it perfect day nor night.
5   Now sways it this way, like a mighty sea
    Forced by the tide to combat with the wind.
    Now sways it that way, like the selfsame sea
    Forced to retire by fury of the wind.
    Sometime the flood prevails, and then the wind;
10   Now one the better, then another best;
    Both tugging to be victors, breast to breast,
    Yet neither conqueror nor conquerèd:
    So is the equal poise of this fell war.
    Here on this molehill will I sit me down.
15   To whom God will, there be the victory!
    For Margaret my queen, and Clifford too,
    Have chid me from the battle, swearing both
    They prosper best of all when I am thence.
    Would I were dead, if God's good will were so!
20   For what is in this world but grief and woe?
    O God! methinks it were a happy life,
    To be no better than a homely swain;
    To sit upon a hill, as I do now,
    To carve out dials quaintly, point by point,
25   Thereby to see the minutes how they run—
    How many makes the hour full complete,
    How many hours brings about the day,

II.v.3 **of his nails** on his fingers   13 **poise** weight (as in the scales of a
balance)   22 **swain** shepherd   24 **quaintly** ingeniously   27 **brings about**
completes

How many days will finish up the year,
How many years a mortal man may live;
When this is known, then to divide the times—   30
So many hours must I tend my flock,
So many hours must I take my rest,
So many hours must I contemplate,
So many hours must I sport myself,
So many days my ewes have been with young,   35
So many weeks ere the poor fools will ean,
So many years ere I shall shear the fleece.
So minutes, hours, days, months, and years,
Passed over to the end they were created,
Would bring white hairs unto a quiet grave.   40
Ah, what a life were this! how sweet! how lovely!
Gives not the hawthorn-bush a sweeter shade
To shepherds looking on their silly sheep,
Than doth a rich embroidered canopy
To kings that fear their subjects' treachery?   45
O, yes, it doth! a thousand-fold it doth!
And to conclude, the shepherd's homely curds,
His cold thin drink out of his leather bottle,
His wonted sleep under a fresh tree's shade,
All which secure and sweetly he enjoys,   50
Is far beyond a prince's delicates,
His viands sparkling in a golden cup,
His body couchèd in a curious bed,
When care, mistrust, and treason waits on him.

*Alarum. Enter a Son that hath killed his Father, at
one door; and [later] a Father that hath killed
his Son at another door.*

SON Ill blows the wind that profits nobody.   55
This man, whom hand to hand I slew in fight,
May be possessèd with some store of crowns;
And I, that haply take them from him now,
May yet, ere night, yield both my life and them
To some man else, as this dead man doth me.   60

36 **ean** bring forth lambs   43 **silly** helpless   50 **secure** free from care
51 **delicates** delicacies   53 **curious** exquisite   58 **haply** by chance

293

Who's this? O God! it is my father's face,
Whom in this conflict I, unwares, have killed.
O heavy times, begetting such events!
From London by the King was I pressed forth;
65   My father, being the Earl of Warwick's man,
Came on the part of York, pressed by his master;
And I, who at his hands received my life,
Have by my hands of life bereavèd him.
Pardon me, God! I knew not what I did.
70   And pardon, father, for I knew not thee!
My tears shall wipe away these bloody marks;
And no more words till they have flowed their fill.

KING HENRY   O piteous spectacle! O bloody times!
Whiles lions war and battle for their dens,
75   Poor harmless lambs abide their enmity.
Weep, wretched man! I'll aid thee tear for tear;
And let our hearts and eyes, like civil war,
Be blind with tears, and break o'ercharged with
      grief.

Enter Father, bearing of his Son.

FATHER   Thou that so stoutly hath resisted me,
80   Give me thy gold, if thou hast any gold;
For I have bought it with an hundred blows.
But let me see: is this our foeman's face?
Ah, no, no, no! It is mine only son!
Ah, boy, if any life be left in thee,
85   Throw up thine eye! See, see what show'rs arise,
Blown with the windy tempest of my heart
Upon thy wounds, that kills mine eye and heart!
O, pity, God, this miserable age!
What stratagems, how fell, how butcherly,
90   Erroneous, mutinous and unnatural,
This deadly quarrel daily doth beget!
O boy, thy father gave thee life too soon,
And hath bereft thee of thy life too late!

62 **unwares** unawares   66 **part** party, side   89 **stratagems** violent deeds
90 **Erroneous** criminal   93 **late** recently

KING HENRY Woe above woe! grief more than com-
        mon grief!
    O that my death would stay these ruthful deeds!   95
    O, pity, pity, gentle heaven, pity!
    The red rose and the white are on his face,
    The fatal colors of our striving houses:
    The one his purple blood right well resembles;
    The other his pale cheeks, methinks, presenteth: 100
    Wither one rose, and let the other flourish!
    If you contend, a thousand lives must wither.

SON How will my mother for a father's death
    Take on with me and ne'er be satisfied!

FATHER How will my wife for slaughter of my son   105
    Shed seas of tears and ne'er be satisfied!

KING HENRY How will the country for these woeful
        chances
    Misthink the King and not be satisfied!

SON Was ever son so rued a father's death?

FATHER Was ever father so bemoaned his son?   110

KING HENRY Was ever king so grieved for subjects'
        woe?
    Much is your sorrow; mine ten times so much.

SON I'll bear thee hence, where I may weep my fill.
                                    [*Exit with the body.*]

FATHER These arms of mine shall be thy winding-
        sheet;
    My heart, sweet boy, shall be thy sepulcher,   115
    For from my heart thine image ne'er shall go;
    My sighing breast shall be thy funeral bell;
    And so obsequious will thy father be,
    Even for the loss of thee, having no more,
    As Priam was for all his valiant sons.   120

---

95 **ruthful** lamentable 108 **Misthink** think ill of 118 **obsequious** dutiful
(particularly toward the dead)

I'll bear thee hence; and let them fight that will,
For I have murdered where I should not kill.

Exit [with the body].

KING HENRY Sad-hearted men, much overgone with
     care,
Here sits a king more woeful than you are.

*Alarums. Excursions. Enter the Queen [Margaret],
the Prince [of Wales], and Exeter.*

125 PRINCE Fly, father, fly! for all your friends are fled
     And Warwick rages like a chafèd bull:
     Away! for death doth hold us in pursuit.

QUEEN MARGARET Mount you, my lord, towards
     Berwick post amain.
     Edward and Richard, like a brace of greyhounds
130 Having the fearful flying hare in sight,
     With fiery eyes sparkling for very wrath,
     And bloody steel grasped in their ireful hands,
     Are at our backs; and therefore hence amain!

EXETER Away! for vengeance comes along with them:
135 Nay, stay not to expostulate; make speed!
     Or else come after. I'll away before.

KING HENRY Nay, take me with thee, good sweet
     Exeter.
     Not that I fear to stay, but love to go
     Whither the Queen intends. Forward, away!

Exeunt.

---

123 **overgone** overcome   128, 133 **amain** with full speed

Scene VI. [*Another part of the field.*]

A loud alarum. Enter Clifford, wounded.

CLIFFORD Here burns my candle out; ay, here it dies,
Which, whiles it lasted, gave King Henry light.
O Lancaster! I fear thy overthrow
More than my body's parting with my soul.
My love and fear glued many friends to thee,   5
And now I fall, thy tough commixtures melts,
Impairing Henry, strength'ning misproud York.
The common people swarm like summer flies;
And whither fly the gnats but to the sun?
And who shines now but Henry's enemies?   10
O Phoebus, hadst thou never given consent
That Phaëthon should check thy fiery steeds,
Thy burning car never had scorched the earth!
And, Henry, hadst thou swayed as kings should do,
Or as thy father and his father did,   15
Giving no ground unto the house of York,
They never then had sprung like summer flies;
I and ten thousand in this luckless realm
Had left no mourning widows for our death;
And thou this day hadst kept thy chair in peace.   20
For what doth cherish weeds but gentle air?
And what makes robbers bold but too much lenity?
Bootless are plaints, and cureless are my wounds;
No way to fly, nor strength to hold out flight;
The foe is merciless, and will not pity;   25
For at their hands I have deserved no pity.
The air hath got into my deadly wounds,
And much effuse of blood doth make me faint.

II.vi.5 **My love and fear glued** both love and fear of me attached
6 **commixtures** compound 7 **misproud** arrogant 14 **swayed** ruled
28 **effuse** pouring out

Come, York and Richard, Warwick and the rest;
30   I stabbed your fathers' bosoms; split my breast.
                                                    [*Faints.*]

*Alarum and retreat. Enter Edward, Warwick, Richard,
and Soldiers; Montague and Clarence.*

EDWARD Now breathe we, lords: good fortune bids
            us pause,
        And smooth the frowns of war with peaceful looks.
        Some troops pursue the bloody-minded Queen,
        That led calm Henry, though he were a king,
35   As doth a sail, filled with a fretting gust,
        Command an argosy to stem the waves.
        But think you, lords, that Clifford fled with them?

WARWICK No, 'tis impossible he should escape;
        For, though before his face I speak the words,
40   Your brother Richard marked him for the grave:
        And whereso'er he is, he's surely dead.
                                Clifford groans [and dies].

EDWARD Whose soul is that which takes her heavy
            leave?

RICHARD A deadly groan, like life and death's
            departing.

EDWARD See who it is: and, now the battle's ended,
45   If friend or foe, let him be gently used.

RICHARD Revoke that doom of mercy, for 'tis Clif-
            ford;
        Who not contented that he lopped the branch
        In hewing Rutland when his leaves put forth,
        But set his murdering knife unto the root
50   From whence that tender spray did sweetly spring:
        I mean our princely father, Duke of York.

WARWICK From off the gates of York fetch down the
            head,

31 **Now breathe we** now let us rest 36 **Command** compel 36 **argosy**
merchant vessel of the largest size and burden 43 **departing** separation
46 **doom** sentence

Your father's head, which Clifford placèd there;
Instead whereof let this supply the room:
Measure for measure must be answerèd.   55

EDWARD Bring forth that fatal screech-owl to our
    house,
That nothing sung but death to us and ours.
Now death shall stop his dismal threat'ning sound
And his ill-boding tongue no more shall speak.

WARWICK I think his understanding is bereft.   60
Speak, Clifford, dost thou know who speaks to
    thee?
Dark cloudy death o'ershades his beams of life,
And he nor sees nor hears us what we say.

RICHARD O, would he did! and so perhaps he doth:
'Tis but his policy to counterfeit,   65
Because he would avoid such bitter taunts
Which in the time of death he gave our father.

CLARENCE If so thou think'st, vex him with eager
    words.

RICHARD Clifford, ask mercy and obtain no grace.

EDWARD Clifford, repent in bootless penitence.   70

WARWICK Clifford, devise excuses for thy faults.

CLARENCE While we devise fell tortures for thy faults.

RICHARD Thou didst love York, and I am son to York.

EDWARD Thou pitied'st Rutland, I will pity thee.

CLARENCE Where's Captain Margaret, to fence you
    now?   75

WARWICK They mock thee, Clifford. Swear as thou
    wast wont.

RICHARD What! not an oath? Nay, then the world goes
    hard

54 room place 60 his understanding is bereft he is deprived of his
understanding 68 vex torment 68 eager sharp 75 fence protect

When Clifford cannot spare his friends an oath.
I know by that he's dead; and, by my soul,
80   If this right hand would buy two hours' life,
That I in all despite might rail at him,
This hand should chop it off, and with the issuing
        blood
Stifle the villain whose unstanchèd thirst
York and young Rutland could not satisfy.

WARWICK Ay, but he's dead. Off with the traitor's
85   head,
And rear it in the place your father's stands.
And now to London with triumphant march,
There to be crownèd England's royal king:
From whence shall Warwick cut the sea to France,
90   And ask the Lady Bona for thy queen.
So shalt thou sinew both these lands together;
And, having France thy friend, thou shalt not dread
The scattered foe that hopes to rise again;
For though they cannot greatly sting to hurt,
95   Yet look to have them buzz to offend thine ears.
First will I see the coronation.
And then to Brittany I'll cross the sea,
To effect this marriage, so it please my lord.

EDWARD Even as thou wilt, sweet Warwick, let it be;
100   For in thy shoulder do I build my seat,
And never will I undertake the thing
Wherein thy counsel and consent is wanting.
Richard, I will create thee Duke of Gloucester;
And George, of Clarence: Warwick, as ourself,
105   Shall do and undo as him pleaseth best.

RICHARD Let me be Duke of Clarence, George of
        Gloucester;
For Gloucester's dukedom is too ominous.

WARWICK Tut, that's a foolish observation.
Richard, be Duke of Gloucester. Now to London,
110   To see these honors in possession.   *Exeunt.*

86 **rear** erect   104 **ourself** (note the royal "we")   107 **For ... ominous** (refers
to the disgrace and murder of Humphrey, Duke of Gloucester, Lord Protector; see
2 Henry VI)

ACT III

Scene I. [*A forest in the North of England.*]

Enter [two Keepers] with cross-bows in their hands.

FIRST KEEPER Under this thick-grown brake we'll
    shroud ourselves;
  For through this laund anon the deer will come,
  And in this covert will we make our stand,
  Culling the principal of all the deer.

SECOND KEEPER I'll stay above the hill, so both may
    shoot.   5

FIRST KEEPER That cannot be; the noise of thy cross-
    bow
  Will scare the herd, and so my shoot is lost.
  Here stand we both, and aim we at the best;
  And, for the time shall not seem tedious,
  I'll tell thee what befell me on day   10
  In this self place where now we mean to stand.

SECOND KEEPER Here comes a man, let's stay till he
    be past.

III.i.1 **brake** thicket 1 **shroud** conceal 2 **laund** glade 3 **covert** thicket
3 **stand** hiding place 4 **Culling** picking out 8 **at the best** as well as we can
9 **for** so that 11 **self** same

Enter the King [Henry, disguised] with a prayer-book.

KING HENRY From Scotland am I stol'n, even of pure
    love,
    To great mine own land with my wishful sight.
15   No, Harry, Harry, 'tis no land of thine;
    Thy place is filled, thy scepter wrung from thee,
    Thy balm washed off wherewith thou wast
    anointed:
    No bending knee will call thee Caesar now,
    No humble suitors press to speak for right,
20   No, not a man comes for redress of thee;
    For how can I help them, and not myself?

FIRST KEEPER Ay, here's a deer whose skin's a keeper's
    fee!
    This is the quondam king; let's seize upon him.

KING HENRY Let me embrace thee, sour Adversity,
25   For wise men say it is the wisest course.

SECOND KEEPER Why linger we? let us lay hands upon
    him.

FIRST KEEPER Forbear awhile; we'll hear a little more.

KING HENRY My queen and son are gone to France for
    aid;
    And, as I hear, the great commanding Warwick
30   Is thither gone, to crave the French king's sister
    To wife for Edward. If this news be true,
    Poor queen and son, your labor is but lost;
    For Warwick is a subtle orator,
    And Lewis a prince soon won with moving words.
35   By this account, then, Margaret may win him;
    For she's a woman to be pitied much.
    Her sighs will make a batt'ry in his breast;
    Her tears will pierce into a marble heart;
    The tiger will be mild whiles she doth mourn;
40   And Nero will be tainted with remorse

20 of from   23 quondam former   37 batt'ry bombardment

To hear and see her plaints, her brinish tears.
Ay, but she's come to beg, Warwick, to give;
She on his left side, craving aid for Henry,
He on his right, asking a wife for Edward.
She weeps, and says her Henry is deposed;   45
He smiles, and says his Edward is installed;
That she (poor wretch) for grief can speak no
    more;
Whiles Warwick tells his title, smooths the wrong,
Inferreth arguments of mighty strength,
And in conclusion wins the King from her,   50
With promise of his sister, and what else,
To strengthen and support King Edward's place.
O Margaret, thus 'twill be; and thou (poor soul)
Art then forsaken, as thou went'st forlorn!

SECOND KEEPER Say, what art thou that talk'st of kings
    and queens?   55

KING HENRY More than I seem, and less than I was
    born to:
A man at least, for less I should not be;
And men may talk of kings, and why not I?

SECOND KEEPER Ay, but thou talk'st as if thou wert a
    king.

KING HENRY Why, so I am (in mind) and that's
    enough.   60

SECOND KEEPER But, if thou be a king, where is thy
    crown?

KING HENRY My crown is in my heart, not on my
    head;
Not decked with diamonds and Indian stones,
Nor to be seen. My crown is called content:
A crown it is that seldom kings enjoy.   65

SECOND KEEPER Well, if you be a king crowned with
    content,
Your crown content and you must be contented
To go along with us; for (as we think)

You are the king King Edward hath deposed;
70 And we his subjects sworn in all allegiance
Will apprehend you as his enemy.

KING HENRY But did you never swear, and break an
oath?

SECOND KEEPER No, never such an oath; nor will not
now.

KING HENRY Where did you dwell when I was King
of England?

SECOND KEEPER Here in this country, where we now
75   remain.

KING HENRY I was anointed king at nine months old;
My father and my grandfather were kings,
And you were sworn true subjects unto me:
And tell me, then, have you not broke your oaths?

80 FIRST KEEPER No;
For we were subjects but while you were king.

KING HENRY Why, am I dead? Do I not breathe a
man?
Ah, simple men, you know not what you swear!
Look, as I blow this feather from my face,
85 And as the air blows it to me again,
Obeying with my wind when I do blow,
And yielding to another when it blows,
Commanded always by the greater gust—
Such is the lightness of you common men.
90 But do not break your oaths; for of that sin
My mild entreaty shall not make you guilty.
Go where you will, the King shall be commanded;
And be you kings, command, and I'll obey.

FIRST KEEPER We are true subjects to the king, King
Edward.

95 KING HENRY So would you be again to Henry,
If he were seated as King Edward is.

FIRST KEEPER We charge you, in God's name, and in the
    King's,
  To go with us unto the officers.

KING HENRY In God's name, lead. Your king's name
    be obeyed:
  And what God will, that let your king perform;   100
  And what he will, I humbly yield unto.

                            Exeunt.

Scene II. [*London. The Palace.*]

Enter King Edward, [Richard, Duke of] Gloucester,
[George, Duke of] Clarence, Lady [Elizabeth] Grey.

KING EDWARD Brother of Gloucester, at Saint Albans
    field
  This lady's husband, Sir Richard Grey, was slain,
  His land then seized on by the conqueror.
  Her suit is now to repossess those lands;
  Which we in justice cannot well deny,   5
  Because in quarrel of the house of York
  The worthy gentleman did lose his life.

RICHARD Your Highness shall do well to grant her
    suit;
  It were dishonor to deny it her.

KING EDWARD It were no less; but yet I'll make a
    pause.   10

RICHARD [*Aside to Clarence*] Yea, is it so?
  I see the lady hath a thing to grant,
  Before the King will grant her humble suit.

III.ii.5 **deny** refuse

305

CLARENCE [*Aside to Richard*] He knows the game:
     how true he keeps the wind!

15 RICHARD [*Aside to Clarence*] Silence!

KING EDWARD Widow, we will consider of your suit;
     And come some other time to know our mind.

LADY GREY Right gracious lord, I cannot brook
     delay:
     May it please your Highness to resolve me now,
20   And what your pleasure is shall satisfy me.

RICHARD [*Aside to Clarence*] Ay, widow? then I'll
     warrant you all your lands,
     And if what pleases him shall pleasure you.
     Fight closer, or, good faith, you'll catch a blow.

CLARENCE [*Aside to Richard*] I fear her not, unless she
     chance to fall.

RICHARD [*Aside to Clarence*] God forbid that! for he'll
25   take vantages.

KING EDWARD How many children hast thou, widow?
     tell me.

CLARENCE [*Aside to Richard*] I think he means to beg
     a child of her.

RICHARD [*Aside to Clarence*] Nay then, whip me: he'll
     rather give her two.

LADY GREY Three, my most gracious lord.

RICHARD [*Aside to Clarence*] You shall have four, if
30   you'll be ruled by him.

KING EDWARD 'Twere pity they should lose their
     father's lands.

LADY GREY Be pitiful, dread lord, and grant it then.

---

14 **keeps the wind** (metaphor from hunting) keeps to the windward side of the
game   18 **brook** endure   21 **warrant** guarantee   25 **take vantages** take advantage of opportunities

KING EDWARD Lords, give us leave: I'll try this
    widow's wit.

RICHARD [*Aside to Clarence*] Ay, good leave have
    you; for you will have leave,
Till youth take leave and leave you to the crutch.   35
                [*Richard and Clarence withdraw.*]

KING EDWARD Now tell me, madam, do you love your
    children?

LADY GREY Ay, full as dearly as I love myself.

KING EDWARD And would you not do much to do
    them good?

LADY GREY To do them good, I would sustain some
    harm.

KING EDWARD Then get your husband's lands, to do
    them good.   40

LADY GREY Therefore I came unto your Majesty.

KING EDWARD I'll tell you how these lands are to be
    got.

LADY GREY So shall you bind me to your Highness'
    service.

KING EDWARD What service wilt thou do me, if I give
    them?

LADY GREY What you command, that rests in me
    to do.   45

KING EDWARD But you will take exceptions to my
    boon.

LADY GREY No, gracious lord, except I cannot do it.

KING EDWARD Ay, but thou canst do what I mean to
    ask.

---

33 wit intelligence   34-35 for ... crutch for you will take liberties until youth
departs and leaves you infirm   45 rests in me is in my power   46 boon favor

LADY GREY Why, then I will do what your grace
commands.

RICHARD [*Aside to Clarence*] He plies her hard; and
50   much rain wears the marble.

CLARENCE [*Aside to Richard*] As red as fire! Nay, then
her wax must melt.

LADY GREY Why stops my lord? shall I not hear my
task?

KING EDWARD An easy task; 'tis but to love a king.

LADY GREY That's soon performed, because I am a
subject.

KING EDWARD Why, then, thy husband's lands I freely
55   give thee.

LADY GREY I take my leave with many thousand
thanks.

RICHARD [*Aside to Clarence*] The match is made; she
seals it with a curtsy.

KING EDWARD But stay thee, 'tis the fruits of love I
mean.

LADY GREY The fruits of love I mean, my loving
liege.

60   KING EDWARD Ay, but, I fear me, in another sense.
What love, think'st thou, I sue so much to get?

LADY GREY My love till death, my humble thanks,
my prayers;
That love which virtue begs and virtue grants.

KING EDWARD No, by my troth, I did not mean such
love.

LADY GREY Why, then you mean not as I thought you
65   did.

KING EDWARD But now you partly may perceive my
mind.

LADY GREY My mind will never grant what I perceive
    Your Highness aims at, if I aim aright.

KING EDWARD To tell thee plain, I aim to lie with thee.

LADY GREY To tell you plain, I had rather lie in
    prison.   70

KING EDWARD Why, then thou shalt not have thy
    husband's lands.

LADY GREY Why, then mine honesty shall be my
    dower;
    For by that loss I will not purchase them.

KING EDWARD Therein thou wrong'st thy children
    mightily.

LADY GREY Herein your Highness wrongs both them
    and me.   75
    But, mighty lord, this merry inclination
    Accords not with the sadness of my suit.
    Please you dismiss me, either with "ay" or "no."

KING EDWARD Ay, if thou wilt say "ay" to my re-
    quest;
    No, if thou dost say "no" to my demand.   80

LADY GREY Then, no, my lord. My suit is at an end.

RICHARD [*Aside to Clarence*] The widow likes him
    not, she knits her brows.

CLARENCE [*Aside to Richard*] He is the bluntest wooer
    in Christendom.

KING EDWARD [*Aside*] Her looks doth argue her re-
    plete with modesty;
    Her words doth show her wit incomparable;   85
    All her perfections challenge sovereignty:
    One way or other, she is for a king;
    And she shall be my love, or else my queen—

72 **honesty** chastity   77 **sadness of my suit** seriousness of my request
86 **challenge** lay claim to

[*aloud*] Say that King Edward take thee for his
    queen?

LADY GREY 'Tis better said than done, my gracious
90   lord:
    I am a subject fit to jest withal,
    But far unfit to be a sovereign.

KING EDWARD Sweet widow, by my state I swear to
    thee
    I speak no more than what my soul intends;
95   And that is, to enjoy thee for my love.

LADY GREY And that is more than I will yield unto.
    I know I am too mean to be your queen,
    And yet too good to be your concubine.

KING EDWARD You cavil, widow: I did mean, my
    queen.

LADY GREY 'Twill grieve your Grace my sons should
100   call you father.

KING EDWARD No more than when my daughters call
    thee mother.
    Thou art a widow, and thou hast some children;
    And, by God's Mother, I, being but a bachelor,
    Have other some: why, 'tis a happy thing
105   To be the father unto many sons.
    Answer no more, for thou shalt be my queen.

RICHARD [*Aside to Clarence*] The ghostly father now
    hath done his shrift.

CLARENCE [*Aside to Richard*] When he was made a
    shriver, 'twas for shift.

KING EDWARD Brothers, you muse what chat we two
    have had.

RICHARD The widow likes it not, for she looks very
110   sad.

97 **mean** low in rank 104 **other some** others 104 **happy** fortunate
107 **ghostly** spiritual 108 **for shift** (1) to serve a purpose (2) for a woman's
undergarment

KING EDWARD You'd think it strange if I should marry
    her.

CLARENCE To who, my lord?

KING EDWARD   Why, Clarence, to myself.

RICHARD That would be ten days' wonder at the least.

CLARENCE That's a day longer than a wonder lasts.

RICHARD By so much is the wonder in extremes.   115

KING EDWARD Well, jest on, brothers. I can tell you
    both
    Her suit is granted for her husband's lands.

                    Enter a Nobleman.

NOBLEMAN My gracious lord, Henry your foe is taken,
    And brought your prisoner to your palace gate.

KING EDWARD See that he be conveyed unto the
    Tower: 120
    And go we, brothers, to the man that took him,
    To question of his apprehension.
    Widow, go you along. Lords, use her honorably.
                    Exeunt. Manet Richard.

RICHARD Ay, Edward will use women honorably.
    Would he were wasted, marrow, bones and all,   125
    That from his loins no hopeful branch may spring,
    To cross me from the golden time I look for!
    And yet, between my soul's desire and me—
    The lustful Edward's title buried—
    Is Clarence, Henry, and his son young Edward,   130
    And all the unlooked-for issue of their bodies,
    To take their rooms, ere I can place myself:
    A cold premeditation for my purpose!
    Why then, I do but dream on sovereignty;
    Like one that stands upon a promontory,   135
    And spies a far-off shore where he would tread,

114 **That's ... lasts** (proverbially a wonder lasts only nine days)   122 **apprehension** arrest   123 s.d. **Manet** remains (Latin)   131 **unlooked for** (1) unforeseen
(2) undesired

Wishing his foot were equal with his eye,
And chides the sea that sunders him from thence,
Saying, he'll lade it dry to have his way:
140 So do I wish the crown, being so far off;
And so I chide the means that keeps me from it;
And so (I say) I'll cut the causes off,
Flattering me with impossibilities.
My eye's too quick, my heart o'erweens too much,
145 Unless my hand and strength could equal them.
Well, say there is no kingdom then for Richard:
What other pleasure can the world afford?
I'll make my heaven in a lady's lap,
And deck my body in gay ornaments
150 And witch sweet ladies with my words and looks.
O miserable thought! and more unlikely
Than to accomplish twenty golden crowns!
Why, Love forswore me in my mother's womb:
And, for I should not deal in her soft laws,
155 She did corrupt frail Nature with some bribe,
To shrink mine arm up like a withered shrub;
To make an envious mountain on my back,
Where sits deformity to mock my body;
To shape my legs of an unequal size;
160 To disproportion me in every part,
Like to a chaos, or an unlicked bear-whelp
That carries no impression like the dam.
And am I then a man to be beloved?
O monstrous fault, to harbor such a thought!
165 Then, since this earth affords no joy to me,
But to command, to check, to o'erbear such
As are of better person than myself,
I'll make my heaven to dream upon the crown,
And, whiles I live, t' account this world but hell,
170 Until my misshaped trunk that bears this head
Be round impalèd with a glorious crown.

139 lade bail   144 o'erweens too much is too presumptuous   150 witch
bewitch   152 accomplish obtain   153 forwore abjured   154 for so that
157 envious spiteful   161 chaos shapeless mass   164 fault error   167 person
appearance

And yet I know not how to get the crown,
For many lives stand between me and home:
And I—like one lost in a thorny wood,
That rends the thorns and is rent with the thorns,   175
Seeking a way and straying from the way,
Not knowing how to find the open air,
But toiling desperately to find it out—
Torment myself to catch the English crown:
And from that torment I will free myself,   180
Or hew my way out with a bloody ax.
Why, I can smile, and murder whiles I smile,
And cry "Content" to that which grieves my heart,
And wet my cheeks with artificial tears,
And frame my face to all occasions.   185
I'll drown more sailors than the mermaid shall;
I'll slay more gazers than the basilisk;
I'll play the orator as well as Nestor,
Deceive more slily than Ulysses could,
And, like a Sinon, take another Troy.   190
I can add colors to the chameleon,
Change shapes with Proteus for advantages,
And set the murderous Machiavel to school.
Can I do this, and cannot get a crown?
Tut, were it farther off, I'll pluck it down.   *Exit.*   195

---

173 **home** my goal   187 **basilisk** fabulous reptile said to kill by its look and
breath   190 **Sinon** Greek warrior who devised the stratagem of the wooden horse,
by which the Greeks ultimately captured and destroyed Troy   192 **Proteus** sea-
deity who assumed various forms   193 **Machiavel** Niccolò Machiavelli, author of
The Prince (1513), whose name became synonymous with sinister intrigue and the
worship of power

Scene III. [*France. The King's Palace.*]

*Flourish. Enter Lewis the French King, his sister Bona,
his Admiral, called Bourbon; Prince Edward, Queen
Margaret, and the Earl of Oxford. Lewis sits, and riseth
up again.*

KING LEWIS Fair Queen of England, worthy Margaret,
Sit down with us: it ill befits thy state
And birth, that thou should'st stand while Lewis
   doth sit.

QUEEN MARGARET No, mighty King of France: now
   Margaret
5   Must strike her sail and learn awhile to serve
Where kings command. I was (I must confess)
Great Albion's Queen in former golden days;
But now mischance hath trod my title down,
And with dishonor laid me on the ground;
10   Where I must take like seat unto my fortune,
And to my humble seat conform myself.

KING LEWIS Why, say, fair Queen, whence springs
   this deep despair?

QUEEN MARGARET From such a cause as fills mine eyes
   with tears
And stops my tongue, while heart is drowned in
   cares.

15   KING LEWIS Whate'er it be, be thou still like thyself,
And sit thee by our side. (*Seats her by him.*) Yield
   not thy neck
To Fortune's yoke, but let thy dauntless mind
Still ride in triumph over all mischance.

III.iii.5 **strike her sail** humble herself   7 **Albion** ancient name of Britain

Be plain, Queen Margaret, and tell thy grief;
It shall be eased, if France can yield relief.   20

QUEEN MARGARET Those gracious words revive my
    drooping thoughts
And give my tongue-tied sorrows leave to speak.
Now, therefore, be it known to noble Lewis,
That Henry, sole possessor of my love,
Is of a king become a banished man,   25
And forced to live in Scotland a forlorn;
While proud ambitious Edward, Duke of York,
Usurps the regal title and the seat
Of England's true-anointed lawful King.
This is the cause that I, poor Margaret,   30
With this my son, Prince Edward, Henry's heir,
Am come to crave thy just and lawful aid;
And if thou fail us, all our hope is done.
Scotland hath will to help, but cannot help;
Our people and our peers are both misled,   35
Our treasure seized, our soldiers put to flight,
And, as thou seest, ourselves in heavy plight.

KING LEWIS Renownèd Queen, with patience calm the
    storm,
While we bethink a means to break it off.

QUEEN MARGARET The more we stay, the stronger
    grows our foe.   40

KING LEWIS The more I stay, the more I'll succor
    thee.

QUEEN MARGARET O, but impatience waiteth on true
    sorrow.
And see where comes the breeder of my sorrow!

                    Enter Warwick.

KING LEWIS What's he approacheth boldly to our
    presence?

26 **a forlorn** a forlorn man   37 **heavy** sad   39 **break it off** end it   41 **stay**
(with pun on the meaning "support")   42 **waiteth on** accompanies

315

QUEEN MARGARET Our Earl of Warwick, Edward's
45   greatest friend.

KING LEWIS Welcome, brave Warwick! What brings
       thee to France?   *He descends. She ariseth.*

QUEEN MARGARET [*Aside*] Ay, now begins a second
       storm to rise,
    For this is he that moves both wind and tide.

WARWICK From worthy Edward, King of Albion,
50   My lord and sovereign, and thy vowèd friend,
    I come, in kindness and unfeignèd love,
    First, to do greetings to thy royal person;
    And then to crave a league of amity;
    And lastly, to confirm that amity
55   With nuptial knot, if thou vouchsafe to grant
    That virtuous Lady Bona, thy fair sister,
    To England's King in lawful marriage.

QUEEN MARGARET [*Aside*] If that go forward, Henry's
       hope is done.

WARWICK (*Speaking to Bona*) And, gracious madam,
       in our king's behalf,
60   I am commanded, with your leave and favor,
    Humbly to kiss your hand, and with my tongue
    To tell the passion of my sovereign's heart;
    Where fame, late ent'ring at his heedful ears,
    Hath placed thy beauty's image and thy virtue.

QUEEN MARGARET King Lewis and Lady Bona, hear
65   me speak,
    Before you answer Warwick. His demand
    Springs not from Edward's well-meant honest love,
    But from deceit, bred by necessity;
    For how can tyrants safely govern home,
70   Unless abroad they purchase great alliance?
    To prove him tyrant this reason may suffice,
    That Henry liveth still; but were he dead,
    Yet here Prince Edward stands, King Henry's son.

60 **leave and favor** kind permission   62 **passion** suffering   63 **fame** rumor
69 **tyrants** usurpers   70 **purchase** obtain

Look, therefore, Lewis, that by this league and
    marriage
Thou draw not on thy danger and dishonor;   75
For though usurpers sway the rule awhile,
Yet heavens are just, and time suppresseth wrongs.

WARWICK Injurious Margaret!

PRINCE   And why not Queen?

WARWICK Because thy father Henry did usurp;
And thou no more art Prince than she is Queen.   80

OXFORD Then Warwick disannuls great John of
    Gaunt,
Which did subdue the greatest part of Spain;
And, after John of Gaunt, Henry the Fourth,
Whose wisdom was a mirror to the wisest;
And, after that wise prince, Henry the Fifth,   85
Who by his prowess conquerèd all France:
From these our Henry lineally descends.

WARWICK Oxford, how haps it, in this smooth
    discourse,
You told not how Henry the Sixth hath lost
All that which Henry the Fifth had gotten?   90
Methinks these peers of France should smile at
    that.
But for the rest: you tell a pedigree
Of threescore and two years—a silly time
To make prescription for a kingdom's worth.

OXFORD Why, Warwick, canst thou speak against thy
    liege,   95
Whom thou obeyèdst thirty and six years,
And not bewray thy treason with a blush?

WARWICK Can Oxford, that did ever fence the right,
Now buckler falsehood with a pedigree?
For shame! leave Henry, and call Edward king.   100

81 **disannuls** again cancels 84 **mirror** model 92 **tell** (1) relate (2) count
93 **silly** scanty 94 **prescription** claim 97 **bewray** reveal 98 **fence** defend
99 **buckler** shield

OXFORD Call him my king by whose injurious doom
　　My elder brother, the Lord Aubrey Vere,
　　Was done to death? and more than so, my father,
　　Even in the downfall of his mellowed years,
105　When nature brought him to the door of death?
　　No, Warwick, no; while life upholds this arm,
　　This arm upholds the house of Lancaster.

WARWICK And I the house of York.

KING LEWIS Queen Margaret, Prince Edward, and
　　Oxford,
110　Vouchsafe, at our request, to stand aside,
　　While I use further conference with Warwick.

　　　　　　　　　　　　　　　　They stand aloof.

QUEEN MARGARET Heavens grant that Warwick's words
　　bewitch him not!

KING LEWIS Now, Warwick, tell me, even upon thy
　　conscience,
　　Is Edward your true king? for I were loath
115　To link with him that were not lawful chosen.

WARWICK Thereon I pawn my credit and mine honor.

KING LEWIS But is he gracious in the people's eye?

WARWICK The more that Henry was unfortunate.

KING LEWIS Then further, all dissembling set aside,
120　Tell me for truth the measure of his love
　　Unto our sister Bona.

WARWICK　　　　　　　Such it seems
　　As may beseem a monarch like himself.
　　Myself have often heard him say and swear
　　That this his love was an eternal plant,
125　Whereof the root was fixed in virtue's ground,
　　The leaves and fruit maintained with beauty's sun,
　　Exempt from envy, but not from disdain,
　　Unless the Lady Bona quit his pain.

101 **injurious doom** unjust sentence　117 **gracious** favored, popular　128 **quit** requite

KING LEWIS Now, sister, let us hear your firm resolve.

BONA Your grant, or your denial, shall be mine: 130
   Yet I confess that often ere this day
                           (Speaks to Warwick),
   When I have heard your king's desert recounted,
   Mine ear hath tempted judgment to desire.

KING LEWIS Then, Warwick, thus: our sister shall be
   Edward's;
   And now forthwith shall articles be drawn   135
   Touching the jointure that your king must make,
   Which with her dowry shall be counterpoised.
   Draw near, Queen Margaret, and be a witness
   That Bona shall be wife to the English king.

PRINCE To Edward, but not to the English king.   140

QUEEN MARGARET Deceitful Warwick! it was thy device
   By this alliance to make void my suit:
   Before thy coming Lewis was Henry's friend.

KING LEWIS And still is friend to him and Margaret:
   But if your title to the crown be weak,   145
   As may appear by Edward's good success,
   Then 'tis but reason that I be released
   From giving aid which late I promisèd.
   Yet shall you have all kindness at my hand
   That your estate requires and mine can yield.   150

WARWICK Henry now lives in Scotland at his ease,
   Where having nothing, nothing can he lose.
   And as for you yourself, our quondam queen,
   You have a father able to maintain you,
   And better 'twere you troubled him than France.   155

QUEEN MARGARET Peace, impudent and shameless
   Warwick, peace,
   Proud setter up and puller down of kings!
   I will not hence, till with my talk and tears
   (Both full of truth) I make King Lewis behold

136 **jointure** marriage settlement   153 **quondam** former

160   Thy sly conveyance and thy lord's false love;
       For both of you are birds of selfsame feather.
                         Post blowing a horn within.

KING LEWIS Warwick, this is some post to us or thee.

                       Enter the Post.

POST (*Speaks to Warwick*) My lord ambassador,
       these letters are for you,
       Sent from your brother, Marquess Montague;
       (*To Lewis*) These from our King unto your
165   Majesty;
       (*To Margaret*) And, madam, these for you; from
       whom I know not.   *They all read their letters.*

OXFORD I like it well that our fair Queen and mistress
       Smiles at her news, while Warwick frowns at his.

PRINCE Nay, mark how Lewis stamps, as he were
170   nettled.
       I hope all's for the best.

KING LEWIS Warwick, what are thy news? and yours,
       fair Queen?

QUEEN MARGARET Mine, such as fill my heart with
       unhoped joys.

WARWICK Mine, full of sorrow and heart's discontent.

KING LEWIS What! has your king married the Lady
       Grey?
175   And now, to soothe your forgery and his,
       Sends me a paper to persuade me patience?
       Is this th' alliance that he seeks with France?
       Dare he presume to scorn us in this manner?

QUEEN MARGARET I told your Majesty as much before:
180   This proveth Edward's love and Warwick's honesty!

---

160 **conveyance** (1) transfer of property (here, Lewis's promise of aid) (2) trickery

WARWICK King Lewis, I here protest, in sight of
   heaven,
   And by the hope I have of heavenly bliss,
   That I am clear from this misdeed of Edward's,
   No more my king, for he dishonors me,
   But most himself, if he could see his shame.   185
   Did I forget that by the house of York
   My father came untimely to his death?
   Did I let pass th' abuse done to my niece?
   Did I impale him with the regal crown?
   Did I put Henry from his native right?   190
   And am I guerdoned at the last with shame?
   Shame on himself! for my desert is honor:
   And to repair my honor lost for him,
   I here renounce him and return to Henry.
   My noble Queen, let former grudges pass,   195
   And henceforth I am thy true servitor:
   I will revenge his wrong to Lady Bona
   And replant Henry in his former state.

QUEEN MARGARET Warwick, these words have turned
   my hate to love;
   And I forgive and quite forget old faults,   200
   And joy that thou becom'st King Henry's friend.

WARWICK So much his friend, ay, his unfeignèd
   friend,
   That, if King Lewis vouchsafe to furnish us
   With some few bands of chosen soldiers,
   I'll undertake to land them on our coast   205
   And force the tyrant from his seat by war.
   'Tis not his new-made bride shall succor him:
   And as for Clarence, as my letters tell me,
   He's very likely now to fall from him,
   For matching more for wanton lust than honor,   210
   Or than for strength and safety of our country.

BONA Dear brother, how shall Bona be revenged
   But by thy help to this distressèd queen?

189 impale encircle   191 guerdoned rewarded   210 matching marrying

QUEEN MARGARET Renownèd prince, how shall poor
    Henry live,
215   Unless thou rescue him from foul despair?

BONA My quarrel and this English queen's are one.

WARWICK And mine, fair Lady Bona, joins with yours.

KING LEWIS And mine with hers, and thine, and
    Margaret's.
    Therefore at last I firmly am resolved
220   You shall have aid.

QUEEN MARGARET Let me give humble thanks for all
    at once.

KING LEWIS Then, England's messenger, return in
    post,
    And tell false Edward, thy supposèd king,
    That Lewis of France is sending over masquers
225   To revel it with him and his new bride:
    Thou seest what's passed, go fear thy king withal.

BONA Tell him, in hope he'll prove a widower shortly,
    I'll wear the willow garland for his sake.

QUEEN MARGARET Tell him, my mourning weeds are
    laid aside,
230   And I am ready to put armor on.

WARWICK Tell him from me that he hath done me
    wrong,
    And therefore I'll uncrown him ere't be long.
    There's thy reward. Be gone.   *Exit Post.*

KING LEWIS   But, Warwick,
    Thou and Oxford, with five thousand men,
235   Shall cross the seas, and bid false Edward battle;
    And, as occasion serves, this noble Queen
    And Prince shall follow with a fresh supply.
    Yet, ere thou go, but answer me one doubt,
    What pledge have we of thy firm loyalty?

222 **post** haste 224 **masquers** performers 226 **fear** (verb) frighten
228 **willow garland** sign of disappointed love 229 **weeds** garments
236 **serves** is opportune

WARWICK This shall assure my constant loyalty,   240
    That if our Queen and this young Prince agree,
    I'll join mine eldest daughter and my joy
    To him forthwith in holy wedlock bands.

QUEEN MARGARET Yes, I agree, and thank you for
        your motion.
    Son Edward, she is fair and virtuous,   245
    Therefore delay not, give thy hand to Warwick;
    And, with thy hand, thy faith irrevocable,
    That only Warwick's daughter shall be thine.

PRINCE Yes, I accept her, for she well deserves it;
    And here, to pledge my vow, I give my hand.   250
                        He gives his hand to Warwick.

KING LEWIS Why stay we now? These soldiers shall
        be levied,
    And thou, Lord Bourbon, our High Admiral,
    Shall waft them over with our royal fleet.
    I long till Edward fall by war's mischance,
    For mocking marriage with a dame of France.   255
                        Exeunt. Manet Warwick.

WARWICK I came from Edward as ambassador,
    But I return his sworn and mortal foe:
    Matter of marriage was the charge he gave me,
    But dreadful war shall answer his demand.
    Had he none else to make a stale but me?   260
    Then none but I shall turn his jest to sorrow.
    I was the chief that raised him to the crown,
    And I'll be chief to bring him down again;
    Not that I pity Henry's misery,
    But seek revenge on Edward's mockery.   *Exit.* 265

244 motion offer   254 long till Edward fall am impatient for Edward to fall
255 s.d. Manet remains   259 demand request   260 stale (1) dupe (2) tool

ACT IV

Scene I. [*London. The Palace.*]

Enter Richard, Clarence, Somerset, and Montague.

RICHARD Now tell me, brother Clarence, what think
    you
    Of this new marriage with the Lady Grey?
    Hath not our brother made a worthy choice?

CLARENCE Alas, you know 'tis far from hence to
    France!
5   How could he stay till Warwick made return?

SOMERSET My Lords, forbear this talk; here comes the
    King.

RICHARD And his well-chosen bride.

CLARENCE I mind to tell him plainly what I think.

*Flourish. Enter King Edward, Lady Grey [as Queen],
Pembroke, Stafford, Hastings, [and others]. Four stand
on one side and four on the other.*

KING EDWARD Now, brother of Clarence, how like
    you our choice,
10   That you stand pensive, as half malcontent?

CLARENCE As well as Lewis of France, or the Earl of
    Warwick,

IV.i.10 **malcontent** discontented, dissatisfied

324

Which are so weak of courage and in judgment
That they'll take no offense at our abuse.

KING EDWARD Suppose they take offense without a
    cause:
They are but Lewis and Warwick; I am Edward,   15
Your King and Warwick's, and must have my will.

RICHARD And shall have your will, because our King.
Yet hasty marriage seldom proveth well.

KING EDWARD Yea, brother Richard, are you offended
    too?

RICHARD Not I.   20
No, God forbid that I should wish them severed
Whom God hath joined together; ay, and 'twere pity
To sunder them that yoke so well together.

KING EDWARD Setting your scorns and your mislike
    aside,
Tell me some reason why the Lady Grey   25
Should not become my wife and England's Queen.
And you too, Somerset and Montague,
Speak freely what you think.

CLARENCE Then this is mine opinion, that King Lewis
Becomes your enemy for mocking him   30
About the marriage of the Lady Bona.

RICHARD And Warwick, doing what you gave in
    charge,
Is now dishonorèd by this new marriage.

KING EDWARD What if both Lewis and Warwick be
    appeased
By such invention as I can devise?   35

MONTAGUE Yet, to have joined with France in such
    alliance

13 **abuse** deceit

Would more have strengthened this our common-
    wealth
'Gainst foreign storms than any home-bred
    marriage.

40 HASTINGS Why, knows not Montague that of itself
England is safe, if true within itself?

MONTAGUE But the safer when 'tis backed with France.

HASTINGS 'Tis better using France than trusting
    France:
Let us be backed with God and with the seas
Which He hath given for fence impregnable,
45 And with their helps only defend ourselves;
In them and in ourselves our safety lies.

CLARENCE For this one speech Lord Hastings well
    deserves
To have the heir of the Lord Hungerford.

KING EDWARD Ay, what of that? It was my will and
    grant;
50 And for this once my will shall stand for law.

RICHARD And yet methinks your Grace hath not done
    well,
To give the heir and daughter of Lord Scales
Unto the brother of your loving bride.
She better would have fitted me or Clarence;
55 But in your bride you bury brotherhood.

CLARENCE Or else you would not have bestowed the
    heir
Of the Lord Bonville on your new wife's son,
And leave your brothers to go speed elsewhere.

KING EDWARD Alas, poor Clarence! Is it for a wife
60 That thou art malcontent? I will provide thee.

CLARENCE In choosing for yourself, you showed your
    judgment,
Which being shallow, you shall give me leave

45 only alone   58 speed prosper

To play the broker in mine own behalf;
And to that end I shortly mind to leave you.

KING EDWARD Leave me or tarry, Edward will be
    King,   65
And not be tied unto his brother's will.

QUEEN ELIZABETH My lords, before it pleased his
    Majesty
To raise my state to title of a queen,
Do me but right, and you must all confess
That I was not ignoble of descent;   70
And meaner than myself have had like fortune.
But as this title honors me and mine,
So your dislikes, to whom I would be pleasing,
Doth cloud my joys with danger and with sorrow.

KING EDWARD My love, forbear to fawn upon their
    frowns.   75
What danger or what sorrow can befall thee,
So long as Edward is thy constant friend
And their true sovereign, whom they must obey?
Nay, whom they shall obey, and love thee too,
Unless they seek for hatred at my hands;   80
Which if they do, yet will I keep thee safe,
And they shall feel the vengeance of my wrath.

RICHARD [Aside] I hear, yet say not much, but think
    the more.

Enter a Post.

KING EDWARD Now, messenger, what letters or what
    news
From France?   85

POST My sovereign liege, no letters; and few words,
But such as I, without your special pardon,
Dare not relate.

KING EDWARD Go to, we pardon thee. Therefore, in
    brief,

63 **play the broker** act as go-between   71 **meaner** persons of lower rank
87 **pardon** permission   89 **Go to** (exclamation of impatience)

327

Tell me their words as near as thou canst guess
90   them.
What answer makes King Lewis unto our letters?

POST At my depart, these were his very words:
"Go tell false Edward, thy supposèd King,
That Lewis of France is sending over masquers
95 To revel it with him and his new bride."

KING EDWARD Is Lewis so brave? Belike he thinks
me Henry.
But what said Lady Bona to my marriage?

POST These were her words, uttered with mild
disdain:
"Tell him, in hope he'll prove a widower shortly,
100 I'll wear the willow garland for his sake."

KING EDWARD I blame not her, she could say little less;
She had the wrong. But what said Henry's queen?
For I have heard that she was there in place.

POST "Tell him," quoth she, "my mourning weeds
are done,
105 And I am ready to put armor on."

KING EDWARD Belike she minds to play the Amazon.
But what said Warwick to these injuries?

POST He, more incensed against your Majesty
Than all the rest, discharged me with these words:
110 "Tell him from me that he hath done me wrong,
And therefore I'll uncrown him ere't be long."

KING EDWARD Ha! durst the traitor breathe out so
proud words?
Well, I will arm me, being thus forewarned.
They shall have wars and pay for their presumption.
115 But say, is Warwick friends with Margaret?

POST Ay, gracious sovereign. They are so linked in
friendship

96 **brave** defiant   107 **injuries** insults

That young Prince Edward marries Warwick's
  daughter.

CLARENCE Belike the elder; Clarence will have the
  younger.
Now, brother king, farewell, and sit you fast,
For I will hence to Warwick's other daughter,   120
That, though I want a kingdom, yet in marriage
I may not prove inferior to yourself.
You that love me and Warwick, follow me.
                   Exit Clarence, and Somerset follows.

RICHARD [*Aside*] Not I:
My thoughts aim at a further matter. I   125
Stay not for the love of Edward, but the crown.

KING EDWARD Clarence and Somerset both gone to
  Warwick!
Yet am I armed against the worst can happen;
And haste is needful in this desp'rate case.
Pembroke and Stafford, you in our behalf   130
Go levy men, and make prepare for war.
They are already, or quickly will be, landed.
Myself in person will straight follow you.
                   Exeunt Pembroke and Stafford.
But, ere I go, Hastings and Montague,
Resolve my doubt. You twain, of all the rest,   135
Are near to Warwick by blood and by alliance.
Tell me if you love Warwick more than me.
If it be so, then both depart to him;
I rather wish you foes than hollow friends.
But if you mind to hold your true obedience,   140
Give me assurance with some friendly vow,
That I may never have you in suspect.

MONTAGUE So God help Montague as he proves true!

HASTINGS And Hastings as he favors Edward's cause!

KING EDWARD Now, brother Richard, will you stand
  by us?   145

118 **Belike** probably   121 **want** lack

RICHARD Ay, in despite of all that shall withstand you.

KING EDWARD Why, so! then am I sure of victory.
    Now therefore let us hence, and lose no hour,
    Till we meet Warwick with his foreign pow'r.

                                             Exeunt.

Scene II. [*A plain in Warwickshire.*]

*Enter Warwick and Oxford in England, with
French Soldiers.*

WARWICK Trust me, my lord, all hitherto goes well;
    The common people by numbers swarm to us.

            Enter Clarence and Somerset.

    But see where Somerset and Clarence comes!
    Speak suddenly, my lords, are we all friends?

5   CLARENCE Fear not that, my lord.

WARWICK Then, gentle Clarence, welcome unto
        Warwick;
    And welcome, Somerset: I hold it cowardice
    To rest mistrustful where a noble heart
    Hath pawned an open hand in sign of love.
10 Else might I think that Clarence, Edward's brother,
    Were but a feignèd friend to our proceedings:
    But welcome, sweet Clarence; my daughter shall be
        thine.
    And now what rests but, in night's coverture,
    Thy brother being carelessly encamped,
15 His soldiers lurking in the towns about,
    And but attended by a simple guard,

IV.ii.1 **hitherto** thus far   4 **suddenly** at once   5 **Fear not that** do not doubt
it   8 **rest** remain   9 **pawned** pledged   13 **in night's coverture** under cover of
night

330

We may surprise and take him at our pleasure?
Our scouts have found the adventure very easy:
That as Ulysses and stout Diomede
With sleight and manhood stole to Rhesus' tents,   20
And brought from thence the Thracian fatal
    steeds,
So we, well covered with the night's black mantle,
At unawares may beat down Edward's guard
And seize himself. I say not, slaughter him,
For I intend but only to surprise him.   25
You that will follow me to this attempt,
Applaud the name of Henry with your leader.
                            They all cry, "Henry!"
Why, then, let's on our way in silent sort.
For Warwick and his friends, God and Saint
    George!   *Exeunt.*

Scene III. [*Edward's camp, near Warwick.*]

Enter three Watchmen, to guard the King's tent.

FIRST WATCHMAN Come on, my masters, each man
    take his stand.
    The King by this is set him down to sleep.

SECOND WATCHMAN What, will he not to bed?

FIRST WATCHMAN Why, no; for he hath made a solemn
    vow
    Never to lie and take his natural rest   5
    Till Warwick or himself be quite suppressed.

---

19 stout valiant 20 sleight trickery 19-21 That as Ulysses ... fatal steeds
Iliad, X. (because an oracle had said that Troy could not be taken if Rhesus' horses
grazed on Trojan plains, the Greeks sent Ulysses and Diomede to capture the
horses before they reached Troy) 28 in silent sort silently IV.iii.2 by this by
this time

SECOND WATCHMAN Tomorrow then belike shall be
    the day,
  If Warwick be so near as men report.

THIRD WATCHMAN But say, I pray, what nobleman is
    that
10   That with the King here resteth in his tent?

FIRST WATCHMAN 'Tis the Lord Hastings, the King's
  chiefest friend.

THIRD WATCHMAN O, is it so? But why commands the
    King
  That his chief followers lodge in towns about him,
  While he himself keeps in the cold field?

SECOND WATCHMAN 'Tis the more honor, because more
15   dangerous.

THIRD WATCHMAN Ay, but give me worship and
    quietness;
  I like it better than a dangerous honor.
  If Warwick knew in what estate he stands,
  'Tis to be doubted he would waken him.

FIRST WATCHMAN Unless our halberds did shut up his
20   passage.

SECOND WATCHMAN Ay, wherefore else guard we his
  royal tent,
  But to defend his person from night-foes?

Enter Warwick, Clarence, Oxford, Somerset, and
French Soldiers, silent all.

WARWICK This is his tent; and see where stand his
    guard.
  Courage, my masters! honor now or never!
25 But follow me, and Edward shall be ours.

FIRST WATCHMAN Who goes there?

SECOND WATCHMAN Stay, or thou diest!

14 **keeps** lives 16 **worship** ease and dignity 18 **he** i.e., the King 19 **doubted**
suspected 20 **halberds** battle-axes on poles

332

Warwick and the rest cry all, "Warwick! Warwick!"
and set upon the Guard, who fly, crying, "Arm! arm!",
Warwick and the rest following them.

The Drum playing and Trumpet sounding, enter
Warwick, Somerset, and the rest, bringing the King out
in his gown, sitting in a chair. Richard and Hastings flies
over the stage.

SOMERSET What are they that fly there?

WARWICK Richard and Hastings. Let them go. Here is
The Duke.

KING EDWARD The Duke! Why, Warwick, when we
    parted,   30
Thou call'dst me King.

WARWICK   Ay, but the case is altered:
When you disgraced me in my embassade,
Then I degraded you from being King,
And come now to create you Duke of York.
Alas, how should you govern any kingdom,   35
That know not how to use ambassadors,
Nor how to be contented with one wife,
Nor how to use your brothers brotherly,
Nor how to study for the people's welfare,
Nor how to shroud yourself from enemies?   40

KING EDWARD Yea, brother of Clarence, art thou here
    too?
Nay, then I see that Edward needs must down.
Yet, Warwick, in despite of all mischance,
Of thee thyself and all thy complices,
Edward will always bear himself as King: 45
Though fortune's malice overthrow my state,
My mind exceeds the compass of her wheel.

WARWICK Then, for his mind, be Edward England's
    King: *Takes off his crown.*
But Henry now shall wear the English crown,

32 **embassade** ambassadorial errand 46 **state** sovereignty 47 **compass**
range 48 **for his mind** i.e., in Edward's mind (but not otherwise)

50   And be true king indeed, thou but the shadow.
      My Lord of Somerset, at my request,
      See that forthwith Duke Edward be conveyed
      Unto my brother, Archbishop of York.
      When I have fought with Pembroke and his fellows,
55   I'll follow you, and tell what answer
      Lewis and the Lady Bona send to him.
      Now, for a while farewell, good Duke of York.
                              They lead him out forcibly.

    KING EDWARD What fates impose, that men must
      needs abide;
      It boots not to resist both wind and tide.   *Exeunt.*

60 OXFORD What now remains, my lords, for us to do
      But march to London with our soldiers?

    WARWICK Ay, that's the first thing that we have to do,
      To free King Henry from imprisonment
      And see him seated in the regal throne.   *Exeunt.*

                Scene IV. [*London. The Palace.*]

            Enter Rivers and Lady Grey [as Queen].

    RIVERS Madam, what makes you in this sudden
      change?

    QUEEN ELIZABETH Why, brother Rivers, are you yet to
      learn
      What late misfortune is befall'n King Edward?

    RIVERS What, loss of some pitched battle against War-
      wick?

    QUEEN ELIZABETH No, but the loss of his own royal
5   person.

IV.iv.1 **Madam ... change?** What is the cause of this sudden change in you?

RIVERS Then is my sovereign slain?

QUEEN ELIZABETH Ay, almost slain, for he is taken
    prisoner,
  Either betrayed by falsehood of his guard
  Or by his foe surprised at unawares;
  And, as I further have to understand,   10
  Is new committed to the Bishop of York,
  Fell Warwick's brother and by that our foe.

RIVERS These news, I must confess, are full of grief;
  Yet, gracious madam, bear it as you may:
  Warwick may lose, that now hath won the day.   15

QUEEN ELIZABETH Till then fair hope must hinder life's
    decay.
  And I the rather wean me from despair
  For love of Edward's offspring in my womb.
  This is it that makes me bridle passion
  And bear with mildness my misfortune's cross.   20
  Ay, ay, for this I draw in many a tear
  And stop the rising of blood-sucking sighs,
  Lest with my sighs or tears I blast or drown
  King Edward's fruit, true heir to th' English crown.

RIVERS But, madam, where is Warwick then become?   25

QUEEN ELIZABETH I am informèd that he comes
    towards London,
  To set the crown once more on Henry's head.
  Guess thou the rest; King Edward's friends must
    down.
  But, to prevent the tyrant's violence—
  (For trust not him that hath once broken faith)   30
  I'll hence forthwith unto the sanctuary,
  To save at least the heir of Edward's right.
  There shall I rest secure from force and fraud.
  Come, therefore, let us fly while we may fly.
  If Warwick take us we are sure to die.   *Exeunt.*   35

8 **falsehood** treachery 9 **surprised at** captured 25 **where … become** what
has become of Warwick 29 **prevent** forestall

Scene V. [*A park near Middleham Castle in
Yorkshire.*]

*Enter Richard, Lord Hastings, and Sir William
Stanley.*

RICHARD Now, my Lord Hastings and Sir William
    Stanley,
    Leave off to wonder why I drew you hither,
    Into this chiefest thicket of the park.
    Thus stands the case: you know our King, my
    brother,
5   Is prisoner to the Bishop here, at whose hands
    He hath good usage and great liberty,
    And often but attended with weak guard,
    Comes hunting this way to disport himself.
    I have advertised him by secret means
10   That if about this hour he make this way
    Under the color of his usual game,
    He shall here find his friends with horse and men
    To set him free from his captivity.

Enter King Edward and a Huntsman with him.

HUNTSMAN This way, my lord, for this way lies the
    game.

KING EDWARD Nay, this way, man! See where the
15   huntsmen stand.
    Now, brother of Gloucester, Lord Hastings, and
    the rest,
    Stand you thus close, to steal the Bishop's deer?

RICHARD Brother, the time and case requireth haste:
    Your horse stands ready at the park-corner.

IV.v.9 **advertised** informed 11 **color** pretext 14 **game** quarry 17 **close**
concealed

KING EDWARD But whither shall we then?

HASTINGS   To Lynn, my lord,   20
  And ship from thence to Flanders.

RICHARD Well guessed, believe me; for that was my
    meaning.

KING EDWARD Stanley, I will requite thy forwardness.

RICHARD But wherefore stay we? 'tis no time to talk.

KING EDWARD Huntsman, what say'st thou? wilt thou
    go along?   25

HUNTSMAN Better do so than tarry and be hanged.

RICHARD Come then, away; let's ha' no more ado.

KING EDWARD Bishop, farewell. Shield thee from War-
    wick's frown
  And pray that I may repossess the crown.   *Exeunt*.

Scene VI. [*London. The Tower.*]

Flourish. Enter King Henry the Sixth, Clarence,
Warwick, Somerset, young Henry [Earl of Richmond],
Oxford, Montague, and Lieutenant [of the Tower].

KING HENRY Master Lieutenant, now that God and
    friends
  Have shaken Edward from the regal seat
  And turned my captive state to liberty,
  My fear to hope, my sorrows unto joys,
  At our enlargement what are thy due fees?   5

LIEUTENANT Subjects may challenge nothing of their
    sovereigns;

23 forwardness zeal   24 stay delay   IV.vi.5 enlargement liberation   6 challenge demand

But, if an humble prayer may prevail,
I then crave pardon of your Majesty.

KING HENRY For what, Lieutenant? for well using me?
10 Nay, be thou sure I'll well requite thy kindness
For that it made my imprisonment a pleasure;
Ay, such a pleasure as incagèd birds
Conceive when after many moody thoughts
At last by notes of household harmony
15 They quite forget their loss of liberty.
But, Warwick, after God, thou set'st me free,
And chiefly therefore I thank God and thee;
He was the author, thou the instrument.
Therefore, that I my conquer Fortune's spite
20 By living low, where Fortune cannot hurt me,
And that the people of this blessèd land
May not be punished with my thwarting stars,
Warwick, although my head still wear the crown,
I here resign my government to thee,
25 For thou art fortunate in all thy deeds.

WARWICK Your Grace hath still been famed for
      virtuous;
And now may seem as wise as virtuous,
By spying and avoiding Fortune's malice,
For few men rightly temper with the stars:
30 Yet in this one thing let me blame your Grace,
For choosing me when Clarence is in place.

CLARENCE No, Warwick, thou art worthy of the sway,
To whom the heavens in thy nativity
Adjudged an olive branch and laurel crown,
35 As likely to be blest in peace and war;
And therefore I yield thee my free consent.

WARWICK And I choose Clarence only for Protector.

KING HENRY Warwick and Clarence, give me both
      your hands:

20 **low** humbly   22 **thwarting stars** ill fortune   26 **still** always   26 **famed for**
reputed   29 **temper** blend, accord   31 **in place** present   32 **sway** power
33 **nativity** horoscope

Now join your hands, and with your hands your
   hearts,
That no dissension hinder government: 40
I make you both Protectors of this land,
While I myself will lead a private life,
And in devotion spend my latter days,
To sin's rebuke and my Creator's praise.

WARWICK What answers Clarence to his sovereign's
   will?   45

CLARENCE That he consents, if Warwick yield consent,
For on thy fortune I repose myself.

WARWICK Why, then, though loath, yet must I be
   content:
We'll yoke together, like a double shadow
To Henry's body, and supply his place;   50
I mean, in bearing weight of government,
While he enjoys the honor and his ease.
And, Clarence, now then it is more than needful
Forthwith that Edward be pronounced a traitor,
And all his lands and good be confiscate.   55

CLARENCE What else? And that succession be
   determined.

WARWICK Ay, therein Clarence shall not want his
   part.

KING HENRY But, with the first of all your chief affairs,
Let me entreat (for I command no more)
That Margaret your queen and my son Edward   60
Be sent for, to return from France with speed;
For, till I see them here, by doubtful fear
My joy of liberty is half eclipsed.

CLARENCE It shall be done, my sovereign, with all
   speed.

KING HENRY My Lord of Somerset, what youth is that,   65
Of whom you seem to have so tender care?

47 **repose myself** rely   57 **want his part** lack his share

SOMERSET My liege, it is young Henry, Earl of
   Richmond.

KING HENRY Come hither, England's hope. *(Lays his
   hand on his head.)* If secret powers
   Suggest but truth to my divining thoughts,
70 This pretty lad will prove our country's bliss.
   His looks are full of peaceful majesty,
   His head by nature framed to wear a crown,
   His hand to wield a scepter, and himself
   Likely in time to bless a regal throne.
75 Make much of him, my lords, for this is he
   Must help you more than you are hurt by me.

Enter a Post.

WARWICK What news, my friend?

POST The Edward is escapèd from your brother,
   And fled, as he hears since, to Burgundy.

80 WARWICK Unsavory news! but how made he escape?

POST He was conveyed by Richard Duke of
   Gloucester
   And the Lord Hastings, who attended him
   In secret ambush on the forest side
   And from the Bishop's huntsmen rescued him;
85 For hunting was his daily exercise.

WARWICK My brother was too careless of his charge.
   But let us hence, my sovereign, to provide
   A salve for any sore that may betide.
             Exeunt. Manet Somerset, Richmond, and Oxford.

SOMERSET My lord, I like not of this flight of Edward's,
90 For doubtless Burgundy will yield him help,
   And we shall have more wars before't be long.
   As Henry's late presaging prophecy
   Did glad my heart with hope of this young
   Richmond,

81 **conveyed** stolen away   82 **attended** waited for   88 s.d. **Manet** remains (the
Latin singular is often used in Elizabethan directions with a plural subject)

So doth my heart misgive me, in these conflicts
What may befall him, to his harm and ours: 95
Therefore, Lord Oxford, to prevent the worst,
Forthwith we'll send him hence to Brittany,
Till storms be past of civil enmity.

OXFORD Ay, for if Edward repossess the crown,
'Tis like that Richmond with the rest shall down.   100

SOMERSET It shall be so; he shall to Brittany.
Come, therefore, let's about it speedily.   *Exeunt*.

Scene VII. [*Before York*.]

*Flourish. Enter [King] Edward, Richard, Hastings,
and Soldiers.*

KING EDWARD Now, brother Richard, Lord Hastings,
   and the rest,
Yet thus far Fortune maketh us amends,
And says that once more I shall interchange
My wanèd state for Henry's regal crown.
Well have we passed and now repassed the seas   5
And brought desirèd help from Burgundy.
What then remains, we being thus arrived
From Ravenspurgh haven before the gates of York,
But that we enter, as into our dukedom?

RICHARD The gates made fast! Brother, I like not this. 10
For many men that stumble at the threshold
Are well foretold that danger lurks within.

KING EDWARD Tush, man, abodements must not now
   affright us:
By fair or foul means we must enter in,
For hither will our friends repair to us.   15

IV.vii.13 **abodements** omens   15 **repair** come

341

HASTINGS My liege, I'll knock once more to summon
    them.

Enter, on the walls, the Mayor of York and his
Brethren.

MAYOR My lords, we were forewarnèd of your
    coming,
  And shut the gates for safety of ourselves;
  For now we owe allegiance unto Henry.

KING EDWARD But, Master Mayor, if Henry be your
20   king,
  Yet Edward at the least is Duke of York.

MAYOR True, my good lord; I know you for no less.

KING EDWARD Why, and I challenge nothing but my
    dukedom,
  As being well content with that alone.

25 RICHARD But when the fox hath once got in his nose,
  He'll soon find means to make the body follow.

HASTINGS Why, Master Mayor, why stand you in a
    doubt?
  Open the gates; we are King Henry's friends.

MAYOR Ay, say you so? the gates shall then be opened.
                    He descends [with the Aldermen].

30 RICHARD A wise stout captain, and soon persuaded!

HASTINGS The good old man would fain that all were
    well,
  So 'twere not long of him; but being entered,
  I doubt not, I, but we shall soon persuade
  Both him and all his brothers unto reason.

Enter the Mayor and two Aldermen, [below].

KING EDWARD So, Master Mayor: these gates must
35   not be shut

30 **stout** valiant (here ironic)　32 **long of** because of

But in the night or in the time of war.
What! fear not, man, but yield me up the keys;
                                        Takes his keys.
For Edward will defend the town and thee,
And all those friends that deign to follow me.

March. Enter Montgomery, with Drum and Soldiers.

RICHARD Brother, this is Sir John Montgomery,   40
Our trusty friend, unless I be deceived.

KING EDWARD Welcome, Sir John! But why come you
in arms?

MONTGOMERY To help King Edward in his time of
storm,
As every loyal subject ought to do.

KING EDWARD Thanks, good Montgomery. But we
now forget   45
Our title to the crown and only claim
Our dukedom till God please to send the rest.

MONTGOMERY Then fare you well, for I will hence
again:
I came to serve a king and not a duke.
Drummer, strike up, and let us march away.   50
                        The Drum begins to march.

KING EDWARD Nay stay, Sir John, awhile, and we'll
debate
By what safe means the crown may be recovered.

MONTGOMERY What talk you of debating? in few
words,
If you'll not here proclaim yourself our King,
I'll leave you to your fortune and be gone   55
To keep them back that come to succor you.
Why shall we fight, if you pretend no title?

RICHARD Why, brother, wherefore stand you on nice
points?

57 **pretend** claim   58 **nice points** subtle distinctions

343

KING EDWARD When we grow stronger, then we'll
    make our claim;
60   Till then, 'tis wisdom to conceal our meaning.

HASTINGS Away with scrupulous wit! Now arms must
    rule.

RICHARD And fearless minds climb soonest unto
    crowns.
    Brother, we will proclaim you out of hand;
    The bruit thereof will bring you many friends.

65 KING EDWARD Then be it as you will; for 'tis my right,
    And Henry but usurps the diadem.

MONTGOMERY Ay, now my sovereign speaketh like
    himself;
    And now will I be Edward's champion.

HASTINGS Sound trumpet; Edward shall be here
    proclaimed.
70   Come, fellow-soldier, make thou proclamation.
                        Flourish. Sound.

SOLDIER Edward the Fourth, by the grace of God, King
    of England and France, and Lord of Ireland, &c.

MONTGOMERY And whosoe'er gainsays King Edward's
    right,
    By this I challenge him to single fight.
                   Throws down his gauntlet.

75 ALL Long live Edward the Fourth!

KING EDWARD Thanks, brave Montgomery; and thanks
    unto you all:
    If fortune serve me, I'll requite this kindness.
    Now, for this night, let's harbor here in York;
    And when the morning sun shall raise his car
80   Above the border of this horizon,
    We'll forward towards Warwick and his mates;

---

64 **bruit** rumor   71-72 **Edward ... &c.** (this is the only prose passage in the play.
The use of prose here represents the language of proclamations, official documents,
and formal statements)   79 **car** chariot (of Phoebus Apollo)

For well I wot that Henry is no soldier.
Ah, froward Clarence! how evil it beseems thee,
To flatter Henry and forsake thy brother!
Yet, as we may, we'll meet both thee and Warwick.   85
Come on, brave soldiers. Doubt not of the day,
And, that once gotten, doubt not of large pay.

                                                    Exeunt.

                  Scene VIII. [*London.*
           The Bishop of London's Palace.]

         Flourish. Enter the King [*Henry*], *Warwick,
         Montague, Clarence, Oxford, and Exeter.*

WARWICK What counsel, lords? Edward from Belgia,
    With hasty Germans and blunt Hollanders,
    Hath passed in safety through the Narrow Seas,
    And with his troops doth march amain to London;
    And many giddy people flock to him.   5

KING HENRY Let's levy men, and beat him back again.

CLARENCE A little fire is quickly trodden out;
    Which, being suffered, rivers cannot quench.

WARWICK In Warwickshire I have true-hearted friends,
    Not mutinous in peace, yet bold in war;   10
    Those will I muster up: and thou, son Clarence,
    Shalt stir up in Suffolk, Norfolk and in Kent,
    The knights and gentlemen to come with thee.
    Thou, brother Montague, in Buckingham,
    Northampton, and in Leicestershire shalt find   15
    Men well inclined to hear what thou command'st.
    And thou, brave Oxford, wondrous well beloved,
    In Oxfordshire shalt muster up thy friends.
    My sovereign, with the loving citizens,

82 **wot** know   83 **froward** rebellious   IV.viii.2 **blunt** rude   4 **amain** with full
speed   8 **suffered** allowed (to grow)

20   Like to his island girt in with the ocean,
       Or modest Dian circled with her nymphs,
       Shall rest in London till we come to him.
       Fair lords, take leave and stand not to reply.
       Farewell, my sovereign.

KING HENRY   Farewell, my Hector, and my Troy's true
25   hope.

CLARENCE   In sign of truth, I kiss your Highness' hand.

KING HENRY   Well-minded Clarence, be thou
           fortunate!

MONTAGUE   Comfort, my lord! and so I take my leave.

OXFORD   And thus I seal my truth and bid adieu.

30   KING HENRY   Sweet Oxford, and my loving Montague,
           And all at once, once more a happy farewell.

WARWICK   Farewell, sweet lords; let's meet at
           Coventry.
                           Exeunt [all but King Henry and Exeter].

KING HENRY   Here at the palace will I rest awhile.
           Cousin of Exeter, what thinks your lordship?
35   Methinks the power that Edward hath in field
           Should not be able to encounter mine.

EXETER   The doubt is that he will seduce the rest.

KING HENRY   That's not my fear. My meed hath got
           me fame.
           I have not stopped mine ears to their demands,
40   Nor posted off their suits with slow delays.
           My pity hath been balm to heal their wounds,
           My mildness hath allayed their swelling griefs,
           My mercy dried their water-flowing tears.
           I have not been desirous of their wealth
45   Nor much oppressed them with great subsidies,
           Nor forward of revenge, though they much erred.

21 **Dian** Diana, goddess of chastity   27 **Well-minded** well-disposed   37 **doubt** fear   38 **meed** merit, worth   40 **posted off** postponed   45 **subsidies** taxes 46 **forward of** eager for

Then why should they love Edward more than me?
No, Exeter, these graces challenge grace;
And when the lion fawns upon the lamb,
The lamb will never cease to follow him.   50
　　　　Shout within, "A Lancaster! A Lancaster!"

EXETER Hark, hark, my lord! what shouts are these?

　　Enter [King] Edward, [Richard,] and his Soldiers.

KING EDWARD Seize on the shamefaced Henry, bear
　　him hence;
And once again proclaim us King of England.
You are the fount that makes small brooks to flow.
Now stops thy spring; my sea shall suck them dry   55
And swell so much the higher by their ebb.
Hence with him to the Tower. Let him not speak.
　　　　　　　Exit [some] with King Henry.
And, lords, towards Coventry bend we our course,
Where peremptory Warwick now remains:
The sun shines hot; and, if we use delay,   60
Cold biting winter mars our hoped-for hay.

RICHARD Away betimes, before his forces join,
And take the great-grown traitor unawares.
Brave warriors, march amain towards Coventry.
　　　　　　　　　　　　　　Exeunt.

48 **graces challenge grace** virtues claim favor   50 s.d. **A ... Lancaster!** (so in F.
Many editors read: "A York! A York!" as signalizing entrance of King Edward)
52 **shamefaced** modest, bashful   59 **peremptory** overbearing   64 **amain**
swiftly

347

ACT V.

Scene I. [*Coventry.*]

Enter Warwick, the Mayor of Coventry, two
Messengers, and others upon the walls.

WARWICK Where is the post that came from valiant
    Oxford?
    How far hence is thy lord, mine honest fellow?

FIRST MESSENGER By this at Dunsmore, marching
    hitherward.

WARWICK How far off is our brother Montague?
5   Where is the post that came from Montague?

SECOND MESSENGER By this at Daintry, with a puissant
    troop.

Enter [Sir John] Somerville.

WARWICK Say, Somerville, what says my loving son?
    And, by thy guess, how nigh is Clarence now?

SOMERVILLE At Southam I did leave him with his
    forces,
10   And do expect him here some two hours hence.
                          [*Drum heard.*]

WARWICK Then Clarence is at hand; I hear his drum.

SOMERVILLE It is not his, my lord. Here Southam lies.
    The drum your Honor hears marcheth from
    Warwick.

V.i.3,6 **By this** by this time

348

WARWICK Who should that be? Belike, unlooked-for
    friends.

SOMERVILLE They are at hand, and you shall quickly
    know.   15

March. Flourish. Enter [King] Edward, Richard,
                      and Soldiers.

KING EDWARD Go, trumpet, to the walls, and sound
    a parle.

RICHARD See how the surly Warwick mans the wall!

WARWICK O unbid spite! Is sportful Edward come?
    Where slept our scouts, or how are they seduced,
    That we could hear no news of his repair?   20

KING EDWARD Now, Warwick, wilt thou ope the city
    gates,
    Speak gentle words and humbly bend thy knee,
    Call Edward King, and at his hands beg mercy?
    And he shall pardon thee these outrages.

WARWICK Nay, rather, wilt thou draw thy forces
    hence,   25
    Confess who set thee up and plucked thee down,
    Call Warwick patron and be penitent?
    And thou shalt still remain the Duke of York.

RICHARD I thought, at least, he would have said "the
    King";
    Or did he make the jest against his will?   30

WARWICK Is not a dukedom, sir, a goodly gift?

RICHARD Ay, by my faith, for a poor earl to give!
    I'll do thee service for so good a gift.

WARWICK 'Twas I that gave the kingdom to thy
    brother.

KING EDWARD Why then 'tis mine, if but by Warwick's
    gift.   35

WARWICK Thou art no Atlas for so great a weight;

16 **trumpet** trumpeter   18 **sportful** wanton   20 **repair** return

And, weakling, Warwick takes his gift again,
And Henry is my king, Warwick his subject.

KING EDWARD But Warwick's king is Edward's
    prisoner;
40   And, gallant Warwick, do but answer this:
What is the body when the head is off?

RICHARD Alas, that Warwick had no more forecast,
But, whiles he thought to steal the single ten,
The king was slily fingered from the deck!
45   You left poor Henry at the Bishop's palace,
And ten to one you'll meet him in the Tower.

KING EDWARD 'Tis even so. Yet you are Warwick
    still.

RICHARD Come, Warwick, take the time. Kneel down,
    kneel down!
Nay, when? Strike now, or else the iron cools.

50 WARWICK I had rather chop this hand off at a blow,
And with the other fling it at thy face,
Than bear so low a sail to strike to thee.

KING EDWARD Sail how thou canst, have wind and
    tide thy friend,
This hand, fast wound about thy coal-black hair,
55   Shall, whiles thy head is warm and new cut off,
Write in the dust this sentence with thy blood,
"Wind-changing Warwick now can change no
    more."

Enter Oxford, with Drum and Colors.

WARWICK O cheerful colors! see where Oxford comes!

OXFORD Oxford, Oxford, for Lancaster!
                         [He and his forces enter the city].

60 RICHARD The gates are open, let us enter too.

42 **forecast** foresight   43 **single ten** mere ten (not a court card)   48 **take the
time** seize the opportunity   49 **when** (exclamation of impatience)   49 **Strike**
(1) act (i.e., while the iron is hot) (2) yield   52 **bear ... thee** be so humble as to
surrender to you

KING EDWARD So other foes may set upon our backs.
  Stand we in good array, for they no doubt
  Will issue out again and bid us battle.
  If not, the city being but of small defense,
  We'll quickly rouse the traitors in the same.   65

WARWICK O, welcome, Oxford! for we want thy help.

  Enter Montague, with Drum and Colors.

MONTAGUE Montague, Montague, for Lancaster!
                    [*He and his forces enter the city.*]

RICHARD Thou and thy brother both shall buy this
    treason
  Even with the dearest blood your bodies bear.

KING EDWARD The harder matched, the greater vic-
    tory: 70
  My mind presageth happy gain and conquest.

  Enter Somerset, with Drum and Colors.

SOMERSET Somerset, Somerset, for Lancaster!
                    [*He and his forces enter the city.*]

RICHARD Two of thy name, both Dukes of Somerset,
  Have sold their lives unto the house of York;
  And thou shalt be the third, if this sword hold.   75

  Enter Clarence, with Drum and Colors.

WARWICK And lo, where George of Clarence sweeps
    along,

---

65 **rouse** flush (as an animal from its lair)   75 s.d. (at this point Q introduces the
following dialogue and business:

Warwick And loe where *George* of *Clarence* sweepes
  Along, of power enough to bid his brother battell.
Clarence. Clarence, Clarence, for *Lancaster.*
Edward Et tu Brute, wilt thou stab *Cæsar* too?
  A parlie sirra to *George* of Clarence.
  Sound a Parlie, and *Richard* and *Clarence* whispers togither, and then Clarence
takes his red Rose out of his hat and throwes it at *Warwike.*

This passage, and especially the stage direction, follows closely the account in the
chronicles of both Hall and Holinshed of Clarence's final change of allegiance.)

Of force enough to bid his brother battle;
With whom an upright zeal to right prevails
More than the nature of a brother's love!
80   Come, Clarence, come! Thou wilt, if Warwick call.

CLARENCE Father of Warwick, know you what this
        means?   [*Takes his red rose out of his hat.*]
    Look here, I throw my infamy at thee.
    I will not ruinate my father's house,
    Who gave his blood to lime the stones together,
    And set up Lancaster. Why, trowest thou,
85   Warwick,
    That Clarence is so harsh, so blunt, unnatural,
    To bend the fatal instruments of war
    Against his brother and his lawful king?
    Perhaps thou wilt object my holy oath.
90   To keep that oath were more impiety
    Than Jephthah, when he sacrificed his daughter.
    I am so sorry for my trespass made
    That, to deserve well at my brother's hands,
    I here proclaim myself thy mortal foe,
95   With resolution, whereso'er I meet thee
    (As I will meet thee, if thou stir abroad)
    To plague thee for thy foul misleading me.
    And so, proud-hearted Warwick, I defy thee,
    And to my brother turn my blushing cheeks.
100   Pardon me, Edward! I will make amends;
    And, Richard, do not frown upon my faults,
    For I will henceforth be no more unconstant.

KING EDWARD Now welcome more, and ten times
        more beloved,
    Than if thou never hadst deserved our hate.

RICHARD Welcome, good Clarence! This is brother-
105   like.

WARWICK O passing traitor, perjured and unjust!

81s.d. **Takes ... hat** i.e., removes the symbol of his allegiance to the House of
Lancaster 84 **lime** join with mortar 85 **trowest thou** do you think 89 **object**
invoke 91 **Jephthah ... daughter** (see Judges xi.30) 106 **passing** extreme

KING EDWARD What, Warwick, wilt thou leave the
    town, and fight?
    Or shall we beat the stones about thine ears?

WARWICK Alas, I am not cooped here for defense!
    I will away towards Barnet presently,   110
    And bid thee battle, Edward, if thou dar'st.

KING EDWARD Yes, Warwick, Edward dares, and
    leads the way.
    Lords, to the field. Saint George and victory!
             Exeunt [King Edward and his company].
             March. Warwick and his company follows.

Scene II. [*A field of battle near Barnet.*]

*Alarum and excursions. Enter [King] Edward,
bringing forth Warwick wounded.*

KING EDWARD So, lie thou there! Die thou, and die our
    fear!
    For Warwick was a bug that feared us all.
    Now, Montague, sit fast! I seek for thee,
    That Warwick's bones may keep thine company.
                          Exit.

WARWICK Ah, who is nigh? Come to me, friend or foe,   5
    And tell me who is victor, York or Warwick.
    Why ask I that? My mangled body shows,
    My blood, my want of strength, my sick heart
        shows,
    That I must yield my body to the earth
    And, by my fall, the conquest to my foe.   10
    Thus yields the cedar to the ax's edge,
    Whose arms gave shelter to the princely eagle,

109 **cooped** prepared 110 **presently,** immediately V.ii.2 **bug** bug-bear
2 **feared** terrified 3 **sit fast** watch out

Under whose shade the ramping lion slept,
Whose top-branch overpeered Jove's spreading
    tree
15 And kept low shrubs from winter's pow'rful wind.
These eyes, that now are dimmed with death's
    black veil,
Have been as piercing as the mid-day sun
To search the secret treasons of the world.
The wrinkles in my brows, now filled with blood,
20 Were likened oft to kingly sepulchers;
For who lived king but I could dig his grave?
And who durst smile when Warwick bent his brow?
Lo, now my glory smeared in dust and blood!
My parks, my walks, my manors that I had,
25 Even now forsake me, and of all my lands
Is nothing left me but my body's length.
Why, what is pomp, rule, reign, but earth and dust?
And, live we how we can, yet die we must.

Enter Oxford and Somerset.

SOMERSET Ah, Warwick, Warwick! wert thou as we
    are,
30 We might recover all our loss again!
The Queen from France hath brought a puissant
    power.
Even now we heard the news. Ah, couldst thou fly!

WARWICK Why, then I would not fly. Ah, Montague,
If thou be there, sweet brother, take my hand,
35 And with thy lips keep in my soul awhile!
Thou lov'st me not; for, brother, if thou didst,
Thy tears would wash this cold congealèd blood
That glues my lips and will not let me speak.
Cone quickly, Montague, or I am dead.

SOMERSET Ah, Warwick! Montague hath breathed his
40   last,
And to the latest gasp cried out for Warwick
And said "Commend me to my valiant brother."

13 **ramping** rearing   14 **Jove's spreading tree** the oak

354

And more he would have said, and more he spoke,
Which sounded like a cannon in a vault,
That mought not be distinguished; but at last   45
I well might hear, delivered with a groan,
"O, farewell, Warwick!"

WARWICK Sweet rest his soul! Fly, lords, and save
     yourselves;
For Warwick bids you all farewell, to meet in
     heaven.   [*Dies.*]

OXFORD Away, away, to meet the Queen's great
     power!   *Here they bear away his body.*   50
                                    Exeunt.

Scene III. [*Another part of the field.*]

*Flourish. Enter King Edward in triumph,
with Richard, Clarence, and the rest.*

KING EDWARD Thus far our fortune keeps an upward
     course
And we are graced with wreaths of victory.
But, in the midst of this bright-shining day
I spy a black, suspicious, threat'ning cloud
That will encounter with our glorious sun   5
Ere he attain his easeful western bed.
I mean, my lords, those powers that the Queen
Hath raised in Gallia have arrived our coast,
And, as we hear, march on to fight with us.

CLARENCE A little gale will soon disperse that cloud   10
And blow it to the source from whence it came.
Thy very beams will dry those vapors up,
For every cloud engenders not a storm.

45 mought might   V.iii.5 sun badge of York   8 arrived landed on

355

RICHARD The Queen is valued thirty thousand
          strong,
15   And Somerset, with Oxford, fled to her:
          If she have time to breathe, be well assured
          Her faction will be full as strong as ours.

KING EDWARD We are advertised by our loving
              friends
          That they do hold their course toward Tewksbury.
20   We, having now the best at Barnet field,
          Will thither straight, for willingness rids way;
          And, as we march, our strength will be augmented
          In every county as we go along.
          Strike up the drum. Cry "Courage!" and away.
                                                    Exeunt.

Scene IV. [*Plains near Tewkesbury.*]

*Flourish. March. Enter the Queen [Margaret], young
[Prince] Edward, Somerset, Oxford, and Soldiers.*

QUEEN MARGARET Great lords, wise men ne'er sit and
                 wail their loss,
          But cheerly seek how to redress their harms.
          What though the mast be now blown overboard,
          The cable broke, the holding-anchor lost,
5   And half our sailors swallowed in the flood?
          Yet lives our pilot still. Is't meet that he
          Should leave the helm, and like a fearful lad
          With tearful eyes add water to the sea,
          And give more strength to that which hath too
              much,
10   Whiles, in his moan, the ship splits on the rock,

14 **valued** estimated   18 **advertised** informed   21 **straight** at once   21 **rids
way** covers ground quickly   V.iv.4 **holding-anchor** sheet anchor (largest of
ship's anchors)   6 **Is't meet** is it suitable

Which industry and courage might have saved?
Ah, what a shame! ah, what a fault were this!
Say Warwick was our anchor. What of that?
And Montague our topmast. What of him?
Our slaughtered friends the tackles; what of these?   15
Why, is not Oxford here another anchor?
And Somerset another goodly mast?
The friends of France our shrouds and tacklings?
And, though unskilful, why not Ned and I
For once allowed the skilful pilot's charge?   20
We will not from the helm to sit and weep,
But keep our course (though the rough wind say no)
From shelves and rocks that threaten us with wrack.
As good to chide the waves as speak them fair.
And what is Edward but a ruthless sea?   25
What Clarence but a quicksand of deceit?
And Richard but a ragged fatal rock?
All these the enemies to our poor bark.
Say you can swim—alas, 'tis but a while!
Tread on the sand—why, there you quickly sink!   30
Bestride the rock—the tide will wash you off,
Or else you famish: that's a threefold death.
This speak I, lords, to let you understand,
In case some one of you would fly from us,
That there's no hoped-for mercy with the brothers   35
More than with ruthless waves, with sands and
      rocks.
Why, courage then! What cannot be avoided
'Twere childish weakness to lament or fear.

PRINCE Methinks a woman of this valiant spirit
      Should, if a coward heard her speak these words,   40
      Infuse his breast with magnanimity,
      And make him, naked, foil a man at arms.
      I speak not this as doubting any here;
      For did I but suspect a fearful man,
      He should have leave to go away betimes,   45
      Lest in our need he might infect another

11 **industry** labor   20 **charge** duty   42 **naked** unarmed

357

And make him of like spirit to himself.
If any such be here (as God forbid!)
Let him depart before we need his help.

50   OXFORD   Women and children of so high a courage,
And warriors faint! why, 'twere perpetual shame.
O brave young prince! thy famous grandfather
Doth live again in thee: long mayst thou live
To bear his image and renew his glories!

55   SOMERSET   And he that will not fight for such a hope,
Go home to bed, and like the owl by day,
If he arise, be mocked and wondered at.

QUEEN MARGARET   Thanks, gentle Somerset. Sweet
        Oxford, thanks.

PRINCE   And take his thanks that yet hath nothing else.

Enter a Messenger.

60   MESSENGER   Prepare you, lords, for Edward is at hand
Ready to fight; therefore be resolute.

OXFORD   I thought no less: it is his policy
To haste thus fast, to find us unprovided.

SOMERSET   But he's deceived; we are in readiness.

QUEEN MARGARET   This cheers my heart, to see your
65   forwardness.

OXFORD   Here pitch our battle; hence we will not
        budge.

*Flourish and march. Enter [King] Edward,
Richard, Clarence, and Soldiers.*

KING EDWARD   Brave followers, yonder stands the
        thorny wood,
Which, by the heavens' assistance and your
        strength,
Must by the roots be hewn up yet ere night.
70   I need not add more fuel to your fire,

52 **grandfather** Henry V   54 **image** likeness   62 **policy** craft

For well I wot ye blaze to burn them out.
Give signal to the fight, and to it, lords!

QUEEN MARGARET Lords, knights, and gentlemen, what
    I should say
My tears gainsay; for every word I speak,
Ye see I drink the water of my eye.   75
Therefore, no more but this: Henry, your sovereign,
Is prisoner to the foe; his state usurped,
His realm a slaughterhouse, his subjects slain,
His statutes canceled, and his treasure spent;
And yonder is the wolf that makes this spoil.   80
You fight in justice. Then, in God's name, lords,
Be valiant, and give signal to the fight.
    Alarum. Retreat. Excursions. Exeunt.

Scene V. [*Another part of the field.*]

*Flourish. Enter [King] Edward, Richard, Clarence, [and
Soldiers; with] Queen [Margaret], Oxford, Somerset [as
prisoners].*

KING EDWARD Now here a period of tumultuous
    broils.
Away with Oxford to Hames Castle straight.
For Somerset, off with his guilty head.
Go bear them hence. I will not hear them speak.

OXFORD For my part, I'll not trouble thee with words.   5

SOMERSET Nor I, but stoop with patience to my for-
    tune.   *Exeunt [Oxford and Somerset, guarded].*

QUEEN MARGARET So part we sadly in this troublous
    world,
To meet with joy in sweet Jerusalem.

80 **spoil** destruction   V.v.1 **a period of** an end to   2 **straight** immediately

KING EDWARD Is proclamation made, that who finds
　　Edward
10　Shall have a high reward, and he his life?

RICHARD It is: and lo, where youthful Edward comes!

KING EDWARD Bring forth the gallant, let us hear him
　　speak.

Enter the Prince [Edward].

　　What! Can so young a thorn begin to prick?
　　Edward, what satisfaction canst thou make
15　For bearing arms, for stirring up my subjects,
　　And all the trouble thou hast turned me to?

PRINCE Speak like a subject, proud ambitious York!
　　Suppose that I am now my father's mouth;
　　Resign thy chair, and where I stand kneel thou,
20　Whilst I propose the selfsame words to thee,
　　Which, traitor, thou wouldst have me answer to.

QUEEN MARGARET Ah, that thy father had been so
　　resolved!

RICHARD That you might still have worn the petticoat,
　　And ne'er have stol'n the breech from Lancaster.

25　PRINCE Let Aesop fable in a winter's night;
　　His currish riddles sorts not with this place.

RICHARD By heaven, brat, I'll plague ye for that word.

QUEEN MARGARET Ay, thou wast born to be a plague
　　to men.

RICHARD For God's sake, take away this captive scold.

30　PRINCE Nay, take away this scolding crookback rather.

KING EDWARD Peace, wilful boy, or I will charm your
　　tongue.

CLARENCE Untutored lad, thou art too malapert.

---

14 **satisfaction** amends　24 **breech** breeches　26 **currish** (because Aesop was
sometimes thought to be a hunchback, because the fables talk of animals, and
because their morality resembles that of Cynic [from a Greek word for "dog"]
philosophy)　31 **charm** silence　32 **malapert** impudent

PRINCE I know my duty; you are all undutiful:
   Lascivious Edward, and thou perjured George,
   And thou misshapen Dick, I tell ye all   35
   I am your better, traitors as ye are:
   And thou usurp'st my father's right and mine.

KING EDWARD Take that, the likeness of this railer
    here.   *Stabs him.*

RICHARD Sprawl'st thou? Take that, to end thy agony.
                Richard stabs him.

CLARENCE And there's for twitting me with perjury.   40
                Clarence stabs him.

QUEEN MARGARET O, kill me too!

RICHARD Marry, and shall.   *Offers to kill her.*

KING EDWARD Hold, Richard, hold; for we have done
    too much.

RICHARD Why should she live, to fill the world with
    words?

KING EDWARD What! doth she swoon? use means for
    her recovery.   45

RICHARD Clarence, excuse me to the King my brother;
   I'll hence to London on a serious matter:
   Ere ye come there, be sure to hear some news.

CLARENCE What? what?

RICHARD The Tower, the Tower!   *Exit.*   50

QUEEN MARGARET O Ned, sweet Ned! speak to thy
    mother, boy!
   Canst thou not speak? O traitors! murderers!
   They that stabbed Caesar shed no blood at all,
   Did not offend, nor were not worthy blame,
   If this foul deed were by to equal it.   55
   He was a man; this (in respect) a child,
   And men ne'er spend their fury on a child.

42 **Marry** indeed (light oath, from "By Mary")   56 **in respect** in comparison

What's worse than murderer, that I may name it?
No, no, my heart will burst, and if I speak!
60   And I will speak, that so my heart may burst.
Butchers and villains! bloody cannibals!
How sweet a plant have you untimely cropped!
You have no children, butchers! If you had,
The thought of them would have stirred up remorse:
65   But if you ever chance to have a child,
Look in his youth to have him so cut off
As, deathsmen, you have rid this sweet young prince!

KING EDWARD Away with her! Go bear her hence
perforce.

QUEEN MARGARET Nay, never bear me hence! Dispatch
me here.
70   Here sheathe thy sword, I'll pardon thee my death:
What, wilt thou not? Then, Clarence, do it thou.

CLARENCE By heaven, I will not do thee so much ease.

QUEEN MARGARET Good Clarence, do! Sweet Clarence,
do thou do it!

CLARENCE Didst thou not hear me swear I would not
do it?

QUEEN MARGARET Ay, but thou usest to forswear
75   thyself.
'Twas sin before, but now 'tis charity.
What wilt thou not? Where is that devil's butcher,
Hard-favored Richard? Richard, where art thou?
Thou art not here. Murder is thy alms-deed.
80   Petitioners for blood thou ne'er put'st back.

KING EDWARD Away, I say. I charge ye bear her
hence.

QUEEN MARGARET So come to you and yours, as to this
prince!   *Exit Queen.*

78 **Hard-favored** ugly 80 **put'st back** refuse

KING EDWARD Where's Richard gone?

CLARENCE To London, all in post; and, as I guess,
To make a bloody supper in the Tower.   85

KING EDWARD He's sudden if a thing comes in his
head.
Now march we hence, discharge the common sort
With pay and thanks, and let's away to London,
And see our gentle Queen how well she fares:
By this, I hope, she hath a son for me.   *Exeunt.*   90

Scene VI. [*London. The Tower.*]

*Enter [King] Henry the Sixth and Richard, with the
Lieutenant [of the Tower], on the walls.*

RICHARD Good day, my lord. What, at your book so
hard?

KING HENRY Ay, my good lord—"my lord," I should
say rather.
'Tis sin to flatter. "Good" was little better.
"Good Gloucester" and "good devil" were alike,
And both preposterous; therefore, not "good
lord."   5

RICHARD Sirrah, leave us to ourselves: we must con-
fer.   [*Exit Lieutenant.*]

KING HENRY So flies the reckless shepherd from the
wolf;
So first the harmless sheep doth yield his fleece,

84 all in post in haste   86 sudden swift in action   90 By this by this time
V.vi.5 preposterous an inversion of the natural order   6 Sirrah (form of address
used to an inferior)

And next his throat unto the butcher's knife.
10   What scene of death hath Roscius now to act?

RICHARD Suspicion always haunts the guilty mind;
The thief doth fear each bush an officer.

KING HENRY The bird that hath been limèd in a
        bush,
With trembling wings misdoubteth every bush;
15   And I, the hapless male to one sweet bird,
Have now the fatal object in my eye
Where my poor young was limed, was caught and
        killed.

RICHARD Why, what a peevish fool was that of Crete,
That taught his son the office of a fowl!
20   And yet, for all his wings, the fool was drowned.

KING HENRY I, Daedalus; my poor boy, Icarus;
Thy father, Minos, that denied our course;
The sun that seared the wings of my sweet boy
Thy brother Edward, and thyself the sea
25   Whose envious gulf did swallow up his life.
Ah, kill me with thy weapon, not with words!
My breast can better brook thy dagger's point
Than can my ears that tragic history.
But wherefore dost thou come? Is't for my life?

30   RICHARD Think'st thou I am an executioner?

KING HENRY A persecutor, I am sure, thou art:
If murdering innocents be executing,
Why, then thou art an executioner.

RICHARD Thy son I killed for his presumption.

KING HENRY Hadst thou been killed when first thou
35   didst presume,

---

10 **Roscius** great Roman actor (d. 62 B.C.) 13 **limèd** caught with bird-lime
(a sticky substance smeared on twigs) 14 **misdoubteth** mistrusts 15-17 **And I**
... killed i.e., I, the father of one sweet child, have in my eye the death-dealing
substance by which my son was trapped and slain 19 **office** function
22 **denied our course** barred our way 25 **gulf** whirlpool

Thou hadst not lived to kill a son of mine.
And thus I prophesy, that many a thousand,
Which now mistrust no parcel of my fear,
And many an old man's sigh and many a widow's,
And many an orphan's water-standing eye—   40
Men for their sons, wives for their husbands,
Orphans for their parents' timeless death—
Shall rue the hour that ever thou wast born.
The owl shrieked at thy birth—an evil sign;
The night-crow cried, aboding luckless time;   45
Dogs howled, and hideous tempest shook down
    trees;
The raven rooked her on the chimney's top,
And chatt'ring pies in dismal discords sung.
Thy mother felt more than a mother's pain,
And yet brought forth less than a mother's hope,   50
To wit, an indigested and deformèd lump,
Not like the fruit of such a goodly tree.
Teeth hadst thou in thy head when thou wast born,
To signify thou cam'st to bite the world;
And, if the rest be true which I have heard,   55
Thou cam'st—

RICHARD I'll hear no more. Die, prophet, in thy
    speech.   *Stabs him.*
For this, amongst the rest, was I ordained.

KING HENRY Ay, and for much more slaughter after
    this.
O God forgive my sins, and pardon thee!   *Dies.* 60

RICHARD What? Will the aspiring blood of Lancaster
Sink in the ground? I thought it would have
    mounted.
See how my sword weeps for the poor King's
    death!
O may such purple tears be alway shed
From those that wish the downfall of our house!   65

___

40 **water-standing** flooded with tears   42 **timeless** untimely   45 **aboding**
foreboding   47 **rooked her** squatted   48 **pies** magpies

If any spark of life be yet remaining,
Down, down to hell; and say I sent thee thither—
                              Stabs him again.
I, that have neither pity, love, nor fear.
Indeed, 'tis true that Henry told me of;
70 For I have often heard my mother say
I came into the world with my legs forward.
Had I not reason, think ye, to make haste
And seek their ruin that usurped our right?
The midwife wondered, and the women cried
75 "O Jesus bless us, he is born with teeth!"
And so I was, which plainly signified
That I should snarl and bite and play the dog.
Then, since the heavens have shaped my body so,
Let hell make crook'd my mind to answer it.
80 I have no brother, I am like no brother;
And this word "love," which graybeards call
        divine,
Be resident in men like one another
And not in me: I am myself alone.
Clarence, beware. Thou keep'st me from the light;
85 But I will sort a pitchy day for thee;
For I will buzz abroad such prophecies
That Edward shall be fearful of his life,
And then, to purge his fear, I'll be thy death.
King Henry and the Prince his son are gone:
90 Clarence, thy turn is next, and then the rest,
Counting myself but bad till I be best.
I'll throw thy body in another room
And triumph, Henry, in thy day of doom.
                              Exit [with the body].

79 **answer** correspond to   85 **I ... thee** I shall arrange a black future for you
86 **buzz abroad** spread

366

Scene VII. [*London. The Palace.*]

Flourish. Enter King [Edward], Queen [Elizabeth],
Clarence, Richard, Hastings, [a] Nurse [with the young
Prince], and Attendants.

KING EDWARD Once more we sit in England's royal
    throne,
    Repurchased with the blood of enemies.
    What valiant foemen, like to autumn's corn,
    Have we mowed down in tops of all their pride!
    Three Dukes of Somerset, threefold renowned   5
    For hardy and undoubted champions;
    Two Cliffords, as the father and the son,
    And two Northumberlands—two braver men
    Ne'er spurred their coursers at the trumpet's
    sound;
    With them, the two brave bears, Warwick and
    Montague,   10
    That in their chains fettered the kingly lion
    And made the forest tremble when they roared.
    Thus have we swept suspicion from our seat
    And made our footstool of security.
    Come hither, Bess, and let me kiss my boy.   15
    Young Ned, for thee, thine uncles and myself
    Have in our armors watched the winter's night,
    Went all afoot in summer's scalding heat,
    That thou mightst repossess the crown in peace:
    And of our labors thou shalt reap the gain.   20

RICHARD [*Aside*] I'll blast his harvest, if your head
    were laid,
    For yet I am not looked on in the world.

V.vii.7 **as** namely   9 **coursers** horses   10 **bears** (alluding to the family emblem)
13 **suspicion** anxiety   17 **watched** stayed awake   21 **laid** i.e., in the grave

367

This shoulder was ordained so thick to heave,
And heave it shall some weight, or break my back.
25 Work thou the way, and that shalt execute.

KING EDWARD Clarence and Gloucester, love my
      lovely queen;
And kiss your princely nephew, brothers both.

CLARENCE The duty that I owe unto your majesty
I seal upon the lips of this sweet babe.

KING EDWARD Thanks, noble Clarence; worthy
30   brother, thanks.

RICHARD And, that I love the tree from whence thou
      sprang'st,
Witness the loving kiss I give the fruit.
[*Aside*] To say the truth, so Judas kissed his
      master,
And cried, "All hail!" whenas he meant all harm.

35 KING EDWARD Now am I seated as my soul delights,
Having my country's peace and brother's loves.

CLARENCE What will your Grace have done with
      Margaret?
Reignier, her father, to the King of France
Hath pawned the Sicils and Jerusalem,
40 And hither have they sent it for her ransom.

KING EDWARD Away with her, and waft her hence
      to France!
And now what rests but that we spend the time
With stately triumphs, mirthful comic shows,
Such as befits the pleasure of the court?
45 Sound drums and trumpets! Farewell sour annoy!
For here, I hope, begins our lasting joy.
                              Exeunt omnes.

FINIS

42 **rests** remains   43 **triumphs** public processions

368

Textual Note

Henry VI, Part Three, has come down to us in two major texts: the so-called "Bad Quarto" (actually a "Bad Octavo"), called Q—*The true Tragedie of Richard | Duke of Yorke, and the death of | good King Henrie the Sixt, | with the whole contention betweene | the two Houses Lancaster | and Yorke, as it was sundrie times | acted by the Right Honoura- | ble the Earle of Pem- | brooke his seruants*—and the First Folio of 1623 (called F). Q, which is about two-thirds the length of F and imperfect in numerous respects, was published in 1595 by P[eter] S[hort] for Thomas Millington. The copy was not entered in the Stationers' Register. Q was long considered (principally on the authority of the noted eighteenth-century editor Edmond Malone) to be the source of Shakespeare's play; but in the past four decades there has come into fairly general acceptance the view that Q represents a reported version (perhaps by the actors who played Warwick and Clifford) of the text of an early production of the play that was later printed as F. Such, at any rate, is the opinion of the most important modern editors of the play (A. S. Cairncross, John Dover Wilson, George Lyman Kittredge, and Peter Alexander, among others). The technical studies that were largely responsible for tipping the balance in favor of this view include J. S. Smart: *Shakespeare: Truth and Tradition* (1928); Madeleine Doran: *Henry VI, Parts II and III* (1928); and Peter Alexander: *Shakespeare's Henry VI and Richard III* (1929). A. S. Cairncross's introductions to his Arden editions of *Henry VI, Part Two,* and *Henry VI, Part Three,* summarize much useful information bearing on the relation between *Henry VI, Part Two,* and *The First Part of the Contention betwixt the two famous Houses of Yorke and Lancaster* ... and between *Henry VI, Part Three,* and *The true Tragedie of Richard Duke of Yorke.*

TEXTUAL NOTE

Apart from the initial "*Actus Primus. Scœna Prima*," no act or scene divisions appear in F, and none at all appear in Q. The act and scene divisions in the present edition are those of the Globe edition. All divisions and stage directions that have been added are enclosed in square brackets.

A number of the stage directions in Q, like stage directions in other Shakespeare quartos, reflect stage business in actual performance, for example:

> Enter *Richard* Duke of Yorke, The Earle of *Warwicke*, *The Duke of* Norffolke, *Marquis Montague*, *Edward Earle of March*, *Crookeback Richard*, and the yong *Earle of Rutland*, with Drumme and Souldiers, with white Roses in their hats.[1]

> Sound a Parlie, and *Richard* and *Clarence* whispers togither, and then Clarence takes his red Rose out of his hat, and throws it at *Warwike*.[2]

> Alarmes to the battell, *Yorke* flies, then the chambers be discharged. Then enter the king, *Cla.* & *Glo.* & the rest, & make a great shout, and crie, for *Yorke*, for *Yorke*, and then the *Queene* is taken, & the prince, & *Oxf.* & *Sum.* and then found and enter all againe.[3]

In the second direction quoted above, some effort has obviously been made to motivate Clarence's betrayal of Warwick—for which F does nothing to prepare us—and the stage business here echoes the accounts in the chronicles. Another stage direction of interest is at III.i., which reads: "Enter Sinklo, and Humfrey, with Crosse-bowes in their hands." (The Quarto reads: "Enter two keepers with bow and arrowes.") The names Sinklo and Humfrey appear to be those of actors in Shakespeare's company— John Sincler, and Humphrey Jeffes—incorporated into the text by error. Possibly Shakespeare wrote the names as he composed, possibly a prompter added them

---

1 W. W. Greg, ed., *The True Tragedy of Richard Duke of York* (*Henry the Sixth, Part III*). Shakespeare Quarto Facsimiles No. 11 (Oxford, 1958), Sig. A2.

2 *Ibid.*, Sig. E2.

3 *Ibid.*, Sig. E4.

TEXTUAL NOTE

to the company's copy. "Gabriel" in the stage direction at I.ii.47 is probably a similar error, naming the actor Gabriel Spencer.

Speech prefixes have been silently regularized, and the position of a few stage directions slightly altered. The following list includes emendations and corrections of F. In each case, the altered reading appears first, in bold; the original reading follows, in roman. When the alteration is derived from Q, that fact is indicated.

I.i.69 **Exeter** [Q] Westm.   105 **Thy** [Q] My   259 **stay with** [Q] stay   261 **from** [Q] to   273 s.d. **Exeunt** Exit

I.ii.24 **Enter [a Messenger]** [Q] Enter   75 s.d. **Exeunt** Exit

I.iv.180 **Exeunt** Exit

II.i.113 **And very well appointed, as I thought** [Q; F omits]   131 **an idle** [Q] a lazie   158 **makes** make   182 **amain** [Q; F omits]

II.ii.89–92 **Since … in** [F assigns to Clarence]   133 **Richard** [Q] War.   172 **deniest** [Q] denied'st

II.v.119 **Even** Men

II.vi.44 **See who it is** [Q; F gives to Richard]   60 **his** [Q] is

III.i. s.d. **Enter two Keepers** [Q] Enter Sinklo, and Humfrey   12 *Second Keeper* Sink. [i.e., First Keeper]   18 **wast** was   24 **thee, sour** Adversity the sower Aduersaries   55 **thou that** [Q] thou

III.ii.123 **honorably** [Q] honourable

III.iii.124 **eternal** [Q] externall   156 **peace** [added in F2]   228 **I'll** [Q] I

IV.i.89–90 [three lines in F, ending **thee, words, them**]   93 **thy** [Q] the

IV.ii.15 **towns** Towne

IV.iii.64 s.d. **Exeunt** exit

IV.iv.17 **wean** waine

IV.v.4 **stands** stand   8 **Comes** Come   12 **ship** shipt

IV.vi.55 **be confiscate** confiscate

IV.viii. s.d. **Exeter** Somerset

V.i.75 s.d. (see note in text)   78 **an** in

V.v. s.d. **Clarence … prisoners** Queene, Clarence, Oxford, Somerset 78 **butcher** butcher Richard   90 s.d. **Exeunt** Exit

V.vii.5 **renowned** [Q] Renowne   30 **King Edward** Cla.   30 **Thanks** [Q] Thanke   38 **Reignier** Reynard

371

WILLIAM SHAKESPEARE

THE TRAGEDY
OF RICHARD
THE THIRD

Edited by Mark Eccles

[*Dramatis Personae*

KING EDWARD IV
EDWARD, Prince of Wales, afterwards King Edward V ⎫
RICHARD, Duke of York ⎬ sons of the King
GEORGE, Duke of Clarence ⎫
RICHARD, Duke of Gloucester, afterwards King Richard III ⎬ brothers of the King
A YOUNG SON OF CLARENCE (EDWARD)
HENRY, Earl of Richmond, afterwards King Henry VII
CARDINAL BOURCHIER, Archbishop of Canterbury
THOMAS ROTHERHAM, Archbishop of York
JOHN MORTON, Bishop of Ely
DUKE OF BUCKINGHAM
DUKE OF NORFOLK
EARL OF SURREY, his son
ANTHONY WOODVILLE, Earl Rivers, brother of Queen Elizabeth
MARQUIS OF DORSET and LORD GREY, sons of Queen Elizabeth
EARL OF OXFORD
LORD STANLEY, called also Earl of Derby
LORD HASTINGS
LORD WOODVILLE   SIR RICHARD RATCLIFFE
LORD SCALES   SIR JAMES TYRREL
LORD LOVELL   SIR JAMES BLUNT
SIR ROBERT BRAKENBURY,   SIR WALTER HERBERT
   Lieutenant of the Tower   SIR WILLIAM BRANDON
SIR THOMAS VAUGHAN   WILLIAM CATESBY
LORD MAYOR OF LONDON
CHRISTOPHER URSWICK, a chaplain
TRESSEL and BARKLEY, gentlemen attending on Lady Anne
QUEEN ELIZABETH, wife of King Edward IV
QUEEN MARGARET, widow of King Henry VI
DUCHESS OF YORK, mother of King Edward IV, Clarence, and Gloucester
LADY ANNE, widow of Edward Prince of Wales, son of King Henry VI; afterwards married to Richard
A YOUNG DAUGHTER OF CLARENCE (MARGARET)
GHOSTS OF RICHARD'S VICTIMS, LORDS and OTHER ATTENDANTS, BISHOPS, PRIEST, SHERIFF, KEEPER, TWO MURDERERS, PURSUIVANT, SCRIVENER, PAGE, CITIZENS, MESSENGERS, SOLDIERS, &c.

Scene: England]

THE TRAGEDY OF
RICHARD THE THIRD

ACT I

Scene I. [*London. A street.*]

Enter Richard, Duke of Gloucester, solus.

RICHARD Now is the winter of our discontent
Made glorious summer by this sun of York;
And all the clouds that loured upon our house
In the deep bosom of the ocean buried.
Now are our brows bound with victorious wreaths,   5
Our bruisèd arms hung up for monuments,
Our stern alarums changed to merry meetings,
Our dreadful marches to delightful measures.
Grim-visaged War hath smoothed his wrinkled
    front,
And now, instead of mounting barbèd steeds   10
To fright the souls of fearful adversaries,
He capers nimbly in a lady's chamber
To the lascivious pleasing of a lute.
But I, that am not shaped for sportive tricks
Nor made to court an amorous looking glass;   15

Text references are printed in **bold** type; the annotation follows in roman type.
I.i. s.d. **solus** alone   2 **sun** (1) emblem of King Edward (2) son   6 **monuments**
memorials   7 **alarums** calls to arms   8 **measures** dances   9 **front** forehead
10 **barbèd** armored

I, that am rudely stamped, and want love's
  majesty
To strut before a wanton ambling nymph;
I, that am curtailed of this fair proportion,
Cheated of feature by dissembling Nature,
20 Deformed, unfinished, sent before my time
Into this breathing world scarce half made up,
And that so lamely and unfashionable
That dogs bark at me as I halt by them;
Why, I, in this weak piping time of peace,
25 Have no delight to pass away the time,
Unless to spy my shadow in the sun
And descant on mine own deformity.
And therefore, since I cannot prove a lover
To entertain these fair well-spoken days,
30 I am determinèd to prove a villain
And hate the idle pleasures of these days.
Plots have I laid, inductions dangerous,
By drunken prophecies, libels, and dreams,
To set my brother Clarence and the King
35 In deadly hate the one against the other;
And if King Edward be as true and just
As I am subtle, false, and treacherous,
This day should Clarence closely be mewed up
About a prophecy which says that *G*
40 Of Edward's heirs the murderer shall be.
Dive, thoughts, down to my soul. Here Clarence
  comes.

Enter Clarence, guarded, and Brakenbury,
  [Lieutenant of the Tower].

Brother, good day. What means this armèd guard
That waits upon your Grace?

CLARENCE   His Majesty,
Tend'ring my person's safety, hath appointed
45 This conduct to convey me to the Tower.

16 **want** lack   19 **feature** good shape   23 **halt** limp   24 **piping time** i.e., time
when shepherds play their pipes   27 **descant** comment   29 **entertain** while away
32 **inductions** first steps   38 **mewed up** caged in prison   44 **Tend'ring** taking
care of   45 **conduct** escort

RICHARD Upon what cause?

CLARENCE   Because my name is George.

RICHARD Alack, my lord, that fault is none of yours;
He should for that commit your godfathers.
O, belike his Majesty hath some intent
That you should be new christ'ned in the Tower.   50
But what's the matter, Clarence? May I know?

CLARENCE Yea, Richard, when I know; for I protest
As yet I do not. But, as I can learn,
He harkens after prophecies and dreams,
And from the crossrow plucks the letter *G*,   55
And says a wizard told him that by *G*
His issue disinherited should be;
And, for my name of George begins with *G*,
It follows in his thought that I am he.
These (as I learn) and suchlike toys as these   60
Hath moved his Highness to commit me now.

RICHARD Why, this it is when men are ruled by
   women.
'Tis not the King that sends you to the Tower.
My Lady Grey his wife, Clarence, 'tis she
That tempers him to this extremity.   65
Was it not she, and that good man of worship,
Anthony Woodeville her brother there,
That made him send Lord Hastings to the Tower,
From whence this present day he is deliverèd?
We are not safe, Clarence, we are not safe.   70

CLARENCE By heaven, I think there is no man secure
But the Queen's kindred, and night-walking
   heralds
That trudge betwixt the King and Mistress Shore.

---

49 belike probably 55 crossrow alphabet 58 for because 60 toys trifles
65 tempers persuades 65 extremity extreme severity 66 good man of
worship (play on "goodman," common man, raised to "worship," honor, as Earl
Rivers 67 Woodeville (trisyllabic, play on "would evil") 72 heralds king's
messengers (ironic) 73 Mistress Shore Jane Shore, wife of a London citizen;
Edward IV's mistress

Heard you not what an humble suppliant

75   Lord Hastings was to her for his delivery?

RICHARD Humbly complaining to her deity
Got my Lord Chamberlain his liberty.
I'll tell you what, I think it is our way,
If we will keep in favor with the King,

80   To be her men and wear her livery.
The jealous o'erworn widow and herself,
Since that our brother dubbed them gentlewomen,
Are mighty gossips in our monarchy.

BRAKENBURY I beseech your Graces both to pardon me.

85   His Majesty hath straitly given in charge
That no man shall have private conference,
Of what degree soever, with your brother.

RICHARD Even so? And please your worship, Brakenbury,
You may partake of anything we say.

90   We speak no treason, man; we say the King
Is wise and virtuous, and his noble queen
Well struck in years, fair, and not jealous;
We say that Shore's wife hath a pretty foot,
A cherry lip, a bonny eye, a passing pleasing
tongue;

95   And that the Queen's kindred are made gentlefolks.
How say you, sir? Can you deny all this?

BRAKENBURY With this, my lord, myself have nought
to do.

RICHARD Naught to do with Mistress Shore! I tell
thee, fellow,
He that doth naught with her, excepting one,

100   Were best to do it secretly alone.

BRAKENBURY What one, my lord?

RICHARD Her husband, knave. Wouldst thou betray
me?

81 **widow** Queen Elizabeth, widow of Sir John Grey   83 **gossips** chattering
women, busybodies   85 **straitly** strictly   87 **degree** rank   88 **And** if   92 **struck**
advanced   98 **Naught** evil

BRAKENBURY I beseech your Grace to pardon me, and
    withal
    Forbear your conference with the noble Duke.

CLARENCE We know thy charge, Brakenbury, and will
    obey.   105

RICHARD We are the Queen's abjects, and must obey.
    Brother, farewell. I will unto the King;
    And whatsoe'er you will employ me in,
    Were it to call King Edward's widow sister,
    I will perform it to enfranchise you.   110
    Meantime, this deep disgrace in brotherhood
    Touches me deeper than you can imagine.

CLARENCE I know it pleaseth neither of us well.

RICHARD Well, your imprisonment shall not be long;
    I will deliver you, or else lie for you.   115
    Meantime, have patience.

CLARENCE   I must perforce. Farewell.
              Exit Clarence, [with Brakenbury and Guard].

RICHARD Go tread the path that thou shalt ne'er
    return.
    Simple plain Clarence, I do love thee so
    That I will shortly send thy soul to heaven,
    If heaven will take the present at our hands.   120
    But who comes here? The new-deliverèd Hastings!

                Enter Lord Hastings.

HASTINGS Good time of day unto my gracious lord.

RICHARD As much unto my good Lord Chamberlain.
    Well are you welcome to the open air.
    How hath your lordship brooked imprisonment?   125

HASTINGS With patience, noble lord, as prisoners must.
    But I shall live, my lord, to give them thanks
    That were the cause of my imprisonment.

103 **withal** moreover 106 **abjects** abject slaves 110 **enfranchise** set free
115 **lie for** (1) go to prison instead of (2) tell lies about 125 **brooked** endured

RICHARD No doubt, no doubt; and so shall Clarence
          too,
130   For they that were your enemies are his
          And have prevailed as much on him as you.

HASTINGS More pity that the eagles should be mewed
          Whiles kites and buzzards prey at liberty.

RICHARD What news abroad?

135 HASTINGS No news so bad abroad as this at home:
          The King is sickly, weak, and melancholy,
          And his physicians fear him mightily.

RICHARD Now, by Saint John, that news is bad
          indeed.
          O, he hath kept an evil diet long
140   And overmuch consumed his royal person.
          'Tis very grievous to be thought upon.
          What, is he in his bed?

HASTINGS He is.

RICHARD Go you before, and I will follow you.
                                        Exit Hastings.
145   He cannot live, I hope, and must not die
          Till George be packed with post horse up to
          heaven.
          I'll in to urge his hatred more to Clarence
          With lies well steeled with weighty arguments;
          And, if I fail not in my deep intent,
150   Clarence hath not another day to live.
          Which done, God take King Edward to his mercy
          And leave the world for me to bustle in!
          For then I'll marry Warwick's youngest daughter.
          What though I killed her husband and her father?
155   The readiest way to make the wench amends
          Is to become her husband and her father.

133 **kites** birds of the hawk family   137 **fear** fear for   139 **diet** way of living
146 **packed with post horse** sent off in a hurry   148 **steeled** reinforced
153 **Warwick's youngest daughter** Lady Anne   154 **father** father-in-law
(Henry VI)

The which will I, not all so much for love
As for another secret close intent
By marrying her which I must reach unto.
But yet I run before my horse to market.   160
Clarence still breathes, Edward still lives and reigns;
When they are gone, then must I count my gains.

                                                Exit.

Scene II. [*A street.*]

*Enter the corse of Henry the Sixth, with Hal-
berds to guard it, Lady Anne being the mourner.*

ANNE Set down, set down your honorable load—
If honor may be shrouded in a hearse—
Whilst I awhile obsequiously lament
Th' untimely fall of virtuous Lancaster.
                    [*The Bearers set down the hearse.*]
Poor key-cold figure of a holy king,   5
Pale ashes of the house of Lancaster,
Thou bloodless remnant of that royal blood,
Be it lawful that I invocate thy ghost
To hear the lamentations of poor Anne,
Wife to thy Edward, to thy slaught'red son,   10
Stabbed by the selfsame hand that made these
      wounds!
Lo, in these windows that let forth thy life
I pour the helpless balm of my poor eyes.
O, cursèd be the hand that made these holes!
Cursèd the heart that had the heart to do it!   15
Cursèd the blood that let this blood from hence!
More direful hap betide that hated wretch
That makes us wretched by the death of thee
Than I can wish to wolves, to spiders, toads,

I.ii. s.d. **corse** corpse s.d. **Halberds** guards armed with long poleaxes 3 **obsequiously** like a mourner at a funeral 13 **helpless** unavailing 17 **hap betide**
fortune happen to

20   Or any creeping venomed thing that lives!
       If ever he have child, abortive be it,
       Prodigious and untimely brought to light,
       Whose ugly and unnatural aspect
       May fright the hopeful mother at the view,
25   And that be heir to his unhappiness!
       If ever he have wife, let her be made
       More miserable by the life of him
       Than I am made by my young lord and thee!
       Come, now towards Chertsey with your holy load,
30   Taken from Paul's to be interrèd there;
                        [*The Bearers take up the hearse.*]
       And still as you are weary of this weight,
       Rest you, whiles I lament King Henry's corse.

                   Enter Richard, Duke of Gloucester.

RICHARD Stay, you that bear the corse, and set it
       down.

ANNE What black magician conjures up this fiend
35   To stop devoted charitable deeds?

RICHARD Villains, set down the corse, or, by Saint
       Paul,
       I'll make a corse of him that disobeys.

GENTLEMAN My lord, stand back and let the coffin
       pass.

RICHARD Unmannered dog, stand thou when I
       command!
40   Advance thy halberd higher than my breast,
       Or, by Saint Paul, I'll strike thee to my foot
       And spurn upon thee, beggar, for thy boldness.
                        [*The Bearers set down the hearse.*]

ANNE What, do you tremble? Are you all afraid?
       Alas, I blame you not, for you are mortal,
45   And mortal eyes cannot endure the devil.
       Avaunt, thou dreadful minister of hell!

22 **Prodigious** monstrous   25 **unhappiness** wickedness   30 **Paul's** St. Paul's
Cathedral   31 **Still as** whenever   39 **stand** halt   42 **spurn** trample   46 **Avaunt**
begone

382

Thou hadst but power over his mortal body,
His soul thou canst not have; therefore, begone.

RICHARD Sweet saint, for charity, be not so curst.

ANNE Foul devil, for God's sake hence, and trouble
    us not,   50
For thou hast made the happy earth thy hell,
Filled it with cursing cries and deep exclaims.
If thou delight to view thy heinous deeds,
Behold this pattern of thy butcheries.
O gentlemen, see, see dead Henry's wounds   55
Open their congealed mouths and bleed afresh!
Blush, blush, thou lump of foul deformity,
For 'tis thy presence that exhales this blood
From cold and empty veins where no blood dwells.
Thy deed inhuman and unnatural   60
Provokes this deluge most unnatural.
O God, which this blood mad'st, revenge his death!
O earth, which this blood drink'st, revenge his
    death!
Either heav'n, with lightning strike the murd'rer
    dead,
Or earth, gape open wide and eat him quick,   65
As thou dost swallow up this good King's blood
Which his hell-governed arm hath butcherèd!

RICHARD Lady, you know no rules of charity,
Which renders good for bad, blessings for curses.

ANNE Villain, thou know'st nor law of God nor man.   70
No beast so fierce but knows some touch of pity.

RICHARD But I know none, and therefore am no beast.

ANNE O wonderful, when devils tell the truth!

RICHARD More wonderful, when angels are so angry.
Vouchsafe, divine perfection of a woman,   75
Of these supposèd crimes to give me leave
By circumstance but to acquit myself.

49 **curst** sharp-tongued   54 **pattern** example   58 **exhales** causes to flow
65 **quick** alive   77 **By circumstance** in detail

ANNE Vouchsafe, diffused infection of a man,
Of these known evils but to give me leave
80   By circumstance to accuse thy cursèd self.

RICHARD Fairer than tongue can name thee, let me
have
Some patient leisure to excuse myself.

ANNE Fouler than heart can think thee, thou canst
make
No excuse current but to hang thyself.

85   RICHARD By such despair I should accuse myself.

ANNE And by despairing shalt thou stand excusèd
For doing worthy vengeance on thyself
That didst unworthy slaughter upon others.

RICHARD Say that I slew them not?

ANNE   Then say they were not slain.
90   But dead they are, and, devilish slave, by thee.

RICHARD I did not kill your husband.

ANNE   Why, then he is alive.

RICHARD Nay, he is dead, and slain by Edward's hands.

ANNE In thy foul throat thou li'st! Queen Margaret
saw
Thy murd'rous falchion smoking in his blood;
95   The which thou once didst bend against her breast,
But that thy brothers beat aside the point.

RICHARD I was provokèd by her sland'rous tongue,
That laid their guilt upon my guiltless shoulders.

ANNE Thou wast provokèd by thy bloody mind,
100   That never dream'st on aught but butcheries.
Didst thou not kill this king?

RICHARD   I grant ye.

78 **diffused** shapeless   84 **current** genuine   94 **falchion** curved sword

ANNE Dost grant me, hedgehog? Then God grant me
  too
  Thou mayst be damnèd for that wicked deed!
  O, he was gentle, mild, and virtuous!

RICHARD The better for the King of heaven that hath
  him.   105

ANNE He is in heaven, where thou shalt never come.

RICHARD Let him thank me that holp to send him
  thither;
  For he was fitter for that place than earth.

ANNE And thou unfit for any place but hell.

RICHARD Yes, one place else, if you will hear me name
  it.   110

ANNE Some dungeon.

RICHARD   Your bedchamber.

ANNE Ill rest betide the chamber where thou liest!

RICHARD So will it, madam, till I lie with you.

ANNE I hope so.

RICHARD   I know so. But, gentle Lady Anne,
  To leave this keen encounter of our wits   115
  And fall something into a slower method,
  Is not the causer of the timeless deaths
  Of these Plantagenets, Henry and Edward,
  As blameful as the executioner?

ANNE Thou wast the cause and most accursed affect.   120

RICHARD Your beauty was the cause of that effect;
  Your beauty, that did haunt me in my sleep
  To undertake the death of all the world,
  So I might live one hour in your sweet bosom.

ANNE If I thought that, I tell thee, homicide,   125

---

107 holp helped   117 timeless untimely   120 effect effective agent

These nails should rend that beauty from my
    cheeks.

RICHARD These eyes could not endure that beauty's
    wrack.
You should not blemish it if I stood by.
As all the world is cheerèd by the sun,
130   So I by that; it is my day, my life.

ANNE Black night o'ershade thy day, and death thy
    life!

RICHARD Curse not thyself, fair creature; thou art both.

ANNE I would I were, to be revenged on thee.

RICHARD It is a quarrel most unnatural
135   To be revenged on him that loveth thee.

ANNE It is a quarrel just and reasonable
    To be revenged on him that killed my husband.

RICHARD He that bereft thee, lady, of thy husband,
    Did it to help thee to a better husband.

140 ANNE His better doth not breathe upon the earth.

RICHARD He lives that loves thee better than he could.

ANNE Name him.

RICHARD   Plantagenet.

ANNE   Why, that was he.

RICHARD The selfsame name, but one of better nature.

ANNE Where is he?

RICHARD   Here.   [*She*] *spits at him.*
    Why dost thou spit at me?

145 ANNE Would it were mortal poison for thy sake!

RICHARD Never came poison from so sweet a place.

ANNE Never hung poison on a fouler toad.
    Out of my sight! Thou dost infect mine eyes.

127 **wrack** destruction

RICHARD Thine eyes, sweet lady, have infected mine.

ANNE Would they were basilisks to strike thee dead!   150

RICHARD I would they were, that I might die at once;
For now they kill me with a living death.
Those eyes of thine from mine have drawn salt tears,
Shamed their aspect with store of childish drops,
These eyes which never shed remorseful tear,   155
No, when my father York and Edward wept
To hear the piteous moan that Rutland made
When black-faced Clifford shook his sword at him,
Nor when thy warlike father, like a child,
Told the sad story of my father's death   160
And twenty times made pause to sob and weep,
That all the standers-by had wet their cheeks
Like trees bedashed with rain. In that sad time
My manly eyes did scorn an humble tear;
And what these sorrows could not thence exhale   165
Thy beauty hath, and made them blind with weeping.
I never sued to friend nor enemy;
My tongue could never learn sweet smoothing word;
But now thy beauty is proposed my fee,
My proud heart sues, and prompts my tongue to speak.   170
                      She looks scornfully at him.
Teach not thy lip such scorn, for it was made
For kissing, lady, not for such contempt.
If thy revengeful heart cannot forgive,
Lo, here I lend thee this sharp-pointed sword;
Which if thou please to hide in this true breast   175
And let the soul forth that adoreth thee,
I lay it naked to the deadly stroke

---

150 **basilisks** fabulous monsters believed to kill by a look   151 **at once** once and for all   154 **aspect** appearance   155 **remorseful** pitying   157 **Rutland** a young brother of Richard (see *3 Henry VI*, I.iii)   158 **black-faced** cruel-looking 168 **smoothing** flattering

And humbly beg the death upon my knee.

He lays his breast open.
She offers at [it] with his sword.

Nay, do not pause, for I did kill King Henry,
180   But 'twas thy beauty that provokèd me.
Nay, now dispatch; 'twas I that stabbed young
    Edward,
But 'twas thy heavenly face that set me on.

She falls the sword.

Take up the sword again, or take up me.

ANNE Arise, dissembler; though I wish thy death,
185   I will not be thy executioner.

RICHARD Then bid me kill myself, and I will do it.

ANNE I have already.

RICHARD   That was in thy rage.
Speak it again, and even with the word
This hand, which for thy love did kill thy love,
190   Shall for thy love kill a far truer love.
To both their deaths shalt thou be accessary.

ANNE I would I knew thy heart.

RICHARD 'Tis figured in my tongue.

ANNE I fear me both are false.

195   RICHARD Then never was man true.

ANNE Well, well, put up your sword.

RICHARD Say, then, my peace is made.

ANNE That shalt thou know hereafter.

RICHARD But shall I live in hope?

200   ANNE All men, I hope, live so.

RICHARD Vouchsafe to wear this ring.

ANNE To take is not to give.

[Richard puts the ring on her finger.]

182 s.d. **falls** lets fall   191 **accessary** sharing in guilt   193 **figured** pictured
201 **Vouchsafe** consent

388

RICHARD Look how my ring encompasseth thy finger,
   Even so thy breast encloseth my poor heart.
   Wear both of them, for both of them are thine.   205
   And if thy poor devoted servant may
   But beg one favor at thy gracious hand,
   Thou dost confirm his happiness forever.

ANNE What is it?

RICHARD That it may please you leave these sad
     designs   210
   To him that hath most cause to be a mourner,
   And presently repair to Crosby House,
   Where, after I have solemnly interred
   At Chertsey monast'ry this noble king
   And wet his grave with my repentant tears,   215
   I will with all expedient duty see you.
   For divers unknown reasons, I beseech you,
   Grant me this boon.

ANNE With all my heart; and much it joys me too
   To see you are become so penitent.   220
   Tressel and Barkley, go along with me.

RICHARD Bid me farewell.

ANNE   'Tis more than you deserve;
   But since you teach me how to flatter you,
   Imagine I have said farewell already.
                     Exit two with Anne.

RICHARD Sirs, take up the corse.

GENTLEMAN   Towards Chertsey, noble lord?   225

RICHARD No, to Whitefriars; there attend my coming.
            Exit [Bearers and Gentlemen with] corse.
   Was ever woman in this humor wooed?
   Was ever woman in this humor won?
   I'll have her, but I will not keep her long.
   What! I that killed her husband and his father   230
   To take her in her heart's extremest hate,

203 **Look how** just as   212 **presently** immediately   216 **expedient** speedy
217 **unknown** secret   226 **attend** await   227 **humor** mood

With curses in her mouth, tears in her eyes,
The bleeding witness of my hatred by,
Having God, her conscience, and these bars against
    me,
235 And I no friends to back my suit at all
But the plain devil and dissembling looks,
And yet to win her, all the world to nothing!
Ha!
Hath she forgot already that brave prince,
240 Edward her lord, whom I, some three months since,
Stabbed in my angry mood at Tewkesbury?
A sweeter and a lovelier gentleman,
Framed in the prodigality of nature,
Young, valiant, wise, and, no doubt, right royal,
245 The spacious world cannot again afford.
And will she yet abase her eyes on me,
That cropped the golden prime of this sweet
    prince
And made her widow to a woeful bed?
On me, whose all not equals Edward's moi'ty?
250 On me, that halts and am misshapen thus?
My dukedom to a beggarly denier,
I do mistake my person all this while.
Upon my life, she finds, although I cannot,
Myself to be a marv'lous proper man.
255 I'll be at charges for a looking glass
And entertain a score or two of tailors
To study fashions to adorn my body.
Since I am crept in favor with myself,
I will maintain it with some little cost.
260 But first I'll turn yon fellow in his grave,
And then return lamenting to my love.
Shine out, fair sun, till I have bought a glass
That I may see my shadow as I pass.   *Exit.*

---

241 **Tewkesbury** scene of a Yorkist victory 243 **prodigality** lavishness
245 **afford** supply 247 **prime** springtime 249 **moi'ty** half 251 **denier**
French coin worth a tenth of an English penny 254 **marv'lous proper** wonder-
fully handsome 255 **at charges for** at the expense of 256 **entertain**
engage 260 **in** into

Scene III. [*The palace.*]

Enter Queen [Elizabeth,] Lord Rivers, [Dorset,]
and Lord Grey.

RIVERS Have patience, madam; there's no doubt his
    Majesty
Will soon recover his accustomed health.

GREY In that you brook it ill, it makes him worse.
    Therefore for God's sake entertain good comfort
    And cheer his Grace with quick and merry eyes.   5

QUEEN ELIZABETH If he were dead, what would betide
    on me?

GREY No other harm but loss of such a lord.

QUEEN ELIZABETH The loss of such a lord includes all
    harms.

GREY The heavens have blessed you with a goodly son
    To be your comforter when he is gone.   10

QUEEN ELIZABETH Ah, he is young, and his minority
    Is put unto the trust of Richard Gloucester,
    A man that loves not me, nor none of you.

RIVERS Is it concluded he shall be Protector?

QUEEN ELIZABETH It is determined, not concluded yet;   15
    But so it must be if the King miscarry.

Enter Buckingham and [Stanley, Earl of] Derby.

GREY Here come the lords of Buckingham and Derby.

BUCKINGHAM Good time of day unto your royal Grace!

I.iii.3 **brook** endure 6 **betide on** happen to 15 **determined, not concluded**
decided, not finally decreed 16 **miscarry** die

391

STANLEY God make your Majesty joyful as you have
been!

QUEEN ELIZABETH The Countess Richmond, good my
20   Lord of Derby,
To your good prayer will scarcely say "Amen."
Yet, Derby, notwithstanding she's your wife
And loves not me, be you, good lord, assured
I hate not you for her proud arrogance.

25 STANLEY I do beseech you, either not believe
The envious slanders of her false accusers,
Or, if she be accused on true report,
Bear with her weakness, which I think proceeds
From wayward sickness and no grounded malice.

QUEEN ELIZABETH Saw you the King today, my Lord
30   of Derby?

STANLEY But now the Duke of Buckingham and I
Are come from visiting his Majesty.

QUEEN ELIZABETH What likelihood of his amendment,
lords?

BUCKINGHAM Madam, good hope; his Grace speaks
cheerfully.

QUEEN ELIZABETH God grant him health! Did you
35   confer with him?

BUCKINGHAM Ay, madam; he desires to make atone-
ment
Between the Duke of Gloucester and your brothers,
And between them and my Lord Chamberlain,
And sent to warn them to his royal presence.

QUEEN ELIZABETH Would all were well! But that will
40   never be.
I fear our happiness is at the height.

20 **Countess Richmond** Margaret Tudor, mother of the Earl of Richmond (later
Henry VII) and wife of Lord Stanley   31 **But now** just now   36 **atonement**
reconciliation   38 **Lord Chamberlain** Hastings   39 **warn** summon

Enter Richard [and Hastings].

RICHARD They do me wrong, and I will not endure it!
Who is it that complains unto the King
That I, forsooth, am stern, and love them not?
By holy Paul, they love his Grace but lightly   45
That fill his ears with such dissentious rumors.
Because I cannot flatter and look fair,
Smile in men's faces, smooth, deceive, and cog,
Duck with French nods and apish courtesy,
I must be held a rancorous enemy.   50
Cannot a plain man live and think no harm
But thus his simple truth must be abused
With silken, sly, insinuating Jacks?

GREY To who in all this presence speaks your Grace?

RICHARD To thee, that hast nor honesty nor grace.   55
When have I injured thee? When done thee wrong?
Or thee? Or thee? Or any of your faction?
A plague upon you all! His royal Grace—
Whom God preserve better than you would wish!—
Cannot be quiet scarce a breathing while   60
But you must trouble him with lewd complaints.

QUEEN ELIZABETH Brother of Gloucester, you mistake
    the matter.
The King on his own royal disposition,
And not provoked by any suitor else,
Aiming, belike, at your interior hatred   65
That in your outward action shows itself
Against my children, brothers, and myself,
Makes him to send that he may learn the ground.

RICHARD I cannot tell; the world is grown so bad
That wrens make prey where eagles dare not perch.   70
Since every Jack became a gentleman,
There's many a gentle person made a Jack.

48 cog fawn 53 Jacks knaves 55 grace virtue 60 breathing while time to
take a breath 61 lewd wicked 68 Makes (the subject has shifted from The
King to your interior hatred) 72 gentle wellborn

QUEEN ELIZABETH Come, come, we know your
meaning, brother Gloucester.
You envy my advancement and my friends'.
75   God grant we never may have need of you!

RICHARD Meantime, God grants that I have need of
you.
Our brother is imprisoned by your means,
Myself disgraced, and the nobility
Held in contempt, while great promotions
80   Are daily given to ennoble those
That scarce, some two days since, were worth a
noble.

QUEEN ELIZABETH By him that raised me to this
careful height
From that contented hap which I enjoyed,
I never did incense his Majesty
85   Against the Duke of Clarence, but have been
An earnest advocate to plead for him.
My lord, you do me shameful injury
Falsely to draw me in these vile suspects.

RICHARD You may deny that you were not the mean
90   Of my Lord Hastings' late imprisonment.

RIVERS She may, my lord, for—

RICHARD She may, Lord Rivers! Why, who knows not
so?
She may do more, sir, than denying that:
She may help you to many fair preferments,
95   And then deny her aiding hand therein
And lay those honors on your high desert.
What may she not? She may, ay, marry, may she!

RIVERS What, marry, may she?

RICHARD What, marry, may she! Marry with a king,
100   A bachelor and a handsome stripling too.

81 **noble** coin worth a third of a pound 82 **careful** care-filled 83 **hap** fortune
88 **in** into 88 **suspects** suspicions 94 **preferments** promotions 97 **marry**
indeed (from "By the virgin Mary")

Iwis your grandam had a worser match.

QUEEN ELIZABETH My Lord of Gloucester, I have too
    long borne
Your blunt upbraidings and your bitter scoffs.
By heaven, I will acquaint his Majesty
Of those gross taunts that oft I have endured.   105
I had rather be a country servant maid
Than a great queen with this condition,
To be so baited, scorned, and stormèd at.

       Enter old Queen Margaret, [behind].

Small joy have I in being England's Queen.

QUEEN MARGARET [*Aside*] And less'ned be that small,
    God I beseech him!   110
Thy honor, state, and seat is due to me.

RICHARD What! Threat you me with telling of the
    King?
Tell him and spare not. Look what I have said
I will avouch in presence of the King.
I dare adventure to be sent to th' Tow'r.   115
'Tis time to speak; my pains are quite forgot.

QUEEN MARGARET [*Aside*] Out, devil! I do remember
    them too well.
Thou kill'dst my husband Henry in the Tower
And Edward, my poor son, at Tewkesbury.

RICHARD Ere you were queen, ay, or your husband
    king,   120
I was a packhorse in his great affairs,
A weeder-out of his proud adversaries,
A liberal rewarder of his friends;
To royalize his blood I spent mine own.

QUEEN MARGARET [*Aside*] Ay, and much better blood
    than his or thine.   125

RICHARD In all which time you and your husband Grey

101 **Iwis** certainly   108 **baited** tormented   113 **Look what** whatever   116 **pains**
efforts

Were factious for the house of Lancaster;
And, Rivers, so were you. Was not your husband
In Margaret's battle at Saint Albans slain?
130   Let me put in your minds, if you forget,
What you have been ere this, and what you are;
Withal, what I have been, and what I am.

QUEEN MARGARET   [*Aside*] A murd'rous villain, and so
    still thou art.

RICHARD   Poor Clarence did forsake his father
    Warwick;
135   Ay, and forswore himself—which Jesu pardon!—

QUEEN MARGARET   [*Aside*] Which God revenge!

RICHARD   To fight on Edward's party for the crown;
And for his meed, poor lord, he is mewèd up.
I would to God my heart were flint like Edward's,
140   Or Edward's soft and pitiful like mine.
I am too childish-foolish for this world.

QUEEN MARGARET   [*Aside*] Hie thee to hell for shame
    and leave this world,
Thou cacodemon! There thy kingdom is.

RIVERS   My Lord of Gloucester, in those busy days
145   Which here you urge to prove us enemies,
We followed then our lord, our sovereign king.
So should we you, if you should be our King.

RICHARD   If I should be! I had rather be a peddler.
Far be it from my heart, the thought thereof!

150   QUEEN ELIZABETH   As little joy, my lord, as you suppose
You should enjoy were you this country's king,
As little joy you may suppose in me
That I enjoy, being the queen thereof.

QUEEN MARGARET   [*Aside*] A little joy enjoys the queen
    thereof;
155   For I am she, and altogether joyless.
I can no longer hold me patient. [*Comes forward.*]

129 battle army   134 father father-in-law   138 **meed** reward   143 **caco-**
demon evil spirit

Hear me, you wrangling pirates, that fall out
In sharing that which you have pilled from me!
Which of you trembles not that looks on me?
If not, that I am queen, you bow like subjects,   160
Yet that, by you deposed, you quake like rebels.
Ah, gentle villain, do not turn away!

RICHARD Foul wrinkled witch, what mak'st thou in
    my sight?

QUEEN MARGARET But repetition of what thou hast
    marred;
    That will I make before I let thee go.   165

RICHARD Wert thou not banishèd on pain of death?

QUEEN MARGARET I was; but I do find more pain in
    banishment
    Than death can yield me here by my abode.
    A husband and a son thou ow'st to me;
    And thou a kingdom; all of you allegiance.   170
    This sorrow that I have, by right is yours,
    And all the pleasures you usurp are mine.

RICHARD The curse my noble father laid on thee
    When thou didst crown his warlike brows with
      paper
    And with thy scorns drew'st rivers from his eyes   175
    And then to dry them gav'st the Duke a clout
    Steeped in the faultless blood of pretty Rutland,
    His curses then from bitterness of soul
    Denounced against thee are all fall'n upon thee;
    And God, not we, hath plagued thy bloody deed.   180

QUEEN ELIZABETH So just is God to right the innocent.

HASTINGS O, 'twas the foulest deed to slay that babe
    And the most merciless that e'er was heard of!

RIVERS Tyrants themselves wept when it was reported.

DORSET No man but prophesied revenge for it.   185

158 **pilled** plundered   160–61 **that ... that** because ... because   162 **gentle**
(1) wellborn (2) kindly (ironic)   163 **mak'st thou** are you doing   176 **clout**
piece of cloth

BUCKINGHAM Northumberland, then present, wept to
　　see it.

QUEEN MARGARET What! Were you snarling all before I
　　came,
　　Ready to catch each other by the throat,
　　And turn you all your hatred now on me?
　　Did York's dread curse prevail so much with
190　　heaven
　　That Henry's death, my lovely Edward's death,
　　Their kingdom's loss, my woeful banishment,
　　Should all but answer for that peevish brat?
　　Can curses pierce the clouds and enter heaven?
　　Why then, give way, dull clouds, to my quick
195　　curses!
　　Though not by war, by surfeit die your king,
　　As ours by murder, to make him a king!
　　Edward thy son, that now is Prince of Wales,
　　For Edward our son, that was Prince of Wales,
200　　Die in his youth by like untimely violence!
　　Thyself a queen, for me that was a queen,
　　Outlive thy glory like my wretched self!
　　Long mayst thou live to wail thy children's death
　　And see another, as I see thee now,
205　　Decked in thy rights as thou art stalled in mine!
　　Long die thy happy days before thy death,
　　And, after many length'ned hours of grief,
　　Die neither mother, wife, nor England's Queen!
　　Rivers and Dorset, you were standers-by,
210　　And so wast thou, Lord Hastings, when my son
　　Was stabbed with bloody daggers. God I pray him
　　That none of you may live his natural age,
　　But by some unlooked accident cut off!

RICHARD Have done thy charm, thou hateful withered
　　hag!

QUEEN MARGARET And leave out thee? Stay, dog, for
215　　thou shalt hear me.

193 **but answer** only pay back 193 **peevish** foolish 195 **quick** full of life
205 **stalled** installed 214 **charm** spell, curse

If heaven have any grievous plague in store
Exceeding those that I can wish upon thee,
O let them keep it till thy sins be ripe
And then hurl down their indignation
On thee, the troubler of the poor world's peace!   220
The worm of conscience still begnaw thy soul!
Thy friends suspect for traitors while thou liv'st,
And take deep traitors for thy dearest friends!
No sleep close up that deadly eye of thine,
Unless it be while some tormenting dream   225
Affrights thee with a hell of ugly devils!
Thou elvish-marked, abortive, rooting hog!
Thou that wast sealed in thy nativity
The slave of nature and the son of hell!
Thou slander of thy heavy mother's womb!   230
Thou loathèd issue of thy father's loins!
Thou rag of honor! Thou detested—

RICHARD Margaret.

QUEEN MARGARET Richard!

RICHARD   Ha?

QUEEN MARGARET   I call thee not.

RICHARD I cry thee mercy then, for I did think
    That thou hadst called me all these bitter names.   235

QUEEN MARGARET Why, so I did, but looked for no
    reply.
    O, let me make the period to my curse!

RICHARD 'Tis done by me, and ends in "Margaret."

QUEEN ELIZABETH Thus have you breathed your curse
    against yourself.

QUEEN MARGARET Poor painted queen, vain flourish
    of my fortune,   240
    Why strew'st thou sugar on that bottled spider

227 elvish-marked disfigured by evil fairies 227 hog (the boar was Richard's emblem) 228 sealed marked 230 heavy sorrowful 234 cry thee mercy beg your pardon 237 period end 240 painted unreal 240 vain flourish useless decoration 241 bottled swollen

Whose deadly web ensnareth thee about?
Fool, fool, thou whet'st a knife to kill thyself.
The day will come that thou shalt wish for me
To help thee curse this poisonous bunch-backed
245   toad.

HASTINGS False-boding woman, end thy frantic curse,
Lest to thy harm thou move our patience.

QUEEN MARGARET Foul shame upon you! You have all
moved mine.

RIVERS Were you well served, you would be taught
250   your duty.

QUEEN MARGARET To serve me well, you all should do
me duty,
Teach me to be your queen and you my subjects.
O, serve me well and teach yourselves that duty!

DORSET Dispute not with her; she is lunatic.

QUEEN MARGARET Peace, Master Marquis, you are
malapert.
255   Your fire-new stamp of honor is scarce current.
O that your young nobility could judge
What 'twere to lose it and be miserable!
They that stand high have many blasts to shake
them,
And if they fall, they dash themselves to pieces.

RICHARD Good counsel, marry! Learn it, learn it,
260   Marquis.

DORSET It touches you, my lord, as much as me.

RICHARD Ay, and much more; but I was born so high.
Our aerie buildeth in the cedar's top
And dallies with the wind and scorns the sun.

QUEEN MARGARET And turns the sun to shade, alas!
265   alas!
Witness my son, now in the shade of death,

254 **malapert** impudent   255 **fire-new stamp** newly coined title   263 **aerie**
brood of eagles

Whose bright outshining beams thy cloudy wrath
Hath in eternal darkness folded up.
Your aerie buildeth in our aerie's nest.
O God, that seest it, do not suffer it!   270
As it is won with blood, lost be it so!

BUCKINGHAM Peace, peace, for shame, if not for
    charity.

QUEEN MARGARET Urge neither charity nor shame to
    me.
Uncharitably with me have you dealt,
And shamefully my hopes by you are butchered.   275
My charity is outrage, life my shame,
And in that shame still live my sorrow's rage!

BUCKINGHAM Have done, have done.

QUEEN MARGARET O princely Buckingham, I'll kiss thy
    hand
In sign of league and amity with thee.   280
Now fair befall thee and thy noble house!
Thy garments are not spotted with our blood,
Nor thou within the compass of my curse.

BUCKINGHAM Nor no one here; for curses never pass
The lips of those that breathe them in the air.   285

QUEEN MARGARET I will not think but they ascend the
    sky
And there awake God's gentle-sleeping peace.
O Buckingham, take heed of yonder dog!
Look when he fawns he bites; and when he bites,
His venom tooth will rankle to the death.   290
Have not to do with him, beware of him.
Sin, death, and hell have set their marks on him
And all their ministers attend on him.

RICHARD What doth she say, my Lord of Buckingham?

BUCKINGHAM Nothing that I respect, my gracious
    lord.   295

289 **Look when** whenever   295 **respect** pay heed to

QUEEN MARGARET What, dost thou scorn me for my
    gentle counsel
    And soothe the devil that I warn thee from?
    O, but remember this another day,
    When he shall split thy very heart with sorrow,
300   And say poor Margaret was a prophetess.
    Live each of you the subjects to his hate,
    And he to yours, and all of you to God's!   *Exit.*

BUCKINGHAM My hair doth stand on end to hear her
    curses.

RIVERS And so doth mine. I muse why she's at
    liberty.

305 RICHARD I cannot blame her. By God's holy mother,
    She hath had too much wrong, and I repent
    My part thereof that I have done to her.

QUEEN ELIZABETH I never did her any to my
    knowledge.

RICHARD Yet you have all the vantage of her wrong:
310   I was too hot to do somebody good
    That is too cold in thinking of it now.
    Marry, as for Clarence, he is well repaid;
    He is franked up to fatting for his pains.
    God pardon them that are the cause thereof!

315 RIVERS A virtuous and a Christianlike conclusion,
    To pray for them that have done scathe to us.

RICHARD So do I ever—[*speaks to himself*] being well
    advised;
    For had I cursed now, I had cursed myself.

Enter Catesby.

CATESBY Madam, his Majesty doth call for you;
320   And for your Grace; and yours, my gracious lord.

QUEEN ELIZABETH Catesby, I come. Lords, will you go
    with me?

304 **muse** wonder   313 **franked up** shut up (like an animal to be slaughtered)
316 **scathe** harm

RIVERS We wait upon your Grace.

               Exeunt all but [Richard of] Gloucester.

RICHARD I do the wrong, and first begin to brawl.
  The secret mischiefs that I set abroach
  I lay unto the grievous charge of others.   325
  Clarence, who I indeed have cast in darkness,
  I do beweep to many simple gulls,
  Namely to Derby, Hastings, Buckingham,
  And tell them 'tis the Queen and her allies
  That stir the King against the Duke my brother.   330
  Now they believe it, and withal whet me
  To be revenged on Rivers, Dorset, Grey.
  But then I sigh, and with a piece of Scripture
  Tell them that God bids us do good for evil;
  And thus I clothe my naked villainy   335
  With odd old ends stol'n forth of holy writ,
  And seem a saint when most I play the devil.

            Enter two Murderers.

  But soft! Here come my executioners.
  How now, my hardy, stout-resolvèd mates!
  Are you now going to dispatch this thing?   340

FIRST MURDERER We are, my lord, and come to have
    the warrant
  That we may be admitted where he is.

RICHARD Well thought upon; I have it here about me.

               [Gives the warrant.]
  When you have done, repair to Crosby Place.
  But, sirs, be sudden in the execution,   345
  Withal obdurate, do not hear him plead;
  For Clarence is well-spoken, and perhaps
  May move your hearts to pity if you mark him.

FIRST MURDERER Tut, tut, my lord, we will not stand
    to prate.
  Talkers are no good doers; be assured   350
  We go to use our hands and not our tongues.

324 **set abroach** originate   327 **gulls** dupes   329 **allies** kindred

RICHARD Your eyes drop millstones when fools' eyes
        fall tears.
     I like you, lads; about your business straight.
     Go, go, dispatch.

FIRST MURDERER   We will, my noble lord.   *Exeunt*.

Scene IV. [*The Tower*.]

Enter Clarence and Keeper.

KEEPER Why looks your Grace so heavily today?

CLARENCE O, I have passed a miserable night,
        So full of fearful dreams, of ugly sights,
        That, as I am a Christian faithful man,
5   I would not spend another such a night
        Though 'twere to buy a world of happy days,
        So full of dismal terror was the time.

KEEPER What was your dream, my lord? I pray you
        tell me.

CLARENCE Methoughts that I had broken from the
        Tower
10   And was embarked to cross to Burgundy,
        And in my company my brother Gloucester,
        Who from my cabin tempted me to walk
        Upon the hatches. Thence we looked toward
        England
        And cited up a thousand heavy times,
15   During the wars of York and Lancaster,
        That had befall'n us. As we paced along
        Upon the giddy footing of the hatches,
        Methought that Gloucester stumbled, and in falling
        Struck me (that thought to stay him) overboard

352 **fall** let fall   353 **straight** at once I.iv.1 **heavily** sadly   9 **Methoughts** it
seemed to me   19 **stay** support

Into the tumbling billows of the main.   20
O Lord, methought what pain it was to drown!
What dreadful noise of water in mine ears!
What sights of ugly death within mine eyes!
Methoughts I saw a thousand fearful wracks;
A thousand men that fishes gnawed upon;   25
Wedges of gold, great anchors, heaps of pearl,
Inestimable stones, unvalued jewels,
All scatt'red in the bottom of the sea.
Some lay in dead men's skulls, and in the holes
Where eyes did once inhabit there were crept,   30
As 'twere in scorn of eyes, reflecting gems
That wooed the slimy bottom of the deep
And mocked the dead bones that lay scatt'red by.

KEEPER Had you such leisure in the time of death
   To gaze upon these secrets of the deep?   35

CLARENCE Methought I had; and often did I strive
   To yield the ghost, but still the envious flood
   Stopped in my soul and would not let it forth
   To find the empty, vast, and wand'ring air,
   But smothered it within my panting bulk,   40
   Who almost burst to belch it in the sea.

KEEPER Awaked you not in this sore agony?

CLARENCE No, no, my dream was lengthened after life.
   O, then began the tempest to my soul!
   I passed, methought, the melancholy flood,   45
   With that sour ferryman which poets write of,
   Unto the kingdom of perpetual night.
   The first that there did greet my stranger soul
   Was my great father-in-law, renownèd Warwick,
   Who spake aloud, "What scourge for perjury   50
   Can this dark monarchy afford false Clarence?"
   And so he vanished. Then came wand'ring by
   A shadow like an angel, with bright hair
   Dabbled in blood, and he shrieked out aloud,

20 **main** ocean   27 **unvaluèd** priceless   40 **bulk** body   46 **ferryman** Charon,
who ferried the dead across the Styx

"Clarence is come, false, fleeting, perjured
55   Clarence,
That stabbed me in the field by Tewkesbury.
Seize on him, Furies, take him unto torment!"
With that, methought, a legion of foul fiends
Environed me and howlèd in mine ears
60   Such hideous cries that with the very noise
I, trembling, waked, and for a season after
Could not believe but that I was in hell,
Such terrible impression made my dream.

KEEPER No marvel, lord, though it affrighted you.
65   I am afraid, methinks, to hear you tell it.

CLARENCE Ah, keeper, keeper, I have done these things
That now give evidence against my soul
For Edward's sake, and see how he requites me!
O God! If my deep pray'rs cannot appease thee,
70   But thou wilt be avenged on my misdeeds,
Yet execute thy wrath in me alone.
O, spare my guiltless wife and my poor children!
Keeper, I prithee sit by me awhile.
My soul is heavy, and I fain would sleep.

KEEPER I will, my lord. God give your Grace good
75   rest!   [Clarence sleeps.]

            Enter Brakenbury, the Lieutenant.

BRAKENBURY Sorrow breaks seasons and reposing
      hours,
Makes the night morning and the noontide night.
Princes have but their titles for their glories,
An outward honor for an inward toil,
80   And for unfelt imaginations
They often feel a world of restless cares;
So that between their titles and low name
There's nothing differs but the outward fame.

            Enter two Murderers.

FIRST MURDERER Ho! Who's here?

55 fleeting fickle   80 unfelt imaginations pleasures imagined but not felt

BRAKENBURY What wouldst thou, fellow? And how
    cam'st thou hither?   85

FIRST MURDERER I would speak with Clarence, and I
    came hither on my legs.

BRAKENBURY What, so brief?

SECOND MURDERER 'Tis better, sir, than to be tedious.
    Let him see our commission, and talk no more.   90
                          [Brakenbury] reads [it].

BRAKENBURY I am in this commanded to deliver
    The noble Duke of Clarence to your hands.
    I will not reason what is meant hereby,
    Because I will be guiltless from the meaning.
    There lies the Duke asleep, and there the keys.   95
    I'll to the King and signify to him
    That thus I have resigned to you my charge.

FIRST MURDERER You may, sir, 'tis a point of wisdom.
    Fare you well.
                 Exit [Brakenbury with Keeper].

SECOND MURDERER What, shall we stab him as he   100
    sleeps?

FIRST MURDERER No, he'll say 'twas done cowardly
    when he wakes.

SECOND MURDERER Why, he shall never wake until the
    great Judgment Day.   105

FIRST MURDERER Why, then he'll say we stabbed him
    sleeping.

SECOND MURDERER The urging of that word "judgment"
    hath bred a kind of remorse in me.

FIRST MURDERER What, art thou afraid?   110

SECOND MURDERER Not to kill him, having a warrant;
    but to be damned for killing him, from the which
    no warrant can defend me.

FIRST MURDERER I thought thou hadst been resolute.

115 SECOND MURDERER So I am—to let him live.

FIRST MURDERER I'll back to the Duke of Gloucester
and tell him so.

SECOND MURDERER Nay, I prithee stay a little. I hope
this passionate humor of mine will change; it was
120 wont to hold me but while one tells twenty.

FIRST MURDERER How dost thou feel thyself now?

SECOND MURDERER Faith, some certain dregs of conscience are yet within me.

FIRST MURDERER Remember our reward when the
125 deed's done.

SECOND MURDERER Zounds, he dies! I had forgot the
reward.

FIRST MURDERER Where's thy conscience now?

SECOND MURDERER O, in the Duke of Gloucester's
130 purse.

FIRST MURDERER When he opens his purse to give us
our reward, thy conscience flies out.

SECOND MURDERER 'Tis no matter, let it go. There's
few or none will entertain it.

135 FIRST MURDERER What if it come to thee again?

SECOND MURDERER I'll not meddle with it; it makes a
man a coward. A man cannot steal, but it accuseth
him; a man cannot swear, but it checks him; a man
cannot lie with his neighbor's wife, but it detects
140 him. 'Tis a blushing shamefaced spirit that mutinies
in a man's bosom. It fills a man full of obstacles.
It made me once restore a purse of gold that, by
chance, I found. It beggars any man that keeps it.
It is turned out of towns and cities for a dangerous
145 thing, and every man that means to live well endeavors to trust to himself and live without it.

119 **passionate humor** compassionate mood   120 **tells** counts   126 **Zounds**
(an oath, from "By God's wounds")

FIRST MURDERER Zounds, 'tis even now at my elbow,
persuading me not to kill the Duke.

SECOND MURDERER Take the devil in thy mind, and
believe him not. He would insinuate with thee but   150
to make thee sigh.

FIRST MURDERER I am strong-framed; he cannot prevail with me.

SECOND MURDERER Spoke like a tall man that respects
thy reputation. Come, shall we fall to work?   155

FIRST MURDERER Take him on the costard with the
hilts of thy sword, and then throw him into the
malmsey butt in the next room.

SECOND MURDERER O excellent device! And make a
sop of him.   160

FIRST MURDERER Soft, he wakes.

SECOND MURDERER Strike!

FIRST MURDERER No, we'll reason with him.

CLARENCE Where art thou, keeper? Give me a cup of
wine.

SECOND MURDERER You shall have wine enough, my
lord, anon.   165

CLARENCE In God's name, what art thou?

FIRST MURDERER A man, as you are.

CLARENCE But not as I am, royal.

FIRST MURDERER Nor you as we are, loyal.

CLARENCE Thy voice is thunder, but thy looks are
humble.   170

FIRST MURDERER My voice is now the King's, my looks
mine own.

150 **him** i.e., conscience   154 **tall** brave   156 **costard** head   158 **malmsey
butt** cask of malmsey, a Greek wine   160 **sop** piece of bread soaked in wine
163 **reason** talk

CLARENCE How darkly and how deadly dost thou
        speak!
      Your eyes do menace me. Why look you pale?
      Who sent you hither? Wherefore do you come?

175 SECOND MURDERER To, to, to—

CLARENCE To murder me?

BOTH Ay, ay.

CLARENCE You scarcely have the hearts to tell me so,
      And therefore cannot have the hearts to do it.
180   Wherein, my friends, have I offended you?

FIRST MURDERER Offended us you have not, but the
        King.

CLARENCE I shall be reconciled to him again.

SECOND MURDERER Never, my lord; therefore prepare
        to die.

CLARENCE Are you drawn forth among a world of men
185   To slay the innocent? What is my offense?
      Where is the evidence that doth accuse me?
      What lawful quest have given their verdict up
      Unto the frowning judge? Or who pronounced
      The bitter sentence of poor Clarence' death?
190   Before I be convict by course of law,
      To threaten me with death is most unlawful.
      I charge you, as you hope to have redemption
      By Christ's dear blood shed for our grievous sins,
      That you depart, and lay no hands on me.
195   The deed you undertake is damnable.

FIRST MURDERER What we will do, we do upon com-
        mand.

SECOND MURDERER And he that hath commanded is our
        king.

CLARENCE Erroneous vassals! The great King of kings
      Hath in the table of his law commanded
200   That thou shalt do no murder. Will you then

187 **quest** jury   195 **damnable** i.e., one which will damn your souls

    Spurn at his edict and fulfill a man's?
    Take heed; for he holds vengeance in his hand
    To hurl upon their heads that break his law.

SECOND MURDERER And that same vengeance doth he
      hurl on thee
    For false forswearing and for murder too.   205
    Thou didst receive the sacrament to fight
    In quarrel of the house of Lancaster.

FIRST MURDERER And like a traitor to the name of God
    Didst break that vow, and with thy treacherous
      blade
    Unrip'st the bowels of thy sov'reign's son.   210

SECOND MURDERER Whom thou wast sworn to cherish
      and defend.

FIRST MURDERER How canst thou urge God's dreadful
      law to us
    When thou hast broke it in such dear degree?

CLARENCE Alas! For whose sake did I that ill deed?
    For Edward, for my brother, for his sake.   215
    He sends you not to murder me for this,
    For in that sin he is as deep as I.
    If God will be avengèd for the deed,
    O, know you yet he doth it publicly.
    Take not the quarrel from his pow'rful arm.   220
    He needs no indirect or lawless course
    To cut off those that have offended him.

FIRST MURDERER Who made thee then a bloody
      minister
    When gallant-springing brave Plantagenet,
    That princely novice, was struck dead by thee?   225

CLARENCE My brother's love, the devil, and my rage.

FIRST MURDERER Thy brother's love, our duty, and thy
      faults
    Provoke us hither now to slaughter thee.

CLARENCE If you do love my brother, hate not me.

213 **dear** high   225 **princely novice** young prince

230 I am his brother, and I love him well.
If you are hired for meed, go back again,
And I will send you to my brother Gloucester,
Who shall reward you better for my life
Than Edward will for tidings of my death.

SECOND MURDERER You are deceived; your brother
235   Gloucester hates you.

CLARENCE O, no, he loves me and he holds me dear.
Go you to him from me.

FIRST MURDERER   Ay, so we will.

CLARENCE Tell him, when that our princely father York
Blessed his three sons with his victorious arm
240 And charged us from his soul to love each other,
He little thought of this divided friendship.
Bid Gloucester think on this, and he will weep.

FIRST MURDERER Ay, millstones, as he lessoned us to
weep.

CLARENCE O, do not slander him, for he is kind.

FIRST MURDERER Right as snow in harvest. Come, you
245   deceive yourself.
'Tis he that sends us to destroy you here.

CLARENCE It cannot be, for he bewept my fortune
And hugged me in his arms and swore with sobs
That he would labor my delivery.

250 FIRST MURDERER Why so he doth, when he delivers you
From this earth's thralldom to the joys of heaven.

SECOND MURDERER Make peace with God, for you must
die, my lord.

CLARENCE Have you that holy feeling in your souls
To counsel me to make my peace with God,
255 And are you yet to your own souls so blind
That you will war with God by murd'ring me?

231 **meed** reward   243 **lessoned** taught   245 **Right as** just like   249 **labor** work for

O, sirs, consider, they that set you on
To do this deed will hate you for the deed.

SECOND MURDERER What shall we do?

CLARENCE   Relent, and save your souls.

FIRST MURDERER Relent! No. 'Tis cowardly and woman-
    ish.   260

CLARENCE Not to relent is beastly, savage, devilish.
    [*To Second Murderer*] My friend, I spy some pity
    in thy looks.
  O, if thine eye be not a flatterer,
  Come thou on my side and entreat for me.
  A begging prince what beggar pities not?   265
  Which of you, if you were a prince's son,
  Being pent from liberty as I am now,
  If two such murderers as yourselves came to you,
  Would not entreat for life? As you would beg,
  Were you in my distress—   270

SECOND MURDERER Look behind you, my lord!

FIRST MURDERER Take that! And that! (*Stabs him.*) If
    all this will not do,
  I'll drown you in the malmsey butt within.
                        Exit [with the body].

SECOND MURDERER A bloody deed and desperately
    dispatched!
  How fain, like Pilate, would I wash my hands   275
  Of this most grievous murder!

          Enter First Murderer.

FIRST MURDERER How now? What mean'st thou that
    thou help'st me not?
  By heaven, the Duke shall know how slack you
    have been.

SECOND MURDERER I would he knew that I had saved
    his brother!
  Take thou the fee, and tell him what I say,   280
  For I repent me that the Duke is slain.   *Exit.*

FIRST MURDERER So do not I. Go, coward as thou art.
Well, I'll go hide the body in some hole
Till that the Duke give order for his burial;
285   And when I have my meed, I will away,
For this will out, and then I must not stay.   *Exit.*

ACT II

Scene I. [*The palace.*]

Flourish. Enter the King, sick, the Queen, Lord Marquis Dorset, [Grey,] Rivers, Hastings, Catesby, Buckingham, Woodville, [and Scales].

KING EDWARD Why, so. Now have I done a good day's work.
You peers, continue this united league.
I every day expect an embassage
From my Redeemer to redeem me hence;
And more in peace my soul shall part to heaven,   5
Since I have made my friends at peace on earth.
Rivers and Hastings, take each other's hand;
Dissemble not your hatred, swear your love.

RIVERS By heaven, my soul is purged from grudging hate,
And with my hand I seal my true heart's love.   10

HASTINGS So thrive I as I truly swear the like!

KING EDWARD Take heed you dally not before your king,
Lest he that is the supreme King of kings

II.i. s.d. **Flourish** fanfare of trumpets   8 **Dissemble** disguise by false pretense
12 **dally** trifle

Confound your hidden falsehood and award
15   Either of you to be the other's end.

HASTINGS So prosper I as I swear perfect love!

RIVERS And I as I love Hastings with my heart!

KING EDWARD Madam, yourself is not exempt from this;
Nor you, son Dorset; Buckingham, nor you;
20   You have been factious one against the other.
Wife, love Lord Hastings, let him kiss your hand,
And what you do, do it unfeignedly.

QUEEN ELIZABETH There, Hastings. I will never more remember
Our former hatred, so thrive I and mine!

KING EDWARD Dorset, embrace him; Hastings, love
25   Lord Marquis.

DORSET This interchange of love, I here protest,
Upon my part shall be inviolable.

HASTINGS And so swear I.

KING EDWARD Now, princely Buckingham, seal thou this league
30   With thy embracements to my wife's allies,
And make me happy in your unity.

BUCKINGHAM [*To the Queen*] Whenever Buckingham doth turn his hate
Upon your Grace, but with all duteous love
Doth cherish you and yours, God punish me
35   With hate in those where I expect most love!
When I have most need to employ a friend,
And most assurèd that he is a friend,
Deep, hollow, treacherous, and full of guile
Be he unto me! This do I beg of God,
40   When I am cold in zeal to you or yours.   *Embrace.*

KING EDWARD A pleasing cordial, princely Bucking-ham,

33 but (the meaning calls for "and not")

416

Is this thy vow unto my sickly heart.
There wanteth now our brother Gloucester here
To make the blessèd period of this peace.

BUCKINGHAM And in good time,   45
Here comes Sir Richard Ratcliffe and the Duke.

Enter Ratcliffe and [Richard, Duke of] Gloucester.

RICHARD Good morrow to my sovereign king and
    queen;
And, princely peers, a happy time of day!

KING EDWARD Happy indeed, as we have spent the
    day.
Gloucester, we have done deeds of charity,   50
Made peace of enmity, fair love of hate,
Between these swelling wrong-incensèd peers.

RICHARD A blessèd labor, my most sovereign lord.
Among this princely heap if any here
By false intelligence or wrong surmise   55
Hold me a foe;
If I unwittingly, or in my rage,
Have aught committed that is hardly borne
By any in this presence, I desire
To reconcile me to his friendly peace.   60
'Tis death to me to be at enmity;
I hate it, and desire all good men's love.
First, madam, I entreat true peace of you,
Which I will purchase with my duteous service;
Of you, my noble cousin Buckingham,   65
If ever any grudge were lodged between us;
Of you and you, Lord Rivers and of Dorset,
That all without desert have frowned on me;
Of you, Lord Woodville, and, Lord Scales, of you;
Dukes, earls, lords, gentlemen; indeed, of all.   70
I do not know that Englishman alive
With whom my soul is any jot at odds

44 **period** conclusion   54 **heap** company, group   58 **hardly borne** resented
68 **all without desert** wholly without my deserving it   69 **Lord Woodville,
and, Lord Scales** (historically, these are both other titles of Anthony Woodville,
Earl Rivers)

More than the infant that is born tonight.
I thank my God for my humility.

QUEEN ELIZABETH A holy day shall this be kept here-
75   after.
I would to God all strifes were well compounded.
My sovereign lord, I do beseech your Highness
To take our brother Clarence to your Grace.

RICHARD Why, madam, have I off'red love for this,
80   To be so flouted in this royal presence?
Who knows not that the gentle Duke is dead?

                                        They all start.

You do him injury to scorn his corse.

KING EDWARD Who knows not he is dead! Who knows
he is?

QUEEN ELIZABETH All-seeing heaven, what a world is
this!

85 BUCKINGHAM Look I so pale, Lord Dorset, as the rest?

DORSET Ay, my good lord; and no man in the presence
But his red color hath forsook his cheeks.

KING EDWARD Is Clarence dead? The order was
reversed.

RICHARD But he, poor man, by your first order died,
90   And that a wingèd Mercury did bear;
Some tardy cripple bare the countermand,
That came too lag to see him buried.
God grant that some, less noble and less loyal,
Nearer in bloody thoughts, and not in blood,
95   Deserve not worse than wretched Clarence did,
And yet go current from suspicion!

                Enter [Lord Stanley,] Earl of Derby.

STANLEY A boon, my sovereign, for my service done!

KING EDWARD I prithee peace. My soul is full of
sorrow.

76 compounded settled   92 lag late   94 and if   96 go current from are taken
at face value without

418

STANLEY I will not rise unless your Highness hear me.

KING EDWARD Then say at once what is it thou requests. 100

STANLEY The forfeit, sovereign, of my servant's life,
Who slew today a riotous gentleman
Lately attendant on the Duke of Norfolk.

KING EDWARD Have I a tongue to doom my brother's
        death,
And shall that tongue give pardon to a slave? 105
My brother killed no man, his fault was thought,
And yet his punishment was bitter death.
Who sued to me for him? Who, in my wrath,
Kneeled at my feet and bid me be advised?
Who spoke of brotherhood? Who spoke of love? 110
Who told me how the poor soul did forsake
The mighty Warwick and did fight for me?
Who told me, in the field at Tewkesbury
When Oxford had me down, he rescuèd me
And said, "Dear brother, live, and be a king"? 115
Who told me, when we both lay in the field
Frozen almost to death, how he did lap me
Even in his garments, and did give himself
All thin and naked, to the numb-cold night?
All this from my remembrance brutish wrath 120
Sinfully plucked, and not a man of you
Had so much grace to put it in my mind.
But when your carters or your waiting vassals
Have done a drunken slaughter and defaced
The precious image of our dear Redeemer, 125
You straight are on your knees for "Pardon,
        pardon!"
And I, unjustly too, must grant it you.
                                        [Stanley rises.]
But for my brother not a man would speak,
Nor I, ungracious, speak unto myself
For him, poor soul. The proudest of you all 130
Have been beholding to him in his life;

101 forfeit ... life i.e., forfeited life 109 be advised consider carefully
117 lap wrap

Yet none of you would once beg for his life.
O God, I fear thy justice will take hold
On me and you, and mine and yours, for this!
Come, Hastings, help me to my closet. Ah, poor
135   Clarence!   *Exeunt some with King and Queen.*

RICHARD This is the fruits of rashness. Marked you not
How that the guilty kindred of the Queen
Looked pale when they did hear of Clarence'
        death?
O, they did urge it still unto the King!
140   God will revenge it. Come, lords, will you go
To comfort Edward with our company?

BUCKINGHAM We wait upon your Grace.   *Exeunt.*

Scene II. [*The palace.*]

*Enter the old Duchess of York, with the two
Children of Clarence.*

BOY Good grandam, tell us, is our father dead?

DUCHESS OF YORK No, boy.

DAUGHTER Why do you weep so oft, and beat your
        breast,
And cry, "O Clarence, my unhappy son"?

5   BOY Why do you look on us, and shake your head,
And call us orphans, wretches, castaways,
If that our noble father were alive?

DUCHESS OF YORK My pretty cousins, you mistake me
        both.
I do lament the sickness of the King,
10   As loath to lose him, not your father's death.
It were lost sorrow to wail one that's lost.

135 **closet** private room   II.ii.8 **cousins** relatives

420

BOY Then you conclude, my grandam, he is dead.
   The King mine uncle is too blame for it.
   God will revenge it, whom I will importune
   With earnest prayers all to that effect.   15

DAUGHTER And so will I.

DUCHESS OF YORK Peace, children, peace! The King
    doth love you well.
   Incapable and shallow innocents,
   You cannot guess who caused your father's death.

BOY Grandam, we can; for my good uncle Gloucester   20
   Told me the King, provoked to it by the Queen,
   Devised impeachments to imprison him;
   And when my uncle told me so, he wept,
   And pitied me, and kindly kissed my cheek;
   Bade me rely on him as on my father,   25
   And he would love me dearly as a child.

DUCHESS OF YORK Ah, that deceit should steal such
    gentle shape
   And with a virtuous visor hide deep vice!
   He is my son, ay, and therein my shame;
   Yet from my dugs he drew not this deceit.   30

BOY Think you my uncle did dissemble, grandam?

DUCHESS OF YORK Ay, boy.

BOY I cannot think it. Hark! What noise is this?

*Enter the Queen, [Elizabeth,] with her hair about
her ears, Rivers and Dorset after her.*

QUEEN ELIZABETH Ah, who shall hinder me to wail and
    weep,
   To chide my fortune, and torment myself?   35
   I'll join with black despair against my soul
   And to myself become an enemy.

DUCHESS OF YORK What means this scene of rude
    impatience?

13 **too blame** too blameworthy 18 **Incapable** unable to understand
22 **impeachments** accusations 27 **shape** disguise 28 **visor** mask

QUEEN ELIZABETH To make an act of tragic violence.
40   Edward, my lord, thy son, our king, is dead!
       Why grow the branches when the root is gone?
       Why wither not the leaves that want their sap?
       If you will live, lament; if die, be brief,
       That our swift-wingèd souls may catch the King's,
45   Or like obedient subjects follow him
       To his new kingdom of ne'er-changing night.

DUCHESS OF YORK Ah, so much interest have I in thy
           sorrow
       As I had title in thy noble husband!
       I have bewept a worthy husband's death,
50   And lived with looking on his images;
       But now two mirrors of his princely semblance
       Are cracked in pieces by malignant death,
       And I for comfort have but once false glass
       That grieves me when I see my shame in him.
55   Thou art a widow, yet thou art a mother
       And hast the comfort of thy children left;
       But death hath snatched my husband from mine
           arms
       And plucked two crutches from my feeble hands,
       Clarence and Edward. O, what cause have I,
60   Thine being but a moi'ty of my moan,
       To overgo thy woes and drown thy cries!

BOY Ah, aunt, you wept not for our father's death.
     How can we aid you with our kindred tears?

DAUGHTER Our fatherless distress was left unmoaned;
65   Your widow-dolor likewise be unwept!

QUEEN ELIZABETH Give me no help in lamentation;
       I am not barren to bring forth complaints.
       All springs reduce their currents to mine eyes,
       That I, being governed by the watery moon,
70   May send forth plenteous tears to drown the world.
       Ah for my husband, for my dear lord Edward!

47 **interest** share 48 **title** legal right 50 **images** i.e., children 51 **semblance**
appearance 59 **what** how much 60 **moi'ty of my moan** half of my grief
68 **reduce** bring

CHILDREN Ah for our father, for our dear lord
    Clarence!

DUCHESS OF YORK Alas for both, both mine, Edward
    and Clarence!

QUEEN ELIZABETH What stay had I but Edward? And
    he's gone.

CHILDREN What stay had we but Clarence? And he's
    gone.   75

DUCHESS OF YORK What stays had I but they? And
    they are gone.

QUEEN ELIZABETH Was never widow had so dear a loss.

CHILDREN Were never orphans had so dear a loss.

DUCHESS OF YORK Was never mother had so dear a
    loss.
  Alas, I am the mother of these griefs!   80
  Their woes are parceled, mine is general.
  She for an Edward weeps, and so do I;
  I for a Clarence weep, so doth not she.
  These babes for Clarence weep, and so do I;
  I for an Edward weep, so do not they.   85
  Alas, you three on me, threefold distressed,
  Pour all your tears! I am your sorrow's nurse,
  And I will pamper it with lamentation.

DORSET Comfort, dear mother; God is much
    displeased
  That you take with unthankfulness his doing.   90
  In common worldly things 'tis called ungrateful
  With dull unwillingness to repay a debt
  Which with a bounteous hand was kindly lent;
  Much more to be thus opposite with heaven
  For it requires the royal debt it lent you.   95

RIVERS Madam, bethink you like a careful mother
  Of the young prince your son. Send straight for him;

74 stay support 81 parceled particular 94 opposite with opposed to
95 For because

Let him be crowned; in him your comfort lives.
Drown desperate sorrow in dead Edward's grave
100   And plant your joys in living Edward's throne.

Enter Richard, Buckingham, [Stanley, Earl of]
Derby, Hastings, and Ratcliffe.

RICHARD Sister, have comfort. All of us have cause
To wail the dimming of our shining star;
But none can help our harms by wailing them.
Madam, my mother, I do cry you mercy;
105   I did not see your Grace. Humbly on my knee
I crave your blessing.

DUCHESS OF YORK God bless thee, and put meekness
in thy breast,
Love, charity, obedience, and true duty!

RICHARD Amen! [*Aside*] And make me die a good old
man!
110   That is the butt-end of a mother's blessing;
I marvel that her Grace did leave it out.

BUCKINGHAM You cloudy princes and heart-sorrowing
peers
That bear this heavy mutual load of moan,
Now cheer each other in each other's love.
115   Though we have spent our harvest of this king,
We are to reap the harvest of his son.
The broken rancor of your high-swol'n hates,
But lately splintered, knit, and joined together,
Must gently be preserved, cherished, and kept.
120   Me seemeth good that with some little train
Forthwith from Ludlow the young prince be fet
Hither to London, to be crowned our king.

RIVERS Why with some little train, my Lord of Buckingham?

BUCKINGHAM Marry, my lord, lest by a multitude

118 **splintered** set in splints 119 **Must ... kept** (the subject has shifted from
rancor to its opposite) 120 **Me seemeth** it seems to me 121 **fet** fetched

424

The new-healed wound of malice should break out,   125
Which would be so much the more dangerous
By how much the estate is green and yet un-
    governed.
Where every horse bears his commanding rein
And may direct his course as please himself,
As well the fear of harm as harm apparent,   130
In my opinion, ought to be prevented.

RICHARD I hope the King made peace with all of us;
And the compact is firm and true in me.

RIVERS And so in me; and so (I think) in all.
Yet, since it is but green, it should be put   135
To no apparent likelihood of breach,
Which haply by much company might be urged.
Therefore I say with noble Buckingham
That it is meet so few should fetch the Prince.

HASTINGS And so say I.   140

RICHARD Then be it so; and go we to determine
Who they shall be that straight shall post to
    Ludlow.
Madam, and you, my sister, will you go
To give your censures in this business?

QUEEN AND DUCHESS OF YORK With all our hearts.   145
            Exeunt. Manet Buckingham and Richard.

BUCKINGHAM My lord, whoever journeys to the
    Prince,
For God sake let not us two stay at home;
For by the way I'll sort occasion,
As index to the story we late talked of,
To part the Queen's proud kindred from the Prince.   150

RICHARD My other self, my counsel's consistory,

127 **estate is green** regime is new   130 **apparent** seen clearly   137 **haply**
perhaps   139 **meet** fitting   144 **censures** judgments   145 s.d. **Manet** (Latin for
"remains." The third person plural is **manent**, but the Elizabethans commonly
used the third person singular—like "exit"—for the plural)   148 **sort occasion**
contrive opportunity   149 **index** preface   151 **consistory** council chamber

My oracle, my prophet, my dear cousin,
I, as a child, will go by thy direction.
Toward Ludlow then, for we'll not stay behind.

Exeunt.

Scene III. [*A street.*]

Enter one Citizen at one door and another at the other.

FIRST CITIZEN Good morrow, neighbor. Whither away
so fast?

SECOND CITIZEN I promise you, I scarcely know myself.
Hear you the news abroad?

FIRST CITIZEN   Yes, that the King is dead.

SECOND CITIZEN Ill news, by'r Lady; seldom comes the
better.
5   I fear, I fear 'twill prove a giddy world.

Enter another Citizen.

THIRD CITIZEN Neighbors, Godspeed!

FIRST CITIZEN   Give you good morrow, sir.

THIRD CITIZEN Doth the news hold of good King
Edward's death?

SECOND CITIZEN Ay, sir, it is too true, God help the
while!

THIRD CITIZEN Then, masters, look to see a troublous
world.

FIRST CITIZEN No, no; by God's good grace his son
10   shall reign.

II.iii.4 **seldom comes the better** change for the better is rare (a proverb)

426

THIRD CITIZEN Woe to that land that's governed by a
   child!

SECOND CITIZEN In him there is a hope of government,
   Which in his nonage counsel under him,
   And, in his full and ripened years, himself,
   No doubt shall then and till then govern well.   15

FIRST CITIZEN So stood the state when Henry the Sixth
   Was crowned in Paris but at nine months old.

THIRD CITIZEN Stood the state so? No, no, good
   friends, God wot!
   For then this land was famously enriched
   With politic grave counsel; then the King   20
   Had virtuous uncles to protect his Grace.

FIRST CITIZEN Why, so hath this, both by his father and
   mother.

THIRD CITIZEN Better it were they all came by his
   father,
   Or by his father there were none at all;
   For emulation who shall now be nearest   25
   Will touch us all too near, if God prevent not.
   O, full of danger is the Duke of Gloucester,
   And the Queen's sons and brothers haught and
   proud!
   And were they to be ruled, and not to rule,
   This sickly land might solace as before.   30

FIRST CITIZEN Come, come, we fear the worst. All will
   be well.

THIRD CITIZEN When clouds are seen, wise men put on
   their cloaks;
   When great leaves fall, then winter is at hand;
   When the sun sets, who doth not look for night?
   Untimely storms makes men expect a dearth.   35

12-13 **In him ... counsel** there is hope of good rule in him, during whose
minority advisers   18 **wot** knows   25 **emulation** rivalry   28 **haught** haughty
29 **were they to be ruled** if they could be controlled   30 **solace** take comfort
35 **dearth** famine

All may be well; but if God sort it so,
'Tis more than we deserve or I expect.

SECOND CITIZEN Truly, the hearts of men are full of
fear.
You cannot reason, almost, with a man
40   That looks not heavily and full of dread.

THIRD CITIZEN Before the days of change, still is it so.
By a divine instinct men's minds mistrust
Ensuing danger, as by proof we see
The water swell before a boist'rous storm.
45   But leave it all to God. Whither away?

SECOND CITIZEN Marry, we were sent for to the justices.

THIRD CITIZEN And so was I. I'll bear you company.
Exeunt.

Scene IV. [*The palace.*]

*Enter [the] Archbishop [of York], [the] young [Duke
of] York, the Queen, [Elizabeth,] and the Duchess [of
York].*

ARCHBISHOP Last night, I hear, they lay at Stony
Stratford;
And at Northampton they do rest tonight;
Tomorrow or next day they will be here.

DUCHESS OF YORK I long with all my heart to see the
Prince.
5   I hope he is much grown since last I saw him.

QUEEN ELIZABETH But I hear no; they say my son of
York
Has almost overta'en him in his growth.

YORK Ay, mother, but I would not have it so.

36 **sort** arrange   39 **reason** talk   43 **proof** experience

DUCHESS OF YORK Why, my good cousin? It is good to
   grow.

YORK Grandam, one night as we did sit at supper,   10
   My uncle Rivers talked how I did grow
   More than my brother. "Ay," quoth my uncle
      Gloucester,
   "Small herbs have grace, great weeds do grow
      apace."
   And since, methinks, I would not grow so fast,
   Because sweet flow'rs are slow and weeds make
      haste.   15

DUCHESS OF YORK Good faith, good faith, the saying
      did not hold
   In him that did object the same to thee.
   He was the wretched'st thing when he was young,
   So long a-growing and so leisurely,
   That, if his rule were true, he should be gracious.   20

ARCHBISHOP And so no doubt he is, my gracious
   madam.

DUCHESS OF YORK I hope he is; but yet let mothers
   doubt.

YORK Now, by my troth, if I had been rememb'red,
   I could have given my uncle's grace a flout
   To touch his growth nearer than he touched mine.   25

DUCHESS OF YORK How, my young York? I prithee let
   me hear it.

YORK Marry, they say, my uncle grew so fast
   That he could gnaw a crust at two hours old.
   'Twas full two years ere I could get a tooth.
   Grandam, this would have been a biting jest.   30

DUCHESS OF YORK I prithee, pretty York, who told thee
   this?

YORK Grandam, his nurse.

II.iv.13 grace virtue 13 apace quickly 17 object bring as a reproach
20 gracious virtuous 23 been rememb'red thought 24 flout taunt

DUCHESS OF YORK His nurse! Why, she was dead ere
    thou wast born.

YORK If 'twere not she, I cannot tell who told me.

QUEEN ELIZABETH A parlous boy! Go to, you are too
35   shrewd.

DUCHESS OF YORK Good madam, be not angry with the
    child.

QUEEN ELIZABETH Pitchers have ears.

Enter a Messenger.

ARCHBISHOP Here comes a messenger. What news?

MESSENGER Such news, my lord, as grieves me to
    report.

QUEEN ELIZABETH How doth the Prince?

40 MESSENGER   Well, madam, and in health.

DUCHESS OF YORK What is thy news?

MESSENGER Lord Rivers and Lord Grey are sent to
    Pomfret,
And with them Sir Thomas Vaughan, prisoners.

DUCHESS OF YORK Who hath committed them?

MESSENGER   The mighty dukes,
    Gloucester and Buckingham.

45 ARCHBISHOP   For what offense?

MESSENGER The sum of all I can I have disclosed.
Why or for what the nobles were committed
Is all unknown to me, my gracious lord.

QUEEN ELIZABETH Ay me! I see the ruin of my house.
50   The tiger now hath seized the gentle hind;
Insulting tyranny begins to jut
Upon the innocent and aweless throne.
Welcome destruction, blood, and massacre!

35 **parlous** terribly quick-witted 35 **shrewd** sharp-tongued 37 **Pitchers have ears** (a proverb: small pitchers have great ears) 50 **hind** doe 51 **jut** encroach 52 **aweless** inspiring no awe

I see, as in a map, the end of all.

DUCHESS OF YORK Accursèd and unquiet wrangling
    days,   55
How many of you have mine eyes beheld!
My husband lost his life to get the crown,
And often up and down my sons were tossed
For me to joy and weep their gain and loss;
And being seated, and domestic broils   60
Clean overblown, themselves, the conquerors,
Make war upon themselves, brother to brother,
Blood to blood, self against self. O preposterous
And frantic outrage, end thy damnèd spleen,
Or let me die, to look on death no more!   65

QUEEN ELIZABETH Come, come, my boy; we will to
    sanctuary.
Madam, farewell.

DUCHESS OF YORK Stay, I will go with you.

QUEEN ELIZABETH You have no cause.

ARCHBISHOP   [*To the Queen*] My gracious lady, go,
And thither bear your treasure and your goods.
For my part, I'll resign unto your Grace   70
The seal I keep; and so betide to me
As well I tender you and all of yours!
Go, I'll conduct you to the sanctuary.   *Exeunt*.

60 **domestic broils** civil wars 63 **preposterous** inverting natural order
64 **spleen** malice 66 **sanctuary** refuge on church property 72 **tender** care for

ACT III

Scene I. [*A street.*]

The trumpets sound. Enter [the] young Prince, the Dukes of Gloucester and Buckingham, Lord Cardinal, [Catesby,] with others.

BUCKINGHAM Welcome, sweet Prince, to London, to your chamber.

RICHARD Welcome, dear cousin, my thoughts' sovereign.
The weary way hath made you melancholy.

PRINCE EDWARD No, uncle, but our crosses on the way
5   Have made it tedious, wearisome, and heavy.
I want more uncles here to welcome me.

RICHARD Sweet Prince, the untainted virtue of your years
Hath not yet dived into the world's deceit;
Nor more can you distinguish of a man
10   Than of his outward show, which, God he knows,
Seldom or never jumpeth with the heart.
Those uncles which you want were dangerous;

III.i.1 **chamber** capital   4 **crosses** vexations   6 **want** (1) lack (2) wish for
11 **jumpeth** agrees

Your Grace attended to their sug'red words
But looked not on the poison of their hearts.
God keep you from them, and from such false
    friends!   15

PRINCE EDWARD God keep me from false friends!
    But they were none.

RICHARD My lord, the Mayor of London comes to
    greet you.

Enter Lord Mayor [and Citizens].

LORD MAYOR God bless your Grace with health and
    happy days!

PRINCE EDWARD I thank you, good my lord, and thank
    you all.   *[Mayor and Citizens stand aside.]*
I thought my mother and my brother York   20
Would long ere this have met us on the way.
Fie, what a slug is Hastings that he comes not
To tell us whether they will come or no!

Enter Lord Hastings.

BUCKINGHAM And in good time here comes the sweat-
    ing lord.

PRINCE EDWARD Welcome, my lord. What, will our
    mother come?   25

HASTINGS On what occasion God he knows, not I,
The Queen your mother and your brother York
Have taken sanctuary. The tender Prince
Would fain have come with me to meet your Grace,
But by his mother was perforce withheld.   30

BUCKINGHAM Fie, what an indirect and peevish
    course
Is this of hers! Lord Cardinal, will your Grace
Persuade the Queen to send the Duke of York
Unto his princely brother presently?

22 slug sluggard 26 On what occasion for what cause 30 perforce by
force 31 indirect and peevish devious and obstinate 34 presently at once

35   If she deny, Lord Hastings, go with him
      And from her jealous arms pluck him perforce.

CARDINAL My Lord of Buckingham, if my weak
          oratory
      Can from his mother win the Duke of York,
      Anon expect him here; but if she be obdurate
40   To mild entreaties, God in heaven forbid
      We should infringe the holy privilege
      Of blessèd sanctuary! Nor for all this land
      Would I be guilty of so deep a sin.

BUCKINGHAM You are too senseless-obstinate, my lord,
45   Too ceremonious and traditional.
      Weigh it but with the grossness of this age,
      You break not sanctuary in seizing him.
      The benefit thereof is always granted
      To those whose dealings have deserved the place
50   And those who have the wit to claim the place.
      This prince hath neither claimed it nor deserved it,
      And therefore, in mine opinion, cannot have it.
      Then, taking him from thence that is not there,
      You break no privilege nor charter there.
55   Oft have I heard of sanctuary men,
      But sanctuary children ne'er till now.

CARDINAL My lord, you shall o'errule my mind for
          once.
      Come on, Lord Hastings, will you go with me?

HASTINGS I go, my lord.

PRINCE EDWARD Good lords, make all the speedy haste
60   you may.   *Exit Cardinal and Hastings.*
      Say, uncle Gloucester, if our brother come,
      Where shall we sojourn till our coronation?

RICHARD Where it seems best unto your royal self.
      If I may counsel you, some day or two
65   Your Highness shall repose you at the Tower;
      Then where you please, and shall be thought most
          fit

36 **jealous** suspicious   45 **ceremonious** punctilious   46 **grossness** coarseness

For your best health and recreation.

PRINCE EDWARD I do not like the Tower, of any place.
Did Julius Caesar build that place, my lord?

BUCKINGHAM He did, my gracious lord, begin that
    place,   70
Which since succeeding ages have re-edified.

PRINCE EDWARD Is it upon record, or else reported
Successively from age to age, he built it?

BUCKINGHAM Upon record, my gracious lord.

PRINCE EDWARD But say, my lord, it was not
    regist'red,   75
Methinks the truth should live from age to age,
As 'twere retailed to all posterity,
Even to the general all-ending day.

RICHARD [Aside] So wise so young, they say do ne'er
    live long.

PRINCE EDWARD What say you, uncle?   80

RICHARD I say, without characters fame lives long.
[Aside] Thus, like the formal Vice, Iniquity,
I moralize two meanings in one word.

PRINCE EDWARD That Julius Caesar was a famous man.
With what his valor did enrich his wit,   85
His wit set down to make his valor live.
Death makes no conquest of this conqueror,
For now he lives in fame, thou not in life.
I'll tell you what, my cousin Buckingham—

BUCKINGHAM What, my gracious lord?   90

PRINCE EDWARD And if I live until I be a man,
I'll win our ancient right in France again
Or die a soldier as I lived a king.

68 **of any place** of all places   71 **re-edified** rebuilt   77 **retailed** reported
81 **characters** written letters   82 **formal** careful to observe forms (i.e.,
hypocritical)   82 **Vice** mischief-maker in a morality play   83 **moralize** interpret
85 **With what** that with which

RICHARD [*Aside*] Short summers lightly have a forward spring.

Enter [the] young [Duke of] York, Hastings, and
Cardinal.

BUCKINGHAM Now in good time here comes the Duke
95   of York.

PRINCE EDWARD Richard of York, how fares our loving
brother?

YORK Well, my dread lord—so must I call you now.

PRINCE EDWARD Ay, brother, to our grief, as it is yours.
Too late he died that might have kept that title,
100   Which by his death hath lost much majesty.

RICHARD How fares our cousin, noble Lord of York?

YORK I thank you, gentle uncle. O, my lord,
You said that idle weeds are fast in growth.
The Prince my brother hath outgrown me far.

RICHARD He hath, my lord.

105 YORK   And therefore is he idle?

RICHARD O my fair cousin, I must not say so.

YORK Then he is more beholding to you than I.

RICHARD He may command me as my sovereign,
But you have power in me as in a kinsman.

110 YORK I pray you, uncle, give me this dagger.

RICHARD My dagger, little cousin? With all my heart.

PRINCE EDWARD A beggar, brother?

YORK Of my kind uncle, that I know will give,
And being but a toy, which is no grief to give.

115 RICHARD A greater gift than that I'll give my cousin.

94 **Short ... spring** i.e., the short-lived are usually (**lightly**) precocious
97 **dread** revered   99 **late** recently   103 **idle** useless   114 **toy** trifle

RICHARD THE THIRD   III.i.

YORK A greater gift? O, that's the sword to it.

RICHARD Ay, gentle cousin, were it light enough.

YORK O, then I see you will part but with light gifts!
    In weightier things you'll say a beggar nay.

RICHARD It is too heavy for your Grace to wear.   120

YORK I weigh it lightly, were it heavier.

RICHARD What, would you have my weapon, little
    lord?

YORK I would, that I might thank you as you call me.

RICHARD How?

YORK Little.   125

PRINCE EDWARD My Lord of York will still be cross
    in talk.
    Uncle, your Grace knows how to bear with him.

YORK You mean, to bear me, not to bear with me.
    Uncle, my brother mocks both you and me;
    Because that I am little, like an ape,   130
    He thinks that you should bear me on your
    shoulders.

BUCKINGHAM [*Aside*] With what a sharp, provided
    wit he reasons!
    To mitigate the scorn he gives his uncle
    He prettily and aptly taunts himself.
    So cunning and so young is wonderful.   135

RICHARD My lord, will't please you pass along?
    Myself and my good cousin Buckingham
    Will to your mother, to entreat of her
    To meet you at the Tower and welcome you.

YORK What, will you go unto the Tower, my lord?   140

118 **light** slight   121 **weigh** value   126 **still be cross** always be contrary
131 **bear me on your shoulders** i.e., carry me on your hunchback   132 **provided**
ready

PRINCE EDWARD My Lord Protector needs will have it
so.

YORK I shall not sleep in quiet at the Tower.

RICHARD Why, what should you fear?

YORK Marry, my uncle Clarence' angry ghost.
145   My grandam told me he was murd'red there.

PRINCE EDWARD I fear no uncles dead.

RICHARD Nor none that live, I hope.

PRINCE EDWARD And if they live, I hope I need not
fear.
But come, my lord; with a heavy heart,
150   Thinking on them, go I unto the Tower.
            A sennet. Exeunt Prince [Edward], York, Hastings,
            [Cardinal, and others]. Manet Richard,
            Buckingham, and Crosby.

BUCKINGHAM Think you, my lord, this little prating
York
Was not incensèd by his subtle mother
To taunt and scorn you thus opprobriously?

RICHARD No doubt, no doubt. O, 'tis a parlous boy,
155   Bold, quick, ingenious, forward, capable:
He is all the mother's, from the top to toe.

BUCKINGHAM Well, let them rest. Come hither,
Catesby.
Thou art sworn as deeply to effect what we
intend
As closely to conceal what we impart.
160   Thou knowest our reasons urged upon the way.
What thinkest thou? Is it not an easy matter
To make William Lord Hastings of our mind
For the installment of this noble duke
In the seat royal of this famous isle?

165 CATESBURY He for his father's sake so loves the Prince

150 s.d. **sennet** trumpet signal   152 **incensèd** stirred up   158 **effect** carry out
163 **installment** installation as a king

438

That he will not be won to aught against him.

BUCKINGHAM What thinkest thou then of Stanley?
What will he?

CATESBY He will do all in all as Hastings doth.

BUCKINGHAM Well then, no more but this: go, gentle
Catesby,
And, as it were far off, sound thou Lord Hastings   170
How he doth stand affected to our purpose,
And summon him tomorrow to the Tower
To sit about the coronation.
If thou dost find him tractable to us,
Encourage him, and tell him all our reasons.   175
If he be leaden, icy-cold, unwilling,
Be thou so too, and so break off the talk,
And give us notice of his inclination;
For we tomorrow hold divided councils,
Wherein thyself shalt highly be employed.   180

RICHARD Commend me to Lord William. Tell him,
Catesby,
His ancient knot of dangerous adversaries
Tomorrow are let blood at Pomfret Castle,
And bid my lord, for joy of this good news,
Give Mistress Shore one gentle kiss the more.   185

BUCKINGHAM Good Catesby, go effect this business
soundly.

CATESBY My good lords both, with all the heed I can.

RICHARD Shall we hear from you, Catesby, ere we
sleep?

CATESBY You shall, my lord.

RICHARD At Crosby House, there shall you find us
both.   190
Exit Catesby.

171 **affected** inclined   173 **sit** meet with the council   179 **divided councils**
i.e., meetings of the council in two separate groups   182 **ancient knot** long-
standing clique

BUCKINGHAM Now, my lord, what shall we do if we perceive
Lord Hastings will not yield to our complots?

RICHARD Chop off his head. Something we will determine.
And look when I am king, claim thou of me
195   The earldom of Hereford and all the movables
Whereof the King my brother was possessed.

BUCKINGHAM I'll claim that promise at your Grace's hand.

RICHARD And look to have it yielded with all kindness.
Come, let us sup betimes, that afterwards
200   We may digest our complots in some form.

                                        Exeunt.

Scene II. [*Before Lord Hastings' house.*]

Enter a Messenger to the door of Hastings.

MESSENGER My lord! My lord!

HASTINGS [*Within*] Who knocks?

MESSENGER One from the Lord Stanley.

HASTINGS [*Within*] What is't o'clock?

5   MESSENGER Upon the stroke of four.

                        Enter Lord Hastings.

HASTINGS Cannot my Lord Stanley sleep these tedious nights?

MESSENGER So it appears by that I have to say:

192 **complots** plots 194 **look when** whenever 195 **movables** goods
198 **look** expect 199 **betimes** early 200 **digest** arrange

First, he commends him to your noble self.

HASTINGS What then?

MESSENGER Then certifies your lordship that this night   10
He dreamt the boar had rasèd off his helm.
Besides, he says there are two councils kept,
And that may be determined at the one
Which may make you and him to rue at th' other.
Therefore he sends to know your lordship's
      pleasure,   15
If you will presently take horse with him
And with all speed post with him toward the
      north
To shun the danger that his soul divines.

HASTINGS Go, fellow, go return unto thy lord;
Bid him not fear the separated council.   20
His honor and myself are at the one,
And at the other is my good friend Catesby;
Where nothing can proceed that toucheth us
Whereof I shall not have intelligence.
Tell him his fears are shallow, without instance;   25
And for his dreams, I wonder he's so simple
To trust the mock'ry of unquiet slumbers.
To fly the boar before the boar pursues
Were to incense the boar to follow us
And make pursuit where he did mean no chase.   30
Go bid thy master rise and come to me,
And we will both together to the Tower,
Where he shall see the boar will use us kindly.

MESSENGER I'll go, my lord, and tell him what you
      say.   *Exit.*

Enter Catesby.

CATESBY Many good morrows to my noble lord!   35

HASTINGS Good morrow, Catesby; you are early
      stirring.
What news, what news, in this our tott'ring state?

III.ii.11 **the boar ... helm** i.e., Richard had cut off his head   25 **instance** cause

441

CATESBY It is a reeling world indeed, my lord,
And I believe will never stand upright
40   Till Richard wear the garland of the realm.

HASTINGS How! Wear the garland! Dost thou mean
the crown?

CATESBY Ay, my good lord.

HASTINGS I'll have this crown of mine cut from my
shoulders
Before I'll see the crown so foul misplaced.
45   But canst thou guess that he doth aim at it?

CATESBY Ay, on my life, and hopes to find you
forward
Upon his party for the gain thereof;
And thereupon he sends you this good news,
That this same very day your enemies,
50   The kindred of the Queen, must die at Pomfret.

HASTINGS Indeed I am no mourner for that news,
Because they have been still my adversaries;
But that I'll give my voice on Richard's side
To bar my master's heirs in true descent,
55   God knows I will not do it, to the death!

CATESBY God keep your lordship in that gracious
mind!

HASTINGS But I shall laugh at this a twelvemonth
hence,
That they which brought me in my master's hate,
I live to look upon their tragedy.
60   Well, Catesby, ere a fortnight make me older,
I'll send some packing that yet think not on't.

CATESBY 'Tis a vile thing to die, my gracious lord,
When men are unprepared and look not for it.

HASTINGS O monstrous, monstrous! And so falls it out
65   With Rivers, Vaughan, Grey; and so 'twill do
With some men else that think themselves as safe

47 **party** side   56 **gracious** virtuous   61 **send some packing** get rid of some

As thou and I, who, as thou know'st, are dear
To princely Richard and to Buckingham.

CATESBY The Princes both make high account of
    you—
[*Aside*] For they account his head upon the Bridge.   70

HASTINGS I know they do, and I have well deserved it.

Enter Lord Stanley.

Come on, come on! Where is your boarspear, man?
Fear you the boar, and go so unprovided?

STANLEY My lord, good morrow; good morrow,
    Catesby.
You may jest on, but, by the holy rood,   75
I do not like these several councils, I.

HASTINGS My lord, I hold my life as dear as yours,
And never in my days, I do protest,
Was it so precious to me as 'tis now.
Think you, but that I know our state secure,   80
I would be so triumphant as I am?

STANLEY The lords at Pomfret, when they rode from
    London,
Were jocund and supposed their states were sure,
And they indeed had no cause to mistrust;
But yet you see how soon the day o'ercast.   85
This sudden stab of rancor I misdoubt.
Pray God, I say, I prove a needless coward!
What, shall we toward the Tower? The day is
    spent.

HASTINGS Come, come, have with you. Wot you what,
    my lord?
Today the lords you talk of are beheaded.   90

STANLEY They, for their truth, might better wear
    their heads

70 **the Bridge** London Bridge (where traitors' heads were displayed)   75 **rood**
cross   76 **several** separate   77 **as yours** i.e., as you do yours   80 **state** position
86 **misdoubt** have misgivings about   88 **spent** wasted   89 **Wot** know   91 **truth**
loyalty

Than some that have accused them wear their hats.
But come, my lord, let's away.

Enter a Pursuivant.

HASTINGS Go on before. I'll talk with this good fellow.
Exit Lord Stanley, and Catesby.

95   How now, sirrah? How goes the world with thee?

PURSUIVANT The better that your lordship please to
ask.

HASTINGS I tell thee, man, 'tis better with me now
Than when thou met'st me last where now we meet.
Then was I going prisoner to the Tower
100   By the suggestion of the Queen's allies;
But now I tell thee—keep it to thyself—
This day those enemies are put to death,
And I in better state than e'er I was.

PURSUIVANT God hold it, to your honor's good content!

105   HASTINGS Gramercy, fellow; there, drink that for me.
Throws him his purse.

PURSUIVANT I thank your honor.   *Exit Pursuivant.*

Enter a Priest.

PRIEST Well met, my lord; I am glad to see your honor.

HASTINGS I thank thee, good Sir John, with all my
heart.
I am in your debt for your last exercise;
110   Come the next Sabbath, and I will content you.
He whispers in his ear.

Enter Buckingham.

BUCKINGHAM What, talking with a priest, Lord Chamberlain?
Your friends at Pomfret, they do need the priest;

93 s.d. **Pursuivant** royal messenger with power to execute warrants   95 **sirrah**
(common form of address to an inferior)   100 **suggestion** instigation
105 **Gramercy** much thanks   108 **Sir** (used for a priest, as well as for a knight)
109 **exercise** sermon   110 **content** reward

Your honor hath no shriving work in hand.

HASTINGS Good faith, and when I met this holy man
The men you talk of came into my mind.   115
What, go you toward the Tower?

BUCKINGHAM I do, my lord, but long I cannot stay
there.
I shall return before your lordship thence.

HASTINGS Nay, like enough, for I stay dinner there.

BUCKINGHAM [*Aside*] And supper too, although thou
know'st it not.   120
Come, will you go?

HASTINGS   I'll wait upon your lordship.
                                          Exeunt.

Scene III. [*Pomfret Castle.*]

*Enter Sir Richard Ratcliffe, with Halberds, carrying
the Nobles, [Rivers, Grey, and Vaughan,] to death at
Pomfret.*

RIVERS Sir Richard Ratcliffe, let me tell thee this:
Today shalt thou behold a subject die
For truth, for duty, and for loyalty.

GREY God bless the Prince from all the pack of you!
A knot you are of damnèd bloodsuckers.   5

VAUGHAN You live that shall cry woe for this hereafter.

RATCLIFFE Dispatch; the limit of your lives it out.

RIVERS O Pomfret, Pomfret! O thou bloody prison,
Fatal and ominous to noble peers!
Within the guilty closure of thy walls   10

113 **shriving** confessing   III.iii.10 **closure** circuit

Richard the Second here was hacked to death;
And, for more slander to thy dismal seat,
We give to thee our guiltless blood to drink.

GREY Now Margaret's curse is fall'n upon our heads,
15   When she exclaimed on Hastings, you, and I,
For standing by when Richard stabbed her son.

RIVERS Then cursed she Richard, then cursed she
    Buckingham,
Then cursed she Hastings. O, remember, God,
To hear her prayer for them, as now for us!
20   And for my sister and her princely sons,
Be satisfied, dear God, with our true blood,
Which, as thou know'st, unjustly must be spilt.

RATCLIFFE Make haste; the hour of death is expiate.

RIVERS Come, Grey, come, Vaughan, let us here
    embrace.
25   Farewell, until we meet again in heaven.   *Exeunt.*

Scene IV. [*The Tower.*]

*Enter Buckingham, [Lord Stanley, Earl of] Derby,
Hastings, Bishop of Ely, Norfolk, Ratcliffe, Lovell, with
others, at a table.*

HASTINGS Now, noble peers, the cause why we are
    met
Is to determine of the coronation.
In God's name, speak, when is the royal day?

BUCKINGHAM Is all things ready for the royal time?

5   STANLEY It is, and wants but nomination.

12 **slander** disgrace 23 **expiate** come for suffering III.iv.5 **nomination**
naming

446

BISHOP OF ELY Tomorrow then I judge a happy day.

BUCKINGHAM Who knows the Lord Protector's mind
  herein?
Who is most inward with the noble Duke?

BISHOP OF ELY Your grace, we think, should soonest
  know his mind.

BUCKINGHAM We know each other's faces; for our
  hearts,   10
He knows no more of mine than I of yours;
Or I of his, my lord, than you of mine.
Lord Hastings, you and he are near in love.

HASTINGS I thank his Grace, I know he loves me well;
But for his purpose in the coronation   15
I have not sounded him, nor he delivered
His gracious pleasure any way therein.
But you, my honorable lords, may name the time,
And in the Duke's behalf I'll give my voice,
Which I presume he'll take in gentle part.   20

    Enter [Richard, Duke of] Gloucester.

BISHOP OF ELY In happy time here comes the Duke
  himself.

RICHARD My noble lords and cousins all, good
  morrow.
I have been long a sleeper, but I trust
My absence doth neglect no great design
Which by my presence might have been concluded. 25

BUCKINGHAM Had you not come upon your cue, my
  lord,
William Lord Hastings had pronounced your part,
I mean your voice for crowning of the King.

RICHARD Than my Lord Hastings no man might be
  bolder.
His lordship knows me well and loves me well. 30
My Lord of Ely, when I was last in Holborn
I saw good strawberries in your garden there.

8 inward intimate   24 neglect cause neglect of

I do beseech you send for some of them.

BISHOP OF ELY Marry, and will, my lord, with all my
    heart.   *Exit Bishop.*

35 RICHARD Cousin of Buckingham, a word with you.
                                    [*Takes him aside.*]
    Catesby hath sounded Hastings in our business
    And finds the testy gentleman so hot
    That he will lose his head ere give consent
    His master's child, as worshipfully he terms it,
40   Shall lose the royalty of England's throne.

BUCKINGHAM Withdraw yourself awhile. I'll go with
    you.   *Exeunt [Richard and Buckingham].*

STANLEY We have not yet set down this day of
    triumph.
    Tomorrow, in my judgment, is too sudden;
    For I myself am not so well provided
45   As else I would be, were the day prolonged.

Enter the Bishop of Ely.

BISHOP OF ELY Where is my lord the Duke of
    Gloucester?
    I have sent for these strawberries.

HASTINGS His Grace looks cheerfully and smooth this
    morning;
    There's some conceit or other likes him well
50   When that he bids good morrow with such spirit.
    I think there's never a man in Christendom
    Can lesser hide his love or hate than he,
    For by his face straight shall you know his heart.

STANLEY What of his heart perceive you in his face
55   By any livelihood he showed today?

HASTINGS Marry, that with no man here he is offended;
    For were he, he had shown it in his looks.

39 **worshipfully** respectfully 45 **prolonged** postponed 49 **conceit** idea
49 **likes** pleases 55 **livelihood** liveliness

Enter Richard and Buckingham.

RICHARD I pray you all, tell me what they deserve
That do conspire my death with devilish plots
Of damnèd witchcraft, and that have prevailed   60
Upon my body with their hellish charms.

HASTINGS The tender love I bear your Grace, my lord,
Makes me most forward in this princely presence
To doom th' offenders, whosoe'er they be.
I say, my lord, they have deservèd death.   65

RICHARD Then be your eyes the witness of their evil.
Look how I am bewitched. Behold, mine arm
Is like a blasted sapling withered up;
And this is Edward's wife, that monstrous witch,
Consorted with that harlot strumpet Shore,   70
That by their witchcraft thus have markèd me.

HASTINGS If they have done this deed, my noble lord—

RICHARD If! Thou protector of this damnèd strumpet,
Talk'st thou to me of if's? Thou art a traitor.
Off with his head! Now by Saint Paul I swear   75
I will not dine until I see the same.
Lovell and Ratcliffe, look that it be done.
The rest that love me, rise and follow me.
                    Exeunt. Manet Lovell and Ratcliffe, with
                              the Lord Hastings.

HASTINGS Woe, woe for England, not a whit for me!
For I, too fond, might have prevented this.   80
Stanley did dream the boar did rase our helms,
And I did scorn it and disdain to fly.
Three times today my footcloth horse did stumble,
And started when he looked upon the Tower,
As loath to bear me to the slaughterhouse.   85
O, now I need the priest that spake to me!
I now repent I told the pursuivant,
As too triumphing, how mine enemies
Today at Pomfret bloodily were butchered,

80 **fond** foolish   83 **footcloth horse** richly decorated horse

449

90   And I myself secure in grace and favor.
        O Margaret, Margaret, now thy heavy curse
        Is lighted on poor Hastings' wretched head!

RATCLIFFE Come, come, dispatch; the Duke would be
        at dinner.
        Make a short shrift; he longs to see your head.

95 HASTINGS O momentary grace of mortal men,
        Which we more hunt for than the grace of God!
        Who builds his hope in air of your good looks
        Lives like a drunken sailor on a mast,
        Ready with every nod to tumble down
100   Into the fatal bowels of the deep.

LOVELL Come, come, dispatch; 'tis bootless to
        exclaim.

HASTINGS O bloody Richard! Miserable England!
        I prophesy the fearful'st time to thee
        That ever wretched age hath looked upon.
105   Come, lead me to the block; bear him my head.
        They smile at me who shortly shall be dead.

                                        Exeunt.

                    Scene V. [*The Tower walls.*]

        *Enter Richard, [Duke of Gloucester,] and Buckingham,
            in rotten armor, marvelous ill-favored.*

RICHARD Come, cousin, canst thou quake and change
        thy color,
        Murder thy breath in middle of a word,
        And then again begin, and stop again,
        As if thou wert distraught and mad with terror?

94 **shrift** confession   95 **grace** favor   101 **bootless** useless   III.v. s.d. **rotten**
worn-out   s.d. **ill-favored** bad-looking

BUCKINGHAM Tut, I can counterfeit the deep
    tragedian,   5
  Speak and look back, and pry on every side,
  Tremble and start at wagging of a straw,
  Intending deep suspicion. Ghastly looks
  Are at my service, like enforcèd smiles;
  And both are ready in their offices   10
  At any time to grace my stratagems.
  But what, is Catesby gone?

RICHARD He is; and see, he brings the Mayor along.

Enter the Mayor and Catesby.

BUCKINGHAM Lord Mayor—

RICHARD Look to the drawbridge there!   15

BUCKINGHAM Hark! A drum.

RICHARD Catesby, o'erlook the walls.

BUCKINGHAM Lord Mayor, the reason we have sent—

RICHARD Look back, defend thee! Here are enemies.

BUCKINGHAM God and our innocency defend and
    guard us!   20

Enter Lovell and Ratcliffe, with Hastings' head.

RICHARD Be patient, they are friends, Ratcliffe and
  Lovell.

LOVELL Here is the head of that ignoble traitor,
  The dangerous and unsuspected Hastings.

RICHARD So dear I loved the man that I must weep:
  I took him for the plainest harmless creature   25
  That breathed upon the earth a Christian;
  Made him my book, wherein my soul recorded
  The history of all her secret thoughts.
  So smooth he daubed his vice with show of virtue
  That, his apparent open guilt omitted,   30

8 **Intending** pretending   10 **offices** functions   17 **o'erlook** watch over
27 **book** notebook   29 **daubed** whitewashed

I mean his conversation with Shore's wife,
He lived from all attainder of suspects.

BUCKINGHAM Well, well, he was the covert'st shelt'red
      traitor
That ever lived.

35 Would you imagine, or almost believe,
Were't not that by great preservation
We live to tell it, that the subtle traitor
This day had plotted, in the council house,
To murder me and my good Lord of Gloucester?

40 MAYOR Had he done so?

RICHARD What! Think you we are Turks or infidels?
Or that we would, against the form of law,
Proceed thus rashly in the villain's death
But that the extreme peril of the case,
45 The peace of England, and our persons' safety
Enforced us to this execution?

MAYOR Now fair befall you! He deserved his death,
And your good Graces both have well proceeded
To warn false traitors from the like attempts.

50 BUCKINGHAM I never looked for better at his hands
After he once fell in with Mistress Shore.
Yet had we not determined he should die
Until your lordship came to see his end,
Which now the loving haste of these our friends,
55 Something against our meanings, have prevented;
Because, my lord, I would have had you heard
The traitor speak, and timorously confess
The manner and the purpose of his treasons,
That you might well have signified the same
60 Unto the citizens, who haply may
Misconster us in him and wail his death.

MAYOR But, my good lord, your Grace's words shall
      serve
As well as I had seen and heard him speak;

31 **conversation** intercourse   32 **from . . . suspects** free from all stain of suspicions
33 **covert'st** most secret   55 **prevented** forestalled   61 **Misconster** misjudge

And do not doubt, right noble princes both,
But I'll acquaint our duteous citizens   65
With all your just proceedings in this case.

RICHARD And to that end we wished your lordship
          here,
T' avoid the censures of the carping world.

BUCKINGHAM Which, since you come too late of our
          intent,
Yet witness what you hear we did intend.   70
And so, my good Lord Mayor, we did farewell.
                                            Exit Mayor.

RICHARD Go after, after, cousin Buckingham.
The Mayor towards Guildhall hies him in all post.
There, at your meetest vantage of the time,
Infer the bastardy of Edward's children.   75
Tell them how Edward put to death a citizen
Only for saying he would make his son
Heir to the Crown, meaning indeed his house,
Which by the sign thereof was termèd so.
Moreover, urge his hateful luxury   80
And bestial appetite in change of lust,
Which stretched unto their servants, daughters,
          wives,
Even where his raging eye or savage heart,
Without control, lusted to make a prey.
Nay, for a need, thus far come near my person: 85
Tell them, when that my mother went with child
Of that insatiate Edward, noble York
My princely father then had wars in France,
And by true computation of the time
Found that the issue was not his begot;   90
Which well appearèd in his lineaments,
Being nothing like the noble Duke my father.
Yet touch this sparingly, as 'twere far off,
Because, my lord, you know my mother lives.

69 **Which** as to which 69 **of** for 73 **Guildhall** the city hall of London
73 **post** haste 74 **meetest** fittest 75 **Infer** bring forward as an argument
80 **luxury** lechery

453

95 BUCKINGHAM Doubt not, my lord, I'll play the orator
       As if the golden fee for which I plead
       Were for myself; and so, my lord, adieu.

   RICHARD If you thrive well, bring them to Baynard's
           Castle,
       Where you shall find me well accompanied
100   With reverend fathers and well-learnèd bishops.

   BUCKINGHAM I go; and towards three or four o'clock
       Look for the news that the Guildhall affords.
                                         Exit Buckingham.

   RICHARD Go, Lovell, with all speed to Doctor Shaw.
       [*To Catesby*] Go thou to Friar Penker. Bid them
           both
105   Meet me within this hour at Baynard's Castle.
                       Exeunt [*Lovell, Catesby, and Ratcliffe*].
       Now will I go to take some privy order
       To draw the brats of Clarence out of sight,
       And to give order that no manner person
       Have any time recourse unto the Princes.   *Exit.*

               Scene VI. [*A street.*]

       Enter a Scrivener [*with a paper in his hand*].

   SCRIVENER Here is the indictment of the good Lord
           Hastings,
       Which in a set hand fairly is engrossed
       That it may be today read o'er in Paul's.
       And mark how well the sequel hangs together:
5   Eleven hours I have spent to write it over,
       For yesternight by Catesby was it sent me;
       The precedent was full as long a-doing;

106 **privy order** secret arrangement   108 **no manner** no sort of   III.vi.2 **set** formal   2 **fairly is engrossed** is written clearly   3 **Paul's** St. Paul's   7 **precedent** original draft

454

And yet within these five hours Hastings lived,
Untainted, unexamined, free, at liberty.
Here's a good world the while! Who is so gross   10
That cannot see this palpable device?
Yet who so bold but says he sees it not?
Bad is the world, and all will come to nought
When such ill dealing must be seen in thought.

                                                    Exit.

Scene VII. [*Baynard's Castle.*]

*Enter Richard, [Duke of Gloucester,] and Buck-
ingham at several doors.*

RICHARD How now, how now? What say the citizens?

BUCKINGHAM Now, by the holy Mother of our Lord,
  The citizens are mum, say not a word.

RICHARD Touched you the bastardy of Edward's
  children?

BUCKINGHAM I did, with his contract with Lady Lucy   5
  And his contract by deputy in France;
  Th' unsatiate greediness of his desire
  And his enforcement of the city wives;
  His tyranny for trifles; his own bastardy,
  As being got, your father then in France,   10
  And his resemblance, being not like the Duke.
  Withal I did infer your lineaments,
  Being the right idea of your father
  Both in your form and nobleness of mind;
  Laid open all your victories in Scotland,   15

9 **Untainted** not accused   10 **gross** dull   11 **palpable device** obvious trick
14 **in thought** i.e., in silence   III.vii. s.d. **several** separate   5 **Lady Lucy**
Elizabeth Lucy (whose betrothal to Edward was never proved)   6 **by deputy**
(Edward had sent Warwick to arrange a French marriage)   10 **got** begotten
11 **resemblance** appearance   13 **right idea** exact image

Your discipline in war, wisdom in peace,
Your bounty, virtue, fair humility;
Indeed, left nothing fitting for your purpose
Untouched or slightly handlèd in discourse;
20 And when my oratory drew toward end,
I bid them that did love their country's good
Cry, "God save Richard, England's royal king!"

RICHARD And did they so?

BUCKINGHAM No, so God help me, they spake not a
    word,
25 But like dumb statues or breathing stones
Stared each on other and looked deadly pale.
Which when I saw, I reprehended them
And asked the Mayor what meant this willful
    silence.
His answer was, the people were not usèd
30 To be spoke to but by the Recorder.
Then he was urged to tell my tale again:
"Thus saith the Duke, thus hath the Duke
    inferred";
But nothing spoke in warrant from himself.
When he had done, some followers of mine own
35 At lower end of the hall hurled up their caps,
And some ten voices cried, "God save King
    Richard!"
And thus I took the vantage of those few:
"Thanks, gentle citizens and friends," quoth I.
"This general applause and cheerful shout
40 Argues your wisdom and your love to Richard";
And even here brake off and came away.

RICHARD What tongueless blocks were they! Would
    they not speak?
Will not the Mayor then and his brethren come?

BUCKINGHAM The Mayor is here at hand. Intend
    some fear;
45 Be not you spoke with but by mighty suit;

25 **statues** (pronounced "stat-u-es")   30 **Recorder** chief legal official of the city
44 **Intend** pretend   45 **suit** petition

And look you get a prayer book in your hand
And stand between two churchmen, good my lord,
For on that ground I'll make a holy descant;
And be not easily won to our requests.
Play the maid's part: still answer nay, and take it.   50

RICHARD I go; and if you plead as well for them
As I can say nay to thee for myself,
No doubt we bring it to a happy issue.

BUCKINGHAM Go, go up to the leads. The Lord
     Mayor knocks.   [*Exit Richard.*]

Enter the Mayor, and Citizens.

Welcome, my lord. I dance attendance here.   55
I think the Duke will not be spoke withal.

Enter Catesby.

Now, Catesby, what says your lord to my request?

CATESBY He doth entreat your Grace, my noble lord,
To visit him tomorrow or next day.
He is within, with two right reverend fathers,   60
Divinely bent to meditation,
And in no worldly suits would he be moved
To draw him from his holy exercise.

BUCKINGHAM Return, good Catesby, to the gracious
     Duke.
Tell him, myself, the Mayor and Aldermen,   65
In deep designs, in matter of great moment,
No less importing than our general good,
Are come to have some conference with his Grace.

CATESBY I'll signify so much unto him straight.   *Exit.*

BUCKINGHAM Ah ha, my lord, this prince is not an
     Edward!   70
He is not lulling on a lewd love-bed,

48 **ground** (1) melody (2) basis 48 **descant** (1) musical variation
(2) argument 50 **still answer nay** always say no (a proverb) 54 **leads** flat roof
covered with lead 56 **withal** with 63 **exercise** act of devotion 71 **lulling**
lounging

But on his knees at meditation;
Not dallying with a brace of courtesans,
But meditating with two deep divines;
75   Not sleeping, to engross his idle body,
But praying, to enrich his watchful soul.
Happy were England, would this virtuous prince
Take on his Grace the sovereignty thereof;
But sure I fear we shall not win him to it.

MAYOR Marry, God defend his Grace should say us
80   nay!

BUCKINGHAM I fear he will. Here Catesby comes
again.

Enter Catesby.

Now, Catesby, what says his Grace?

CATESBY He wonders to what end you have assemblèd
Such troops of citizens to come to him,
85   His Grace not being warned thereof before.
He fears, my lord, you mean no good to him.

BUCKINGHAM Sorry I am my noble cousin should
Suspect me that I mean no good to him.
By heaven, we come to him in perfect love;
90   And so once more return and tell his Grace.
Exit [Catesby].
When holy and devout religious men
Are at their beads, 'tis much to draw them thence,
So sweet is zealous contemplation.

Enter Richard aloft, between two Bishops.
[Catesby returns.]

MAYOR See where his Grace stands 'tween two
clergymen!

BUCKINGHAM Two props of virtue for a Christian
95   prince,
To stay him from the fall of vanity;
And see, a book of prayer in his hand—

75 **engross** make fat   80 **defend** forbid   92 **much** hard   96 **fall** falling into sin

458

True ornaments to know a holy man.
Famous Plantagenet, most gracious Prince,
Lend favorable ear to our requests,   100
And pardon us the interruption
Of thy devotion and right Christian zeal.

RICHARD My lord, there needs no such apology.
I do beseech your Grace to pardon me,
Who, earnest in the service of my God,   105
Deferred the visitation of my friends.
But, leaving this, what is your Grace's pleasure?

BUCKINGHAM Even that, I hope, which pleaseth God
    above
And all good men of this ungoverned isle.

RICHARD I do suspect I have done some offense   110
That seems disgracious in the city's eye,
And that you come to reprehend my ignorance.

BUCKINGHAM You have, my lord. Would it might
    please your Grace,
On our entreaties, to amend your fault!

RICHARD Else wherefore breathe I in a Christian
    land?   115

BUCKINGHAM Know then it is your fault that you
    resign
The supreme seat, the throne majestical,
The scept'red office of your ancestors,
Your state of fortune and your due of birth,
The lineal glory of your royal house,   120
To the corruption of a blemished stock;
Whiles, in the mildness of your sleepy thoughts,
Which here we waken to our country's good,
The noble isle doth want his proper limbs;
His face defaced with scars of infamy,   125
His royal stock graft with ignoble plants,
And almost should'red in the swallowing gulf
Of dark forgetfulness and deep oblivion.

111 **disgracious** displeasing 119 **state** high position 126 **graft** grafted
127 **should'red in** jostled into

459

Which to recure, we heartily solicit
130   Your gracious self to take on you the charge
And kingly government of this your land;
Not as protector, steward, substitute,
Or lowly factor for another's gain,
But as successively, from blood to blood,
135   Your right of birth, your empery, your own.
For this, consorted with the citizens,
Your very worshipful and loving friends,
And by their vehement instigation,
In this just cause come I to move your Grace.

140   RICHARD I cannot tell if to depart in silence
Or bitterly to speak in your reproof
Best fitteth my degree or your condition.
If not to answer, you might haply think
Tongue-tied ambition, not replying, yielded
145   To bear the golden yoke of sovereignty
Which fondly you would here impose on me.
If to reprove you for this suit of yours,
So seasoned with your faithful love to me,
Then, on the other side, I checked my friends.
150   Therefore, to speak, and to avoid the first,
And then, in speaking, not to incur the last,
Definitively thus I answer you.
Your love deserves my thanks, but my desert
Unmeritable shuns your high request.
155   First, if all obstacles were cut away
And that my path were even to the crown
As the ripe revenue and due of birth,
Yet so much is my poverty of spirit,
So mighty and so many my defects,
160   That I would rather hide me from my greatness,
Being a bark to brook no mighty sea,
Than in my greatness covet to be hid
And in the vapor of my glory smothered.

129 **recure** remedy 133 **factor** agent 134 **successively** by inheritance
135 **empery** supreme power 142 **degree** rank 142 **condition** status
148 **seasoned** given relish 149 **checked** should be rebuking 152 **Definitively**
once and for all 156 **even** clear 158 **poverty of spirit** lack of self-confidence
161 **bark to brook** small ship able to endure

But, God be thanked, there is no need of me,
And much I need to help you, were there need.   165
The royal tree hath left us royal fruit,
Which, mellowed by the stealing hours of time,
Will well become the seat of majesty
And make, no doubt, us happy by his reign.
On him I lay that you would lay on me,   170
The right and fortune of his happy stars,
Which God defend that I should wring from him!

BUCKINGHAM My lord, this argues conscience in your
    Grace,
But the respects thereof are nice and trivial,
All circumstances well considerèd.   175
You say that Edward is your brother's son.
So say we too, but not by Edward's wife;
For first was he contract to Lady Lucy—
Your mother lives a witness to his vow—
And afterward by substitute betrothed   180
To Bona, sister to the King of France.
These both put off, a poor petitioner,
A care-crazed mother to a many sons,
A beauty-waning and distressèd widow,
Even in the afternoon of her best days,   185
Made prize and purchase of his wanton eye,
Seduced the pitch and height of his degree
To base declension and loathed bigamy.
By her, in his unlawful bed, he got
This Edward, whom our manners call the Prince.   190
More bitterly could I expostulate,
Save that for reverence to some alive
I give a sparing limit to my tongue.
Then, good my lord, take to your royal self
This proffered benefit of dignity;   195
If not to bless us and the land withal,
Yet to draw forth your noble ancestry

165 **need** lack   172 **defend** forbid   174 **respects thereof are nice** consider-
ations about it are too scrupulous   186 **purchase** booty   187 **pitch** high point
(of a hawk's flight)   188 **base declension** ignoble falling low   195 **benefit of
dignity** gift of greatness

From the corruption of abusing times
Unto a lineal true-derivèd course.

200 MAYOR Do, good my lord; your citizens entreat you.

BUCKINGHAM Refuse not, mighty lord, this proffered
    love.

CATESBY O, make them joyful, grant their lawful suit!

RICHARD Alas, why would you heap this care on me?
    I am unfit for state and majesty.
205 I do beseech you take it not amiss,
    I cannot nor I will not yield to you.

BUCKINGHAM If you refuse it, as in love and zeal
    Loath to depose the child, your brother's son—
    As well we know your tenderness of heart
210 And gentle, kind, effeminate remorse,
    Which we have noted in you to your kindred
    And egally indeed to all estates—
    Yet know, whe'r you accept our suit or no,
    Your brother's son shall never reign our king,
215 But we will plant some other in the throne
    To the disgrace and downfall of your house;
    And in this resolution here we leave you.
    Come, citizens. Zounds, I'll entreat no more!

RICHARD O, do not swear, my lord of Buckingham.
            Exeunt [Buckingham, Mayor and Citizens].

CATESBY Call him again, sweet Prince, accept their
220   suit.
    If you deny them, all the land will rue it.

RICHARD Will you enforce me to a world of cares?
    Call them again. I am not made of stone,
    But penetrable to your kind entreaties,
225   Albeit against my conscience and my soul.

            Enter Buckingham and the rest.

Cousin of Buckingham, and sage grave men,

210 **effeminate remorse** softhearted pity   212 **egally** equally   213 **whe'r**
whether

Since you will buckle fortune on my back,
To bear her burden, whe'r I will or no,
I must have patience to endure the load;
But if black scandal or foul-faced reproach   230
Attend the sequel of your imposition,
Your mere enforcement shall acquittance me
From all the impure blots and stains thereof;
For God doth know, and you may partly see,
How far I am from the desire of this.   235

MAYOR God bless your Grace! We see it and will say
    it.

RICHARD In saying so you shall but say the truth.

BUCKINGHAM Then I salute you with this royal title:
    Long live King Richard, England's worthy king!

ALL Amen.   240

BUCKINGHAM Tomorrow may it please you to be
    crowned?

RICHARD Even when you please, for you will have
    it so.

BUCKINGHAM Tomorrow then we will attend your
    Grace,
    And so most joyfully we take our leave.

RICHARD [*To the Bishops*] Come, let us to our holy
    work again.   245
    Farewell, my cousin; farewell, gentle friends.
                                            Exeunt.

231 imposition laying on the burden   232 Your mere enforcement the simple
fact of your compulsion   232 acquittance release

463

ACT IV

Scene I. [*Before the Tower.*]

*Enter the Queen, [Elizabeth,] the Duchess of York, and
Marquis [of] Dorset [at one door]; Anne, Duchess of
Gloucester, [with Clarence's daughter, at another door].*

DUCHESS OF YORK   Who meets us here? My niece
      Plantagenet,
   Led in the hand of her kind aunt of Gloucester!
   Now, for my life, she's wand'ring to the Tower
   On pure heart's love to greet the tender Prince.
   Daughter, well met.

5   ANNE   God give your Graces both
      A happy and a joyful time of day!

QUEEN ELIZABETH   As much to you, good sister!
      Whither away?

ANNE   No farther than the Tower, and, as I guess,
   Upon the like devotion as yourselves,
10   To gratulate the gentle princes there.

QUEEN ELIZABETH   Kind sister, thanks. We'll enter all
      together.

IV.i.1 **niece** granddaughter   9 **devotion** purpose   10 **gratulate** greet with joy

Enter the Lieutenant [Brakenbury].

And in good time here the Lieutenant comes.
Master Lieutenant, pray you, by your leave,
How doth the Prince, and my young son of York?

LIEUTENANT Right well, dear madam. By your patience,   15
I may not suffer you to visit them;
The King hath strictly charged the contrary.

QUEEN ELIZABETH The King? Who's that?

LIEUTENANT   I mean the Lord Protector.

QUEEN ELIZABETH The Lord protect him from that
    kingly title!
Hath he set bounds between their love and me?   20
I am their mother; who shall bar me from them?

DUCHESS OF YORK I am their father's mother; I will
    see them.

ANNE Their aunt I am in law, in love their mother.
Then bring me to their sights; I'll bear thy blame
And take thy office from thee on my peril.   25

LIEUTENANT No, madam, no; I may not leave it so.
I am bound by oath, and therefore pardon me.
                    Exit Lieutenant.

Enter Stanley, [Earl of Derby].

STANLEY Let me but meet you, ladies, one hour hence,
And I'll salute your Grace of York as mother
And reverend looker-on of two fair queens.   30
[*To Anne*] Come, madam, you must straight to
    Westminster,
There to be crownèd Richard's royal queen.

QUEEN ELIZABETH Ah, cut my lace asunder,
That my pent heart may have some scope to beat,
Or else I swoon with this dead-killing news!   35

ANNE Despiteful tidings! O unpleasing news!

25 take thy office take over your duty 26 leave abandon 33 lace bodice string
36 Despiteful cruel

DORSET Be of good cheer; mother, how fares your
    Grace?

QUEEN ELIZABETH O Dorset, speak not to me, get thee
    gone!
    Death and destruction dogs thee at thy heels;
40   Thy mother's name is ominous to children.
    If thou wilt outstrip death, go cross the seas
    And live with Richmond, from the reach of hell.
    Go hie thee, hie thee from this slaughterhouse,
    Lest thou increase the number of the dead
45   And make me die the thrall of Margaret's curse,
    Nor mother, wife, nor England's counted queen.

STANLEY Full of wise care is this your counsel, madam.
    Take all the swift advantage of the hours.
    You shall have letters from me to my son
50   In your behalf, to meet you on the way.
    Be not ta'en tardy by unwise delay.

DUCHESS OF YORK O ill-dispersing wind of misery!
    O my accursèd womb, the bed of death!
    A cockatrice hast thou hatched to the world,
55   Whose unavoided eye is murderous.

STANLEY Come, madam, come; I in all haste was sent.

ANNE And I with all unwillingness will go.
    O, would to God that the inclusive verge
    Of golden metal that must round my brow
60   Were red-hot steel to sear me to the brains!
    Anointed let me be with deadly venom
    And die ere men can say, "God save the Queen!"

QUEEN ELIZABETH Go, go, poor soul! I envy not thy
    glory.
    To feed my humor wish thyself no harm.

65 ANNE No? Why, when he that is my husband now

42 **from** away from   45 **thrall** slave   46 **England's counted queen** regarded as
Queen of England   49 **son** i.e., his wife's son, Richmond   51 **ta'en tardy** caught
napping   52 **ill-dispersing** scattering evil   54 **cockatrice** fabulous monster,
basilisk (see I.ii.150)   58 **inclusive verge** enclosing rim   59 **round** encircle
64 **feed my humor** satisfy my mood

Came to me as I followed Henry's corse,
When scarce the blood was well washed from his
  hands
Which issuèd from my other angel husband
And that dear saint which then I weeping
  followed—
O, when, I say, I looked on Richard's face,   70
This was my wish: "Be thou," quoth I, "accursed
For making me, so young, so old a widow!
And when thou wed'st, let sorrow haunt thy bed;
And be thy wife, if any be so mad,
More miserable by the life of thee   75
Than thou hast made me by my dear lord's death!"
Lo, ere I can repeat this curse again,
Within so small a time, my woman's heart
Grossly grew captive to his honey words
And proved the subject of mine own soul's curse,   80
Which hitherto hath held mine eyes from rest;
For never yet one hour in his bed
Did I enjoy the golden dew of sleep,
But with his timorous dreams was still awaked.
Besides, he hates me for my father Warwick,   85
And will, no doubt, shortly be rid of me.

QUEEN ELIZABETH Poor heart, adieu! I pity thy
  complaining.

ANNE No more than with my soul I mourn for yours.

DORSET Farewell, thou woeful welcomer of glory!

ANNE Adieu, poor soul that tak'st thy leave of it!   90

DUCHESS OF YORK [*To Dorset*] Go thou to Richmond,
  and good fortune guide thee!
  [*To Anne*] Go thou to Richard, and good angels
  tend thee!
  [*To Queen Elizabeth*] Go thou to sanctuary, and
  good thoughts possess thee!
  I to my grave, where peace and rest lie with me!
  Eighty odd years of sorrow have I seen,   95

72 **so old a widow** a widow so aged by grief   84 **still** continually

And each hour's joy wracked with a week of teen.

QUEEN ELIZABETH Stay, yet look back with me unto the
        Tower.
      Pity, you ancient stones, those tender babes
      Whom envy hath immured within your walls,
100   Rough cradle for such little pretty ones!
      Rude ragged nurse, old sullen playfellow
      For tender princes, use my babies well!
      So foolish sorrow bids your stones farewell.

Exeunt.

Scene II. [*The palace.*]

*Sound a sennet. Enter Richard, in pomp, Buckingham,
Catesby, Ratcliffe, Lovell, [a Page, and others].*

KING RICHARD Stand all apart. Cousin of Buckingham!

BUCKINGHAM My gracious sovereign?

KING RICHARD Give me thy hand.
                    Sound. [He ascends the throne.]
                      Thus high, by thy advice
      And thy assistance, is King Richard seated.
5   But shall we wear these glories for a day?
      Or shall they last, and we rejoice in them?

BUCKINGHAM Still live they, and forever let them last!

KING RICHARD Ah, Buckingham, now do I play the
        touch
      To try if thou be current gold indeed.
      Young Edward lives—think now what I would
10   speak.

BUCKINGHAM Say on, my loving lord.

96 **wracked** ruined   96 **teen** grief   IV.ii.8 **touch** touchstone (used to test gold)

468

KING RICHARD Why, Buckingham, I say I would be
    king.

BUCKINGHAM Why, so you are, my thrice-renownèd
    lord.

KING RICHARD Ha! Am I king? 'Tis so; but Edward
    lives.

BUCKINGHAM True, noble Prince.

KING RICHARD   O bitter consequence,   15
    That Edward still should live true noble prince!
    Cousin, thou wast not wont to be so dull.
    Shall I be plain? I wish the bastards dead,
    And I would have it suddenly performed.
    What say'st thou now? Speak suddenly, be brief.   20

BUCKINGHAM Your Grace may do your pleasure.

KING RICHARD Tut, tut, thou art all ice, thy kindness
    freezes.
    Say, have I thy consent that they shall die?

BUCKINGHAM Give me some little breath, some pause,
    dear lord,
    Before I positively speak in this.   25
    I will resolve you herein presently.
                      Exit Buckingham.

CATESBY [*Aside to another*] The King is angry. See,
    he gnaws his lip.

KING RICHARD I will converse with iron-witted fools
    And unrespective boys. None are for me
    That look into me with considerate eyes.   30
    High-reaching Buckingham grows circumspect.
    Boy!

PAGE My lord?

KING RICHARD Know'st thou not any whom corrupting
    gold

15 **consequence** sequel 26 **resolve** answer 28 **converse** keep company
28 **iron-witted** dull-witted 29 **unrespective** heedless 30 **considerate**
thoughtful

35   Will tempt unto a close exploit of death?

PAGE I know a discontented gentleman
    Whose humble means match not his haughty spirit.
    Gold were as good as twenty orators
    And will, no doubt, tempt him to anything.

KING RICHARD What is his name?

40 PAGE   His name, my lord, is Tyrrel.

KING RICHARD I partly know the man. Go call him
    hither, boy.   *Exit [Page].*
    The deep-revolving witty Buckingham
    Nor more shall be the neighbor to my counsels.
    Hath he so long held out with me, untired,
45 And stops he now for breath? Well, be it so.

Enter Stanley, [Earl of Derby].

How now, Lord Stanley? What's the news?

STANLEY   Know, my loving lord,
    The Marquis Dorset, as I hear, is fled
    To Richmond in the parts where he abides.
                              [Stands aside.]

KING RICHARD Come hither, Catesby. Rumor it abroad
50 That Anne my wife is very grievous sick;
    I will take order for her keeping close.
    Inquire me out some mean poor gentleman,
    Whom I will marry straight to Clarence' daughter.
    The boy is foolish, and I fear not him.
55 Look how thou dream'st! I say again, give out
    That Anne my queen is sick and like to die.
    About it; for it stands me much upon
    To stop all hopes whose growth may damage me.
                              [Exit Catesby.]
    I must be married to my brother's daughter,
60 Or else my kingdom stands on brittle glass.
    Murder her brothers and then marry her!

35 **close exploit** secret deed 42 **deep-revolving** witty deeply-pondering
clever 44 **held out** kept up 54 **foolish** an idiot 57 **stands me much upon** is
very important to me

Uncertain way of gain! But I am in
So far in blood that sin will pluck on sin.
Tear-falling pity dwells not in this eye.

Enter Tyrrel.

Is thy name Tyrrel?   65

TYRREL James Tyrrel, and your most obedient subject.

KING RICHARD Art thou indeed?

TYRREL   Prove me, my gracious lord.

KING RICHARD Dar'st thou resolve to kill a friend of
    mine?

TYRREL Please you;
    But I had rather kill two enemies.   70

KING RICHARD Why, there thou hast it! Two deep
    enemies,
Foes to my rest and my sweet sleep's disturbers,
Are they that I would have thee deal upon.
Tyrrel, I mean those bastards in the Tower.

TYRREL Let me have open means to come to them,   75
    And soon I'll rid you from the fear of them.

KING RICHARD Thou sing'st sweet music. Hark, come
    hither, Tyrrel.
Go, by this token. Rise, and lend thine ear. *Whispers.*
There is no more but so. Say it is done,
And I will love thee and prefer thee for it.   80

TYRREL I will dispatch it straight.   *Exit.*

Enter Buckingham.

BUCKINGHAM My lord, I have considered in my mind
    The late request that you did sound me in.

KING RICHARD Well, let that rest. Dorset is fled to
    Richmond.

BUCKINGHAM I hear the news, my lord.   85

69 **Please** If it pleases   80 **prefer** advance

KING RICHARD Stanley, he is your wife's son. Well,
      look unto it.

BUCKINGHAM My lord, I claim the gift, my due by
      promise,
      For which your honor and your faith is pawned:
      Th' earldom of Hereford and the movables
90   Which you have promisèd I shall possess.

KING RICHARD Stanley, look to your wife; if she convey
      Letters to Richmond, you shall answer it.

BUCKINGHAM What says your Highness to my just
      request?

KING RICHARD I do remember me, Henry the Sixth
95   Did prophesy that Richmond should be king
      When Richmond was a little peevish boy.
      A king! Perhaps, perhaps.

BUCKINGHAM My lord!

KING RICHARD How chance the prophet could not at
      that time
100   Have told me, I being by, that I should kill him?

BUCKINGHAM My lord, your promise for the earldom!

KING RICHARD Richmond! When last I was at Exeter,
      The Mayor in courtesy showed me the castle,
      And called it Rugemont; at which name I started,
105   Because a bard of Ireland told me once
      I should not live long after I saw Richmond.

BUCKINGHAM My lord!

KING RICHARD Ay, what's o'clock?

BUCKINGHAM I am thus bold to put your Grace in
      mind
      Of what you promised me.

110 KING RICHARD   Well, but what's o'clock?

BUCKINGHAM Upon the stroke of ten.

88 **pawned** pledged   96 **peevish** childish

KING RICHARD   Well, let it strike.

BUCKINGHAM Why let it strike?

KING RICHARD Because that like a Jack thou keep'st
  the stroke
  Betwixt thy begging and my meditation.
  I am not in the giving vein today.   115

BUCKINGHAM May it please you to resolve me in my
  suit.

KING RICHARD Thou troublest me; I am not in the vein.
              Exit [King Richard, and all but Buckingham].

BUCKINGHAM And is it thus? Repays he my deep
  service
  With such contempt? Made I him king for this?
  O, let me think on Hastings, and be gone   120
  To Brecknock while my fearful head is on!   *Exit.*

Scene III. [*The palace*.]

Enter Tyrrel.

TYRREL The tyrannous and bloody act is done,
  The most arch deed of piteous massacre
  That ever yet this land was guilty of.
  Dighton and Forrest, who I did suborn
  To do this piece of ruthful butchery,   5
  Albeit they were fleshed villains, bloody dogs,
  Melted with tenderness and mild compassion,
  Wept like to children in their death's sad story.
  "O thus," quoth Dighton, "lay the gentle babes."
  "Thus, thus," quoth Forrest, "girdling one another 10

---

113 **Jack** (1) figure of a man on a clock, striking the hour (2) knave 113 **thou
keep'st the stroke** you keep on making a noise IV.iii.2 **arch** extreme 5 **piece**
masterpiece 5 **ruthful** piteous 6 **fleshed** experienced

Within their alabaster innocent arms.
Their lips were four red roses on a stalk
And in their summer beauty kissed each other.
A book of prayers on their pillow lay,
Which once," quoth Forrest, "almost changed my
15   mind;
But O, the devil"—there the villain stopped;
When Dighton thus told on: "We smotherèd
The most replenishèd sweet work of Nature
That from the prime creation e'er she framèd."
20   Hence both are gone with conscience and remorse
They could not speak; and so I left them both,
To bear this tidings to the bloody King.

Enter [King] Richard.

And here he comes. All health, my sovereign lord!

KING RICHARD Kind Tyrrel, am I happy in thy news?

25   TYRREL If to have done the thing you gave in charge
Beget your happiness, be happy then,
For it is done.

KING RICHARD But didst thou see them dead?

TYRREL I did, my lord.

KING RICHARD   And buried, gentle Tyrrel?

TYRREL The chaplain of the Tower hath buried them;
30   But where (to say the truth) I do not know.

KING RICHARD Come to me, Tyrrel, soon at after-
supper,
When thou shalt tell the process of their death.
Meantime, but think how I may do thee good
And be inheritor of thy desire.
Farewell till then.

35   TYRREL   I humbly take my leave.   [*Exit.*]

---

18 **replenishèd** complete   19 **prime** first   21 **They** i.e., which they   26 **Beget**
cause   31 **aftersupper** late supper   32 **process** story

KING RICHARD The son of Clarence have I pent up
    close;
  His daughter meanly have I matched in marriage;
  The sons of Edward sleep in Abraham's bosom,
  And Anne my wife hath bid this world good night.
  Now, for I know the Britain Richmond aims   40
  At young Elizabeth, my brother's daughter,
  And by that knot looks proudly on the crown,
  To her go I, a jolly thriving wooer.

               Enter Ratcliffe.

RATCLIFFE My lord!

KING RICHARD Good or bad news, that thou com'st in
    so bluntly?   45

RATCLIFFE Bad news, my lord. Morton is fled to Rich-
    mond,
  And Buckingham, backed with the hardy Welsh-
    men,
  Is in the field, and still his power increaseth.

KING RICHARD Ely with Richmond troubles me more
    near
  Than Buckingham and his rash-levied strength.   50
  Come, I have learned that fearful commenting
  Is leaden servitor to dull delay;
  Delay leads impotent and snail-paced beggary.
  Then fiery expedition be my wing,
  Jove's Mercury, and herald for a king!   55
  Go muster men. My counsel is my shield;
  We must be brief when traitors brave the field.
                    Exeunt.

---

38 **Abraham's bosom** paradise 40 **for** because 40 **Britain** Breton 42 **knot**
marriage tie 50 **rash-levied** hastily raised 51 **fearful commenting** timorous
meditating 53 **beggary** bankruptcy 54 **expedition** speed

Scene IV. [*The palace.*]

Enter old Queen Margaret.

QUEEN MARGARET So now prosperity begins to mellow
  And drop into the rotten mouth of death.
  Here in these confines slily have I lurked
  To watch the waning of mine enemies.
5 A dire induction am I witness to,
  And will to France, hoping the consequence
  Will prove as bitter, black, and tragical.
  Withdraw thee, wretched Margaret. Who comes
  here?   [*Retires.*]

Enter Duchess [of York] and Queen [Elizabeth].

QUEEN ELIZABETH Ah, my poor princes, ah, my tender
  babes!
10 My unblown flow'rs, new-appearing sweets!
  If yet your gentle souls fly in the air
  And be not fixed in doom perpetual,
  Hover about me with your airy wings
  And hear your mother's lamentation!

QUEEN MARGARET [*Aside*] Hover about her, say that
15 right for right
  Hath dimmed your infant morn to agèd night.

DUCHESS OF YORK So many miseries have crazed my
  voice
  That my woe-wearied tongue is still and mute.
  Edward Plantagenet, why art thou dead?

QUEEN MARGARET [*Aside*] Plantagenet doth quit
20 Plantagenet,

IV.iv.5 **induction** opening scene 6 **consequence** following part 10 **unblown**
unblossomed 17 **crazed** cracked 20 **quit** make up for

476

Edward for Edward pays a dying debt.

QUEEN ELIZABETH Wilt thou, O God, fly from such
    gentle lambs
And throw them in the entrails of the wolf?
When didst thou sleep when such a deed was done?

QUEEN MARGARET [*Aside*] When holy Harry died, and
    my sweet son.   25

DUCHESS OF YORK Dead life, blind sight, poor mortal
    living ghost,
Woe's scene, world's shame, grave's due by life
    usurped,
Brief abstract and record of tedious days,
Rest thy unrest on England's lawful earth,
                          [*Sits down.*]
Unlawfully made drunk with innocent blood!   30

QUEEN ELIZABETH Ah that thou wouldst as soon afford
    a grave
As thou canst yield a melancholy seat!
Then would I hide my bones, not rest them here.
Ah, who hath any cause to mourn but we?
                        [*Sit down by her.*]

QUEEN MARGARET [*Comes forward*] If ancient sorrow
    be most reverend,   35
Give mine the benefit of seniory
And let my griefs frown on the upper hand.
If sorrow can admit society, [*Sits down with them.*]
Tell o'er your woes again by viewing mine.
I had an Edward, till a Richard killed him;   40
I had a husband, till a Richard killed him.
Thou hadst an Edward, till a Richard killed him;
Thou hadst a Richard, till a Richard killed him.

DUCHESS OF YORK I had a Richard too, and thou didst
    kill him;
I had a Rutland too, thou holp'st to kill him.   45

28 **abstract** summary   36 **seniory** seniority   37 **on the upper hand** i.e., above
all others   39 **Tell** count   45 **holp'st** helpedst

QUEEN MARGARET Thou hadst a Clarence too, and
    Richard killed him.
    From forth the kennel of thy womb hath crept
    A hellhound that doth hunt us all to death.
    That dog that had his teeth before his eyes
50   To worry lambs and lap their gentle blood,
    That foul defacer of God's handiwork,
    That excellent grand tyrant of the earth
    That reigns in gallèd eyes of weeping souls,
    Thy womb let loose to chase us to our graves.
55   O upright, just, and true-disposing God,
    How do I thank thee that this carnal cur
    Preys on the issue of his mother's body
    And makes her pewfellow with others' moan!

DUCHESS OF YORK O Harry's wife, triumph not in my
    woes!
60   God witness with me I have wept for thine.

QUEEN MARGARET Bear with me; I am hungry for
    revenge,
    And now I cloy me with beholding it.
    Thy Edward he is dead, that killed my Edward;
    Thy other Edward dead, to quit my Edward;
65   Young York he is but boot, because both they
    Matched not the high perfection of my loss.
    Thy Clarence he is dead that stabbed my Edward,
    And the beholders of this frantic play,
    Th' adulterate Hastings, Rivers, Vaughan, Grey,
70   Untimely smothered in their dusky graves.
    Richard yet lives, hell's black intelligencer,
    Only reserved their factor to buy souls
    And send them thither. But at hand, at hand,
    Ensues his piteous and unpitied end.
75   Earth gapes, hell burns, fiends roar, saints pray,
    To have him suddenly conveyed from hence.

52 **excellent grand** surpassingly chief   53 **gallèd** sore from rubbing   55 **true-disposing** justly ordaining   56 **carnal** carnivorous   58 **pewfellow** companion   65 **but boot** only a makeweight   69 **adulterate** adulterous   71 **intelligencer** secret agent   72 **Only reserved their factor** kept alive merely as agent for the powers of hell

Cancel his bond of life, dear God, I pray,
That I may live and say, "The dog is dead."

QUEEN ELIZABETH O, thou didst prophesy the time
   would come
That I should wish for thee to help me curse   80
That bottled spider, that foul bunch-backed toad!

QUEEN MARGARET I called thee then vain flourish of
   my fortune;
I called thee then poor shadow, painted queen,
The presentation of but what I was,
The flattering index of a direful pageant,   85
One heaved a-high to be hurled down below,
A mother only mocked with two fair babes,
A dream of what thou wast, a garish flag
To be the aim of every dangerous shot,
A sign of dignity, a breath, a bubble,   90
A queen in jest, only to fill the scene.
Where is thy husband now? Where be thy brothers?
Where be thy two sons? Wherein dost thou joy?
Who sues and kneels and says, "God save the
   Queen"?
Where be the bending peers that flatterèd thee?   95
Where be the thronging troops that followèd thee?
Decline all this, and see what now thou art:
For happy wife, a most distressèd widow;
For joyful mother, one that wails the name;
For one being sued to, one that humbly sues;   100
For queen, a very caitiff crowned with care;
For she that scorned at me, now scorned of me;
For she being feared of all, now fearing one;
For she commanding all, obeyed of none.
Thus hath the course of justice whirled about   105
And left thee but a very prey to time,
Having no more but thought of what thou wast
To torture thee the more, being what thou art.

84 presentation of but image only of 85 flattering index deceptive prologue
85 pageant stage show 86 a-high on high 88 garnish showy 97 Decline
recite in order 101 very caitiff truly unhappy wretch

Thou didst usurp my place, and dost thou not
110   Usurp the just proportion of my sorrow?
Now thy proud neck bears half my burdened yoke,
From which even here I slip my wearied head
And leave the burden of it all on thee.
Farewell, York's wife, and queen of sad mischance!
115   These English woes shall make me smile in France.

QUEEN ELIZABETH O thou well skilled in curses, stay
        awhile
And teach me how to curse mine enemies!

QUEEN MARGARET Forbear to sleep the nights, and fast
        the days;
Compare dead happiness with living woe;
120   Think that thy babes were sweeter than they were
And he that slew them fouler than he is.
Bett'ring thy loss makes the bad causer worse;
Revolving this will teach thee how to curse.

QUEEN ELIZABETH My words are dull; O, quicken
        them with thine!

QUEEN MARGARET Thy woes will make them sharp and
125   pierce like mine.   Exit [Queen] Margaret.

DUCHESS OF YORK Why should calamity be full of
        words?

QUEEN ELIZABETH Windy attorneys to their client's
        woes,
Airy succeeders of intestate joys,
Poor breathing orators of miseries,
130   Let them have scope! Though what they will impart
Help nothing else, yet do they ease the heart.

DUCHESS OF YORK If so, then be not tongue-tied. Go
        with me
And in the breath of bitter words let's smother
My damnèd son that thy two sweet sons smothered.

110 **just proportion** exact extent   122 **Bett'ring** magnifying   123 **Revolving**
meditating on   124 **quicken** give life to   127 **attorneys to their client's woes**
spokesmen for the griefs of the one who employs them (i.e., words)
128 **succeeders of intestate joys** successors of joys which died without leaving a
will

The trumpet sounds. Be copious in exclaims.   135

*Enter King Richard and his Train, [marching
with Drums and Trumpets].*

KING RICHARD Who intercepts me in my expedition?

DUCHESS OF YORK O, she that might have intercepted
thee,
By strangling thee in her accursèd womb,
From all the slaughters, wretch, that thou hast done!

QUEEN ELIZABETH Hid'st thou that forehead with a
golden crown   140
Where should be branded, if that right were right,
The slaughter of the prince that owed that crown
And the dire death of my poor sons and brothers?
Tell me, thou villain-slave, where are my children?

DUCHESS OF YORK Thou toad, thou toad, where is thy
brother Clarence?   145
And little Ned Plantagenet, his son?

QUEEN ELIZABETH Where is the gentle Rivers, Vaughan,
Grey?

DUCHESS OF YORK Where is kind Hastings?

KING RICHARD A flourish, trumpets! Strike alarum,
drums!
Let not the heavens hear these telltale women   150
Rail on the Lord's anointed. Strike, I say!
                                    Flourish. Alarums.
Either be patient and entreat me fair,
Or with the clamorous report of war
Thus will I drown your exclamations.

DUCHESS OF YORK Art thou my son?   155

KING RICHARD Ay, I thank God, my father, and yourself.

DUCHESS OF YORK Then patiently hear my impatience.

136 **expedition** (1) campaign (2) haste   142 **owed** owned   152 **entreat me fair**
treat me courteously

KING RICHARD Madam, I have a touch of your
        condition
    That cannot brook the accent of reproof.

DUCHESS OF YORK O, let me speak!

160 KING RICHARD   Do then; but I'll not hear.

DUCHESS OF YORK I will be mild and gentle in my
        words.

KING RICHARD And brief, good mother, for I am in
        haste.

DUCHESS OF YORK Art thou so hasty? I have stayed
        for thee,
    God knows, in torment and in agony.

165 KING RICHARD And came I not at last to comfort you?

DUCHESS OF YORK No, by the holy rood, thou know'st
        it well,
    Thou cam'st on earth to make the earth my hell.
    A grievous burden was thy birth to me;
    Tetchy and wayward was thy infancy;
    Thy schooldays frightful, desp'rate, wild, and
170   furious;
    Thy prime of manhood daring, bold, and venturous;
    Thy age confirmed, proud, subtle, sly, and bloody,
    More mild, but yet more harmful, kind in hatred.
    What comfortable hour canst thou name
175 That ever graced me with thy company?

KING RICHARD Faith, none but Humphrey Hour, that
        called your Grace
    To breakfast once forth of my company.
    If I be so disgracious in your eye,
    Let me march on and not offend you, madam.
    Strike up the drum.

180 DUCHESS OF YORK   I prithee hear me speak.

158 **condition** disposition   163 **stayed** waited   169 **Tetchy** fretful   172 **age
confirmed** maturity   176 **Humphrey Hour** (apparently the name of a man,
chosen for the play on *comfortable hour*)   178 **disgracious** displeasing

KING RICHARD You speak too bitterly.

DUCHESS OF YORK   Hear me a word;
  For I shall never speak to thee again.

KING RICHARD So.

DUCHESS OF YORK Either thou wilt die by God's just
    ordinance
  Ere from this war thou turn a conqueror,   185
  Or I with grief and extreme age shall perish
  And never more behold thy face again.
  Therefore take with thee my most grievous curse,
  Which in the day of battle tire thee more
  Than all the complete armor that thou wear'st!   190
  My prayers on the adverse party fight!
  And there the little souls of Edward's children
  Whisper the spirits of thine enemies
  And promise them success and victory!
  Bloody thou art, bloody will be thy end;   195
  Shame serves thy life and doth thy death attend.
                                        Exit.

QUEEN ELIZABETH Though far more cause, yet much
    less spirit to curse
  Abides in me. I say amen to her.

KING RICHARD Stay, madam; I must talk a word with
    you.

QUEEN ELIZABETH I have no moe sons of the royal
    blood   200
  For thee to slaughter. For my daughters, Richard,
  They shall be praying nuns, not weeping queens;
  And therefore level not to hit their lives.

KING RICHARD You have a daughter called Elizabeth,
  Virtuous and fair, royal and gracious.   205

QUEEN ELIZABETH And must she die for this? O, let her
    live,
  And I'll corrupt her manners, stain her beauty,

185 **turn** return   200 **moe** more (in number)   203 **level** aim   207 **manners**
habits

483

Slander myself as false to Edward's bed,
Throw over her the veil of infamy;
210 So she may live unscarred of bleeding slaughter,
I will confess she was not Edward's daughter.

KING RICHARD Wrong not her birth; she is a royal
princess.

QUEEN ELIZABETH To save her life, I'll say she is not so.

KING RICHARD Her life is safest only in her birth.

QUEEN ELIZABETH And only in that safety died her
215 brothers.

KING RICHARD Lo, at their birth good stars were
opposite.

QUEEN ELIZABETH No, to their lives ill friends were
contrary.

KING RICHARD All unavoided is the doom of destiny.

QUEEN ELIZABETH True, when avoided grace makes
destiny.
220 My babes were destined to a fairer death
If grace had blessed thee with a fairer life.

KING RICHARD You speak as if that I had slain my
cousins!

QUEEN ELIZABETH Cousins indeed, and by their uncle
cozened
Of comfort, kingdom, kindred, freedom, life.
225 Whose hand soever lanced their tender hearts,
Thy head (all indirectly) gave direction.
No doubt the murd'rous knife was dull and blunt
Till it was whetted on thy stone-hard heart
To revel in the entrails of my lambs.
230 But that still use of grief makes wild grief tame,
My tongue should to thy ears not name my boys
Till that my nails were anchored in thine eyes;

218 **unavoided** inevitable 218 **doom** decree 219 **avoided grace** i.e., the
rejection of God's grace (by Richard) 223 **cozened** defrauded 226 **indirectly**
underhandedly 230 **still use** continued habit

And I, in such a desp'rate bay of death,
Like a poor bark of sails and tackling reft,
Rush all to pieces on thy rocky bosom.   235

KING RICHARD Madam, so thrive I in my enterprise
And dangerous success of bloody wars
As I intend more good to you and yours
Than ever you and yours by me were harmed!

QUEEN ELIZABETH What good is covered with the face
    of heaven,   240
To be discovered, that can do me good?

KING RICHARD Th' advancement of your children,
    gentle lady.

QUEEN ELIZABETH Up to some scaffold, there to lose
    their heads!

KING RICHARD Unto the dignity and height of fortune,
The high imperial type of this earth's glory.   245

QUEEN ELIZABETH Flatter my sorrow with report of it.
Tell me, what state, what dignity, what honor
Canst thou demise to any child of mine?

KING RICHARD Even all I have—ay, and myself and all
Will I withal endow a child of thine,   250
So in the Lethe of thy angry soul
Thou drown the sad remembrance of those wrongs
Which thou supposest I have done to thee.

QUEEN ELIZABETH Be brief, lest that the process of
    thy kindness
Last longer telling than thy kindness' date.   255

KING RICHARD Then know that from my soul I love
    thy daughter.

QUEEN ELIZABETH My daughter's mother thinks it with
    her soul.

---

237 **success** result   245 **type** symbol   248 **demise** convey legally   250 **withal**
with   251 **Lethe** river of oblivion   254 **process** story   255 **date** duration

KING RICHARD What do you think?

QUEEN ELIZABETH That thou dost love my daughter
        from thy soul.
260   So from thy soul's love didst thou love her brothers,
        And from my heart's love I do thank thee for it.

KING RICHARD Be not so hasty to confound my
        meaning.
        I mean that with my soul I love thy daughter
        And do intend to make her Queen of England.

QUEEN ELIZABETH Well then, who dost thou mean shall
265   be her king?

KING RICHARD Even he that makes her queen. Who
        else should be?

QUEEN ELIZABETH What, thou?

KING RICHARD   Even so. How think you of it?

QUEEN ELIZABETH How canst thou woo her?

KING RICHARD   That would I learn of you,
        As one being best acquainted with her humor.

QUEEN ELIZABETH And wilt thou learn of me?

270   KING RICHARD   Madam, with all my heart.

QUEEN ELIZABETH Send to her by the man that slew her
        brothers
        A pair of bleeding hearts; thereon engrave
        "Edward" and "York." Then haply will she weep;
        Therefore present to her—as sometimes Margaret
275   Did to thy father, steeped in Rutland's blood—
        A handkerchief, which, say to her, did drain
        The purple sap from her sweet brother's body,
        And bid her wipe her weeping eyes withal.
        If this inducement move her not to love,
280   Send her a letter of thy noble deeds:
        Tell her thou mad'st away her uncle Clarence,
        Her uncle Rivers; ay, and for her sake

259 **from** apart from (i.e., not with)   269 **humor** disposition   274 **sometimes**
once   278 **withal** with (it)

Mad'st quick conveyance with her good aunt
Anne.

KING RICHARD You mock me, madam, this is not the
way
To win your daughter.

QUEEN ELIZABETH   There is no other way,   285
Unless thou couldst put on some other shape
And not be Richard that hath done all this.

KING RICHARD Say that I did all this for love of her.

QUEEN ELIZABETH Nay, then indeed she cannot choose
but hate thee,
Having bought love with such a bloody spoil.   290

KING RICHARD Look what is done cannot be now
amended.
Men shall deal unadvisedly sometimes,
Which afterhours gives leisure to repent.
If I did take the kingdom from your sons,
To make amends I'll give it to your daughter.   295
If I have killed the issue of your womb,
To quicken your increase I will beget
Mine issue of your blood upon your daughter.
A grandam's name is little less in love
Than is the doting title of a mother;   300
They are as children but one step below,
Even of your metal, of your very blood,
Of all one pain, save for a night of groans
Endured of her for whom you bid like sorrow.
Your children were vexation to your youth,   305
But mine shall be a comfort to your age.
The loss you have is but a son being king,
And by that loss your daughter is made queen.
I cannot make you what amends I would;
Therefore accept such kindness as I can.   310
Dorset your son, that with a fearful soul

283 conveyance (1) carrying off (2) underhand dealing   290 spoil destruction
291 Look what whatever   292 shall deal unadvisedly are bound to act
thoughtlessly   297 quicken your increase give life to your offspring   302 metal
substance   304 of by   304 bid suffered

Leads discontented steps in foreign soil,
This fair alliance quickly shall call home
To high promotions and great dignity.
315   The king that calls your beauteous daughter wife
Familiarly shall call thy Dorset brother.
Again shall you be mother to a king,
And all the ruins of distressful times
Repaired with double riches of content.
320   What! We have many goodly days to see.
The liquid drops of tears that you have shed
Shall come again, transformed to orient pearl,
Advantaging their loan with interest
Of ten times double gain of happiness.
325   Go then, my mother, to thy daughter go;
Make bold her bashful years with your experience;
Prepare her ears to hear a wooer's tale.
Put in her tender heart th' aspiring flame
Of golden sovereignty; acquaint the Princess
330   With the sweet silent hours of marriage joys.
And when this arm of mine hath chastisèd
The petty rebel, dull-brained Buckingham,
Bound with triumphant garlands will I come
And lead thy daughter to a conqueror's bed;
335   To whom I will retail my conquest won,
And she shall be sole victoress, Caesar's Caesar.

QUEEN ELIZABETH What were I best to say? Her father's
brother
Would be her lord? Or shall I say her uncle?
Or he that slew her brothers and her uncles?
340   Under what title shall I woo for thee
That God, the law, my honor, and her love
Can make seem pleasing to her tender years?

KING RICHARD Infer fair England's peace by this
alliance.

QUEEN ELIZABETH Which she shall purchase with still-
lasting war.

313 **alliance** marriage   322 **orient** shining   335 **retail** recount   343 **Infer**
bring forward as an argument

KING RICHARD Tell her the King, that may command, entreats.   345

QUEEN ELIZABETH That at her hands which the King's King forbids.

KING RICHARD Say she shall be a high and mighty queen.

QUEEN ELIZABETH To wail the title, as her mother doth.

KING RICHARD Say I will love her everlastingly.

QUEEN ELIZABETH But how long shall that title "ever" last?   350

KING RICHARD Sweetly in force unto her fair life's end.

QUEEN ELIZABETH But how long fairly shall her sweet life last?

KING RICHARD As long as heaven and nature lengthens it.

QUEEN ELIZABETH As long as hell and Richard likes of it.

KING RICHARD Say I, her sovereign, am her subject low.   355

QUEEN ELIZABETH But she, your subject, loathes such sovereignty.

KING RICHARD Be eloquent in my behalf to her.

QUEEN ELIZABETH An honest tale speeds best being plainly told.

KING RICHARD Then plainly to her tell my loving tale.

QUEEN ELIZABETH Plain and not honest is too harsh a style.   360

KING RICHARD Your reasons are too shallow and too quick.

358 **speeds best being** succeeds best when it is   360 **harsh** discordant

QUEEN ELIZABETH O no, my reasons are too deep and
    dead;
    Too deep and dead, poor infants, in their graves.

KING RICHARD Harp not on that string, madam; that
    is past.

QUEEN ELIZABETH Harp on it still shall I till heart-
365   strings break.

KING RICHARD Now, by my George, my garter, and
    my crown—

QUEEN ELIZABETH Profaned, dishonored, and the third
    usurped.

KING RICHARD I swear—

QUEEN ELIZABETH   By nothing, for this is no oath:
    Thy George, profaned, hath lost his lordly honor;
370   Thy garter, blemished, pawned his knightly virtue;
    Thy crown, usurped, disgraced his kingly glory.
    If something thou wouldst swear to be believed,
    Swear then by something that thou hast not
    wronged.

KING RICHARD Then by myself—

QUEEN ELIZABETH   Thyself is self-misused.

KING RICHARD Now by the world—

375 QUEEN ELIZABETH   'Tis full of thy foul wrongs.

KING RICHARD My father's death—

QUEEN ELIZABETH   Thy life hath it dishonored.

KING RICHARD Why then, by God—

QUEEN ELIZABETH   God's wrong is most of all.
    If thou didst fear to break an oath with him,
    The unity the King my husband made
380   Thou hadst not broken, nor my brothers died.
    If thou hadst feared to break an oath by him,

366 **George ... garter** insignia of the Order of the Garter (a figure of St. George
and a velvet ribbon)

Th' imperial metal circling now thy head
Had graced the tender temples of my child,
And both the Princes had been breathing here,
Which now, two tender bedfellows for dust,   385
Thy broken faith hath made the prey for worms.
What canst thou swear by now?

KING RICHARD   The time to come.

QUEEN ELIZABETH That thou hast wrongèd in the time
   o'erpast;
For I myself have many tears to wash
Hereafter time, for time past wronged by thee.   390
The children live whose fathers thou hast
   slaughtered,
Ungoverned youth, to wail it in their age;
The parents live whose children thou hast
   butchered,
Old barren plants, to wail it with their age.
Swear not by time to come, for that thou hast   395
Misused ere used, by times ill-used o'erpast.

KING RICHARD As I intend to prosper and repent,
So thrive I in my dangerous affairs
Of hostile arms! Myself myself confound!
Heaven and fortune bar me happy hours!   400
Day, yield me not thy light, nor, night, thy rest!
Be opposite all planets of good luck
To my proceeding if, with dear heart's love,
Immaculate devotion, holy thoughts,
I tender not thy beauteous princely daughter!   405
In her consists my happiness and thine;
Without her, follows to myself and thee,
Herself, the land, and many a Christian soul,
Death, desolation, ruin, and decay.
It cannot be avoided but by this;   410
It will not be avoided but by this.
Therefore, dear mother—I must call you so—
Be the attorney of my love to her.
Plead what I will be, not what I have been;

390 **Hereafter** future 392 **Ungoverned** unguided 399 **confound** ruin
405 **tender** look after tenderly

415   Not my deserts, but what I will deserve.
       Urge the necessity and state of times,
       And be not peevish-fond in great designs.

       QUEEN ELIZABETH Shall I be tempted of the devil thus?

       KING RICHARD Ay, if the devil tempt you to do good.

420   QUEEN ELIZABETH Shall I forget myself to be myself?

       KING RICHARD Ay, if yourself's remembrance wrong
             yourself.

       QUEEN ELIZABETH Yet thou didst kill my children.

       KING RICHARD But in your daughter's womb I'll bury
             them,
       Where in that nest of spicery they will breed
425   Selves of themselves, to your recomforture.

       QUEEN ELIZABETH Shall I go win my daughter to thy
             will?

       KING RICHARD And be a happy mother by the deed.

       QUEEN ELIZABETH I go. Write to me very shortly,
       And you shall understand from me her mind.

       KING RICHARD Bear her my truelove's kiss; and so
430   farewell.
                                    Exit Queen [*Elizabeth*].
       Relenting fool, and shallow, changing woman!

             Enter Ratcliffe, [*Catesby following*].

       How now! What news?

       RATCLIFFE Most mighty sovereign, on the western coast
       Rideth a puissant navy; to our shores
435   Throng many doubtful hollow-hearted friends,
       Unarmed, and unresolved to beat them back.
       'Tis thought that Richmond is their admiral;

416 **state of times** condition of affairs   417 **peevish-fond** obstinately foolish
420 **myself to be myself** that I am I   424 **next of spicery** (alludes to the
nest of the phoenix, a bird that periodically returned to its fragrant nest, where it
was consumed in flame and arose renewed)   425 **recomforture** consolation
434 **puissant** powerful   436 **unresolved** irresolute

And there they hull, expecting but the aid
Of Buckingham to welcome them ashore.

KING RICHARD Some light-foot friend post to the
  Duke of Norfolk: 440
  Ratcliffe, thyself—or Catesby; where is he?

CATESBY Here, my good lord.

KING RICHARD   Catesby, fly to the Duke.

CATESBY I will, my lord, with all convenient haste.

KING RICHARD Ratcliffe, come hither. Post to
  Salisbury.
  When thou com'st thither—[*To Catesby*] Dull un-
  mindful villain,   445
  Why stay'st thou here and go'st not to the Duke?

CATESBY First, mighty liege, tell me your Highness'
  pleasure
  What from your Grace I shall deliver to him.

KING RICHARD O, true, good Catesby. Bid him levy
  straight
  The greatest strength and power that he can make   450
  And meet me suddenly at Salisbury.

CATESBY I go.   *Exit.*

RATCLIFFE What, may it please you, shall I do at
  Salisbury?

KING RICHARD Why, what wouldst thou do there
  before I go?

RATCLIFFE Your Highness told me I should post before. 455

KING RICHARD My mind is changed.

          Enter Lord Stanley, [Earl of Derby].

                    Stanley, what news with you?

STANLEY None good, my liege, to please you with the
  hearing,

438 **hull** drift with the wind   438 **expecting** awaiting   440 **post** hasten
443 **convenient** appropriate

493

Nor none so bad but well may be reported.

KING RICHARD Hoyday, a riddle! Neither good nor
         bad!
460   What need'st thou run so many miles about
         When thou mayest tell thy tale the nearest way?
         One more, what news?

STANLEY   Richmond is on the seas.

KING RICHARD There let him sink, and be the seas on
         him!
         White-livered runagate, what doth he there?

465   STANLEY I know not, mighty sovereign, but by guess.

KING RICHARD Well, as you guess?

STANLEY Stirred up by Dorset, Buckingham, and
         Morton,
         He makes for England, here to claim the crown.

KING RICHARD Is the chair empty? Is the sword
         unswayed?
470   Is the King dead, the empire unpossessed?
         What heir of York is there alive but we?
         And who is England's King but great York's heir?
         Then tell me, what makes he upon the seas?

STANLEY Unless for that, my liege, I cannot guess.

KING RICHARD Unless for that he comes to be your
475   liege,
         You cannot guess wherefore the Welshman comes.
         Thou wilt revolt and fly to him, I fear.

STANLEY No, my good lord; therefore mistrust me not.

KING RICHARD Where is thy power then to beat him
         back?
480   Where be thy tenants and thy followers?
         Are they not now upon the western shore,
         Safe-conducting the rebels from their ships?

464 **runagate** fugitive

STANLEY No, my good lord, my friends are in the
    north.

KING RICHARD Cold friends to me! What do they in
    the north
    When they should serve their sovereign in the west?   485

STANLEY They have not been commanded, mighty
    King.
    Pleaseth your Majesty to give me leave,
    I'll muster up my friends and meet your Grace
    Where and what time your Majesty shall please.

KING RICHARD Ay, thou wouldst be gone to join with
    Richmond.   490
    But I'll not trust thee.

STANLEY   Most mighty sovereign,
    You have no cause to hold my friendship doubtful.
    I never was nor never will be false.

KING RICHARD Go then and muster men; but leave
    behind
    Your son George Stanley. Look your heart be firm,   495
    Or else his head's assurance is but frail.

STANLEY So deal with him as I prove true to you.
                                        Exit Stanley.

                    Enter a Messenger.

FIRST MESSENGER My gracious sovereign, now in
    Devonshire,
    As I by friends am well advertisèd,
    Sir Edward Courtney and the haughty prelate,   500
    Bishop of Exeter, his elder brother,
    With many moe confederates, are in arms.

                Enter another Messenger.

SECOND MESSENGER In Kent, my liege, the Guilfords
    are in arms,

496 **assurance** security   499 **advertisèd** informed

And every hour more competitors
505 Flock to the rebels, and their power grows strong.

Enter another Messenger.

THIRD MESSENGER My lord, the army of great Buckingham—

KING RICHARD Out on ye, owls! Nothing but songs of
death?   *He striketh him.*
There, take thou that, till thou bring better news.

THIRD MESSENGER The news I have to tell your
Majesty
510 Is that by sudden floods and fall of waters
Buckingham's army is dispersed and scattered,
And he himself wand'red away alone,
No man knows whither.

KING RICHARD   I cry thee mercy.
There is my purse to cure that blow of thine.
515 Hath any well-advisèd friend proclaimed
Reward to him that brings the traitor in?

THIRD MESSENGER Such proclamation hath been made,
my lord.

Enter another Messenger.

FOURTH MESSENGER Sir Thomas Lovell and Lord
Marquis Dorset,
'Tis said, my liege, in Yorkshire are in arms.
520 But this good comfort bring I to your Highness:
The Britain navy is dispersed by tempest.
Richmond in Dorsetshire sent out a boat
Unto the shore to ask those on the banks
If they were his assistants, yea or no;
525 Who answered him they came from Buckingham
Upon his party. He, mistrusting them,
Hoised sail and made his course again for Britain.

504 **competitors** associates 521 **Britain** Breton 527 **Hoised** hoisted
527 **Britain** Brittany

KING RICHARD March on, march on, since we are up
    in arms,
  If not to fight with foreign enemies,
  Yet to beat down these rebels here at home.   530

Enter Catesby.

CATESBY My liege, the Duke of Buckingham is taken.
  That is the best news. That the Earl of Richmond
  Is with a mighty power landed at Milford
  Is colder news, but yet they must be told.

KING RICHARD Away towards Salisbury! While we
    reason here,   535
  A royal battle might be won and lost.
  Someone take order Buckingham be brought
  To Salisbury; the rest march on with me.

                  Flourish. Exeunt.

Scene V. [*Lord Stanley's house.*]

*Enter [Lord Stanley, Earl of] Derby, and
Sir Christopher [Urswick, a chaplain].*

STANLEY Sir Christopher, tell Richmond this from me:
  That in the sty of the most deadly boar
  My son George Stanley is franked up in hold;
  If I revolt, off goes young George's head;
  The fear of that holds off my present aid.   5
  So get thee gone; commend me to thy lord.
  Withal say that the Queen hath heartily consented
  He should espouse Elizabeth her daughter.
  But tell me, where is princely Richmond now?

IV.v.3. **franked up in hold** penned up in custody (**frank** = sty)

CHRISTOPHER At Pembroke or at Harfordwest in
10   Wales.

STANLEY What men of name resort to him?

CHRISTOPHER Sir Walter Herbert, a renownèd soldier,
      Sir Gilbert Talbot, Sir William Stanley,
      Oxford, redoubted Pembroke, Sir James Blunt,
15   And Rice ap Thomas, with a valiant crew,
      And many other of great name and worth;
      And towards London do they bend their power,
      If by the way they be not fought withal.

STANLEY Well, hie thee to thy lord. I kiss his hand;
20   My letter will resolve him of my mind.
                                          [*Gives letter.*]
      Farewell.   *Exeunt.*

10 **Harfordwest** Haverfordwest   20 **resolve** inform

ACT V

Scene I. [*Salisbury. An open place.*]

Enter Buckingham with [Sheriff and] Halberds,
led to execution.

BUCKINGHAM Will not King Richard let me speak with
    him?

SHERIFF No, my good lord; therefore be patient.

BUCKINGHAM Hastings, and Edward's children, Grey
    and Rivers,
  Holy King Henry and thy fair son Edward,
  Vaughan, and all that have miscarrièd   5
  By underhand corrupted foul injustice,
  If that your moody discontented souls
  Do through the clouds behold this present hour,
  Even for revenge mock my destruction!
  This is All Souls' day, fellow, is it not?   10

SHERIFF It is, my lord.

BUCKINGHAM Why, then All Souls' day is my body's
    doomsday.
  This is the day which in King Edward's time
  I wished might fall on me when I was found
  False to his children and his wife's allies.   15

V.i. s.d. **Halberds** guards armed with long poleaxes

499

This is the day wherein I wished to fall
By the false faith of him whom most I trusted.
This, this All Souls' day to my fearful soul
Is the determined respite of my wrongs.
20   That high All-seer which I dallied with
Hath turned my feignèd prayer on my head
And given in earnest what I begged in jest.
Thus doth he force the swords of wicked men
To turn their own points in their masters' bosoms.
25   Thus Margaret's curse falls heavy on my neck:
"When he," quoth she, "shall split thy heart with
        sorrow,
Remember Margaret was a prophetess."
Come lead me, officers, to the block of shame;
Wrong hath but wrong, and blame the due of
        blame.

Exeunt Buckingham with Officers.

Scene II. [*Camp near Tamworth.*]

*Enter Richmond, Oxford, Blunt, Herbert,
and others, with Drum and Colors.*

RICHMOND Fellows in arms and my most loving
        friends,
Bruised underneath the yoke of tyranny,
Thus far unto the bowels of the land
Have we marched on without impediment;
5   And here receive we from our father Stanley
Lines of fair comfort and encouragement.
The wretched, bloody, and usurping boar,
That spoiled your summer fields and fruitful vines,
Swills your warm blood like wash, and makes his
        trough

19 **determined respite of my wrongs** end of reprieve for my unjust acts
V.ii.3. **bowels** center

500

In your emboweled bosoms, this foul swine   10
Is now even in the center of this isle,
Near to the town of Leicester, as we learn.
From Tamworth thither is but one day's march.
In God's name cheerly on, courageous friends,
To reap the harvest of perpetual peace   15
By this one bloody trial of sharp war.

OXFORD Every man's conscience is a thousand men
To fight against this guilty homicide.

HERBERT I doubt not but his friends will turn to us.

BLUNT He hath no friends but what are friends for
fear,   20
Which in his dearest need will fly from him.

RICHMOND All for our vantage. Then in God's name
march!
True hope is swift and flies with swallow's wings;
Kings it makes gods, and meaner creatures kings.
                                        Exeunt omnes.

Scene III. [*Bosworth Field.*]

*Enter King Richard in arms, with Norfolk, Ratcliffe,
and the Earl of Surrey, [and Soldiers].*

KING RICHARD Here pitch our tent, even here in
Bosworth field.
My Lord of Surrey, why look you so sad?

SURREY My heart is ten times lighter than my looks.

KING RICHARD My Lord of Norfolk!

NORFOLK   Here, most gracious liege.

10 **emboweled** ripped up

KING RICHARD Norfolk, we must have knocks; ha,
5   must we not?

NORFOLK We must both give and take, my loving lord.

KING RICHARD Up with my tent! Here will I lie
    tonight;
                    [*Soldiers begin to set up the King's tent.*]
    But where tomorrow? Well, all's one for that.
    Who hath descried the number of the traitors?

10 NORFOLK Six or seven thousand is their utmost power.

KING RICHARD Why, our battalia trebles that account;
    Besides, the King's name is a tower of strength,
    Which they upon the adverse faction want.
    Up with the tent! Come, noble gentlemen,
15   Let us survey the vantage of the ground.
    Call for some men of sound direction.
    Let's lack no discipline, make no delay,
    For, lords, tomorrow is a busy day.   *Exeunt.*

    *Enter Richmond, Sir William Brandon, Oxford,
        and Dorset, [Herbert, and Blunt].*

RICHMOND The weary sun hath made a golden set
20   And by the bright tract of his fiery car
    Gives token of a goodly day tomorrow.
    Sir William Brandon, you shall bear my standard.
    Give me some ink and paper in my tent.
    I'll draw the form and model of our battle,
25   Limit each leader to his several charge,
    And part in just proportion our small power.
    My Lord of Oxford, you, Sir William Brandon,
    And you, Sir Walter Herbert, stay with me.
    The Earl of Pembroke keeps his regiment;
30   Good Captain Blunt, bear my good-night to him,
    And by the second hour in the morning
    Desire the Earl to see me in my tent.
    Yet one thing more, good Captain, do for me:

V.iii.11 **Battalia** army   13 **want** lack   16 **direction** ability to give orders
20 **tract** track   20 **car** chariot   25 **Limit** assign   29 **keeps** stays with

Where is Lord Stanley quartered, do you know?

BLUNT Unless I have mista'en his colors much,   35
Which well I am assured I have not done,
His regiment lies half a mile at least
South from the mighty power of the King.

RICHMOND If without peril it be possible,
Sweet Blunt, make some good means to speak with
him   40
And give him from me this most needful note.

BLUNT Upon my life, my lord, I'll undertake it;
And so God give you quiet rest tonight!

RICHMOND Good night, good Captain Blunt. [*Exit
Blunt.*] Come, gentlemen,
Let us consult upon tomorrow's business.   45
Into my tent; the dew is raw and cold.
                         They withdraw into the tent.

         *Enter, [to his tent, King] Richard, Ratcliffe,
                Norfolk, and Catesby.*

KING RICHARD What is't o'clock?

         CATESBY   It's suppertime, my lord;
It's nine o'clock.

KING RICHARD   I will not sup tonight.
Give me some ink and paper.
What, is my beaver easier than it was?   50
And all my armor laid into my tent?

CATESBY It is, my liege, and all things are in readiness.

KING RICHARD Good Norfolk, hie thee to thy charge;
Use careful watch, choose trusty sentinels.

NORFOLK I go, my lord.   55

KING RICHARD Stir with the lark tomorrow, gentle
Norfolk.

NORFOLK I warrant you, my lord.   *Exit.*

50 **beaver** face-guard of a helmet

KING RICHARD Catesby!

CATESBY My lord?

KING RICHARD Send out a pursuivant-at-arms
60   To Stanley's regiment; bid him bring his power
        Before sunrising, lest his son George fall
        Into the blind cave of eternal night.   [*Exit Catesby*.]
        Fill me a bowl of wine. Give me a watch.
        Saddle white Surrey for the field tomorrow.
65   Look that my staves be sound and not too heavy.
        Ratcliffe!

RATCLIFFE My lord?

KING RICHARD Saw'st thou the melancholy Lord
        Northumberland?

RATCLIFFE Thomas the Earl of Surrey and himself,
70   Much about cockshut time, from troop to troop
        Went through the army, cheering up the soldiers.

KING RICHARD So, I am satisfied. Give me a bowl of
        wine.
        I have not that alacrity of spirit
        Nor cheer of mind that I was wont to have.
                                    [*Wine brought*.]
75   Set it down. Is ink and paper ready?

RATCLIFFE It is, my lord.

KING RICHARD Bid my guard watch. Leave me.
        Ratcliffe,
        About the mid of night come to my tent
        And help to arm me. Leave me, I say.
                        Exit Ratcliffe. [*King Richard sleeps*.]

        Enter [*Stanley, Earl of*] *Derby, to Richmond in
        his tent,* [*Lords and Gentlemen attending*].

80   STANLEY Fortune and victory sit on thy helm!

---

59 pursuivant-at-arms minor herald   63 watch timepiece   64 Surrey (the
name of a horse)   65 staves lances   70 cockshut time twilight

RICHMOND All comfort that the dark night can afford
    Be to thy person, noble father-in-law!
    Tell me, how fares our loving mother?

STANLEY I by attorney bless thee from thy mother,
    Who prays continually for Richmond's good.   85
    So much for that. The silent hours steal on
    And flaky darkness breaks within the east.
    In brief, for so the season bids us be,
    Prepare thy battle early in the morning
    And put thy fortune to the arbitrament   90
    Of bloody strokes and mortal-staring war.
    I, as I may—that which I would I cannot—
    With best advantage will deceive the time
    And aid thee in this doubtful shock of arms.
    But on thy side I may not be too forward,   95
    Lest, being seen, thy brother, tender George,
    Be executed in his father's sight.
    Farewell; the leisure and the fearful time
    Cuts off the ceremonious vows of love
    And ample interchange of sweet discourse   100
    Which so long sund'red friends should dwell upon.
    God give us leisure for these rites of love!
    Once more adieu; be valiant, and speed well.

RICHMOND Good lord, conduct him to his regiment.
    I'll strive with troubled thoughts to take a nap,   105
    Lest leaden slumber peise me down tomorrow
    When I should mount with wings of victory.
    Once more, good night, kind lords and gentlemen.
                    Exeunt. Manet Richmond.
    O thou whose captain I account myself,
    Look on my forces with a gracious eye!   110
    Put in their hands thy bruising irons of wrath,
    That they may crush down with a heavy fall
    The usurping helmets of our adversaries!
    Make us thy ministers of chastisement,

87 **flaky** streaked with light   88 **season** time   91 **mortal-staring** fatally glaring
93 **advantage** opportunity   93 **the time** the people of this time   98 **leisure**
time available   105 **with** against   106 **peise** weigh

115   That we may praise thee in the victory!
      To thee I do commend my watchful soul
      Ere I let fall the windows of mine eyes.
      Sleeping and waking, O defend me still!   *Sleeps.*

        *Enter the Ghost of Prince Edward, son to Henry
                      the Sixth.*

      GHOST (*To Richard*) Let me sit heavy on thy soul
        tomorrow!
120   Think how thou stab'st me in my prime of youth
      At Tewkesbury. Despair therefor and die!
      (*To Richmond*) Be cheerful, Richmond; for the
        wrongèd souls
      Of butchered princes fight in thy behalf.
      King Henry's issue, Richmond, comforts thee.
                                              [*Exit.*]

          Enter the Ghost of Henry the Sixth.

      GHOST (*To Richard*) When I was mortal, my anointed
125   body
      By thee was punchèd full of deadly holes.
      Think on the Tower and me. Despair and die!
      Harry the Sixth bids thee despair and die!
      (*To Richmond*) Virtuous and holy, be thou
        conqueror!
130   Harry, that prophesied thou shouldst be king,
      Doth comfort thee in thy sleep. Live and flourish!
                                              [*Exit.*]

            Enter the Ghost of Clarence.

      GHOST [*To Richard*] Let me sit heavy in thy soul
        tomorrow,
      I that was washed to death with fulsome wine,
      Poor Clarence, by thy guile betrayed to death.
135   Tomorrow in the battle think on me,
      And fall thy edgeless sword. Despair and die!

      117 **windows** eyelids   121 **therefor** because of that   124 **issue** offspring
      136 **fall** let fall

(*To Richmond*) Thou offspring of the house of
    Lancaster,
The wrongèd heirs of York do pray for thee.
Good angels guard thy battle! Live and flourish!
                                                [*Exit.*]

Enter the Ghosts of Rivers, Grey, and Vaughan.

RIVERS [*To Richard*] Let me sit heavy in thy soul
    tomorrow,   140
Rivers, that died at Pomfret! Despair and die!

GREY Think upon Grey, and let thy soul despair!

VAUGHAN Think upon Vaughan and with guilty fear
    Let fall thy lance: despair, and die!

ALL (*To Richmond*) Awake, and think our wrongs in
    Richard's bosom   145
Will conquer him! Awake, and win the day!
                                                [*Exeunt.*]

Enter the Ghost of Hastings.

GHOST [*To Richard*] Bloody and guilty, guiltily awake,
    And in a bloody battle end thy days!
    Think on Lord Hastings. Despair and die!
    (*To Richmond*) Quiet untroubled soul, awake,
        awake!   150
    Arm, fight, and conquer for fair England's sake!
                                                [*Exit.*]

Enter the Ghosts of the two young Princes.

GHOSTS (*To Richard*) Dream on thy cousins
    smotherèd in the Tower.
Let us be lead within thy bosom, Richard,
And weigh thee down to ruin, shame, and death.
Thy nephews' souls bid thee despair and die!   155
(*To Richmond*) Sleep, Richmond, sleep in peace
    and wake in joy.
Good angels guard thee from the boar's annoy!

157 **annoy** disturbance

Live, and beget a happy race of kings!
Edward's unhappy sons do bid thee flourish.

[*Exeunt*.]

Enter the Ghost of Lady Anne his wife.

GHOST (*To Richard*) Richard, thy wife, that wretched
160   Anne thy wife,
That never slept a quiet hour with thee,
Now fills thy sleep with perturbations.
Tomorrow in the battle think on me,
And fall thy edgeless sword. Despair and die!
(*To Richmond*) Thou quiet soul, sleep thou a quiet
165   sleep.
Dream of success and happy victory!
Thy adversary's wife doth pray for thee.   [*Exit*.]

Enter the Ghost of Buckingham.

GHOST (*To Richard*) The first was I that helped thee
      to the crown;
The last was I that felt thy tyranny.
170 O, in the battle think on Buckingham,
And die in terror of thy guiltiness!
Dream on, dream on, of bloody deeds and death;
Fainting, despair; despairing, yield thy breath!
(*To Richmond*) I died for hope ere I could lend
      thee aid;
175 But cheer thy heart and be thou not dismayed.
God and good angels fight on Richmond's side,
And Richard falls in height of all his pride.   [*Exit*.]

Richard starteth up out of a dream.

KING RICHARD Give me another horse! Bind up my
      wounds!
Have mercy, Jesu! Soft! I did but dream.
180 O coward conscience, how dost thou afflict me!
The lights burn blue. It is now dead midnight.
Cold fearful drops stand on my trembling flesh.

174 **for hope** because of hope (to help)

What do I fear? Myself? There's none else by.
Richard loves Richard: that is, I am I.
Is there a murderer here? No. Yes, I am.   185
Then fly. What, from myself? Great reason why!
Lest I revenge. What, myself upon myself?
Alack, I love myself. Wherefore? For any good
That I myself have done unto myself?
O no! Alas, I rather hate myself   190
For hateful deeds committed by myself.
I am a villain. Yet I lie, I am not.
Fool, of thyself speak well. Fool, do not flatter.
My conscience hath a thousand several tongues,
And every tongue brings in a several tale,   195
And every tale condemns me for a villain.
Perjury, perjury in the highest degree,
Murder, stern murder in the direst degree,
All several sins, all used in each degree,
Throng to the bar, crying all, "Guilty! Guilty!"   200
I shall despair. There is no creature loves me;
And if I die, no soul will pity me.
Nay, wherefore should they, since that I myself
Find in myself no pity to myself?
Methought the souls of all that I had murdered   205
Came to my tent, and every one did threat
Tomorrow's vengeance on the head of Richard.

Enter Ratcliffe.

RATCLIFFE My lord!

KING RICHARD Zounds, who is there?

RATCLIFFE Ratcliffe, my lord; 'tis I. The early village
     cock   210
Hath twice done salutation to the morn.
Your friends are up and buckle on their armor.

KING RICHARD O Ratcliffe, I have dreamed a fearful
     dream!
What think'st thou, will our friends prove all true?

194 **several** separate

RATCLIFFE No doubt, my lord.

215 KING RICHARD   O Ratcliffe, I fear, I fear!

RATCLIFFE Nay, good my lord, be not afraid of
    shadows.

KING RICHARD By the apostle Paul, shadows tonight
    Have struck more terror to the soul of Richard
    Than can the substance of ten thousand soldiers
220   Armèd in proof and led by shallow Richmond.
    'Tis not yet near day. Come, go with me.
    Under our tents I'll play the easedropper
    To see if any mean to shrink from me.
                    Exeunt Richard and Ratcliffe.

Enter the Lords to Richmond sitting in his tent.

LORDS Good morrow, Richmond.

RICHMOND Cry mercy, lords and watchful gentle-
225   men,
    That you have ta'en a tardy sluggard here.

LORDS How have you slept, my lord?

RICHMOND The sweetest sleep and fairest-boding
    dreams
    That ever ent'red in a drowsy head
230   Have I since your departure had, my lords.
    Methought their souls whose bodies Richard
    murdered
    Came to my tent and cried on victory.
    I promise you my heart is very jocund
    In the remembrance of so fair a dream.
235   How far into the morning is it, lords?

LORDS Upon the stroke of four.

RICHMOND Why, then 'tis time to arm and give
    direction.

220 proof tested armor 222 **easedropper** eavesdropper 225 **Cry mercy** (1)
beg pardon 232 **cried** called aloud

His Oration to his Soldiers.

More than I have said, loving countrymen,
The leisure and enforcement of the time
Forbids to dwell upon; yet remember this: 240
God and our good cause fight upon our side;
The prayers of holy saints and wrongèd souls,
Like high-reared bulwarks, stand before our faces.
Richard except, those whom we fight against
Had rather have us win than him they follow.   245
For what is he they follow? Truly, gentlemen,
A bloody tyrant and a homicide;
One raised in blood and one in blood established;
One that made means to come by what he hath,
And slaughterèd those that were the means to help
    him;   250
A base foul stone, made precious by the foil
Of England's chair, where he is falsely set;
One that hath ever been God's enemy.
Then if you fight against God's enemy,
God will in justice ward you as his soldiers;   255
If you do sweat to put a tyrant down,
You sleep in peace, the tyrant being slain;
If you do fight against your country's foes,
Your country's fat shall pay your pains the hire;
If you do fight in safeguard of your wives,   260
Your wives shall welcome home the conquerors;
If you do free your children from the sword,
Your children's children quits it in your age.
Then in the name of God and all these rights,
Advance your standards, draw your willing swords.   265
For me, the ransom of my bold attempt
Shall be this cold corpse on the earth's cold face;
But if I thrive, the gain of my attempt
The least of you shall share his part thereof.   270
Sound drums and trumpets boldly and cheerfully;
God and Saint George! Richmond and victory!

                                        [*Exeunt.*]

249 **made means** contrived ways   251 **foil** setting for a gem   255 **ward** protect
259 **fat** abundance   263 **quits** repays   266 **the ransom** i.e., the price paid
(if defeated)

Enter King Richard, Ratcliffe, and [Soldiers].

KING RICHARD What said Northumberland as touching
    Richmond?

RATCLIFFE That he was never trainèd up in arms.

KING RICHARD He said the truth; and what said
    Surrey then?

RATCLIFFE He smiled and said, "The better for our
275   purpose."

KING RICHARD He was in the right, and so indeed it is.
                        The clock striketh.
Tell the clock there. Give me a calendar.
Who saw the sun today?

RATCLIFFE   Not I, my lord.

KING RICHARD Then he disdains to shine; for by the
    book
280   He should have braved the east an hour ago.
A black day will it be to somebody.
Ratcliffe!

RATCLIFFE My lord?

KING RICHARD   The sun will not be seen today;
The sky doth frown and lour upon our army.
285   I would these dewy tears were from the ground.
Not shine today! Why, what is that to me
More than to Richmond? For the selfsame heaven
That frowns on me looks sadly upon him.

Enter Norfolk.

NORFOLK Arm, arm, my lord; the foe vaunts in the
    field.

KING RICHARD Come, bustle, bustle. Caparison my
290   horse.
Call up Lord Stanley, bid him bring his power.
I will lead forth my soldiers to the plain,
And thus my battle shall be orderèd:

277 **Tell** count   280 **braved** made glorious

My foreward shall be drawn out all in length,
Consisting equally of horse and foot;   295
Our archers shall be placèd in the midst;
John Duke of Norfolk, Thomas Earl of Surrey,
Shall have the leading of this foot and horse.
They thus directed, we will follow
In the main battle, whose puissance on either side   300
Shall be well wingèd with our chiefest horse.
This, and Saint George to boot! What think'st
    thou, Norfolk?

NORFOLK A good direction, warlike sovereign.
    This found I on my tent this morning.
                            He showeth him a paper.
    "Jockey of Norfolk, be not so bold,   305
    For Dickon thy master is bought and sold."

KING RICHARD A thing devisèd by the enemy.
    Go, gentlemen, every man unto his charge.
    Let not our babbling dreams affright our souls;
    Conscience is but a word that cowards use,   310
    Devised at first to keep the strong in awe;
    Our strong arms be our conscience, swords our
        law!
    March on, join bravely, let us to it pell-mell,
    If not to heaven, then hand in hand to hell.

            His Oration to his Army.

What shall I say more than I have inferred?   315
Remember whom you are to cope withal,
A sort of vagabonds, rascals, and runaways,
A scum of Britains and base lackey peasants,
Whom their o'ercloyèd country vomits forth
To desperate ventures and assured destruction.   320
You sleeping safe, they bring to you unrest;
You having lands, and blest with beauteous wives,
They would distrain the one, distain the other.

299 **directed** arranged   300 **puissance** power   302 **to boot** to our help
305 **Jockey** (nickname for John)   306 **bought and sold** betrayed for a bribe
317 **sort** set   323 **distrain** confiscate   323 **distain** dishonor

And who doth lead them but a paltry fellow,
325   Long kept in Britain at our mother's cost,
A milksop, one that never in his life
Felt so much cold as over shoes in snow?
Let's whip these stragglers o'er the seas again,
Lash hence these overweening rags of France,
330   These famished beggars, weary of their lives,
Who, but for dreaming on this fond exploit,
For want of means, poor rats, had hanged them-
      selves.
If we be conquerèd, let men conquer us,
And not these bastard Britains, whom our fathers
Have in their own land beaten, bobbed, and
335   thumped,
And in record left them the heirs of shame.
Shall these enjoy our lands? Lie with our wives?
Ravish our daughters? (*Drum afar off.*) Hark! I
      hear their drum.
Fight, gentlemen of England! Fight, bold yeomen!
340   Draw, archers, draw your arrows to the head!
Spur your proud horses hard and ride in blood!
Amaze the welkin with your broken staves!

Enter a Messenger.

What says Lord Stanley? Will he bring his power?

MESSENGER   My lord, he doth deny to come.

345   KING RICHARD   Off with his son George's head!

NORFOLK   My lord, the enemy is past the marsh.
After the battle let George Stanley die.

KING RICHARD   A thousand hearts are great within my
      bosom.
Advance our standards, set upon our foes!
350   Our ancient word of courage, fair Saint George,
Inspire us with the spleen of fiery dragons!
Upon them! Victory sits on our helms.   *Exeunt.*

325 **Britain** Brittany   331 **fond** foolish   342 **welkin** sky   351 **spleen** fierce
spirit

514

Scene IV. [*Bosworth Field.*]

Alarum; excursions. Enter Catesby
[and Norfolk].

CATESBY Rescue, my Lord of Norfolk, rescue, rescue!
    The King enacts more wonders than a man,
    Daring an opposite to every danger.
    His horse is slain, and all on foot he fights,
    Seeking for Richmond in the throat of death.   5
    Rescue, fair lord, or else the day is lost!

Alarums. Enter [King] Richard.

KING RICHARD A horse! A horse! My kingdom for a
    horse!

CATESBY Withdraw, my lord; I'll help you to a horse.

KING RICHARD Slave, I have set my life upon a cast,
    And I will stand the hazard of the die.   10
    I think there be six Richmonds in the field;
    Five have I slain today instead of him.
    A horse! A horse! My kingdom for a horse!

                                     [*Exeunt.*]

V.iv. s.d. **excursions** sallies 3 **opposite** opponent 9 **cast** throw (of dice)
10 **hazard** chance

Scene V. [*Bosworth Field.*]

Alarum. Enter [King] Richard and Richmond;
they fight; Richard is slain.

Retreat and flourish. Enter Richmond, [Stanley, Earl of]
Derby, bearing the crown, with divers other Lords.

RICHMOND God and your arms be praised, victorious
    friends!
    The day is ours; the bloody dog is dead.

STANLEY Courageous Richmond, well hast thou acquit
    thee.
    Lo, here this long-usurpèd royalty
5   From the dead temples of this bloody wretch
    Have I plucked off, to grace thy brows withal.
    Wear it, enjoy it, and make much of it.

RICHMOND Great God of heaven, say amen to all!
    But tell me, is young George Stanley living?

10 STANLEY He is, my lord, and safe in Leicester town,
    Whither, if it please you, we may now withdraw us.

RICHMOND What men of name are slain on either
    side?

STANLEY John Duke of Norfolk, Walter Lord Ferrers,
    Sir Robert Brakenbury, and Sir William Brandon.

15 RICHMOND Inter their bodies as become their births.
    Proclaim a pardon to the soldiers fled
    That in submission will return to us;

V.v. s.d. **Retreat** trumpet signal to recall troops   **12 name** high rank

And then, as we have ta'en the sacrament,
We will unite the White Rose and the Red.
Smile heaven upon this fair conjunction,   20
That long have frowned upon their enmity!
What traitor hears me and says not amen?
England hath long been mad and scarred herself;
The brother blindly shed the brother's blood,
The father rashly slaughtered his own son,   25
The son, compelled, been butcher to the sire.
All this divided York and Lancaster,
Divided in their dire division,
O, now let Richmond and Elizabeth,
The true succeeders of each royal house,   30
By God's fair ordinance conjoin together!
And let their heirs, God, if thy will be so,
Enrich the time to come with smooth-faced peace,
With smiling plenty, and fair prosperous days!
Abate the edge of traitors, gracious Lord,   35
That would reduce these bloody days again
And make poor England weep in streams of blood!
Let them not live to taste this land's increase
That would with treason wound this fair land's
    peace!
Now civil wounds are stopped, peace lives again;   40
That she may long live here, God say amen!

                                        Exeunt.

FINIS

---

18 ta'en the sacrament taken a solemn oath (to marry Elizabeth when he won the crown)   20 conjunction joining in marriage   35 Abate the edge blunt the sharp point   36 reduce bring back

Textual Note

Richard III, one of Shakespeare's most popular plays, appeared in eight quarto editions, more than any other Shakespeare play except *Henry IV, Part 1*. The First Quarto (Q1) was entered for publication on October 20, 1597, as "The tragedie of kinge Richard the Third with the death of the Duke of Clarence." The actors of Shakespeare's company who reconstructed this text from memory left out over 200 lines and made many changes, but they preserved some lines omitted in the Folio, especially IV.ii.98–115. Printers added errors in each of the later quartos, dated 1598, 1602 (Q3), 1605, 1612, 1622 (Q6), 1629, and 1634.

The best text of the play appeared in 1623 in the First Folio (F). The printer, William Jaggard, had his compositors set up *Richard III* from a quarto marked with many corrections from an authentic manuscript. It used to be believed that this quarto was Q6, supplemented by an uncorrected quarto, Q3. In 1955, however, J. K. Walton, in *The Copy for the Folio Text of Richard III*, concluded that Q3, corrected, was the only quarto used for F. My collation of all variants in the first six quartos supports this conclusion. It is possible that both Q3 and Q6 were used, but that remains to be proved.

The present edition follows the readings of the First Folio except for the changes listed below. These changes have been made for definite reasons. First, the part of the Folio text containing III.i.1–168 seems to have been printed from Q3 without any correction from a manuscript, and the Folio text from V.iii.49 to the end of the play makes very few corrections. These few corrections have been accepted, but the rest of the text in these passages is based on Q1, from which Q3 and F are here derived. For example, the right reading "as" in III.i.123 appears in Q1, while "as, as," in F derives from the misprint "as as" in Q3. Second, the reading of Q1 is also

518

preferred, in any part of the play, to a different reading
which F merely reprints from Q 3. Third, the present text
accepts 30 lines from Q1 which are not in F. Finally,
I have corrected errors and have made a few emendations.

The divisions into acts and scenes include all those
in the Folio, translated from Latin, and these further
scenes as marked in modern editions: III.v-vii, IV.iii, and
V.iii.-v. Brackets set off these and other editorial additions.
Spelling, punctuation, and capitalization are modernized,
and speech prefixes are regularized. In the following list
of significant changes from the Folio, and from Q1 where
it is the basic text, the reading of the present text is given
in bold and the alternative reading of the Folio, or of
Q1 or Q 3, in roman.

I.i.26 **spy** [Q1] see   42s.d. **Clarence, guarded, and Brakenbury** Clarence, and
Brakenbury, guarded   45 **the** [Q1] th'   52 **for** [Q1] but   65 **tempers him to
this** [Q1] tempts him to this harsh   75 **to her for his** [Q1] for her   103 **I** [Q1] I
do   124 **the** [Q1] this [Q3]   133 **prey** [Q1] play   142 **What** [Q1] Where

I.ii.27 **life** death (cf. IV.i.75)   39 **stand** [Q1] Stand'st   60 **deed** [Q1]
Deeds   78 **a man** [Q1] man   80 **accuse** curse   154 **aspect** [Q1] Aspects
195 **was man** [Q1] man was [Q3]   201 **Richard** [Q1, not in F]   202 **Anne. To
take ... give** [Q1, not in F]   225 **Richard. Sirs ... corse** [Q1, not in F]   235 **at
all** [Q1] withall [Q3]

I.iii. s.d. **Queen** [Q1] the Queene Mother   17 **come the lords** [Q1] comes the
Lord   108 s.d. **Enter old Queen Margaret** [after 109]   113 **Tell ... said** [Q1,
not in F]   114 **avouch** [Q1] auouch't   308 **Queen Elizabeth** [Q1 Qu.] Mar.
341, 349, 354 **First Murderer** Vil.   354 s.d. **Exeunt** [Q1 after 353, not in F]

I.iv.13 **Thence** [Q1] There   86 **First Murderer** 2 Mur.   89 **Second Murderer** 1
122 **Faith** [Q1, not in F]   126 **Zounds** [Q1] Come   147 **Zounds** [Q1, not in
F]   192-93 **to have ... sins** [Q1] for any goodnesse   240 **And charged ...
other** [Q1, not in F]   266-70 **Which ... distress** [not in Q; F inserts after 259]

II.i.5 **in** [Q1] to   7 **Rivers and Hastings** [Q1] Dorset and Riuers   39 **God** [Q1]
heauen   40 **zeal** [Q1] loue   57 **unwittingly** [Q1] vnwillingly   59 **By** [Q1]
To   109 **at** [Q1] and

II.ii.1 **Boy** [Q1] Edw.   3 **do you** [Q1] do   47 **have** 1 [Q1] haue   83 **weep** [Q1]
weepes   84-85 **and so ... Edward weep** [Q1, not in F]   142, 154 **Ludlow** [Q1]
London   145 **Queen and Duchess of York. With all our hearts** [Q1, not in F]

II.iii.43 **Ensuing** [Q1] Pursuing (catchword "Ensuing")

II.iv.1 **hear** [Q1] heard [Q3]   21 **Archbishop** [Q1 Car.] Yor.   65 **death** [Q1]
earth

TEXTUAL NOTE

III.i. s.d. **with others** [F] &c [Q1]   9 **Nor** [Q1] No   40 **God in heaven** [Q1] God [Q3]   43 **deep** [Q1] great [Q3]   56 **ne'er** [F] neuer [Q1]   57 **o'errule** [F] ouerrule [Q1]   60 s.d. **Exit** [not in Q1; after 59 in Q3 and F]   63 **seems** [Q1] thinkst [Q3]   78 **all-ending** [Q1] ending [Q3]   79 **ne'er** neuer [Q1 F]   87 **this** [Q1] his [Q3]   94 s.d. **and Cardinal** [F] Cardinall [Q1]   96 **loving** [Q1] noble [Q3]   97 **dread** [Q1] deare [Q3]   120 **heavy** [Q1] weightie [Q3]   123 **as** [Q1] as as [Q3]   141 **needs will** [Q1] will [Q3]   145 **grandam** [F] Granam [Q1]   149 **with** [Q1] and with   150 s.d. **A sennet** [F, not in Q1] **Hastings** Hast. Dors [Q1] Hastings, and Dorset [F] **and Catesby** [F, not in Q1]   154 **parlous** perillous [Q1 F]   160 **knowest** [Q1] know'st   161 **thinkest** [Q1] think'st   167 **thinkest** [Q1] think'st   167 **What will he?** [Q1] Will not hee?

III.ii.110 s.d. **He whispers in his ear** [Q1] Priest. Ile wait vpon your Lordship [cf. line 121]

III.iv.78 s.d. **Exeunt** [after 77]   81 **rase** [Q1] rowse

III.v.4. **wert** [Q1] were   104 **Penker** Peuker   105 s.d. **Exeunt** Exit   109 s.d. **Exit** [Q1] Exeunt

III.vii.218 **Zounds, I'll** [Q1] we will   219 **Richard. O ... Buckingham** [Q1, not in F]   223 **stone** Stones   246 **cousin** [Q1] Cousins

IV.i. s.d. **Enter ... another door** Enter the Queene, Anne Duchesse of Gloucester, the Duchesse of Yorke, and Marquesse Dorset   103 **sorrow** Sorrowes

IV.ii.71 **there** [Q1] then   89 **Hereford** [Q1] Hertford   97 **Perhaps, perhaps** [Q1] perhaps   98–115 **Buckingham. My lord ... vein today** [Q1, not in F]

IV.iii.15 **once** [Q1] one   31 **at** [Q1] and

IV.iv.10 **unblown** [Q1] vnblowed   39 **Tell o'er ... mine** Tell ouer ... mine [Q1, not in F]   45 **holp'st** hop'st   52 **That excellent ... earth** [after 53]   64 **Thy** [Q1] The   118 **nights ... days** [Q1] night ... day [Q3]   128 **intestate** [Q1] intestine   141 **Where** [Q1] Where't   200 **moe** [Q1] more [Q3]   268 **would I** [Q1] I would [Q3]   274 **sometimes** [Q1] sometime [Q3]   284 **this is** [Q1] this   323 **loan** Loue   348 **wail** [Q1] vaile   364 **Harp ... past** [after 365]   377 **God ... God's** [Q1] Heuen ... Heanens (so misprinted)   392 **in** [Q1] with   396 **o'erpast** [Q1] repast   417 **peevish-fond** peeuish found   423 **I'll** I   430 s.d. **Exit Queen** [after 429]   431 s.d. **Enter Ratcliffe** [after "newes"]   444 **Ratcliffe** Catesby

IV.v.10 **Harfordwest** [Q1] Hertford-west [Q3]

V.i.11 **it is, my lord** [Q1] It is

V.ii.11 **center** [Q1] Centry

520

TEXTUAL NOTE

V.iii.28 **you** your   54 **sentinels** [F] centinell [Q1]   58 **Catesby** [Q1]
Ratcliffe   59 Catesby Rat. [Q1]   68 Saw'st thou [Q1] Saw'st
[Q1]   83 **loving** [Q1] noble [Q3]   90 **the** [Q1] th'   101 **sund'red** [F] sundried
[Q1]   105 **thoughts** [Q1] noise   108 s.d. **Manet Richmond** [F, not in Q1]
113 **The** [Q1] Th'   115 **the** [Q1] thy [Q3]   118 s.d. **Enter ... Sixth** [F] Enter the
ghost of young Prince Edward, sonne Harry the sixt, to Ri. [Q1]   126 **deadly holes**
[Q1] holes [Q3]   131 **thy sleep** [Q1] sleepe   132 **sit** [Q3] set [Q1]   139 s.d. **and
Vaughan** [F] Vaughan [Q1]   140 **Rivers** [Q3] King [Q1]   146 **Will** [Q3] Wel
[Q1]   146 s.d.–151 **Enter ... sake** [Q3; after line 159 in Q1]   146 s.d. **Hastings**
[Q1]   L. Hastings [Q3]   152 **Ghosts** [F] Ghost [Q1]   153 **lead** [Q1] laid
[Q3]   155 **souls bid** [Q1] soule bids   159 s.d. **Lady Anne** [Q1] Anne
162 **perturbations** [Q3] preturbations [Q1]   177 **falls** [Q1] fall   177 s.d. **starteth
up out of a dream** [Q1] starts out of his dreame   181 **now** [Q1] not [Q3]   184 **I
am I** [Q3] I and I [Q1]   197 **Perjury, perjury** [Q1] Periurie [Q3]   197 **highest**
[Q1] high'st   198 **direst** [Q1] dyr'st   200 **to the** [Q1] all to'th'   202 **will** [Q1]
shall [Q3]   203 **Nay** [F] And [Q1]   209 **Zounds, who is** [Q1] Who's   213–15
King Richard. O Ratcliffe ... my lord [Q1, not in F]   223 **see** [Q1] heare
[Q3]   223 s.d. **Exeunt Richard and Ratcliffe** [F] Exeunt [Q1]   223 s.d. **Enter ...
in his tent** [F] Enter the Lordes to Richmond [Q1]   224 **Lords** [Lo. Q1]
Richm.   233 **heart** [F] soule [Q1]   251 **foil** [Q1] soile [Q3]   256 **sweat** [Q1]
sweare [Q3]   271 s.d. **Ratcliffe, and** [Rat &c Q1] Ratcliffe, and Catesby   276 s.d.
The clock striketh [Q1] Clocke strikes   283 **not** [Q3] nor [Q1]   294 **drawn out
all** [Q1] drawne [Q3]   298 **this** [Q1] the [Q3]   302 **boot** [Q3] bootes
[Q1]   304 s.d. **He ... paper** [Q1, not in F]   308 **unto** [Q1] to   310 **Conscience
is but** [Q1] For Conscience is   313 **to it** [Q1] too't   314 s.d. **His ... Army**
[Q1, not in F]   320 **ventures** aduentures [Q1]   321 **to you** [Q1] you to [Q3]
323 **distrain** restraine [Q1]   336 **in** [Q1] on [Q3]   339 **Fight, gentlemen** [Q1]
Right Gentlemen [Q3]   339 **bold** [Q1] boldly [Q3]   342 s.d. **Enter a Messenger**
[F, not in Q1]   352 **helms** [Q1] helpes [Q3]   352 s.d. **Exeunt** [Q1, not in F]

V.iv.6 s.d. **Alarums.** [F, not in Q1]

V.v. s.d. **Retreat ... Lords** [F] then retrait being sounded. Enter Richmond, Darby,
bearing the crowne, with other Lords, &c [Q1]   4 **this ... royalty** [Q1] these ...
Royalties   7 **Wear it, enjoy it** [Q1] Weare it [Q3]   11 **if it please you, we may
now** [Q1] (if you please) we may   13 **Stanley** [Der. F, not in Q1]   32 **their** [Q1]
thy [Q3]   41 s.d. **Exeunt** [F, not in Q1]

WILLIAM
SHAKESPEARE

THE LIFE
AND DEATH
OF KING JOHN

Edited by William H. Matchett

[Dramatis Personae

KING JOHN
PRINCE HENRY, son to the King
ARTHUR, Duke of Brittany, nephew to the King
BIGOT
ESSEX
PEMBROKE } English Lords
SALISBURY
ROBERT FAULCONBRIDGE, son to Sir Robert Faulconbridge
PHILIP THE BASTARD, his half brother
HUBERT, a citizen of Angiers
JAMES GURNEY, servant to Lady Faulconbridge
PETER OF POMFRET, a prophet
PHILIP, King of France
LEWIS, the Dauphin (Dolphin)
LYMOGES, Duke of Austria
CARDINAL PANDULPH, the Pope's legate
COUNT MELUN (MELOONE), a French Lord
CHATILLION, ambassador from France
QUEEN ELINOR, mother to King John
CONSTANCE, mother to Arthur
BLANCH OF SPAIN, niece to King John
LADY FAULCONBRIDGE, widow to Sir Robert Faulconbridge
LORDS, SHERIFF, HERALDS, OFFICERS, SOLDIERS, EXECUTIONERS,
MESSENGERS, and other ATTENDANTS

Scene: England and France]

THE LIFE
AND DEATH
OF KING JOHN

ACT I

Scene I. [*England. King John's court.*]

*Enter King John, Queen Elinor, Pembroke, Essex, and
Salisbury, with Chatillion of France.*

KING JOHN Now say, Chatillion, what would France with us?

CHATILLION Thus, after greeting, speaks the King of
France
In my behavior to the majesty,
The borrowed majesty, of England here.

ELINOR A strange beginning: "borrowed majesty"!   5

KING JOHN Silence, good mother; hear the embassy.

CHATILLION Philip of France, in right and true behalf
Of thy deceasèd brother Geoffrey's son,
Arthur Plantagenet, lays most lawful claim
To this fair island and the territories: 10
To Ireland, Poictiers, Anjou, Touraine, Maine,

Footnotes are keyed to the text by line number. Text references are printed in
boldface type; the annotation follows in roman type.
I.i.3 In my behavior through me   **4 borrowed** usurped

Desiring thee to lay aside the sword
Which sways usurpingly these several titles,
And put the same into young Arthur's hand,
15   Thy nephew and right royal sovereign.

KING JOHN What follows if we disallow of this?

CHATILLION The proud control of fierce and bloody war,
To enforce these rights so forcibly withheld.

KING JOHN Here have we war for war and blood for blood,
20   Controlment for controlment: so answer France.

CHATILLION Then take my king's defiance from my mouth,
The farthest limit of my embassy.

KING JOHN Bear mine to him, and so depart in peace.
Be thou as lightning in the eyes of France,
25   For, ere thou canst report, I will be there:
The thunder of my cannon shall be heard.
So, hence! Be thou the trumpet of our wrath
And sullen presage of your own decay.
An honorable conduct let him have:
30   Pembroke, look to 't. Farewell, Chatillion.
                          Exit Chatillion and Pembroke.

ELINOR What now, my son! Have I not ever said
How that ambitious Constance would not cease
Till she had kindled France and all the world
Upon the right and party of her son?
35   This might have been prevented and made whole
With very easy arguments of love,
Which now the manage of two kingdoms must
With fearful bloody issue arbitrate.

---

16 **disallow of** deny 17 **proud control** resolute compulsion 20 **Controlment**
compulsion 22 **farthest limit of** most extreme measure permitted by
25 **report** (1) give an account (2) make a noise like a gun (cf. line 26 "thunder")
27 **trumpet** herald 28 **sullen presage ... decay** gloomy foreteller of your own
destruction 29 **conduct** escort 36 **arguments of love** (1) expressions of love
(2) friendly discussions (?) 37 **manage** government(s)

KING JOHN Our strong possession and our right for us.

ELINOR Your strong possession much more than your
    right,   40
  Or else it must go wrong with you and me;
  So much my conscience whispers in your ear,
  Which none but God, and you, and I, shall hear.

Enter a Sheriff.

ESSEX My liege, here is the strangest controversy,
  Come from the country to be judged by you,   45
  That e'er I heard. Shall I produce the men?

KING JOHN Let them approach.
  Our abbeys and our priories shall pay
  This expeditious charge.

Enter Robert Faulconbridge, and Philip
[his bastard brother].

What men are you?

BASTARD Your faithful subject, I, a gentleman,   50
  Born in Northamptonshire, and eldest son,
  As I suppose, to Robert Faulconbridge,
  A soldier, by the honor-giving hand
  Of Cordelion knighted in the field.

KING JOHN What art thou?   55

ROBERT The son and heir to that same Faulconbridge.

KING JOHN Is that the elder, and art thou the heir?
  You came not of one mother then, it seems.

BASTARD Most certain of one mother, mighty king;
  That is well known; and, as I think, one father: 60
  But for the certain knowledge of that truth
  I put you o'er to God and to my mother;
  Of that I doubt, as all men's children may.

---

49 **expeditious charge** (1) sudden expense (2) speedy attack 49 **What men**
who (of what name) 54 **Cordelion** *Coeur de lion* (Lion-hearted), i.e., King
Richard I, John's older brother 62 **put you o'er** refer you

ELINOR Out on thee, rude man! Thou dost shame thy
          mother,
65   And wound her honor with this diffidence.

BASTARD I, madam? No, I have no reason for it;
          That is my brother's plea and none of mine;
          The which if he can prove, 'a pops me out
          At least from fair five hundred pound a year.
70   Heaven guard my mother's honor and my land!

KING JOHN A good blunt fellow. Why, being younger
            born,
          Doth he lay claim to thine inheritance?

BASTARD I know not why, except to get the land.
          But once he slandered me with bastardy.
75   But whe'r I be as true begot or no,
          That still I lay upon my mother's head;
          But that I am as well begot, my liege –
          Fair fall the bones that took the pains for me –
          Compare our faces and be judge yourself.
80   If old Sir Robert did beget us both,
          And were our father, and this son like him,
          O old Sir Robert, father, on my knee
          I give heaven thanks I was not like to thee!

KING JOHN Why, what a madcap hath heaven lent us
            here!

85   ELINOR He hath a trick of Cordelion's face;
          The accent of his tongue affecteth him:
          Do you not read some tokens of my son
          In the large composition of this man?

KING JOHN Mine eye hath well examinèd his parts,
90   And finds them perfect Richard. Sirrah, speak,
          What doth move you to claim your brother's land?

65 **diffidence** mistrust 68 **'a** he 75 **whe'r** whether 76 **lay upon my
mother's head** leave up to my mother 78 **Fair fall** may good befall 85 **trick**
distinctive trait 86 **affecteth** tends towards, resembles 88 **large composition**
(1) large size (2) general features 91 **you** Robert (John shows his partiality for
the Bastard by the shift of pronoun—cf. line 55—and by his use of the slightly
contemptuous "Sirrah")

528

BASTARD Because he hath a half-face like my father!
  With half that face would he have all my land—
  A half-faced groat five hundred pound a year!

ROBERT My gracious liege, when that my father lived,   95
  Your brother did employ my father much—

BASTARD Well sir, by this you cannot get my land:
  Your tale must be how he employed my mother.

ROBERT And once dispatched him in an embassy
  To Germany, there with the emperor   100
  To treat of high affairs touching that time.
  Th' advantage of his absence took the King,
  And in the mean time sojourned at my father's,
  Where how he did prevail I shame to speak—
  But truth is truth: large lengths of seas and shores   105
  Between my father and my mother lay,
  As I have heard my father speak himself,
  When this same lusty gentleman was got.
  Upon his deathbed he by will bequeathed
  His lands to me, and took it on his death   110
  That this my mother's son was none of his;
  And if he were, he came into the world
  Full fourteen weeks before the course of time.
  Then, good my liege, let me have what is mine,
  My father's land, as was my father's will.   115

KING JOHN Sirrah, your brother is legitimate.
  Your father's wife did after wedlock bear him;
  And if she did play false, the fault was hers;
  Which fault lies on the hazards of all husbands
  That marry wives. Tell me, how if my brother,   120
  Who, as you say, took pains to get this son,
  Had of your father claimed this son for his?
  In sooth, good friend, your father might have kept

92 half-face (1) profile (2) imperfect or emaciated face 93 With half that face (1) with a face like that (2) with such impudence 94 half-faced groat (1) small silver coin with a profile stamped on it (2) imperfect or clipped coin 99 dispatched (1) sent (2) disposed of 108 lusty merry got conceived 110 took it on his death swore at the peril of his soul 112 And if if (a frequent Elizabethan usage) 119 lies on is among

This calf, bred from his cow, from all the world.
125 In sooth he might; then, if he were my brother's,
My brother might not claim him, nor your father,
Being none of his, refuse him: this concludes.
My mother's son did get your father's heir;
Your father's heir must have your father's land.

130 ROBERT Shall then my father's will be of no force
To dispossess that child which is not his?

BASTARD Of no more force to dispossess me, sir,
Than was his will to get me, as I think.

ELINOR Whether hadst thou rather be, a Faulconbridge,
135 And like thy brother, to enjoy thy land,
Or the reputed son of Cordelion,
Lord of thy presence and no land beside?

BASTARD Madam, and if my brother had my shape
And I had his, Sir Robert's his, like him,
140 And if my legs were two such riding-rods,
My arms such eel-skins stuffed, my face so thin
That in mine ear I durst not stick a rose
Lest men should say, "Look, where three-farthings
goes!"
And, to his shape, were heir to all this land,
145 Would I might never stir from off this place,
I would give it every foot to have this face:
I would not be Sir Nob in any case.

ELINOR I like thee well: wilt thou forsake thy fortune,

127 **concludes** is decisive 134 **Whether hadst thou** which would you
135 **like thy brother** resembling Robert (in physique and character) 137 **Lord
of thy presence** master of your own physique and character 139 **Sir Robert's
his** Sir Robert's (a double genitive) 140 **riding-rods** switches for horses
143 **three-farthings** (the smallest of a number of coins which were distinguished
from coins of similar sizes by the presence of a rose behind the ear in Queen
Elizabeth's portrait) 144 **to** in addition to 147 **Nob** nickname for Robert (?—
perhaps with puns on "head" and "knob," continuing mockery of his brother's
appearance) 147 **in any case** (1) under any circumstances (2) in any covering
(clothing, body)

Bequeath thy land to him, and follow me?
I am a soldier and now bound to France.   150

BASTARD Brother, take you my land, I'll take my
    chance.
Your face hath got five hundred pound a year,
Yet sell your face for five pence and 'tis dear.
Madam, I'll follow you unto the death.

ELINOR Nay, I would have you go before me thither.   155

BASTARD Our country manners give our betters way.

KING JOHN What is thy name?

BASTARD Philip, my liege, so is my name begun—
Philip, good old Sir Robert's wife's eldest son.

KING JOHN From henceforth bear his name whose
    form thou bearest: 160
Kneel thou down Philip, but rise more great,
Arise Sir Richard, and Plantagenet.

BASTARD Brother by th' mother's side, give me your
    hand:
My father gave me honor, yours gave land.
Now blessèd be the hour, by night or day,   165
When I was got, Sir Robert was away!

ELINOR The very spirit of Plantagenet!
I am thy grandam, Richard; call me so.

BASTARD Madam, by chance but not by truth; what
    though?
Something about, a little from the right,   170
In at the window, or else o'er the hatch:
Who dares not stir by day must walk by night,
And have is have, however men do catch.
Near or far off, well won is still well shot,
And I am I, howe'er I was begot.   175

149 **Bequeath** legally transfer (immediately; his death is not implied)
162 **Plantagenet** (surname of the royal family) 165 **hour** (1) hour (2) whore
(then identically pronounced) 169 **truth** virtue 170 **Something about** a bit
off course 171-74 **In at the window … well shot** (all proverbial expressions)

KING JOHN Go, Faulconbridge. Now hast thou thy
            desire:
          A landless knight makes thee a landed squire.
          Come, madam, and come, Richard, we must speed
          For France, for France, for it is more than need.

180 BASTARD Brother, adieu: good fortune come to thee!
              For thou wast got i' th' way of honesty.
                                    Exeunt all but Bastard.

          A foot of honor better than I was,
          But many a many foot of land the worse.
          Well, now can I make any Joan a lady.
185   "Good den, Sir Richard!"—"God-a-mercy, fellow"—
          And if his name be George, I'll call him Peter,
          For new-made honor doth forget men's names:
          'Tis too respective and too sociable
          For your conversion. Now your traveler,
190   He and his toothpick at my worship's mess,
          And when my knightly stomach is sufficed,
          Why then I suck my teeth and catechize
          My pickèd man of countries: "My dear sir"—
          Thus, leaning on mine elbow, I begin—
195   "I shall beseech you"—that is Question now;
          And then comes Answer like an Absey-book:
          "O, sir," says Answer, "at your best command,
          At your employment, at your service, sir";
          "No, sir," says Question, "I, sweet sir, at yours";
200   And so, ere Answer knows what Question would,
          Saving in dialogue of compliment,
          And talking of the Alps and Apennines,

177 **A landless knight makes** (1) the Bastard makes (2) making the Bastard
landless makes   184 **Joan** common girl   185 **Good den, God-a-mercy** (usual
greetings, elisions of "God give you good evening" and "God have mercy on
you")   185 **fellow** (used for one of lower rank)   188–89 **'Tis too respective ...
conversion** it (remembering names) is too respectful and too amiable for my
change in rank ("your" is general and vague: any conversion)   190 **Toothpick**
(an un-English affectation)   190 **mess** dinner table   192 **suck my teeth** (scorning a toothpick)   193 **pickèd** (1) affected (2) with his teeth picked   196 **Absey-
book** A B C book, a child's question-and-answer primer

The Pyrenean and the river Po,
It draws toward supper in conclusion so.
But this is worshipful society, 205
And fits the mounting spirit like myself;
For he is but a bastard to the time
That doth not smack of observation.
And so am I, whether I smack or no:
And not alone in habit and device, 210
Exterior form, outward accoutrement,
But from the inward motion to deliver
Sweet, sweet, sweet poison for the age's tooth,
Which, though I will not practice to deceive,
Yet, to avoid deceit, I mean to learn; 215
For it shall strew the footsteps of my rising.
But who comes in such haste in riding-robes?
What woman-post is this? Hath she no husband
That will take pains to blow a horn before her?

Enter Lady Faulconbridge and James Gurney.

O me! 'Tis my mother. How now, good lady! 220
What brings you here to court so hastily?

LADY FAULCONBRIDGE Where is that slave, thy brother?
    Where is he,
That holds in chase mine honor up and down?

BASTARD My brother Robert? Old Sir Robert's son?
Colbrand the giant, that same mighty man? 225
Is it Sir Robert's son that you seek so?

207 **but a bastard to the time** not a true child of his time 208 **observation** (1) paying attention (2) obsequiousness 210 **habit and device** dress and emblem (the heraldic symbol of his shield will be crossed by a black band, the "bar sinister" denoting a bastard) 212 **motion** incitement, intention 213 **sweet poison** flattery 215 **deceit** deception (i.e. being deceived) 216 **it shall strew ... rising** flattery will be thrown before me as I rise just as flowers are thrown to welcome a great man 218 **woman-post** female messenger 219 **blow a horn before her** (1) clear the way for her (as a herald announced an important arrival, or as the speeding post blew his post horn) (2) announce her adultery (the cuckold was said to wear horns) 223 **holds in chase** pursues (as a huntsman) 225 **Colbrand the giant** (Guy of Warwick's final opponent in the popular old romances)

LADY FAULCONBRIDGE Sir Robert's son? Aye, thou
    unreverend boy,
        Sir Robert's son! Why scorn'st thou at Sir Robert?
        He is Sir Robert's son, and so art thou.

230 BASTARD James Gurney, wilt thou give us leave awhile?

GURNEY Good leave, good Philip.

BASTARD   Philip, sparrow! James,
        There's toys abroad; anon I'll tell thee more.
                                        Exit James.
        Madam, I was not old Sir Robert's son.
        Sir Robert might have eat his part in me
235   Upon Good Friday and ne'er broke his fast:
        Sir Robert could do well—marry, to confess—
        Could he get me! Sir Robert could not do it.
        We know his handiwork: therefore, good mother,
        To whom am I beholding for these limbs?
240   Sir Robert never holp to make this leg.

LADY FAULCONBRIDGE Hast thou conspirèd with thy
    brother too,
        That for thine own gain shouldst defend mine
            honor?
        What means this scorn, thou most untoward
            knave?

BASTARD Knight, knight, good mother, Basilisco-like.
245   What! I am dubbed; I have it on my shoulder.
        But, mother, I am not Sir Robert's son;
        I have disclaimed Sir Robert and my land;
        Legitimation, name, and all is gone.
        Then, good my mother, let me know my father;
250   Some proper man I hope: who was it, mother?

231 **Good leave** willingly   231 **Philip, sparrow!** (Philip, a common name for a
pet sparrow, is too paltry for the newly knighted Bastard)   232 **toys** trifling gifts,
i.e., knighthoods, or rumors (?)   236 **marry, to confess** indeed, to speak the
truth   240 **holp** helped   240 **to make this leg** (1) to form a leg like mine (2) to
give me courtly manners like this ("to make a leg" is to bow; the Bastard must
bow, perhaps ironically, as he requests her answer)   243 **untoward** perverse,
ill-mannered   244 **Basilisco** (a bragging knight in an earlier play, *Soliman and
Perseda*)   250 **proper** handsome, respectable

LADY FAULCONBRIDGE Hast thou denied thyself a
    Faulconbridge?

BASTARD As faithfully as I deny the devil.

LADY FAULCONBRIDGE King Richard Cordelion was thy
    father.
  By long and vehement suit I was seduced
  To make room for him in my husband's bed.   255
  Heaven lay not my transgression to my charge,
  That art the issue of my dear offense,
  Which was so strongly urged past my defense.

BASTARD Now, by this light, were I to get again,
  Madam, I would not wish a better father.   260
  Some sins do bear their privilege on earth,
  And so doth yours: your fault was not your folly.
  Needs must you lay your heart at his dispose,
  Subjected tribute to commanding love,
  Against whose fury and unmatchèd force   265
  The aweless lion could not wage the fight,
  Nor keep his princely heart from Richard's hand.
  He that perforce robs lions of their hearts
  May easily win a woman's. Ay, my mother,
  With all my heart I thank thee for my father!   270
  Who lives and dares but say thou didst not well
  When I was got, I'll send his soul to hell.
  Come, lady, I will show thee to my kin,
  And they shall say, when Richard me begot,
  If thou hadst said him nay, it had been sin.   275
  Who says it was, he lies; I say 'twas not!   *Exeunt.*

---

257 **That art** thou that art   259 **get** be conceived   261 **bear their privilege**
carry their immunity (because of their good results?)   264 **Subjected tribute**
tribute required of a vassal   266-67 **The aweless lion ... Richard's hand** (the
legend was that Richard's epithet came from his having eaten the heart he tore out
by reaching, bare-handed, down the throat of a living lion)   270 **for my father**
(1) on behalf of my father (2) for the father you have given me   276 **not** (1) not
(2) naught, i.e., nothing (3) naught, i.e., wickedness (sexual immorality; cf. *Richard
III* I.i.97–100)

ACT II

Scene I. [*France.*]

Enter before [the gate of] Angiers, King Philip of
France, Lewis the Dauphin, Constance, Arthur, and their
Attendants and, from the other side, Austria and his
Attendants.

KING PHILIP Before Angiers well met, brave Austria.
Arthur, that great forerunner of thy blood,
Richard, that robbed the lion of his heart
And fought the holy wars in Palestine,
5 By this brave duke came early to his grave;
And for amends to his posterity,
At our importance hither is he come
To spread his colors, boy, in thy behalf,
And to rebuke the usurpation
10 Of thy unnatural uncle, English John:
Embrace him, love him, give him welcome hither.

ARTHUR God shall forgive you Cordelion's death
The rather that you give his offspring life,

II.i.2 **forerunner of thy blood** predecessor in your line (Arthur was Richard's
nephew) 5 **this brave duke** Austria (that Austria killed Richard is not historical,
but see note to III.i.40) 7 **importance** importunity 8 **spread his colors**
unfurl his battle flags

536

Shadowing their right under your wings of war.
I give you welcome with a powerless hand,   15
But with a heart full of unstainèd love:
Welcome before the gates of Angiers, Duke.

LEWIS Ah, noble boy, who would not do thee right?

AUSTRIA Upon thy cheek lay I this zealous kiss,
As seal to this indenture of my love: 20
That to my home I will no more return
Till Angiers, and the right thou hast in France,
Together with that pale, that white-faced shore,
Whose foot spurns back the ocean's roaring tides
And coops from other lands her islanders,   25
Even till that England, hedged in with the main,
That water-wallèd bulwark, still secure
And confident from foreign purposes,
Even till that utmost corner of the west
Salute thee for her king; till then, fair boy,   30
Will I not think of home, but follow arms.

CONSTANCE O take his mother's thanks, a widow's
    thanks,
Till your strong hand shall help to give him strength
To make a more requital to your love.

AUSTRIA The peace of heaven is theirs that lift their
    swords   35
In such a just and charitable war.

KING PHILIP Well then, to work: our cannon shall be
    bent
Against the brows of this resisting town.
Call for our chiefest men of discipline,
To cull the plots of best advantages.   40

---

14 **Shadowing** sheltering 20 **indenture** sealed agreement 23 **that pale, that white-faced shore** (reference to the chalk cliffs on England's southern coast; a "pale" is also a limited territory) 25 **coops** encloses for protection 27 **still** always 34 **a more requital** to a larger recompense for 37 **bent** aimed (as is a bow) 39 **discipline** military training 40 **To cull ... advantages** to choose the best location (for the cannons)

We'll lay before this town our royal bones,
Wade to the marketplace in Frenchmen's blood:
But we will make it subject to this boy.

CONSTANCE Stay for an answer to your embassy,
45   Lest unadvised you stain your swords with blood.
My Lord Chatillion may from England bring
That right in peace which here we urge in war,
And then we shall repent each drop of blood
That hot rash haste so indirectly shed.

Enter Chatillion.

50   KING PHILIP A wonder, lady! Lo, upon thy wish,
Our messenger Chatillion is arrived!
What England says, say briefly, gentle lord;
We coldly pause for thee; Chatillion, speak.

CHATILLION Then turn your forces from this paltry siege
55   And stir them up against a mightier task:
England, impatient of your just demands,
Hath put himself in arms; the adverse winds,
Whose leisure I have stayed, have given him time
To land his legions all as soon as I;
60   His marches are expedient to this town,
His forces strong, his soldiers confident.
With him along is come the mother-queen,
An Ate, stirring him to blood and strife;
With her her niece, the Lady Blanch of Spain;
65   With them a bastard of the king's deceased;
And all th' unsettled humors of the land,
Rash, inconsiderate, fiery voluntaries,
With ladies' faces and fierce dragons' spleens,
Have sold their fortunes at their native homes,
70   Bearing their birthrights proudly on their backs,

---

49 **indirectly** wrongly 60 **expedient** speedy 63 **Ate** goddess of vengeance
65 **of the king's deceased** of the deceased king 66 **unsettled humors** unsteady
rabble ("humors" were bodily fluids, the balance of which supposedly determined
a man's disposition) 67 **voluntaries** volunteers 68 **spleens** (the spleen was
considered the location of the emotions) 70 **Bearing ... backs,** i.e., having
invested their patrimonies in armor

To make a hazard of new fortunes here.
In brief, a braver choice of dauntless spirits
Than now the English bottoms have waft o'er
Did never float upon the swelling tide,
To do offense and scathe in Christendom.   75

Drum beats.

The interruption of their churlish drums
Cuts off more circumstance: they are at hand,
To parley or to fight; therefore prepare.

KING PHILIP How much unlooked for is this expedition!

AUSTRIA By how much unexpected, by so much   80
We must awake endeavor for defense,
For courage mounteth with occasion:
Let them be welcome then; we are prepared.

*Enter King [John] of England, Bastard, Queen
[Elinor], Blanch, Pembroke, and others.*

KING JOHN Peace be to France, if France in peace
permit
Our just and lineal entrance to our own;   85
If not, bleed France, and peace ascend to heaven,
Whiles we, God's wrathful agent, do correct
Their proud contempt that beats His peace to heaven.

KING PHILIP Peace be to England, if that war return
From France to England, there to live in peace.   90
England we love, and for that England's sake
With burden of our armor here we sweat.
This toil of ours should be a work of thine,
But thou from loving England art so far
That thou hast underwrought his lawful king,   95
Cut off the sequence of posterity,
Outfacèd infant state, and done a rape
Upon the maiden virtue of the crown.
Look here upon thy brother Geoffrey's face:

71 **make a hazard of** take a chance on winning 73 **bottoms** ships
77 **circumstance** detailed information 79 **expedition** speed 85 **lineal**
inherited 87 **correct** chastise 95 **underwrought** undermined 97 **Outfacèd
infant state** arrogantly defiled the child king

100   These eyes, these brows, were molded out of his;
      This little abstract doth contain that large
      Which died in Geoffrey, and the hand of time
      Shall draw this brief into as huge a volume.
      That Geoffrey was thy elder brother born,
105   And this his son; England was Geoffrey's right
      And this is Geoffrey's in the name of God.
      How comes it then that thou art called a king,
      When living blood doth in these temples beat,
      Which owe the crown that thou o'ermasterest?

      KING JOHN From whom hast thou this great commis-
110   sion, France,
      To draw my answer from thy articles?

      KING PHILIP From that supernal judge that stirs good
         thoughts
      In any breast of strong authority
      To look into the blots and stains of right;
115   That judge hath made me guardian to this boy,
      Under whose warrant I impeach thy wrong
      And by whose help I mean to chastise it.

      KING JOHN Alack, thou dost usurp authority.

      KING PHILIP Excuse it is to beat usurping down.

120   ELINOR Who is it thou dost call usurper, France?

      CONSTANCE Let me make answer: thy usurping son.

      ELINOR Out, insolent! Thy bastard shall be king
      That thou mayst be a queen and check the world!

      CONSTANCE My bed was ever to thy son as true
125   As thine was to thy husband, and this boy
      Liker in feature to his father Geoffrey
      Than thou and John in manners, being as like
      As rain to water, or devil to his dam.

---

101 **abstract** summary, abridgment (cf. "brief" and "volume" in line 103)
106 **this** (possibly the English crown, which John is wearing, the city of Angiers,
or Arthur himself)   109 **owe** own   111 **To draw ... articles** to compel me to
answer your accusations   123 **queen** (1) queen (2) quean = whore (3) queen in
chess (cf. "check")

My boy a bastard! Be my soul I think
His father never was so true begot: 130
It cannot be and if thou wert his mother.

ELINOR There's a good mother, boy, that blots thy
father.

CONSTANCE There's a good grandam, boy, that would
blot thee.

AUSTRIA Peace!

BASTARD   Hear the crier.

AUSTRIA   What the devil art thou?

BASTARD One that will play the devil, sir, with you,   135
And 'a may catch your hide and you alone:
You are the hare of whom the proverb goes,
Whose valor plucks dead lions by the beard.
I'll smoke your skin-coat, and I catch you right;
Sirrah, look to 't; i' faith, I will, i' faith.   140

BLANCH O well did he become that lion's robe,
That did disrobe the lion of that robe!

BASTARD It lies as sightly on the back of him
As great Alcides' shoes upon an ass.
But, ass, I'll take that burden from your back,   145
Or lay on that shall make your shoulders crack.

AUSTRIA What cracker is this same that deafs our ears
With this abundance of superfluous breath?
King Philip, determine what we shall do straight.

KING PHILIP Women and fools, break off your   150
conference.
King John, this is the very sum of all:

---

134 **crier** law-court official who called for silence   136 **And 'a** if he   136 **hide**
Richard's lion-skin, which Austria is wearing   139 **smoke** (1) disinfect (2) beat
143 **sightly** handsomely   144 **Alcides' shoes upon an ass** (1) Hercules' shoes
(proverbial) on an ass (2) Hercules appears (Folio's "shooes" may also=shows)
mounted on an ass (3) Hercules' lion-skin (he wore the skin of the Nemean lion
which he had killed) appears on an ass   147 **cracker** (1) braggart (2) firecracker

    England and Ireland, Anjou, Touraine, Maine,
    In right of Arthur do I claim of thee:
    Wilt thou resign them and lay down thy arms?

155 KING JOHN My life as soon! I do defy thee, France.
    Arthur of Britain, yield thee to my hand,
    And out of my dear love I'll give thee more
    Than e'er the coward hand of France can win;
    Submit thee, boy.

    ELINOR   Come to thy grandam, child.

160 CONSTANCE Do, child, go to it grandam, child;
    Give grandam kingdom, and it grandam will
    Give it a plum, a cherry, and a fig;
    There's a good grandam.

    ARTHUR   Good my mother, peace!
    I would that I were low laid in my grave.
165 I am not worth this coil that's made for me.

    ELINOR His mother shames him so, poor boy, he
      weeps.

    CONSTANCE Now shame upon you, whe'r she does
      or no!
    His grandam's wrongs, and not his mother's shames,
    Draws those heaven-moving pearls from his poor
      eyes,
170 Which heaven shall take in nature of a fee:
    Ay, with these crystal beads heaven shall be bribed
    To do him justice and revenge on you.

    ELINOR Thou monstrous slanderer of heaven and
      earth!

    CONSTANCE Thou monstrous injurer of heaven and
      earth!
175 Call not me slanderer; thou and thine usurp

156 **Britain** Brittany 160-63 **Do, child ... grandam** (baby talk) 165 **coil**
fuss 169 **Draws** draw (it is not unusual for a plural subject to have a verb in
-*s*) 170 **in nature of** in place of, as though it were 171 **with these ... bribed**
i.e., these crystal beads—pearls, tears—will bribe heaven both as precious gems
and as prayer beads

The dominations, royalties, and rights
Of this oppressèd boy: this is thy eldest son's son,
Infortunate in nothing but in thee:
Thy sins are visited in this poor child;
The canon of the law is laid on him, 180
Being but the second generation
Removèd from thy sin-conceiving womb.

KING JOHN Bedlam, have done.

CONSTANCE   I have but this to say,
That he is not only plaguèd for her sin,
But God hath made her sin and her the plague 185
On this removèd issue, plagued for her
And with her plague; her sin his injury,
Her injury the beadle to her sin,
All punished in the person of this child,
And all for her; a plague upon her! 190

ELINOR Thou unadvisèd scold, I can produce
A will that bars the title of thy son.

CONSTANCE Aye, who doubts that? A will! A wicked
will;
A woman's will; a cankered grandam's will!

KING PHILIP Peace, lady! Pause, or be more temperate: 195
It ill beseems this presence to cry aim
To these ill-tunèd repetitions.
Some trumpet summon hither to the walls
These men of Angiers. Let us hear them speak
Whose title they admit, Arthur's or John's. 200
                              Trumpet sounds.

176 dominations dominions   177 eldest son's son oldest grandson (*not* oldest-son's son)   179 visited punished   180 canon of the law i.e., Exodus 20:5   183 Bedlam lunatic   185 her sin John (?)   185 the plague (the great plagues were commonly explained as punishment for a sinful nation—Elinor is both the cause of Arthur's punishment and that punishment itself)   186 this removèd issue this remote descendant, i.e., Arthur   188 beadle parish official who whipped sinners   192 A will (Richard's will named John his heir; Shakespeare plays this down to present John as a usurper)   194 A woman's will (Constance suggests that Elinor wrote the will, and women's wills were not legal)   196 presence royal assembly   196-97 cry aim/To encourage

Enter Hubert upon the walls.

HUBERT Who is it that hath warned us to the walls?

KING PHILIP 'Tis France, for England.

KING JOHN   England for itself.
　　You men of Angiers, and my loving subjects—

KING PHILIP You loving men of Angiers, Arthur's
　　subjects,
205　Our trumpet called you to this gentle parle—

KING JOHN For our advantage; therefore hear us first:
　　These flags of France, that are advancèd here
　　Before the eye and prospect of your town,
　　Have hither marched to your endamagement.
210　The cannons have their bowels full of wrath,
　　And ready mounted are they to spit forth
　　Their iron indignation 'gainst your walls.
　　All preparation for a bloody siege
　　And merciless proceeding by these French
215　Confronts your city's eyes, your winking gates,
　　And but for our approach those sleeping stones,
　　That as a waist doth girdle you about,
　　By the compulsion of their ordinance
　　By this time from their fixèd beds of lime
220　Had been dishabited, and wide havoc made
　　For bloody power to rush upon your peace.
　　But on the sight of us your lawful king,
　　Who painfully with much expedient march
　　Have brought a countercheck before your gates,
225　To save unscratched your city's threatened cheeks,
　　Behold, the French, amazed, vouchsafe a parle;
　　And now, instead of bullets wrapped in fire,
　　To make a shaking fever in your walls,
　　They shoot but calm words folded up in smoke,
230　To make a faithless error in your ears;
　　Which trust accordingly, kind citizens,

201 **warned** summoned 205 **parle** parley 207 **advancèd** raised 215 **winking** able to open and shut (the gates are like eyelids) 217 **waist** belt or sash
218 **ordinance** cannons 220 **dishabited** disinhabited, dislodged 230 **faithless error** treacherous lie

And let us in, your king, whose labored spirits,
Forwearied in this action of swift speed,
Craves harborage within your city walls.

KING PHILIP When I have said, make answer to us
    both.   235
Lo, in this right hand, whose protection
Is most divinely vowed upon the right
Of him it holds, stands young Plantagenet,
Son to the elder brother of this man,
And king o'er him and all that he enjoys: 240
For this downtrodden equity we tread
In warlike march these greens before your town,
Being no further enemy to you
Than the constraint of hospitable zeal
In the relief of this oppressèd child   245
Religiously provokes. Be pleasèd then
To pay that duty which you truly owe
To him that owes it, namely this young prince;
And then our arms, like to a muzzled bear,
Save in aspect, hath all offense sealed up: 250
Our cannons' malice vainly shall be spent
Against th' invulnerable clouds of heaven,
And with a blessèd and unvexed retire,
With unhacked swords and helmets all unbruised,
We will bear home that lusty blood again   255
Which here we came to spout against your town,
And leave your children, wives, and you in peace.
But if you fondly pass our proffered offer,
'Tis not the roundure of your old-faced walls
Can hide you from our messengers of war,   260
Though all these English and their discipline
Were harbored in their rude circumference.
Then tell us, shall your city call us lord,

232 labored overworked 233 Forwearied tired out 235 said finished speaking
241 equity right 244 the constraint of hospitable zeal the obligations of
generous resolution 248 owes owns 250 hath will have 253 unvexed retire
orderly departure 258 fondly pass foolishly disregard 259 roundure
roundness 259 old-faced walls walls so well built they had not required
refacing 263 us i.e., King Philip (England, with Arthur as king, would be
subordinate to France)

In that behalf which we have challenged it?
265 Or shall we give the signal to our rage
And stalk in blood to our possession?

HUBERT In brief, we are the King of England's
subjects:
For him, and in his right, we hold this town.

KING JOHN Acknowledge then the King, and let me in.

HUBERT That can we not; but he that proves the
270 King,
To him will we prove loyal: till that time
Have we rammed up our gates against the world.

KING JOHN Doth not the crown of England prove the
King?
And if not that, I bring you witnesses,
275 Twice fifteen thousand hearts of England's breed—

BASTARD Bastards, and else.

KING JOHN To verify our title with their lives.

KING PHILIP As many and as well-born bloods as
those—

BASTARD Some bastards, too.

280 KING PHILIP Stand in his face to contradict his claim.

HUBERT Till you compound whose right is worthiest,
We for the worthiest hold the right from both.

KING JOHN Then God forgive the sin of all those souls
That to their everlasting residence,
285 Before the dew of evening fall, shall fleet,
In dreadful trial of our kingdom's king!

KING PHILIP Amen, amen! Mount, chevaliers! To
arms!

---

264 In that behalf which on behalf of him for whom 270 proves proves to
be 272 rammed up barricaded 276 else others 278 bloods (1) men of
courage (2) men of good family 281 compound settle 285 fleet pass away, fly

BASTARD Saint George, that swinged the dragon, and
    e'er since
  Sits on's horseback at mine hostess' door,
  Teach us some fence! [*To Austria*] Sirrah, were I
    at home   290
  At your den, sirrah, with your lioness,
  I would set an ox head to your lion's hide,
  And make a monster of you.

AUSTRIA   Peace! No more.

BASTARD O tremble, for you hear the lion roar.

KING JOHN Up higher to the plain, where we'll set
    forth   295
  In best appointment all our regiments.

BASTARD Speed then, to take advantage of the field.

KING PHILIP It shall be so; and at the other hill
  Command the rest to stand. God, and our right!
                                     Exeunt.

   *Here, after excursions, enter the Herald of France
          with Trumpets, to the gates.*

FRENCH HERALD You men of Angiers, open wide your
    gates,   300
  And let young Arthur, Duke of Britain, in,
  Who by the hand of France this day hath made
  Much work for tears in many an English mother,
  Whose sons lie scattered on the bleeding ground:
  Many a widow's husband groveling lies,   305
  Coldly embracing the discolored earth,
  And victory with little loss doth play
  Upon the dancing banners of the French,
  Who are at hand, triumphantly displayed,
  To enter conquerors and to proclaim   310
  Arthur of Britain England's king, and yours.

288 **swinged** beat   289 **Sits ... hostess' door** i.e., painted on an inn sign
290 **fence** skill with the sword   293 **monster** (1) ox-headed lion (2) cuckold
299 s.d. **excursions** sallies, raids (in the theater, stage-crossings and clashes to
represent a battle)   309 **displayed** spread out (for a parade, not for a battle)

Enter English Herald, with Trumpet.

ENGLISH HERALD Rejoice, you men of Angiers, ring
    your bells:
    King John, your king and England's, doth approach.
    Commander of this hot malicious day.
315   Their armors, that marched hence so silver-bright,
    Hither return all gilt with Frenchmen's blood;
    There stuck no plume in any English crest
    That is removèd by a staff of France.
    Our colors do return in those same hands
320   That did display them when we first marched forth,
    And, like a jolly troop of huntsmen, come
    Our lusty English, all with purpled hands,
    Dyed in the dying slaughter of their foes.
    Open your gates and give the victors way.

325 HUBERT Heralds, from off our tow'rs we might behold,
    From first to last, the onset and retire
    Of both your armies, whose equality
    By our best eyes cannot be censurèd.
    Blood hath bought blood, and blows have answered
       blows,
    Strength matched with strength, and power con-
330   fronted power.
    Both are alike, and both alike we like:
    One must prove greatest. While they weigh so even,
    We hold our town for neither, yet for both.

Enter the two Kings, with their powers,
at several doors.

KING JOHN France, hast thou yet more blood to cast
    away?
335   Say, shall the current of our right roam on?
    Whose passage, vexed with thy impediment,

316 **gilt** gilded, i.e., reddened (gold was considered red, as in "his golden blood," *Macbeth* II.iii.114) 318 **staff** spear, lance 323 **Dyed in the dying slaughter** hunters customarily dipped their hands in the deer's blood, cf. *Julius Caesar* III.i.106 ff.) 326 **retire** withdrawal 328 **censurèd** judged 333 s.d. **several** separate

Shall leave his native channel and o'erswell,
With course disturbed, even thy confining shores,
Unless thou let his silver water keep
A peaceful progress to the ocean.   340

KING PHILIP England, thou hast not saved one drop of
      blood.
   In this hot trial more than we of France;
   Rather, lost more. And by this hand I swear,
   That sways the earth this climate overlooks,
   Before we will lay down our just-borne arms,   345
   We'll put thee down, 'gainst whom these arms we
      bear,
   Or add a royal number to the dead,
   Gracing the scroll that tells of this war's loss.
   With slaughter coupled to the name of kings.

BASTARD Ha, majesty! How high thy glory tow'rs   350
   When the rich blood of kings is set on fire!
   O now doth death line his dead chaps with steel;
   The swords of soldiers are his teeth, his fangs;
   And now he feasts, mousing the flesh of men
   In undetermined differences of kings.   355
   Why stand these royal fronts amazèd thus?
   Cry "Havoc!" kings; back to the stainèd field,
   You equal potents, fiery kindled spirits!
   Then let confusion of one part confirm
   The other's peace; till then, blows, blood, and death! 360

KING JOHN Whose party do the townsmen yet admit?

KING PHILIP Speak, citizens, for England: who's your
      King?

HUBERT The King of England, when we know the King.

347 **royal number** king's name as one item in the list   329 **With slaughter ...
kings** with a king slaughtered as well as slaughtering   350 **tow'rs** soars (hawking
jargon)   352 **chaps** jaws   354 **mousing** tearing, biting   355 **undetermined
differences** unsettled disputes   356 **fronts** foreheads   357 **"Havoc!"** (the call
for general slaughter with no taking of prisoners)   358 **potents** potentates, powers
359 **confusion** defeat   359 **part** party   361 **yet** now

KING PHILIP Know him in us, that here hold up his
right.

365 KING JOHN In us, that are our own great deputy,
And bear possession of our person here,
Lord of our presence, Angiers, and of you.

HUBERT A greater pow'r than we denies all this,
And, till it be undoubted, we do lock
370 Our former scruple in our strong-barred gates,
Kings of our fear, until our fears, resolved,
Be by some certain king purged and deposed.

BASTARD By heaven, these scroyles of Angiers flout
you, kings,
And stand securely on their battlements
375 As in a theater, whence they gape and point
At your industrious scenes and acts of death.
Your royal presences be ruled by me:
Do like the mutines of Jerusalem,
Be friends awhile and both conjointly bend
380 Your sharpest deeds of malice on this town.
By east and west let France and England mount
Their battering cannon chargèd to the mouths,
Till their soul-fearing clamors have brawled down
The flinty ribs of this contemptuous city.
385 I'd play incessantly upon these jades,
Even till unfencèd desolation
Leave them as naked as the vulgar air.
That done, dissever your united strengths,
And part your mingled colors once again;
390 Turn face to face and bloody point to point.

---

366 **bear possession of our person** owe no allegiance to anyone else (unlike
Arthur, who has apparently done homage to Philip—cf. line 263) 367 **presence**
person 371 **Kings of our fear** kings as a result of our fear (forced by our fears to
be our own kings) 373 **scroyles** scoundrels 378 **mutines** mutineers (factions
fighting each other in Jerusalem in 70 A.D. united to fight the Romans) 383 **soul-
fearing** causing the soul to fear 383 **brawled down** noisily laid waste
385 **play ... upon** (1) play guns upon (2) make sport of 385 **jades** wretches (a
"jade" is a worn-out horse or wanton woman) 386 **unfencèd** unfortified
387 **vulgar** common

Then, in a moment, fortune shall cull forth
Out of one side her happy minion,
To whom in favor she shall give the day,
And kiss him with a glorious victory.
How like you this wild counsel, mighty states?   395
Smacks it not something of the policy?

KING JOHN Now, by the sky that hangs above our
   heads,
I like it well. France, shall we knit our pow'rs
And lay this Angiers even with the ground,
Then after fight who shall be king of it?   400

BASTARD And if thou hast the mettle of a king,
Being wronged as we are by this peevish town,
Turn thou the mouth of thy artillery,
As we will ours, against these saucy walls;
And when that we have dashed them to the ground,   405
Why then defy each other, and, pell-mell,
Make work upon ourselves, for heaven or hell.

KING PHILIP Let it be so. Say, where will you assault?

KING JOHN We from the west will send destruction
Into this city's bosom.   410

AUSTRIA I from the north.

KING PHILIP   Our thunder from the south
Shall rain their drift of bullets on this town.

BASTARD [*Aside*] O prudent discipline! From north to
   south
Austria and France shoot in each other's mouth.
I'll stir them to it: come, away, away!   415

HUBERT Hear us, great kings: vouchsafe a while to
   stay
And I shall show you peace and fair-faced league,

---

391 **cull** (1) choose (2) fondle, hug   392 **minion** darling, favorite   395 **states** kings   396 **the policy** political skill, perhaps specifically Machiavellian political cunning   406 **pell-mell** headlong, tumultuously   407 **Make work** work havoc   407 **for heaven or hell** to the death   411 **thunder** cannons   412 **drift** shower

Win you this city without stroke or wound,
Rescue those breathing lives to die in beds,
420　That here come sacrifices for the field.
Persever not, but hear me, mighty kings.

KING JOHN　Speak on with favor; we are bent to hear.

HUBERT　That daughter there of Spain, the Lady
Blanch,
Is near to England: look upon the years
425　Of Lewis the Dolphin and that lovely maid.
If lusty love should go in quest of beauty,
Where should he find it fairer than in Blanch?
If zealous love should go in search of virtue,
Where should he find it purer than in Blanch?
430　If love, ambitious, sought a match of birth,
Whose veins bound richer blood than Lady
Blanch?
Such as she is, in beauty, virtue, birth,
Is the young Dolphin every way complete;
If not complete of, say he is not she,
435　And she again wants nothing, to name want,
If want it be not that she is not he.
He is the half part of a blessèd man,
Left to be finishèd by such as she,
And she a fair divided excellence,
440　Whose fullness of perfection lies in him.
O, two such silver currents when they join
Do glorify the banks that bound them in;
And two such shores, to two such streams made
one,
Two such controlling bounds shall you be, kings,
445　To these two princes, if you marry them.

---

422 bent determined　424 near to England closely related to King John (she
was the daughter of John's sister and of the King of Castile)　425 Dolphin
Dauphin　428 zealous sanctified　431 bound hold　433 complete fully endowed
434 of therein　435 wants lacks　435 to name want to speak of defects
436 If want it be not if it is not a deficiency (the verbal quibbling of these lines is
more to the Elizabethan taste than to ours, but it marks also the impersonal
formality of Hubert's proposal)　445 If you marry them i.e., to each other

This union shall do more than battery can
To our fast-closèd gates: for at this match,
With swifter spleen than powder can enforce,
The mouth of passage shall we fling wide ope,
And give you entrance. But without this match,   450
The sea enragèd is not half so deaf,
Lions more confident, mountains and rocks
More free from motion, no, not death himself
In mortal fury half so peremptory,
As we to keep this city.

BASTARD   Here's a stay   455
That shakes the rotten carcass of old death
Out of his rags! Here's a large mouth, indeed,
That spits forth death and mountains, rocks and
    seas,
Talks as familiarly of roaring lions
As maids of thirteen do of puppy-dogs.   460
What cannoneer begot this lusty blood?
He speaks plain cannon fire, and smoke, and
    bounce;
He gives the bastinado with his tongue:
Our ears are cudgeled; not a word of his
But buffets better than a fist of France.   465
Zounds! I was never so bethumped with words
Since I first called my brother's father dad.

ELINOR Son, list to this conjunction, make this match;
Give with our niece a dowry large enough,
For by this knot thou shalt so surely tie   470
Thy now unsured assurance to the crown
That yon green boy shall have no sun to ripe
The bloom that promiseth a mighty fruit.
I see a yielding in the looks of France:
Mark how they whisper. Urge them while their souls   475
Are capable of this ambition,

447 **match** (1) marriage (2) wick for igniting powder   448 **spleen** impetuosity
454 **peremptory** resolute   455 **stay** check, hindrance   462 **bounce** explosive
noise   463 **bastinado** cudgeling   466 **Zounds!** by God's wounds!   468 **list to
this conjunction** listen to (accept) this union   471 **unsured assurance** uncertain
title   476 **capable of this ambition** ready to accept this desire for alliance

Lest zeal, now melted by the windy breath
Of soft petitions, pity, and remorse,
Cool and congeal again to what it was.

480 HUBERT Why answer not the double majesties
This friendly treaty of our threatened town?

KING PHILIP Speak England first, that hath been
forward first
To speak unto this city: what say you?

KING JOHN If that the Dolphin there, thy princely son,
485 Can in this book of beauty read "I love,"
Her dowry shall weigh equal with a queen:
For Anjou and fair Touraine, Maine, Poictiers,
And all that we upon this side the sea—
Except this city now by us besieged—
490 Find liable to our crown and dignity,
Shall gild her bridal bed and make her rich
In titles, honors, and promotions,
As she in beauty, education, blood,
Holds hand with any princess of the world.

KING PHILIP What sayst thou, boy? Look in the lady's
495 face.

LEWIS I do, my lord, and in her eye I find
A wonder, or a wondrous miracle,
The shadow of myself formed in her eye,
Which, being but the shadow of your son,
500 Becomes a sun, and makes your son a shadow:
I do protest I never loved myself
Till now infixèd I beheld myself,
Drawn in the flattering table of her eye.
                                                    Whispers with Blanch.

BASTARD Drawn in the flattering table of her eye!

477 **zeal** i.e., King Philip's eagerness to support Arthur   481 **treaty** proposal
488 **sea** i.e., the English Channel   490 **liable** subject   494 **Holds hands with** is
the equal of   498 **shadow** image   503 **Drawn in the flattering table** portrayed
on the flattering surface (the whole of the Dauphin's speech—eye, sun, son,
shadow—is conventional; he simply says what is expected of him)   504 **Drawn**
(1) portrayed (2) disemboweled

Hanged in the frowning wrinkle of her brow!   505
And quartered in her heart! He doth espy
Himself love's traitor; this is pity now,
That, hanged and drawn and quartered, there
  should be
In such a love so vile a lout as he.

BLANCH [*To Lewis*] My uncle's will in this respect is
  mine: 510
If he see aught in you that makes him like,
That anything he sees which moves his liking,
I can with ease translate it to my will;
Or, if you will, to speak more properly,
I will enforce it eas'ly to my love.   515
Further I will not flatter you, my lord,
That all I see in you is worthy love,
Than this: that nothing do I see in you,
Though churlish thoughts themselves should be
  your judge,
That I can find should merit any hate.   520

KING JOHN What say these young ones? What say you,
  my niece?

BLANCH That she is bound in honor still to do
What you in wisdom still vouchsafe to say.

KING JOHN Speak then, Prince Dolphin: can you love
  this lady?

LEWIS Nay, ask me if I can refrain from love,   525
For I do love her most unfeignedly.

KING JOHN Then do I give Volquessen, Touraine,
  Maine,
Poictiers, and Anjou, these five provinces,
With her to thee; and this addition more,
Full thirty thousand marks of English coin.   530

506 **quartered** (1) lodged (2) cut or torn in four parts (traitors were hanged, drawn and quartered)   513 **translate it to my will** i.e., I can bend my will to my uncle's desires (Blanch is much less conventional, and much more honest, than Lewis)   522 **still** always

Philip of France, if thou be pleased withal,
Command thy son and daughter to join hands.

KING PHILIP   It likes us well. Young princes, close
your hands.

AUSTRIA   And your lips too, for I am well assured
535   That I did so when I was first assured.

KING PHILIP   Now, citizens of Angiers, ope your gates;
Let in that amity which you have made,
For at Saint Mary's chapel presently
The rites of marriage shall be solemnized.
540   Is not the Lady Constance in this troop?
I know she is not, for this match made up
Her presence would have interrupted much.
Where is she and her son? Tell me, who knows.

LEWIS   She is sad and passionate at your Highness'
tent.

KING PHILIP   And, by my faith, this league that we
545   have made
Will give her sadness very little cure.
Brother of England, how may we content
This widow lady? In her right we came,
Which we, God knows, have turned another way,
To our own vantage.

550   KING JOHN   We will heal up all,
For we'll create young Arthur Duke of Britain
And Earl of Richmond, and this rich fair town
We make him lord of. Call the Lady Constance.
Some speedy messenger bid her repair
555   To our solemnity. I trust we shall,
If not fill up the measure of her will,
Yet in some measure satisfy her so
That we shall stop her exclamation.

---

533 **It likes us** we like it   535 **assured** engaged to be married   544 **passionate** enraged   555 **solemnity** ceremony (the wedding and the granting of titles to Arthur)   558 **stop her exclamation** silence her complaining

Go we, as well as haste will suffer us,
To this unlooked for, unpreparèd pomp.   560
                    Exeunt [all but the Bastard].

BASTARD Mad world! Mad kings! Mad composition!
    John, to stop Arthur's title in the whole,
    Hath willingly departed with a part,
    And France, whose armor conscience buckled on,
    Whom zeal and charity brought to the field   565
    As God's own soldier, rounded in the ear
    With that same purpose-changer, that sly devil,
    That broker that still breaks the pate of faith,
    That daily break-vow, he that wins of all,
    Of kings, of beggars, old men, young men, maids,   570
    Who, having no external thing to lose
    But the word "maid," cheats the poor maid of that,
    That smooth-faced gentleman, tickling commodity,
    Commodity, the bias of the world,
    The world, who of itself is peisèd well,   575
    Made to run even upon even ground,
    Till this advantage, this vile drawing bias,
    This sway of motion, this commodity,
    Makes it take head from all indifference,
    From all direction, purpose, course, intent.   580
    And this same bias, this commodity,
    This bawd, this broker, this all-changing word,
    Clapped on the outward eye of fickle France,

560 **pomp** ceremony 561 **composition** compromise 563 **departed with** given away 566-67 **rounded in the ear/With** whispered to by 568 **broker** pander 571 **Who** (elliptical; begins by referring to "maids," ends, as the subject of "cheats," by referring to "commodity," the subject of this whole series of appositions) 573 **smooth-faced** ingratiating, deceitful 573 **tickling** (1) teasing—the maids (2) flattering—anyone 573 **commodity** self-interest 574 **bias** oblique course (in bowling, the bowl went on an oblique course because of the weight built into one side; "bias" was the word for either the course or the weight itself) 575 **peisèd** weighted 577 **vile drawing** (two adjectives, but also "vile-drawing," drawing to evil) 578 **sway** (that which sways) diverter, corrupter 578 **motion** (1) movement (2) intention 579 **take head** run 579 **indifferency** impartiality, disinterestedness 583 **outward eye** (1) physical vision, as opposed to moral vision or conscience (2) in bowling, the bowl had an "eye" which received the weight, the bias

Hath drawn him from his own determined aid,
585   From a resolved and honorable war,
To a most base and vile-concluded peace.
And why rail I on this commodity?
But for because he hath not wooed me yet:
Not that I have the power to clutch my hand,
590   When his fair angels would salute my palm,
But for my hand, as unattempted yet,
Like a poor beggar, raileth on the rich.
Well, whiles I am a beggar, I will rail
And say there is no sin but to be rich;
595   And being rich, my virtue then shall be
To say there is no vice but beggary.
Since kings break faith upon commodity,
Gain, be my lord, for I will worship thee!   *Exit.*

Scene II. [*King Philip's tent.*]

Enter Constance, Arthur, and Salisbury.

CONSTANCE Gone to be married! Gone to swear a
peace!
False blood to false blood joined! Gone to be
friends!
Shall Lewis have Blanch, and Blanch those
provinces?
It is not so; thou hast misspoke, misheard;
5   Be well advised, tell o'er thy tale again.
It cannot be; thou dost but say 'tis so.
I trust I may not trust thee, for thy word

---

585 **resolved** the decision to undertake it having been made 588 **But for
because** only because 589 **clutch my hand** i.e., refuse the bribe 590 **angels**
(1) commodity's agents, the fallen angels (2) gold coins called "angels" because
they carried a picture of the archangel Michael killing a dragon 591 **unattempted** untested, untempted 597 **upon** as a result of

Is but the vain breath of a common man;
Believe me, I do not believe thee, man:
I have a king's oath to the contrary.   10
Thou shalt be punished for thus frighting me,
For I am sick and capable of fears,
Oppressed with wrongs, and therefore full of fears,
A widow, husbandless, subject to fears,
A woman naturally born to fears;   15
And though thou now confess thou didst but jest,
With my vexed spirits I cannot take a truce,
But they will quake and tremble all this day.
What dost thou mean by shaking of thy head?
Why dost thou look so sadly on my son?   20
What means that hand upon that breast of thine?
Why holds thine eye that lamentable rheum,
Like a proud river peering o'er his bounds?
Be these sad signs confirmers of thy words?
Then speak again, not all thy former tale,   25
But this one word, whether thy tale be true.

SALISBURY As true as I believe you think them false
That give you cause to prove my saying true.

CONSTANCE O if thou teach me to believe this sorrow,
Teach thou this sorrow how to make me die!   30
And let belief and life encounter so
As doth the fury of two desperate men
Which in the very meeting fall and die.
Lewis marry Blanch! O boy, then where art thou?
France friend with England, what becomes of me?   35
Fellow, be gone! I cannot brook thy sight.
This news hath made thee a most ugly man.

SALISBURY What other harm have I, good lady, done,
But spoke the harm that is by others done?

II.ii.14 **A widow, husbandless** (not necessarily a tautology: the historical Constance, though Geoffrey's widow, was at this time married to her third husband;
his presence would, however, be a dramatic confusion, and Shakespeare simplifies
to increase her isolation) 17 **take a truce** make peace 22 **that lamentable
rheum** those sorrowful tears 23 **peering o'er** overflowing

40 CONSTANCE Which harm within itself so heinous is
        As it makes harmful all that speak of it.

    ARTHUR I do beseech you, madam, be content.

    CONSTANCE If thou, that bid'st me be content, wert
        grim,
        Ugly and sland'rous to thy mother's womb,
45   Full of unpleasing blots and sightless stains,
        Lame, foolish, crooked, swart, prodigious,
        Patched with foul moles and eye-offending marks,
        I would not care, I then would be content,
        For then I should not love thee: no, nor thou
50   Become thy great birth, nor deserve a crown.
        But thou art fair, and at thy birth, dear boy,
        Nature and fortune joined to make thee great.
        Of nature's gifts thou mayst with lilies boast
        And with the half-blown rose. But fortune, O,
55   She is corrupted, changed, and won from thee;
        Sh' adulterates hourly with thine uncle John,
        And with her golden hand hath plucked on
            France
        To tread down fair respect of sovereignty,
        And made his majesty the bawd to theirs.
60   France is a bawd to fortune and King John,
        That strumpet fortune, that usurping John!
        Tell me, thou fellow, is not France forsworn?
        Envenom him with words, or get thee gone
        And leave those woes alone which I alone
        Am bound to underbear.

65 SALISBURY   Pardon me, madam,
        I may not go without you to the kings.

    CONSTANCE Thou mayst; thou shalt: I will not go with
        thee.

---

42 **content** calm, satisfied 44 **sland'rous** a disgrace, giving cause for slander
45 **blots** spots, disfigurements 45 **sightless** unsightly 46 **prodigious**
deformed, hence a prodigy or bad omen 54 **half-blown** half-opened
56 **hourly** (1) every hour (2) like a whore (cf. I.i.165) 57 **golden hand** hand
which dispenses gold 57 **plucked on** drawn along 63 **Envenom** (1) poison
(2) curse 65 **underbear** endure, suffer

I will instruct my sorrows to be proud,
For grief is proud and makes his owner stoop.
To me and to the state of my great grief   70
Let kings assemble, for my grief's so great
That no supporter but the huge firm earth
Can hold it up: here I and sorrows sit;
Here is my throne, bid kings come bow to it.

> *[Seats herself on the ground.*
> *Exeunt Salisbury and Arthur.]*

68, 69 **proud** (1) proud (2) prou'd = proved = tested   69 **stoop** bow down
(Constance is made to bow down under her grief, but she will also make the kings
bow down to it)   70 **state** (1) condition (2) high rank (3) government
(4) throne   74 s.d. **Exeunt Salisbury and Arthur** (it is not clear whether
Salisbury should lead Arthur off or they should go in opposite directions; it is only
clear that they are not present during the next scene and that Arthur next appears,
in III.ii, as John's prisoner)

ACT III

Scene I. [*King Philip's tent.*]

Enter King John, [King Philip of] France, [Lewis, the]
Dauphin, Blanch, Elinor, Philip [the Bastard], Austria
[and Attendants, to] Constance, [seated on the ground].

KING PHILIP 'Tis true, fair daughter, and this blessèd
    day
    Ever in France shall be kept festival:
    To solemnize this day the glorious sun
    Stays in his course and plays the alchemist,
5   Turning with splendor of his precious eye
    The meager cloddy earth to glittering gold.
    The yearly course that brings this day about
    Shall never see it but a holy day.

CONSTANCE [*Rising*] A wicked day, and not a holy day!
10   What hath this day deserved? what hath it done
    That it in golden letters should be set
    Among the high tides in the calendar?

III.i. s.d. **seated on the ground** (the action is of course continuous from the end
of the second act)   2 **festival** as a holiday   12 **high tides** principal anniversaries

Nay, rather turn this day out of the week,
This day of shame, oppression, perjury.
Or, if it must stand still, let wives with child   15
Pray that their burdens may not fall this day,
Lest that their hopes prodigiously be crossed:
But on this day let seamen fear no wrack;
No bargains break that are not this day made;
This day all things begun come to ill end,   20
Yea, faith itself to hollow falsehood change!

KING PHILIP By heaven, lady, you shall have no cause
To curse the fair proceedings of this day:
Have I not pawned to you my majesty?

CONSTANCE You have beguiled me with a counterfeit   25
Resembling majesty, which, being touched and
    tried,
Proves valueless: you are forsworn, forsworn!
You came in arms to spill mine enemies' blood,
But now, in arms, you strengthen it with yours.
The grappling vigor and rough frown of war   30
Is cold in amity and painted peace,
And our oppression hath made up this league.
Arm, arm, you heavens, against these perjured
    kings!
A widow cries; be husband to me, heavens!
Let not the hours of this ungodly day   35
Wear out the day in peace; but, ere sunset,
Set armèd discord 'twixt these perjured kings!
Hear me! O, hear me!

AUSTRIA   Lady Constance, peace!

CONSTANCE War! War! No peace! Peace is to me a war.

15 **stand still** always remain 17 **prodigiously be crossed** be denied by the
birth of a deformed child 18 **But** except 18 **wrack** disaster (here, of course,
shipwreck) 19 **bargains** agreements 24 **pawned to you my majesty** pledged
you my word as a king 25 **counterfeit** false coin 26 **touched and tried** its
gold tested on a touchstone 28-29 **in arms ... in arms** armed ...
embracing 31 **Is cold ... peace** lies dead in your friendship and false peace
32 **our oppression** your oppression of us 36 **Wear out** last through

40   O, Lymoges! O, Austria! Thou dost shame
     That bloody spoil: thou slave, thou wretch, thou
       coward!
     Thou little valiant, great in villainy!
     Thou ever strong upon the stronger side!
     Thou fortune's champion, that dost never fight
45   But when her humorous ladyship is by
     To teach thee safety! Thou art perjured too,
     And sooth'st up greatness. What a fool art thou,
     A ramping fool, to brag and stamp and swear
     Upon my party! Thou cold-blooded slave,
50   Hast thou not spoke like thunder on my side?
     Been sworn my soldier, bidding me depend
     Upon thy stars, thy fortune, and thy strength,
     And dost thou now fall over to my foes?
     Thou wear a lion's hide! Doff it for shame,
55   And hang a calfskin on those recreant limbs.

AUSTRIA   O that a man should speak those words to
     me!

BASTARD   And hang a calfskin on those recreant limbs.

AUSTRIA   Thou dar'st not say so, villain, for thy life!

BASTARD   And hang a calfskin on those recreant limbs.

60 KING JOHN   We like not this; thou dost forget thyself.

Enter Pandulph.

KING PHILIP   Here comes the holy legate of the Pope.

PANDULPH   Hail, you anointed deputies of heaven!
     To thee, King John, my holy errand is.
     I Pandulph, of fair Milan cardinal,

---

40 **Lymoges** (Limoges and Austria were, historically, two men, but are here combined; Richard *Coeur de lion* was actually killed, not by Austria, but while besieging Limoges)   41 **bloody spoil** i.e., the lion-skin   45 **humorous** full of humors, capricious   47 **sooth'st up** flatterest   48 **ramping** (1) raging (2) threatening—chiefly said of lions (3) standing on the hind legs, like a heraldic lion   49 **Upon my party** as one of my supporters   53 **fall over** go over   55 **calfskin** (1) indicating a calf, or meek, cowardly fellow, in sharpest contrast with a lion (2) traditional coat (?) for a household fool or idiot kept for amusement   55 **recreant** cowardly

And from Pope Innocent the legate here,   65
Do in his name religiously demand
Why thou against the church, our holy mother,
So willfully dost spurn; and force perforce
Keep Stephen Langton, chosen Archbishop
Of Canterbury, from that holy see: 70
This, in our foresaid holy father's name,
Pope Innocent, I do demand of thee.

KING JOHN What earthy name to interrogatories
Can task the free breath of a sacred king?
Thou canst not, Cardinal, devise a name   75
So slight, unworthy and ridiculous,
To charge me to an answer, as the Pope.
Tell him this tale, and from the mouth of England
Add thus much more, that no Italian priest
Shall tithe or toll in our dominions;   80
But as we, under God, are supreme head,
So under Him that great supremacy
Where we do reign, we will alone uphold
Without th' assistance of a mortal hand:
So tell the Pope, all reverence set apart   85
To him and his usurped authority.

KING PHILIP Brother of England, you blaspheme in
    this.

KING JOHN Though you and all the kings of Christen-
    dom
Are led so grossly by this meddling priest,
Dreading the curse that money may buy out,   90
And by the merit of vile gold, dross, dust,
Purchase corrupted pardon of a man,
Who in that sale sells pardon from himself:
Though you and all the rest, so grossly led,

68 **spurn** kick contemptuously   68 **force perforce** by violent means   73 **inter-rogatories** questions asked formally in a law court   73-74 **What earthy name ... king** what mortal can force a king to answer charges   77 **charge me to an answer** command an answer from me   80 **tithe or toll** collect church revenues   89 **grossly** (1) stupidly (2) materially—as opposed to spiritually   89 **this med-dling priest** i.e., the Pope   90 **buy out** remove   93 **sells pardon from himself** (1) i.e., not from God (2) loses his own pardon through the transaction

95   This juggling witchcraft with revenue cherish,
        Yet I alone, alone do me oppose
        Against the Pope, and count his friends my foes.

PANDULPH Then, by the lawful power that I have,
        Thou shalt stand curst and excommunicate:
100   And blessèd shall he be that doth revolt
        From his allegiance to an heretic;
        And meritorious shall that hand be called,
        Canonized and worshiped as a saint,
        That takes away by any secret course
        Thy hateful life.

105 CONSTANCE   O lawful let it be
        That I have room with Rome to curse awhile!
        Good Father Cardinal, cry thou "Amen"
        To my keen curses, for without my wrong
        There is no tongue hath power to curse him right.

110 PANDULPH There's law and warrant, lady, for my curse.

CONSTANCE And for mine too: when law can do no
        right,
        Let it be lawful that law bar no wrong!
        Law cannot give my child his kingdom here,
        For he that holds his kingdom holds the law;
115   Therefore, since law itself is perfect wrong,
        How can the law forbid my tongue to curse?

PANDULPH Philip of France, on peril of a curse,
        Let go the hand of that arch-heretic,
        And raise the power of France upon his head,
120   Unless he do submit himself to Rome.

ELINOR Look'st thou pale, France? Do not let go thy
        hand.

CONSTANCE Look to that, Devil, lest that France
        repent,
        And by disjoining hands, hell lose a soul.

95 **This juggling ... cherish** cling to, and nourish financially, this deceptive
wickedness 106 **room with Rome** (the words were presumably homonyms)
119 **upon his head** against him

AUSTRIA King Philip, listen to the Cardinal.

BASTARD And hang a calfskin on his recreant limbs. 125

AUSTRIA Well, ruffian, I must pocket up these wrongs,
  Because—

BASTARD   Your breeches best may carry them.

KING JOHN Philip, what sayst thou to the Cardinal?

CONSTANCE What should he say, but as the Cardinal?

LEWIS Bethink you, father, for the difference 130
  Is purchase of a heavy curse from Rome,
  Or the light loss of England for a friend:
  Forgo the easier.

BLANCH   That's the curse of Rome.

CONSTANCE O Lewis, stand fast! The devil tempts thee
  here
  In likeness of a new untrimmèd bride. 135

BLANCH The Lady Constance speaks not from her
  faith,
  But from her need.

CONSTANCE   O, if thou grant my need,
  Which only lives but by the death of faith,
  That need must needs infer this principle,
  That faith would live again by death of need. 140
  O then tread down my need, and faith mounts up;
  Keep my need up, and faith is trodden down!

KING JOHN The King is moved, and answers not to
  this.

CONSTANCE O be removed from him, and answer well!

AUSTRIA Do so, King Philip; hang no more in doubt. 145

BASTARD Hang nothing but a calfskin, most sweet lout.

---

133 **the easier** the lighter, the less oppressive   135 **untrimmèd** still possessing
her maidenhead   136-37 **speaks not ... need** is not interested in truth but in
advancing her cause   139 **infer** imply

KING PHILIP I am perplexed, and know not what to say.

PANDULPH What canst thou say but will perplex thee more,
If thou stand excommunicate and cursed?

KING PHILIP Good reverend Father, make my person
150   yours,
And tell me how you would bestow yourself.
This royal hand and mine are newly knit,
And the conjunction of our inward souls
Married in league, coupled and linked together
155   With all religious strength of sacred vows;
The latest breath that gave the sound of words
Was deep-sworn faith, peace, amity, true love
Between our kingdoms and our royal selves;
And even before this truce, but new before,
160   No longer than we well could wash our hands
To clap this royal bargain up of peace,
Heaven knows, they were besmeared and over-
      stained
With slaughter's pencil, where revenge did paint
The fearful difference of incensèd kings:
165   And shall these hands, so lately purged of blood,
So newly joined in love, so strong in both,
Unyoke this seizure and this kind regreet?
Play fast and loose with faith? so jest with heaven,
Make such unconstant children of ourselves
170   As now again to snatch our palm from palm,
Unswear faith sworn, and on the marriage bed
Of smiling peace to march a bloody host,
And make a riot on the gentle brow
Of true sincerity? O holy sir,
175   My reverend Father, let it not be so!

150 **make my person yours** put yourself in my place 159 **new** just 161 **clap
... peace** shake hands on this agreement, this royal peace treaty 163 **pencil**
paintbrush 164 **difference** dissension 166 **so strong in both** (1) hands so
strong in both blood and love (2) love so strong in both kings (?) 167 **Unyoke ...
regreet** release their clasp and friendly counterclasp 168 **Play fast and loose**
cheat 170 **palm** (1) hand (2) symbol of peace

Out of your grace, devise, ordain, impose
Some gentle order, and then we shall be blessed
To do your pleasure and continue friends.

PANDULPH All form is formless, order orderless,
Save what is opposite to England's love.   180
Therefore to arms! Be champion of our church,
Or let the church, our mother, breathe her curse,
A mother's curse, on her revolting son.
France, thou mayst hold a serpent by the tongue,
A casèd lion by the mortal paw,   185
A fasting tiger safer by the tooth,
Than keep in peace that hand which thou dost hold.

KING PHILIP I may disjoin my hand, but not my faith.

PANDULPH So mak'st thou faith an enemy to faith,
And like a civil war set'st oath to oath,   190
Thy tongue against thy tongue. O, let thy vow,
First made to heaven, first be to heaven performed,
That is, to be the champion of our church.
What since thou swor'st is sworn against thyself
And may not be performèd by thyself,   195
For that which thou hast sworn to do amiss
Is not amiss when it is truly done;
And being not done, where doing tends to ill,
The truth is then most done not doing it.
The better act of purposes mistook   200
Is to mistake again; though indirect,
Yet indirection thereby grows direct,
And falsehood falsehood cures, as fire cools fire
Within the scorchèd veins of one new burned.
It is religion that doth make vows kept,   205
But thou hast sworn against religion

185 casèd caged (?) wearing its own hide, i.e., living (?)   185 mortal deadly
189 So mak'st ... to faith thus you make your loyalty to your oath to John an
enemy to your loyalty to the true faith, the church   194 What since thou
swor'st what you have sworn at any time after your original vow to the church
197 truly done done as it ought to be done, rather than done in accordance with
your unsound oath (this argument for swearing one thing and doing another is the
so-called "doctrine of equivocation" for which Elizabethan Protestants particularly
hated and feared the Jesuits)

    (By what thou swear'st against the thing thou
       swear'st)
    And mak'st an oath the surety for thy truth
    (Against an oath the truth); thou art unsure
210   To swear—swears only not to be forsworn,
    Else what a mockery should it be to swear!
    But thou dost swear only to be forsworn,
    And most forsworn, to keep what thou dost swear;
    Therefore thy later vows against thy first
215   Is in thyself rebellion to thyself:
    And better conquest never canst thou make
    Than arm thy constant and thy nobler parts
    Against these giddy loose suggestions;
    Upon which better part our prayers come in,
220   If thou vouchsafe them. But if not, then know
    The peril of our curses light on thee
    So heavy as thou shalt not shake them off,
    But in despair die under their black weight.

AUSTRIA Rebellion, flat rebellion!

BASTARD   Will 't not be?
225   Will not a calfskin stop that mouth of thine?

LEWIS Father, to arms!

BLANCH   Upon thy wedding day?
    Against the blood that thou hast marrièd?
    What, shall our feast be kept with slaughtered men?
    Shall braying trumpets and loud churlish drums,
230   Clamors of hell, be measures to our pomp?

207 **(By what ... swear'st)** by your oath to John against your religion
209 **(Against an oath the truth)** the truth itself (religion) stands against the oath
(to John) which you make the basis of your loyalty   209–10 **thou art unsure/To
swear** you are untrustworthy in your oaths   210 **swears ... forsworn** one swears
in the first place to ensure that one will not later swear the opposite (the complex,
paranthetical style of Pandulph's argument creates a dramatic effect of quibbling
ingenuity as opposed to an effect of plain-spoken truth)   213 **And most forsworn, to keep** and you would be most forsworn if you were to keep   217 **arm** to
arm   218 **giddy loose suggestions** inconstant, unrestrained temptations
219 **Upon which better part** in behalf of which preferable party or faction
220 **vouchsafe** permit   224 **Will't not be** will this not cease   230 **measures**
melodies

O husband, hear me! Ay, alack, how new
Is "husband" in my mouth! Even for that name,
Which till this time my tongue did ne'er pronounce,
Upon my knee I beg, go not to arms
Against mine uncle.

CONSTANCE   O, upon my knee,   235
Made hard with kneeling, I do pray to thee,
Thou virtuous Dolphin, alter not the doom
Forethought by God!

BLANCH Now shall I see thy love: what motive may
Be stronger with thee than the name of wife?   240

CONSTANCE That which upholdeth him that thee
          upholds,
His honor: O thine honor, Lewis, thine honor!

LEWIS I muse your Majesty doth seem so cold,
When such profound respects do pull you on!

PANDULPH I will denounce a curse upon his head.   245

KING PHILIP Thou shalt not need. England, I will fall
          from thee.

CONSTANCE O fair return of banished majesty!

ELINOR O foul revolt of French inconstancy!

KING JOHN France, thou shalt rue this hour within
          this hour.

BASTARD Old Time the clock-setter, that bald sexton
          Time,   250
Is it as he will? Well then, France shall rue.

BLANCH The sun's o'ercast with blood: fair day, adieu!
Which is the side that I must go withal?
I am with both: each army hath a hand,
And in their rage, I having hold of both,   255
They whirl asunder and dismember me.

237-38 **alter not ... God** don't interfere with divine intervention   244 **respects**
inducements   245 **denounce** pronounce   246 **fall from** desert   250 **sexton**
gravedigger and bell-ringer   251 **Is it all he will** is that the way he wants it

Husband, I cannot pray that thou mayst win;
Uncle, I needs must pray that thou mayst lose;
Father, I may not wish the fortune thine;
260   Grandam, I will not wish thy wishes thrive:
Whoever wins, on that side shall I lose;
Assurèd loss before the match be played.

LEWIS Lady, with me, with me thy fortune lies.

BLANCH There where my fortune lives, there my life
dies.

265   KING JOHN Cousin, go draw our puissance together.
                              [*Exit Bastard.*]
France, I am burned up with inflaming wrath,
A rage whose heat hath this condition,
That nothing can allay, nothing but blood,
The blood, and dearest-valued blood, of France.

KING PHILIP Thy rage shall burn thee up, and thou
270   shalt turn
To ashes, ere our blood shall quench that fire!
Look to thyself, thou art in jeopardy.

KING JOHN No more than he that threats. To arms
let's hie!   *Exeunt.*

259 **Father** father-in-law (King Philip)   265 **Cousin** kinsman (commonly, as
here, nephew)   265 **puissance** army   267 **condition** characteristic

Scene II. [*Battlefield near Angiers.*]

Alarums, excursions. Enter Bastard, with
Austria's head.

BASTARD Now, by my life, this day grows wondrous
  hot.
  Some airy devil hovers in the sky
  And pours down mischief. Austria's head lie there,

  Enter [King] John, Arthur, Hubert.

  While Philip breathes.

KING JOHN Hubert, keep this boy. Philip, make up: 5
  My mother is assailèd in our tent,
  And ta'en, I fear.

BASTARD   My lord, I rescued her;
  Her Highness is in safety, fear you not:
  But on, my liege, for very little pains
  Will bring this labor to an happy end.   *Exit [all]*.   10

  Alarums, excursions, retreat. [Re-]enter [King]
  John, Elinor, Arthur, Bastard, Hubert, Lords.

KING JOHN [*To Elinor*] So shall it be: your Grace shall
  stay behind
  So strongly guarded. [*To Arthur*] Cousin, look not
  sad:

III.ii.s.d. **Alarums** trumpets, battle cries s.d. **with Austria's head** (though there
is no mention of the lion-skin, the Bastard should presumably wear it in this scene
and perhaps from now on; his complaint of the heat may be in part a comic
reference to this addition to his costume) 1 **this day** (1) the day itself (2) the
battle 2-3 **Some airy ... mischief** some invisible devil has made the day so hot,
or the battle so fierce 4 **breathes** catches his breath 5 **make up** advance, press
on 7 **I rescued her** (Shakespeare gives the Bastard credit for a rescue historically
effected by John) 10 s.d. **Exit [all]** (because the stage is cleared, many editors
begin a new scene here)

Thy grandam loves thee, and thy uncle will
As dear be to thee as thy father was.

15 ARTHUR O this will make my mother die with grief!

KING JOHN [*To the Bastard*] Cousin, away for
     England! Haste before,
And, ere our coming, see thou shake the bags
Of hoarding abbots; imprisoned angels
Set at liberty: the fat ribs of peace
20 Must by the hungry now be fed upon!
Use our commission in his utmost force.

BASTARD Bell, book, and candle shall not drive me
     back
When gold and silver becks me to come on.
I leave your Highness. Grandam, I will pray
25 (If ever I remember to be holy)
For your fair safety; so I kiss your hand.

ELINOR Farewell, gentle cousin.

KING JOHN   Coz, farewell. [*Exit Bastard.*]

ELINOR Come hither, little kinsman. Hark, a word.
                    [*She takes Arthur aside.*]

KING JOHN Come hither, Hubert. O my gentle Hubert,
30 We owe thee much! Within this wall of flesh
There is a soul counts thee her creditor,
And with advantage means to pay thy love;
And, my good friend, thy voluntary oath
Lives in this bosom, dearly cherishèd.
35 Give me thy hand. I had a thing to say,
But I will fit it with some better tune.

16 **Before** ahead of us 17 **shake the bags** empty the moneybags ("Shak[e]bag" is a "desperate ruffi[a]n" in *Arden of Feversham*, 1592) 18 **angels** coins; cf. II.i.590 21 **his** its 22 **Bell, book, and candle** excommunication 23 **becks** beckons 27 **Coz** cousin, kinsman 30 **We owe thee much** (perhaps the entry after line 3 indicates that Hubert is responsible for the capture of Arthur. At any rate, Hubert is now clearly loyal to John, not to France) 32 **advantage** interest 32 **pay** recompense, repay 36 **fit it ... tune** (1) set it to more appropriate music (2) render it in a better style (i.e., reward you with more than words)

By heaven, Hubert, I am almost ashamed
To say what good respect I have of thee.

HUBERT   I am much bounden to your Majesty.

KING JOHN Good friend, thou hast no cause to say
    so yet,   40
But thou shalt have; and creep time ne'er so slow,
Yet it shall come for me to do thee good.
I had a thing to say, but let it go.
The sun is in the heaven, and the proud day,
Attended with the pleasures of the world,   45
Is all too wanton and too full of gauds
To give me audience. If the midnight bell
Did, with his iron tongue and brazen mouth,
Sound on into the drowsy race of night;
If this same were a churchyard where we stand,   50
And thou possessèd with a thousand wrongs;
Or if that surly spirit, melancholy,
Had baked thy blood and made it heavy, thick,
Which else runs tickling up and down the veins,
Making that idiot, laughter, keep men's eyes   55
And strain their cheeks to idle merriment,
A passion hateful to my purposes;
Or if that thou couldst see me without eyes,
Hear me without thine ears, and make reply
Without a tongue, using conceit alone,   60
Without eyes, ears, and harmful sound of words;
Then, in despite of brooded watchful day,
I would into thy bosom pour my thoughts:
But, ah, I will not; yet I love thee well,
And, by my troth, I think thou lov'st me well.   65

HUBERT So well, that what you bid me undertake,

---

38 **good respect** high regard   39 **bounden** bound, indebted   46–47 **too full ...
audience** (1) the mind of the day is too full of trinkets to listen to me (2) the day is
too full of florid beauties for you to pay proper attention to my harsh meaning
49 **race** course, progress (many editors substitute "ear" for "race," but this
destroys the oxymoron, "drowsy race")   55 **keep** employ for its own
purposes   56 **strain** constrain, limit   60 **conceit** imagination, understanding
62 **brooded** brooding

Though that my death were adjunct to my act,
By heaven, I would do it.

KING JOHN   Do not I know thou wouldst?
Good Hubert, Hubert, Hubert, throw thine eye
70 On yon young boy; I'll tell thee what, my friend,
He is a very serpent in my way,
And wheresoe'er this foot of mine doth tread
He lies before me: dost thou understand me?
Thou art his keeper.

HUBERT   And I'll keep him so
75 That he shall not offend your Majesty.

KING JOHN Death.

HUBERT   My lord.

KING JOHN   A grave.

HUBERT   He shall not live.

KING JOHN   Enough.
I could be merry now. Hubert, I love thee.
Well, I'll not say what I intend for thee:
Remember. Madam, fare you well.
80 I'll send those powers o'er to your Majesty.

ELINOR My blessing go with thee!

KING JOHN   For England, cousin, go.
Hubert shall be your man, attend on you
With all true duty. On toward Calais, ho!   *Exeunt.*

67 **adjunct** to an essential constituent of 82 **man** servant 83 **Calais** (pronounced to rhyme with "palace")

Scene III. [*King Philip's tent.*]

Enter [King Philip of] France, [Lewis, the] Dauphin,
Pandulph, Attendants.

KING PHILIP So, by a roaring tempest on the flood,
A whole armado of convicted sail
Is scattered and disjoined from fellowship.

PANDULPH Courage and comfort! All shall yet go well.

KING PHILIP What can go well, when we have run
     so ill?   5
Are we not beaten? Is not Angiers lost?
Arthur ta'en prisoner? divers dear friends slain?
And bloody England into England gone,
O'erbearing interruption, spite of France?

LEWIS What he hath won, that hath he fortified.   10
So hot a speed with such advice disposed,
Such temperate order in so fierce a cause,
Doth want example: who hath read or heard
Of any kindred action like to this?

KING PHILIP Well could I bear that England had this
     praise,   15
So we could find some pattern of our shame.

Enter Constance.

Look, who comes here! a grave unto a soul,
Holding th' eternal spirit, against her will,

III.iii.1 **flood** sea 2 **armado** armada, fleet of armed ships 2 **convicted** doomed
5 **run** (1) proceeded (2) run away 7 **divers** various 9 **spite of** in spite of
11 **with such advice disposed** carried out with such determination 13 **Doth
want example** is without parallel 16 **So** if 16 **pattern** example, parallel

In the vile prison of afflicted breath.
20 I prithee, lady, go away with me.

CONSTANCE Lo, now! now see the issue of your peace!

KING PHILIP Patience, good lady! Comfort, gentle
    Constance!

CONSTANCE No, I defy all counsel, all redress,
    But that which ends all counsel, true redress:
25 Death, death, O, amiable, lovely death!
    Thou odoriferous stench! sound rottenness!
    Arise forth from the couch of lasting night,
    Thou hate and terror to prosperity,
    And I will kiss thy detestable bones,
30 And put my eyeballs in thy vaulty brows,
    And ring these fingers with thy household worms,
    And stop this gap of breath with fulsome dust,
    And be a carrion monster like thyself:
    Come, grin on me, and I will think thou smil'st
35 And buss thee as thy wife! Misery's love,
    O, come to me!

KING PHILIP   O fair affliction, peace!

CONSTANCE No, no, I will not, having breath to cry!
    O that my tongue were in the thunder's mouth!
    Then with a passion would I shake the world,
40 And rouse from sleep that fell anatomy
    Which cannot hear a lady's feeble voice,
    Which scorns a modern invocation.

PANDULPH Lady, you utter madness, and not sorrow.

CONSTANCE Thou art holy to belie me so!
45 I am not mad: this hair I tear is mine;

19 **afflicted breath** tormented life 23 **defy** reject 27 **couch of lasting night**
lair of eternal night, i.e., Hell 30 **vaulty** (1) arched (2) tomblike 32 **stop this
gap of breath** stop up this mouth 32 **fulsome** loathsome 35 **buss** kiss
36 **affliction** (1) afflicted one (2) one who now afflicts us 40 **fell anatomy** cruel
skeleton, i.e., death 42 **modern invocation** common or ordinary entreaty
44 **Thou ... so** (as it stands, the line must be sarcastic; it is short a syllable, and
many editors follow the fourth edition of the Folio, 1685, in supplying "not"
before "holy")

My name is Constance; I was Geoffrey's wife;
Young Arthur is my son, and he is lost!
I am not mad: I would to heaven I were,
For then 'tis like I should forget myself!
O, if I could, what grief should I forget!   50
Preach some philosophy to make me mad,
And thou shalt be canonized, Cardinal.
For, being not mad but sensible of grief,
My reasonable part produces reason
How I may be delivered of these woes,   55
And teaches me to kill or hang myself:
If I were mad, I should forget my son,
Or madly think a babe of clouts were he.
I am not mad: too well, too well I feel
The different plague of each calamity.   60

KING PHILIP Bind up those tresses! O, what love I note
In the fair multitude of those her hairs!
Where but by chance a silver drop hath fall'n,
Even to that drop ten thousand wiry friends
Do glue themselves in sociable grief,   65
Like true, inseparable, faithful loves,
Sticking together in calamity.

CONSTANCE To England, if you will.

KING PHILIP   Bind up your hairs.

CONSTANCE Yes, that I will; and wherefore will I do it?
I tore them from their bonds and cried aloud,   70
"O that these hands could so redeem my son,
As they have given these hairs their liberty!"
But now I envy at their liberty,
And will again commit them to their bonds,

49 like likely   53 sensible of capable of feeling   54-55 reason/How the idea of
a way in which   55 be delivered of (1) give birth to (2) be delivered from
58 babe of clouts rag doll   63 drop tear   64 wiry friends hairs ("wiry" was a
common, and not pejorative, epithet for hair)   65 glue sympathetically
attach   68 To England, if you will (Constance here responds to King Philip's
invitation at line 20; the separation is often taken as evidence that her "mad scene"
is an interpolation, though the leap back to an earlier subject may simply be
another symptom of her agitation)   73 envy at am envious of

75   Because my poor child is a prisoner.
        And, Father Cardinal, I have heard you say
        That we shall see and know our friends in heaven:
        If that be true, I shall see my boy again,
        For since the birth of Cain, the first male child,
80   To him that did but yesterday suspire,
        There was not such a gracious creature born.
        But now will canker-sorrow eat my bud
        And chase the native beauty from his cheek,
        And he will look as hollow as a ghost,
85   As dim and meager as an ague's fit,
        And so he'll die; and rising so again,
        When I shall meet him in the court of heaven
        I shall not know him: therefore never, never
        Must I behold my pretty Arthur more.

90   PANDULPH You hold too heinous a respect of grief.

     CONSTANCE He talks to me that never had a son.

     KING PHILIP You are as fond of grief as of your child.

     CONSTANCE Grief fills the room up of my absent child,
        Lies in his bed, walks up and down with me,
95   Puts on his pretty looks, repeats his words,
        Remembers me of all his gracious parts,
        Stuffs out his vacant garments with his form;
        Then have I reason to be fond of grief!
        Fare you well: had you such a loss as I,
100   I could give better comfort than you do.
        I will not keep this form upon my head,
        When there is such disorder in my wit!
        O Lord! My boy, my Arthur, my fair son!
        My life, my joy, my food, my all the world!
105   My widow-comfort, and my sorrows' cure!   *Exit.*

     KING PHILIP I fear some outrage, and I'll follow
            her.   *Exit.*

81 **gracious** (1) attractive, pleasing (2) holy, expressing and meriting divine
grace 82 **canker-sorrow** sorrow as a cankerworm 89 **Must I** can I
90 **heinous a respect** atrocious a conception 92 **fond of** foolishly enamored
with 96 **Remembers** reminds 101 **form** order (she had bound up her hair at
lines 69-75, and now unbinds it again) 102 **wit** mind

LEWIS There's nothing in this world can make me joy;
    Life is as tedious as a twice-told tale,
    Vexing the dull ear of a drowsy man,
    And bitter shame hath spoiled the sweet words'
       taste,   110
    That it yields nought but shame and bitterness.

PANDULPH Before the curing of a strong disease,
    Even in the instant of repair and health,
    The fit is strongest: evils that take leave,
    On their departure most of all show evil.   115
    What have you lost by losing of this day?

LEWIS All days of glory, joy, and happiness.

PANDULPH If you had won it, certainly you had.
    No, no; when fortune means to men most good,
    She looks upon them with a threat'ning eye: 120
    'Tis strange to think how much King John hath lost
    In this which he accounts so clearly won—
    Are not you grieved that Arthur is his prisoner?

LEWIS As heartily as he is glad he hath him.

PANDULPH Your mind is all as youthful as your blood.   125
    Now hear me speak with a prophetic spirit,
    For even the breath of what I mean to speak
    Shall blow each dust, each straw, each little rub,
    Out of the path which shall directly lead
    Thy foot to England's throne. And therefore mark: 130
    John hath seized Arthur, and it cannot be
    That, whiles warm life plays in that infant's veins,
    The misplaced John should entertain an hour,
    One minute, nay, one quiet breath of rest.
    A scepter snatched with an unruly hand   135
    Must be as boisterously maintained as gained,

110 **the sweet words' taste** (the words of the tale, sweet on first telling, are bitter on second telling. Many editors follow Pope in emending the Folio's "words" to "world's") 113 **repair** recovery 116 **losing of this day** losing today's battle 128 **dust** particle of dust 128 **rub** obstacle (from bowling, a roughness in the path of the bowl) 133 **misplaced** out of his proper place, i.e. usurping 136 **boisterously** violently

And he that stands upon a slipp'ry place
Makes nice of no vile hold to stay him up:
That John may stand, then Arthur needs must fall;
140 So be it, for it cannot be but so.

LEWIS But what shall I gain by young Arthur's fall?

PANDULPH You, in the right of Lady Blanch your wife,
May then make all the claim that Arthur did.

LEWIS And lose it, life and all, as Arthur did.

PANDULPH How green you are and fresh in this old
145   world!
John lays you plots; the times conspire with you,
For he that steeps his safety in true blood
Shall find but bloody safety and untrue.
This act so evilly borne shall cool the hearts
150 Of all his people, and freeze up their zeal,
That none so small advantage shall step forth
To check his reign, but they will cherish it;
No natural exhalation in the sky,
No scope of nature, no distempered day,
155 No common wind, no customèd event,
But they will pluck away his natural cause
And call them meteors, prodigies, and signs,
Abortives, presages, and tongues of heaven,
Plainly denouncing vengeance upon John.

160 LEWIS May be he will not touch young Arthur's life,
But hold himself safe in his prisonment.

PANDULPH O sir, when he shall hear of your approach,
If that young Arthur be not gone already,

138 **Makes nice … up** is not fastidious about his means of holding himself
up 146 **lays you plots** prepares the course for you to follow 147 **steeps his
safety in true blood** saturates his own security in loyal, or legitimate, blood (the
specific aim of Pandulph's generalization is, of course, John's inevitable need to
murder the true king, Arthur) 149 **borne** (1) born (2) carried out 151 **none so
small advantage** no opportunity, however small 153 **exhalation** meteor
154 **scope of nature** event at the limit of natural possibility 154 **distempered**
stormy 156 **his** its 157 **meteors** supernatural omens (opposed to the "natural
exhalation" of line 153) 158 **Abortives** misshaped creations (also considered
omens)

Even at that news he dies; and then the hearts
Of all his people shall revolt from him 165
And kiss the lips of unacquainted change,
And pick strong matter of revolt and wrath
Out of the bloody fingers' ends of John.
Methinks I see this hurly all on foot;
And, O, what better matter breeds for you 170
Than I have named! The bastard Faulconbridge
Is now in England ransacking the church,
Offending charity: if but a dozen French
Were there in arms, they would be as a call
To train ten thousand English to their side, 175
Or as a little snow, tumbled about,
Anon becomes a mountain. O noble Dolphin,
Go with me to the King: 'tis wonderful
What may be wrought out of their discontent,
Now that their souls are topful of offense. 180
For England go; I will whet on the King.

LEWIS Strong reasons makes strange actions! Let us
go:
If you say aye, the King will not say no. *Exeunt.*

---

166 kiss ... change amorously welcome any alteration   167 matter (1) reason, cause (2) corrupt matter, pus   169 hurly turmoil   169 on foot under way 170 breeds is being prepared   173 charity right feeling among Christians 174 call decoy   175 train entice   177 Anon at once   180 topful of offense (1) filled to the brim with John's offenses (2) thoroughly offended   181 whet on urge 182 makes make (the verb form may imply "having strong reasons")

ACT IV

Scene I. [*England. A room in a castle.*]

Enter Hubert and Executioners.

HUBERT Heat me these irons hot, and look thou stand
　　　Within the arras. When I strike my foot
　　　Upon the bosom of the ground, rush forth
　　　And bind the boy which you shall find with me
5　　Fast to the chair. Be heedful. Hence, and watch.

EXECUTIONER I hope your warrant will bear out the
　　　deed.

HUBERT Uncleanly scruples! Fear not you! Look to 't.
　　　　　　　　　　　　　　　[*Executioners hide.*]
　　　Young lad, come forth; I have to say with you.

Enter Arthur.

ARTHUR Good morrow, Hubert.

HUBERT　　　　　　　　Good morrow, little prince.

IV.i.2 **Within the arras** behind the curtain　6 **bear out** vindicate, give authority
for　7 **Uncleanly** improper　8 **to say with** something to say to

ARTHUR As little prince, having so great a title   10
  To be more prince, as may be. You are sad.

HUBERT Indeed, I have been merrier.

ARTHUR   Mercy on me!
  Methinks nobody should be sad but I:
  Yet I remember, when I was in France,
  Young gentlemen would be as sad as night,   15
  Only for wantonness. By my Christendom,
  So I were out of prison, and kept sheep,
  I should be as merry as the day is long;
  And so I would be here, but that I doubt
  My uncle practices more harm to me.   20
  He is afraid of me, and I of him:
  Is it my fault that I was Geoffrey's son?
  No, indeed, is 't not; and I would to heaven
  I were your son, so you would love me, Hubert.

HUBERT [Aside] If I talk to him, with his innocent
    prate   25
  He will awake my mercy, which lies dead:
  Therefore I will be sudden and dispatch.

ARTHUR Are you sick, Hubert? You look pale today.
  In sooth, I would you were a little sick,
  That I might sit all night and watch with you.   30
  I warrant I love you more than you do me.

HUBERT [Aside] His words do take possession of my
    bosom.
  [To Arthur] Read here, young Arthur.
                              [Showing a paper.]
                    [Aside] How now, foolish rheum!
  Turning dispiteous torture out of door!
  I must be brief, lest resolution drop   35

10-11 As little ... may be considering my title (King) to be even greater, I am
presently as little prince as may be 16 wantonness whim 16 By my
Christendom as I am a Christian (perhaps literally "by my baptism") 17 So if
only 19 doubt fear 20 practices schemes 25 prate prattle 27 dispatch
finish the job quickly 33 rheum (1) tears (2) room (in his bosom, Arthur's words
threatening to displace the torture there) 34 dispiteous torture merciless
torture (1) threatened to Arthur (2) now tormenting Hubert

Out at mine eyes in tender womanish tears.
[*To Arthur*] Can you not read it? Is it not fair writ?

ARTHUR Too fairly, Hubert, for so foul effect:
Must you with hot irons burn out both mine eyes?

HUBERT Young boy, I must.

ARTHUR   And will you?

40 HUBERT   And I will.

ARTHUR Have you the heart? When your head did but ache,
I knit my handkercher about your brows
(The best I had, a princess wrought it me—
And I did never ask it you again)
45 And with my hand at midnight held your head,
And like the watchful minutes to the hour,
Still and anon cheered up the heavy time,
Saying, "What lack you?" and "Where lies your grief?"
Or "What good love may I perform for you?"
50 Many a poor man's son would have lien still,
And ne'er have spoke a loving word to you:
But you at your sick service had a prince.
Nay, you may think my love was crafty love,
And call it cunning. Do and if you will.
55 If heaven be pleased that you must use me ill,
Why then you must. Will you put out mine eyes?
These eyes that never did nor never shall
So much as frown on you?

HUBERT   I have sworn to do it,
And with hot irons must I burn them out.

60 ARTHUR Ah, none but in this iron age would do it!
The iron of itself, though heat red-hot,

37 **fair writ** written clearly   38 **effect** purpose   43 **wrought it me** worked (embroidered) it for me   44 **ask it you** ask you for it   46 **like the ... hour** as frequently as there are observable minutes in an hour (?)   47 **Still and anon** continually   49 **love** labor of love   50 **lien** (two syllables) lain   52 **you at your sick service had** you, sick, had at your service   53 **crafty** feigned   61 **heat** heated

Approaching near these eyes, would drink my tears
And quench his fiery indignation
Even in the matter of mine innocence!
Nay, after that, consume away in rust, 65
But for containing fire to harm mine eye!
Are you more stubborn-hard than hammered iron?
And if an angel should have come to me
And told me Hubert should put out mine eyes,
I would not have believed him—no tongue but
    Hubert's. 70

HUBERT [*Stamps*] Come forth.

    [*Executioners come forth with a cord, irons, etc.*]

                Do as I bid you do.

ARTHUR O save me, Hubert, save me! My eyes are out
Even with the fierce looks of these bloody men.

HUBERT Give me the iron, I say, and bind him here.

ARTHUR Alas, what need you be so boist'rous rough? 75
I will not struggle; I will stand stone still!
For God's sake, Hubert, let me not be bound!
Nay, hear me, Hubert! Drive these men away,
And I will sit as quiet as a lamb.
I will not stir, nor winch, nor speak a word, 80
Nor look upon the iron angerly:
Thrust but these men away, and I'll forgive you,
Whatever torment you do put me to.

HUBERT Go, stand within; let me alone with him.

EXECUTIONER I am best pleased to be from such a
    deed. [*Exeunt Executioners.*] 85

ARTHUR Alas, I then have chid away my friend!
He hath a stern look, but a gentle heart:
Let him come back, that his compassion may
Give life to yours.

HUBERT   Come, boy, prepare yourself.

64 **matter** substance, i.e., tears 66 **But for** merely as a result of 80 **winch** wince 85 **from** away from

ARTHUR Is there no remedy?

90 HUBERT   None, but to lose your eyes.

ARTHUR O heaven, that there were but a mote in
        yours,
    A grain, a dust, a gnat, a wandering hair,
    Any annoyance in that precious sense:
    Then feeling what small things are boisterous there,
95 Your vile intent must needs seem horrible.

HUBERT Is this your promise? Go to, hold your
        tongue.

ARTHUR Hubert, the utterance of a brace of tongues
    Must needs want pleading for a pair of eyes:
    Let me not hold my tongue! let me not, Hubert!
100 Or, Hubert, if you will, cut out my tongue,
    So I may keep mine eyes. O, spare mine eyes,
    Though to no use but still to look on you!
    Lo, by my troth, the instrument is cold
    And would not harm me.

HUBERT   I can heat it, boy.

105 ARTHUR No, in good sooth; the fire is dead with grief,
    Being create for comfort, to be used
    In undeserved extremes. See else yourself.
    There is no malice in this burning coal.
    The breath of heaven hath blown his spirit out
110 And strewed repentant ashes on his head.

HUBERT But with my breath I can revive it, boy.

ARTHUR And if you do, you will but make it blush
    And glow with shame of your proceedings, Hubert:
    Nay, it perchance will sparkle in your eyes,

94 **boisterous** painful 96 **Go to** (disapproving exclamation, equivalent, perhaps
to "come, come") 97 **brace** pair 98 **want** be insufficient 99 **let me not**
(1) repeating the previous plea (2) hinder me not 101 So if thereby 104 **would
not** (1) would not be able to (2) does not wish to 106 **create** created 106 **to be
used** at the prospect of being used 107 **In undeserved extremes** for undeserved cruelties (with pun on Latin *in extremis*, in the final agonies of dying)
107 **else** further 114 **sparkle in** throw sparks into

And, like a dog that is compelled to fight,   115
Snatch at his master that doth tarre him on.
All things that you should use to do me wrong
Deny their office: only you do lack
That mercy which fierce fire and iron extends,
Creatures of note for mercy-lacking uses.   120

HUBERT Well, see to live: I will not touch thine eye
For all the treasure that thine uncle owes;
Yet am I sworn and I did purpose, boy,
With this same very iron to burn them out.

ARTHUR O, now you look like Hubert! All this while   125
You were disguisèd.

HUBERT   Peace! No more. Adieu.
Your uncle must not know but you are dead.
I'll fill these doggèd spies with false reports;
And, pretty child, sleep doubtless and secure
That Hubert, for the wealth of all the world,   130
Will not offend thee.

ARTHUR   O heaven! I thank you, Hubert.

HUBERT Silence! No more! Go closely in with me.
Much danger do I undergo for thee.   *Exeunt.*

---

116 **tarre him on** incite him   118 **Deny their office** contradict their customary
functions   119 **extends** extend, grant   120 **Creatures … uses** creatures (i.e.,
fire and iron) famous for cruel uses   122 **owes** owns   127 **but** anything but
that   128 **doggèd** surly   129 **doubtless and secure** certain and assured
132 **closely** secretly

Scene II. [*King John's court.*]

*Enter [King] John, Pembroke, Salisbury,
and other Lords.*

KING JOHN Here once again we sit, once again
    crowned,
And looked upon, I hope, with cheerful eyes.

PEMBROKE This "once again," but that your Highness
    pleased,
Was once superfluous: you were crowned before,
5   And that high royalty was ne'er plucked off,
The faiths of men ne'er stainèd with revolt;
Fresh expectation troubled not the land
With any longed-for change or better state.

SALISBURY Therefore, to be possessed with double
    pomp,
10   To guard a title that was rich before,
To gild refinèd gold, to paint the lily,
To throw a perfume on the violet,
To smooth the ice, or add another hue
Unto the rainbow, or with taper-light
15   To seek the beauteous eye of heaven to garnish,
Is wasteful and ridiculous excess.

IV.ii.1 **once again crowned** (John has just had a second coronation, enforcing new oaths of allegiance to counteract the excommunication which freed his followers from their original oaths. See III.i.100–01) 4 **once superfluous** one time more than necessary 7 **Fresh expectation** (1) eager anticipation (2) anticipation of something new 8 **state** (1) government (2) condition 9 **pomp** ceremony, i.e., coronation 10 **guard** (1) ornament (2) defend 14–15 **with taper-light … garnish** to seek to embellish the sun's beauty with a candle 16 **excess** extravagance ("excess" also = usury—see *Merchant of Venice* I.iii.59—and may here connote Salisbury's sense that John is extorting too much money from his subjects)

PEMBROKE But that your royal pleasure must be done,
    This act is as an ancient tale new told,
    And, in the last repeating, troublesome,
    Being urgèd at a time unseasonable.   20

SALISBURY In this the antique and well-noted face
    Of plain old form is much disfigurèd,
    And like a shifted wind unto a sail,
    It makes the course of thoughts to fetch about,
    Startles and frights consideration,   25
    Makes sound opinion sick and truth suspected,
    For putting on so new a fashioned robe.

PEMBROKE When workmen strive to do better than
        well,
    They do confound their skill in covetousness,
    And oftentimes excusing of a fault   30
    Doth make the fault the worse by th' excuse,
    As patches set upon a little breach
    Discredit more in hiding of the fault
    Than did the fault before it was so patched.

SALISBURY To this effect, before you were new
        crowned,   35
    We breathed our counsel: but it pleased your
        Highness
    To overbear it, and we are all well pleased,
    Since all and every part of what we would
    Doth make a stand at what your Highness will.

21 **well-noted** well-known   22 **old form** customary methods   24 **fetch about**
(nautical) take a new tack   25 **frights consideration** frightens contemplation
(raising the whole question of his right to the crown)   27 **so new a fashioned
robe** (1) a robe so newly made, as opposed to John's original coronation robe (2) a
robe of such new style, as opposed to "plain old form," line 22   29 **confound**
disrupt, destroy   29 **covetousness** (1) desire to do better (2) greed   32 **breach**
tear in a garment, perhaps with a pun on the garment itself   36 **breathed** uttered
quietly or hesitantly   37 **we are all well pleased** (it is becoming increasingly
clear that they are not in the least pleased)   38 **would** would do, wish   39 **Doth
make a stand at** stops at (the limits of)   39 **will** wishes to do

40　KING JOHN Some reasons of this double coronation
　　　　　　　I have possessed you with, and think them strong;
　　　　　　　And more, more strong, when lesser is my fear,
　　　　　　　I shall indue you with. Meantime but ask
　　　　　　　What you would have reformed that is not well,
45　　　　　　And well shall you perceive how willingly
　　　　　　　I will both hear and grant you your requests.

　　　PEMBROKE Then I, as one that am the tongue of these
　　　　　　　To sound the purposes of all their hearts,
　　　　　　　Both for myself and them—but, chief of all,
50　　　　　　Your safety, for the which, myself and them
　　　　　　　Bend their best studies—heartily request
　　　　　　　Th' enfranchisement of Arthur, whose restraint
　　　　　　　Doth move the murmuring lips of discontent
　　　　　　　To break into this dangerous argument:
55　　　　　　If what in rest you have, in right you hold,
　　　　　　　Why then your fears, which, as they say, attend
　　　　　　　The steps of wrong, should move you to mew up
　　　　　　　Your tender kinsman, and to choke his days
　　　　　　　With barbarous ignorance, and deny his youth
60　　　　　　The rich advantage of good exercise?
　　　　　　　That the time's enemies may not have this
　　　　　　　To grace occasions, let it be our suit,
　　　　　　　That you have bid us ask his liberty,
　　　　　　　Which for our goods we do no further ask
65　　　　　　Than whereupon our weal, on you depending,
　　　　　　　Counts it your weal he have his liberty.

41 **possessed you with** given you 43 **indue** endow, supply 48 **sound the purposes** give sound to the intentions 50 **them** they (themselves?) 51 **Bend their best studies** exert their (our?) hardest efforts 55 **rest** peace 56 **Why then** why, then, is it that 60 **exercise** education in those qualities befitting a gentleman 61 **the time's enemies** those opposed to present arrangements 62 **grace occasions** embellish their excuses or opportunities (for rebellion) 63 **That you ... liberty** (as punctuated here—and in the Folio—Pembroke asks that it be given out that John encouraged them to ask for Arthur's liberty. Many editors, following Rowe, place a comma after "ask" to mean: "let his liberty be the suit you have offered to grant us") 64 **our goods** our own good 65 **whereupon our weal** in so far as our own well-being

Enter Hubert.

KING JOHN Let it be so: I do commit his youth
To your direction. Hubert, what news with you?
                              [*Takes him aside.*]

PEMBROKE This is the man should do the bloody deed:
He showed his warrant to a friend of mine.   70
The image of a wicked heinous fault
Lives in his eye; that close aspect of his
Does show the mood of a much troubled breast,
And I do fearfully believe 'tis done,
What we so feared he had a charge to do.   75

SALISBURY The color of the King doth come and go
Between his purpose and his conscience,
Like heralds 'twixt two dreadful battles set:
His passion is so ripe, it needs must break.

PEMBROKE And when it breaks, I fear will issue thence   80
The foul corruption of a sweet child's death.

KING JOHN We cannot hold mortality's strong hand.
Good lords, although my will to give is living,
The suit which you demand is gone and dead.
He tells us Arthur is deceased tonight.   85

SALISBURY Indeed we feared his sickness was past
cure.

PEMBROKE Indeed we heard how near his death he
was,
Before the child himself felt he was sick:
This must be answered either here or hence.

KING JOHN Why do you bend such solemn brows
on me?   90

67 **Let it be so** (John, seeing Hubert, grants their request on the supposition that Arthur is already dead. Many editors, following Dr. Johnson, have destroyed this detail by moving the entry to the middle of line 68) 72 **close aspect** severe appearance, guarded look 78 **battles** armies drawn up for battle 81 **corruption** pus 82 **hold** restrain 89 **This must ... hence** amends must be made for this either in this world or the next 90 **bend .. brows** scowl

Think you I bear the shears of destiny?
Have I commandment on the pulse of life?

SALISBURY It is apparent foul play, and 'tis shame
That greatness should so grossly offer it:
95   So thrive it in your game! and so, farewell.

PEMBROKE Stay yet, Lord Salisbury. I'll go with thee
And find th' inheritance of this poor child,
His little kingdom of a forcèd grave.
That blood which owed the breadth of all this isle,
100   Three foot of it doth hold: bad world the while!
This must not be thus borne; this will break out
To all our sorrows, and ere long, I doubt.
Exeunt [*Lords*].

KING JOHN They burn in indignation. I repent.

Enter Messenger.

There is no sure foundation set on blood,
105   No certain life achieved by others' death.
A fearful eye thou hast. Where is that blood
That I have seen inhabit in those cheeks?
So foul a sky clears not without a storm;
Pour down thy weather: how goes all in France?

MESSENGER From France to England; never such a
110   pow'r
For any foreign preparation
Was levied in the body of a land.
The copy of your speed is learned by them:
For when you should be told they do prepare,
115   The tidings comes that they are all arrived.

KING JOHN O, where hath our intelligence been
      drunk?

91 **shears of destiny** with which Atropos, one of the three Fates, cuts the thread of life 94 **so grossly offer it** present [such foul play] so flagrantly 95 **So thrive it in your game** may your schemes come to the same end 98 **forcèd** enforced, violently brought about 99 **blood which owed** life which owned 100 **the while** during the time this can be true 102 **doubt** fear 111 **foreign preparation** force for foreign invasion 113 **The copy ... by them** they have learned to copy your speed 116 **intelligence** spy service

Where hath it slept? Where is my mother's care,
That such an army could be drawn in France
And she not hear of it?

MESSENGER   My liege, her ear
Is stopped with dust: the first of April died   120
Your noble mother; and, as I hear, my lord,
The Lady Constance in a frenzy died
Three days before—but this from rumor's tongue
I idly heard; if true or false I know not.

KING JOHN Withhold thy speed, dreadful occasion!   125
O, make a league with me, till I have pleased
My discontented peers. What! Mother dead!
How wildly then walks my estate in France!
Under whose conduct came those pow'rs of
     France
That thou for truth giv'st out are landed here?   130

MESSENGER Under the Dolphin.

Enter Bastard and Peter of Pomfret.

KING JOHN   Thou hast made me giddy
With these ill tidings. [*To Bastard*] Now, what
     says the world
To your proceedings? Do not seek to stuff
My head with more ill news, for it is full.

BASTARD But if you be afeard to hear the worst,   135
Then let the worst unheard fall on your head.

KING JOHN Bear with me, cousin, for I was amazed
Under the tide; but now I breathe again
Aloft the flood, and can give audience
To any tongue, speak it of what it will.   140

BASTARD How I have sped among the clergymen,
The sums I have collected shall express.

123 **Three days** (Shakespeare compresses three years to three days) 124 **idly**
carelessly, without paying attention 125 **occasion** course of events
137 **amazed** in a maze, bewildered 139 **Aloft** on top of 141 **sped** fared

595

But as I travailed hither through the land,
I find the people strangely fantasied,
145   Possessed with rumors, full of idle dreams,
Not knowing what they fear, but full of fear.
And here's a prophet that I brought with me
From forth the streets of Pomfret, whom I found
With many hundreds treading on his heels,
150   To whom he sung, in rude harsh-sounding rhymes,
That ere the next Ascension-day at noon,
Your Highness should deliver up your crown.

KING JOHN Thou idle dreamer, wherefore didst thou
    so?

PETER Foreknowing that the truth will fall out so.

155   KING JOHN Hubert, away with him: imprison him,
And on that day at noon, whereon he says
I shall yield up my crown, let him be hanged.
Deliver him to safety and return,
For I must use thee.

                                [*Exit Hubert with Peter.*]

                        O my gentle cousin,
160   Hear'st thou the news abroad, who are arrived?

BASTARD The French, my lord; men's mouths are full
    of it—
Besides, I met Lord Bigot and Lord Salisbury,
With eyes as red as new-enkindled fire,
And others more, going to seek the grave
165   Of Arthur, whom they say is killed tonight
On your suggestion.

KING JOHN   Gentle kinsman, go,
And thrust thyself into their companies.
I have a way to win their loves again;
Bring them before me.

BASTARD   I will seek them out.

143 **travailed** (1) labored (2) traveled (the words had not yet been separated)
144 **strangely fantasied** filled with strange fancies   148 **Pomfret** Pontefract, in
the West Riding of Yorkshire   158 **safety** close custody   159 **gentle** noble,
wellborn

596

KING JOHN Nay, but make haste: the better foot
    before!   170
  O, let me have no subject enemies,
  When adverse foreigners affright my towns
  With dreadful pomp of stout invasion.
  Be Mercury, set feathers to thy heels,
  And fly, like thought, from them to me again.   175

BASTARD The spirit of the time shall teach me speed.

                                  Exit.

KING JOHN Spoke like a sprightful noble gentleman.
  Go after him, for he perhaps shall need
  Some messenger betwixt me and the peers,
  And be thou he.

MESSENGER   With all my heart, my liege. [*Exit.*] 180

KING JOHN My mother dead!

                 Enter Hubert.

HUBERT My lord, they say five moons were seen
    tonight:
  Four fixèd, and the fifth did whirl about
  The other four in wondrous motion.

KING JOHN Five moons?

HUBERT   Old men and beldams in the streets 185
  Do prophesy upon it dangerously;
  Young Arthur's death is common in their mouths,
  And, when they talk of him, they shake their heads
  And whisper one another in the ear,
  And he that speaks doth gripe the hearer's wrist, 190
  Whilst he that hears makes fearful action,
  With wrinkled brows, with nods, with rolling eyes.
  I saw a smith stand with his hammer, thus,
  The whilst his iron did on the anvil cool,
  With open mouth swallowing a tailor's news, 195

---

170 **the better foot before** as fast as you can 174 **Mercury** messenger of the
gods, who wore winged sandals 177 **sprightful** full of spirit 185 **beldams**
grandmothers 186 **prophesy upon it** expound its meaning

Who, with his shears and measure in his hand,
Standing on slippers, which his nimble haste
Had falsely thrust upon contrary feet,
Told of a many thousand warlike French,
200   That were embattailèd and ranked in Kent.
Another lean unwashed artificer
Cuts off his tale and talks of Arthur's death.

KING JOHN Why seek'st thou to possess me with these
      fears?
Why urgest thou so oft young Arthur's death?
205   Thy hand hath murdered him: I had a mighty cause
To wish him dead, but thou hadst none to kill him.

HUBERT No had, my lord? Why, did you not provoke
      me?

KING JOHN It is the curse of kings to be attended
By slaves that take their humors for a warrant
210   To break within the bloody house of life,
And on the winking of authority
To understand a law, to know the meaning
Of dangerous majesty, when perchance it frowns
More upon humor than advised respect.

215   HUBERT Here is your hand and seal for what I did.

KING JOHN O, when the last accompt twixt heaven
      and earth
Is to be made, then shall this hand and seal
Witness against us to damnation!
How oft the sight of means to do ill deeds
220   Make deeds ill done! Hadst not thou been by,
A fellow by the hand of nature marked,
Quoted and signed to do a deed of shame,

200 **embattailèd** marshaled for battle   207 **No had** had I not   207 **provoke**
urge (order?)   209 **humors** moods, whims   211–12 **on the winking ... a law**
take as law the mere hints (or oversights) of one in authority   214 **advised
respect** deliberate consideration   216 **accompt** account   220 **deeds ill done** (1)
evil deeds done (2) deeds done badly   222 **Quoted** (1) marked, as with a line in
the margin of a book (2) noted, recorded   222 **signed** (1) marked with some
distinguishing characteristic, such as, e.g. the sign of Cain (2) assigned, appointed

This murder had not come into my mind;
But taking note of thy abhorred aspect,
Finding thee fit for bloody villainy,   225
Apt, liable to be employed in danger,
I faintly broke with thee of Arthur's death;
And thou, to be endearèd to a king,
Made it no conscience to destroy a prince.

HUBERT My lord—   230

KING JOHN Hadst thou but shook thy head or made a
      pause
When I spake darkly what I purposèd,
Or turned an eye of doubt upon my face,
As bid me tell my tale in express words,
Deep shame had struck me dumb, made me break
      off,   235
And those thy fears might have wrought fears in me.
But thou didst understand me by my signs
And didst in signs again parley with sin;
Yea, without stop, didst let thy heart consent,
And consequently thy rude hand to act   240
The deed, which both our tongues held vile to name.
Out of my sight, and never see me more!
My nobles leave me, and my state is braved,
Even at my gates, with ranks of foreign pow'rs;
Nay, in the body of this fleshly land,   245
This kingdom, this confine of blood and breath,
Hostility and civil tumult reigns
Between my conscience and my cousin's death.

HUBERT Arm you against your other enemies:
I'll make a peace between your soul and you.   250
Young Arthur is alive! This hand of mine
Is yet a maiden and an innocent hand,
Not painted with the crimson spots of blood.

226 **liable** suitable 227 **broke with thee of** disclosed to thee my desire for
229 **Made it no conscience to destroy** had no scruples about destroying
232 **darkly** obscurely 234 **As** as to 238 **sin** (1) sin (2) sign 239 **stop**
hesitation 243 **braved** challenged 245 **the body of this fleshly land** my own
body (conceived as a microcosm) 246 **confine** limited territory

Within this bosom never entered yet
255   The dreadful motion of a murderous thought,
And you have slandered nature in my form,
Which, howsoever rude exteriorly,
Is yet the cover of a fairer mind
Than to be butcher of an innocent child.

KING JOHN Doth Arthur live? O, haste thee to the
260   peers!
Throw this report on their incensèd rage,
And make them tame to their obedience.
Forgive the comment that my passion made
Upon thy feature, for my rage was blind,
265   And foul imaginary eyes of blood
Presented thee more hideous than thou art.
O, answer not, but to my closet bring
The angry lords with all expedient haste.
I conjure thee but slowly: run more fast.   *Exeunt*.

Scene III. [*Before a castle*.]

Enter Arthur, on the walls.

ARTHUR The wall is high, and yet will I leap down.
Good ground, be pitiful and hurt me not!
There's few or none do know me; if they did,
This ship-boy's semblance hath disguised me quite.
5   I am afraid, and yet I'll venture it.
If I get down, and do not break my limbs,
I'll find a thousand shifts to get away.
As good to die and go, as die and stay.
                                        [*Leaps down*.]

255 **motion** impulse, inclination 256 **form** features 262 **tame to their obedience** subject to their oaths 265 **imaginary eyes of blood** (1) John's eyes, imagining bloodshed (2) Hubert's eyes, imagined bloodthirsty (3) Arthur's eyes, imagined as empty sockets 267 **closet** private council-chamber 269 **conjure** entreat IV.iii.7 **shifts** tricks

O me! my uncle's spirit is in these stones!
Heaven take my soul, and England keep my bones!   10

Dies.

Enter Pembroke, Salisbury, and Bigot.

SALISBURY Lords, I will meet him at Saint Edmunds-
bury.
It is our safety, and we must embrace
This gentle offer of the perilous time.

PEMBROKE Who brought that letter from the Cardinal?

SALISBURY The Count Meloone, a noble lord of France,   15
Whose private with me of the Dolphin's love
Is much more general than these lines import.

BIGOT Tomorrow morning let us meet him then.

SALISBURY Or rather then set forward, for 'twill be
Two long days' journey, lords, or ere we meet.   20

Enter Bastard.

BASTARD Once more today well met, distempered
lords!
The King by me requests your presence straight.

SALISBURY The King hath dispossessed himself of us;
We will not line his thin bestainèd cloak
With our pure honors, nor attend the foot   25
That leaves the print of blood where'er it walks.
Return and tell him so: we know the worst.

BASTARD Whate'er you think, good words, I think,
were best.

SALISBURY Our griefs, and not our manners, reason
now.

BASTARD But there is little reason in your grief!   30
Therefore 'twere reason you had manners now.

11 **Saint Edmundsbury** Bury St. Edmunds, in Suffolk   16 **private with** private
message to   17 **general** comprehensive   20 **or ere** before   21 **distempered**
peevish   22 **straight** immediately   29 **reason** control our conduct

PEMBROKE Sir, sir, impatience hath his privilege.

BASTARD 'Tis true, to hurt his master, no man else.

SALISBURY This is the prison. [*Sees Arthur.*] What is
he lies here?

PEMBROKE O death, made proud with pure and
35   princely beauty!
The earth had not a hole to hide this deed.

SALISBURY Murder, as hating what himself hath done,
Doth lay it open to urge on revenge.

BIGOT Or when he doomed this beauty to a grave,
40   Found it too precious princely for a grave.

SALISBURY Sir Richard, what think you? You have
beheld:
Or have you read or heard, or could you think,
Or do you almost think, although you see,
That you do see? Could thought, without this
object,
45   Form such another? This is the very top,
The height, the crest, or crest unto the crest,
Of murder's arms: this is the bloodiest shame,
The wildest savagery, the vilest stroke,
That ever wall-eyed wrath or staring rage
50   Presented to the tears of soft remorse.

PEMBROKE All murders past do stand excused in this:
And this, so sole and so unmatchable,
Shall give a holiness, a purity,
To the yet unbegotten sin of times,
55   And prove a deadly bloodshed but a jest,
Exampled by this heinous spectacle.

BASTARD It is a damnèd and a bloody work,

---

40 **too ... princely for a grave** (the bodies of royalty were not buried but placed
in monuments) 42 **Or have you** have you either 44 **That** that which
47 **arms** (1) heraldic insignia (2) power 49 **wall-eyed** glaring 49 **rage** insanity
50 **remorse** pity 54 **times** future times 56 **Exampled by** in comparison with

The graceless action of a heavy hand,
If that it be the work of any hand.

SALISBURY If that it be the work of any hand!   60
We had a kind of light what would ensue:
It is the shameful work of Hubert's hand,
The practice and the purpose of the King—
From whose obedience I forbid my soul,
Kneeling before this ruin of sweet life,   65
And breathing to his breathless excellence
The incense of a vow, a holy vow,
Never to taste the pleasures of the world,
Never to be infected with delight,
Nor conversant with ease and idleness,   70
Till I have set a glory to this hand,
By giving it the worship of revenge.

PEMBROKE ⎫
BIGOT   ⎬ Our souls religiously confirm thy words.

Enter Hubert.

HUBERT Lords, I am hot with haste in seeking you:
Arthur doth live; the King hath sent for you.   75

SALISBURY O, he is bold and blushes not at death.
Avaunt, thou hateful villain, get thee gone!

HUBERT I am no villain.

SALISBURY [*Drawing his sword*] Must I rob the law?

BASTARD Your sword is bright, sir; put it up again.

SALISBURY Not till I sheathe it in a murderer's skin.   80

HUBERT Stand back, Lord Salisbury, stand back, I say!

---

58 **graceless** lacking divine sanction, damned 58 **heavy** oppressive, evil
61 **light** intimation (perhaps with the sarcastic connotation of "divinely inspired,"
following upon the Bastard's "damnèd" and "graceless") 63 **practice** plot
69 **infected with delight** (given these circumstances, delight would be
unhealthy) 71-72 **set a glory to ... revenge** put a halo around Arthur's hand
(as opposed to Hubert's, in line 62) by showing my veneration through revenge (he
will make Arthur a saint by worshiping him as one. Some editors would read "this
hand" as Salisbury's own, but that causes difficulties with the religious imagery)

By heaven, I think my sword's as sharp as yours.
I would not have you, lord, forget yourself,
Nor tempt the danger of my true defense,
85 Lest I, by marking of your rage, forget
Your worth, your greatness, and nobility.

BIGOT Out, dunghill! dar'st thou brave a nobleman?

HUBERT Not for my life: but yet I dare defend
My innocent life against an emperor.

SALISBURY Thou art a murderer.

90 HUBERT   Do not prove me so:
Yet I am none. Whose tongue soe'er speaks false,
Not truly speaks; who speaks not truly, lies.

PEMBROKE Cut him to pieces!

BASTARD   Keep the peace, I say.

SALISBURY Stand by, or I shall gall you, Faulconbridge.

95 BASTARD Thou wert better gall the devil, Salisbury.
If thou but frown on me, or stir thy foot,
Or teach thy hasty spleen to do me shame,
I'll strike thee dead. Put up thy sword betime,
Or I'll so maul you and your toasting-iron
100 That you shall think the devil is come from hell.

BIGOT What wilt thou do, renownèd Faulconbridge?
Second a villain and a murderer?

HUBERT Lord Bigot, I am none.

BIGOT   Who killed this prince?

---

84 **tempt** test 85 **marking of** (1) observing (2) striking at 87 **brave**
challenge 90 **Do not prove me so** (by forcing me to kill you) 91 **Yet** up to
now 93 **Cut him to pieces** (Hubert, as a mere citizen, is not considered worthy
of the dueling code. The lords' honor demands that they kill him for calling them
liars, but they will not bother to kill him as a gentleman) 94 **by** aside 94 **gall**
wound 97 **spleen** ill temper 97 **do me shame** treat me contemptuously (as
you have Hubert) 98 **betime** soon, before it is too late

HUBERT 'Tis not an hour since I left him well:
　　I honored him, I loved him, and will weep   105
　　My date of life out for his sweet life's loss.

SALISBURY Trust not those cunning waters of his eyes,
　　For villainy is not without such rheum,
　　And he, long traded in it, makes it seem
　　Like rivers of remorse and innocency.   110
　　Away with me, all you whose souls abhor
　　Th' uncleanly savors of a slaughterhouse,
　　For I am stifled with this smell of sin.

BIGOT Away toward Bury, to the Dolphin there!

PEMBROKE There tell the King he may inquire us out.   115
                              Exeunt Lords.

BASTARD Here's a good world! Knew you of this fair
　　work?
　　Beyond the infinite and boundless reach
　　Of mercy, if thou didst this deed of death,
　　Art thou damned, Hubert.

HUBERT Do but hear me, sir—

BASTARD   Ha! I'll tell thee what: 120
　　Thou'rt damned as black—nay, nothing is so
　　black—
　　Thou art more deep damned than Prince Lucifer:
　　There is not yet so ugly a fiend of hell
　　As thou shalt be, if thou didst kill this child.

HUBERT Upon my soul—

BASTARD   If thou didst but consent   125
　　To this most cruel act, do but despair,
　　And if thou want'st a cord, the smallest thread
　　That ever spider twisted from her womb
　　Will serve to strangle thee! A rush will be a beam
　　To hang thee on. Or wouldst thou drown thyself,   130
　　Put but a little water in a spoon

106 **date** period 109 **traded** practiced 126 **do but despair** do nothing other
than commit suicide (you are damned already; it is your only choice)

And it shall be as all the ocean,
Enough to stifle such a villain up.
I do suspect thee very grievously.

135 HUBERT If I in act, consent, or sin of thought,
Be guilty of the stealing that sweet breath
Which was embounded in this beauteous clay,
Let hell want pains enough to torture me!
I left him well.

BASTARD   Go, bear him in thine arms.
140 I am amazed, methinks, and lose my way
Among the thorns and dangers of this world.
How easy dost thou take all England up!
From forth this morsel of dead royalty,
The life, the right and truth of all this realm
145 Is fled to heaven, and England now is left
To tug and scamble and to part by th' teeth
The unowed interest of proud swelling state.
Now for the bare-picked bone of majesty
Doth dogged war bristle his angry crest
150 And snarleth in the gentle eyes of peace:
Now powers from home and discontents at home
Meet in one line, and vast confusion waits,
As doth a raven on a sick-fall'n beast,
The imminent decay of wrested pomp.
155 Now happy he whose cloak and center can

---

133 **such a villain** (apparently, the greater the villain, the easier suicide)
140 **amazed** in a maze, bewildered   142 **all England** (in calling Arthur "England," the Bastard acknowledges his right to the throne)   146 **scamble** scramble
146 **part by th' teeth** tear apart as would a pack of dogs or wolves   147 **unowed interest** (1) unowned title (2) the interest (duty, obedience) not owed to any king
149 **dogged** cruel   151-52 **powers from home ... one line** (a confusing image: it may mean either that English deserters fight face to face with English defenders who are themselves discontented, or that foreign invaders—powers away from their homes—are allied in a single army with English rebels. Both senses are apt, and the conplexity is an appropriate preparation for the "vast confusion" which impends)   154 **wrested pomp** (1) the royal magnificence John usurped from Arthur (2) the position which his enemies threaten to wrest from John
155 **center** cincture, belt

Hold out this tempest. Bear away that child,
And follow me with speed: I'll to the King.
A thousand businesses are brief in hand,
And heaven itself doth frown upon the land.

Exit [*both*].

---

158 **brief in hand** immediately demanded ("brief," used here in some apparently
unique adjectival sense, is perhaps related to the noun meaning "a royal mandate"
or "a summary statement")

ACT V

Scene I. [*King John's court.*]

Enter King John and Pandulph [with] Attendants.

[*King John gives Pandulph his crown.*]

KING JOHN Thus have I yielded up into your hand
    The circle of my glory.

PANDULPH [*Returning him the crown*] Take again
    From this my hand, as holding of the Pope,
    Your sovereign greatness and authority.

KING JOHN Now keep your holy word: go meet the
5   French,
    And from his Holiness use all your power
    To stop their marches 'fore we are enflamed.
    Our discontented counties do revolt;
    Our people quarrel with obedience,
10   Swearing allegiance and the love of soul
    To stranger blood, to foreign royalty.

V.i.3 **as holding of** as a leasehold from   8 **counties** shires; nobles (?)   10 **love of soul** soul's love, loyalty

This inundation of mistempered humor
Rests by you only to be qualified.
Then pause not, for the present time's so sick
That present med'cine must be ministered,   15
Or overthrow incurable ensues.

PANDULPH It was my breath that blew this tempest up,
Upon your stubborn usage of the Pope,
But since you are a gentle convertite,
My tongue shall hush again this storm of war   20
And make fair weather in your blust'ring land.
On this Ascension-day, remember well,
Upon your oath of service to the Pope,
Go I to make the French lay down their arms. *Exit*.

KING JOHN Is this Ascension-day? Did not the prophet   25
Say that before Ascension-day at noon
My crown I should give off? Even so I have!
I did suppose it should be on constraint,
But, heaven be thanked, it is but voluntary.

Enter Bastard.

BASTARD All Kent hath yielded—nothing there holds
out   30
But Dover Castle—London hath received,
Like a kind host, the Dolphin and his powers.
Your nobles will not hear you, but are gone
To offer service to your enemy;
And wild amazement hurries up and down   35
The little number of your doubtful friends.

KING JOHN Would not my lords return to me again
After they heard young Arthur was alive?

12-13 **This inundation ... qualified** only you can moderate this flooding of the body (of the state) with turbulent humor (in medieval physiology, health and disposition were considered dependent upon the balance maintained among four bodily fluids, called humors) 18 **Upon** as a result of 19 **convertite** convert 27 **give off** relinquish 35 **amazement** confusion, uncertainty 36 **doubtful** (1) fearful (2) untrustworthy 35-36 **hurries ... friends** (either "hurries them up and down" or "hurries among them")

BASTARD They found him dead and cast into the
                streets,
40   An empty casket, where the jewel of life
          By some damned hand was robbed and ta'en away.

KING JOHN That villain Hubert told me he did live.

BASTARD So, on my soul, he did, for aught he knew.
          But wherefore do you droop? Why look you sad?
45   Be great in act, as you have been in thought;
          Let not the world see fear and sad distrust
          Govern the motion of a kingly eye;
          Be stirring as the time; be fire with fire.
          Threaten the threat'ner, and outface the brow
50   Of bragging horror: so shall inferior eyes,
          That borrow their behaviors from the great,
          Grow great by your example and put on
          The dauntless spirit of resolution.
          Away, and glister like the god of war
55   When he intendeth to become the field:
          Show boldness and aspiring confidence!
          What, shall they seek the lion in his den,
          And fright him there? and make him tremble there?
          O, let it not be said! Forage, and run
60   To meet displeasure farther from the doors,
          And grapple with him ere he come so nigh.

KING JOHN The legate of the Pope hath been with me,
          And I have made a happy peace with him,
          And he hath promised to dismiss the powers
          Led by the Dolphin.

65   BASTARD   O inglorious league!
          Shall we, upon the footing of our land,
          Send fair-play orders and make compromise,
          Insinuation, parley, and base truce
          To arms invasive? Shall a beardless boy,

---

46 **sad distrust** sorrowful lack of self-confidence 48 **stirring** energetic
49 **outface** defy, stare down 50 **bragging** threatening 55 **become** grace
59 **Forage** sally forth 63 **happy** blessed, favorable 66 **upon the footing of
our land** based upon our native land 67 **fair-play orders** challenges and
injunctions following the rules of chivalry 68 **Insinuation** ingratiating actions

A cockered silken wanton, brave our fields   70
And flesh his spirit in a warlike soil,
Mocking the air with colors idly spread,
And find no check? Let us, my liege, to arms!
Perchance the Cardinal cannot make your peace;
Or if he do, let it at least be said   75
They saw we had a purpose of defense.

KING JOHN Have thou the ordering of this present
     time.

BASTARD Away then, with good courage! Yet, I know,
     Our party may well meet a prouder foe.   *Exeunt.*

Scene II. [*Bury St. Edmunds. The Dauphin's camp.*]

*Enter, in arms, [Lewis, the] Dauphin, Salisbury,
Melun, Pembroke, Bigot, [and] Soldiers.*

LEWIS My Lord Meloone, let this be copied out,
     And keep it safe for our remembrance;
     Return the precedent to those lords again,
     That, having our fair order written down,
     Both they and we, perusing o'er these notes,   5
     May know wherefore we took the sacrament,
     And keep our faiths firm and inviolable.

SALISBURY Upon our sides it never shall be broken.
     And, noble Dolphin, albeit we swear
     A voluntary zeal and an unurged faith   10
     To your proceedings, yet believe me, Prince,
     I am not glad that such a sore of time

70 **cockered** pampered   70 **wanton** spoiled child   70 **brave** (1) defy (2) display
his splendid outfit in   71 **flesh** initiate   72 **idly** (1) carelessly (2) uselessly (if they
meet no defense)   79 **prouder** (1) more powerful (2) more splendid (a last scoff at
the Dauphin) V.ii.3 **precendent** original (the "this" of line 1)   4 **fair order**
reasonable terms of agreement

Should seek a plaster by contemnèd revolt,
And heal the inveterate canker of one wound
15 By making many. O, it grieves my soul
That I must draw this metal from my side
To be a widow-maker! O, and there
Where honorable rescue and defense
Cries out upon the name of Salisbury!
20 But such is the infection of the time
That, for the health and physic of our right,
We cannot deal but with the very hand
Of stern injustice and confusèd wrong.
And is 't not pity, O my grievèd friends,
25 That we, the sons and children of this isle,
Were born to see so sad an hour as this
Wherein we step after a stranger, march
Upon her gentle bosom, and fill up
Her enemies' ranks—I must withdraw and weep
30 Upon the spot of this enforcèd cause—
To grace the gentry of a land remote,
And follow unacquainted colors here?
What, here? O nation, that thou couldst remove!
That Neptune's arms, who clippeth thee about,
35 Would bear thee from the knowledge of thyself,
And cripple thee, unto a pagan shore
Where these two Christian armies might combine
The blood of malice in a vein of league,
And not to spend it so unneighborly!

40 LEWIS A noble temper dost thou show in this,

---

13 **plaster** medical dressing   13 **contemned** despised   14 **inveterate canker**
persistent ulcer   16 **metal** (1) sword (2) mettle, courage   18 **where honorable
rescue** (England) where (the need for) honorable rescue (or, where noblemen
needing rescue)   19 **Cries out upon** appeal to   21 **physic** medical
treatment   22 **deal** contend   30 **Upon the spot** (1) on the location (2) because
of the disgrace   31 **grace** (1) embellish (2) be gracious to, welcome, honor
32 **unacquainted colors** foreign flags   33 **remove** go somewhere else   34 **clippeth** embraces   35 **bear** (1) carry (2) bare, strip   36 **cripple** disable (playing
upon the sound-echo of "clippeth")   38 **vein** (1) blood vessel (2) inclination
39 **unneighborly** (meiosis, or under-statement for rhetorical effect—Salisbury has
created the image of a brutal rape by Neptune which would be preferable to the
present "unneighborly" prospect)

And great affections wrestling in thy bosom
Doth make an earthquake of nobility.
O, what a noble combat has thou fought
Between compulsion and a brave respect!
Let me wipe off this honorable dew,   45
That silverly doth progress on thy cheeks:
My heart hath melted at a lady's tears,
Being an ordinary inundation,
But this effusion of such manly drops,
This show'r, blown up by tempest of the soul,   50
Startles mine eyes, and makes me more amazed
Than had I seen the vaulty top of heaven
Figured quite o'er with burning meteors.
Lift up thy brow, renownèd Salisbury,
And with a great heart heave away this storm.
Command these waters to those baby eyes   55
That never saw the giant-world enraged,
Nor met with fortune, other than at feasts,
Full warm of blood, of mirth, of gossiping.
Come, come; for thou shalt thrust thy hand as deep   60
Into the purse of rich prosperity
As Lewis himself: so, nobles, shall you all,
That knit your sinews to the strength of mine.

Enter Pandulph.

And even there, methinks, an angel spake.   65
Look where the holy legate comes apace,
To give us warrant from the hand of God,

41 **affections** passions (perhaps "affection's" to make "wrestling" the subject of
"Doth")   44 **Between ... respect** between what you were compelled to do and a
courageous (or ostentatious?) consideration (or carefulness)   46 **progress** make a
ceremonious journey   53 **Figured ... o'er with** with a complete pattern of
56 **Commend** entrust, deliver to the keeping of   57 **giant-world** (1) the baby's
world of giants (2) the large world beyond the baby's perception   59 **Full warm
of blood** fully warmed with human feeling   64 **angel** various possibilities: (1)
Lewis himself, punning on "angel" as a coin (following "purse" and "nobles," a
"noble" also being a coin) and attesting his sincerity (2) Pandulph, who has just
arrived with, Lewis thinks, heavenly assistance (3) a trumpet, which has just
announced Pandulph's arrival

And on our actions set the name of right
With holy breath.

PANDULPH   Hail, noble prince of France!
The next is this: King John hath reconciled
70   Himself to Rome; his spirit is come in,
That so stood out against the holy church,
The great metropolis and see of Rome.
Therefore thy threat'ning colors now wind up,
And tame the savage spirit of wild war,
75   That, like a lion fostered up at hand,
It may lie gently at the foot of peace,
And be no further harmful than in show.

LEWIS   Your Grace shall pardon me, I will not back:
I am too high-born to be propertied,
80   To be a secondary at control,
Or useful servingman and instrument
To any sovereign state throughout the world.
Your breath first kindled the dead coal of wars
Between this chastised kingdom and myself,
85   And brought in matter that should feed this fire;
And now 'tis far too huge to be blown out
With that same weak wind which enkindled it!
You taught me how to know the face of right,
Acquainted me with interest to this land,
90   Yea, thrust this enterprise into my heart;
And come ye now to tell me John hath made
His peace with Rome? What is that peace to me?
I, by the honor of my marriage bed,
After young Arthur, claim this land for mine,
95   And, now it is half-conquered, must I back
Because that John hath made his peace with Rome?
Am I Rome's slave? What penny hath Rome borne?
What men provided? what munition sent,
To underprop this action? Is 't not I

67 set place, as an official seal   70 is come in has submitted   78 shall must
78 back go back   79 propertied treated as a property, made a means to some
other end   80 a secondary at control a subordinate under the control of another
85 matter (1) fuel (2) arguments   89 interest title

That undergo this charge? Who else but I,   100
And such as to my claim are liable,
Sweat in this business and maintain this war?
Have I not heard these islanders shout out,
"*Vive le roi!*" as I have banked their towns?
Have I not here the best cards for the game   105
To win this easy match played for a crown?
And shall I now give o'er the yielded set?
No, no, on my soul, it never shall be said.

PANDULPH You look but on the outside of this work.

LEWIS Outside or inside, I will not return   110
Till my attempt so much be glorified
As to my ample hope was promisèd
Before I drew this gallant head of war,
And culled these fiery spirits from the world,
To outlook conquest and to win renown   115
Even in the jaws of danger and of death.
                          [*Trumpet sounds.*]
What lusty trumpet thus doth summon us?

Enter Bastard.

BASTARD According to the fair-play of the world,
Let me have audience; I am sent to speak:
My holy Lord of Milan, from the King   120
I come, to learn how you have dealt for him,
And, as you answer, I do know the scope
And warrant limited unto my tongue.

PANDULPH The Dolphin is too willful-opposite,
And will not temporize with my entreaties: 125
He flatly says he'll not lay down his arms.

---

100 **charge** burden, expense   101 **liable** subject   104 **banked** coasted past (?)
built military embankments around (?) (with *Vive le roi!* this is also part of the
card-playing metaphor)   107 **set** contest   113 **drew this gallant head of war**
assembled this gallant army   114 **culled** selected   115 **outlook** stare down
118 **fair-play** accepted rules for battle   122–23 **as you answer ... tongue**
depending upon your answer, I know what I am authorized to say   124 **willful-
opposite** obstinately quarrelsome   125 **temporize** make terms

BASTARD By all the blood that ever fury breathed,
　　　　The youth says well. Now hear our English king,
　　　　For thus his royalty doth speak in me:
130　　　He is prepared, and reason to he should—
　　　　This apish and unmannerly approach,
　　　　This harnessed masque and unadvisèd revel,
　　　　This unhaired sauciness and boyish troops,
　　　　The King doth smile at, and is well prepared
135　　　To whip this dwarfish war, this pigmy arms,
　　　　From out the circle of his territories.
　　　　That hand which had the strength, even at your
　　　　　　door,
　　　　To cudgel you and make you take the hatch,
　　　　To dive like buckets in concealèd wells,
140　　　To crouch in litter of your stable planks,
　　　　To lie like pawns, locked up in chests and trunks,
　　　　To hug with swine, to seek sweet safety out
　　　　In vaults and prisons, and to thrill and shake
　　　　Even at the crying of your nation's crow,
145　　　Thinking this voice an armèd Englishman—
　　　　Shall that victorious hand be feebled here
　　　　That in your chambers gave you chastisement?
　　　　No! Know the gallant monarch is in arms
　　　　And, like an eagle, o'er his aerie tow'rs,
150　　　To souse annoyance that comes near his nest.
　　　　And you degenerate, you ingrate revolts,
　　　　You bloody Neroes, ripping up the womb
　　　　Of your dear mother England, blush for shame:
　　　　For your own ladies and pale-visaged maids,

130 **reason to he should** there is reason also (too) that he should be prepared (?)
reason to be prepared he indeed has (?) he should also debate, or give his reasons (?)
132 **harnessed ... revel** masque performed in armor and misguided
entertainment 133 **unhaired** beardless 135 **this** these 138 **take the hatch**
jump over the bottom of a half-door without pausing to open it (cf. I.i.171)
140 **litter** bedding 141 **pawns** articles pawned 144 **crow** cock (the Frenchmen
were frightened, so the Bastard claims, by the crowing of the very Gallic cock
which symbolizes France) 149 **tow'rs** (hawking term) mounts up, soars
150 **souse** (1) dive, swoop down on (2) beat severely 150 **annoyance** any threat
151 **ingrate revolts** ungrateful rebels 152 **Neroes** (among his other crimes,
Nero, the Roman emperor, was said not only to have murdered his mother but to
have torn open her womb)

Like Amazons, come tripping after drums,   155
Their thimbles into armèd gauntlets change,
Their needles to lances, and their gentle hearts
To fierce and bloody inclination.

LEWIS There end thy brave, and turn thy face in
    peace.
We grant thou canst outscold us: fare thee well;   160
We hold our time too precious to be spent
With such a brabbler.

PANDULPH   Give me leave to speak.

BASTARD No, I will speak.

LEWIS   We will attend to neither.
Strike up the drums, and let the tongue of war
Plead for our interest and our being here.   165

BASTARD Indeed, your drums, being beaten, will cry
    out;
And so shall you, being beaten: do but start
An echo with the clamor of thy drum,
And, even at hand, a drum is ready braced.
That shall reverberate all, as loud as thine.   170
Sound but another, and another shall,
As loud as thine, rattle the welkin's ear
And mock the deep-mouthed thunder: for at hand—
Not trusting to this halting legate here,
Whom he hath used rather for sport than need—   175
Is warlike John; and in his forehead sits
A bare-ribbed death, whose office is this day
To feast upon whole thousands of the French.

LEWIS Strike up our drums to find this danger out.

BASTARD And thou shalt find it, Dolphin, do not doubt.   180
                            Exeunt.

---

157 **needles** (monosyllabic, "neels") 159 **brave** bravado, defiant boasting
162 **brabbler** brawler 169 **braced** stretched taut (the drumhead) 170 **reverberate** drive back (both the army and the echo) 174 **halting** imperfect, shifting

Scene III. [*A battlefield.*]

Alarums. Enter [King] John and Hubert.

KING JOHN How goes the day with us? O, tell me,
    Hubert.

HUBERT Badly, I fear. How fares your Majesty?

KING JOHN This fever, that hath troubled me so long,
    Lies heavy on me: O, my heart is sick!

Enter a Messenger.

MESSENGER My lord, your valiant kinsman, Faulcon-
5   bridge,
    Desires your Majesty to leave the field
    And send him word by me which way you go.

KING JOHN Tell him, toward Swinstead, to the
    abbey there.

MESSENGER Be of good comfort, for the great supply
10   That was expected by the Dolphin here,
    Are wracked three nights ago on Goodwin sands.
    This news was brought to Richard but even now:
    The French fight coldly and retire themselves.

KING JOHN Ay me! this tyrant fever burns me up,
15   And will not let me welcome this good news.
    Set on toward Swinstead; to my litter straight:
    Weakness possesseth me, and I am faint.   *Exeunt.*

V.iii.8 **Swinstead** (a mistake, historically, for Swineshead Abbey, in Lincolnshire)
9 **supply** i.e., of men   11 **Goodwin sands** shoals in the Straits of Dover

Scene IV. [*Elsewhere on the field.*]

Enter Salisbury, Pembroke, and Bigot.

SALISBURY I did not think the King so stored with
    friends.

PEMBROKE Up once again: put spirit in the French;
    If they miscarry, we miscarry too.

SALISBURY That misbegotten devil, Faulconbridge,
    In spite of spite, alone upholds the day.   5

PEMBROKE They say King John, sore sick, hath left
    the field.

Enter Melun wounded.

MELUN Lead me to the revolts of England here.

SALISBURY When we were happy, we had other names.

PEMBROKE It is the Count Meloone.

SALISBURY   Wounded to death.

MELUN Fly, noble English, you are bought and sold;   10
    Unthread the rude eye of rebellion,
    And welcome home again discarded faith.
    Seek out King John and fall before his feet:
    For if the French be lords of this loud day,
    He means to recompense the pains you take   15
    By cutting off your heads! Thus hath he sworn,
    And I with him, and many moe with me,
    Upon the altar at Saint Edmundsbury,

V.iv.5 **In spite of spite** despite any opposition 10 **bought and sold** duped
11 **Unthread ... rebellion** (rebellion as a needle into which they have threaded
themselves) 12 **discarded** (1) cast off (2) badly carded (their faith as ill-made
thread) 15 He Lewis 17 **moe** more

Even on that altar where we swore to you
20   Dear amity and everlasting love.

SALISBURY May this be possible? May this be true?

MELUN Have I not hideous death within my view,
Retaining but a quantity of life,
Which bleeds away, even as a form of wax
25   Resolveth from his figure 'gainst the fire?
What in the world should make me now deceive,
Since I must lose the use of all deceit?
Why should I then be false, since it is true
That I must die here, and live hence, by Truth?
30   I say again, if Lewis do win the day,
He is forsworn if e'er those eyes of yours
Behold another day break in the east:
But even this night, whose black contagious breath
Already smokes about the burning crest
35   Of the old, feeble, and day-wearied sun,
Even this ill night, your breathing shall expire,
Paying the fine of rated treachery
Even with a treacherous fine of all your lives,
If Lewis by your assistance win the day.
40   Commend me to one Hubert, with your king:
The love of him, and this respect besides,
For that my grandsire was an Englishman,
Awakes my conscience to confess all this.
In lieu whereof, I pray you bear me hence
45   From forth the noise and rumor of the field,
Where I may think the remnant of my thoughts
In peace, and part this body and my soul
With contemplation and devout desires.

23 **quantity** fragment   24 **form of wax** wax image (such, perhaps, as might be used by a witch to represent her victim)   25 **Resolveth from his figure** relaxes its form, melts   27 **use** advantage   29 **die here ... by Truth** (only if he dies undissembling and serving God can he hope for eternal life in heaven)   31 **is forsworn** will be perjured   34 **smokes** spreads like smoke   37 **fine** penalty (but in the next line "fine"=end)   37 **rated** (1) evaluated (2) chided   41 **respect** consideration   42 **For that** because   44 **lieu whereof** exchange for which   45 **rumor** tumult

SALISBURY We do believe thee, and beshrew my soul
   But I do love the favor and the form   50
   Of this most fair occasion, by the which
   We will untread the steps of damnèd flight,
   And like a bated and retirèd flood,
   Leaving our rankness and irregular course,
   Stoop low within those bounds we have o'erlooked,   55
   And calmly run on in obedience
   Even to our ocean, to our great King John.
   My arm shall give thee help to bear thee hence,
   For I do see the cruel pangs of death
   Right in thine eye. Away, my friends! New flight,   60
   And happy newness, that intends old right.
                    Exeunt [assisting Melun].

Scene V. [*The Dauphin's camp.*]

Enter [Lewis, the] Dauphin, and his train.

LEWIS The sun of heaven methought was loath to set,
   But stayed and made the western welkin blush,
   When English measured backward their own ground
   In faint retire! O, bravely came we off,
   When with a volley of our needless shot,   5
   After such bloody toil, we bid good night
   And wound our tott'ring colors clearly up,
   Last in the field, and almost lords of it!

---

49 **beshrew** a curse upon 60 **But I do** if I do not 50 **favor ... form**
appearance 52 **untread** retrace 53 **bated** subsided 54 **rankness** (1) excessive
size (2) impetuous violence (3) offensive odor 55 **Stoop ... o'erlooked**
(1) contract within those banks we have overflowed (2) kneel to accept those
obligations we have disregarded 60 **Right** clearly 61 **happy newness** appropriate and favorable change V.v.4 **faint retire** cowardly retreat 4 **bravely
came we off** (1) fearlessly and (2) worthily we left the field 7 **wound our
tott'ring colors clearly up** rolled up our (1) tattered (2) flapping banners without
interference

Enter a Messenger.

MESSENGER Where is my prince, the Dolphin?

LEWIS   Here. What news?

MESSENGER The Count Meloone is slain; the English
10   lords
          By his persuasion are again fall'n off,
          And your supply, which you have wished so long,
          Are cast away and sunk on Goodwin sands.

LEWIS Ah, foul, shrewd news! Beshrew thy very
          heart!
15   I did not think to be so sad tonight
          As this hath made me. Who was he that said
          King John did fly an hour or two before
          The stumbling night did part our weary pow'rs?

MESSENGER Whoever spoke it, it is true, my lord.

LEWIS Well! keep good quarter and good care
20   tonight:
          The day shall not be up so soon as I
          To try the fair adventure of tomorrow.   *Exeunt.*

Scene VI. [*Near Swinstead.*]

Enter Bastard and Hubert, severally.

HUBERT Who's there? Speak, ho! speak quickly, or I
          shoot.

BASTARD A friend. What art thou?

HUBERT   Of the part of England.

---

14 **shrewd** grievous, cursed 18 **stumbling** stumbling-causing 20 **Well!**
Good! V.vi. s.d. **severally** i.e., from opposite sides 2 **Of the part** on the side

BASTARD Whither dost thou go?

HUBERT What's that to thee? Why may not I demand
Of thine affairs as well as thou of mine?   5

BASTARD Hubert, I think?

HUBERT   Thou has a perfect thought.
I will upon all hazards well believe
Thou art my friend, that know'st my tongue so well.
Who art thou?

BASTARD   Who thou wilt: and if thou please,
Thou mayst befriend me so much as to think   10
I come one way of the Plantagenets.

HUBERT Unkind remembrance! thou and endless
   night
Have done me shame. Brave soldier, pardon me,
That any accent breaking from thy tongue
Should scape the true acquaintance of mine ear.   15

BASTARD Come, come! sans compliment, what news
   abroad?

HUBERT Why, here walk I, in the black brow of
   night,
To find you out.

BASTARD   Brief, then; and what's the news?

HUBERT O, my sweet sir, news fitting to the night,
Black, fearful, comfortless, and horrible.   20

BASTARD Show me the very wound of this ill news:
I am no woman; I'll not swound at it.

HUBERT The King, I fear, is poisoned by a monk:
I left him almost speechless, and broke out

---

6 **perfect** correct   9 **Who art thou?** (given John's weakness and Arthur's death, this is now a key question)   12 **remembrance** (1) reminder (2) memory   12–13 **thou ... shame** (the Bastard, by recognizing Hubert's voice though Hubert did not recognize his; the night, by concealing his features)   16 **sans compliment** without courtly flattery   17 **in the black brow** under the threatening countenance   22 **swound** faint   24 **broke out** left abruptly

25   To acquaint you with this evil, that you might
          The better arm you to the sudden time
          Than if you had at leisure known of this.

      BASTARD How did he take it? Who did taste to him?

      HUBERT A monk, I tell you, a resolvèd villain
30   Whose bowels suddenly burst out. The King
          Yet speaks, and peradventure may recover.

      BASTARD Who didst thou leave to tend his Majesty?

      HUBERT Why, know you not? The lords are all come
             back,
          And brought Prince Henry in their company,
35   At whose request the King hath pardoned them,
          And they are all about his Majesty.

      BASTARD Withhold thine indignation, mighty God,
          And tempt us not to bear above our power!
          I'll tell thee, Hubert, half my power this night,
40   Passing these flats, are taken by the tide;
          These Lincoln Washes have devourèd them;
          Myself, well mounted, hardly have escaped.
          Away before! Conduct me to the King;
          I doubt he will be dead or ere I come.   *Exeunt.*

---

26 **arm you ... time** prepare yourself (both psychologically and materially) for
the crisis   27 **at leisure** without haste   28 **7 taste** to act as taster for (the taster
sampled each dish to detect possible poison)   29 **resolvèd** resolute (he poisoned
himself, by tasting, in order to poison the King)   30 **Whose bowels ... out** (cf.
the death of Judas in Acts 1:18)   31 **peradventure** perhaps   34 **Prince Henry**
John's son (this is the first mention of him in the play)   38 **tempt us not ...**
power (1) do not tempt us to undertake more than we can accomplish (2) do not
test us by imposing more suffering than we can endure   39 **power** army
40 **these flats** the tidal flats at the mouth of the River Welland in The Wash, a
large inlet between Lincolnshire and Norfolk   44 **doubt** fear   44 **or ere** before

Scene VII. [*An orchard at Swinstead Abbey.*]

Enter Prince Henry, Salisbury, and Bigot.

PRINCE HENRY It is too late: the life of all his blood
　　Is touched corruptibly, and his pure brain,
　　Which some suppose the soul's frail dwelling house,
　　Doth by the idle comments that it makes,
　　Foretell the ending of mortality.　　　　　　　　　5

Enter Pembroke.

PEMBROKE His Highness yet doth speak, and holds
　　　belief
　　That, being brought into the open air,
　　It would allay the burning quality
　　Of that fell poison which assaileth him.

PRINCE HENRY Let him be brought into the orchard
　　　here.　　　　　　　　　　　　　　　　　10
　　Doth he still rage?

PEMBROKE　　　　　　He is more patient
　　Than when you left him; even now he sung.
　　　　　　　　　　　　　　　　[*Exit Pembroke.*]

PRINCE HENRY O, vanity of sickness! fierce extremes
　　In their continuance will not feel themselves.
　　Death, having preyed upon the outward parts,　　15
　　Leaves them invisible, and his siege is now
　　Against the mind, the which he pricks and wounds
　　With many legions of strange fantasies,
　　Which, in their throng and press to that last hold,

V.vii.2 **touched corruptibly** infected to the point of decomposition　2 **pure**
lucid　4 **idle** irrational　9 **fell** cruel　11 **rage** rave　13-14 **fierce ... themselves** as the sufferings of a dying man continue he loses awareness of them
16 **invisible** (modifies "Death," but suggests also, as modifying "outward parts,"
John's present disregard of his pains)　19 **hold** stronghold

Confound themselves. 'Tis strange that death
20   should sing!
I am the cygnet to this pale faint swan,
Who chants a doleful hymn to his own death,
And from the organ-pipe of frailty sings
His soul and body to their lasting rest.

SALISBURY Be of good comfort, Prince, for you are
25   born
To set a form upon that indigest
Which he hath left so shapeless and so rude.

[King] John brought in.

KING JOHN Ay, marry, now my soul hath elbow-room,
It would not out at windows, nor at doors;
30   There is so hot a summer in my bosom
That all my bowels crumble up to dust!
I am a scribbled form, drawn with a pen
Upon a parchment, and against this fire
Do I shrink up.

PRINCE HENRY   How fares your Majesty?

KING JOHN Poisoned—ill fare! dead, forsook, cast
35   off,
And none of you will bid the winter come
To thrust his icy fingers in my maw,
Nor let my kingdom's rivers take their course
Through my burned bosom, nor entreat the north
40   To make his bleak winds kiss my parchèd lips
And comfort me with cold. I do not ask you
        much—
I beg cold comfort—and you are so strait,
And so ingrateful, you deny me that.

---

20 **Confound themselves** defeat or destroy one another (the fantasies seeking to
capture John's mind so get in each other's way that no one of them succeeds)
22 **Who ... death** (the swan was fabled to sing only as it died)   26 **indigest**
shapeless confusion   28–29 **now ... doors** either (1) now my soul has room to
escape me, which it did not have inside the Abbey, or (2) now that my soul has
room, it still refuses to leave my body   35 **ill fare** (1) ill fortune (2) bad food
42 **strait** narrow, severe, stingy

PRINCE HENRY O, that there were some virtue in my
     tears
   That might relieve you!

KING JOHN   The salt in them is hot.   45
   Within me is a hell, and there the poison
   Is as a fiend confined to tyrannize
   On unreprievable condemnèd blood.

              Enter Bastard.

BASTARD O, I am scalded with my violent motion
   And spleen of speed to see your Majesty!   50

KING JOHN O cousin, thou art come to set mine eye!
   The tackle of my heart is cracked and burnt,
   And all the shrouds wherewith my life should sail
   Are turnèd to one thread, one little hair:
   My heart hath one poor string to stay it by,   55
   Which holds but till thy news be utterèd,
   And then all this thou seest is but a clod
   And module of confounded royalty.

BASTARD The Dolphin is preparing hitherward,
   Where God He knows how we shall answer him,   60
   For in a night the best part of my pow'r,
   As I upon advantage did remove,
   Were in the Washes all unwarily
   Devourèd by the unexpected flood.   [*The King dies.*]

SALISBURY You breathe these dead news in as dead
     an ear.   65
   My liege! my lord!—but now a king, now thus!

PRINCE HENRY Even so must I run on, and even so
     stop.

44 **virtue** healing power   49 **scalded** overheated, covered with hot liquid
(perspiration)   50 **spleen** impetuous violence, eagerness   51 **set mine eye** close
my eyes after I die   53 **shrouds** (1) ropes holding a mast in place; with a
contextually, but not syntactically, appropriate reminder of (2) winding sheets
58 **module** image   58 **confounded** defeated, destroyed   60 **God He knows**
God only knows   62 **upon advantage did remove** seizing the chance changed
my location   63 **unwarily** without warning   65 **dead news** (1) deadly news (2)
news of death

What surety of the world, what hope, what stay,
When this was now a king, and now is clay?

70 BASTARD Art thou gone so? I do but stay behind
To do the office for thee of revenge,
And then my soul shall wait on thee to heaven,
As it on earth hath been thy servant still.
Now, now, you stars that move in your right
    spheres,
Where be your pow'rs? Show now your mended
75   faiths,
And instantly return with me again,
To push destruction and perpetual shame
Out of the weak door of our fainting land:
Straight let us seek, or straight we shall be sought.
80 The Dolphin rages at our very heels.

SALISBURY It seems you know not, then, so much as we:
The Cardinal Pandulph is within at rest,
Who half an hour since came from the Dolphin,
And brings from him such offers of our peace
85 As we with honor and respect may take,
With purpose presently to leave this war.

BASTARD He will the rather do it when he sees
Ourselves well sinewèd to our defense.

SALISBURY Nay, 'tis in a manner done already,
90 For many carriages he hath dispatched
To the seaside, and put his cause and quarrel
To the disposing of the Cardinal,
With whom yourself, myself, and other lords,
If you think meet, this afternoon will post
95 To consummate this business happily.

---

68 **surety** guarantee, certainty   68 **stay** (1) support (2) continuance   73 **still** constantly   74 **stars ... spheres** noblemen who have returned to your proper positions   75 **pow'rs** (1) armed troops (2) astral influences   79 **Straight** immediately   90 **carriages** wagons   94 **post** hasten

BASTARD Let it be so; and you, my noble prince,
    With other princes that may best be spared,
    Shall wait upon your father's funeral.

PRINCE HENRY At Worcester must his body be interred,
    For so he willed it.

BASTARD   Thither shall it then.   100
    And happily may your sweet self put on
    The lineal state and glory of the land!
    To whom, with all submission, on my knee,
    I do bequeath my faithful services
    And true subjection everlastingly.   105

SALISBURY And the like tender of our love we make,
    To rest without a spot for evermore.

PRINCE HENRY I have a kind soul that would give you
      thanks,
    And knows not how to do it but with tears.

BASTARD O, let us pay the time but needful woe,   110
    Since it hath been beforehand with our griefs.
    This England never did, nor never shall,
    Lie at the proud foot of a conqueror
    But when it first did help to wound itself.
    Now these her princes are come home again,   115
    Come the three corners of the world in arms,
    And we shall shock them! Naught shall make us
      rue
    If England to itself do rest but true!   *Exeunt.*

FINIS

98 **wait upon** escort ceremonially   101 **happily** fittingly   102 **lineal state**
directly inherited rank (as king), or the crown, etc., denoting that rank
106 **tender** offer   107 **spot** stain (of disloyalty)   110-11 **let us pay ... griefs** let
us weep no more than necessary since time has anticipated our griefs (providing
compensation: the French abandonment of the invasion offsetting the English
losses; Henry replacing John)   116 **the three corners** (presumably England is
the fourth)   117 **shock them** (1) meet them in battle (2) throw them into
confusion (3) tie them in bundles like sheaves (?)

Textual Note

Though mentioned by Francis Meres in 1598, *King John* was not printed until 1623, in the Folio. It has usually been thought that it must have been written between 1591, the publication date of *The Troublesome Reign of King John*, upon which many consider Shakespeare's play to have been based, and 1598, when Meres mentioned it. Since I am convinced that it preceded *The Troublesome Reign*, I naturally date Shakespeare's play before 1591, somewhere, probably, between 1588 and 1590. I would think that the writing of the three parts of *Henry VI*, certainly, and of *Richard III*, probably, preceded it. *King John* should be seen as belonging with these early plays but, in its conception, a long step forward from them.

To see *The Troublesome Reign* as based upon Shakespeare's play is not to make it a trustworthy quarto. Its author imitates Shakespeare's plot but has little memory for his lines. The Folio remains the only substantive text.

Such inconsistencies as the Folio text contains suggest that the play was printed from author's manuscript and not from a theatrical promptbook. The chief of these inconsistencies is the Act II entry of "a Citizen upon the walls" of Angiers, followed by the speech-heading "Cit." for his first four speeches, after which, in midscene, he becomes "Hubert" for one speech, and then "Hub." Presumably this change represents the author's decision, while writing, to develop the anonymous Citizen into a character of importance to the plot, and such confusion of speech-heading would have been removed from the promptbook. To the detriment of the play, most editors have carried the unnamed Citizen through the act, thus introducing Hubert as a new character in III.ii. Hubert's development as a man forced to take a stand is only clear when we recognize his attempt to avoid involvement during Act II.

TEXTUAL NOTE

The errors in act and scene headings were presumably made by the compositor. His repetition of "Actus Quartus" where he needed "Actus Quintus" may have been carried over from his copy, but a less obvious confusion would seem most simply explained on the basis of his having misunderstood what he found. "Actus Primus, Scaena Prima" is followed by a "Scaena Secunda" covering more than four double-column pages, to be followed in turn by an "Actus Secundus" covering little more than half of one page, which makes for a total first act of more than seven pages, and a second act of less than one. Editors, following Theobald, have generally turned the "Scaena Secunda" into Act II, and "Actus Secundus" into Act III, Scene i, which necessitates considering the Folio's "Actus Tertius, Scaena prima" a further error. Since Constance throws herself to the ground at the conclusion of "Actus Secundus" and is apparently still there at the opening of "Actus Tertius" (in spite of her being listed as entering with the others), editors have felt justified in making those scenes continuous in spite of the indicated division.

It is much more likely, as Honigmann suggests in the Arden edition, that the compositor mistook a simple manuscript *two* (or *2*, or *II*), meaning Act II, as indicating Scene ii, reversing the process when he came to the next *two* (or *2*, or *II*) and labeling an intended second scene of Act II as though it were the whole act. This edition therefore follows Honigmann and differs from other editors by including a II.ii and thus beginning III.i in accordance with the Folio. Given the continuous action of an Elizabethan production, the presence of Constance seated onstage from one act to the next is not a serious challenge to following the Folio at that point.

Several scholars have noted that, at III.i.81, the Folio prints "heaven" where the context clearly demands the word "God," and they have suggested that censorship intervened at some point between the original manuscript and the Folio. But editors have not considered the implications of this argument.

TEXTUAL NOTE

In only one other history play, *Henry VIII*, does "heaven" appear more frequently than "God" ("heaven" 44 times, "God" 21); in *1 Henry VI* and *3 Henry VI* they appear an equal number of times (16 times each in the first, 20 times each in the second); in the other five history plays "heaven" appears 115 times to "God's" 270, with the greatest discrepancy in *Richard III* (29 to 79). In all these plays, the lowest frequency of appearance of the word "God" is the 16 times it appears in *1 Henry VI*, and the highest frequency of the word "heaven" is the 44 times in *Henry VIII*. Compare with these figures the fact that "heaven" appears 51 times in the Folio text of *King John*, while "God" appears only 5 times, and the suggestion of censorship is greatly strengthened.

Such being likely, each appearance of the word "heaven" in this play becomes suspect. V.vii.60 is, as clearly as III.i.81, an instance in which "God" was the original word. In phrases like "heaven and earth" (II.i.173), "clouds of heaven" (II.i.252), or "heaven or hell" (II.i.407), it is obvious that no change should be made. But this leaves a large group of doubtful instances. On the basis of context (verbal, rhythmic, and dramatic) I have made the change from "heaven" to "God" eight times where it seems thoroughly justified, as noted below. Eleven places where I would also prefer to make the change but, in line with the conservative textual policy of this series, have not done so are: I.i.83, 84, 256; II.i. 373; III.i.162, 168, 192 (twice); IV.i.55; IV.iii.82; and V.i.29. Eighteen other places where the change would be possible but where, for contextual reasons (with which others might disagree), I would not make it are: I.i.70; II.i.35, 86, 170, 171; III.i.22, 33, 34, 62; III.ii.37, 68; III.iii.48; IV.i.23, 91, 109; and IV.iii.10, 145, 159. (In addition to the three instances mentioned previously, I consider "heaven" obviously correct in II.i.174; III.ii.44; III.iii.77, 87, 158; IV.ii.15, 216; V.ii.52; V.v.1; and V.vii.72.)

Speech-headings in this edition are regularized by spelling them out in full. Spelling and punctuation have been modernized (conservatively), and obvious typographical

TEXTUAL NOTE

errors have been corrected. I have changed to *Dauphin* and *Melun* in stage directions, but have left the old spellings, *Dolphin* and *Meloone*, in the speeches for the sake of pronunciation. Other than these changes, departures from the Folio text are listed below, the adopted reading first, in bold, followed by the original, in roman.

I.i.1 s.d. **with Chatillion** with the Chattylion   43 **God** heauen   62 **God** heauen   147 **I would** It would   203 **Pyrenean** Perennean   208 **smack** smoake   237 **Could he get me** Could get me

II.i. **ACT II** Scaena Secunda s.d. **King Philip ... Austria and his Attendants** Philip King of France, Lewis, Daulphin, Austria, Constance, Arthur   1 **King Philip** Lewis [the text several times confuses the French king's name]   18 **Ah, noble boy** A noble boy   63 **Ate** Ace   127 **Than thou and John in manners, being as like** Then thou and Iohn, in manners being as like,   149 **Philip** Lewis   150 **King Philip** Lew.   152 **Anjou** Angiers   201 s.d. **Hubert** a Citizen [not identified as Hubert until the speech-heading at line 325]   215 **Confronts your** Comfort yours   259 **roundure** rounder   368 **Hubert.** Fra[nce].   485 **Anjou** Angiers [the error—see also II.i.152—is probably not the author's, for Angiers is the city excepted in line 489; cf. also line 528, where Folio has "Aniow"]

II.ii. **Scene II** Actus Secundus

III.i.36 **day** daies   74 **task** tast   81 **God** heauen   238 **God** heauen

III.iii.64 **friends** fiends

IV.i.77 **God's** heauen   91 **mote** moth

IV.ii.1 **again crowned** against crowned   42 **when** then   73 **Does** Do

IV.iii.33 **man** mans

V. **ACT V** Actus Quartus

V.ii.26 **Were** Was   43 **hast thou fought** hast fought   66 **God** heauen

V.v.3 **measured** measure

V.vi.37 **God** heauen

V.vii.17 **mind** winde   21 **cygnet** Symet   42 **strait** straight   60 **God** heauen

THE HOUSES OF LANCASTER AND YORK
(Simplified)

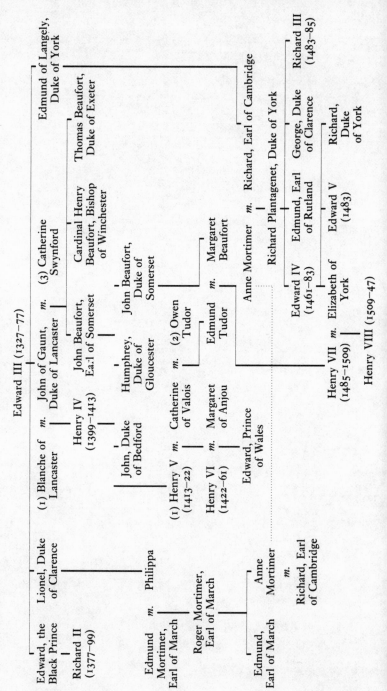

ABOUT THE INTRODUCER

TONY TANNER is Professor of English and American Literature in Cambridge University, and Fellow of King's College. Previous publications include *The Reign of Wonder, City of Words, Adultery and the Novel*, and *Venice Desired*. He has also published studies of Jane Austen, Henry James, Saul Bellow and Thomas Pynchon.

TITLES IN EVERYMAN'S LIBRARY

GEORGE ELIOT
Adam Bede
Middlemarch
The Mill on the Floss
Silas Marner

WILLIAM FAULKNER
The Sound and the Fury

HENRY FIELDING
Tom Jones

F. SCOTT FITZGERALD
The Great Gatsby

GUSTAVE FLAUBERT
Madame Bovary

FORD MADOX FORD
The Good Soldier
Parade's End

E. M. FORSTER
Howards End
A Passage to India

ELIZABETH GASKELL
Mary Barton

EDWARD GIBBON
The Decline and Fall of the
Roman Empire
Vols 1 to 3: The Western Empire
Vols 4 to 6: The Eastern Empire

IVAN GONCHAROV
Oblomov

GÜNTER GRASS
The Tin Drum

GRAHAM GREENE
Brighton Rock
The Human Factor

THOMAS HARDY
Far From The Madding Crowd
Jude the Obscure
The Mayor of Casterbridge
The Return of the Native
Tess of the d'Urbervilles

JAROSLAV HAŠEK
The Good Soldier Švejk

NATHANIEL HAWTHORNE
The Scarlet Letter

ERNEST HEMINGWAY
A Farewell to Arms
Collected Stories

HINDU SCRIPTURES
(tr. R. C. Zaehner)

JAMES HOGG
Confessions of a Justified Sinner

HOMER
The Iliad
The Odyssey

HENRY JAMES
The Awkward Age
The Bostonians
The Golden Bowl
The Portrait of a Lady
The Princess Casamassima

JAMES JOYCE
Dubliners
A Portrait of the Artist as
a Young Man
Ulysses

FRANZ KAKFA
The Castle
The Trial
Collected Stories

JOHN KEATS
The Poems

SØREN KIERKEGAARD
Fear and Trembling and
The Book on Adler

RUDYARD KIPLING
Collected Stories

THE KORAN
(tr. Marmaduke Pickthall)

CHODERLOS DE LACLOS
Les Liaisons dangereuses

GIUSEPPE TOMASI DI
LAMPEDUSA
The Leopard

D. H. LAWRENCE
Collected Stories
The Rainbow
Sons and Lovers
Women in Love

MIKHAIL LERMONTOV
A Hero of Our Time

NICCOLÒ MACHIAVELLI
The Prince

THOMAS MANN
Buddenbrooks
Death in Venice and Other Stories
Doctor Faustus

KATHERINE MANSFIELD
The Garden Party and Other
Stories

ANDREW MARVELL
The Complete Poems

HERMAN MELVILLE
Moby-Dick

JOHN STUART MILL
On Liberty and Utilitarianism

JOHN MILTON
The Complete English Poems

YUKIO MISHIMA
The Temple of the
Golden Pavilion

MARY WORTLEY MONTAGU
Letters

THOMAS MORE
Utopia

MURASAKI SHIKIBU
The Tale of Genji

VLADIMIR NABOKOV
Lolita
Pale Fire
Speak, Memory

GEORGE ORWELL
Animal Farm
Nineteen Eighty-Four

THOMAS PAINE
Rights of Man
and Common Sense

BORIS PASTERNAK
Doctor Zhivago

PLATO
The Republic

EDGAR ALLAN POE
The Complete Stories

ALEXANDER PUSHKIN
The Captain's Daughter
and Other Stories

FRANÇOIS RABELAIS
Gargantua and Pantagruel

JEAN-JACQUES ROUSSEAU
Confessions
The Social Contract and
the Discourses

WILLIAM SHAKESPEARE
Sonnets and Narrative Poems
Histories Vols 1 and 2
Tragedies Vols 1 and 2

MARY SHELLEY
Frankenstein

ADAM SMITH
The Wealth of Nations

STENDHAL
The Charterhouse of Parma
Scarlet and Black

JOHN STEINBECK
The Grapes of Wrath

LAURENCE STERNE
Tristram Shandy

ROBERT LOUIS STEVENSON
The Master of Ballantrae and Weir of
Hermiston
⁄ Dr Jekyll and Mr Hyde
and Other Stories

JONATHAN SWIFT
Gulliver's Travels

Everyman's Library, founded in 1906 and relaunched in 1991, aims to offer the most complete library in the English language of the world's classics. Each volume is printed in a classic typeface on acid-free, cream-wove paper with a sewn full cloth binding.